PRODUCTION/OPERATIONS MANAGEMENT

Concepts and Situations

Third Edition

ROGER W. SCHMENNER

School of Business

Indiana University

SCIENCE RESEARCH ASSOCIATES, INC.

Chicago, Henley-on-Thames, Sydney, Toronto

To my father, a helluva operations manager

Acquisition Editor	Robert Horan
Project Editor	Geof Garvey
Copy Editor	Lynn Brown
Text Design	Judith Olson
Cover Design	Paul Adams Design
Production Director	Steve Leonardo
Composition	Carlisle Graphics
Illustrations	House of Graphics/Carlisle Graphics

Library of Congress Cataloging-in-Publication Data

Schmenner, Roger W., 1947–
    Production/operations management.

    Bibliography: p.
    Includes index.
    1. Production management—Case studies. I. Title.
TS155.S322 1987   658.5   86-13957
ISBN 0-574-19570-X

The author wishes to thank the following companies for reviewing the relevant manuscript pages and authorizing use of the process descriptions: Arthur Andersen & Co.; Burger King Corporation; General Motors Corporation (Chevrolet-Pontiac-Canada Group Headquarters); Howard Ford-Isuzu Peugeot; International Paper Company; Joseph A. Bank Mfg. Co., Inc.; Norcen Industries; Stroh Brewery Company; and Thalhimer Brothers, Inc. Tour opening photos are courtesy of these companies.

Page 348, Note 3:   List adapted from "QWL Indicators—Prospects and Problems" by Richard E. Walton in *Studies in Personnel Psychology 6*, no. 1 (Spring 1974). Used by permission.
Page 501, Situation 5-5:   Courtesy of Black & Decker Corporation.
Page 610:   Case Study of Jung Products, Inc. by Roger W. Schmenner. Copyright © 1977 by the President and Fellows of Harvard College. All rights reserved. Reprinted by permission.

Table 3-1:   Marvin E. Mundel, *Motion and Time Study: Improving Productivity*, © 1978, pp. 230–231. Reprinted by permission of Prentice-Hall, Englewood Cliffs, New Jersey.
Table 3-4:   Reprinted with permission of Richard B. Freeman and James L. Medoff from: *The Public Interest*, No. 57 (Fall 1979), p. 75. © 1979 by National Affairs, Inc.

Table 5-7:   Reprinted with permission of Council of Logistics Management (formerly National Council of Physical Distribution Management) from *Customer Service: Meaning and Management* by B. J. LaLonde and P. H. Zinszer. Copyright © 1976.
Table 6-4:   Reprinted with permission of McGraw Hill from *Quality Control Handbook* by J. M. Juran (ed.). Copyright © 1979.
Table 6-6:   Robert E. Cole, *Work, Mobility, and Participation: A Comparative Study of American and Japanese Industry* (Berkeley: University of California Press, 1979). Reprinted with permission by U. C. Press. © 1979 Regents of the University of California.
Table 8-1:   Reprinted by permission of *Technology Review*. Figure from "Patterns of Industrial Innovation" by William J. Abernathy and James M. Utterback (June–July 1978), p. 40.

Figure I1:   Courtesy of International Paper Company. "Report of Independent Public Accountants to the Share Owners of International Paper Company," 1985.
Figures 4-14 and 4-15:   Reprinted with permission of Dow Jones-Irwin from *Zero Inventories* by Robert W. Hall. Copyright © 1983.

CONTENTS

iii

PREFACE

The reception that the first two editions of this text have enjoyed is very gratifying. With this third edition, I have had the opportunity to approach again the original vision that I had for the book. I saw it as combining and unifying the best elements of two schools of thought about production/operations management (POM): one anchored in the application of techniques to POM problems; the other anchored in the dilemmas and decision making of the operating manager. With this edition, the text has taken a step closer to accomplishing that original vision. At the same time, the book remains true to the point of view that production/operations management is best appreciated when grounded in the study of manufacturing and service processes—their characters, their advantages and disadvantages, their implications for management, and the dynamics of their change.

The third edition has undergone several significant alterations. A recounting of them is instructive:

A Revamped and Expanded Segment II

Perhaps the weakest portion of the previous editions were those that dealt with the traditional, core aspects of POM: production planning, scheduling, inventory management, production control, queuing, forecasting, project management, quality control, and related topics. In this edition, the treatment of these important subjects is both greatly expanded and much improved. Discussions of these issues are richer and better stated, with more examples and situations worked through.

The organization of Segment II has also changed dramatically. The chapter on production planning and control now precedes that on materials management, and several appendixes have been broken out to deal more effectively with specialized topics.

Enhanced Treatment of Service Operations

The third edition treats service operations even more explicitly than the second edition did. Segment I now includes four service tours to complement the plant tours that have been the cornerstones of the previous editions.

Among the service tours, the Burger King operations have been updated, and these three have been added: Thalhimers—Cloverleaf Mall (a department store); Howard Ford-Isuzu-Peugeot (auto repair), and Arthur Andersen & Co.—Charlotte (a Big Eight accounting firm).

Service operations also receive separate treatment in several of the theoretical chapters.

Reorganization and Updating of the Tours

Not only have three new tours been added to Segment I, but the other six have been updated

ix

considerably to reflect the continued changes their capable managers have made.

The plant and service tours are now lettered and not listed as numbered chapters. This was done to lessen the chance that people would feel compelled to study all nine tours before embarking on the remainder of the text.

The tours of Segment I can easily be used in a variety of ways and for a variety of purposes. They span many distinctions that separate both manufacturing and service processes and can serve either as introductions to POM or as references.

ACKNOWLEDGMENTS

This edition has benefited greatly from the co-operation I have received from a number of companies. While I cannot acknowledge the contributions of everyone in those companies, I would like to mention some who have been especially helpful with this edition: Michael Ippolito of International Paper, Joseph and Lillian Gehret of Norcen Industries, Edward Jecelin and Bohdan Oleksiuk of Jos. A. Bank, James Kovacs of General Motors (C-P-C Group—Tarrytown), David Stephens and Thomas Faust of Burger King, Roy Fischer of Stroh Brewery, Dex Howard and Ty Hamby of Howard Ford, W. Kimball Price of Thalhimers, Frank Jonas of Arthur Andersen & Co., Kenneth Good of Black & Decker, and Frank Coyne, Victor Baldridge, and Kathy Wilkerson. My deep thanks to them and their colleagues.

I have also benefited from a number of thoughtful and perceptive reviews. I am grateful to Don Edwards (Baylor University), Allen Kartchner (Utah State University), Blaine McCormick (Eastern Tennessee State University), Duncan McDougall (Boston University), Craig McLanahan (Salem State College), Willbann Terpening (Gonzaga University), and Jerome Weist (University of Utah) for reviewing this edition.

Many of the problems and situations for study are the work of Joseph R. Biggs (University of Wisconsin—Whitewater) and Thomas F. Callarman (Arizona State University). They reduced the burden for me at an important time in this text's development.

Judy Clow did a marvelous job in preparing the manuscript, putting in many long hours. I am deeply grateful for her efforts and devotion.

My wife, Barbie, was again most forgiving of me and my attachment to this book. She listened to me alternately curse it and rejoice in it. She understood the need to disrupt evenings and weekends with it. She endured patiently the travel this revision required of me. I owe her much.

Roger W. Schmenner

INTRODUCTION

Operations. For many people, mentioning the word brings on a rush of disagreeable feelings and sensations. Details. Pressure. Long hours. Inhospitable working conditions. Dull colleagues. For these people, a company's operating managers—usually typed as engineers who could not hack it in the "more creative" design aspects of the business—lead very unromantic careers. Moreover, operations is viewed as a dead-end job with no future in the upper layers of management.

This description is an exaggeration, of course, but it conveys some of the impressions that people hold about operations. This text is a crusade against that kind of stereotype of the operations manager. In fact, operations offers an exciting and dynamic management challenge that is as absorbing and rewarding as any marketing or finance can offer. After all, for the typical company, most of its assets and people are devoted to the production function. Moreover, a badly run operation can be a staggering drain on corporate profits and morale, as a number of even large corporations can attest; conversely, a well-run operation can be a competitive weapon every bit as potent as any in the corporate arsenal.

For many senior managers, the path to the top snaked through operations—even for those whose climb has been in so-called "marketing companies." Many others would admit that a tour of duty in operations was an important part of their general management education and background. The point is that operations is and rightly should be a key concern for most companies and one that all students of business who aspire to general management responsibilities ought to know about.

The importance of operations has been highlighted in recent years. Numerous articles have appeared in business periodicals stressing the need for young managers, especially those fresh from business schools, to seek out careers in operations jobs. The success of the Japanese has reinforced this view in many people's eyes, since the prowess of the Japanese is widely recognized to be in manufacturing.

What makes for an outstanding operating manager is an elusive concept that no doubt will be debated for years to come. One recent thoughtful analysis, however, was made by Wickham Skinner and Earl Sasser.* Citing a study of a number of managers thrust into some very different situations, they suggest that the managers who are real achievers demonstrate four distinct characteristics:

- They employ analytical tools with discipline and consistency and are careful to keep information and data flowing.

- They truly motivate their subordinates and know what satisfies their own superiors.

- They manage themselves—their time, their temper, their clout, their thinking.

- They focus on one task of prime importance at a time.

*Wickham Skinner and W. Earl Sasser, "Managers with Impact: Versatile and Inconsistent," *Harvard Business Review* 55, no. 6 (November–December 1977): 140–48.

This text cannot hope to teach you, the reader, how to manage yourself or all the subtleties in the interpersonal interactions that abound in business organizations. It can, however, open the doors to some useful ways of looking at operations, of identifying and analyzing their problems, and of judging what merits chief concern and attention as well as to possible means of solving problems. Instilling this awareness is the goal of this text.

This Text's Philosophy and Organization

This text approaches operations management from the bottom up. I am convinced that a sound grounding in the nitty-gritty of existing operations is a prerequisite to a fuller understanding of what it means to alter a production system or to design a new one. Therefore, Segment I of this text describes in detail nine manufacturing and service processes that differ from one another in important ways and represent the entire spectrum of process choice. Each process is analyzed in turn, and then all of them are compared and contrasted against one another, so as to highlight the particular features that define a production process. The remainder of the text builds on the foundation provided by these processes.

Segment II considers some of the typical problems of ongoing operations and how these operations can be improved over the short run. The areas of management concern addressed in Segment II include breaking production bottlenecks; managing the workforce; planning, scheduling, and controlling production over the near term (say, six to 18 months); managing materials (purchasing, inventories, and logistics); and making quality happen.

Segment III takes operations one step further, by considering more drastic changes to the production process—capacity change, technological change, change in the span of process undertaken (vertical integration)—all of which require advance planning and, usually, a year or more to implement.

Segment IV then ties together Segments I, II, and III by focusing on the broad issue of operations strategy and organization. It is only here that the design of a production system—its facilities, technology, policies, and organization—is discussed in full. It is here too that the use of operations as a competitive weapon can be appreciated most keenly.

It has been my experience that nothing serves better to stimulate interest in a problem or topic than seeing it come to life in a real world situation. With this in mind, Segments II through IV of this book are liberally sprinkled with production and operations situations demanding management decisions and derived from the travails of managers in a host of industries; these situations supplement and reinforce the process descriptions in Segment I. In fact, several of them revisit the companies described in Segment I to provide a more detailed picture of selected aspects of their operations. All of these situations are like small case studies that make very specialized points about operations. They serve as a touchstone for both the reader's understanding of the nature and importance of a particular concept and the text's ensuing discussion of possible resolutions of the problems and opportunities exposed by each situation. Thus, much of the format of this text consists of a particular situation followed by discussion of that situation and its more general implications.

For the situations that initiate the discussion of operations concepts, this text draws on both manufacturing and nonmanufacturing company experience. At regular intervals throughout the text the similarities and differences between manufacturing and nonmanufacturing industry operations are highlighted.

With this as a prologue, let us begin our exploration of various production processes.

SEGMENT

I

PLANT AND SERVICE TOURS

Each of the following nine tours introduces a particular kind of production or service process. All of the processes described are different in important respects. Together they span the entire range of process choice and fall into two categories: manufacturing and service. The manufacturing tours describe the following types of processes:

- Job shop
- Batch flow process
- Worker-paced line flow process
- Machine-paced line flow process
- Continuous flow process
- Hybrid process (part batch and part continuous flow)

Included in the service tours are

- Service factory
- Service shop
- Mass service
- Professional service

The models for each of these process types are drawn from actual operations as they were functioning in the latter half of 1985. Naturally, I am greatly indebted to the cooperating companies for spending a good deal of time with me discussing their processes and walking me around them, and also for reviewing and cor-

recting my written descriptions of their operations. Each tour consists of a process description followed by a discussion of the salient features of the process. The sequence of tours highlights the differences among the processes. For example, the description of a continuous flow process (Tour A) is followed immediately by the description of a job shop, which lies at the opposite extreme of the process spectrum. By playing up these contrasts, the unique features of each process may be kept more clearly in mind.

Chapter 1 of this text, also in this segment, compares and contrasts all the processes and in so doing pinpoints the key realms of management choice and concern in each.

These plant and service tours and their comparison anchor this text. They introduce few, if any, techniques of analysis since they are essentially descriptive. Rather, they provide the background against which the usefulness of the concepts and techniques discussed in Chapters 2 through 10 can best be seen. Aspects of these tours are referred to on numerous occasions elsewhere in the text. The plant and service tours taken in this segment are a constant reminder of the diversity, complexity, and challenge of the operations decisions faced by managers every day in hosts of industries.

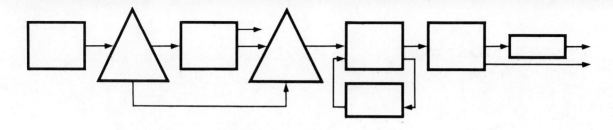

A CONTINUOUS FLOW PROCESS
International Paper Company, Androscoggin Mill Jay, Maine

The Androscoggin Mill, situated along the Androscoggin River in central Maine, was one of 17 pulp and paper mills that the International Paper Company operated worldwide. It was one of the largest and most modern, having been built originally in 1965 with significant additions in 1968 and 1977. The plant occupied 478 acres of land, had 20 acres under roof, and represented a book value investment of nearly $400 million.

The mill, part of International Paper's Pulp and Paper Group, produced three distinctly different kinds of paper: (1) forms bond, envelope, tablet, and offset paper for office or computer use; (2) paper tissue for use as carbon paper in business forms; and (3) publication gloss for magazine printing.

Androscoggin was a fully integrated mill; that is, it produced all the wood pulp it needed to make its paper. The mill was laid out to receive logs or chips of wood at one end and, about a mile farther down, to ship packaged "logs" of paper from the other end. (See Figure A1 for a layout of the mill; the production flow is from left to right.)

PART ONE
PROCESS DESCRIPTION

A Brief And Simplified Description of Papermaking

The paper we use today is created from individual wood fibers that are first suspended in water and then pressed and dried into sheets. The process of converting the wood to a suspension of wood fibers in water is known as *pulpmaking,* while the manufacture of the dried and pressed sheets of paper is formally termed *papermaking.* The process of making paper has undergone a steady evolution, and larger and more sophisticated equipment and better technology continue to improve it.

The Woodyard and Woodrooms

The process at Androscoggin began with receiving wood in the form of chips or of logs 4 or 8 feet in length. From 6 A.M. to 10 P.M. a steady

FIGURE A1 Layout of International Paper Company's Androscroggin Mill.

stream of trucks and railroad cars were weighed and unloaded. About 40 percent of the deliveries were of wood cut from International Paper's own land (over 1 million acres in Maine), while the other 60 percent were supplied by independents who were paid by weight for their logs. The mill also received wood chips from lumber mills in the area. The chips and logs were stored in mammoth piles with separate piles for wood of different species (such as pine, spruce, hemlock).

When needed, logs were floated in flumes from the woodyard into one of the mill's three woodrooms. There bark was rubbed off in long, ribbed debarking drums by tumbling the logs against one another. The logs then fell into a chipper; within seconds a large log was reduced to a pile of chips approximately 1 inch by 1 inch by $\frac{1}{4}$ inch. The wood chips were then sorted through large, flat vibrating screens. Oversized chips were rechipped, and ones that were too small were collected for burning in the power

house. (The mill provided approximately 50 percent of all its own steam and electricity needs from burning waste. An additional 50 percent of total electricity needs was produced by harnessing the river for hydroelectric power.)

The chips were then stored in silos. There were separate silos for spruce and fir, pine and hemlock, and hardwoods (maple, beech, and birch). This separate and temporary storage of chips permitted the controlled mixing of chips of these three main types into the precise recipe for the grade of paper being produced. Once drawn from the silo into the digesters, there was no stopping the flow of chips into paper.

Pulpmaking

The pulp made at Androscoggin was of two types: Kraft pulp (produced chemically) and groundwood pulp (produced mechanically). Kraft pulp was far more important to the high-quality white papers produced at Androscoggin, accounting for 80 percent of all the pulp used. Kraft pulp makes strong paper. (*Kraft* is German for strength. A German invented the Kraft pulp process in 1884.) A paper's strength generally comes from the overlap and binding of long fibers of softwood; only chemically was it initially possible to separate long wood fibers for suspension in water. Hardwood fibers are generally smaller and thinner and help smooth the paper and make it less porous.

The groundwood pulping process was simpler and less expensive than the Kraft process. It took high-quality spruce and fir logs and pressed them continuously against a revolving stone that broke apart the wood's fibers. The fibers, however, were smaller than those produced by the Kraft process and, although used to make newsprint, were useful at Androscoggin in providing "fill" for the coated publication gloss papers of machines 2 and 3, as will be described later.

The chemical Kraft process worked by dissolving the lignin that bonds wood fibers together. It did this in a tall pressure cooker, called a *digester*, by "cooking" the chips in a solution of caustic soda (NaOH) and sodium sulfide (Na_2S), which was termed the "white liquor." The two digesters at Androscoggin were continuous digesters; chips and liquor went into the top, were cooked together as they slowly settled down to the bottom, and were drawn off the bottom after about three hours. By this time, the white liquor had changed chemically to "black liquor"; the digested chips were then separated from this black liquor.

Upon leaving the digester, the digested chips entered the blow tank, which was maintained at a significantly lower pressure than the pressurized continuous digester. The pressure difference literally exploded the wood fibers apart, since there was no lignin left to bond them together.

The black liquor entered a separate four-step recovery process. Over 95 percent of the black liquor could be reconstituted as white liquor, thereby saving on chemical costs and significantly lowering pollution. The four-step process involved (1) washing the black liquor from the cooked fiber to produce weak black liquor, (2) evaporating the weak black liquor to a thicker consistency, (3) combustion of this heavy black liquor with sodium sulfate (Na_2So_4), and redissolving the smelt, yielding a "green liquor" (sodium carbonate), and (4) adding lime, which reacted with the green liquor to produce white liquor. The last step was known as recaust.

Meanwhile, the wood-fiber pulp was purged of impurities like bark and dirt by spinning the mixture in centrifugal cleaners. The pulp was then concentrated by removing water from it so that it could be stored and bleached more economically.

By this time, depending on the type of pulp being made, it had been between three and a half and five hours since the chips had entered the pulp mill. Over 90 percent of all the Kraft pulp was bleached; carbonizing tissue was the key product using unbleached pulp. Bleaching took between seven and eight hours. It consisted of a five-step process in which (1) chlorine (Cl_2) was introduced to the pulp and then washed; (2) sodium hydroxide (NaOH) was then added to the pulp and washed; (3) chlorine dioxide (ClO_2) was introduced; (4) the ClO_2 was extracted once again with sodium hydroxide; and then (5) ClO_2 was reintroduced to the pulp. The result was like fluffy cream of wheat. By this time the pulp was nearly ready to made into paper.

From the bleachery, the stock of pulp was held for a short time in storage so that a string of additives (for example, filler clay, resins, brighteners, alum, dyes) could be mixed into the pulp according to the recipe for the paper grade being produced. Here, too, "broke" (paper wastes from the mill itself) was recycled into the pulp. The pulp was then once again cleaned

Continuous digesters at the pulp mill. These work like pressure cookers, dissolving the lignin bonds between wood fibers. (*Courtesy of International Paper Company*)

and blended into an even consistency before moving to the papermaking machine itself.

Papermaking

The paper machine was a simply awesome engineering creation, stretching hundreds of feet. At Androscoggin, there were five of varying size. The paper machine had a wet end and a dry end. The pulp entered the machine at the head-box, which released the heavily diluted pulp through a slit onto a moving belt of synthetic fabric. This belt was called the "wire" because originally it was made of bronze mesh. Many paper machines still used the bronze "wire."

As the wire with its deposit of pulp stock moved away from the headbox, water drained through it. Suction was also applied. Within 60 feet after the headbox slit, so much water had been removed that it could be said the wire carried paper, rather than a suspension of pulp in water. From the wire, huge woolen felts picked up the paper "web" and started it through a series of rollers and steam-heated drying drums, which pressed and evaporated even more water out of the web. If the paper was to be coated, the coating would be applied first to one side of the paper and then to the other and more drying done. If the paper was to be shiny, it would be pressed on smooth, shiny rollers called calenders. Drying and pressing having been done, the paper was essentially finished and was picked up from the machine on winders.

The speeds at which all this happened were incredible. The fastest machines (#2 and #3, devoted to publication gloss) produced over a mile of paper every two minutes. This great speed was made possible by continual improvements made by the machine's builders and by computerized process controls, which constantly adjusted the machine's settings based on the values registered by numerous electronic sensors scattered along the length of the machine.

Once on the winders, the "logs" of paper could be slit directly into widths the customers had ordered, or they could be slit into two logs of equal width and stored until needed. These stored logs, called "parent logs," were then placed on rewinders for successive slitting to customer order. Once cut to order, rolls were packaged, labeled, and then shipped.

MAINTAINING THE ENVIRONMENT

Being a relatively new mill, Androscoggin had environmental control equipment designed into it. Pulp and paper mills were large users of water. Androscoggin took water from the river, filtered it, and then used it in the process. Before being released back to the river, the water was treated in three stages to remove the effluent it had picked up.

1. A primary clarifier (two large cone-shaped basins) allowed particles to settle to the bottom. A slow-moving rake forced the settled sludge to the middle, where it was removed to be burned.
2. In a 37-acre lagoon the clarified effluent was aerated by a collection of churning fountains, and a special collection of microorganisms broke down the effluent over the course of seven or eight days.
3. A secondary clarifier (two more large basins) settled more solids from the water.

The entire treatment process took about 10 days.

Since waste water treatment at paper mills was still a relatively new enterprise, it was not as well understood as it would be in the years to come. While the water released to the river met the standard, there were variations in the quality of the discharge that were not completely understood. This was a source of management concern and technological effort.

Air pollution control was another area where great strides had been made since the early 1960s. Gas collection systems to collect and burn noncondensible gases from the digester and evaporators had helped to eliminate the rotten egg smell that had been characteristic of paper mills. Scrubbers on the stacks at An-droscoggin had gone even further in removing sulphur and other particulates from the smoke and air at the mill. Also, using black liquor oxidation had helped in odor removal.

THE DESIGN OF THE ANDROSCOGGIN MILL

Vertical Integration

The Androscoggin Mill was vertically integrated; that is, it combined pulpmaking and papermaking at the same site. Not all mills, especially not the older ones, were designed to combine both activities. Several advantages argued strongly in favor of vertical integration:

1. Integration removed the transportation costs of transporting pulp between a pulp mill and a paper mill. Vertical integration eliminated the double handling of pulp, a cost saving in any event. In addition, because the mill shipped all over the country, transportation costs for finished paper were not affected significantly by the mill's location; and so a location near the supply of pulp was highly desirable. Pulp drying and reslushing costs were also eliminated.
2. Integration provided for better quality control. Since the quality of the paper produced depended heavily on the quality of the pulp, vertical integration permitted hour-by-hour control over the quality of pulp entering each paper machine. Such control greatly reduced the chances for paper breaks on the machine and eliminated any quality problems caused by old pulp or other deficiencies.
3. The wood preparation and pulpmaking operations generated sawdust, bark, chemicals, and wood chips that could be burned as fuel

for the whole plant, thus cutting down on plant-wide energy costs.

Although the Androscoggin Mill integrated pulpmaking and papermaking, the extent of the mill's vertical integration could have been even broader. For example, only about 40 percent of the wood used at the mill was cut from land owned by International Paper. The company could have integrated backward even more by raising that 40 percent figure. It chose not to do so, however, because the 40 percent figure, and modest variations around it, (1) permitted good forest management of International Paper's own land and (2) meant that the company could add directly to the area's economy by purchasing from independents. There were no substantial cost differences between independent and company tree harvesting. Only if independent loggers could not supply the mill's needs would the company have harvested more from its own land.

By the same token, the operations at Androscoggin could have been extended by forward integration, so that the plant converted more of its paper into end uses (for example, sheets of bond paper rather than rolls of it, carbonizing of the tissue rather than simply its base stock fabrication). The company chose not to do this as well. For one thing, adding converting facilities would have greatly increased Androscoggin's already large size and would have diluted management's attention from the mission of producing quality paper efficiently. Converting operations were also best located closer to markets, since the nature of conversion often placed the paper in bulkier and more awkward packages that were harder to ship and were often shipped in smaller quantities than Androscoggin's full truck and rail carloads. Splitting conversion from papermaking, at least for white papers, meant lower overall transport costs, whereas

there were no real economies in the linking of the two operations.

Capacity

Over time, the size and capacity of individual paper machines had grown enormously. There were distinct advantages to this large scale of operation, since the largest and latest machines could produce more tons of paper per worker, thus reducing costs. At Androscoggin, for example, before 1981, machines 2 and 5 both manufactured carbonizing tissue. Machine 2, built in 1965, could produce paper 208 inches wide at a speed of 1750 feet per minute. Machine 5, in contrast, built in 1977, could produce paper 230 inches wide at a rate of 1800 feet per minute. In only 12 years, the capacity of the machine per unit of time had increased by nearly 26 percent. The capacity difference between machines 1 and 4 was even more striking—31 percent. The increases in machine size and speed enabled the newer mills to house fewer paper machines and employ fewer workers than older mills and yet produce more paper.

At its current size, the Androscoggin Mill was about as large as it was likely to grow. In 1980, the company rebuilt paper machine 2 and converted its production from carbonizing tissue to lightweight publication gloss. The project, which cost $71 million, included the addition of some groundwood pulping, supercalenders, and coating preparation processes. The output rates of its five paper machines (over 500,000 tons per year, up from approximately 410,000 tons per year before the conversion of machine 2), its two continuous digesters, its groundwood mill, and its three woodrooms were all reasonably well balanced. As it was, the pulp mill had been deliberately built larger so that another mill down the river and other International Paper mills could be supplied with pulp.

Paper machine 5, built in 1977. (*Courtesy of International Paper Company*)

Location

The Androscoggin Mill's general location in central Maine was attributable largely to three factors:

1. The production of strong, quality white office papers demanded long wood fibers. This demand favored a Maine location because cold winter weather favors the production of longer fibers in both the softwood and hardwood trees that Maine grows in abundance.

2. A paper mill uses so much water that it has to be located on either a lake or a river, and preferably a river because of environmental factors.

3. This part of central Maine enjoyed the availability of a good supply of labor.

Technology

In pulpmaking and papermaking, keeping abreast of the latest changes in process equipment and technology is critical to a company's continued success. At International Paper the main responsibility for keeping up with technology rested with the corporate staff. The staff was also instrumental in the selection of major new equipment or process changes. The plant, however, did play an important role by providing managers (such as the plant engineer or the paper mill superintendent) who joined the corporate staff in studying any new capacity addition or process technology change. This team was responsible for developing the capital appropriation request and its supporting documents. (More will be said about this capital appropriation request procedure in Chapter 7.)

Loading the Factory

Production Planning

Orders for any of the white papers produced at Androscroggin would be taken by the company's central order department in New York. Orders, as they were received, were placed in the next available open time in the planned weekly production cycles. One week before the start of the next weekly cycle, the manager of operations control planned the production schedule for that cycle. This production schedule allocated the types and weights of paper to be produced at each mill by each machine for every day of the weekly cycle. These machine assignments and the orders they represented were then transmitted to each of the company's plants.

Each quarter a linear program was run to develop the optimum schedule. Marketing and customer constraints were factored into the quarterly plan by operations control. This plan was reviewed with product line managers and was used to establish weekly cycles.

The assignment of types and weights of paper to each paper machine was a sophisticated en-

terprise. Because the company's machines were all slightly different from one another, due primarily to their different vintages, their capabilities differed. That is, they were often relatively more successful and/or more cost efficient at making certain types and weights of paper than others. In assigning products to machines, therefore, the corporation took care to make the assignments in such a way that the company's total contribution to profits and overhead was maximized. This assigning required not only information on the mix of papers demanded for the period and on machine capabilities, but on distribution and transportation costs as well. Thus, for some grades, colors, or weights of paper, depending on the situation, Androscoggin might have filled an order that might otherwise have been filled by a mill much closer to the customer.

At present, Androscoggin's five paper machines were likely to be assigned the following "paper machine products":

- Machine 1—various types of bond or offset paper in white or colors
- Machine 2—coated publication gloss
- Machine 3—coated publication gloss
- Machine 4—various types of bond, ledger, envelope, and tablet paper (all white)
- Machine 5—carbonizing tissue

Since machine 4 was both larger and faster than machine 1, it was devoted to fewer different kinds of paper and thus to longer production runs than machine 1. In that way, the mill could produce more total paper than if machine 4 continually had to be stopped and reset for different colors, grades, or weights. Better to stop and start machine 1 for such changes.

Demand for paper products was cyclical in nature. Volume requirements tracked the general economy very closely, although lagging it slightly both upward and downward. In good economic times, Androscoggin and other mills

Paper machine 4 (Courtesy of International Paper Company)

could be running flat out, with sales so strong that customers had to be put on allocation and orders monitored very closely. This situation was far different from some recessionary times when mills took any order and still had to cut back production.

While the company's central order department (operations control) decided what would be produced on what machine on which days, the mill still had its own considerable production planning problems. Customer orders not only specified the type of paper but also the size (width) to be cut, the quantity (the diameter of the roll), and some other features. In planning

for any specific run on a paper machine, the mill wanted to group together all those orders calling for the same diameter and in such a way that the entire width of the paper machine's output was accounted for. The mill did not like to leave any waste, since even an inch of paper unaccounted for could cost the company forgone revenue of several thousand dollars. The mill used a computer program to optimize paper machine trim.

The mill also wanted to schedule slitting the rolls to minimize additional handling. This goal meant slitting as much off the winder as possible; small widths, however, should be cut from the center portion to reduce the risk of distortion in slitting.

Three production planners scheduled orders on the mill's five machines. They had to remain flexible enough to allow at least some changes in customer orders as late as the Wednesday before the start of the next week's production. The mill also had to schedule trucks and railcars for order shipments.

Inventories and Purchasing

Most of the wood the Androscoggin Mill used was provided by contract for 10,000 to 100,000 cords per year. International Paper did not cut its own wood, but contracted that task out as well. The company's woodlands division was responsible for purchasing the mill's wood and managing the woodyard at economical inventory levels. In addition, the mill stood ready to purchase, by weight, the wood of small, independent loggers without prior commitments being made. The mill did, however, deliberately seek the building up of wood in inventory in the fall and winter so that the spring thaw and the mud it brought did not disrupt the mill as it disrupted logging. It was not uncommon to have 30 days of production in pulp wood inventory.

All the work-in-process inventories were small and temporary, used mainly to permit the mixing of different types of wood chips or pulp.

The extent of finished goods inventory varied. Comparatively few finished goods were held for the products of machines 2, 3, and 5 (publication gloss and carbonizing tissue). Some were kept to permit stray order fulfillment or order amendments, but most paper production was soon headed out the door, waiting only long enough for all items in the order to be gathered together. The parent log and finished goods inventories for machine 1 (bond and offset papers) were very much larger, typically about 15 days

of production. Such a large inventory was required to meet customer needs on any of the 48 paper machine products that machine 1 was qualified to manufacture, while keeping to a minimum the number of machine setups over the course of a year.

At Androscoggin, all responsibilities for production planning, loading machines, product distribution to customers, and finished goods inventories rested with the planning, scheduling, and distribution department because it was felt that all of these items affected one another at the plant and should be controlled by the same authority.

THE WORKFORCE

The Androscoggin Mill employed about 1200 people, about 175 of whom were salaried. The 1000 or so hourly employees (paid according to the hours worked), were represented by three international unions. The United Paper Workers International Union represented the woodyard, woodroom, pulp mill, paper mill, maintenance, finishing, and shipping workers; the International Brotherhood of Firemen and Oilers represented the power house employees and plant electricians; and the Office and Professional Employees International Union represented many of the office and clerical workers at the mill. The agreements were specific to Androscoggin and had been negotiated by the plant's management.

Work was defined as either day work or tour (shift) work. Most work was in fact tour work. The first tour or shift worked from 7 A.M. to 3 P.M., the second from 3 P.M. to 11 P.M., and the third from 11 P.M. to 7 A.M. Each worker remained at his or her position until relieved by the next shift's worker so that continuity of production was ensured. The three shifts were manned by four separate crews; on any given

	Monday Tuesday Wednesday Thursday Friday Saturday Sunday	Monday Tuesday Wednesday Thursday Friday Saturday Sunday	Monday Tuesday Wednesday Thursday Friday Saturaday Sunday	Monday Tuesday Wednesday Thursday Friday Saturday Sunday
7:00 A.M.— 3:00 P.M.	A A A A A D D	D D D D D C C	C C C C C B B	B B B B B A A
3:00 P.M.—11:00 P.M.	(1) D D D D C C C	(2) C C C C B B B	(3) B B B B A A A	(4) A A A A D D D
11:00 P.M.— 7:00 A.M.	C C B B B B B	B B A A A A A	A A D D D D D	D D C C C C C
OFF DAY	B B C C D A A	A A B B C D D	D D A A B C C	C C D D A B B

Notes:
1. Schedule repeats every 4 weeks.
2. Three out of every 4 weeks each shift works 5 days and is off 2.
3. One out of every 4 weeks each shift works 6 days and is off 1.
4. One out of every 4 weeks each shift works 5 days and has a 4-day weekend.
5. Average hours worked, 42.
6. Average hours paid, 48.

FIGURE A2   Shift schedule for International Paper Company's Androscoggin Mill. (From Labor Agreement, p. 57)

day, one crew would be off. Each crew worked an average of 42 hours each week, scheduled as three work weeks of five days and one work week of six days in every four weeks. The crews rotated among the shifts; over the span of four weeks, each crew worked seven consecutive days on each shift separated by breaks of four days, two days, and one day. (See the shift schedule in Figure A2.) Sunday work was paid at a rate of time and one-half; second and third shift work was awarded a special "shift differential" increase. In total, these rate increases added six hours worth of regular pay to the average of 42 hours worked.

Even though one crew or another was at the mill 24 hours a day, there were still some occasions that warranted overtime pay. Sometimes, for example, a worker's failure to report on time would precipitate an overtime situation for another worker. Other times—generally extra work situations—management would request overtime work of some individuals—

for example, to help during a machine changeover.

All of the jobs in the mill were classified and assigned different rates of pay according to the hierarchy of knowledge and responsibilities required. When job openings came up, usually precipitated by a worker's transferring or terminating for one reason or another, workers in the next lower position were advanced according to seniority, assuming they demonstrated the abilities required of the new job. When a high-level job became vacant, a cascading of open positions was triggered, as workers moved up in the hierarchy. Transfers within the mill were permitted, in addition to promotions within the same department. Seniority governed transfers as well. For most hourly workers, the typical career path would entail transfers and promotions up to the highest paying jobs and/or from tour work to day work.

Management's relations with the unions were harmonious and constructive. Worker com-

Very few people were needed to work in the power plant control room. (*Courtesy of International Paper Company*)

plaints were relatively few and, if not adjusted on the job, could be adjusted by a four-step grievance procedure involving successively higher levels of union and management officials. The fourth and final step was arbitration, which was seldom invoked—perhaps once a year. About three-quarters of the complaints involved the procedures for assigning overtime or emergency work. Overtime had to be distributed more or less equally among the workers when and where an overtime situation was created.

Over the years, as papermaking equipment grew in size, speed, and sophistication (particularly with the advent of computerized process controls), papermaking became less and less an art and more and more a science. This change left its imprint on the workforce. Not only could a new paper mill be operated with fewer work-

ers than an old one, but the requisite worker skills were less manual and more cerebral. The latest breed of papermakers were more highly educated, in general, and more analytical. As one would expect, some of the older workers were frightened by the automation and its demands on them. Management had to be understanding of this, and considerable resources were expended on training. Fortunately, any worker anxiety about automation was not evident in labor-management relations.

CONTROLLING THE OPERATION

The entire papermaking process at Androscoggin was designed to manufacture paper with as little downtime as possible. Equipment maintenance could generally be scheduled during the periodic changing of the paper machine's "clothing" (that is, changing the worn wire and felt). Process control equipment and workforce skills were geared to react instantly to production disruptions, like paper breaks, or to product changes in weight or color. The time it took to correct a disruption like a paper break varied enormously (from, say, three minutes to an hour). But the average break time was in the 10- to 15-minute range. A color change normally took about 10 minutes, and a careful weight change could be done without any downtime.

Paper was continually being tested for quality, and the feedback to the workforce was swift so that any needed adjustments could be made. In general, however, operations at the mill could be described as quiet and watchful. Because the elements of the process were so interdependent, skilled managers and workers were required in every phase of the mill's operations. Indeed, many of the mill's supervisors had been promoted out of the ranks and were thus intimately familiar with the mill's operations.

Changes in the process, routine capital acquisition and maintenance were the province of plant engineering. Plant engineering was constantly engaged in projects. Here is a sampling:

- A new, larger storage tank for broke (waste paper) for machine 4.
- A proposal to dry bark with exhaust gases.
- Converting boilers from oil to coal fuel.
- Replacing a worn section of a debarking drum.

- Installing steam meters.
- Overseeing the repair of a roof.
- Laying out specifications for a new gas scrubber.
- Replacing winders and supercalenders with state-of-the-art equipment.

EVALUATING MILL PERFORMANCE

The mill was evaluated as a cost center; it had no control or authority over prices, markets, or revenues. The mill operated to a budget. Given a sales forecast from marketing in New York, prices, and a product mix, the mill developed standard costs for producing the quantity of each paper product forecasted. The budget reflected these standard costs and the mill was held to the budget. However, if the product mix changed, the resulting cost changes were charged to marketing, not the mill. The mill was accountable only for those costs over which it had control.

While the efficient production of paper was an important goal, it was by no means the only aspect of mill operations that was evaluated. Others played an important role: employee safety; management and worker training; commitment to environmental controls (not only meeting present standards, but keeping the environmental control equipment balanced in capacity with the rest of mill operations and advancing in technology); expenditures for new capital appropriations and for maintenance; and industrial relations.

PART TWO
DISCUSSION

The International Paper Company is in no way responsible for the following views and presentation. They remain solely the responsibility of the author.

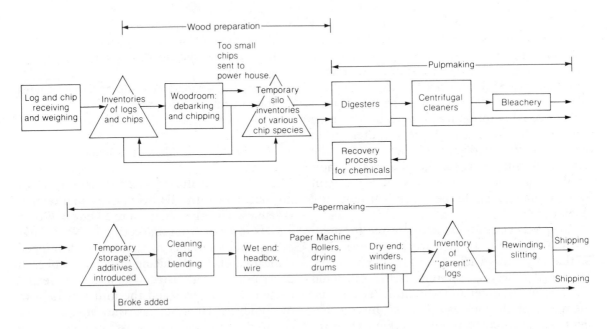

FIGURE A3   Process flow diagrams for International Paper Company's Androscoggin Mill.

THE PROCESS FLOW

The process of making paper, while a frightfully complicated endeavor, follows a clear-cut and rigid pattern. All of the paper that the Andro-scoggin Mill produces—however different in appearance, weight, and feel—proceeds through essentially the same production steps, from logs of wood in the woodyard to "logs" of paper at the shipping dock. This kind of production process can be readily portrayed in a diagram like Figure A3, which is commonly called a *process flow diagram*.

The process flow diagram of Figure A3 is a fairly general one and could be made considerably more detailed. Whether more detail is desirable depends, naturally, on the use to which a process portrait like Figure A3 is put. Several points about the diagram ought to be noted:

1. Actual processing operations are usually distinguished from storage points in the process. In the diagram, processing operations are indicated by rectangles and inventories by triangles. (Rectangles are used here because it is easier to fit the descriptions in them. However, typically in industrial enginering, circles are used to indicate processing operations and rectangles are used to indicate tests and inspections. See Figure 3-1 for the standard conventions.)

2. Several operations could be bypassed and are indicated by two arrows emanating from one operation and pointing to others. For example, all of the woodroom's output need not have gone directly to the silos but could have been placed in the woodyard for storage. Similarly, the bleachery was bypassed by pulp destined to become carbonizing tis-

FIGURE A4   Information flow diagram for International Paper Company's Androscoggin Mill.

sue, and the rewinders were superfluous for those orders that could be slit directly from the main winders.

3. The continuous nature of the process is evident by the very low level of inventories and by the designation of the silo chip and pulp additive inventories as temporary.

INFORMATION IN THE PROCESS

A production process is more than a series of operations performed on a collection of materials. What a process flow diagram can depict—the sequencing of process steps, the choice of equipment and technology, the capacity of process steps, the tasks required of the workforce—while critical, is only part of the story. Another part of the story involves the procedures that have been put in place to direct the process flow. We can usefully think of a companion to the process flow diagram—namely, an information flow diagram. Figure A4 provides an example of what might be placed in such a diagram. Note how the actions of different layers of managers and workers are distinguished in the diagram and how information is fed back up the channels of communication.

Most of the information flow in this continuous flow process is directed from the top down. Feedback is needed only to acknowledge receipt of information and to signal significant problems in the actual workings of the process. The process is designed with such care and the workforce so carefully trained that workers do not have to be in repeated touch with management to do their jobs well. The information needs of the process simply are not great, although the thought and effort standing behind that information (such as scheduling tasks of both the corporate office and the mill itself) are considerable and sophisticated.

CAPACITY

Capacity in this continuous flow process is fairly well defined and can be spoken of in physical terms—namely, tons of pulp and paper manufactured and cords of wood consumed. Likewise, there is a straightforward meaning to the term *capacity utilization*. In fact, all one needs to do is check to see whether the paper machines are running. If they are, capacity (all of it) is being used. Simply compiling the time the paper machines have run over some period of time and dividing that sum by the total available machine-hours gives a splendid indication of capacity utilization. Indeed, only when sales are insufficient or when the machine is broken or down temporarily for a setup or a change of "clothing" would we expect capacity utilization that was less than 100 percent.

Despite the relative ease with which we can talk of capacity and capacity utilization in this continuous flow process, on closer inspection of the concept a number of disquieting ambiguities surface. The ambiguities surface largely because the capacity of the mill is dependent on a number of factors. Among them:

1. *Product mix.* Some grades and weights of paper are more difficult to produce than others. The Androscoggin Mill's carbonizing tissue, a very thin paper, must run at a slower speed than the stronger, thicker publication gloss. Newer machines, of course, are apt to run at faster speeds than older machines, given the same kind of paper. But, given similar vintage paper machines, thin papers and high-quality finish papers have to run at slower speeds than others. Thus comparing

the capacity of the Androscoggin Mill with that of other paper mills or with its own in other years can only be done with some understanding of the product mixes involved.

2. *Run lengths.* Every time a paper machine must be set up for a different grade, weight, or color of paper, capacity is lost. Although some changes are inherently more time-consuming than others, every change implies at least a small reduction in theoretical capacity. The capacity of machine 1 was somewhat lower than that of machine 4 at least in part because machine 1 was scheduled to produce 48 different paper machine products in white and in colors, whereas machine 4 was primarily devoted to white.

3. *Maintenance.* A paper machine might also lose capacity because it was being repaired or because its "clothing" was being changed. The machines that could be kept running until only regularly scheduled maintenance interrupted production were those that lost the least capacity.

4. *Slitting schedule.* Slitting paper "logs" from the winders and rewinders was purposely scheduled so that as little waste as possible resulted. The more successful the schedule, the less waste there was.

For these reasons, the terms *capacity* and *capacity utilization* were not as unambiguous as might have been anticipated. Nevertheless, the process was extraordinarily well balanced and smooth-running, and this made discussion of capacity and capacity utilization easy.

DEMANDS OF THE PROCESS
ON WORKERS

Over the years, papermaking, like other continuous flow processes, has become a process where increasingly machinery "does it all."

Pulpmakers and papermakers have been systematically removed from playing their traditional direct "hands-on" roles in the process. Instead, papermakers are more and more "indirect" labor—setters, monitors, and repairers of equipment that makes paper much faster and more reliably than any crew of traditional papermakers could using the older technology and their own skills. Where papermaking was "art," it is now "science." The lengthy apprenticeships from sixth hand on a paper machine to machine tender are no longer so easily justified by the need to learn the art. Despite the change to science, the level of skill required in the process remains high. The workforce may have been removed to gazing at control panels, adjusting knobs, and throwing switches, but the technical demands of the process are even higher in a modern, as compared to traditional, paper mill. Training is therefore an important consideration and an apprenticeship, while different from before, is still required. The lines of worker progression in the mill are clear (in fact, they are diagrammed for each department in the labor agreement), and workers are paid accordingly.

What comprises any job in the mill is fairly restricted. That is, the content of most jobs is small, although it widens as one approaches the prestige jobs in the mill (such as machine tender, pulp mill operator, control room operator). Pay is invariably by the hour worked.

Skilled workers are needed everywhere in the process, largely because the process is so interdependent. If one aspect of the process falls down (for example, quality of the pulp), another aspect is likely to suffer (increased risk of a paper break).

DEMANDS OF THE PROCESS ON MANAGEMENT

The interdependence and capital intensity (a high ratio of plant and equipment value to labor payroll) of a continuous flow process like papermaking place tremendous demands on management, especially in the realms of coordination and of the choice and care of equipment. Furthermore, these demands are made not only of the mill's own management but of the corporation as a whole. Profitability in such processes largely rests on (1) assuring that the proper technology is selected, (2) balancing the capacities of all segments of the process so that as little capacity goes to waste as possible, (3) scheduling the use of that capacity as completely as possible, (4) keeping the equipment running up to speed and up to quality standards. Let us review these points in turn, and (5) an ever-continuing effort to improve in all areas of the operation.

Choice of Technology

The march of technological change is inexorable. While the output of continuous flow processes seldom changes by much, there can be upheavals in how that output is manufactured. The introduction of process control equipment to papermaking is a case in point. Management must be constantly aware of equipment advances across the industry, and savvy manufacturers engage in regular dialogues with equipment makers so that their own ideas and needs can be tried out in new equipment designs. The impact of technology is so fundamental that the corporate staffs of continuous flow process industries are usually charged with monitoring and selecting major new technology for all the plants of the company. Individual plants may have representatives on any plant and equipment choice studies, but corporate level managers are apt to take the lead in the study and decision-making process.

What is true for technology decisions is also true for decisions on how vertically integrated the process should be. This is generally also a corporate decision and one that is the province of corporate staff.

Balancing Capacities

The papermaking process, as we have seen, can be broken down into distinct segments (as in the process flow diagram); associated with each of these segments are machines and other equipment, often very large. Frequently, these machines and equipment are manufactured by different companies and do not come in just any size. It is management's responsibility to select the equipment for each process segment that represents both the suitable technology and size for the contemplated plant or plant expansion. One segment's capacity should be balanced, as well as possible, against that of other segments, so that as little extra capacity as possible has to be financed. After all, in an integrated, continuous flow process the capacity of the entire process is determined by the lowest capacity segment.

In reality, balancing process segment capacities is a difficult chore, and choices have to be made as to which process segments are to be assigned whatever excess capacity may exist. Often such a choice entails an investigation of equipment costs, with the relatively cheaper equipment being assigned any excess capacity. In papermaking, for example, the big bucks get chewed up in financing paper machines and bleacheries. Woodrooms, digesters, and rewinders are relatively less expensive. Thus, frequently, the spare capacity is to be found at the ends of the process (woodrooms, rewinders) rather than in the middle (bleacheries, paper machines). Having spare capacity at the rewinders increases the flexibility of the process as well to modifications of the product mix or order specifications. With excess capacity in place, unusual orders can be serviced without undue strain or delay.

The need for, and the expense of, maintaining a balance of capacities in a continuous flow process like the Androscoggin Mill are dramatically highlighted by the recent rebuilding of paper machine 2 and its conversion from carbonizing tissue to publication gloss. That conversion speeded up the flow of paper from about 20 miles per hour to nearly 35 miles per hour and raised the mill's net yearly tonnage by about 100,000 tons. To accommodate a change of that magnitude meant altering the pulpmaking capabilities of the mill as well as its papermaking capabilities. When process segments are tightly coupled, capacity changes echo throughout the entire process.

Scheduling

Large, high-speed continuous flow processes are geared to high-volume production of standard items. Typically, they are low-cost processes, but they often sacrifice the ability to respond quickly to changing customer specifications without introducing a lot of waste and thus destroying their low-cost character. In order then to satisfy customer orders at low cost, continuous flow processes must schedule their capacity well in advance, offering their customers longer lead times than may be common in other types of processes or else filling orders out of in-process or finished goods inventories.

At International Paper, as we saw, the broad "paper machine products" scheduling proceeded one week in advance of production and the schedule devised was for a one-week period. The customer orders that were produced in each run, however, were set at the plant level only two days in advance of the production cycle. As many customer orders as could be slit right off the winder were scheduled, to eliminate rehandling of paper logs. More exotic orders for special colors, grades, or weights from machine 1 were often filled out of finished goods inventory to avoid having to schedule special production runs. Scheduling at International Paper, as these observations indicate, was a sophisticated enterprise.

The idea, of course, behind such sophisticated scheduling is to keep the process flowing as continuously as possible. Generally, the process could be more responsive to customer orders, but to do so would necessarily mean interrupting production to set up equipment. Capacity would be reduced and costs increased. By stretching out deliveries or by keeping finished goods inventories, the continuous flow process can keep its costs down.

Equipment Maintenance

Most continuous flow process plants are evaluated as cost centers. As with the Androscog-gin Mill, such plants are not given authority over revenues (no sales forces are tied to them), and so the plant is judged by how well it can adhere to a budget. The plant has an incentive then to keep its equipment well maintained; if it does not, it risks assuming costs that can be very high (equipment breakdowns force high repair costs and expensive makeup work). Given such an evaluation scheme, most managers would opt to spend all of their budget for maintenance to avoid the chance, however slim, of suffering a huge cost increase and an instantly bad reputation for plant management.

QUESTIONS

1. The changeover of machine 2 from carbonizing tissue to publication gloss involved changes in other parts of the process. Why was this so? Speculate in as much detail as possible about the kinds of changes that would have had to occur as a consequence of such a paper machine changeover.

2. Much of the "higher level" production planning for the Androscoggin Mill occurs in International Paper's New York headquarters, whereas "lower level" production planning occurs at the mill itself. Why is there this division of responsibilities? What would happen if New York handled all the production planning or if Androscoggin did it all?

3. If you were a production planner at the Androscoggin Mill, what might you be most likely to consider important? Why? How would these priorities affect your production plans?

4. Why did the Androscoggin Mill choose vertical integration for its design? What would some of the advantages and disadvantages of increased forward integration for the mill be?

5. How is the workforce organized at the mill? What are some of the operational implications of this workforce composition?

6. As a manager, which aspects of a continuous flow process appeal to you? Which aspects might not?

SITUATION FOR STUDY A-1
BEACON GLASS WORKS

Beacon Glass Works, located in Marysville, West Virginia, manufactures hollow glass tubing for use in catalytic converters. Beacon is a large division of one of the leading glass manufacturers, and was founded when the Environmental Protection Agency strongly urged the development of antipollution devices for trucks and automobiles. The hollow glass tubing manufactured at Beacon comes in around 30 different size combinations. The lengths are from 6 to 12 inches, and the inside diameter ranges from 1/32 inch to 1/16 inch.

These tubes are produced by extrusion. The molten glass is first forced through a die that determines the inside diameter of the tube. The tube then is cooled and cut to the proper length. After the cut edges have been finished so that they are smooth, the product is sent to a holding area where it waits to be packaged. Once the tubing is packaged, it is again stored, this time awaiting shipment to Beacon's customers, the four major domestic motor vehicle manufacturers.

The extrusion process is basically a make-to-stock operation driven by production scheduling. Based upon anticipated stock shortages, Jose Torrez, the production manager, schedules the next week's production, and the necessary dies are readied. Each die is used until about one month's demand has been produced. Then, the dies are changed and another product with a different inside diameter is run. Actually, since several lengths have the same inside diameter,

several products can be extruded with one extrusion run.

Once the product cools to the proper cutting temperature, the cutting area cuts the proper lengths, again based upon the stock needs determined by the production manager. The product is then stored in a holding area waiting to be packaged. Packaging is usually done to customer order, as different customers want different quantities and want them packaged differently.

Sometimes, however, Jose will schedule the packaging department based on what he believes will be the customer orders, so that he can use the packaging machinery efficiently. This scheduling sometimes results in excess inventory for one customer while another customer's order is backordered because of a stockout.

Jose is concerned that his process scheduling is not as good as it could be and thinks that possibly the first step he should take is to diagram the production flow and the information flow for the process.

1. Diagram the production flow.
2. Diagram the information flow.
3. Discuss possible problem areas for Beacon's production process.

SITUATION FOR STUDY A-2
SUNMEADOW DAIRY

Sunmeadow Dairy produced and distributed a variety of products including whole milk, skim milk, 2 percent milk, ice milk, fruit drinks, buttermilk, eggnog, chocolate milk, and many different mixes used to produce ice cream. The production of milk, however, was 90 percent of the operation.

From 8 A.M. until 5 P.M., raw milk (unpasteurized milk direct from the farm) arrived by refrigerated tanker truck at or below 42° F. The raw milk was pumped from the tanker (capacity 5500 gallons) to one of three refrigerated storage silos (capacity 70,000 gallons total) adjacent to the receiving area. During this transfer, the milk flowed through a plate heat exchanger to lower its temperature to 37°. From these silos, the milk was pumped to the second floor as needed for production and was stored in four of six storage tanks. The empty tanks were used for mixing and diluting the raw milk, which was 3.5 to 4.0 percent butterfat.

Because whole milk contains 3 to 5 percent butterfat (depending on its source) and some skim milk products contain as little as 0.5 percent butterfat, a certain percentage of butterfat had to be removed from the raw milk. A separator was employed to remove the excess butterfat. (A separator is a centrifuge in which raw milk is spun at high speed, forcing the separation of the butterfat from the heavier milk and allowing the isolation of the two fractions.) One by-product of this process contained 40 percent butterfat and was pumped off (at a rate of 1000 to 1500 gallons per day) into nearby holding tanks and shipped to a butter factory once a week. The other by-product was 0.5 percent milk; it was pumped into an empty tank and mixed with 3.5 percent raw milk to obtain the desired butterfat level for the product being packaged next in the plant. This mixing was called "standardizing" the product. From an information chart on obtaining the percentage of butterfat needed for each product, the separator operator determined the exact quantity of each input (3.5 percent milk and 0.5 percent milk) to be mixed in the empty tank.

From the holding tanks the standardized product was pumped into one of two pasteurizers (capacity 1,500 and 4,000 gallons per hour). (Pasteurization is the process of heating raw milk to 161° F for 16 seconds to kill harmful bacteria.) The pasteurized milk was pumped into one of two homogenizers, which blew the milk through a very small opening to break up the fat globules and create a uniform, or homogenous, mixture. The pasteurized, homogenized milk was directed into any one of seven pasteurizing holding tanks to await packaging on the first floor. Because packaging might start as early as 5:30 A.M., pasteurization usually began at midnight—to build a buffer inventory in the holding tanks for the first and second products to be run that day.

Milk could be pumped into one of five packaging processes:

1. The filler filled plastic gallons and half-gallons at a rate of 70 per minute. The plastic containers were made in the blow-molding department and arrived at this machine by overhead conveyor. This conveyor continued through the completely automated processes of filling, capping, and storing the filled containers in metal cases for shipment. These metal cases were stacked six high and sent to the cooler for order filling.

2. The H-75 machine produced paper half-gallons (capacity 75 units per minute) and automatically filled, sealed, and stacked them. Manual attention was needed only to take the wax cardboard containers from the adjacent stockroom and load them into the feed mechanism. Each carton was automatically unfolded, heat-sealed at the bottom, and filled with the product being produced in this run; the excess foam and overfill were drawn off the top, and the carton was heat-sealed. The cartons were then automatically stacked into metal cases and put on the conveyor for the short trip to the cooler.

3. The Q80-110 machine operated the same way as the H-75 but was for half-pints, pints, and quarts (capacity 80 quarts, 110 pints, and 110 half-pints per minute).

4. The NEP 210 machine (capacity 210 half-pints per minute) also operated the same way as the H-75. The unique feature of this process was that it produced only for schools.

5. Using the bag and box filler was a totally manual process for filling five-gallon plastic bags inside boxes. These were shipped to local schools and hospitals for use in self-service milk dispensers.

While each process was running, there was at least one operator with each machine at all times. The high volume of production demanded constant attention and minor adjustments, especially to keep the product from becoming caught in the moving parts.

Once packaged, the product was carried by conveyor from the packaging areas to the 38° F cooler, where it was stored according to how soon it would be used to fill orders on the daily trucks. The cooler operated on a first-in, first-out (FIFO) basis; rotating the product this way kept the buffer stock as fresh as possible, The product was moved to the loading areas on the same conveyor that circulated through the packaging and cooler.

Orders to the dairy were called in by the branches and other customers, usually two or three days in advance. The sales clerks wrote the orders on computer-generated, preaddressed order sheets for each account. Special phone orders and adjustments could be made until shipment, because of the buffer inventory in the cooler. Local orders were written by the drivers of the route trucks while visiting each customer on their daily schedule. The day before shipment, the cooler supervisor scheduled and consolidated all orders for filling based on the usual arrival times of the incoming trucks. Two order copies stayed in the sales office, two copies were sent with the order, and one stayed with the cooler supervisor. After delivery, the signed order copy was compared with the original order and all necessary information was entered into the computer. This update triggered the daily report on actual production, cooler inventory, actual units loaded on all trucks by product line,

and total amount needed for the next day's production. The plant manager received this printout early the following morning.

Two 10-hour shifts were needed to accommodate each day's scheduled production. The same order of production was run each day (such as 2 percent milk first and chocolate last). To accommodate the trucks that started arriving at 4 A.M., the buffer inventory in the cooler at the start of the day for the last two products run might be as high as 60 percent of total production.

The quality control supervisor was responsible for product quality throughout the plant. Quality control was a major factor in the production of milk. As the tankers arrived from the farms, three quality checks were done to make certain the raw milk was within the acceptable range of temperature, bacteria count, and acidity. Except during pasteurization, milk was maintained at 38° F throughout the plant. In addition to the standardization checks for butterfat content, two tests were done after pasteurization to check the bacteria count and type of bacteria still in the milk. Raw milk arrived with a bacteria count of 10,000 to 20,000 per milliliter and was shipped out at about 500 per milliliter. Each worker was acutely aware of the importance of quality control, and all machinery and equipment were thoroughly washed at least once a day to ensure cleanliness. Most of the equipment—including tankers, silos, and storage tanks—was stainless steel to facilitate cleaning and reduce the chances of contamination.

1. Diagram the process and information flows.
2. What do you see as the challenges that the management of the dairy faced?
3. Recently the dairy lost a large contract for supplying milk to a chain of grocery stores. How do you think the loss of sales will affect the operations of the dairy? Be as specific as you can.

A JOB SHOP
Norcen Industries
Jersey Shore, Pennsylvania

It had been years since Joe Gehret finally gave in to his desire to control his own company and resigned his position as general foreman in the machine shop of the Litton Industries plant in Williamsport, Pennsylvania. In July 1967, Joe and a partner (who had since left the firm) began Norcen Industries by selling stock and taking over an old garage in Jersey Shore, about 15 miles west of Williamsport. They initially intended for Norcen to be a plastics distributor and fabricator, but it soon became apparent that both their experience and the demands of industry in north central Pennsylvania dictated a change of course. Norcen quickly became mainly a metal-working machine shop, and the machine shop accounted for almost 90 percent of gross revenues.

The company had experienced reasonably steady growth. In 1981, Norcen moved into a new, 21,000-square-foot building on the outskirts of town. Sales in 1985 had grown to almost $2.25 million and employment to 41.

PART ONE
PROCESS DESCRIPTION

PRODUCTS, SALES, AND
ORDER HANDLING

As a general machine shop, Norcen was capable of producing a seemingly endless succession of small-scale metal and plastic parts that a host of companies typically assembled into machines and other products. Almost all of Norcen's customers were manufacturers, but 95 percent of this business Norcen had to win by submitting low bids. The purchasing departments of Norcen's customer firms generally requested Norcen and at least two other machine shops to "quote" the work they wanted done. The request always specified (1) the number of pieces desired, which varied enormously from ten pieces to over a thousand, (2) the nature of the material required and whether it was supplied by the customer, (3) the design of the piece (a blueprint would be sent), and (4) the date by

29

VARIANCE	PRICE UNIT	PRICE TOTAL	HOURS	MATERIAL	LABOR	SERVICE	COST TOTAL	VOL.	COMP DATE 84	INVOICE	JOB	DATE 84	P.O. NUMBER
	9 20	607 20					13 41	66	2/14	12107	17503	1/4	53368
	9 20	708 40					53 87	77	1/16	11813			
	9 20	57? 60					747 93	63	1/12	11788			
	9 20	322 00					263 14	35	3/19	12419			
	9 20	956 80					37 00	104	3/29	12575			
	9 20	883 20	1369				60 13	96	4/16	12709		84	
	8 90	453 90					483 36	51	4/12	13335	17583	2/8	55590
	8 90	685 30					—	77	4/20	13416			
	9 10	191 10					—	21	8/8	13876			
	9 10	172 40					719 76	19	8/6	13833			
	9 10	464 10					—	51	8/7	13834			
	9 10	336 70					214 59	97	8/15	13911			
	9 10	873 60					222 20	96	8/23	14009			
	9 10	455 00					237 5 50		9/27	14360			
	9 10	1146 60 / 182 40	2181				59 23	126	10/27	14495			
	10 24	1382 40					622 72	135	1/25	15529	18980	10/25	60938
	10 00	1180 00	88.5	Made on 18980			121 79	118	2/8	15668	19206	12/14	61673
	12 24	722 16	26				259 89	59	10/2	18004	20414	9/6	65630

Notes:

1. This record card is for a so-called "transformer" (not what we would ordinarily term a transformer) for a company whose name has been withheld. This part is distinguished at Norcen by its part number, 53147, which also corresponds to a blueprint and a process sheet (see Figure B2).

2. The material to work on is furnished by the customer company.

3. This is a part that Norcen has machined for years. This record card is sheet #3. On this sheet, we can see at the top of the columns that the first order was placed on January 4, 1984, under purchase order (P.O.) number 53368. That job was assigned job number 17503 and consisted of 6 separate shipments of varying shipment dates (such as 2/14, 1/16) and corresponding and separate invoices to the customer (such as 121074, 11813). The shipment quantities varied as well (for example, 66 units, 77 units, 63 units). The total for the entire order is 441 pieces.

   The latest order (#65630), dated 9/10 and shipped 10/2, involved just 59 pieces. It carried job number 20414 and was billed on invoice 18004.

4. The quoted price for the first order on the card (job number 17503) was $9.20 per piece. The total billing for the first invoice (#12107) was $607.20. The total billing for the entire order was the sum of the six relevant invoices, $4,057.20.

5. A total of 136.9 hours of labor were spent fulfilling the first order. The total labor cost of the job was $1,175.44 (the sum of the cost total column).

   For the latest job, a total of 26 hours of labor was expended at a cost of $259.89. The total billing was $722.16 for the 59 pieces shipped, quoted at a price of $12.24 each.

6. Norcen Industries made its charge-out rate in the latest completed job. The labor hours of 26 times the prevailing charge-out rate of $24 per hour equals $624, which is below the actual revenue for the job of $722.16.

7. Two special notations are worth explaining: (1) The latest entry for P.O. number 55590 is a charge of $182.40 for an extra setup. The customer company had not provided the material on time, requiring Norcen Industries to incur an additional, unscheduled setup. Norcen charged the customer for that setup.

   (2) P.O. numbers 60938 and 61673, involving job numbers 18980 and 19206, were able to be run with a single setup. This was advantageous to the shop (denoted by the notation "made on 18980") and resulted in a lower quote for P.O. number 61673.

FIGURE B1   A sample record card for a particiular item manufactured at Norcen Industries.

8. Lillian Gehret used to keep a variance figure for each order, calculated as the difference between the per unit quoted price and the sum of the labor and materials costs on a per unit basis. Joe Gehret found himself using the variance figure less and less in his quote work, so the variance calculation was no longer kept.

9. Record cards such as this one were kept for parts that Norcen expected to work on as repeat business. If it was known for sure that the order was strictly a "one-shot deal," no record was started.

FIGURE B1   (*continued*)

which the order had to be received. During peak years, Norcen bid on as many as 250 such requests each week, knowing that on a long-run average its quote would be accepted about 15 percent of the time. (In the past this figure had sometimes been as high as 40 percent.)

Joe Gehret was responsible for deciding all metalworking quotes. Naturally, it was easier for him to quote jobs that Norcen had done before. Not only did he know the hourly charge-out rate (currently $24–30 per hour), which would cover both direct labor and overhead expenses, but he had a past record of what the piece had actually cost Norcen to make on all previous occasions. (See Figure B1 and the discussion on recordkeeping below.) In addition, Norcen would already have a blueprint of the piece and a "process sheet" (Figure B2), which would outline the steps the shop had previously taken to manufacture it and the time standards for each of those steps. Deciding quotes for pieces Norcen had not previously made was more difficult. In such cases, Joe had to ponder the blueprint and develop,

OFHC Cu					Some company	Transformer	512864			
MATERIAL DESCRIPTION					COMPANY	PART NAME	PART No.			
LINEAL INCHES	AREA (SQ. IN.)	DIMENSIONS			COMPUTATION-MTL. REQD.	PREPARED BY	PG __ OF __		REV.	
EQUIPMENT					OPERATION		ESTIMATED			
FIXTURES & TOOLS	MACH.	SPEED	FEED	No.	DESCRIPTION		No. OF PIECES PER HR.	TIME		
								PER PC.	SET UP	
Arbor, collet				10	Rough face to turn O.D. to size (.972–.974) on Arbor					
				20	Face waterfall drag down off of open end					
				30	Face off other end to .400 long					
				40	Deburr					
Collet, template				50	Dress radius & grind radius in part, holding length to size (.381)					
				60	Deburr					
				70	Inspect					

Notes:
1. A collet holds the workpiece. An arbor is another device to hold the workpiece.
2. A template was used to help guide the grinding.
3. The waterfall was excess metal, a humpline bulge, that had to be machined off the part.
4. Various dimensions were given in steps 10, 30, and 50. They were also available on the blueprint of the part.
5. In the material description, OFHC Cu means oxygen-free copper, which is a very pure copper.

FIGURE B2   A sample process sheet used at Norcen Industries.

ORDER No. _60938_ JOB _18980_

PART No. _53147_ LOT SIZE _____

MATERIAL _Furnished_ _245_

DELIVERY _2/10_

Checked By	Date	Name	Operation	Qty.	Hrs.	Acc. Hrs.
	1/14	R.P.M	255			
DM	1-16	J.L.	Lathe		8.0	8.0
	1-17	JL	LATHE		8.0	16.0
	1-18	JL	"		8.0	24.0
	1-19	JL	"		5.0	29.0
	1-21	JL	"		2.5	31.5
	1-21	Doyle	Deburr		3.9	35.4
	1-22	Doyle	Deburr-Buff		4.2	39.6
DM	1-22	DM.	Set up & Gr.		2.0	41.6
	1-22	O.R.	Gr.		0.7	42.3
JJ	1-23	OR	Gr.		8.0	50.3
DM	1-24	O.R.	Gr		8.0	58.3
JJ	1/25	JJ	Deburr		2.0	60.3
	1-25	Doyle	Wipe-Buff		1.5	61.8
	1/25	JJ	Deburr INSP		1.5	63.3
	135 PCS		To Ship	1/25 JJ		
	1-25	OR	Gr.		8.0	71.3
JJ	1-26	OR	Gr.		2.5	73.8
DM	1-28	OR	Gr.		4.0	77.8
	1-29	OR	Gr.		4.5	82.3
	2-7	Doyle	CLEAN Deburr-Buff		5.2	87.5
	2-8	JJ	INSP		1.0	88.5
	118 Pcs		To Ship	2/8 JJ		

FIGURE B3 A sample of the job sheet used at Norcen Industries.

Notes:

1. This job sheet accompanied job number 18980 around the shop from the initial receipt of materials from the customer (255 pieces on 1/14) until shipments on 1/25 and 2/8 of 135 and 118 pieces, respectively.

2. The lot size on this job changed. It was increased to 245 (253 were actually shipped) when P.O. number 61673 came along, and the shop was able to do both jobs with a single setup.

3. Dates worked, worker initials, operation done, time spent, and total time to date on the order are filled in by each worker after he or she completes working on the job. Periodically, others have checked the order's work (RTM and JJ).

4. The accumulated labor hours are 88.5. This figure is also displayed on the record card.

at least in his mind, a rough-cut process sheet. Sometimes the request for the quote included a process sheet developed by the company itself, and this was a great aid. Other factors such as delivery dates (rush orders, being more trouble, commanded higher margins), and the prevailing load in the shop (the more slack in the shop, the lower the margin) also influenced the quote.

The acceptance of a Norcen quote typically came by phone and was confirmed later by letter. Upon notification of acceptance, Joe's wife,

ORDER No. _60938_   JOB _18980_

PART No. _53147_   LOT SIZE _245_

MATERIAL _____

_____

DELIVERY _2/10_   _10.24_

Checked By	Date	Name	Operation	Qty.	Hrs.	Acc. Hrs.
	1/13	JL	246	50		29
	1/20	GG	33	25	3.5	32.5
		JL	21	25	2.5	35
		OR	231	20	27.2	62.2
		DM	19	00	2	64.2
		DD	71	52	9.6	73.8
			622	72		
		chgd	155.29			
	1/27	OR	72.25		8.5	82.3
	2/3	DD	40.04		5.2	87.5
		GG	9.50		1	88.5
			121.79			
		chgd	15668			

Notes:

1. This job sheet was compiled by Lillian Gehret after job 18980 was completed. The information for the job sheet was derived from (a) the job sheet (Figure B3) that follows the job around the shop, (b) worker time cards (Figure B5), and (c) information on worker hourly rates.

2. The top portion of this job sheet contains the same information as Figure B3 and includes as well the quoted price on the job ($10.24 per piece).

3. Worker times are gathered by the week, with the weeks being dated from their start on a Sunday (1/13, 1/20). Workers' hours spent on this job in each week are listed in the Hrs. column. The cumulative hours for the job as a whole are totaled in the Acc. Hrs. column. In the center columns are listed the worker pay for the week due to the job. By dividing this pay by the hours, one can see that workers have different hourly wages. JL has an hourly wage of $9.50 ($33.25/3.5).

4. The total wage bills for the job are $622.72, charged to invoice 15529, and $121.79, charged to invoice 15668. Recall that job 18980 combined two purchase orders and ran them on the same setup.

FIGURE B4   A sample showing Lillian Gehret's office copy of a job sheet.

Lillian, who was responsible for all bookkeeping, wrote up two copies of a job sheet (Figures B3 and B4). One copy was kept in a record book, and the other was attached to a blueprint and placed in a special tray. Joe was then responsible for looking over each job sheet to see whether any materials not provided by the customer needed to be ordered and whether any tooling needed to be done. Job sheets that awaited materials or tooling were kept in a separate tray. When enough materials were on hand to complete the order, the job sheet and blueprint were placed in a special drawer. This action released the order to the shop.

PLANT AND PERSONNEL

The machine shop operated on two shifts: 6:50 A.M. to 3:20 P.M. and 3:30 P.M. to midnight, with a half-hour break for lunch or dinner and two 10-minute break periods. The day shift consisted of 25 hourly workers, and the evening shift currently ran with only nine workers. (This shift operated primarily the company's direct numerical control (DNC) lathes and mills and was also used to expedite rush jobs.) Norcen's hourly wages (the highest paid by any of the machine shops in the area) started at $8 per hour for unskilled workers and went to $11 per

(Total plant area = 21,000 square feet)

EDM machining area

Coordinate measuring machine

Numeridex computer

General office

First Aid

Packing

Washroom

Lunchroom

Spare, old equipment

Lathes

Warehouse

Saws

Foreman

Tap burner

Milling, drilling tapping

Old mills

Inspection

Drilling

Deburring

Welders

Grinding

Heat treat

Tumble deburring

Loading dock

Workforce (43 total)

1 general manager	2 tool and die makers
1 bookkeeper	31 machine operators
1 foreman	1 inspector/shipper-receiver
3 lead operators	1 utility person
1 computer programmer	1 manager of the plastics business

FIGURE B5 Plant layout and workforce at Norcen Industries.

hour for the most demanding work. This pay was augmented in two ways:

1. Overtime pay at time and a half
2. A bonus plan, payable at Christmas and in the summer

The size of each bonus depended on the fortunes of the company over the previous six months. It was Joe Gehret's policy to distribute as much to the workers as Norcen paid out in dividends to its shareholders; recently this meant an increase of about 40 percent to each worker for 1985, a good year. In leaner years, of course, this bonus was much lower. The size of the bonus for each worker, like the number of vacation days, depended on seniority. The workers recognized this system as an incentive for continued good work. In the words of a lathe and drill press operator: "The better we are to the company, the better the company is to us."

A rough layout of the plant, showing the general groupings of machines, is included as Figure B5. An inventory of the most important machines in the shop, along with their weekly average hours in use, is provided in Table B1.

The Workings of the Shop

Although Joe Gehret spent a good deal of time on the shop floor, responsibility for shop operations rested with Bill Lundy, the shop foreman. Like Joe, Bill had been a shop foreman at Litton Industries. Bill's duties were varied, but his first concern for the smooth running of the shop was to see that all workers were assigned tasks and that they understood these tasks well, both their nature and their time standards. Moreover, Bill knew that it was important to the success of the company that tasks be as-

signed in a way that saved Norcen money. Cost reductions could come about in several ways:

1. Before an operator could machine any of the myriad jobs Norcen was capable of performing, the necessary machine had to be set up. The setup varied from about a half-hour for simple jobs to 8–10 hours for the most complex. An average setup was about 1.5 hours. Since, once set up, the machine could produce any number of pieces with only minor adjustments, it made sense to run full lots whenever possible. In this way, setup costs were spread over all the units in the order.

2. Frequently, especially with automatic equipment, the running time of the machine per piece produced was long enough so that, by staggering operations, a single operator could attend two different machines at the same time. That is, while one piece was being machined, the operator could be working at another machine, typically inserting new material or removing a finished piece. To exploit these possibilities, Joe and Bill had grouped similar kinds of machines together on the shop floor. It was to Norcen's advantage for Bill to identify and to match together those jobs that permitted this kind of labor saving.

3. As might be expected, some operators could perform certain machining tasks relatively better than others and thus held a comparative advantage over other workers in the shop for some jobs. It was worth it for Bill to keep these special capabilities in mind in his assignment of jobs.

4. Cost reductions could also occur through improvements in the process sheets that Bill kept in special binders. Often, changes in the sequence of drilling, cutting, milling, grinding, tapping, threading, deburring, and so on, could have profound effects on the total time Norcen had to allocate to a particular job.

TABLE B1   Inventory of major machines (*Norcen Industries*)

MACHINE AND NUMBER OWNED	HOURS USED PER MACHINE PER WEEK
2 Table saws	6.0
1 Radial saw	0.3
3 Vertical band saws	0.8
2 Automatic cut-off saws	3.0
1 Automatic horizontal band saw	30.0
3 Small surface grinders	26.5
2 Large surface grinders	7.5
1 Large rotary surface grinder	2.0
1 Small centerless grinder	12.0
1 Large grinder	8.0
1 Large cylindrical grinder	4.0
3 Drill grinders	3.0
1 Creep feed grinder	32.0
1 Cutter grinder	10.0
3 Vertical milling machines	32.0
1 Small NC vertical milling machine	41.0
1 Small CNC vertical milling machine	4.1
2 Horizontal milling machines	25.0
1 Jig boring machine	45.0
1 Large DNC milling machine	50.0
2 Small DNC vertical machining centers	36.0
1 Large DNC vertical machining center	38.0
3 Four-spindle drill presses	32.0
4 Single-spindle drill presses	1.0
2 Small precision single-spindle bench drill presses	1.0
1 4 Speed lathe	15.0
1 Second operation lathe	10.0
5 Lathes	49.0
6 Small DNC bar and chucking lathes	51.5
2 Large DNC bar and chucking lathes	55.0
2 Automatic bar and chucking lathes	5.0
1 Hand turret lathe	.5
1 16-inch engine lathe	.5
2 Small vibratory deburring machines	5.0
1 Large vibratory deburring machine	5.0
1 Honing machine	6.0
1 DNC wire EDM machine	50.0
1 Coordinate measuring machine	21.0
3 6-inch abrasive sanding machines	2.7
1 Electric welder-TIG type	1.0
1 Spot welder	0.3
1 Sandblaster	0.5
1 20-ton punch press	0.3
2 Digital 20-inch optical comparators	10.0
1 Shrink wrapping machine	14.0

Miscellaneous inspection equipment: hardness tester, gauge blocks, profilometer, microscopes, precision hand measuring tools, electronic height gauge, etc.

Bill had to be alert for possible improvements he could make in the process.

5. The probability of successfully reducing costs was naturally greater for more complex operations and for repeat business. Furthermore, cost reductions could lie in more than process sequence changes. To cite an example, Norcen machined a part composed of a thin molybdenum strip bonded to steel. The customer's initial process specifications called for cutting two semicircles into the part using a lathe, but Joe Gehret recognized this technique as a high-risk, low-yield way to machine this part. By changing the process to use a specially adapted grinder, Norcen was able to machine the part successfully with much higher yields than would otherwise have been the case. Such dramatic success was not to be found often, but its significance was great enough to demand a good deal of Joe's and Bill's thoughts.

Even more important to Bill than assigning tasks in money-saving ways was seeing to it that the delivery schedule was met. Norcen could not miss deliveries and still expect to receive repeat orders. Bill was constantly aware of the promised delivery dates, and he attached high priorities to imminent deliveries due.

Bill's scheduling of jobs was further influenced by Norcen's cash flow needs. Other things being equal, and particularly at the end of the month, small jobs were given preference so that billing could proceed at once.

As foreman, Bill dealt also with worker morale, training, and development, with materials handling, and with quality control. (As for the latter, workers were responsible for checking their own work; in addition, spot checks were made of all outgoing shipments.) But job scheduling was the most demanding on Bill's energies. He tried to stay one day ahead of his workers, so that he knew precisely which job would go next to every machine, who would work that job, and when they would start on it. As Joe Gehret put it: "Scheduling is the most difficult function we have around here. It's the easiest thing in the world to say no to a customer, that we can't fit his job into the shop. But after a few noes, you may not have a customer."

During the recession period of 1982–84, scheduling was even more difficult than usual. The drop in orders then meant that Bill and Joe had fewer chances to group compatible orders together to avoid bottlenecks or to create labor-

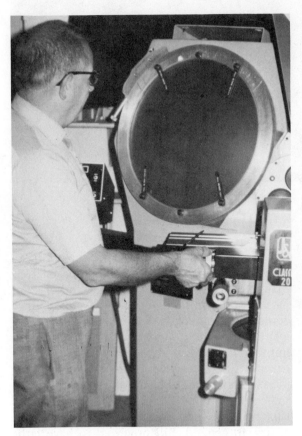

Joe Gehret with some inspection equipment.
(*Courtesy of Norcen Industries*)

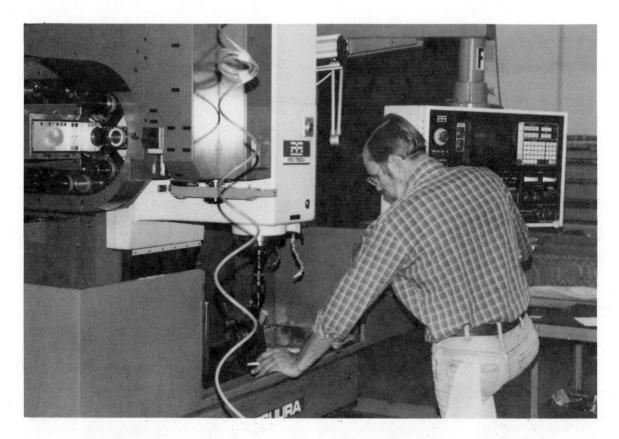

An operator doing some setup on a machining center at Norcen Industries. (*Courtesy of Norcen Industries*)

saving opportunities. In busier times, Joe and Bill could choose among the many orders in the shop, spreading out demand for particular pieces of equipment and taking advantage of the economies possible.

Frequently, planned schedules had to be interrupted because of customer desires for expedited delivery, because materials were received late from the customer, or because of the breakdown of the machine or its tooling. In these cases quick, remedial action had to be taken. Often, this remedial action took the form of adding a new job or rerouting an existing job through the shop. Norcen had enough equipment on hand, typically, to per-

mit a new or rerouted job to be set up on an unused machine. Joe Gehret purchased new machines for the shop with this kind of compatibility in mind. Not all jobs, of course, could be rerouted through the shop if things went awry, but it was possible with a sizable number, especially those that were not too complex. Some jobs could even be machined in an alternative sequence (for example, milling could be done first rather than third), and this helped when remedial action was necessary. In general, Bill preferred to have lathe work performed first, then milling, and only then grinding; but he was willing to abandon this sequence if necessary.

A view of the milling machine area on the plant floor at Norcen Industries. (*Courtesy of Norcen Industries*)

Some aspects of just-in-time manufacturing had repercussions for machine shops like Norcen. Customers were now placing orders that required multiple, time-phased deliveries of smaller-than-usual lots. Even though many of Norcen's new machines were capable of running small lots economically, this trend did serve to complicate scheduling.

RECORDKEEPING

When an operator completed his assigned task on any job, he completed the job sheet (Figure B3) attached to the blueprint. On this sheet he filled in his name, the date, the operation he performed, the quantity he completed, and the length of time it took him to complete the task, including setup time. In addition, at the end of the day, each operator completed a time card (Figure B6), listing the time spent on each job during the day.

In this way, Lillian Gehret had two records of the time each operator spent on each of the jobs done in the shop. Knowing the times and the wages of each operator involved in any job permitted Lillian to calculate the labor cost of that job. She made this calculation weekly and took care to see that any discrepancies in the two time records were resolved. Usually, the

828	Reading Orie Reading / Orie						1-24-85	
EMP. #	EMPLOYEE SIGNATURE						WORK PERIOD	
START	7:00	7:00	7:00	7:00	7:00	7:00		
STOP	3:30	5:30	5:30	5:30	5:30	12:0		
CHARGE NO	SUN	MON	TUE	WED	THUR	FRI	SAT	Total Hours
18980	✓	4	-	4 5				8 5
18593	✓	4	-	2 -		- 3		6 3
18976	✓		3 5	1 5				5
19363	✓			1 2	1 -			2 2
19191	✓			3 6	1 5			5 1
19192	✓			3 7	1 5			5 2
19363	✓				2 5			2 5
19116	✓				4 5	2 5		7 -
19215	✓					6 2	5 -	11 2
TOTAL	8 -	10 -	10 -	10 -	10 -	5 -		53 -

Notes:

1. This is Orie Reading's time card for the week beginning January 24, 1985. This was a busy time at Norcen, and Orie worked 53 total hours during the week, including two hours of overtime from Tuesday through Friday and five hours on Saturday.

2. During the week, Reading worked on nine different jobs. He worked on the job we are most interested in, #18980, on Monday and Tuesday, for 4 and 4.5 hours, respectively. On Monday he also worked 4 hours on job 18593, and on Tuesday, he worked on job 18976 as well.

3. By totaling the hours by each worker on each job as recorded on these time cards, Lillian Gehret has another, independent estimate of the hours worked on any job. These estimates can be compared with the hours totaled on the job sheets.

FIGURE B6   A sample of an operator's time card used at Norcen Industries.

daily time cards were more accurate than the job sheets.

Knowing this information, at the close of every job Lillian would complete the record card (Figure B1) which Joe relied on for making quotes on repeat business. As a rule of thumb for calculating the profitability of a job, Lillian multiplied total labor-hours by the relevant charge-out rate ($24–30 per hour) and compared that total with the total price Norcen had quoted. She alerted Joe to any major deviations in that comparison, either positive or negative. Subsequent bids could be based accordingly.

Technological Advances and Other Trends

Over the years, technological advances, especially in computers, have been revolutionizing the machine tool industry. The fully manual lathes, mills, grinders, and other tools were succeeded first by NC (numerically controlled) machines that could repeat operations exactly by reading punched paper tapes. The paper tapes had to be specially prepared and thus were typically suitable for only high-volume, repetitive jobs. Naturally, in job shops like Norcen with many low-volume, one-of-a-kind jobs, NC machines could find only limited use.

The next generation of equipment, the computer numerically controlled (CNC) machines, found more of a home in job shops like Norcen Industries. Much of this machinery was programmable, enabling operators to enter, at the computer console, the depths, speeds, and feed rates of cuts to be made along X-, Y-, or Z-axes. In addition, they could operate from tapes (paper or magnetic). These newer machine tools were more versatile, more accurate, and faster than previous ones. Their automatic features easily permitted an operator to run more than one machine at a time, although this doubling up was often less feasible for machine shops

One of Norcen Industries' new machining centers in the milling area in operation. (*Courtesy of Norcen Industries*)

running small parts (Norcen) than for shops machining large parts. The versatility and economy of these machines were enhanced by the development of computer hardware and software that could easily prepare tapes for them. For the CNC machines that Norcen already owned, the company had recently purchased the Numeridex system and had trained an operator and two lead men in its use. Given parameters such as lengths and depths of cuts, diameters for drilling, and thread sizes, the Numeridex system constructed a tape and could display on a special plotter what the tape would do, so that the tape could be checked and any modifications made. The combination of CNC machines with tape-making systems like the Numeridex made the use of such sophisticated equipment economical even for low-volume

runs. And if machining curved contours was required, even a production lot of one piece was advantageously run on CNC machines for reasons of quality alone.

The latest generation of equipment, the direct number control (DNC) machines, could be run directly by a computer, eliminating the need for the preparation of tapes. Norcen Industries had upgraded several CNC machines with new controls to make them DNC and had purchased several new DNC machines that were run from the computer. These new machines could spend more time actually running parts than could non-DNC machines. Joe believed that in the future, the entire shop's operations would be computerized: the machines, recordkeeping, scheduling, and quoting—all would be managed with the help of computers.

The new equipment complicated the running of the shop, particularly job quoting. The cost accounting associated with the new machines was much more ambiguous than with the older equipment. Machine costs were high and labor was often split between running two or more jobs at the same time. Determining the true cost of a particular piece was fraught with more and more uncertainty. In response, Norcen had developed different charge-out rates for different pieces of equipment, but that went only so far in solving the problem.

In late 1985, Norcen was planning the introduction of a new kind of machining to its operation, electrical discharge machining. This machining required more of a "clean room" environment, so a separate room was being prepared for the machine that had been purchased.

The movement for just-in-time (JIT) manufacturing and concern for quality and inventory levels were affecting the operation at Norcen Industries. Customers were less lenient about scrap, no longer providing an extra 10 percent of material as a matter of course to cover potential scrap. Customers were also requiring multiple deliveries of their orders, forcing Norcen either to hold the inventory or to set up the job more than once. These trends complicated Norcen's operations.

PART TWO

DISCUSSION

Norcen Industries is in no way responsible for the following views and presentation. They remain solely the responsibility of the author.

THE PROCESS FLOW

Compared with the continuous flow process at International Paper's Androscoggin Mill, the job shop process at Norcen Industries is strikingly loose and ill-defined. A process flow diagram becomes difficult to draw in any precise or meaningful way. For example, we might sketch a process flow diagram such as in Figure B7. Although many of the parts made at Norcen Industries would have passed through exactly this sequence of operations, many more would have required a different set of operations and a different order. Some of the differences might be minor, but there are a host of parts for which the differences are major. At best, Figure B7's flow diagram can be termed a dominant flow or, perhaps, a preferred, simplified flow. For the most part, the job shop process exhibits great product flux and flexibility. Work-in-process can be routed anywhere within the shop so that even extraordinary machining requirements can be met.

THE INFORMATION FLOW

What is not flexible but is almost totally rigid in the job shop is the flow of information through it. In stark contrast to the diversity of paths a machined part can take through the shop, information flows in a prescribed way (see Figure B8). Recordkeeping is done in the same manner for every order; the responsibilities of the workers, bookkeeper, and managers toward information in the process never vary. Everyone has fixed information tasks to perform: quot-

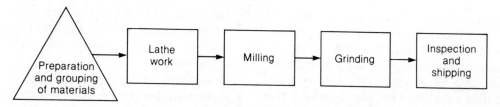

Notes:

1. Other tasks could be sequenced before, in between, or after the three middle tasks.
2. Work-in-process inventories exist between each operation.

FIGURE B7 A dominant, or preferred, process flow diagram for Norcen Industries.

FIGURE B8 An information flow diagram for Norcen Industries.

ing, job sheet and blueprint preparation, release to the shop, filling out of job sheets and time cards, labor cost calculations, updating of quote record cards, and signaling of any variances.

The reason for all this rigidity, of course, is that the job shop lives and dies by its ability to process information. Significantly, too, the information flows in the job shop are as much from worker to management (job sheets, time cards, process suggestions, machine break-

downs) as from management to worker (job and machine assignments, schedules, quality control checks, troubleshooting, training). Without suitable records, there would be no clear or readily available means of routing an order through the shop or of specifying exactly what should be done to satisfy it. Without suitable records, the job shop's managers would have little idea how to bid for various jobs. Without suitable records, advances in productivity would be more sporadic and less well retained for future use. Without suitable records, managers would not be able to load the shop effectively. Information and the responsibility of everyone in a job shop to maintain its accuracy and smooth flow constitute the glue by which this type of process is held together.

CAPACITY IN THE JOB SHOP

In the job shop at Norcen Industries, capacity is as ambiguous as the process flow's pattern. No single measure of capacity makes complete sense. While a paper mill can measure its capacity rather straightforwardly in tons per day or some similar measure, a machine shop like Norcen Industries cannot readily do the same thing. The large and constantly changing mix of products in the typical job shop ensures that a simple count of units produced is a meaningless way to gauge what the shop's effective capacity really is. We must avoid that simple measure in favor of one that transcends the product mix problem. The easiest remedy is to measure capacity in dollar terms, but that still leaves us with a variety of options. Dollars of typical output per unit of time? Dollars of output per worker? Dollars of output per machine? Dollars of output per dollar of machine value (at cost? at replacement cost?)? All of these measures grab a piece of what we mean intuitively when we say *capacity*, and yet no one of them fully describes the concept. Only over the long term, when we can feel comfortable that the mix of products has been representative, can we point at differences in shop output over time or output per worker or output per machine as valid measures of high or low capacity. In the short run, no capacity measure is clearly appropriate. Any measure of the shop's capacity is dependent on a host of factors, such as:

1. *Lot sizes.* The larger the lots ordered, the fewer setups in any one day and the greater the number of pieces produced, other things being equal.

2. *Complexity of the pieces worked on.* The more complex the piece, the more likely it will require a large succession of operations and thus the more likely its manufacture will demand a succession of time-consuming setups and difficult scheduling decisions. Of course, this factor is relatively more important in accounting for differences in the number of units manufactured than it is in accounting for differences in dollar value measures of capacity.

3. *Mix of jobs already on the shop floor.* The number and nature of orders already released to the shop floor affect the capacity of the shop in at least two ways: shifting bottlenecks and worker-machine interference.

   Many of the orders in the shop may require the services of particular machines. We can expect, then, that some orders may back up while awaiting a particular machine or operation. Further, we can expect to see such bottlenecks occurring from time to time all over the shop. That is, we can expect to see work-in-process inventories building up in different places and at different times in the shop. A smooth-runing, well-scheduled job shop will have a low number of such "shifting bottlenecks," but given the diversity of output and run lengths within a job shop process, they are absolutely unavoidable.

   In a typical job shop, there will be many machines that require the constant attention of a worker when they are in operation. Increasingly, however, automatic equipment is entering the shop with its ability to perform without the constant "hands-on" attention of the workforce. This advance is not without a challenge of its own. While automatic equipment frees up worker time, only the (sometimes fortuitous) scheduling of two or more jobs to the same worker actually leads to greater worker productivity apart from any speed advances built into the automatic equipment itself. If the scheduling cannot mesh two or more jobs together, the machine can be said to "interfere" with the worker, and capacity in the shop drops relative to the situation where the worker can easily operate two or more pieces of equipment at once. For this reason, Joe Gehret and Bill Lundy positioned machinery within the shop to maximize the possibilities for reducing worker-machine interference.

4. *Ability to schedule work well.* As Joe Gehret himself put it, "Scheduling is the most difficult function we have around here." The matching of workers to machines and of workers and machines to jobs often separates a profitable job shop from an unprofitable one. Good scheduling lessens shifting bottlenecks and worker-machine interference. Poor scheduling introduces more work-in-process inventory to the shop than is necessary. In particular, if too many rush orders are permitted in the shop, their scheduling will become difficult, often necessitating the interruption of runs on machines already set up.

As was noted in the process description, in recessionary times management has many fewer jobs from which to choose to keep all the shop's machining centers busy and to avoid bottlenecks. In better economic times, management can search through the released orders for jobs that can help smooth the flow of work through the shop.

5. *Process improvements.* Any advances in the methods employed in producing a part at Norcen Industries permitted the shop to increase its capacity and thus its profitability. With so many orders passing through the shop, there are many opportunities for improving the process: resequencing of operations, different use of machines, quicker setups, special jigs or fixtures for increasing speed and/or accuracy, possibly redesign of the piece ordered. Because any of these improvements takes time to work through, it is likely that only the higher volume, repeat business will benefit from such attention.

6. *Number of machines and their condition.* It is obvious that, even without expanding the workforce, the addition of equipment to the shop is likely to increase capacity detectably. For one thing, rush orders will be less likely to necessitate the dismantling of existing machine setups before completion of the run. Having more machines also increases the probability of finding favorable combinations of orders to lessen worker-machine interference. Fewer bottlenecks, too, are likely to occur with the addition of more equipment. It is evident as well that machines in good condition are less likely to break down and thus demand attention both for themselves and for the rescheduling of operations through the shop.

Technological advances, notably the evolution from manual to NC machines to CNC machines and then to DNC machines, have greatly influenced the shop's capacity. Setups are often easier with the more advanced machine tools; more time can be spent actually cutting metal. Moreover, the newer tools permit fancier machining (such as curved shapes) to be done with greater accuracy, higher speed, and less scrap. And given that the machining was accomplished via tape or computer instruction, the new equiment does not tie up workers as long as the older equipment did.

7. *Quantity and quality of labor input.* Another obvious set of factors affecting the capacity of a job shop is drawn from the labor force itself. Overtime and second shift work is a standard way to augment capacity with the same stock of plant and equipment. Employing inexperienced workers and having to train them is a drain on capacity, however.

Obvious in identification but subtle in design and application is an incentive system for the workers. At Norcen Industries, the bonus plan that was dependent on company profits was viewed by the workers as a fair and reasonable spur for continued good work. But it is not the only payment system that could be installed; different systems might have different effects on worker effort and thus on capacity.

Increasing the capacity of a job shop in the way outlined here, at little or no cost, is important to the shop because that is how it makes its money. Of course, the shop must be flexible enough to bid on a tremendous variety of jobs, but the shop's ability to earn any profit, once granted the business, is linked fundamentally to its capacity and its knowledge of that capacity. As we have discussed, these two items are influenced by a number of factors, many of which require the accurate processing of information around the shop.

The Role of Standards and Incentives

Time standards for all of the operations to be performed at Norcen Industries are an integral feature of its cost estimation and bidding responsibilities. Some of the standards are developed internally, mostly through past experience doing the same thing; but others are supplied by the customer when bids are solicited, having been worked out for or by the customer.

The standards are a useful guide for both workers and managers. For the workers, the standards (written on the job sheet) provide continual feedback on how well they are doing the job. For managers, the standards provide information on how long certain jobs should take and thus how they might be scheduled. The standards also provide management with a yardstick for worker performance that is useful not only for making advancement/layoff decisions but also for determining which tasks each worker does relatively better.

Other than by furnishing feedback for each worker, the time standards are not tied formally to any incentive system. Incentives for good work and/or for speedy work are provided either through knowledge that such work often contributes to better company profits (although such work is not the only determinant of profits, by far) or by the prodding and cajoling of the foreman. In job shops like Norcen industries, the foreman carries much of the responsibility for pacing work through the shop and for ensuring that the quality is satisfactory.

QUESTIONS

1. Write up a hypothetical job sheet for an order and briefly explain each column entry. How do the functions of the job sheet and the record card differ?

2. Can you make any generalizations about cost reductions from the example of Norcen Industries? Do these generalizations apply to any other process with which you are already familiar?

3. Why might scheduling be "the most difficult function" in a job shop?

4. "The job shop lives and dies by its ability to process information." Discuss this comment and compare the information flow in the job shop with that in another type of process.

5. Discuss three of the factors that influence a job shop's capacity. What might be "the perfect set of circumstances" in a shop foreman's eyes?

6. As a worker, which would you prefer: the calm predictability of the continuous flow process or the frequently frantic unpredictability of the job shop? As a manager, which

would you prefer? How might your attitude affect the setting of standards and incentives in each process?

7. Norcen's foreman places particular emphasis on meeting customer due dates. Due dates thus significantly affect the scheduling that is done. Suppose, however, that due dates were not so important to you as the foreman. What other factors could take precedence? How could they serve as the basis for scheduling jobs through the shop? Under what circumstances might the different factors take precedence in establishing scheduling rules?

8. Suppose you were forced to justify to upper management the purchase of new technology, such as a CNC machine, for an existing job shop. Where would you look for the benefits of such an addition to the shop? How would you measure the extent of those benefits?

SITUATION FOR STUDY B-1
OWENS INC.

Fred and Ralph own and operate a small machine and metal fabrication shop. Most of their business involves small orders from local industry. These orders are usually ones that the larger customer firms farm out because they do not have the excess capacity. In other words, Fred and Ralph provide "slack" capacity to the larger firms. Figure B9 shows the plant layout.

Fred and Ralph feel that if they can once get an order in their shop, they can learn how to make the part and then underbid on future orders. Moreover, they think they can make most parts more cheaply than the customer can in house.

They are currently considering bidding on part 273. Figure B10 is an engineerng sketch of this part. For the first order the customer will supply a coil of 1⅝-inch cold rolled steel (CRS), but Fred and Ralph are investigating to see whether other processes might use other sizes of raw material more efficiently. The proposed order is for 500 pieces, with possible future orders of 500 per month. The proposed bid must be submitted in two weeks, the bid award determined within one week, and the 500 units delivered one month after that.

Fred has generated the estimates shown in Table B2. The cost estimates used for bids are

FIGURE B9 Plant layout for Owens, Inc.

FIGURE B10 Engineering sketch for part 273, a bracket.

TABLE B2   Process sheet for part 273 (Owens, Inc.)

OPERATION SEQUENCE	MACHINE	OPERATION	SETUP TIME (minutes)	OPERATION TIME PER UNIT (minutes)
1	Shear #3	Shear to length	5	.030
2	Shear #3	Shear 45° corners	8	.050
3	Multispindle Drill press #1	Drill both holes and deburr	15	3.000
4	Brake press	Bend 90°	10	.025
5	Tumbler	Deburr	5	*
6		Pack in boxes		30.000

*The deburr operation can be left unattended, and so the only labor required is to load and unload.

$10.55 per hour for labor and $18.50 per hour for machines—or $29.05 per hour for one worker/one machine operations. Any time "sold" at this rate makes Owens a margin of 25 percent with which to cover indirect costs such as administrative costs.

1. If you were Fred and Ralph, what other aspects of the shop, the market, and the future would you consider regarding the bid for part 273?

2. Analyze the current proposal and generate a bid to the customer and a rough shop schedule.

SITUATION FOR STUDY B-2
STREETER DIE & STAMPING COMPANY

Streeter Tool & Die Company was founded in 1956 by entrepreneur Jack Streeter. For 20 years the small firm flourished, furnishing tools, dies, jigs, and fixtures to metal stamping firms. In 1976 the firm became Streeter Die & Stamping Company (SDS) and began a move toward a new business. Today SDS had two plants in Toledo, Ohio, furnishing metal stampings and assemblies primarily to the major U.S. automakers. In the most recent year, General Motors (GM) accounted for 85 percent of SDS's sales.

The main plant (Plant 1) had 14 presses, ranging in power from 20 to 1000 tons, that stamped out metal parts from raw steel. Production was usually based on firm customer orders, but occasionally some forecasting of future orders was done in an attempt to get longer, more efficient production runs.

The secondary plant (Plant 2), representing a type of forward vertical integration for SDS, was more labor intensive than Plant 1. Plant 2 specialized in the assembly and welding of parts stamped at Plant 1. Extra space at Plant 2 was used as a finished goods warehouse for any parts made at Plant 1 or 2 that would not be shipped within one week.

The orders that SDS normally produced to were contracts that SDS had won by submitting quotes to the customer. In the case of GM contracts, it was known at SDS that price was not always the deciding factor; SDS's record for quality and timeliness played an important role in winning many of these contracts.

Raw materials arriving at SDS, almost all of them coils weighing one to five tons, were stored in a warehouse adjacent to Plant 1. When the steel was needed in the shop, a forklift picked it up and brought it to the press where it was to be used. From this point, the steel could go through many different combinations of presses and operations, depending on the specific part being made.

In general, the first operation involved running the steel through an automatic press. Steel coils were hoisted onto a reel and fed into the press automatically. The stamped parts fell off the press into bins, which the press operators occasionally checked to see whether the parts were being stamped properly. When the order had been completed, the remaining part of the steel coil was removed from the reel and stored against the shop wall. For several parts this operation was the only one necessary; a random sample of these parts was inspected by quality control and, if the parts were good, they were taken to the loading dock and prepared for shipping.

After passing a quality inspection, bins of more complex parts were moved to nonautomatic presses for the rest of their stamping operations, such as piercing, drawing, and forming. These operations were much slower, because the parts had to be placed manually into the dies by the press operators. These operations completed some parts. Other parts were sent to a vendor for sandblasting, painting, heat treating, and/or deburring before being shipped to the customer; still others were sent to Plant 2, where several component parts were welded and/or assembled into the finished product.

The finished goods inventory at SDS was relatively small. Parts that were to be shipped within one week were stacked along the walls of the loading docks at both plants so that fork-lift drivers could easily spot which parts must be loaded onto a certain truck.

Smooth operations at SDS were extremely dependent on a coordinated, accurate information flow. The information flow followed a cycle that began and ended with engineering submitting a quote for a contract. If information was not accurate at one point in the cycle, the results could have a domino effect on the various departments at SDS. To help improve information flow, all departments at SDS used an IBM System 34 computer extensively.

After analyzing customers' blueprints and past SDS results on similar parts, engineering quoted prices per piece for lot sizes ranging from 100 to 600,000 pieces per year. Reflecting the fixed costs of initial tooling, the price per piece decreased as the lot size increased. After winning a contract, SDS had six to eight months before its first shipment was due on a new part and three to four months on a carryover part.

During the six to eight months before the first due date, engineering was responsible for getting the shop ready for production. This included ordering the tooling from a vendor, drawing up process sheets for each subassembly, determining what presses could or should be used to stamp each part, assigning part numbers to new parts, and entering all pertinent data about each part into the computer. Engineering also sent a copy of the contract and process sheets to production planning so that they had a record of parts that had to be scheduled in the near future.

Production planning needed no further information until 13 weeks before the first shipment due date. The data systems manager had designed a computer program that received information directly from GM's computer each Monday morning and printed out a list of SDS's week-by-week requirements over the next 13 weeks; the first two weeks were required by contract to be firm. When new parts showed up on the list, production planning had to (1) check with engineering to see how the tooling was progressing, (2) order materials, and (3) schedule a sample run. No full production runs could be shipped to GM or other top customers until samples had been approved.

The Monday morning printout listed other important information for each part, such as the number pieces on hand, the week in which the number on hand would be insufficient to cover cumulative requirements, and the amount of components and raw materials on hand for each part. The production scheduler used this report to determine which parts would have to be made two weeks into the future. The scheduler filled out a small card for each operation that must be performed and posted the card on a schedule board that enabled him to schedule work on each press for the present week and the next two weeks.

While the scheduler was busy loading the presses, a production planning assistant used another copy of this report to determine raw material requirements over the entire 13 weeks. Any materials that SDS would not have enough of to meet these requirements were written on a material requisition, which was delivered to the purchasing agent for further action.

Each morning, after surveying the progress on the shop floor, analyzing the previous day's production summary, and updating the schedule board, the scheduler brought to the shop foreman (1) a schedule of parts to be stamped in each press, (2) routing cards for each part, and (3) process sheets with pictures of each operation. Press operators used counters on the presses to count the number of pieces stamped each shift, each day, and each production run. When the total count for the run reached the number on the routing card, the operator signed the routing card, wrote on his activity card his shift count and his hours spent on the part, and signaled the foreman for a new job. At the end of each shift, the foreman gathered all the activity cards and summarized the data into the daily production summary. In addition to the scheduler's use of this summary, the inventory control specialist combined this information with shipping and receiving data to update inventories on the computer files daily. Keying

in this inventory data and some additional cost data also updated financial and job cost data, thus completing the information flow cycle and ensuring that accounting and engineering had access to the information necessary for preparing monthly financial statements and accurate quotes on parts contracts.

A somewhat separate line of information flowed between the shipping department and the billing clerks. Each day shipping filled out a list of the parts, with quantities, that it had shipped. This list was delivered to the billing clerks who, at the end of each day, wired these shipments into the customers' computers. With this method, the customers' procurement agents knew exactly from day to day which parts were in transit, and both SDS and its customers had a common reference date if questions arose about a particular shipment.

Often, the information flow was less formal when customers' procurement agents called and asked for early delivery or when SDS was behind schedule on a part. Information flow became a matter of someone from production planning personally expediting these orders through the shop and arranging special rush transportation.

1. To the extent that you can, diagram the process and information flows.

2. Sales at Streeter Die & Stamping recently increased and bottlenecks emerged in the operation, although the exact cause of the bottlenecks was not immediately obvious. How would you determine where any bottlenecks were? Be specific.

3. How would you control the levels of inventory? How would you monitor and, perhaps, change the status of jobs in the company? What kinds of things would you have the computer do?

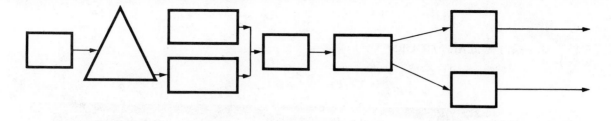

A BATCH FLOW PROCESS
Jos. A. Bank Clothiers, Baltimore Shop Baltimore, Maryland

Jos. A. Bank Clothiers was a maker of high-quality, traditionally styled men's and women's clothes—primarily suits, sport coats, slacks, and skirts. It sold these clothes along with shirts, ties, and other accessories through 29 retail stores* and an extensive mail-order business. Its stores were called "showrooms" and were comfortable and efficient, but avoided a "clubby," pretentious atmosphere. Compared with retailers of similar clothes, the company used lower price markups and had a lower overhead. These features, combined with manufacturing efficiencies, permitted Jos. A. Bank to market its high-quality clothes at prices significantly lower than those of its competitors.

The company employed 1649 people. Approximately half (827) worked in manufacturing. There were three manufacturing plants in Maryland—one in downtown Baltimore, one in uptown Baltimore, and the other in rural Hampstead. The Hampstead plant produced men's coats and all of the women's clothes. The uptown Baltimore plant situated on North Avenue was the company's latest, in operation since November 1984. It produced men's coats—primarily sportcoats—and some pants. The Baltimore shop made only men's clothes and concentrated on suits. All warehousing and distribution were accomplished at a new distribution center on Homeland Avenue in Baltimore, which was opened in July 1983.

In early July 1981, Quaker Oats purchased Jos. A. Bank Clothiers from the Bank family, who had owned and operated the company since its founding in 1902. Members of the family were still active in managing the company, and Quaker Oats took a "hands off" approach toward its operations. The company had been extraordinarily successful. Its sales in 1985 totaled approximately $93 million, almost five times its total in 1978. The company was opening new retail stores at a rate of four or more a year, and its prospects for continued growth in both sales and stores were considered excellent.

*Two stores were in the Baltimore area (on Light Street in downtown Baltimore and in Towson, north of the city), one in Washington, D.C., two in Virginia (Falls Church and Richmond), three in Pennsylvania (Philadelphia, Haverford, and Pittsburgh), three in Illinois (Chicago Loop, Wilmette, and Lombard), two in Massachusetts (Boston and Natick), two in Tennessee (Memphis and Nashville), two in Texas (Dallas and Houston), and other stores in Atlanta; Birmingham, Alabama; Buffalo, New York; Charlotte, North Carolina; Cleveland; Denver; Detroit; and St. Louis.

An early step in the manufacture of a coat or pants was called "spreading" the fabric. (*Courtesy of Jos. A. Bank Mfg. Co.*)

The Baltimore shop of Jos. A. Bank occupied five floors of the Candler Building at the corner of Pratt Street and Market Place in the inner harbor area of downtown Baltimore. About 650 people worked for the company in the Candler Building, 362 of whom were associated with the manufacturing done there (28 managers and 334 operators and other workers).

The Baltimore factory consisted of a coat shop (with a capacity of 450 to 500 coats a day); a pants shop (with a capacity of 900 to 1000 pairs of pants a day); a cutting room, which handled all the cutting for the three Maryland plants; and a matching warehouse, which facilitated the matching of coats and pants for suits. Virtually all the plant's output carried the Jos. A. Bank label. In years past, however, Jos. A. Bank had manufactured clothing that carried other labels, but as the company grew this activity had dwindled.

PART ONE
PROCESS DESCRIPTION

THE PROCESS FLOW

The making of a quality sportcoat or suit coat was a complex endeavor, encompassing 140 to 150 distinct operations. (See Figure C1.) The coat was an assembly of various parts, including sleeves, backs, fronts, facings, collars, and pockets. Each of these parts, in turn, combined the basic fabric for the coat itself (known as piece goods) with 40 to 50 trim items. These

MODEL MASTER LISTING RPT-PAY032

MODEL-S821ACS5BC PLN = 321 VALLEY PLAIN COAT

OPER	DESCRIPTION	WRKCTR	PRICE	S-A-M	SINGLE	SUB-FLAG
SUB ASSEMBLY 00011-SLEEVE						
25	JOIN SLEEVE	00101	.1455	.0000	.1600	
50	PRESS SLEEVE	00101	.0475	.0000	.0523	
75	JN ELBOW MK VT	00101	.4425	.0000	.4868	
125	PRS EBW SLV VT	00101	.1038	.0000	.1142	
175	TN SLV LNG QT	00101	.0807	.0000	.0888	
SUB ASSEMBLY TOTAL			.8200	.0000	.9021	
SUB ASSEMBLY 01003-SLEEVE-LINING -						
225	MK SLV LNG	00102	.1598	.0000	.1751	
275	FELL SLV LNG	00102	.1105	.0000	.1216	
303	MK SLV BT SHK	00102	.0394	.0000	.0435	
325	SW 2BT TRN SL	00102	.1435	.0000	.1579	
375	TK SL LNG TRN	00102	.1515	.0000	.1668	
410	PRS ELB DB BK	00102	.0464	.0000	.0512	N
425	PR IN SLEEVES	00102	.0606	.0000	.0666	Y
SUB ASSEMBLY TOTAL			.7117	.0000	.7827	
SUB ASSEMBLY 02001-YOKE						
525	MK HEM 2PC YK	00103	.0854	.0000	.0939	
SUB ASSEMBLY TOTAL			.0854	.0000	.0939	
SUB ASSEMBLY 03001-VENT-LINING						
625	MK TRN VT LNG	00104	.0342	.0000	.0375	
650	PRESS VNT LNG	00104	.0252	.0000	.0278	
675	PR SRG VT LNG	00104	.0633	.0000	.0699	
SUB ASSEMBLY TOTAL			.1227	.0000	.1352	
SUB ASSEMBLY 04009-BACK						
715	SPONGE BACKS	00105	.0248	.0000	.0275	
725	BOOK SMS BACK	00105	.1262	.0000	.1387	
750	JN BCK CTR VT	00105	.2251	.0000	.2477	N
775	SEW TPE BK NK	00105	.0435	.0000	.0478	
825	PR C/SM & C/V	00105	.0592	.0000	.0660	
850	MCH BST C/V	00105	.0564	.0000	.0619	
875	FEL VT LNG TK	00105	.0953	.0000	.1049	
900	PAIR BACKS	00106	.0699	.0000	.0768	
SUB ASSEMBLY TOTAL			.7004	.0000	.7713	
SUB ASSEMBLY 05004-CANVAS						
950	FSE FRNT W/SB	00106	.0829	.0000	.0908	N

Notes:

1. This portion of a Model Master Listing details the specific operations to perform, in sequence, for various subassemblies for the coat of suit model 321 PN, a plain fabric Valley model. These subassemblies include the sleeve, sleeve lining, yoke, vent-lining, and so on. The entire listing contains 13 different subassemblies.

2. Each line consists of an operation number, a description of the operation, the workcenter number where it is performed, the piece rate price for a standard bundle, the standard allowed minutes (not applicable to these subassemblies), and the piece rate price for a single unit. The Sub-flag column denotes exceptions to the standard that are made for selected coats.

FIGURE C1 Sample operation sheet for coat.

A soabar machine was used to put an identifying ticket on the pieces of fabric. (*Courtesy of Jos. A. Bank Mfg. Co.*)

trim items included linings, fusings (the firm material fused by heat to various parts of the piece goods to help them retain their shape and resist wear), pocketing, stays, tape, thread, and buttons. The assembly of pants was less complex.

The Cutting Room

The assembly of a suit or coat began when a bolt of fabric (the piece goods) was withdrawn from raw materials inventory. This fabric was then carefully laid on long cutting room tables. This task was known as "spreading" the cloth; depending upon the particular order, the num- ber of layers spread ranged from 1 to 110. Once spread, a paper pattern known as a *marker* was placed over the layers of fabric.* The coat, vest, and/or pants pattern pieces were carefully arranged on it so that as little fabric as possible was wasted. This arrangement was generated by a special computer-based instrument (an AM-5, made by Gerber Garment Technologies) and was printed out, ready to be used. The AM-5 could easily adjust sizes and arrange the pieces in the most efficient pattern. For example, certain suit sizes (such as 40 regulars and 41 regulars or 39 regulars and 43 regulars) might be combined efficiently on the marker pattern. The markers were stapled to the layers of fabric and

*Only occasionally would a pattern have to be chalked on fabric by hand.

Shade number
Shop number
Cloth lot number
Model number
Coat size
Variation (e.g., long)
Pants size

FIGURE C2   A sample ticket used by Jos. A. Bank to identify cut fabric.

the fabric was cut using either electric cutters or manual shears, depending on the number of layers and the outline of the pattern.

The pieces that composed the same coat and/or pants were cut from the same layer in the spread fabric. After being cut, they were matched together and assembled (this assembly was termed "fitting") into various groups of materials—one group, for example, for the pants, one group for the coat. These matched and assembled cutouts of fabric were then tagged (using either heat or staples) with special identifying numbers by the Soabar marking and ticketing machine. (See Figure C2). These numbers were critical in ensuring that material cut for the same suit would stay together throughout the process. After being tagged, the pieces destined for coat, pants, or vest were directed to the proper shop.

The Coat Shop

The materials transported to the coat shop were subdivided and assembled, or fitted, into special bundles with an average of 12 units in each bundle. Bundle sizes ranged from 1 to 22. Bundles were

In the cutting room, both electric cutters and manual shears were used. (*Courtesy of Jos. A. Bank Mfg. Co.*)

fitted for various segments of the coat, such as sleeves, fronts, backs, collars, facings, linings, flaps, and welts (pockets). Each bundle (batch) of materials to be processed in the coat shop would have the same operations performed on each of the pieces in the bundle. For the most part, workers in the shop did the same things to successive bundles of materials. A record of what was to be done to each bundle and how many items were in each traveled with the bundle.

Most operations in the coat shop consisted of sewing pieces of the fabric together and/or attaching various trim items to the fabric. The bundles representing parts of the coat were worked on separately in various areas of the coat shop. Periodically, some were brought together to make larger subassemblies before these were joined in the assembly that was the coat itself. At two key places in the shop and at several minor locations, these parts were matched before being sewn into a major subassembly. These matching stations served to control the process, ensuring that all pieces in each bundle were accounted for and that only those pieces of fabric that had been cut together would be assembled into a coat. Once the coat was fully assembled— linings in, welts and flaps sewn, facings fabricated and assembled to fronts, and sleeves assembled to the rest of the coat—it was ready for finishing. In finishing, basting (temporary stitches) was removed, various parts of the coat were pressed, and the coat was thoroughly inspected. Once inspected, it was placed on a rack and transported to the matching warehouse on the 12th floor. At the matching warehouse, pants and coats for the same suit were placed together and then transported to the distribution center on Homeland Avenue in Baltimore. Orders were filled from the distribution center.

The Pants Shop

Pants underwent similar, although simpler, processing. Except for waistbands, materials for a pair of pants traveled together. Fronts, backs, and pockets were clamped together on a specially designed cart, termed the "pants truck." Some sewing—pockets and fly zippers and closings—was done while the materials were clamped to the truck. When the raw edges of the pants, fronts, and backs were to be serged (overcast) to prevent raveling, the truck clamp was undone. The materials then traveled in bundles while side seams were sewn, the waistband was sewn in, and the remaining assembly tasks were done (see Figure C3). Finishing for pants consisted of pressing and inspection. When approved, the pants were sent to the matching warehouse.

The Workforce and the Piece-Rate System

Except for about 50 nonunion clerical workers, all the workers in the Baltimore manufacturing shop were members of the Amalgamated Clothing and Textile Workers Union. These workers were paid an incentive wage, although the type of incentive differed among departments. Workers in the coat and pants shop were paid piece rates. These piece rates were the prices in dollars per piece that the company paid for each piece of sewing, pressing, matching, or inspection.

When workers finished their assigned tasks, they detached the appropriate cardboard coupon from the perforated sheet of coupons (Figure C4) that traveled with the job. On the coupon was an operations number that was uniquely identified with the piece rate for performing the indicated job. By accumulating these coupons and turning them in at the end of the day, workers were paid for exactly what they had done. There was no minimum payment and no maximum payment. In actuality, the wage payment averages in the coat and pants shop ran about 110 percent of the established

MODEL MASTER LISTING   RPT-PAY032

MODEL-S821APS56P PLD

OPER	DESCRIPTION	WRKCTR	PRICE	S-A-M	SINGLE	SUB-FLAG
SUB ASSEMBLY 21000-WAISTBAND		-				
6050	LOOP MAKE PRS	00301	.0260	.0000	.0260	
6076	RL_CAP W/BAND	00301	.0424	.0000	.0424	
6125	CT W/B PR BND	00301	.0265	.0000	.0265	
SUB ASSEMBLY TOTAL			.0949	.0000	.0949	
SUB ASSEMBLY 22062-ASSEMBLY		-				
6225	FIT PANTS	00302	.0775	.0000	.0853	
6275	SET RGT FY LG	00302	.0318	.0000	.0318	
6300	ST LFT ZIP	00302	.0430	.0000	.0430	
6325	JN SRG HIP	00302	.0659	.0000	.0659	
6350	HIP PKT FACE	00302	.0983	.0000	.0983	
6375	FRT PKT FAC	00302	.1285	.0000	.1285	
6400	RGT L LFT FLY	00302	.1038	.0000	.1142	
6426	HANG PKT STRA	00302	.0883	.0000	.0883	
6450	FRTPKT CRDCTK	00302	.1231	.0000	.1354	
6500	SEW 2DARTS	00302	.0345	.0000	.0378	
6525	COMPO SET HIP	00302	.0788	.0000	.0868	
6550	PRS 2HPKTCTRN	00302	.0529	.0000	.0529	
6600	HIP PKT CLSE2	00302	.0817	.0000	.0901	
6603	STIT HIP PKT	00302	.1202	.0000	.1202	
6625	2TKS EAPKT BT	00302	.0948	.0000	.1043	
6650	FRT L BK SERG	00302	.1506	.0000	.1656	Y
6676	PRCJN SIDESMS	00302	.1944	.0000	.2138	Y
6701	PRS S/S NOSTY	00302	.0536	.0000	.0536	
6725	CLSE SIDFPKT	00302	.0881	.0000	.0881	
6751	SW EX WB LPS	00302	.1980	.0000	.2175	Y
6775	WB PRES VIET	00302	.0628	.0000	.0628	
6800	STIT FRT PKT	00302	.0509	.0000	.0509	
6825	SET-2 HOOKCEY	00302	.0324	.0000	.0324	
6850	MKE FRT CRNER	00302	.0825	.0000	.0825	
6900	PRS RTGLFTFLY	00302	.1060	.0000	.1060	
6925	LFT/RGT FY ST	00302	.0775	.0000	.0855	
6951	JN MK/TN/BKCN	00302	.1267	.0000	.1392	
6975	WAISTBAND FEL	00302	.0590	.0000	.0590	
7000	LOOP TK 7TD9	00302	.1582	.0000	.1740	
7025	FLY L PKT B/H	00302	.0592	.0000	.0649	
7051	INSEM SEW PLD	00302	.1267	.0000	.1391	
7076	ZIP LOCK PLD	00302	.0629	.0000	.0629	
7100	CROTCH SEW	00302	.0786	.0000	.0786	
7125	TAIL SEW	00302	.0497	.0000	.0497	
7150	BTN SEW 2	00302	.0593	.0000	.0651	
7175	BLIND TACK B	00302	.0502	.0000	.0502	
7200	CROTCH TACK	00302	.0307	.0000	.0337	
7250	PRS SEAMCTURN	00302	.1134	.0000	.1134	
7275	LEG PRS WOOL	00302	.1252	.0000	.1381	
7324	TOP PRES WOOL	00302	.1558	.0000	.1695	Y
7335	PINKING	00302	.0195	.0000	.0195	
7350	EXAM TR FOLD	00302	.3262	3.0260	.3589	
SUB ASSEMBLY TOTAL			3.9212	3.0260	4.1573	
MODEL TOTAL			4.0161	3.0260	4.2522	

MODEL MASTER LISTING   RPT-PAY032

MODEL-S821APS5BP STP

OPER	DESCRIPTION	WRKCTR	PRICE	S-A-M	SINGLE	SUB-FLAG
SUB ASSEMBLY 00000-		-				
SUB ASSEMBLY TOTAL			.0000	.0000	.0000	
MODEL TOTAL			.0000	.0000	.0000	

Notes:

1. This portion of a Model Master Listing details the specific operations to perform, in sequence, for the two subassemblies making up the pants for suit model 321 PN, a plain fabric Valley model.

2. Like the Model Master Listing for the coat, each line indicates operation number, operation description, work-center number, standard bundle piecerate price, standard allowed minutes (only applicable to the last operation), single unit piecerate price, and the sub-flag (exceptions) indication.

FIGURE C3   Sample operation sheet for pants.

```
001  03211  0282   14   |              | 001  03211  0376   14   | 001  03211  2488   14   |             | 001  03211  2505   14
UNDLE  CUT  OPER  QTY    |              | BUNDLE  CUT  OPER  QTY   | BUNDLE  CUT  OPER  QTY   |             | BUNDLE  CUT  OPER  QTY
A011032110010405 4      | SLEEVE-LINI  | A012032110010427 6      | A078032110012585 0      | FRONT-CONTR | A079032110012705 2
      U/PR ELB SEAM     |              |      MATCH SLEEVE        | 9884    2ND POCKET       |             |      BAG 3 PKTS.
001  03211  0405   14   |              | 001  03211  0427   14   | 001  03211  2585   14   |             | 001  03211  2705   14
UNDLE  CUT  OPER  QTY    |              | BUNDLE  CUT  OPER  QTY   | BUNDLE  CUT  OPER  QTY   |             | BUNDLE  CUT  OPER  QTY
                        | SLEEVE-LINI  |                         | A080032110012777 9      | FRONT-CONTR | A081032110012802 3
******* ************    |              | ******* ************    |      PRS PKT RT&LF       |             |      MATCH CHESTPC
001  03211  ****   14   |              | 001  03211  ****   14   | 001  03211  2777   14   |             | 001  03211  2802   14
UNDLE  CUT  OPER  QTY    |              | BUNDLE  CUT  OPER  QTY   | BUNDLE  CUT  OPER  QTY   |             | BUNDLE  CUT  OPER  QTY
A014032110010526 1      | YOKE         |                         | A082032110012827 8      | FRONT-CONTR | A083032110012852 4
      MAKE YOKE         |              | ******* ************    |      BSTE CHESTPC.       |             |      TACK BRIDLE
001  03211  0526   14   |              | 001  03211  ****   14   | 001  03211  2827   14   |             | 001  03211  2852   14
UNDLE  CUT  OPER  QTY    |              | BUNDLE  CUT  OPER  QTY   | BUNDLE  CUT  OPER  QTY   |             | BUNDLE  CUT  OPER  QTY
A016032110010626 4      | VENT-LINING  | A017032110010651 0      | A084032110012905 8      | FRONT-CONTR | A085032110012932 9
      MK VENT LIN       |              |      PRE VENT LIN        |      JOIN SIDESEAM       |             |      TAPE BACK A/H
001  03211  0626   14   |              | 001  03211  0651   14   | 001  03211  2905   14   |             | 001  03211  2932   14
UNDLE  CUT  OPER  QTY    |              | BUNDLE  CUT  OPER  QTY   | BUNDLE  CUT  OPER  QTY   |             | BUNDLE  CUT  OPER  QTY
A018032110010676 5      | VENT-LINING  |                         | A086032110012955 8      | FRONT-CONTR | A087032110013002 6
      SERGE VT LIN      |              | ******* ************    |      PRESS SIDESEM       |             |      PRESS FRONTS
001  03211  0676   14   |              | 001  03211  ****   14   | 001  03211  2955   14   |             | 001  03211  3002   14
UNDLE  CUT  OPER  QTY    |              | BUNDLE  CUT  OPER  QTY   | BUNDLE  CUT  OPER  QTY   |             | BUNDLE  CUT  OPER  QTY
A020032110010728 0      | BACK         | A021032110010740 3      | A088032110013051 1      | FRONT-CONTR | A089032110013080 8
      BOOK BACKS        |              |      MK BK PLAIN         |      MEASURE             |             |      SHAPE FRONTS
001  03211  0728   14   |              | 001  03211  0740   14   | 001  03211  3051   14   |             | 001  03211  3080   14
UNDLE  CUT  OPER  QTY    |              | BUNDLE  CUT  OPER  QTY   | BUNDLE  CUT  OPER  QTY   |             | BUNDLE  CUT  OPER  QTY
```

Notes:

1. This is a portion of the sheet of coupons that follows a job through the coat shop. Whenever a piecerate worker completes a bundle, she detaches the coupon. The payroll department then wands the top row with a laser scanning wand.

2. The top row is used for payroll purposes only and indicates the shop number, bundle number, and operator number.

3. The middle row provides a description of the operation and, where appropriate, indicates what trim items are to be used.

4. The bottom indicates the bundle number, the cut number (same as shop number), the operation number, and the quantity in the bundle.

FIGURE C4   Coupon sheet.

standard, with a range for experienced workers from 80 percent of the standard to 160 percent. The coupons that workers turned in were read by a laser wand so that payroll and work-in-process were tracked automatically.

This piece rate system was modified somewhat for the cutting room workers. Before about 1978, workers in the cutting room were paid by the hour. At that time, however, it was felt that the output of the cutting room could be increased if it too were put on some incentive plan. A consulting firm was brought in, and standards were set for all operations in the cutting room—spreading the fabric, cutting the patterns, and other tasks. The standards set were called "standard allowed minutes" for doing particular jobs. All the jobs in the cutting room were studied and rates were set. Thus, workers in the cutting room were paid for the standard allowed minutes that they acquired rather than for the pieces of work that they were able to finish. However, a pay floor was established; workers who did not accumulate eight hours of standard allowed minutes during the day earned a set minimum wage. Workers who accumulated more than eight hours of standard allowed minutes were paid for those minutes. In fact, the average in the cutting room ran between 110 percent and 115 percent of the established standards, with the range being between 80 and 160 percent for experienced workers. Workers were paid by filing incentive declarations that documented start and stop times for various operations. There were no coupons to detach as in the coat or pants shop. This incentive system did in fact increase the productivity of the cutting room dramatically.

There were times when workers were not paid piece rates but were paid the average of their work. This occurred whenever a worker was taken off his or her standard job to do something else. For example, if a worker was asked to fill in for an absent colleague, that worker was taken off the piece rate system. Similarly, if a worker was asked to work on something new or something special, piece rates were removed.

Once a piece rate had been established, it could not be changed without some change in model, materials, methods, or machinery. There were literally thousands of piece rates that could apply in the shop, and typically less than 10 percent of them were changed each year. Some had remained unchanged for years. Many changes were, in fact, triggered by a worker's retirement. (Turnover was only 2 to 3 percent a year.)

Management recognized that the piece-rate system caused some wage inequities in the factory, but there seemed to be no clear solutions. It was known, for example, that some piece rates were tight while others were loose; but if no changes were contemplated to those jobs,

management could not remedy those inequities easily without union consent. Spotting such inequities was not always simple. Variations in performance across operators doing the same job could range from 90 percent of the standard to 150 percent. Given such variations, it was often hard to say that a particular piece rate was loose when for at least some workers it might be considered tight.

Setting New Piece Rates

Establishing new piece rates was the responsibility of the factory's industrial engineer, who spent about 60 percent of his time determining piece rates and the rest of his time calculating the factory's unit costs and following up on special projects (such as investigating whether pockets should be die cut by an outside vendor). The first step the industrial engineer took in setting a new piece rate in the coat or pants shop was to meet with the foreman in charge to discuss the procedure that the foreman thought was required to do a quality job. An operator was then brought in and informed of the new task. He or she was given some time to become familiar with the work. After that time the industrial engineer observed the operator for about an hour and a half, informing the operator that this study would result in the establishment of the piece rate. During this observation period, the industrial engineer used an electronic time study board—a clipboard to which was attached a special digital readout stopwatch that kept track of various times. By pressing a lever the engineer could indicate the beginning of one element of the job (jobs were composed of 2 to 30 elements) or the end of another. The time study board would then freeze the duration measured so that the engineer could write it down while at the same time accumulating the time of the next element of the job. In this way the industrial engineer isolated particular movements and tasks. The engineer could also evaluate whether the operator was working as efficiently as possible and just where improvements could be made.

Setting piece rates was complicated by an agreement the company had with the union. That agreement specified that workers would maintain the same average wage no matter where they worked in the shop. Abiding by this agreement meant that new piece rates for established workers in the company had to be constructed specifically for those workers. This agreement, coupled with the tendency for piece rates to become more loose over time, meant that older workers received higher average wages than younger workers doing the same job as well or even better than the older workers. As could be expected, new jobs with new piece rates were generally assigned to new workers, since that was one means by which costs could be kept under control.

This company-union agreement made setting piece rates in the coat and pants shops somewhat more difficult than setting rates in the cutting room. To comply with the agreement in the cutting room, all that needed to be changed was the base pay of the operator. The standard allowed minutes for a task remained the same.

However, for average wages in the coat and pants shops to be maintained, some juggling of the piece rates normally assigned to a worker had to be done. The old piece rate system was not as "clean" as the newer standard allowed minutes system. (In fact, the new North Avenue factory and the Homeland distribution center had adopted the standard allowed minute system from the start.)

Once the piece rate was established, the industrial engineer informed the worker of it. The union was also notified. Often this was all that was needed, although many times some negotiation with the union ensued. Sometimes a restudy of the job was done to dispel any disagreements. Some restudies lasted as long as eight hours. When a piece rate was first changed, it was deemed "unapproved," but usually after a month the union and management would agree that the piece rate was fair. Then the rate was formally approved until it had to be changed because of changes in model, materials, methods, or machinery. Not all rates were formally approved; some stayed unapproved for years. Whether the rate was approved or unapproved did not matter unless some problem came up about it. The company wanted to set rates that could be beat if the workers worked hard—but not so tight that the workers felt they were not earning a fair incentive wage. In nine out of ten cases there was little problem in establishing a piece rate, although company and union both had to compromise their initial positions to some degree.

The Nature of the Workforce

Most of the workforce had had years of experience in the apparel industry. The decline of segments of the apparel industry in this country had left a pool of experienced workers in most metropolitan areas. Skilled operators were so readily available that management could specify that it needed someone to sew collars and be assured that someone with experience sewing collars would be hired. The union was a great help in recommending skilled workers to the company. Thus, there was little problem in educating new workers to tasks. They already knew fairly well what was required of them; with a little training and help from supervision, these workers were able to meet Jos. A. Bank's high quality standards.

For the most part, once a new operator was assigned a job, it was likely that he or she stayed at that job until retirement. Almost all of the workers spent many years at the same level in

Each sewing machine operator became very skilled at a particular task. (*Courtesy of Jos. A. Bank Mfg. Co.*)

the company; only about 10 percent attempted to elevate their grade. Advancement was possible, and workers could request transfers to higher rate jobs, although there was no formal job posting for vacancies. Management usually filled any vacancies from the outside by informing the union of its needs, although management did not have to go to the union to find new people.

The company's relations with the union were good. It helped that the company was growing in an industry that, for the most part, had suffered severe employment declines. In the last 10 to 15 years there had been only one strike, and it was resolved very quickly. Worker complaints were few—only two or three informal complaints each week, and these were usually resolved quickly. In general, complaints related to earnings; such as:

- A piece rate was set too low.

- Bundles were not large enough. With bundles of less than 12, the operator suffered some inefficiencies, and so a high number of low-count bundles sometimes sparked complaints.

- Too many plaids were put through the factory in a week. Plaids required a great deal of pattern matching and slowed up work in the factory considerably.

- Changes to a new model should require a new piece rate.

As many as 90 percent of these complaints were resolved by the factory's first-line supervision. There was, however, a formal grievance procedure, which involved supervision at the first level, the plant manager at the second level, the vice-president of manufacturing at the third level, and then arbitration at the fourth level. There had been only one arbitration proceeding in the last three years. Most of the complaints taken to higher levels of the grievance procedure related to firings, which typically occurred for absenteeism or poor quality. For the most part, union involvement could save a worker from the first threat of firing; but if the worker did not improve, management could fire the worker without union intercession. The only instant and uncontested dismissals were for theft, gross insubordination, or fighting in the factory.

Dismissal, of course, was the most radical form of discipline that the company used. Other levels of discipline were usually used before a dismissal. The most minor form of discipline was a verbal warning, and in most cases two or three verbal warnings were given before a written warning was issued. This written warning would give the reason for the warning, suggest a way for the worker to correct matters, state what the next step would be if the worker did not improve, and indicate at what future time the worker would be reviewed again. If the worker did not improve, there might be another written warning, and after that would come suspension from work. Some suspensions carried definite starting and ending dates, while others were of indefinite duration. Only if these measures did not resolve matters would the worker be dismissed.

Worker pay depended on the task and the shop. Average hourly wages in the coat shop generally averaged $8.50; in the cutting room, around $9; in the pants shop, around $7.25; in the warehouse, from about $4 for unskilled new labor to $7 for the most experienced worker.

In addition to these wages, Bank paid about 39 percent of base salary in benefits. These included medical and disability insurance, life insurance, a pension plan, an eye care plan, and a prescription plan. All of these plans were administered through the union.

It was the responsibility of the factory's industrial engineer to monitor costs and piece rates once they were set. Foremen also helped monitor tasks, since they had to sign off on all worker summary sheets and were required to calculate the percentage efficiencies for each worker. Thus, the workers who were consistently making well above average on their piece rates were known. If their high pay was a surprise, their jobs and/or quality were sometimes studied to make sure that they were not taking shortcuts.

PRODUCTION AND QUALITY CONTROL

Jos. A. Bank's quality standards were rigid. Not only did the company not tolerate sloppy work in the factory, but it also wanted to make sure that a 40 regular one year exactly matched a 40 regular in every other year.

Quality control started at the beginning of the process. Numerous areas of the factory had their quality checked by the appropriate foremen on every coat or pair of pants processed. The chief inspection area, however, was in pressing, after the coat or pair of pants was fully assembled.

The foremen, who supervised between 30 and 35 people each, were responsible chiefly for

Pressing and inspection were done at the end of the assembly process. (*Courtesy of Jos. A. Bank Mfg. Co.*)

checking quality and for instilling in the workers an appreciation of what quality is and a desire to flag quality problems themselves. It was the foreman's task as well to approach workers with any rework. Workers were responsible for the quality of their own work, and any rework on their portion of a coat or pants was done without pay. It was to the worker's advantage to do things right the first time, every time. The chief role of first-level supervision at Bank was to check and maintain quality. Nothing else took so much time and care.

The control of production, as opposed to quality, was chiefly the responsibility of the production managers to whom the first-level supervisors reported. These production managers were as well known to the workforce as the foremen. It was as if factory supervision had been split in two, with the foreman responsible largely for quality and the production manager responsible largely for materials and production control.

The factory could produce between 450 and 500 coats per day, of which about 25 were usually special orders, single coats that were processed separately. The rest were standard orders batched together into the standard bundles. It generally took six to seven weeks for a coat to travel through the process, from the laying out of fabric in the cutting room to the transport of the finished coat to the shipping department. The primary concern of production control was to make sure that all the parts for a coat moved smoothly through the factory and arrived at the various matching stations at about the same time so that they could be joined with specific other parts for further processing. Naturally, some parts took more labor than other parts to complete. For example, backs might be sewn in five minutes, while fronts might take an hour. To ensure a steady flow of goods through the factory, the workforce on fronts was twelve times larger than the one on backs. If parts were not ready, production had to shift to another lot, and operations were not as smooth as they could be.

Matching

Two critical matching stations helped control the flow of parts through the process and uncover any shortages. The first matching station, located about a quarter of the way through the process, was where backs were matched with fronts. The other key matching station was where sleeves were matched with the front and back subassembly; this occurred when the coat

At a major matching station, sleeves were matched to the body of the coat.
(*Courtesy of Jos. A. Bank Mfg. Co.*)

was about 75 percent complete. Matching was accomplished by looking at the tickets that had been attached to the materials near the start of the process. As we saw in Figure C2, the ticket numbers supplied various information: the model processed, the cloth lot to which it belonged, the size of the coat being fabricated, and the shade (a number for the bolt of cloth, which was the same for all pieces belonging to the same coat). The matching stations collated pieces by using these numbers.

If there were quality problems or if particular parts could not be located, fabric sometimes had to be recut. Naturally, Jos. A. Bank wanted any recuts to be from the same bolt of cloth that the original had come from; thus, lot numbers and shade numbers, as well as shop numbers, were recorded for any item that had to be

recut. One day was allotted to do a recut and to rework the materials so that they could rejoin their bundle in the standard flow of work through the shop. Production control did not want to break apart any bundles of material except for super-rush jobs, which occurred about once a week. For all other jobs the bundles were kept the same.

Formal records were kept showing which lots were started in the shop through the fitting operation, and where the bundles were in the shop. Using the laser wand on the worker coupons provided the information needed to keep this tracking up to date.

Because of rework needed or other problems that might be encountered, the capacities of the upstream operations tended to be slightly higher than the capacities of the downstream operations. In order to avoid the accumulation of work-in-process inventory, the factory wanted to make sure that it could easily recoup the time lost on problems in the early stages of the process. This concern for extra capacity in the early stages of the process was particularly evident when plaids were done. As mentioned previously, plaids were the most difficult fabrics to work with because of pattern alignment for pockets, collars, back seams, and so on. This pattern alignment led to a 10 to 15 percent drop in production and a good bit more rework. (Rework in plain fabrics amounted to only 2 or 3 percent of any production lot, but in plaids the rework figure generally climbed to between 5 and 8 percent.) With this in mind, the target for the easy control of work through the factory was to have 60 percent of the work in plain fabrics, 20 percent in stripes, and the remaining 20 percent in plaids. This grouping was the ideal; sometimes, of course, the percentage of stripes or plaids would have to be increased to meet demand.

Supervision

As noted earlier, the first-level supervisor's prime responsibility was quality. Another of his or her tasks was to deal with absences. The first 15 minutes of the morning were spent determining whether everyone was there (absences averaged only 5 percent) and finding replacements for those absent. A number of the workers were cross-trained to fill in on other tasks; when such a switch occurred, they were paid their average earnings rather than the piece rates for these jobs. (There were also some specified utility workers who were paid their choice of a flat rate or a piece rate for the job.) The workers who were put on absentee work generally came from those who were ahead of the pace of the factory as a whole and could thus afford to take time off from their jobs.

The flow of information to the worker from the foreman generally concerned rework or methods. The flow of information from worker to foreman could be for a variety of problems: machine malfunctions, damaged goods, poor quality upstream. The production manager handled all grievances about piece work and about change in the operation. Sharing the complaint load was another advantage to the split of supervision between the foreman and the production manager. The foreman would, however, handle gripes about the size of the bundles for particular workers.

Loading the Factory

The specific planning for, say, the next year's spring fashions began in March. From March through June, the merchandising department led a group (including manufacturing, production planning, buying for ladies' wear, buying for men's wear, and retail store operations) in determining what would be offered in the spring catalog and in the stores. These meetings were the so-called "layout" meetings, where the numbers of coats, suits, and slacks by model and by fabric were decided. The decisions regarding the percentages of different sizes to be cut took into account the differences between the catalog operations and the store operations. Such decisions in the layout meetings determined how much fabric was needed to satisfy the anticipated demand. (See Figures C5 and C6).

Orders for particular bolts of cloth (piece goods) were then placed with various mills. Jos. A. Bank had long had dealings with many mills and knew exactly which mills it wanted to produce particular fabrics. For many piece goods, about 10 percent extra was purchased so as to give the company some flexibility if demand exceeded the forecast. Since Jos. A. Bank fashions changed in only subtle ways from year

FIGURE C5　A sample percentage sheet, as used at Jos. A. Bank.

Notes:

1. For the fall 1982 line destined for Jos. A. Bank stores, this percentage sheet indicates the percentages of all Valley, Kent, Braddock, and Madison models to be made in each size.

2. Another percentage sheet indicates the size breakdowns for catalog sales.

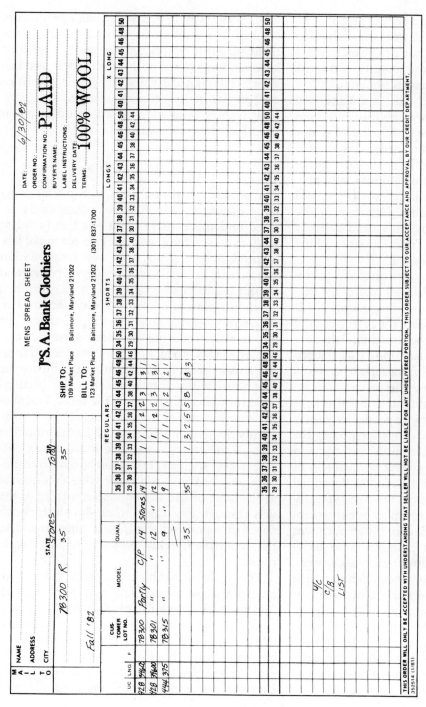

Notes:

1. This men's spread sheet uses the relevant percentage breakdowns into sizes (much as Figure 3-5) to apportion an allocation of 35 coats and pants for portly men that are to be sold through Jos. A. Bank stores.

2. The 35 suits will be cut from three different lots of plaid fabric in quantities of 14, 12, and 9, with the lining (LNG) and undercollar (UC) colors indicated.

3. Note that the same form (in Figure 3-5 and here) is used for two different purposes—as percentage sheet and as spread sheet.

FIGURE C6 A sample men's spread sheet, as used at Jos. A. Bank.

to year, any surplus material could probably be used the following year; being caught with more fabric than required was not nearly as much a problem as being caught with too little. On those rare occasions when there was not enough fabric for a particular model, the merchandising department sometimes was able to purchase fabric from clothiers whose demand may not have been as great. The fabric ordered as a result of the layout meetings for the next year's spring fashions arrived during the summer, any necessary sponging (preshrinking) was done, and cutting began in September. Delivery to the warehouse started in November, and delivery to the stores in January. From January to June or July the spring line was sold.

As noted earlier, manufacturing had no responsibility for the purchase of fabric, the factory's single most important raw material. All responsibility and authority for selection and purchasing rested with the merchandising department. However, manufacturing was charged with the purchase of the numerous trim items that were combined with the piece goods to make coats or pants. Manufacturing also kept track of the status of the piece goods inventory: quantities remaining and their locations. For trim items such as shoulder pads, fusings, and sleeve heads, there were always two sources of supply; the split between the vendors depended upon price. Commitments to vendors typically extended six months in advance, but the shipment of items was specified for much narrower time periods; linings, for example, were delivered every week or two, buttons every six weeks.

Many of the vendors had been dealing with Bank for 15 to 20 years or more. Only if a vendor's price got out of line would the company threaten to reduce the amount of orders placed with it. New vendors were occasionally chosen. Vendor qualification was handled by the chief designer, who tested the item's physical characteristics (such as stretching and pulling) as well as the way it behaved when sewn or dry cleaned. If a vendor was deemed qualified, the plant manager negotiated the price. Typically, new vendors started with small orders as a further check on quality and delivery capabilities and on the stability of the pricing structure. Only if these tests were passed would the order be enlarged for subsequent years.

Production Planning

The production plans began with broad, large-scale decisions, which were subsequently refined and made more detailed. The broadest plans involved ranges—aggregate counts of fabric needs by type. Thus, there were ranges within plains, within stripes, within herringbones, and within plaids. These ranges were then broken down into particular quantities of specified fabrics required; they helped define what was cut and assembled during the entire season. A particular week's production plan was derived from the season plan. It was known that during the first third of the season, most of the cuttings were for the catalog; during the second third of the season, catalog and store sales were more evenly divided; and during the last third of the season, the stores demanded most of any cutting. Using such a rule of thumb, tentative production plans for each week were determined at the start of the season; about a third of the way through the season, there was a thorough check of sales and significant adjustments to the tentative weekly production plans were made.

The production schedule set was typically for an eight-week period. The first week was allocated to planning, the next two weeks to cutting, and the ensuing five weeks to the shop. What was cut in a particular week depended on two key things: the mix of cloth (the 60/20/20 plain/stripe/plaid breakdown mentioned earlier) and customer expectations about delivery.

An automatic sewing machine used for sewing certain parts of the coat.
(*Courtesy of Jos. A. Bank Mfg. Co.*)

Production Planning Paperwork

Once the layout meetings determined the models and quantities for the next season and the necessary bolts of fabric were ordered, received, and in storage, the paperwork was initiated to direct and control the transformation of fabric into suits, coats, and pants. The production plan for any week triggered several actions in the cutting room office. One of them was the issue of a cloth pull sheet (Figure C7), which authorized the withdrawal of fabric from inventory. Authorization to cut the cloth was provided by the cutting slip and the accompanying cutting chart (Figure C8), which indicated, for each lot number, the quantities and the size combinations for the markers or patterns that were actually used to cut the fabric. Cutting was done in groups of fabrics compatible for sewing and for machine setup and operation. (See Figure C9.) The cutting slip and the cutting chart traveled with the job.

After the materials were cut and fitted, the Soabar report (Figure C10) was issued by the cutting room office. This report indicated not only the lot number but also the make, model, and size for all the bundles of fabric to be processed. The data entry for the Soabar report generated, via a special computer program, the fitter's report, which indicated the lot, bundle, and quantities, by size, that were to be run through each shop. The fitter's report in turn generated the coupons that traveled with the job and were critical to the operation of the piece-rate system.

42   (1720

CLOTH PULL SHEET

MODEL: S843A WW253 York Coat & Pant   TYPE OF CLOTH: Plain-Poly-Cotton

DELIVERED BY: RECEIVED BY: DATE: 8-21

Ply No.	Lot No. 1 (3.50)	Ydg. Rec'd.	Shade	Ydg.	Loc.	Shade	Ydg.	Loc.	Shade	Ydg.	Loc.	Shade	Ydg.	Loc.
60½	22400	1775	28	150	P54	30	150	P28	32	150	P28	33	151	P28
			34	105	P28	35	151	P28	38	149	P28	41	151	P28
			42	151	P10	43	151	P10	45	151	P10	44	151	P10
			65	30	530									
	2													
60½	22401	2296	176	149	P50	186	149	P50	179	149	P50	135	94	P18
			189	140	P50	59	150	P27	66	150	P27	67	150	P27
			69	151	P27	173	149	P50	12	151	P24	172	149	P50
			20	151	P24	34	149	P24	40	149	P24	1	30	190
			3	93	251									
	3													
60½	22407	1950	1	149	P14	2	82	P14	3	148	P14	4	145	P14
			5	101	P14	18	71	P14	19	149	P14	20	94	P14
			36	149	P14	37	149	P14	25	135	P5	27	149	P5
			45	147	P5	63	149	494	67	140	495			

Notes:

1. This is the cloth pull sheet for group 42, coats and pants for model WW253.

2. The sheet indicates the yards of fabric cut for each lot, the shade (bolt of fabric), and where that bolt of fabric was located (the bin number).

FIGURE C7   A sample cloth pull sheet, as used at Jos. A. Bank.

Keith Rush F'85   C825A C755A   HW

CUT # _____ MODEL 225 - 265 Coats _____   DATE #2 _____

UNIT _____

Group #33 Delivery 10/1   Dec1   Dec 8 Herringbone   27" goods

LOT NO.	SHADE NO.	40R 42R	43R 48R	44R 46R	41R 41R	43L 48L	44L 46L	38R 39R	40L 41L	42L 50L	42L 42L	37R	39L					
		2	2	2														
D 19400	30	②2	③3	③3	①1												225	S+R	H-Bone
C 19405	30	②2	③3	③3	①1														H-Bone
B 19418	18-25-21	②2	⑨9	⑨9	⑤5	⑤5	⑤5	6	7	2	4	4	5		2044				
A 19409	23-24-15	⑱18	⑫12	⑫12	⑧8	⑩10	⑩10	6	4	8	5	4	34		2040		265	PLN/S+R	
	26-16-20																		
	19-22-84	34	27	27	15	15	15	12	11	10	9	8	89				SHADE	LEFT	
	20														00		30	6	
		4·9¼	4·21¾	4·21	4·9½	4·27½	4·27	40½	4·12¼	4·28¼	4·16½	2·6	2·10		05		30	7	
												NLF			18		25	6	
																	21	6	
																	23	7	
																	24	15	
																	15	6	
			Dec 3					Dec 4									25	6	
																	15	5	
			38S	43XL													2	5	
		42XL	40S	46XL		39S											24	6	
		44XL	42S	48XL	36R	38L	41S	43L	44L	36S	37S	43S	44S				23	15	
19418		4	3	3	2	2	23	3	3	1							225	S+R	

Notes:

1. This is a portion of the cutting chart for a rush order for group 33, coat models 225 and 265. The cutting chart indicates which size combinations will be used for the markers on this order and how many of each lot and shade of fabric are to be cut. The group number and shop number are given in the cutting office.

2. These coats will be cut from 27-inch wide herringbone fabric (Harris tweed). Some of the fabric is plain herringbone, and some is striped.

3. The numbers at the bottom indicate the yards of fabric used by the size combinations listed at the top of the columns.

FIGURE C8 A sample cutting chart, as used at Jos. A. Bank.

PLAID

100% WOOL

REGULAR	SHORT	LONG	X LONG	MODEL	GROUP NUMBER	DESCRIPTION	ISSUED	PAGE	OF
2226				451	207	Portly Coats & Pants	6/30/82	1	1

CUT WITH

COMMENTS: Fall '82

REGULARS

UC	LINING	*	LOT NO	GRAND TOTAL	36	37	38	39	40	41	42	43	44	45	46	48	50	TOTAL
428	34600	T	78300	14					1	1	1	2	2	3	3	1		14
428	34600	T	78301	12					1			2	2	3	3	1		12
444	375	N	78315	9					1	1	1	1	2		2	1		9

SHORTS — 35 36 37 38 39 40 41 42 43 44 TOTAL

LONGS — 37 38 39 40 41 42 43 44 45 46 48 50 TOTAL

X LONGS — 40 41 42 43 44 45 46 48 TOTAL

Jos. A. Bank Clothiers

Group Sales

352504 (9/81)

Notes:

1. This is the group sheet for 35 plaid, 100% wool suits (model 451), cut for portly men. The group number is 207 and the shop number is 2226. After the shop number has been assigned, five copies of this sheet are given to the cutting room floor and one copy to customer service.

2. There are three lots in this group (78300, 78301, and 78315) calling for quantities of 14, 12, and 9, respectively, spread among the regular sizes shown.

3. The colors to be used for UC (undercollars), linings, and * (fusings) are indicated by the numbers or letters in those columns at the left.

4. A separate group sheet is made for plain, stripe, or plaid cloth. Same-color linings are grouped together.

FIGURE C9   A sample group sheet, as used at Jos. A. Bank.

DATE: 6\11\85

VAR: 1. Regular   5. Portley
2. Short   6. Portley Short
3. Long   7. Portley Long
4. X Long

SOABAR REPORT
MEN'S

MAKE: 3

DESCRIPTION: Plain - Poly Wool

H	SHOP NUMBER	261	COAT MODEL	261	PANT MODEL		VEST MODEL	VAR	DATE SOABARED

2|6|0|4 — S|7|5|\|A|C|5|5|8|C   P|N   S|7|5|\|A|9|5|5|8|P   P|N — \ 0|6|/|4|8|5

TYPE: 1. Stock
2. Single
MAKE: 1. ODD
2. 2 PC. SUIT
3. 3 PC. SUIT

UNIT COST
MFG. BC
RETAILER 3

UNIT COST
MFG. BP
RETAILER 3

UNIT COST
MFG.
RETAILER

GRP   DUE DATE
2|0|6   0|8|/|2|8|5

TOTAL QUANTITY

LOT NUMBER	M A K E	T Y P E	COAT	VEST	PANT	29 35	30 36	31 37	32 38	33 39	34 40	35 41	36 42	37 43	38 44	39 45	40 46	41 48	42 50	43 52	44 54	46	48
11403	2	1	131		131	\	\	9	14	23	21	22	13	13	4	5	4	1					
11402	2	1	102		102	2	\	7	11	18	16	18	9	9	3	+	3	1					
tot.			233		233	3	2	16	25	41	37	40	22	22	7	9	7	2					
						3	2	16	16 25	37 41	37	18 36 40	22	22	7	9	7	2					

DATA PROCESSING
JUN 14 1985

6-14-85
Lot C

354012 (3/85)

Notes:

1. This is the Soabar report for shop number 2604 for group 206, 233 coats and pants of model 261, soabared on June 14, 1985 and due out of the shop on August 12, 1985. The BC and BP entered for Mfg. indicate the Baltimore coat shop and Baltimore pants shop, respectively.

2. There are two separate lots. The report indicates the exact sizes and how many of each should be made.

FIGURE C10   A sample Soabar report, as used at Jos. A. Bank.

The paperwork just described served to follow up on the production planning by initiating work in the cutting room and the several shops of the factory. Other paperwork served to help control the movement of materials through the factory and to cope with irregularities (such as rework, recutting, and failed matchings).

TECHNOLOGICAL INNOVATION

Apparel manufacture, especially the manufacture of quality merchandise such as Bank's line, traditionally was not amenable to technological innovation. A quality suit required a good deal of art, since sewing had to be done to contours rather than in straight lines. Reflecting this, the automatic equipment at the Baltimore factory was minimal. There was some automatic undersleeve sewing and some automatic machines for pocket cutting, but other than these, the factory's sewing machines were strictly manually operated.

Some other innovations, however, had been recently accomplished or were underway. The most important of these was the AM-5 machine for automatically generating markers for the cutting room. This innovation eliminated waste in laying out the piece goods, and it automatically increased sizes, saving considerable time in the design of the markers themselves.

Another important innovation was the two-tiered cutting table that permitted cutting and spreading to go on simultaneously, one on each tier of the table. This innovation saved room on the cutting room floor, which was very desirable in the cramped quarters of the Candler Building, but it also meant that workers did not have to travel as far up and down the cutting tables, thereby increasing their productivity.

Other technological innovations involved materials. Fusings for the front of the coat, for example, were comparatively new. Fusing material consisted of firm fabric coated with beads of adhesive that, when heated, fused the material so that it lay properly and did not wrinkle.

Other technological advances were being investigated and showed some promise. One involved the use of sewing machines that could be programmed like machine tools. Future generations of programmable sewing machines might well exhibit the high degree of flexibility required to make quality clothing.

PART TWO

DISCUSSION

Jos. A. Bank Clothiers is in no way responsible for the following views and presentation. They remain solely the responsibility of the author.

The Process and Information Flows

In comparison with the job shop of Norcen Industries, the flow of production at Jos. A. Bank is better defined. While there are some understandable differences between the coat shop and the pants shop, we can compose a process flow diagram for each of those shops that adequately represents the process, at least in general terms (see Figure C11). A more detailed process flow diagram, one that encompasses the actual operations described on the coupons, would reveal that there are still substantial differences between various products (such as suit coat versus sportcoat), models, and materials. Vari-

ations in any one of these lead to the inclusion of certain process steps and the exclusion of others. In general, however, the flow of materials through the process is fairly smooth and easily directed. Concern for materials routing is much less critical in this batch flow process than in a job shop.

Because of the wide variety of materials, models, and sizes, the factory must deal with a vast array of different batches. These variations underscore the still very strong need of the batch flow process for information and control. In their own way, the information flows of the batch flow process are inflexible, although compared with the job shop, the flow of information between workers and management is somewhat reduced. While workers are responsible for notifying management of machine malfunctions and quality problems, the major information flows to and from workers revolve mainly around the coupons that move

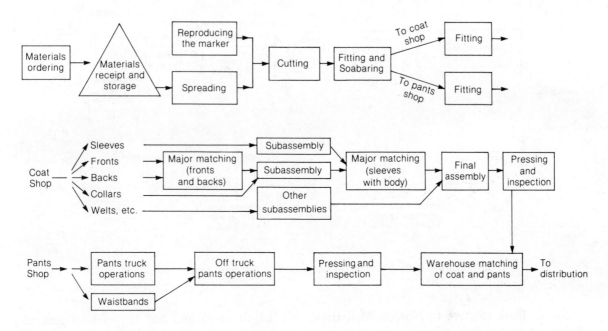

FIGURE C11   A simplified process flow diagram for a Jos. A. Bank suit.

with each bundle, as shown in Figure C12. In essence, the coupons serve as both process sheet and job sheet, to borrow language from the Norcen Industries example. The coupons inform the worker of what must be done to the batch, and they also keep track of who did what to each batch of work.

The increased stability of the batch flow process reduces the amount of information that must be communicated from management to workers. The foreman typically has less troubleshooting and expediting to do and fewer scheduling changes to make. Therefore, it is often possible to supervise more people in a batch flow operation than in a job shop. The foreman at Jos. A. Bank has time to track quality and improve methods rather than having to make schedules and troubleshoot.

The need for continuous flow of information is reduced in the batch flow process, primarily because its product selection, while large, is still lim-

ited and well known in advance. Furthermore, it seldom has to bid for contracts, and so precise, order-specific cost information is not required.

Capacity in the Batch Flow Process

The notion of capacity is only slightly less ambiguous in the batch flow operation than in the job shop. Nevertheless, the wide arrays of products that can be produced in any week make it difficult to specify a batch process's capacity in specific units of output without pegging it first to some standard mix of products.

The capacity of the batch flow process is influenced by many of the same factors that determine the capacity of the job shop.

1. *Batch (or lot) sizes.* Although the setup time for any bundle of materials is low at

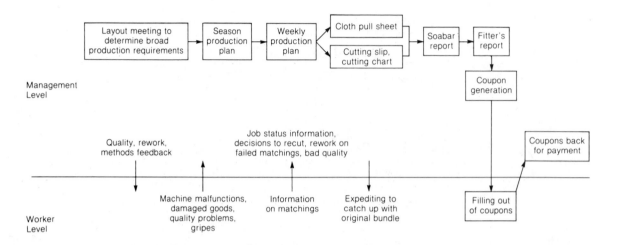

Management
Level

Worker
Level

FIGURE C12   A simplified information flow diagram for Jos. A. Bank.

Jos. A. Bank relative to Norcen Industries, certain procedures are necessary (change of thread and needles) before a new batch can be processed. As mentioned in the process description, the larger the batch, the more satisfied is the worker; too many low-count batches spur complaints from workers.

2. *Complexity of the products run through the operation.* As noted, plaids and stripes are markedly more difficult to handle than plain fabrics; when the production schedule includes a higher-than-normal percentage of these materials, the capacity of the entire coat shop declines.

3. *Nature of the jobs already on the factory floor.* Batch flow operations, like job shops, are subject to shifting bottlenecks and worker-machine interference. However, the definite limits to product diversity in batch flows generally mean that the severity and frequency of these two capacity thieves are reduced.

4. *Scheduling.* Scheduling is still an important consideration with the managers of the

batch operation, but the task is generally simpler than in the job shop. Again, the reduction of products and capabilities offered accounts for the bulk of this difference. With the batch operation, scheduling begins to shed some of its critical importance to the success of the operation as a whole. Given a reasonable composition of orders for the week (for example, the 60/20/20 split of plain/stripe/plaid fabric), scheduling becomes much more routine.

5. *Process improvement.*

6. *Number of machines and their condition.*

7. *Quantity and quality of labor input.*

The last three major influences on capacity, like many of the other influences cited, take on less importance for the typical batch operation than for the typical job shop. This is because the batch flow process itself is better defined, with workers more apt to be assigned to particular machines and less free to float among machines. The transition from job shop to batch operation accounts already for considerable process improvement (such as specific methods, worker aids at the workstation, quicker setups). Considering its routing tickets (coupons), assigned machines, and specialized training, the batch operation is more likely to treat machines and workers as one producing unit. Thus, capacity can be enhanced significantly by increasing both in similar proportions. This is not to say that equipment improvement cannot be made in the typical batch flow operation. Jos. A. Bank, for example, was making substantial investments in new cutting tables and was monitoring advances in sewing machines.

THE ROLE OF STANDARDS AND INCENTIVES

At Jos. A. Bank the role of standards takes on a different function than at Norcen Industries. At Norcen, you will recall, standards were used to estimate times and costs for bidding on jobs and also to provide information for scheduling jobs through the shop. Although the second function for standards is retained at Bank, standards are not used for job cost estimation because there is no bidding for new orders. Rather, standards in the form of piece rates and standard-hour (that is, the standard-allowed-minutes system) incentives are used explicitly to determine worker compensation and thus to spur worker effort and output. In a sense, the piece-rate and standard-hour incentives act to pace work through the factory.

As the process description made plain, the setting of incentives at Jos. A. Bank is serious business. Great care is taken to see that they are both accurate and fair. Considerable time and expense are spent setting new piece rates, observing workers trying out new piece rates, and testing modifications in methods. The procedures for setting and using incentives and for resolving disputes over them are well established and routine.

DEMANDS OF THE PROCESS ON WORKFORCE AND MANAGEMENT

The demands made on the workforce center around the incentive system. The system, rather than foremen, acts to pace production; thus, the demands for worker output are mainly triggered by the incentive system itself. Demands for quality output, on the other hand, come from the foremen. The foremen's most important job is to check the work that has been done and make sure that the methods being followed are proper.

At Jos. A. Bank, the ambition of workers is not great, and so not a lot of effort is expended to provide career paths for the workforce. Some other batch flow operations are more concerned with such issues. Of course, there is cross-training in a batch flow operation like Bank. Not only does cross-training help cope with absenteeism, but it also helps break bottlenecks, particularly chronic ones.

Clearly, one of management's chief concerns in a process like Bank's is the incentive system. The incentive rates should be fair to the workers but not so loose that costs get out of control. Striking a suitable balance is an important endeavor.

Apart from the incentive system, management must also be concerned with keeping the flow of work smooth. This means grouping work well and staying within guidelines for the materials mix. Not only must management be wary of the policies by which it loads the factory, but it must also track jobs through the process and act immediately to remedy any difficulties. While the flow of information is not as rigid and sophisticated as in a job shop, management must still pay considerable attention to the information pertinent to the flow of materials and jobs.

QUESTIONS

1. Compare and contrast the characteristics of the information flow in the batch flow process used by Jos. A. Bank with the information flow characteristics of the two other processes discussed in Tours A and B. Which process requires the least in the way of information flow from its managers? from its workers? Does anything replace the flow of information to workers or managers?

2. The typical duties of first-line supervision at Jos. A. Bank are divided between two people. What are the strengths and/or weaknesses of such an arrangement, as you see them?

3. Discuss the difference between the piece-rate and standard-hour schemes at Jos. A. Bank. Could the cutting room have been put on a piece-rate system? Had that been done, what complications would you have anticipated?

4. Under what conditions do you have the most confidence in the factory's ability to produce 475 coats a week? Under what conditions do you have the least confidence? Why?

5. How would you describe the market for Jos. A. Bank? What relationship, if any, does this market have to the production process chosen by the company?

6. In what ways is the union a help to Jos. A. Bank? A hindrance?

7. Could the low rate of movement of workers among jobs in the factory be related to the activities of the industrial engineer? Elaborate.

SITUATION FOR STUDY C-1

BROWN, SMITH & JONES (BS&J)

Paul Alvarez has just been hired by BS&J as superintendent of the fabricated tank division. Paul's previous experience had been with a leading manufacturer of home heating systems where the processes were highly automated. At the previous firm the goods were also processed in a continuous manner, with a product line being set up for a year or more of production.

The products manufactured by the fabricated tank division were typically oil storage tanks made from sheet steel, which were sent to the customer much like a kit and were erected in remote oil fields. Occasionally, the firm sold the tanks in various sizes to other customers for other uses, such as to the military for the storage of diverse liquids like water and jet airplane fuel. Figure C13 is an example of a tank and some of the parts that must be fabricated. Table C1 is a partial process sheet for these parts. Figure C14 is a layout of the relevant processes.

Many of the smaller parts are common to most tanks, and they are made on a continuous basis to inventory requirements. There are three parts that are unique to each tank size: the tank side parts called staves, the triangular roof, and the bottom sections. The smallest tank, 1500-gallon capacity, requires five staves, five roof sections, and five floor sections. A 55,000-gallon tank, five rows high, requires 13 roof sections, 13 floor sections, and 65 staves. The typical order is for three tanks of the same size,

Typical roof section

Bolts

Access ring

Typical tank stave

Flange bend line

Typical stave with holes punched, rolled, and flanged. All staves are made from cold rolled steel, 4 feet by 8 feet, 1/8 to 1/4 inch thick.

Typical roof or floor section

Bolt holes

Roof and floor sections are made from cold rolled steel, 4 feet by 8 feet (or 4 feet by 12 feet if necessary). Larger requirements are met by making these sections in multiple pieces.

Notes:

1. A typical tank stave (1) is trimmed (if needed), (2) has holes punched on all sides, (3) is rolled to the approximate shape (depending on the tank diameter) on the pyramid roll, and (4) is flanged on both ends in a large brake press. The press is set up with a flanging that also causes the stave to be formed to the final shape according to the tank diameter. There is a flanging tool for each diameter tank.

2. The roof and floor sections are made from material similar to the tank staves, ranging from 1/8 inch to 1/4 inch, per the engineering design. If necessary, these sections can be made from material 4 feet by 12 feet. BS&J uses standard mill sizes to avoid the extra costs involved in having special sizes available; also, pieces that are too big would create construction problems. Two sections are usually cut from a single sheet:

Punch press tool to punch and shear

Circle shear

Bolt holes

8' to 12'

4'

Straight shear

(The view is somewhat exaggerated to demonstrate the method.) If a top or bottom piece were too long, it would be made from two pieces:

Whatever length needed

8' to 12'

Overlap; straight cut to be bolted together at construction site

FIGURE C13 Typical tank and parts.

TABLE C1   Partial outline of the process (Brown, Smith & Jones)

STAVE		ROOF AND FLOOR SECTIONS	
OPERATION	PROCESS	OPERATION	PROCESS
Shear edges true	Sheet shear	Shear edges and split each sheet on diagonal	Sheet shear
Punch bolt holes in both ends	Brake press setup with punches	Punch/shear small end*	Punch press
Punch bolt holes in both sides	Brake press setup with punches	Shear large end	Circle shear
Roll to tank diameter	Pyramid rolls	Clean and paint	Paint line
Flange both ends	Brake press setup with correct flange	Pack and ship	
Clean and paint	Paint line		
Pack and ship			

*For typical tank sizes there were punch press tools for this. Others had to be laid out, circle sheared, and single punched.

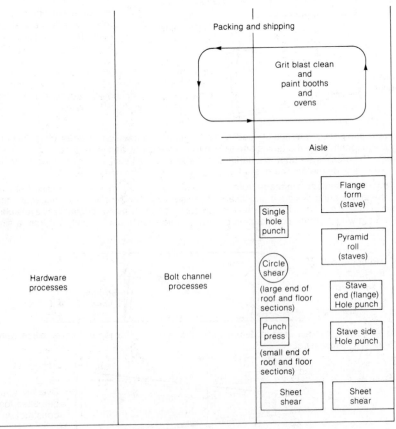

FIGURE C14   Fabricating process layout for a side stave, roof section, or floor section.

but an order can be as small as one tank and has been as large as 15 tanks. The tanks are made to order, but BS&J has a backlog estimated at one and one-half months' production.

Paul was hired because the fabricated tank division has been unable to meet scheduled shipping dates, quality problems are cropping up, and the workers are unhappy about never being able to earn any incentive pay. Paul thought he would focus on the manufacture of the side staves, roof, and floor sections. What

information does he need next? What information should be included on parts routing sheets?

1. Draw a process flow diagram for the two major tank parts.
2. What information would you need in order to set up a production schedule for this shop?
3. What approaches would you suggest to Paul to help him with both his quality problems and his incentive pay problems?

SITUATION FOR STUDY C-2
WELCH'S ICE CREAM

Ice cream production took place every weekday at Welch's, a shop that sold ice cream to the public. The entire process of making the ice cream was performed by Brad Gentry, an hourly employee. In addition, Brad had sole responsibility for inventory maintenance, quality control, and production scheduling. He worked about four hours a day during slow periods and about twice that during the peak season. Because he knew more than anyone else at the shop about production needs at any given time, and because he was decoupled from the sales portion of the business by an inventory of finished ice cream, Brad set his own hours. He usually worked from about 10 A.M. to 2 P.M.

The shop owned one ice cream machine with a 40-quart batch capacity. (The capacity refers to the finished volume rather than the volume of ingredients.) The manufacturing process involved rapid agitation and aeration of the ingredients, which nearly doubled the batch's volume. Hence, a 40-quart batch required approximately 20 quarts of mix.

The machine itself resembled a stainless steel 20-gallon water heater, lying on its side on a

waist-high stand. The cylinder had a refrigeration layer on the outside, through which refrigerants circulated when the machine was in use. At one end of the cylinder was the motor unit, which drove the refrigerant pump and the agitation blades inside the tank. At the other end was a lower spout, through which the finished ice cream was pushed by the rotation of the blades. A table was positioned here so that buckets on it could catch the ice cream. Above the spout were two built-in funnels, through which extracts and flavorings could be added. On top of the cylinder was a stainless steel tub, which held a little over 20 quarts of liquid.

The ice cream machine was located in a small room called the process room, which also contained also a few shelves of supplies, reusable plastic buckets, scales, and a large sink. Three doors in the process room provided access to a walk-in refrigerator where the raw mix was kept, a walk-in freezer ($-30°F$) called the hardening box, and the rest of the premises.

The ingredients used in production were of three general types. The major type was the "mix," which was milk containing sweetener and a high cream content. An order of mix was delivered daily by a local dairy. This order consisted of five 50-pound cartons. Welch's placed an order with the dairy every day for delivery the next day, even though a different quantity was rarely ordered.

The second type of ingredient was the flavor bases: the various syrups and extracts that were added to the mix during agitation. The third type consisted of nuts, cookies, and some syrups that were "marbleized" into the ice cream. (*Marbleization* means that the ingredient is not beaten into the mix, but is poured into the stream of finished ice cream as it comes out the spout.)

The major vendor for the second and third types of ingredients was a company that usually delivered within 7 to 10 days after an order had been placed. This supplier paid freight costs but required a 15-case minimum. Brad took inventory on flavor bases once a month, and on marbleizing ingredients every two weeks. After taking inventory, Brad gave his boss a list of supplies needed and the boss did the ordering.

A production run began with sterilization of the ice cream machine and enough plastic buckets (a bucket equals 10 quarts) to hold the day's batches of ice cream. Each batch required 20 quarts of mix, and Brad usually made six batches a day, so Welch's received about 125 quarts of mix every day. Because the mix doubled during processing and the other ingredients also took up space, Brad used about 25 buckets per day.

While the machine and buckets dried, Brad checked the stock of ice cream in the tempering box, a walk-in freezer (adjacent to the hardening box) kept at 6°F. Ice cream in the hardening box was too cold to scoop, and so a sufficient inventory in the tempering box was necessary to ensure that Welch's did not run out of servable ice cream. After seeing which flavors were running low, Brad rotated those flavors from hardening to tempering box via a doorway connecting the two freezers. A map of ice cream locations was posted in the tempering box so that people who worked out front could easily find whatever flavor they needed. Maintaining this map was important because there were usually about 150 buckets ranging over 40 flavors stocked in this freezer. Welch's complete inventory comprised the contents of (1) the tempering box, (2) the hardening box (also an average of 150 buckets), and (3) the glass-topped refrigerators located in the service area (usually 32 buckets).

After rotating the stock, Brad took from the stock room the flavor bases and any other ingredients he needed that day. On Monday and Friday mornings, he took inventory of the hardening and tempering boxes and on the basis of this decided which flavors to make on a given day. Because he did not work weekends and Welch's sold 65 to 75 percent of their ice cream from Friday to Sunday, Brad had a target inventory for each flavor that he wanted to have on hand by Friday. The Monday inventory informed him how much of each flavor was sold over the weekend and therefore how much he needed to make above daily usage to reach Friday's target. The Friday inventory was a check that enough of each flavor was on hand for the weekend in the tempering box. By comparing usage figures from week to week, Brad could schedule flavor production to reflect demand. The target inventory was not a specific figure but rather a rough number that Brad carried in his head and altered according to his judgment. He did keep track of what he produced during the week, and he used this list to avoid duplicating batches or forgetting needed flavors. It was usually necessary to make two batches of vanilla a day, because about a third of all sales were vanilla.

Brad scheduled the batches from lightest taste and color to heaviest taste and darkest color.

This way he avoided having to rinse the machine after every batch and saved 5 to 10 minutes, plus the ice cream that stuck to the blades. Vanilla was always first, because what little stayed in the machine blended well with the following batch. Brad could usually run three different flavors before having to rinse the machine.

Brad dumped 20 quarts of mix into the tub and allowed it to drain into the tank. He then closed the valve between the two and poured another 20 quarts into the tub, ready for the next batch. He turned on the agitator and added a measured amount of vanilla flavoring and cream tone. Welch's provided a complete index of recipes and instructions, but Brad had those for the most popular flavors memorized. He timed the batch—the first batch of the day for 10 minutes and subsequent batches for 8 minutes. The first took longer because the machine was not yet cold.

When the time was almost up, he took a sample and weighed it. The batch was done if one cup weighed 90 to 95 grams, though chocolate flavors ran a bit denser. When ready, the ice cream was run out into buckets, covered with waxed paper, labeled with flavor and date, and placed in the hardening box, where it stayed for at least 12 hours before being rotated to the tempering box. Ice cream usually stayed in the hardening box for more than 12 hours; it would keep indefinitely at that temperature. When the end of the batch would not fill most of a bucket, Brad filled a few pint and quart cartons which, after freezing, were stored in a confection box at the front of the restaurant and sold. Although not a large business segment, this procedure avoided waste.

Brad repeated this batch process until he had either used up the five cartons of mix or made all he wanted to for the day. Normally he used all the mix, although it could be kept in the refrigerator for several days. When finished, he again sterilized the machine and washed the walls and floor of the process room before leaving. The cleanup took about 45 minutes.

1. Diagram the process and information flows for this process.

2. How would you plan production for such a process (that is, how would you schedule which flavors would be produced and when, both during the day, the week, and the month)?

3. What controls on ice cream production would you use in this ice cream parlor? Why?

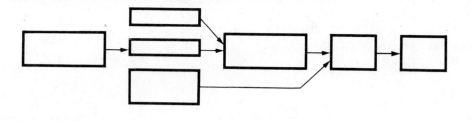

A MACHINE-PACED LINE FLOW PROCESS
General Motors Corporation, Chevrolet-Pontiac-Canada Group Tarrytown, New York

The Tarrytown plant of the Chevrolet-Pontiac-Canada Group (C-P-C), situated on the Hudson River just north of New York City, was the oldest of the 30 domestic and four Canadian assembly plants operated by General Motors (the Tarrytown plant was built in 1914). The plant was huge, stretching over 97 acres, 2,250,000 square feet of space under roof. About 4000 production workers and 475 salaried workers were employed on two production shifts. The plant assembled two models of the body type A car—Pontiac 6000 and Buick Century sedans—and delivered truckloads of these cars to over 5000 auto dealers in United States. The Tarrytown plant was not the only one to assemble cars with body type A. Two sister plants in Oshawa, Canada and sister plants in Doraville, Georgia; Framingham, Massachusetts; and Oklahoma City, Oklahoma produced similar models. Any of these plants could deliver cars to any dealer in the country—however, the model mix schedule dictated dealer delivery, based on customer demand by geographic location.

PART ONE
PROCESS DESCRIPTION

HOW A CAR WAS ASSEMBLED: A SIMPLIFIED DESCRIPTION

The production process at C-P-C—Tarrytown was a classic but modern example of the moving assembly line so closely associated with Henry Ford and the Model T. The essence of the process was to build the car bit by bit by having workers perform the same tasks on each car as it moved through their workstations on a conveyor system. The A body car, with its front-wheel drive, could be viewed as the marriage of two large subassemblies: one for the body of the car and one for the motor cradle (the motor, its support structure, the front axles, and the trailing exhaust system and rear wheel brake lines). The assembly

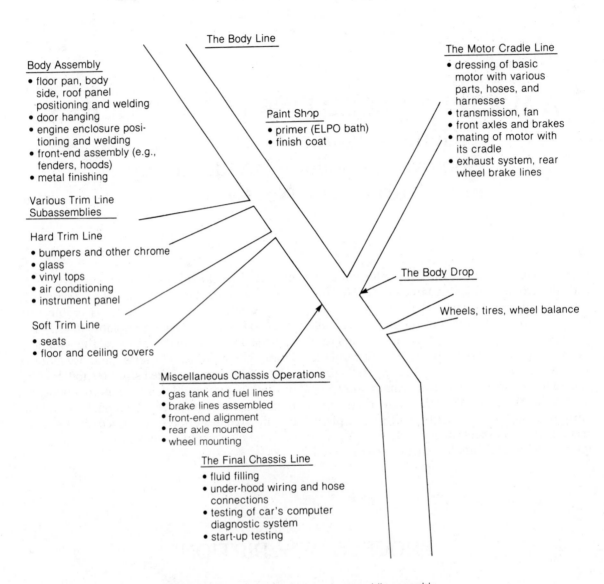

FIGURE D1   A rough diagram of automobile assembly.

plant was organized to build up the body and the motor cradle separately, to "marry" them at the "body drop," and then to finish the car's assembly and inspection. Each of the body and motor cradle lines was fed by smaller subassembly lines, so that pictorially, the process resembled a tree, with a large trunk, one main branch, and many smaller branches. Figure D1 provides just such a rough picture of the entire process; a more detailed version would require more space and explanation than is merited.

The assembly of the front-wheel drive A body cars is very different from the assembly of the traditional rear-wheel drive cars such as the old Chevrolet Nova, which had formerly been assembled at Tarrytown. In the traditional assembly, the body line included assembly of everything from the windshield on back to the tail lights, but not assembly of the enclosure for the engine or any front fenders or hood. The front end's sheet metal parts were assembled after the body was mated with the chassis (everything in front of the windshield) and the undercarriage (including the wheels). In the traditional assembly, the body drop was a spectacular operation where an overhead conveyor system "dropped" the body onto the chassis and undercarriage assembly, triggering a flurry of activity (much of it in a pit under the car) to bolt the two assemblies together.

In the current assembly operation, much of the traditional chassis assembly had been transferred to the body line. The current body drop was actually more of a "motor lift"; the massive overhead conveyor and the pit work were replaced by three workstations to (1) position and lift the motor in the front end, (2) bolt it in place, and (3) bolt the trailing exhaust system to the rear of the body.

The entire line was composed of 1367 cars that took 22.4 hours to progress through the complete assembly process; a rate of about one per minute per workstation. A typical workstation consisted of (1) two workers, one on each side of the line, (2) some space in which to work, (3) equipment specific to the job, and (4) in many stations some racks or bins stocked with parts to be assembled onto the car. A great deal of variety existed from one workstation to another. For example, a typical workstation along the trimline might have the car moving at ground level, while at the body drop the car was raised for work underneath it. An inspection station might have intense lights and raised platforms so that the inspec-

tors could easily identify any flaws and mark them for correction. In the final chassis line there were pits where workers could work on or inspect the cars moving along above them. At workstations that were completely mechanized (robots were in use) all materials handling and all operations were done by special machines; much of the body welding was done at such stations, and the paint shop was soon to be completely automated with painting and materials handling robots. About the only consistent feature across workstations throughout the plant was that the work averaged about a minute per car.

For some options, however, a worker might have to take somewhat over a minute. This deviation was termed "being overcycled." Naturally, a worker could not be continually overcycled without falling behind the pace of the line. To keep up, overcycled jobs had to be quickly balanced off by undercycled jobs for the workers affected. Given the existence of overcycle jobs, then, the sequencing of cars along the line to provide a balance of overcycled and undercycled work was an important endeavor.

Much of the overcycled work occurred along the hard and soft trim lines (see Figure D1), where many of multitude of options were added to the car. Workers were advised what options to include on any car by reading the "broadcast" or "manifest," an instruction sheet attached to the car (usually a copy on each front door). The broadcast was the primary information by which the worker determined what part or component was to be placed on that particular vehicle. In an effort to reduce error, the plant generated about 20 "mini-manifests," which highlighted in large, bold print the proper components for options that were called for in a particular department. The mini-manifests required more paperwork, but they enhanced quality by simplifying the information flow to the workers along the line.

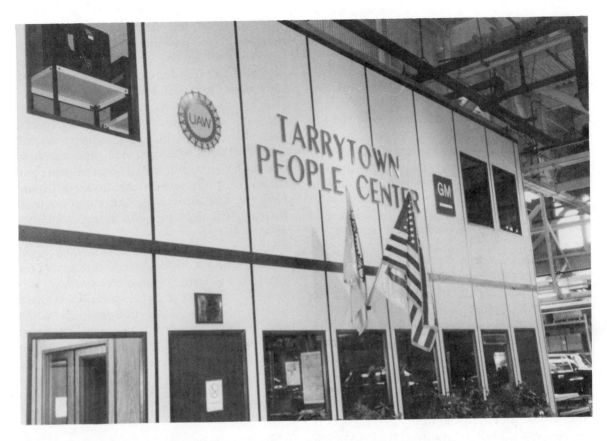

The joint union-management "people center," where the quality-of-work-life programs are housed. (*Courtesy of GM Chevrolet-Pontiac-Canada Group*)

LOADING THE PLANT

Planning Production

Because cars and the parts to make them were both expensive and bulky, considerable thought was given to limiting inventories at the plant. No finished goods inventories were kept; all the cars assembled were trucked to individual dealers within a short time after coming off the production line. Therefore, all the cars destined for a particular dealer had to be scheduled for completion at roughly the same time to avoid significant delays of truck trailers and finished cars.

Furthermore, all the cars produced were to dealer order as to make, model, color, and options. C-P-C—Tarrytown, on its own, was not permitted to ship any dealer a car that the dealer had not ordered. Roughly 30 percent to 50 percent of the dealer's order represented cars that were already sold to particular customers; the remainder represented the dealer's speculation about what the dealership would be able to sell. Such production to order, given the wide range of options permitted in a car, placed tremendous demands on the plant's materials function to schedule the proper mix of cars through the line and to secure enough of the proper parts to fill the order.

The scheduling and the materials procurement functions were characterized by successive tiers of forecasts, orders, and due dates that represented ever more precise refinement. At the broadest level, the corporate office in Detroit determined a rough production schedule for the year. The schedule served as a target for the company's outside suppliers and for its own internal supply groups (such as engine plants, transmission plants). As dealer orders came in, the schedule became increasingly firm.

The C-P-C central office in Warren, Michigan scheduled production in the plant in order to meet a customer promise date known as *target build*. When a dealership received confirmation on an order, it also received word of exactly which week each car ordered was scheduled to be built. Meeting this commitment drove the production plan and the materials schedule.

This target build program represented a change from the production planning used until the early 1980s. It was part of the company's adoption of just-in-time production principles to reduce inventory costs and to improve quality by bringing problems to the surface more readily. Under the former production planning system, Tarrytown knew what cars were to be assembled over the succeeding 10 days, although the firm schedule of which cars were to be assembled on which specific days was known with certainty only 5 days in advance. Moreover, the exact car by car assembly schedule—the manifest—was known only 7 to 8 hours in advance of any shift.

Under the recently adopted system, however, the precise car-by-car assembly schedule (the manifest) was determined for five days in advance. This revised production planning system called for two weeks of frozen orders, so that not only did the assembly plant know in advance what production it was required to do, but the plant's vendors also knew what they were required to make in any week for consumption by the assembly plant in the following week. This change in production planning removed even more slack in the materials pipeline and drove inventory carrying costs and transportation expediting costs even lower. It had the added benefit of revealing vendor problems in quality and delivery more quickly than before. General Motors had already taken strides to aid vendors through longer-term contracts that placed relatively less emphasis on low price and more emphasis on consistently good quality and delivery.

Though the line was flexible in handling many make/model and option variations, there were certain limitations; only so many vinyl tops or air conditioning units, for example, could be produced in an hour without causing imbalance in the system. Thus, restrictions were imposed on what would be assembled during any shift. Vinyl tops, air conditioning units, and other options were typically spread out as evenly as possible along the line so that no worker experienced a string of overcycled conditions. For similar reasons, the line generally alternated four-door and two-door models. However, paint colors were batched as much as possible because color did not affect worker cycle time adversely. In fact, the batching facilitated worker effort and quality control. On a typical day, the batches were large enough so that it was not unusual to have only 3 of the 10 potential exterior colors represented along the line.

Supplies coming to the plant were regulated by the C-P-C central office system. The system took the orders placed and, using information from the bills or materials for each model and option available, "exploded" each order into a list of component parts, each with a distinct part number. This explosion permitted part number specificity for scheduling components. Historically, this level of detail was not scheduled for many long lead time parts. Under the former system, orders were only exploded as far as the body style and option level; some metal and trim items were still scheduled using this old system. However, soon all of the car's components would be scheduled on a part number basis. This promised to improve schedule performance and to reduce the level of inventory in the supply pipeline.

Purchasing and Raw Materials Inventory and Control

There were about 6375 active parts and components that could be assembled into the automobiles at the Tarrytown plant. Most of these parts and components, except for tires and batteries, were purchased by C-P-C's central office. These purchases were generally on long-term contracts; some, of course, came from GM divisions that acted as suppliers to the assembly plant.

To avoid excessive materials inventory, the C-P-C central office scheduled the delivery of materials very tightly. It was essential that suppliers be reliable in their deliveries. For the most part, only between one and three days' worth of production items were kept in inventory at the plant, with two days being typical. For the relatively expensive items, (motors, radiators, alternators), only one to two days' worth of production items were inventoried. Such tight control helped greatly, because the most expensive 100 parts accounted for 70 percent to 80 percent of the dollar value of inventory. Even small items like screws were stocked for only 5 to 10 days. How many days of inventory were held depended on (1) volume (the more regular its use, the tighter the schedule), (2) monetary value (the higher the value, the tighter the schedule), (3) physical size (the larger the part,

the tighter the schedule), and (4) transportation time (the farther away the supplier or the worse the weather, the greater the days of inventory held). C-P-C—Tarrytown unloaded 55 railroad cars and 80 truck trailers a day.

With material deliveries scheduled so tightly, it was necessary to monitor the entire supplier network constantly. Failure to have on hand a key part (such as a side or roof panel) could shut down the plant. Constant vigil was kept on the number and location of all supplies coming to the plant. Every day a list of critical parts that might turn up short (out of stock) for the next two days was developed. The C-P-C central office was notified and ways to expedite the parts were sought. Usually expediting involved securing the part from either the supplier or a C-P-C sister plant and switching delivery to a faster (and generally more expensive) form of transportation. But even a chartered plane was cheap if the alternative was shutting down the plant.

Monitoring materials involved not only the materials department at Tarrytown (staff to tracking shipments, unload and handle the materials) but the line workers and their supervisors as well.

CHANGES IN MATERIALS MANAGEMENT

The high interest rates of the early 1980s increased the costs of carrying inventory. General Motors was also facing intense competition, especially from Japan. Because of these two factors, the corporation was focusing more than ever before on tight materials control as a way to lower costs and improve competitiveness. By late 1985, a number of changes in materials management had been made by the plant and by the entire materials pipeline to the plant. Changes were constantly being made by the plant itself and by the entire C-P-C organization.

Welding robots at work on a car's side panels. (*Courtesy of GM Chevrolet-Pontiac-Canada Group*)

As already discussed, these moves toward just-in-time manufacturing included the elements of "target build," two weeks of frozen orders, manifests developed five days in advance, large batch painting of automobiles, and tight control on the 100 most expensive items. In addition to these, the plant had taken some other actions worth noting:

• Parts received by rail or truck were released to the factory floor the same day as received and not one or two or more days later. The paperwork for parts release had been streamlined to permit immediate release.

• The information about part status and order status was much more accurate. Parts orders were no longer needlessly padded. Stockpiles were drastically reduced. Such policies quickly and dramatically exposed problems such as late vendor delivery and poor quality. No longer were stockpiles of extra parts hiding problems like these.

• Truck transportation was used more and more. Even though truck freight rates were higher than rail, there was a net gain because the speed and reliability of trucks lowered inventory carrying costs. Shipping radios from Delco Electronics, for example, by rail,

The "body drop" where the motor is lifted into the car's body assembly. (*Courtesy of GM Chevrolet-Pontiac-Canada Group*)

might result in 10 days or more of inventory carrying, but shipping them by truck now resulted in only 2 days of inventory carrying (1 day on hand plus 1 day in transit). The plant had greatly reduced the transit times for many other expensive items such as motors, axles, transmissions, carpets, control arms, wheels, drive shafts, and trim items.

• The suppliers were now more responsible for the total product they were shipping. For example, steering columns were now painted outside the plant rather than in the plant.

• The plant had initiated programs whereby some suppliers provided materials in the precise sequence dictated by the manifest. Steering columns, for example, were shipped in the precise order that they were to be installed along the line. The five-day advance notice on the manifest permitted the plant to hold two days inhouse, have one day banked at the vendor, and have two days in transit.

As a result of measures such as these, inventory turns at the plant (annual cost of goods sold divided by the value of inventory) increased from a range of 24 to 28 turns in 1978 to between 35 and 40 turns in 1985.

Controlling the Operation

Although the plant did not have much leeway in the purchase of materials or the mix of makes, models, and options it was to assemble, it did have considerable leeway in the design and management of the assembly line itself. Key roles in this effort were played by the industrial engineering staff, the plant engineering staff, and the quality control group.

Industrial Engineering

The industrial engineering department was charged with (1) translating the engineering design of the automobile into a step-by-step procedure for assembling it; (2) laying out the line, workstations along the line, and any production aids (such as equipment and fixtures) for the workstation; (3) assigning work to each worker on the line and measuring that work so that it was appropriate; (4) establishing the authorized level of the workforce and monitoring that level; and (5) devising methods improvements or other ways to lower costs and/or increase productivity.

The department was continually involved in assessing the functioning of the line. This was a routine commitment, however.

As mentioned earlier, the line was designed in such a way that all workers averaged about a minute's work on each car. Given any major model changes, the line would have to be thoroughly redesigned so that workers, assigned possibly very different work tasks from what they were used to, still had only about a minute's work each on every car. This was what line rebalance was about.

In greater detail, the rebalance of the line followed a number of stages:

1. Given the car's engineering and design, the industrial engineer described what had to be done to assemble the car. This description involved painstaking detail. For example, one could not simply specify "mount headlight" since that task may take either shorter or longer than the desired cycle time. Mounting the headlight would involve a number of separate actions, such as walking five feet to the supply bins, reaching for a headlight and screws, walking back to the line, positioning the headlight in the socket, and using a power screwdriver to screw in two mounting screws.

2. Each of these separate actions (job elements) was assigned a time. These times were primarily determined by reference to standard time data established by C-P-C, although some times were determined by special stopwatch studies where an engineer would time a worker performing the task. The standard time data typically were derived from numerous stopwatch studies, films of workers, and other sampling studies of specific worker tasks.

3. Once times were assigned to specific elements, an industrial engineer would review them with the relevant supervisor on the production line to determine whether they were reasonable. Changes would then be made.

4. Once some agreement was reached, the task, its elements, element time estimates, and whether the task was performed on all cars or only a few were placed in computer-readable form. A computer program then planned the production schedule. It tried to balance workloads among the workers such as by taking job elements from one worker and placing them with another or otherwise shifting assignments to distribute the work properly.

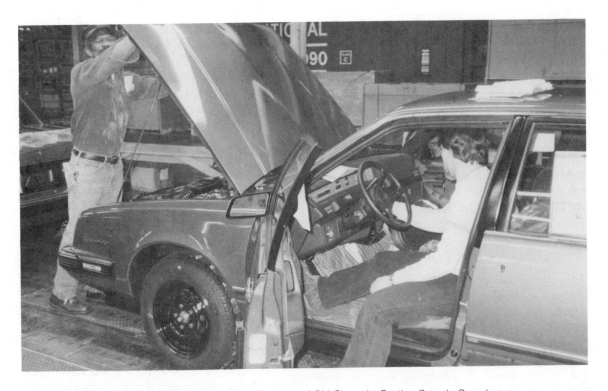

Along the final chassis line. (*Courtesy of GM Chevrolet-Pontiac-Canada Group*)

5. Generally, the initial computer schedule left some workers with either too much or too little to do. What was to be avoided was putting workers in an overcycled condition where they would consistently have too much work to perform for the time cycle decided on. If an imbalance in the line was serious and could not be remedied easily, the task could sometimes be taken off the main line and performed as a separate activity. This course of action was considered a last resort, however.

On the basis of the computer run, tasks and times were adjusted and a subsequent computer run made. This run was then studied for reasonableness and again adjustments were made. Numerous iterations of this adjustment/return process were generally performed before the line was satisfactorily balanced, at least on paper.

6. The "paper" balance of the line was then ready for trial on the factory floor. Industrial engineers, supervisors, and workers all became involved in this activity. The danger was that the predicted and actual times would not mesh. If this in fact occurred, the first thought was to help the worker improve the time—by changing the layout of the workstation, adding fixtures or other equipment, or changing methods. Such action was usually sufficient; but if need be, another operator could be added or a modest rebalance of the line effected.

An inspector along the assembly line. Note the broadcast on the window. (*Courtesy of GM Chevrolet-Pontiac-Canada Group*)

Plant Engineering

The plant engineering department directed all the construction, maintenance, and repair of the Tarrytown site's land, buildings, and equipment (except tooling, which was handled by the quality control group). All the plant's requests for capital appropriations originated with plant engineering.

Plant engineering was constantly on the alert for technological improvement. In recent years, for example, it had introduced electrophoretic painting (ELPO) for the car's initial primer coat. Instead of spraying the first primer coat, the car was now charged electrically and completely submerged into a special pool of primer. The car's electrical charge helped to apply primer to every metal surface in the car in a precisely determined thickness. Every square inch of the car was covered with neither too little nor too much primer. This multimillion dollar investment in electrophoretic painting was justified by the improved quality of painting and the improved pollution control it afforded.

In late 1985, the plant was undertaking a $170 million project to install an entirely new paint shop. The new paint shop was to contain modules that would be completely automated. Robots would open and close doors, hoods, and trunks automatically, and other robots would spray the body with an electrostatic spray, which promised to improve quality and afford better pollution control. The modular paint shop concept permitted one module to be available for maintenance at all times so that maintenance of the paint shop would be greatly facilitated and would not require third shift or weekend effort.

Plant engineering had also been instrumental in the installation of 28 welding robots to weld the body of the car together. Special fixtures had been designed for use by these robots so that all of the car's side panels, for example, were welded with the same fixtures, thus improving the consistency of the positioning and the welding of the body.

Plant engineering sought to anticipate process changes that might be developed over the next five years or so, or that might be forced on the company by competition or by the government. For example, plant engineering had spent considerable effort putting more computer terminals and printers on the line to reduce the flow of paper needed to control the process. Much more could be done in this effort and plant engineering was exploring those possibilities. Maintaining this technological momentum was a continual management concern; it called for many seminars both outside and inside the plant and many personnel development and apprentice programs.

Quality Control

At C-P-C—Tarrytown, quality was a priority. While workers and supervisors could almost take for granted that materials would always be available, quality was the one feature of the product that no one could take for granted.

The quality control department coordinated three distinct functions: inspection, reliability, and audit.

1. *Inspection* referred to those workstations spaced throughout the line where inspectors checked features of every car produced. Often, these inspectors would mark on both car and paper what corrective work ought to be done further down the line. Although situated anywhere in the line, the inspectors were not under the same supervision as the production personnel but rather reported to their own supervisor. Some of the inspection stations were mandated by Detroit, but the plant always added other inspections to the minimum.

   Checking incoming materials was still another aspect of the plant's inspection procedures.

2. The reliability group inspected the work of the inspectors as well as the work of the production workforce to determine whether both were actually doing their jobs according to specifications. The group was also responsible for implementing any engineering changes that Detroit specified for the car and for recommending any changes to specifications.

3. Five cars every shift (1 percent of production), selected at random, were subjected to a thoroughgoing audit that graded all aspects of the car's assembly and performance (body and frame paint, motor, hard trim, soft trim, electrical systems, and others). The audit included a 10-mile road test and a 12-hour cold soak. These processes allowed auditors to check for cold start, transmission, and squeaks and rattles. A scoring system was used, with demerits of varying magnitude assessed for defects of greater or lesser importance. About 10 times a year, unannounced and at random, a quality audit team from Detroit would perform their own audit of 20 cars. This procedure served as a check on the plan's daily audit.

In the past several years, the daily quaility audit briefing had become a focal point for the plant's quality management efforts. At each morning's briefing an hourly employee made a presentation about what his or her section was doing to enhance quality. These presentations, on company time, were typically attended by between 50 and 150 people. This change in the nature and importance of the audit briefing was indicative of the many changes that had been implemented at Tarrytown to promote quality. Among them:

- Any employee could shut down the line if a quality problem cropped up. Shutdowns occurred several times each day, but they generally lasted for only three to four minutes each.

- The factory had initiated a program whereby hourly employees visited dealerships and learned, firsthand, what complaints customers and dealers had with the cars shipped to them. The employees were then able to relate their findings to the specific factory area affected.

- Numerous quality aids had been introduced to the process. In some cases, these aids were protective devices for the car itself (such as to avoid scratches or other damage), and in others they were worker production aids that decreased effort or fatigue or increased precision or reliability.

THE WORKFORCE AND THE PERSONNEL DEPARTMENT

The plant's nonsupervisory personnel were paid by the hour. The plant was currently operating two shifts of production with an hour of scheduled overtime each shift, a total of 18 hours of production a day. The first shift began at 6 A.M. and lasted until 3:30 P.M. with a half hour for lunch. The second shift began at 4:30 P.M. and ended at 2 A.M. In addition, production was being scheduled for about one out of every four Sat-

urdays. During each half of each shift the entire line shut down for 23 minutes so that workers could rest. This was termed "mass relief" and replaced the individual-by-individual "tag relief" that had preceded it.

The hourly employees were represented by the United Auto Workers (UAW) union. Most features of the agreement between GM management and the plant's workers were spelled out in a 487-page national agreement covering a wide range of topics, including wage payments, fringe benefits, seniority, grievance procedures, overtime, layoffs, health and safety, production standard procedures, and numerous other topics. There was also a smaller (less than 100 pages) additional agreement between the local UAW organization and C-P-C's management in Tarrytown. This separate agreement provided detailed information on wages, layoff procedures, health and safety measures, and the like.

Plant relations with the union were extremely cordial and constructive, fostered by daily dialog between the parties and a great deal of mutual respect. Almost all worker complaints (for such problems as a leaky roof, safety problem, or worker discharge) were resolved verbally without recourse to the grievance procedure. Fewer than 100 grievances were formally filed in any month for the plant's 4000 hourly employees; 95 percent of these were resolved at the first of the four levels of the grievance procedure. Only three or four grievances in an entire year would reach the final (arbitration) level.

The plant's personnel department was an essential factor in plant management. Not only did the personnel department oversee labor relations with the UAW, but it was also charged with training responsibilities (such as briefing employees about new models and new safety regulations and programs) and was seeking improvements in the quality-of-work-life effort at the plant. Personnel managers were constantly exploring new ways for the hourly employee to become more involved in the process itself, even if it meant changes in the managerial style at the plant. In addition, the personnel department supervised hiring practices and plant safety and security.

Plant management had not always enjoyed cordial and constructive relations with the UAW. In 1974, however, both sides began a concerted effort to improve communications within the plant and to raise the quality of work life. This ongoing effort involved training both management and the workforce in communications and problem-solving skills. Where once there was suspicion, there was now trust. Both the management and the union recognized that to maintain and to deepen that trust, they must continue to work every day at improving relations and expanding the quality-of-work-life programs already under way.

The cooperation between management and workforce was evident in countless ways around the plant, not the least of which were the smiling people and their pride in the quality of the cars assembled. Notably, too, industrial engineers did not prowl the plant with clipboards and stopwatches, but joined with workers to set up workstation tasks that were both productive and fair.

There were no secrets at the plant. Three union representatives (the president, the vice-president, and the shop chairman) attended the Thursday staff meetings of the plant's top management. From time to time, the entire workforce would meet on company time for presentations on special topics. The union committee room had been relocated to the center of the plant floor and the company had also spent $50,000 constructing a "people center" in the plant that was the home of the union/management quality-of-work-life coordinators. The cafeteria that was formerly only for the salaried personnel was now open to both hourly and salaried people.

The drive for increased competitiveness and for increased worker involvement was exemplified in a new program to formalize problem solving. The quality-of-work-life effort had instituted *PGI teams*, for "people getting involved." These were teams of 8 to 10 hourly employees, together with a supervisor, who were specifically trained in problem solving, group dynamics, team building, and decision making. These teams worked on any problem they chose, but often they chose quality problems in the factory. Their work required problem identification, data collecting, data analysis, and the implementation of a solution. The PGI teams met after work and were paid for only 50 percent of the hours a week that they met. These PGI teams had met with many successes. For example, one team had discovered why one of the chutes down which tires were delivered to the line continually jammed. They were able to institute a $1\frac{1}{4}$-inch widening of the chute, which remedied the problem completely. Another team tracked down damage in taillights and substantiated the problem well enough to compel a vendor to change its packaging.

The spirit of labor-management cooperation and of involvement in the process was strong enough at Tarrytown to have weathered the loss of a shift of people in the fall of 1982 when the plant was producing the X body car. The union was able to stay in contact with all of the people laid off until time came for their recall early in 1985. At that time the A body car was introduced to the plant, at a conversion cost of $22 million. The union took pride that the recall was in part a result of the commitment of the remaining workers to quality, communication, and involvement in the plant's efforts. The conversion to the A body had been very smooth. More than 400 hourly employees had traveled to other A-car assembling plants to find and

FIGURE D2   Organization chart for the Chevrolet-Pontiac-Canada Group, Tarrytown plant.

absorb the best techniques for assembling the car.

C-P-C—Tarrytown offered the hourly employee a number of possibilities for advancement and work preference, from the simple movement from one shift to another to transfers between departments and promotions to higher pay classifications. Hourly employees could also move up to management by becoming supervisors. One key indication of the success of the plant's programs and of management's decentralization of decision-making authority was a recent hefty increase in the number of workers applying for supervisory jobs. Even the union took pride in this increase.

SUPERVISION

Work on the line was directly overseen by first-line supervisors. Typically, the supervisor was directly responsible for about 25 workers on a shift. Supervisors were thoroughly familiar with all aspects of work within their own sections of the line and of what workers could or could

not be expected to do, largely because of having once been one of them. At the start of the shift, the supervisor's immediate concern was manning the production line and making a count of absentees.

Once workers were at all of the line positions, the supervisor spent much of the remainder of the shift in two activities: (1) checking quality and (2) troubleshooting any problems on the line (equipment malfunctions, pending part shortages, or defective materials). Very little of a supervisor's time was spent at a desk. For most of the shift the supervisor would walk the line, talking with the line's workers, trying to solve any problems they might have, and maintaining quality in production.

Four or five supervisors in turn reported to a general supervisor, and the general supervisors reported to one of four superintendents (one each for the body shop, the paint shop, the trim lines, and the chassis (motor cradle) line. In addition, the quality control department had two superintendents, one for each shift (see the organization chart in Figure D2).

The superintendent's job included many aspects of the first line supervisor's, plus other responsibilities. The superintendent was concerned primarily with quality and safety, but also spent considerable time and effort on cost control, human relations, and housekeeping chores. Some of these tasks were routine, such as meeting with union committeemen, checking absenteeism, and conferring with other su-

perintendents, but there were always special plans or meetings and unexpected problems on the line to overcome.

For most supervisors, actually putting the car together posed no headaches. Most of the challenge of the job centered on people: recognizing their achievements and integrity and trying to solve their problems, both on and off the job.

PART TWO
DISCUSSION

The GM C-P-C Group is in no way responsible for the following views and presentation. They remain solely the responsibility of the author.

The Flow of the Process and of Information

The process flow in a factory such as C-P-C—Tarrytown is among the most complex one can encounter. A blizzard of different tasks, equipment, and skills are required to assemble an automobile. Yet the process flow can be diagramed in a very straightforward way. Figure D1 represents a rough-cut process flow diagram. A more detailed version would consist of a recounting of the 1050 workstations along the production line; it is these workstations through which every car passes. Thus, compared with a job shop or a batch flow process, the classic assembly line has a very well-defined process flow.

With a process as complex and as closely scheduled as an automobile assembly plant, it is not surprising that the information flow is complex as well. Figure D3 portrays an information flow diagram for C-P-C—Tarrytown. While the information flow is essentially one-way, from the top down, the need to track materials both inside

and outside the plant implies a great deal of communication between workers and management in the plant and between the plant, corporate level managers, and outside suppliers.

Capacity

The notion of what capacity is in a machine-paced line flow process like C-P-C—Tarrytown is as clear as it ever gets. At C-P-C—Tarrytown, one car rolls off the end of the production line every minute. Everything in the process is geared to making that happen. It is as though the process were a huge on-off switch: when it is on, one car a minute is produced, otherwise, nothing is produced.

Likewise, the notion of capacity utilization is relatively unambiguous. When the plant is up and running, capacity utilization is 100 percent. Otherwise, it is zero. Simply by tallying the hours the plant actually runs and dividing it by a count of hours the plant could be open gives an idea of what capacity utilization is. How many hours the plant could be open is subject to some debate, however. For example, it may very contrary to corporate policy to schedule a third shift of production, and so a

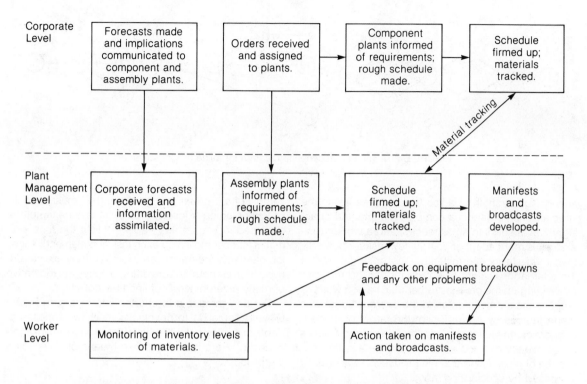

FIGURE D3 An information flow diagram of the Chevrolet-Pontiac-Canada Group, Tarrytown.

capacity utilization measure should be based on two shifts only. Another problem may lie in the determination of how much overtime is the maximum the plant could schedule without antagonizing workers. Is it an hour a day? Two hours a day? Every Saturday? Questions like these make a capacity utilization calculation fuzzy, but it is clear how much the process is capable of producing when it is up and running.

In a machine-paced line flow process, capacity in the short run is severely constrained; it can be modified only by scheduling more or fewer hours. In the medium run, however, capacity can be substantially modified (without huge, new additions of plant and equipment) by adjusting the balance of the production line. Thus, while the machine-paced line flow process cannot modulate its capacity smoothly, as can occur in job shops and batch flow processes, capacity can be adjusted in abrupt steps and by varying amounts. This concept of line balance is worth exploring.

✳ ASIDE ✳

Line Balance

As this description of the line flow process has indicated, the balance of tasks along the line is an important consideration. When products and/or desired rates of production change, the line must be rebal-

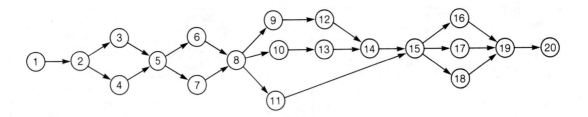

FIGURE D4   A sample precedence diagram for a line flow process.

anced. The strength of a line flow process lies in the specialization of labor: a complex manufacturing assignment is split into small pieces, and a worker (any worker) is more adept at doing a few tasks repeatedly than many tasks intermittently. The observation that the total labor content of a product can be reduced by dividing up the process rather than having workers responsible for manufacturing the entire product was made famous by Adam Smith, the father of modern economics. In his *Inquiry into the Nature and Causes of the Wealth of Nations* (1776), Smith cites the fabrication of pins, noting that pin production was greatly increased by specializing labor.

The keys then to line balance are (1) breaking down a complex product and process into its component pieces and tasks and (2) juggling the coordination of those pieces and tasks so that the process is smooth and no bottlenecks are built into it.

The first of these keys to line balance is greatly aided by a precedence diagram, which portrays the individual elements that make up the fabrication and/or as-

sembly of a product and the order they must logically or technologically follow. Figure D4 is an example of a precedence diagram; Table D1 lists the time estimates for accomplishing each task (job element). These job elements are merely an example (they are not derived from General Motors data), but they are indicative of many different kinds of line flow activities.

Our assignment is to use the information in Figure D4 and Table D1 to develop a line flow process capable of turning out 300 units of the product in an eight-hour day. Here is one possible means of developing the process.

1. By adding up the job element times in Table D1, we know that 14.99 minutes are required to assemble the product.
2. The desired number of units per day is 300, and so 4497 (14.99 × 300) minutes of production are needed in any one day to produce the desired daily output.

TABLE D1   Job elements and estimated times for the process diagramed in Figure D4

JOB ELEMENT	ESTIMATED TIME (minutes)	JOB ELEMENT	ESTIMATED TIME (minutes)
1	0.65	11	1.10
2	0.11	12	1.75
3	0.37	13	0.94
4	0.75	14	0.62
5	0.10	15	0.45
6	0.58	16	0.81
7	0.25	17	0.87
8	1.01	18	1.60
9	1.17	19	0.60
10	0.43	20	0.83

3. Assuming that a worker puts in an 8-hour day with two 15-minute breaks, 450 minutes of production are available from each worker. Dividing the total production time (4497 minutes) by the available minutes per day per worker (450 minutes per worker) suggests that 10 workers are needed to produce 300 units each day.

4. With 10 workers, the 14.99 minutes needed to assemble the product can be divided into 10 segments of 1.5 minutes each. That is, the assembly process can be viewed roughly as a 10 station assembly line with each worker putting in 1.5 minutes per unit. Every 1.5 minutes another unit of the product can be expected to come off the line. This figure (1.5 minutes) is sometimes termed the "control cycle."

5. With the length of the control cycle established, developing the line involves picking 10 sets of job elements from Table D1 so that each of their sums totals 1.5 minutes. In this picking process, the precedence relationships portrayed in Figure D4 must also be adhered to.

Table D2 gives a suggested grouping of job elements into workstations. It prompts several observations:

1. One more workstation than the initial determination of 10 had to be assigned. Because the estimated times for the various job elements differed widely from the control cycle time, the job elements could not be easily grouped so that their times would sum to it.

Naturally, then, some inefficiency is introduced to the line. It was hoped that 10 stations, each with a cycle time of 1.5 minutes, could be assigned—a near-perfect match of 15 minutes of worker time allocated to assemble a product estimated at 14.99 minutes of labor input. Instead, 16.50 minutes of worker time (11 stations × 1.5 minutes per station) have to be allocated. With every unit produced, about 1.5 minutes are extraneous—a loss of about 10 percent relative to a perfect grouping of job elements to match the control cycle.

2. Some workstations are more out-of-kilter than others. The "balance delay" column in Table D2 is the measure of how the total estimated time for the elements comprising each workstation differs from the control cycle. As is readily seen, two workstations (1 and 6) have estimated times in excess of the control cycle. Several other workstations, notably 7, 9, and 10, have slight rest periods built into their work cycles; that is, workers at these stations ought to be able to complete their tasks well before 1.5 minutes go by.

What can be done about such bottlenecks and slack stations? In practice, companies often try to devise work aids or other assistance to lessen the impact of any bottleneck. Both bottlenecks or significant balance delays may trigger a review of the steps in manufacture and/or the product design itself. This review may lead to a new set of job elements and/or times with advantages for the balance of the line.

TABLE D2   A suggested grouping of job elements into workstations

WORKSTATION	JOB ELEMENTS	TOTAL TIME/UNIT (minutes)	BALANCE DELAY (minutes)
1	1,2,4	1.51	−0.01
2	3,5,6,7	1.30	0.20
3	8,10	1.44	0.06
4	9,12	1.46	0.04
5	9,12	1.46	0.04
6	13,14	1.56	−0.06
7	11	1.10	0.40
8	15,17	1.32	0.18
9	16,18	1.21	0.29
10	16,18	1.21	0.29
11	19,20	1.43	0.07

3. This particular assignment of workstations deliberately places four workers "overcycle." Stations 4, 5, 9, and 10 have people working on every other unit instead of every unit that passes down the line. Had not two workers been placed on job elements 12 and 18, significant bottlenecks would have been encountered.

The preceding example of assembly line balance is obviously simpler and more mechanical than that faced by a company like General Motors, but it does serve to introduce the fundamental notions of line balance. A more realistic example of a line balance problem, and one set in an automobile assembly plant, is given in Situation D1.

SITUATION D-1

BUMPER SUBASSEMBLY

Before the front and rear bumpers are put on the automobile, several key parts must first be subassembled to these bumpers. Among these parts are mounting brackets, rub strips (rubberized impact strips that not only affect the car's appearance but also prevent minor damage to the bumpers), and bumper guards. Exactly which of these parts gets subassembled to the standard bumper depends on the style of car being assembled.

The assembly plant produces three different vehicle styles, denoted as car line A, car line B, and car line C. One of these vehicle styles is assembled every minute (that is, 60 per hour) with the following current product mix:

Car line A	20/hour
Car line B	15/hour
Car line C	25/hour
Total	60/hour

Table D3 presents the elements of work and their respective cycle times (the time it takes to perform a designated task on a car) in hundredths of a minute. Note that not all cars receive bumpers subassembled with rub strips or bumper guards.

Because the plant is building 60 cars per hour, an operator's cycle time cannot exceed 1 minute per job; but no one can realistically be expected to work at a production pace of 60 minutes every hour. Thus, an allowance is made so that if an operator's workload falls between 80 and 90 percent of the total time available (in this case 1 minute per job), his cycle is considered "efficient." Therefore, if by combining work elements from each of the three car lines an operator is working somewhere between 48 and 54 seconds (or 80 to 90 hundredths of a minute) per cycle, he is considered efficient.

How many operators are required to subassemble these bumpers and what process considerations could assist the operators in their work?

TABLE D3   Elements of work, front and rear bumpers
Car lines A, B, and C

FRONT BUMPER		REAR BUMPER	
TASK	CYCLE TIME (hundredths of a minute)	TASK	CYCLE TIME (hundredths of a minute)
Car Line A			
1. Transfer bumper from delivery rack to conveyor.	.20	1. Transfer bumper from delivery rack to conveyor.	.20
2. Install 2 rub strips, with 10 clips each, on 15%.	.05/clip	2. Install 1 rub strip, with 20 clips, on 10%.	.05/clip
3. Install 2 bumper guards on 40%. Install loose with required parts. Secure with air motor.	.45/guard .12/guard	3. Install 2 bumper guards on 20%. Install loose with required parts. Secure with air motor.	.45/guard .12/guard
4. Install 2 mounting brackets on all front bumpers.	.65/bracket	4. Install 2 mounting brackets on all rear bumpers.	.65/bracket

TABLE D3   Elements of work, front and rear bumpers (*continued*)

| FRONT BUMPER | | REAR BUMPER | |
TASK	CYCLE TIME (hundredths of a minute)	TASK	CYCLE TIME (hundredths of a minute)
Car Line B			
1. Transfer bumper from delivery rack to conveyor.	.25	Identical to front bumper	
2. Install 1 rub strip, with 8 clips, on each bumper.	.08/clip		
3. Install 6 mounting bolts on each bumper.	.15/bolt		
4. Car line does not require bumper guards.			
Car Line C			
1. Transfer bumper from delivery rack to conveyor.	.20	1. Transfer bumper from delivery rack to conveyor.	.20
2. Install 1 rub strip, with 12 clips, on 50%.	.10/clip	2. Install 1 rub strip, with 12 clips, on 35%.	.10/clip
3. Install 2 bumper guards on 5%. Each guard requires a total of .70, which can be divided into three elements of .20, .30, .20, if necessary.	.70/guard	3. Identical to front bumper (bumper guards)	.70/guard
4. Install 6 mounting bolts on each bumper.	.15/bolt	4. Identical to front bumper (mounting bolts)	.15/bolt

Discussion of Bumper Subassembly

We can use the data given to compute how much total time is required to assemble front and rear bumpers for car lines A, B, and C. Table D4 gives those computations.

These calculations show that, in the aggregate, if two workers were placed on the subassembly of rear bumpers, the efficiency of those workers would fall within the 80 to 90 percent considered appropriate. The calculated required efficiency of two workers on front bumpers, however, exceeds 90 percent; that level of efficiency forces the pace too much, and management must be concerned with whether the workers can sustain the effort over long periods.

Also cause for concern is the variability in what the workers have to perform. Although, on average, the balance delays do not look bad, there are some significant ranges of difference in what a worker may be required to do, depending on whether the bumpers take a certain option or not. Table D5 indicates the range of cycle times implied by the differences between standard and optional bumpers.

This vast range in cycle times per worker suggests that workers would be out of balance in this bumper subassembly area. When standard bumpers were called for, there would be substantial balance delay on car lines A and C. However, when rub strips and bumper guards were called for, the workers would be greatly overcycled. This state of affairs, of course, is a powerful argument for the standardization of product options.

How does a factory solve such a pernicious problem? One possibility is to put more workers on the line

TABLE D4   Computation of total time to subassemble bumpers

	FRONT BUMPER		REAR BUMPER
TASK	TIME NEEDED (minutes)	TASK	TIME NEEDED (minutes)
Car Line A (20/hour)			
1.	4.00	1	4.00
2	3.00	2	2.00
3	9.12	3	4.56
4	26.00	4	26.00
	42.12		36.56
Car Line B (15/hour)			
1	3.75	1	3.75
2	9.60	2	9.60
3	13.50	3	13.50
	26.85		26.85
Car Line C (25/hour)			
1	5.00	1	5.00
2	15.00	2	10.50
3	1.75	3	1.75
4	22.50	4	22.50
	44.25		39.75
Car Lines A, B, and C			
Total	113.22	Total	103.16
Efficiency*	94%	Efficiency*	86%

*Based on two people working and 120 minutes of work time per hour of production.

so that the overcycle conditions can be met, but then the factory must live with vast balance delays (inefficiencies).

A more palatable solution is to improve the times (methods) required to do each task. To do this, the operators could be made more comfortable (for example, by raising or lowering the platform, installing production aids such as air motors or lifts), or the layout of the workstation could be improved (for example, by making materials more accessible).

Another course of action would be to subdivide the tasks required for the options work into many small component tasks and then to spread these component tasks over as many workers as is feasible. In this way, no one worker would be tremendously overcycled. Rather, several workers would be only modestly overcycled. The success of this tactic depends naturally on how neatly the major tasks can be subdivided and over how many other workers it is feasible to spread the component task.

Still another course of action would be to take as much of the options work off the line as possible to decrease the variability in times faced by the worker. In this case, bumper guards could perhaps be mounted to the bumpers or rub strips attached off line, thus leaving to the assembling line merely the transfer and installation of the bumper itself with any options already mounted.

Accuracy of Time Estimates*

Proper line balance depends on accurate estimates of the time it will take to perform each of the job ele-

*More on this topic can be found in Chapter 3.

TABLE D5   Cycle time per worker (minutes) *(assumes two workers each on front and rear bumpers)*

CAR LINE	FRONT BUMPER		REAR BUMPER	
	NO OPTIONS	*ALL OPTIONS*	*NO OPTIONS*	*ALL OPTIONS*
A	.75	1.82	.75	1.82
B	.90	90	.90	90
C	.55	1.85	.55	1.85

ments of the entire assembly process. The time estimates themselves are usually derived from actual observation of the task itself or something very similar. The observation, commonly called a *time and motion study,* can occur in any of a variety of ways; often industrial engineers will use more than one to establish a time standard.

• *Stopwatch studies.*   A traditional but less and less popular means of estimating time standards is to stand by a worker who is performing a task and take stopwatch readings of how long it takes him or her to accomplish the task. As one might expect, the presence of the industrial engineer may cause the worker to slack off somewhat, casting doubts on the estimate. Sometimes this inaccuracy is avoided by having the industrial engineer stand near one worker but actually monitor another worker at a distance. Even this bit of sneakery has not remedied all the problems associated with stopwatch studies, which remain a costly way of setting time standards.

• *Films and videotapes.*   A less obtrusive way of estimating time standards is to film workers in action over an extended period of time and then take time measurements from the film itself. This has become an increasingly popular way to estimate time standards; it reduces the cost and worker-influence problems of stopwatch studies.

• *Work sampling.*   Another, and less expensive, way to determine at least the relative times spent performing various tasks is to take a series of random "snapshots" of a task rather than a "full-length film." If, for example, in every 100 random looks at a particular task, 40 observe a particular action, then we can infer that 40 percent of the cycle time is spent performing that task. This technique is generally termed *work sampling.* It is most appropriate for nonstandard tasks.

• *Task decomposition.*   Since so much information has been accumulated on the time it takes to perform so many bodily movements, sometimes time estimates can be pieced together strictly by breaking the task into its component movements and using stock time estimates for each movement. Summing these individual times is one way to estimate the time standard for a radically new job element, which can then be checked by any of the previous three observational methods.

No matter how individual job element time standards are developed, it is dangerous to expect that adding more than a few together will generate accurate time totals. Table D1's list of 20 job elements totals 14.99 minutes. It is foolish to expect that a single worker could actually work through all 20 steps in 15 minutes, let alone maintain that pace throughout a workday. The strength of a line flow process, as mentioned before, lies in the specialization of labor to a limited number of tasks; the corresponding time standards can be considered accurate only when relatively few job elements are strung together. The rebalance of any line flow process always entails reevaluations of new tasks and/or regroupings of elements, since so many time variations can be introduced to combinations of job elements and the materials handling and positioning requirements that accompany them.

Non-Time-Related Aspects of Line Flow Process Layout

The 20-element example of the line balancing introduced earlier does not assign any special characteristics to any of the job elements listed. In that sense the exercise was mechanical. Often, however, in many line balance situations attention has to be focused on some special features of the process that may constrain the composition of workstations in particular ways. Among these special features can be included:

- Materials handling requirements
- Space constraints within the factory that may force the line into a particular shape
- Special equipment needs
- Product bulkiness or weight, requiring two or more workers to work together
- Segregation of worker skill levels

Any of these features can in themselves define a workstation, quite apart from the simple grouping of job elements according to time estimates alone.

Procedures for Grouping Job Elements

The 20-element example above was simple enough that we can trust a little trial-and-error in selecting the composition of the line's workstations. In more complex situations, however, more formal rules can sometimes be helpful in assigning job elements to specific workstations. Unfortunately, no one means of assigning elements to stations—not even very sophisticated computer techniques—can guarantee a minimum degree of balance delay and inefficiency. It seems that there will always be a role for common sense in line balancing.

At any rate, some procedures have proved helpful in developing candidate line balances:

- Assigning the longest time estimates first
- Assigning first the elements that have the most other elements following them

In addition, there are both heuristic and computer-based methods of generating candidate assembly line balances.[1] It bears repeating that none of the methods by itself is certain to generate an optimum line balance.

Cycle Time Allowances

Some procedures for line balancing, though by no means all, factor in special allowances for fatigue. These allowances lengthen the cycle time. The time standards for individual tasks, under this system, have no slack of any kind built into them, and so it would be inappropriate to expect that they could apply for a full day's workload. Special allowances for fatigue then have to be added to make the computed cycle time realistic. Other line balance procedures try to establish sustainable time standards from the beginning, and so allowances need not be introduced.

Speed versus Balance Delay

As has been mentioned repeatedly, the appeal of a line flow process lies in its ability to reduce the labor time in a product's manufacture by breaking down the fabrication/assembly process into pieces that can be done rapidly and repeatedly by operators along the line. Generally speaking, the smaller the job content of a workstation, the more efficient labor can be. What prevents us from breaking tasks into single job elements? Apart from concern for the mind-numbing character of such jobs, the problem of balance delay militates against such an atomistic approach to line balance. Individual job elements will vary greatly; the greater the variance, the more apt that some combination of job elements will have to occur to prevent high levels of balance delay all down the line. Thus line flow processes with cycle times that are combinations of job elements are typically more efficient than ones with minimum cycle times.

*

A machine-paced assembly line places special demands on a worker. In a sense, the worker is a "slave to the iron monster," which is the moving assembly line. He cannot simply decide to take a break from his work and wander about chatting with co-workers. (But then neither can the second-grade teacher.) Moreover, the assembly line worker must perform the same, fairly routine task repeatedly throughout the workday. Many people view that as monotonous or degrading or worse.

But not all people hold to that view, and therein lies a fundamental point about assembly lines and assembly line workers. Happily, people are very different from one another in tolerances for certain activities and in expectations about their jobs. One class of personality savors proximity to power and influence and will forgo higher salaries to do so (consider many staff workers on Capitol Hill), while another will sacrifice salary for considerable freedom of schedule and the chance to be "their own boss" (such as many college professors). If the assembly line worker can be typed in this way at all, it is that he or she has forgone diversity in the job for relatively high wages and freedom from the anxiety many people suffer when they are confronted with decision making. For many people, that is not a bad trade to make.

Nevertheless, despite the matching of personalities to job types that goes on continuously in our economy, progressive companies like General Motors are constantly searching for ways to improve the quality of work life for their workers. In fact, C-P-C—Tarrytown is a classic example of how management concern for the quality of work life turned around a worsening factory situation. The process description mentioned the commitment of C-P-C—Tarrytown to improve the quality of work life at the plant and how that commitment has grown over the years. Robert H. Guest, writing in the *Harvard Business Review*, tells the story of how C-P-C—Tarrytown, in the space of seven years (1970–77), moved from "one of the poorest labor relations and production records in GM" to its current, enviable position as one of the better run sites in the company.

In the late 1960s and early 1970s, the Tarrytown plant suffered from much absenteeism and labor turnover. Operating costs were high. Frustration, fear, and mistrust characterized the relationship between management and labor. At certain times, as many as 2000 labor grievances were on the docket. As one manager put it, "Management was always in a defensive posture. We were instructed to go by the book, and we played by the book. The way we solved problems was to use our authority and impose discipline." The plant general superintendent acknowledges in retrospect, "For reasons we thought valid, we were very secretive in letting the union and the workers know about changes to be introduced or new programs coming down the pike."

Union officers and committeemen battled constantly with management. As one union officer describes it, "We were always trying to solve yesterday's problems. There was no trust and everybody was putting out fires. The company's attitude was to employ a stupid robot with hands and no face." The union committee chairman describes the situation the way he saw it: "When I walked in each morning I was out to get the personnel director, the committeeman was shooting for the foreman, and the zone committeeman was shooting for the general foreman. Every time a foreman notified a worker that there would be a job change, it resulted in an instant '78 (work standards grievance). It was not unusual to have a hundred '78s hanging fire, more than 300 discipline cases, and many others."[2]

How was the situation at C-P-C—Tarrytown turned around? The process was long and complex, and indeed is still going on. Guest refers, however, to several events and changes of heart:

1. In 1971 a plant manager decided to work with, rather than against, the union on what he recognized as important joint concerns.
2. Shortly after that products in the plant changed, and management was willing to entertain ideas from the workforce in relocating the hard and soft trim lines within the factory and in redesigning their layouts and methods. The workers made hundreds

of worthwhile suggestions, many of which management adopted.

3. In 1973 the plant endorsed a United Auto Workers-General Motors agreement that explicitly addressed ideas and procedures for upgrading the quality of work life as a goal for both the union and the corporation.

4. In 1974 an outside consultant was hired to establish a joint worker-supervisor training program. Two coordinators were selected, one each by management and the union; a small group of workers and supervisors from the Soft Trim Department were brought together on Saturdays to learn about each other and to work on solutions for problems of joint concern.

5. In 1977 this training program was expanded plant-wide, with 11 pairs of worker/supervisor trainers to lead small groups of workers and supervisors in three full days of paid training sessions.

The trainers used printed materials, diagrams, charts, and slides to describe products and model changes, how the plant was laid out, how the production system worked, and what the organizational structures of management and the union are. Time was spent covering safety matters, methods used to measure quality performance, efficiency, and so forth. The work groups were shown how and where they could get any information they wanted about their plant. Special films showed all parts of the plant with a particular worker "conducting the tour" for his part of the operation. To develop effective problem-solving skills, the trainers presented simulated problems and then asked employees to go through a variety of some experiential exercises. The training content enabled the workers to diagnose themselves, their own behavior, how they appeared in competitive situations, how they handled two-way communications, and how they solved problems. By the final day "the groups themselves are carrying the ball," as the trainers put it, "with a minimum of guidance and direction from the two trainers."[3]

It is worth noting that GM's commitment to this program, at a cost of $1.6 million, was not tied to immediate measurable results. In Guest's words, "getting the process of worker involvement going was a primary goal with its own intrinsic rewards. The organizational benefits followed." Nevertheless, there are some perceptible benefits.

The production manager says, for example, "From a strictly production point of view—efficiency and costs—this entire experience has been absolutely positive, and we can't begin to measure the savings that have taken place because of the hundreds of small problems that were solved on the shop floor before they accumulated into big problems."

Although not confirmed by management, the union claims that Tarrytown went from one of the poorest plants in its quality performance (inspection counts or dealer complaints) to one of the best among the 18 plants in the division. It reports that absenteeism went from 7.25 percent to between 2 and 3 percent. In December 1978, at the end of the training sessions, there were only 32 grievances on the docket. Seven years earlier there had been upward of 2000 grievances filed. Such substantial changes can hardly be explained by chance.[4]

We will talk more about quality of work life in Chapter 3. Suffice it here to observe further from the process description (1) the importance that the personnel department at C-P-C—Tarrytown enjoyed and the mandate it bore for worker training, safety, and promoting worker involvement in the process; (2) the challenge supervisors felt for recognizing worker achievement and integrity and for assisting their workers in solving problems both on and off the job; and (3) the care with which the industrial and plant engineers studied the tasks that make up automobile assembly and devised ways to eliminate or simplify more difficult or disagreeable ones.

Within most machine-paced line flow processes, the career path of the worker is much less well defined than it is in many continuous flow processes or in the batch flow process. Lines of progression are not spelled out as directly, and most workers earn about the same pay. Most job changes involve transfers from evening or night work to day work, or from one department to another with what may be perceived as easier or more exciting work. Some promotions in job categories are frequently possible as well.

Demands of the Process on Management

The machine-paced line flow process places a number of taxing demands on management. The products it produces are typically consumed in high volumes; therefore they are likely to compete on price as well as on product performance, workmanship, and perhaps even the reliability of delivery. This is a broad front on which to compete, and it means that line flow managers must devote their attention to cost reduction measures (items 1 through 4 in the following list) and to product performance and workmanship measures (items 5 and 6):

1. *Balance.* The definition and balance of the line, as discussed previously, is a critical aspect in ensuring that as little labor as necessary is placed on the line.

2. *Materials management.* Like the continuous flow process, the line flow process places very regular and steady demands on its suppliers. Because of this regularity, the line flow process can often avoid drawing on large raw materials inventories and paying the necessary finance charges, but only by carefully managing the purchase and logistics of supplies. Such materials management involves the establishment of superb information and control systems so that (1) parts in imminent danger of falling short are iden-

tified and noted and (2) parts from suppliers are tracked thoroughly and delivered on time. The process description noted how recent changes have contributed to coordinating materials more tightly.

3. *Technological change.* In processes as complex as most line flow ones there are always ways to improve their workings. Most such changes are incremental in nature, but periodically more significant steps can be taken either to speed up the process or to eliminate some stations through the introduction of new equipment. Computers, more versatile machine tools, and increased automation have often made significant contributions to process improvement.

4. *Capacity planning.* The managers of a process as rigid in capacity as the machine-paced line flow process must be very careful to plan diligently for its future capacity needs. Line rebalance may be called for or more drastic modifications to the design of the line. Such a drastic revision occurred in the conversion to front-wheel drive cars and in the introduction of ELPO technology. Design changes must be thought through carefully from the beginning of any planning cycle.

5. *Product design.* The high-volume products of the typical line flow process must be designed to be manufactured; the more exotic the demands the product places on the design of the line and the tasks workers perform, the more likely the competition will bury the product on price. Yet, some of the best assembly line products give the impression that they were custom-made, there being so many options for the customer to choose from. Automobiles are often this way. The trick, of course, is to design flexibility into the product so that the same general worker task results in a different appearance or performance in the product.

6. *Workforce management.* In so many line flow processes, quality is fundamentally dependent on the workforce. Fostering pride in workmanship when the tasks performed are as repetitious as they are is a challenge, but an essential one.

QUESTIONS

1. Why is the production process at C-P-C described as "classic but modern"?

2. It has been said that industrial engineering is the most important element of control in a machine-paced line flow process. Do you agree? Why or why not?

3. What are the connections between the workforce and its supervision and product quality at C-P-C—Tarrytown?

4. Discuss in detail the relationship between the notion of capacity in a machine-paced line flow and the technique of line balance.

5. Based on different operations you have so far studied, which operation would you rather work in? In which would you rather be a manager? In which would you like least to be a worker? a manager? Support your answers with specific references to the processes.

6. Various changes in materials management were mentioned in the process description for C-P-C—Tarrytown. Trace the changes in both process and information flows that you would expect to result from these changes.

7. Suppose you had just been designated the plant manager for a new plant about to be completed. You are in charge of assembling your own staff (such as in quality control, plant engineering, supervision, production planning). Based on the process descriptions to date, how would the composition and *relative* strengths of your chosen staff differ from one type of process to another?

SITUATION FOR STUDY D-1
GREAT WESTERN TIME INC.

Adele Welch is a senior at Western Theoretical University, majoring in operations management. The university has a cooperative student-work study arrangement with the local plant of Great Western Time Inc. The students are hired for six months, from June to December of their senior year, as full-time first-line supervisors or the equivalent.

Adele has just started at Great Western as a supervisor over an assembly line for electronic watches. The watch assembly line is a moving belt 25 feet long at which 28 workers assemble, solder, and test watches through the complete assembly process.

Initially, an assembly line balance is developed from the order of operations, the time required for each operation, and the number of units desired. This information is also used to determine the crew size. In order to achieve the required production volume, this line balancing design usually calls for several workstations for some operations. The workstations are simple and require simple tools, and so idle workstations do not represent major losses in terms of equipment.

In the actual operation the watch case is placed on the conveyor belt, and the other subassemblies are added by workers by taking the case off the line, putting it in a fixture, performing their assigned operation, and placing the watch back on the conveyor. If there are five identical workstations, each of the five workers is expected to perform that operation on every fifth watch. Since the product is so small and light, there is little difficulty in returning an unfinished watch to the beginning of the line, if necessary. However, a large number of returns indicates an imbalance in the work arrangement.

Adele has 23 people assigned to her; when one or more does not report for work, she has no labor pool from which to draw. Moreover, if a worker does not feel well and leaves at noon, Adele has to rebalance the assembly line quickly and adjust the belt speed to the rebalanced line. Table D6 shows the sequence of operations and the times involved in the manufacture of the Slinky Slim watch.

Although Great Western would like all assembly operations to go like clockwork, upper management has factored in a value for deter-

TABLE D6 Sequence of operations and times for producing the slinky slim watch (Great Western Time Inc.)

OPERATION	PRECEDING OPERATION(S)	TIME REQUIRED (minutes/unit)
1	—	.2
2	1	.3
3	1	.3
4	1	.5
5	4	.2
6	3	.2
7	4	.4
8	2	.5
9	3, 5, 7	.6
10	8	.6
11	9, 10	.3
12	10, 11	.1
13	9	.2
14	11	.5
15	12, 14	.3
16	15	.2

mining the "average" output requirement. The performance measure used to evaluate Adele and her colleagues is the labor content of each assembled watch compared to an engineered standard. Adele feels that her primary job is to generate a new line balance at any time. In particular, she wants to generate, ahead of time (in case absenteeism forces her to rebalance the line), a set of line balances and work assignments for the following numbers of workers on the Slinky Slim assembly line: 23, 22, 21, 20, 19, 18.

SITUATION FOR STUDY D-2
ABLE RENT-A-CAR

At the Modest Suburban Airport near Metropolis, Able Rent-a-Car shared space with two other car rental companies: Baker and Charlie. Their small, equal-size counters were connected to each other. The rental cars were located in front of the terminal beyond the airport short-term parking and up a steep hill. To get to his rental car, the customer had to walk approximately 150 yards, including 20 steep steps.

Able divided the United States into zones, which varied in size depending on population, number of Able locations, and other practical issues. Each zone was headed by a zone manager, who made all the major administrative decisions, and had its own fleet of cars. The Modest Suburban Able was in the Metropolis zone.

Two telephone numbers were critical to the Able business. One was the main reservation center in Kansas, which served the entire United States and Canada. Kansas made reservations, distributed location business hours and phone numbers, and explained rate structures. The second key number was fleet distribution; the Metropolis fleet center was responsible for ensuring that each location within the zone had enough cars in each size bracket. It was vital in the rental car business that a person who appeared at the counter with a reservation be given a suitable car ready to drive.

There were two types of employee position at Able: the service agent and the rental agent. The service agent's main responsibility was car care. At the start of each shift, the service agent used the computer, stationed behind the customer counter, to get a reservation manifest, which listed the names of customers, when and how each customer would be arriving at the airport, and what size car had been ordered. The service agent had to be sure that there were clean, rentable cars of the correct size ready for each reservation.

After reading the manifest, the service agent put into the computer the identification numbers of the cars that were in the lot and not serviced. The reason for this procedure was to ensure that each car was clear in the computer system. The computer would tell the serviceman whether certain situations preventing immediate servicing existed: (1) the car had been stolen and was now on alert; (2) the car was ready for preventive maintenance, in which case the car must be sent to the city for repair; or (3) the car had mistakenly been entered as present in a different location.

After acquiring the customer manifest and the car clearance forms from the computer, the serviceman walked to the lot to begin servicing cars. The lot was shared with Baker and Charlie; each company had its own gas pumps and parking slots. In addition, Baker and Charlie had an automatic car wash, which could wash the outside of a car in 20 seconds. Servicing cars entailed pumping gas; checking fluid levels, tire pressure, lights, mirrors, safety equipment, spare tire, and jack; and cleaning the inside windows, upholstery, outside windows, and main frame. Whereas Baker and Charlie ran their cars through the car wash, Able used a garden hose and a brush. While servicing cars, the service agent maintained a car control inventory sheet, which listed all Able cars on the lot and divided them into Metropolis zone cars, out-of-service Metropolis zone cars, and non-Metropolis-zone cars. After servicing each car, the service agent filled out a car information form, which listed the number of doors on the car, the make, model, mileage, tire type, number of passengers seated, car identification number and the parking slot number where the car would be parked.

After servicing about five cars, the service agent took the car information forms and the keys to each serviced car down to the counter in the terminal. The rental agent took the keys and the car information forms and put them on the key rack. The service agent then returned to the lot and began servicing more cars.

The responsibilities of the service agent included also inventory regulation; each week the service agent filled out an inventory need list, noting all the car care supplies and counter supplies that were running low. The agent phoned this list in to Metropolis, where another service agent collected the needed supplies from the stockroom and drove them to Modest Suburban Airport. Other service agent duties included picking up customers from the terminal in bad weather and driving them the 150 yards to the parking lot. They also made sure the lot was clear of dirt and snow.

The other employee position at Able was the rental agent, who was stationed behind the counter in the terminal. Responsibilities of the rental agent centered around the customer: transacting rentals and returns; handling reservations that were not made through the Kansas number; answering phone inquiries about rates, car availability, and business hours; and making reservation changes. The renting process began with the customer approaching the counter and identifying himself or herself. The rental agent checked the daily customer manifest to verify the reservation and proceeded to ask the customer for a driver's license and a major credit card. The rental agent then fed the data from the two items into the computer.

Next the rental agent inquired about how long the car would be needed and where it would be returned. Using this information, the agent assigned a rental rate. There were numerous rate structures, which depended on when customers rented, when they returned, where the cars were returned, and how long customers had the cars. After assigning a rate, the rental agent estimated the cost of the rental and called a credit card toll-free number to verify the credit stability of the customer. After the credit check, the rental agent inquired about the desired car make and model, went to the key rack, and chose the appropriate car. The rental agent then entered the data on the car information form into the computer, which printed out all the data from the rental agreement. The customer signed the contract and was given all but one copy of it, with instructions to bring the contract when he or she returned the car. The rental agent gave the keys and the slot number to the

customer with directions to the parking lot. The agent then filed the contract copy.

When returning a rental car, the customer left the car and the keys in the lot, noted the mileage and gas level, and returned with the contract to the terminal. The rental agent entered the present mileage and the gas level into the computer, which then calculated and printed out the bill. The customer got one copy and the rental agent took the remaining three (one was sent to Metropolis, one to billing, and one copy was kept). Almost all business was done with credit cards.

Rental agent duties also included filling out the car count inventory form and sending it through the computer to fleet distribution. This form was crucial because it informed fleet operations about Modest Suburban's car needs for the day. The car count inventory listed data from the present eight-hour period and the next two eight-hour periods. The rental agent used the car control inventory sheet made out by the service agent to list present cars available. He or she then used a forecasting book, written by the Metropolis office using historical data, to estimate how many cars would check in to Modest Suburban Airport during each eight-hour stretch. After adding present available cars and forecasted check-ins, the rental agent subtracted the reservation needs for each of the three eight-hour periods; the result showed either a surplus or a need for each period. The car count inventory form also enabled the rental agent to inform fleet of any special orders such as for station wagons or vans or distant reservations.

1. Diagram the process and information flows for this service operation.

2. How is it like a machine-paced line flow operation? How is it unlike such an operation?

3. What changes would make it more like a machine-paced line flow operation? How many of those changes are dependent on being at a large metropolitan airport to make them effective? (Consider the differences between the rental car operations at large airports and those at small airports.)

REFERENCE NOTES

1. For a discussion of assembly line balance consult the following articles and their bibliographies: R. E. Gunther, G. D. Johnson, and R. S. Peterson, "Currently Practiced Formulations for the Assembly Line Balance Problem," *Journal of Operations Management* 3 (1983): 209–221, and I. Baybars, "On 'Currently Practiced Formulations for the Assembly Line Balance Problem'," *Journal of Operations Management* 5 (1985): 449–453.

2. Robert H. Guest, "Quality of Work Life—Learning from Tarrytown," *Harvard Business Review* 57, no. 4 (July–August 1979): 77. See also William T. Horner, "Tarrytown: A Union Perspective," *National Productivity Review* 1, no. 1 (Winter 1981–1982): 37–41.

3. Ibid., p. 84.

4. Ibid., p. 85.

A HYBRID
(BATCH/CONTINUOUS FLOW) PROCESS
Stroh Brewery Company
Winston-Salem, North Carolina

In 1982, the Stroh Brewery Company of Detroit acquired the Jos. Schlitz Brewing Company of Milwaukee. In the process, Stroh acquired Schlitz's Winston-Salem brewery, which had begun production in June 1969. At the time, the Winston-Salem brewery was the largest brewery ever built at one time. It occupied 1.1 million square feet on 150 acres and cost $130 million.

Originally constructed to produce about 5 million barrels of beer per year (a beer barrel, abbreviated bbl., is equal to 31 gallons), the brewery was now producing about 6 million barrels of beer per year. This increase in capacity was made possible by increases in efficiency (quicker changeovers, better production planning) and by the installation of two new canning lines to replace two older lines. The new lines operated at 1600 cans per minute, 400 cans per minute faster than the lines they replaced.

PART ONE
PROCESS DESCRIPTION

THE BREWING AND PACKAGING OF BEER

Beer is a malt-and-hops-flavored drink that is fermented and carbonated. It has been popular for thousands of years and, in one form or another, exists in almost every society. Although known and enjoyed for so long, the chemistry of brewing is very complex and is still not understood in all its particulars. Brewing remains very much an art, as well as a science, with rapid innovation over the past 20 to 25 years; developments in brewing automation and control have reduced the need for manual labor by 75 percent and placed much of the control of the process on instrument panels.

The brewing process itself can be divided into two main stages: (1) the production of natural cereal sugars, called wort production, and (2) fermentation and finishing. (The process is depicted in Figure E1.) At Stroh, a batch of beer typically took about a month to brew and age.

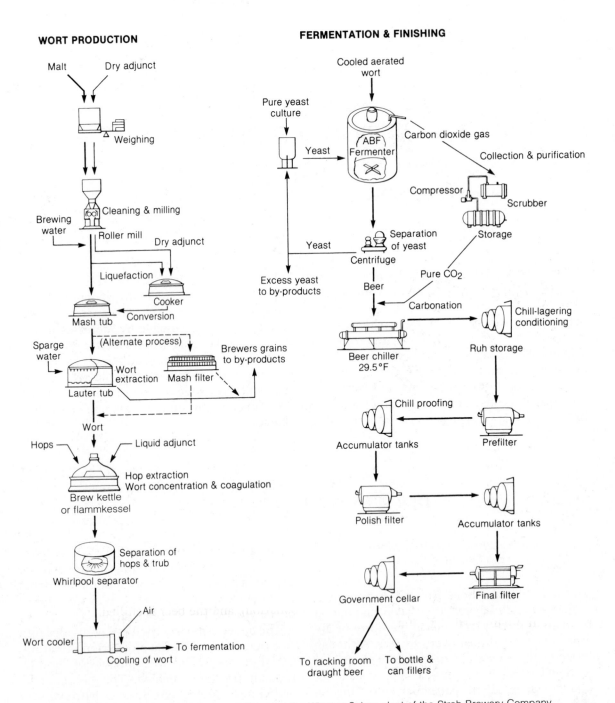

FIGURE E1   The brewing process as followed at the Winston-Salem plant of the Stroh Brewery Company.

Wort Production

Wort production starts with the weighing, cleaning, and milling of the malt, which gives beer its flavor. The malted barley and an adjunct (corn, rice, malt, and/or liquefied corn) are prepared separately. The adjunct is used because malted barley can convert more than its own weight of starch to fermentable sugars. To the milled or crushed barley, malt, and adjunct is added the brewing water, which is specially treated by filtering and pH adjustment to remove impurities. This addition of water to ground malt is known as *mashing* and, at Stroh, was done by the "double mash upward infusion" method. This method demands two separate mashing vessels—an adjunct cooker and a mash tub. These are large, stainless steel vessels in which the ground malt and brewing water can be stirred together and brought to a boil. The double mash upward infusion method ensures that the adjunct is of sufficiently small particle size so that it can best be exposed to the malt and the brewing water for quick and complete breakdown of its starches. The adjunct is therefore mashed separately in the adjunct cooker and then added to the malt mash in the mash tub.

The Stroh's brand and its Stroh Light extension brand are famed for being "fire brewed." Instead of the wort being cooked by heat from steam coils, as was the common practice, the wort for Stroh's and Stroh Light is cooked using direct flame in the flammekessel. This step gives Stroh and Stroh Light its distinctive taste.

After mashing, the mixture is transferred to a lauter tub, which separates the liquid (the wort) from the undissolved solids of the mash. The lauter tub is a large, circular tub with a false bottom and a rotating set of "rakes" that can be raised or lowered. These rotating rakes smooth out the mash as it enters the lauter tub and makes an even filter bed. Undissolved particles in the mash settle to the false floor of the lauter tub. Once settled, the liquid wort can be drawn off with the aid of hot "sparging" water, which rinses the wort off the grain. The undissolved mash is then collected and sent to the nearby Murphy Products Company (formerly a Stroh subsidiary), where it is processed into a highly nutritious live stock feed.

The drawn-off wort then enters the brew kettle where it boils for two hours. This boiling stabilizes the wort by killing off bacteria, deactivating enzymes, and coagulating any still undissolved particles. During this boiling, hops are introduced to the wort to enhance its flavor by extraction of desirable hop components. Boiling also increases the concentration of the wort through evaporation. Once boiled, the hops and trub (coagulated sediment) are separated out by whirlpool action in a special vessel. The hot wort is then cooled and aerated.

Fermentation and Finishing

Only after yeast has been introduced to the cooled wort and fermentation is complete can the product be called beer. The yeast that is introduced to the 50-foot long fermentation tanks transforms maltose, glucose, and other sugars in the wort to alcohol and carbon dioxide. Stroh's fermentation is accomplished by a patented process called "accurate balanced fermentation." During fermentation, carbon dioxide gas is collected and purified. After fermenting has finished and the yeast has been separated from the beer by centrifuge, the carbon dioxide is reintroduced to the beer (carbonation), and the beer is chilled.

Once fermentation is complete and the yeast separated, the remaining finishing consists of a string of storage and filtering steps. The chief aging occurs in the ruh cellar, where the beer is held for between 15 and 21 days. Once properly aged, the beer is filtered several times

A control panel in Stroh's Winston-Salem brewhouse.
(*Courtesy of Stroh Brewery Company*)

through diatomaceous earth. Final storage occurs in what is called the "government cellar," where the next day's production is inventoried and where the quantity of beer subject to federal tax is monitored. Beer typically spends between 9 and 15 days in the government cellar, the time largely dependent on packaging needs.

Out of the government cellar, the beer flows to the keg, canning, and bottling lines.

Canning, Bottling, and Kegging

The Winston-Salem brewery operated five canning lines, three bottling lines, and a keg line. Each line performed essentially the same functions: (1) filling and capping and (2) pasteur-

izing. Cans and bottles were also boxed into six-packs and cases, and cases were placed on pallets for shipping by truck or rail. The process from filling to palletizing ran continuously, with no significant buildup of in-process inventories unless a piece of equipment in the line broke down. The key piece of equipment on the line was the filler (an investment of $400,000)—the limiting element for capacity. All of the machines that followed had rated capacities in excess of the filler; so any equipment breakdown after the filler did not necessitate shutting down the entire line. Small reservoirs of work-in-process were held at several places along the line in order to keep things moving in case one part of the line had to be

A brew kettle in Stroh's Winston-Salem brewhouse. (*Courtesy of Stroh Brewery Company*)

shut down temporarily (such as, a shutdown to remove a broken bottle).

The can lines could run at 1600 cans per minute, the bottling lines at 900 bottles per minute, and the keg line at 340 half-barrels per hour. With five canning lines, several brands brewed at the plant could be canned at the same time. Alternatively, the same beer could be canned with two different types of lid at the same time. Three bottling lines were needed not only to match the demand for bottles but also to permit bottles of different shapes and sizes to be run at the same time. In addition, returnable bottles were separated from new bottles for filling and packaging. A canning line shift required eight workers, while a bottling line shift required 15.

Warehousing

The Winston-Salem plant preferred to load the beer directly from the line into railcars or trucks rather than warehouse it. (See the plant layout in Figure E2.) In fact, about half of the plant's output was shipped without any storage in the warehouse.

The warehouse's fully enclosed railroad docks could store fifty 50-foot freight cars. In addition, 15 truck loading docks were available. The warehouse was designed so that up to 70 percent of capacity output could be shipped by either rail or truck.

The warehouse stored some items that were not produced at the plant. For example, 10-

1. Fuel oil tanks
2. Fire protection water tank and pumps
3. Liquid adjunct tanks
4. Grain storage
5. Grains drying
6. Brew house
7. Brew supplies
8. Government cellar
9. Ruh storage cellar
10. Filtration cellar
11. Fermentation cellar

12. Offices
13. Keg area
14. Warehouse
15. Packaging
16. Can warehouse
17. Can warehouse
18. Truck docks
19. Distribution offices
20. Railroad tracks
21. Schlitz Avenue
22. Parking

FIGURE E2 Layout of the Winston-Salem plant of the Stroh Brewery Company.

ounce and 24-ounce cans were not filled here. These items had to be supplied by other Stroh plants.

Loading the Plant

Order Taking

Stroh's Winston-Salem brewery served approximately 182 wholesalers stretching over the entire Eastern seaboard from New England to some parts of Florida and inland to Ohio, Kentucky, and some parts of Tennessee. A wholesaler generally handled one of the major national brands and perhaps a smaller, regional brand. Each wholesaler serviced a range of retail accounts (such as liquor stores, bars, grocery stores) within a specified geographic area.

At the middle of each month, every wholesaler placed an order for delivery next month. This procedure meant that the brewery had lead times of two to six weeks for each order. The order, entered either directly by computer or mailed in, specified item, quantity, and date (sometimes hour) for delivery of the beer ordered. The brewery offered a remarkable diversity of items.

Thirteen different brands of beer were brewed at the plant (Stroh's, Stroh Light, Old Milwaukee, Old Milwaukee Light, Schlitz, Schlitz Light, Schlitz Malt Liquor, Piels, Piels Light, Goebel, Goebel Light, Schaefer, and Schaefer Light). Old Milwaukee accounted for 37 percent of production and Stroh for 22 percent, with the other brands dividing up the remaining 41 percent of the brewery's capacity. This beer could be packaged in cans, bottles, or kegs of various sizes, with different lids and in different kinds of cardboard cartons. In all, there were about 420 beer and packaging variations that a wholesaler could order. Wholesalers could pick up their order by truck, paying the expenses themselves, or they could have the plant load a special Stroh-assigned rail freight car and direct it to the wholesaler's own rail siding. The truck option offered greater speed and reliability of delivery than rail, thereby cutting down on the inventory the wholesaler had to carry, but it cost considerably more. About 60 percent of the plant's volume was shipped by rail and 40 percent by truck.

The Winston-Salem plant monitored the inventory positions of each of its wholesalers, and it followed trends in the marketplace as well (such as promotional campaigns and their effect). The plant sometimes made suggestions to its wholesalers on what and how much to order, especially if it felt strongly that a wholesaler might not have ordered correctly.

Production Planning

Production planning was intimately related to order taking and was performed in the same department. (See the organization chart in Figure E3.) The role of the production planners was to figure out how the brewery could best fill the orders placed by its wholesalers. A good production plan was one that satisfied all of the wholesalers' demands with (1) little repositioning of the requested delivery dates, (2) few changes in the workforce, and (3) full usage of the existing equipment.

Planning and scheduling production for each month meant determining (1) how much beer of which type was required and the timing of its delivery and packaging and (2) the precise sequencing of lines and beer/packaging combinations on each line.

Because it took a month to brew beer, the brewmaster had to produce to a forecast of sales rather than to customer order. This production to forecast was a key reason why the plant kept close tabs on retail activity and made buying suggestions to its wholesalers. The packaging of beer, on the other hand, could be, and was in fact, done to customer order.

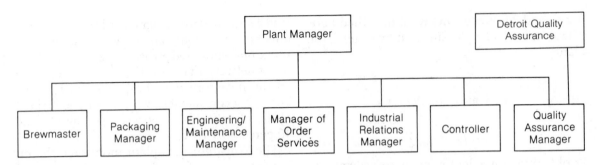

FIGURE E3 Organization chart for the Winston-Salem plant of the Stroh Brewery Company.

In planning packaging for any given month, it was advantageous to:

1. Group runs of the same beers together, such as packaging Old Milwaukee on several lines at the same time.

2. Group similar packaging sizes and types together, such as running all quart bottles at the same time rather than interspersing them among other production runs.

3. Run similar lines at the same time, such as running two can lines in tandem. To run a second line, given the first was running, required only four more workers rather than the eight it took to run the line by itself.

4. Run a canning line together with the keg line, since the joint workforce for such a combination could then be shifted en masse to a bottling line if need be. In that way, the groups working on any line would not have to be split up and reassembled as often.

Once the next month's wholesaler orders were received, the production planners went to work to schedule the production to fulfill that demand. This scheduling was accomplished manually, using trial and error but with reference to decision rules like the four mentioned here. After the production plan became "final," the wholesalers' delivery dates and order quantities were acknowledged on a week-by-week basis, giving the wholesalers two weeks' notice. About 70 percent of the wholesalers' original orders were acknowledged without any changes in dates or quantities. For the other 30 percent, all quantities were filled with timing dislocations that were always less than two weeks. Fully 97 percent of all the acknowledged orders were shipped on time.

Wholesalers could request changes in the schedule after their initial orders had been placed. This meant calling a production coordinator who could change the production plan or arrange swaps between wholesalers (since the brewery was aware of all wholesaler inventory positions). Major modifications of the production plan rarely had to be made. Minor adjustments were made about twice a week, but these occurred normally for production problems such as a machine breakdown. The production plan was declared fixed as to labor content one week in advance of production. It was declared fixed as to packaging variations only one day in advance of production. About one shift's production was kept as a safety stock so that snafus in demand, production, or logistics would not necessarily affect delivery.

The production plan had another role somewhat different from the weekly scheduling of

A bottling line at Stroh's Winston-Salem plant.
(*Courtesy of Stroh Brewery Company*)

machines to match orders exactly. This role had to do with anticipating the seasonality of beer drinking. There was a definite seasonal trend to beer sales. Demand peaked from May through September, with the height of the peak accounting for sales roughly double those of the winter trough.

Because Stroh's pasteurized beer had no living organisms in it (milk had 500 per milliliter), the beer did not spoil. The brewery could therefore cushion itself somewhat for the peak season demand by building up inventories, both in its own warehouse and in the warehouses of its wholesalers. In this way, the brewery did not have to hire or lay off as many workers during the periods when demand was changing abruptly. The brewery and its wholesalers built

up some inventories during the late spring and ran them down as summer progressed.

Because beer tasted best when it was fresh, it was company policy to hold no packaged beer at the brewery that was older than 21 days. The policy for wholesalers was not to hold any beer longer than 60 days. These policies helped to ensure that consumers enjoyed a fresh product.

The precise production schedule for the various lines depended in large measure on the time it took to accomplish various changeovers with the equipment. There were three key types of changeovers:

1. *Beer changeovers.* When a different beer was to be packaged, the pipes leading to the line from the government cellars had to be

The kegging line at Stroh's Winston-Salem plant.
(*Courtesy of Stroh Brewery Company*)

cleaned out by a "blow back" of beer to the cellars, using carbon dioxide. Only then could the new beer travel the pipes to the filling machine. For most beer switches, this changeover could be accomplished in 15 minutes, quicker than that for lines close to the government cellars and longer than that for lines far from the cellars. Because of the significantly different composition of light beers, a changeover to or from light beer involved, in addition to a "blow back" with carbon dioxide, flushing the pipes and the filling machine bowl with water. Thus, when light beer was run, the changeover entailed 20 or 25 minutes to prepare the line for the beer and a similar amount of time to clean up the line once it was run.

2. *Packaging changeovers.* On the canning lines, the chief packaging changeovers involved either a change of can lids or a change of case carton. There were two types of lids: a pop-top, where the tab came off the can, and an ecology lid, where the tab was pushed down into the can and remained attached. (Either of these lids could carry special tax-paid statements for the States of Georgia or Florida.) There were three carton possibilities: (1) a standard case of 24 made up of four six-packs, (2) a fully enclosed box of 24 loose cans, and (3) a fully enclosed box of 12 loose cans. A change of lids took five to ten minutes on average, while a change of case cartons took about five minutes.

The only packaging change for the bottling lines involved a switch of cartons for the 7-ounce bottles, a changeover that averaged 10 minutes.

3. *Container changeovers.* The most complex and time-consuming changeover involved a switch of container sizes—for example, from 14-ounce to 16-ounce cans or from 7-ounce bottles to quarts. (Four can sizes were possible—8, 12, 14, and 16 ounces—and five bottle sizes—7, 12, 16, 32, and 40 ounces.) Such changes involved resetting the filling equipment, the lid placement or bottle crowning equipment, the labeling equipment, and the cartoning equipment. Typically, an entire shift was devoted to these changeovers.

On a typical day, for example, a 12-ounce can line would make eight to ten lid or beer changeovers, a 16-ounce can line would make six such changeovers, and a quart bottling line would make three such changeovers.

The extent of container changeovers depended on the season. There were two basic types of can changeovers and two basic types of bottle changeovers. In the summer, the cycles shown in Table E1 prevailed for these can and bottle lines.

Given changeovers of various sorts and mechanical and other problems, can and bottle lines could not operate all the time. For the most part, the line efficiencies ran about 80–85 percent. Changeovers accounted for between 5 and 8 percent of the difference between these efficiencies and 100 percent.

Purchasing

The purchasing function for the plant was housed in the same department that handled order taking and production planning. This ar-

TABLE E1 Container changeovers for can and bottle lines during summer (Stroh Brewing Company)

LINE	SHIFTS PER CYCLE
Can Line	
Type A (12-ounce cans)	Line devoted to 12-ounce cans; no changes
Type B	
16-ounce cans	15 shifts
14-ounce cans	6 shifts*
Bottle Lines	
Type A	
12-ounce returnables	12 shifts
12-ounce nonreturnables	3 shifts*
Type B	
Quarts	20 shifts
7-ounce bottles	5 shifts
Stroh taper bottles (12 ounces)	12 shifts
Party bottles (12 ounces)	6 shifts*

*Cycle then repeats.

rangement made sense since the production plan implied, in a straightforward way, the material needs for the entire process.

All of the brewery's major materials inputs (malt, adjuncts, cans, bottles, cardboard) were purchased on long-term contracts from major suppliers. These contracts were all negotiated by Stroh's headquarters staff in Detroit. The Winston-Salem plant negotiated on its own only those contracts for materials and services that went into the maintenance of the brewery itself and were not an integral part of the final product. Still, there were plant-specific negotiations for 2500 contracts each year. Also, even though Detroit headquarters may have negotiated for a specific material, there was often a direct supplier-brewery relationship. This was particularly true for cans and bottles. Cans were supplied by Stroh's own can plant located near the brewery, and bottles were provided by three outside sources: Anchor, Foster-Forbes, and Owens-Illinois.

The brewery placed orders for these major materials in much the same way that Stroh's wholesalers placed orders with the brewery. For example, the July order for cans or bottles would be placed on June 10. At that time, the brewery would place a firm 4-week order and an estimate of the succeeding 4 weeks' demand.

The inventory levels for any one of these major materials depended crucially on the dependability of the supplier. If the supplier had proven reliable and no special circumstances intervened, the brewery would want to hold only enough of the material to last until the next delivery. As it was, special circumstances were continually intervening, and so the brewery often adjusted the amount it ordered to take advantage of volume discounts in price or seasonal differences in sales or expectations about a strike in the supplier's plant. Some typical inventory levels for major materials were:

Bottles	2–3 days of production
Malt	5–7 days
Cans	2 weeks
Cardboard cases	2 weeks
Bottle labels	4 months

The Workforce

The brewery currently employed 670 people, producing on three shifts a day, five days a week. Of these, 80 were salaried (managers and staff) and 590 were paid hourly. The hourly workers were represented by a union, the International Brotherhood of Teamsters.

Most of the workforce had been hired from within a 50-mile radius. Half of the salaried workers were drawn from other Stroh breweries, but none of the hourly workers came from other Stroh breweries, mainly because they had to be volunteers and had to pay for their own

move. During plant start-up a strong effort was made to hire persons so that there was a representative mix of ages, ...es, and sexes.

The hourly workers were divided into two main groups: the production workers who brewed and packaged the beer, and the engineering and maintenance workers who cared for and fixed the plant's equipment. The maintenance workers were paid about 5 percent more than the production workers, since their jobs required greater expertise and wider skills.

Once in a department (brewing, packaging, engineering/maintenance), workers tended to stay, often doing the same job. This status quo was frequently by choice, since workers who complained of boredom were generally shifted to more complex jobs or made relief workers (spelling other workers who were taking breaks). Advancement through the ranks and into management was possible, especially in brewing and packaging, although the odds were short. Most movement among the hourly employees was between shifts; such moves were based on seniority.

Control and Evaluation of the Operation

Quality Assurance

Quality assurance (QA) at the brewery was an important activity, employing 38 people in three separate labs: microbiology, brewing, and packaging. The staff at those labs performed 1100 separate tests, many of them repetitions of the same test, on each batch of beer brewed at the plant. QA staff worked round the clock, seven days a week. Quality assurance had the authority to stop operations at any point in the process. The QA manager was responsible for dealing with and rectifying any customer complaints.

A worker inspecting cans of Schlitz along the Stroh's Winston-Salem canning line. (*Courtesy of Stroh Brewery Company*)

Here are two examples of the specifications that the QA staff tested for, one set by the corporation's brewing staff and the other set by the corporation's packaging staff:

1. The brewing staff had set a standard of 16 million yeast cells (± 2 million) per milliliter of beer during fermentation. Quality assurance tested for this standard twice for

every fermentation tank's batch. The test had to be completed within the first four hours of fermentation so that any necessary corrective measures could be taken. The test was accomplished by taking a 4-ounce sample from the tank, diluting it in three steps, and then counting yeast cells by microscope.

2. The packaging staff had established a standard that the air content in a 12-ounce can of beer be no more than 1 cubic centimeter, because oxygen caused flavor instability in the beer. The QA staff tested for this standard by checking each canning line five times per shift, taking three cans from each line each time. If the cans were off specification, the QA staff would quarantine all the line's beer up to the last good check and then systematically inspect the quarantined lot until the beginning of the off-specification beer was encountered. The beer that passed inspection was released, and the beer that failed inspection was discarded. As it turned out, about 98 percent of any quarantined beer was eventually released as good product.

Rarely did any of the batches of beer fail to satisfy standards, but the quality assurance department prided itself on its vigilance. It viewed itself as the early warning station for detecting any encroaching degradations of the process's integrity.

Information Flows within the Process

Most of the information flows within the process were directed from the top down. If the process was working smoothly, workers needed to be informed of only routine things, such as the changeover in a line from one beer to another or the shifting from one line to another. Most jobs did not vary that much anyway, and so the information that was transmitted could be sparse without any detrimental effect.

Top management was eager, however, for the thoughts of the workers on all matters of plant operations. Of particular concern were breakdowns in the process. After worker signals of process breakdown, the engineering and maintenance force would be called in. These troubleshooting jobs were generally regarded as the most complex at the brewery and the most pressure-filled. A good engineering/maintenance department was a real asset and a chief way to keep costs low by maintaining high speed and high yields.

Evaluating Plant Performance

Each week management at the brewery developed an operations summary that listed goals and actual results for an entire list of performance measures such as productivity (barrels per worker), cost per barrel, packaging line efficiencies, material losses, beer losses, beer rejected by QA, deliveries made on time, shipment errors, wholesaler complaints, and worker absenteeism. Each week, too, the plant's beer was evaluated by taste tests in Detroit and elsewhere. More than any other test, this was the one the plant always wanted to pass.

In many respects, the plant's performance could be fine-tuned only from week to week. The major elements of plant performance were either already decided (plant design) or beyond the scope of plant management (the plant's sales volume). As the plant manager admitted: "The heaviest decision in our industry is capital equipment investment." Major cost and quality advances were very much a function of the equipment the company's design people in Detroit decided to incorporate into the plant.

Over the past 20 to 25 years, breweries had also been built larger than before. There were real cost savings implied by larger brewery size: vats and tanks could be larger and still make quality beer at lower cost per barrel, and packaging line speed and capacity could be used fully.

The size for the Winston-Salem brewery was determined as a sort of "lowest common denominator" for different "lumpy" capital investments. Specifically, the plant's lauter tub could process 3 million barrels of beer a year, and the mandatory assortment of packaging lines (lines for kegs, cans, one-way bottles, and returnable bottles) could process 5.2 to 6 million barrels a year. With the addition of other canning lines and another bottling line, packaging capacity could then precisely match the output of two lauter tubs—hence a brewery capacity of 6 million barrels a year.

What the plant manager worried about depended a lot on volume. As he noted, "Volume solves everything." When volume was high, all the manager had to worry about was whether the workers would accept the necessary overtime and whether maintenance could hold everything together. At capacity, quality and meeting shipments were chief concerns, with product cost lower in priority. When sales volume dropped, however, meeting cost targets became relatively more important, and that meant tightening up on staff and laying off workers. The plant was operated as a cost center, since it had no responsibilities for revenue raising (for example, no marketing at the plant) and its geographic market area was fixed. Plant management was concerned chiefly for the maintenance of the plant and the motivation of the workforce; with them came quality beer, high yields, and on-time shipments.

PART TWO

DISCUSSION

The Stroh Brewery Company is in no way responsible for the following views and presentation. They remain solely the responsibility of the author.

THE PROCESS FLOW

Much of the Stroh brewery's operation is reminiscent of the continuous flow process at International Paper's Androscoggin Mill. Even though there are about 420 beer and packaging variations, most of these modifications require setup times that are tiny in comparison with the run length. The process flow is well defined, and every product goes through the same steps in the process. (See Figure E1 for a process flow chart.) Over time, equipment advances have speeded up the process and have driven labor out of the product's value.

The job contents of the direct labor in the process are of two kinds, polar extremes. Most workers have well-delineated tasks, most of which are repeated time and again as the product is manufactured. These jobs, typically, are not very demanding. At the other extreme lies the brewmaster. Despite great strides in automation and control, the brewmaster's duties still lie within the realm of art. Brewing is still imperfectly known enough to require great experience to produce a quality product.

Requiring nearly comparable levels of skill and experience are the plant engineers. Plant engineering and maintenance are crucial to an operation such as a brewery, where the capital investment is enormous and the success of the process depends on meeting quality standards and delivery schedules and on maintaining high yields of output. All of these goals are influenced importantly by the design and upkeep of the equipment in the plant. Moreover, *all* of the equipment must be functioning smoothly for *any* of the product to meet its specifications. Breakdowns or below-specification performance of any of the equipment is likely to lead to poor quality, poor shipment performance, or excessively high costs (such as low packaging speeds).

Despite these important similarities to the continuous flow process at the Androscoggin Mill, the Stroh brewery is not strictly a continuous flow operation. This is true primarily because the brewing phase of the process is done on a batch basis. True, these batches are large, but it is only because of their sequencing and the accumulation of a work-in-process inventory just before packaging that the batch operation in brewing can supply a steady flow of beer to the continuous flow that is packaging. The work-in-process inventories in the ruh and government cellars separate the two different types of processes. Without such an inventory, even though the daily or weekly capacities of the two processes (brewing and packaging) may be matched perfectly, the lumpiness of the batch flow operation's output cycle would cause severe problems for the smooth-running continuous flow operation.

THE INFORMATION FLOW

The inventory between brewing and packaging does more than even out production. It also separates the information needs of the two processes. The brewmaster need only know how much beer of which kind to brew, and the packaging department need only to know what, when, and how much it is to package. Moreover, the timing of the information flows is much different. The precise packaging department schedule is set as final only one day prior to packaging. Up to that time, adjustments to

the schedule can be accepted. Needless to say, the brewmaster cannot react so quickly. Since it takes about a month to brew a batch of beer, the brewmaster can only work to an estimate of demand, not from firm wholesale orders. The work-in-process inventory between brewing and packaging, then, acts as a safety stock of beer as well, so that last-minute changes in demand can be accommodated. It also serves as the dividing line between production triggered by estimate (brewing) and production triggered by firm orders (packaging). This difference in information requirements, as much as anything else, sets aside the Stroh brewery as a hybrid (batch/continuous flow) process.

The separation of information needs and flows at the brewery is depicted in an information flow diagram (Figure E4). Note that the information basically flows in only one direction (top down) except for the usual signaling of equipment breakdowns and acknowledgments of orders shipped. In this way, the information flows are reminiscent of the Androscoggin Mill.

CAPACITY MEASURES

The capacity of the brewery is a firm and easily understood number, 6 million barrels of beer a year. Barring a major breakdown of equipment, the capacity figure is primarily what the existing plant and equipment permit. Neither product mix nor scheduling has much impact on capacity. Other than to maintain the equipment and keep quality up, the plant is limited in what it can do to improve the quantity of good product brewed and packaged.

By the same token, capacity utilization is a well-defined concept. The capacity of any piece of equipment is known because it was engineered that way, and the current capacity is also easily measured. Moreover, because the plant's designers want to leave as little waste or spare

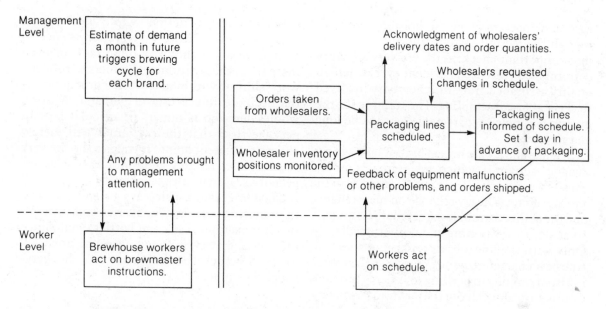

FIGURE E4 An information flow diagram of the Winston-Salem plant of the Stroh Brewery Company.

capacity unused as possible, the capacity utilization for any single piece of equipment is often very close to the capacity utilization figure for the process itself. Since the process's capacity utilization is determined by the bottleneck operation, one can say that all equipment capacities are likely to lie close to the bottleneck capacity.

Standards and Incentives

The standards that matter at the Stroh brewery are not the type of standards that managers of batch or job shop operations get concerned about. Labor standards (output per worker per unit of time) do not exist at the brewery. Rather, it is machine standards (units processed per hour) and quality standards that capture managers' attention and influence their behavior. These are the standards management strives to meet.

Similarly, labor incentives are absent from the brewery. The plant's output is so overwhelmingly related to machine performance rather than worker performance that worker incentive schemes make little sense.

Demands of the Process on the Workers

The process at this Stroh brewery places a variety of demands on a variety of different work groups within the brewery. Art, science, and routine are all found. For the brewhouse workers, even with the panels of controls that now abound, the brewing process still requires art, a "feel" and a "taste" for what makes quality beer. In many breweries, it still is true that the brewmaster's skills have been handed down from generation to generation.

While science may not have overtaken all aspects of the brewing art, it rules the quality assurance operations of the brewery itself (although the Detroit taste test is still the single most important check on the brewery's quality performance.) Science is evident everywhere in quality assurance, from the chemistry involved to the statistical sampling. The training for the quality assurance department can thus be long and rigorous.

Science and art are mixed in the plant's maintenance activities, which are an important and prestigious activity. The capital intensity of the process dictates heavy reliance on maintenance and the ability to troubleshoot problems quickly so as not to waste time and output needlessly. Only with the line jobs in packaging does routine best characterize the process. Still, switching from canning to bottling to kegging provides a measure of diversity in the job from day to day.

DEMANDS OF THE PROCESS ON MANAGEMENT

Stroh's Winston-Salem brewery and International Paper's Androscoggin Mill place many of the same kinds of demands on management. The high degree of capital intensity they both share dictate concern for (1) selection of the proper technology and (2) the balancing of capacities in all segments of the process. Over time, technological advance has dictated numerous advances in the process itself (centrifuges, stainless steel tanks, panels of process controls) and in the scale of the process (larger tanks than ever before). The design, choice, and matching of equipment are critical decisions for a brewer like Stroh.

Scheduling production, while a nontrivial matter, is not as critical to a brewery's success as it is to a job shop. As important, or even more so, as the positioning of orders within any work shift or within any week's production is the accurate forecasting of demand. A Stroh wholesaler who is out of a particular beer or package risks that the consumer will merely choose a different brand. It is up to the brewery to track sales reliably and to forecast sales, especially seasonal sales, accurately.

Good forecasting also plays a significant role in managing suppliers' deliveries and inventories (for example, cans and bottles) well. Since individual breweries do not negotiate price, delivery becomes the key aspect of brewery-supplier contact.

HYBRID PROCESSES

Hybrid processes, mixes of two or more of the purer process types (job shop, batch flow, line flow, continuous flow), are common occurrences. Numerous plants are organized with line or continuous flow processes on their front ends, say, to assemble a product or to package it. On their back ends, these plants often have components fabricated or materials processed by job shop or batch flow processes. Much of food processing, drug manufacture, many complex consumer items (such as, appliances and furniture), and other products combine production in lots with assembly/packaging in lines—the kind of hybrid process represented by the Stroh brewery.

QUESTIONS

1. What similarities are there between the Stroh brewery operation and the Androscoggin Mill operation? What dissimilarities?

2. What did Stroh consider to be the elements of the satisfactory production plan and the requirements for good package planning?

What particular elements of Stroh's hybrid process planning might be applicable to the hybrid process in general? Why?

3. Describe how quality control may differ between the two main processes involved in a brewery.

4. Compare and contrast the demands of the process on Stroh workers and management with the demands on the same groups in two other processes you have studied.

5. It was stated that the brewery had a capacity of 6 million barrels of beer per year. If the plant were to can, bottle, and keg 6 million barrels in a year, what would be the capacity utilization of the packaging equipment, given the speeds mentioned in the case? Feel free to make assumptions about the relative demands for cans, bottles, and kegs.

6. How could the capacity of the brewing process itself be increased without a physical expansion of the brewery? How attractive is such a change?

7. Given the chapter's information on the relative demands of different brands and the summer cycle of container changeovers, concoct a month's production schedule for each major Stroh company brand. In an average week, what fraction of time would be devoted to changeovers of various types?

SITUATION FOR STUDY E-1
COUNTRY GELATIN COMPANY

Thomas Brewer is the plant manager for Country Gelatin Company, maker of powdered gelatins for human consumption. The main component of gelatin is collagen, a fibrous substance that is mostly protein. Steerhide, a major source of collagen, is the main ingredient in the gelatin powder produced at Country's Kansas City, Kansas, plant.

Figure E5 shows the process that Country uses to produce its gelatin. First, the steerhides are treated (acid is added to remove the hair, then neutralized), weighed, and put into storage. Enough steerhide is treated at one time to provide two days' worth of production. The hides are then stored for about two weeks so that they begin to "break down" and can be blended with other ingredients. This storage is called "aging."

Once several batches of steerhides (1500 kilograms each) have aged properly, enough batches are ground (to about the consistency of hamburger) to run one week's production. These mixed batches (5500 kilograms each) are then aged again for a few days before they are mixed into a gel blend (8000 kilograms, of which about half is water). One gel blend is enough for one day's production of gelatin.

After being mixed and aged, the mixed batch undergoes microcutting, a process that cuts the material into very small pieces. It then is mixed with water and an acid to form the gel blend. Next the gel blend is forced through a dryer to make it a powder. Under proper conditions, the powder can be stored almost indefinitely, until it is needed for final production.

Final production consists of two stages. First, the powder is mixed with sugar and a powdered flavoring (unless the final product is to be an unflavored gelatin); second, the product is measured and packaged. Final production, although continuous, is done to customer order. All stages in the process are highly mechanized, and workers are needed only to monitor the machines.

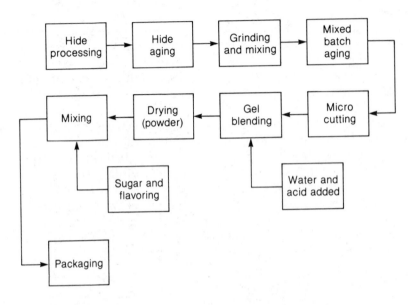

FIGURE E5   The production process at Country Gelatin Company.

Tom feels that quality control at Country can be adequately handled by three types of highly trained process control workers: solutions technicians, powder technicians, and line technicians. The solutions technician is responsible for the proper acid balance, salts, density, percent of solids, and the like of the gel blend. The powder technician's main responsibility is proper mixing of the final product—that is, the proper proportion of powder, sugars, and flavoring. The line technician is responsible for packaging.

Tom is wondering how he should schedule production at the various stages in the process, including the scheduling of labor and machines. In addition, he is uncertain how much inventory should be carried, and in what form. He feels he could begin to answer his concerns about scheduling and inventory control by (1) analyzing the characteristics of the process and (2) asking himself what aspects of the process would help him in scheduling production and controlling inventories and which ones would hinder him.

SITUATION FOR STUDY E-2
BUCHANAN TOBACCO COMPANY

Buchanan Tobacco employed 2000 people in a plant that stretched 15 acres. Ten different cigarette brands were made at the site, each with its own blend of bright, burley, and Turkish tobaccos and various other flavorings.

After the tobacco (the whole dried leaf) had been purchased by the company's buyers at various tobacco markets, it was brought to the stemmeries. Here it was cleaned with moist air and dried, and the stems were removed. The tobacco was then cut into small pieces and stored for two to three years in hogsheads before being brought to the plant for blending. The hogsheads were loaded onto flatbed tractor-trailers, and the tobacco arrived at the west end of the building in the containers in which it was aged.

In the blending area, the tobaccos were blended and flavorants were added in order to produce the correct blend for each brand of cigarettes. At each stage in the blending process, the tobacco was exposed to certain relative humidities and temperatures. At the completion of each stage, the blended tobacco was aged through drying. This aging allowed the tobacco to absorb moisture and flavorants.

After being aged, the tobacco went through the "casing and cutting" process, where certain liquids (casings) were added and the tobacco was shredded and blended for the particular brands being made. A pneumatic vacuum system transported the blended tobaccos to one of the 110 making machines (makers) designated for its brand. Each maker required one operator.

The sealed vacuum tubes ran above the machines, and so the tobacco fell to the bottom of the makers by gravity. The tobacco entered at the rate of 10 pounds per minute. The action of turning drums pulled the tobacco up through the machine. This action also vacuumed out dust and particles such as stems. As the tobacco came out of this section of the maker, it entered a small tube at such a constant rate that one continuous rod of tobacco was formed; this rod stretched almost the length of the machine.

At this point, the paper was wrapped around the tobacco. The paper, which was produced by a subsidiary, came in rolls over six miles long.

Each roll contained enough paper for 95,000 cigarettes. The paper was threaded through the machine, and the cigarette brand name was printed on it. As the paper was folded around the continuous rod of tobacco, a wheel applied glue to one edge. The paper was then sealed around the rod of tobacco. After sealing, the continuous cigarette was cut by a revolving knife, which cut 4100 cigarettes per minute and was timed to cut the exact length required.

The cut cigarettes next went to a drum. Vacuum pressure held the cigarettes on the drum as they slid into pockets. Simultaneously, the filters for the cigarettes, which were made in another area of the building and were precut to the appropriate size, were blown over on a tube. The cigarettes in the pockets were directly opposite each other, and a filter simply fell between them so that a cigarette, double-length filter, and another cigarette were all sealed together. At this point, the double cigarette passed over a sealer, and the filter was sealed to the paper on both ends. At the same time, corking paper, which was fed from a roll into the maker, was cut to the proper length and wrapped around the filter by the action of the drums. The "tipping" picked up enough glue to cause it to adhere to the filter. The double cigarette was then moved to a knife and cut into two 80-millimeter filtered cigarettes.

There were various automatic quality checks during the making process. Any cigarette with a defect would be automatically rejected. Common defects found at this point included air leaks and pin holes. All defective cigarettes were broken down and completely recycled through the process.

Immediately after cutting, the cigarettes that passed inspection were moved on a belt, with cigarettes on the back part of the drum being turned so that all were now facing the same direction. This belt carried the cigarettes to a special reservoir that created a buffer between the making and packing processes. This reservoir loaded cigarettes onto a conveyor for up to 17 minutes. If the maker went down, the packer could continue running for up to 17 minutes by using the reserve cigarettes from overhead. If the packer went down, the process simply reversed and cigarettes fed onto the conveyor directly from the maker. If either machine was inoperable for more than 17 minutes, both machines had to be shut down.

From this point, the cigarettes were fed by gravity into the packing machine or packer. As the cigarettes were fed into the machine, they automatically fell into three rows of seven, six, and seven cigarettes. A plunger pushed the twenty cigarettes into a foil pocket, which was formed as a series of turning drums took the foil that was fed off a roll and wrapped it around a form identical in shape and size to a pack of cigarettes. This foil was the interior of a pack of cigarettes.

Next, the label was taken from the front of the machine and formed into a pack and sealer was applied. Another plunger pushed the foiled pack into the label. A stamper picked up glue and applied a closure (stamp) to the pack. The pack slid on chains to the film machine.

The film fed off of a roll and was cut to the desired length to wrap a pack. Just before the pack was pushed into the film, the tear tape was laid across the film and sealed to it. Mechanical folders folded the film around the pack and electric heaters caused it to seal.

The packer packaged 210 packs of cigarettes a minute (4200 cigarettes); it was operating at a slightly faster rate than the maker. There were approximately 110 packers in the plant, each one operated by one worker.

The packaged cigarettes were then fed on conveyor belts past an inspector. The inspector looked for missing closures, missing tape, or any other defective packaging. Packs were fed to the inspector from two packers; therefore, an inspector saw about 25,000 packs an hour.

After the visual inspection, the packs proceeded on belts to the carton boxer machine. There were approximately 50 carton boxers, each one receiving from two packers; thus, two belts came together at the boxer. The cartons were fed down by a series of rollers and automatically opened. The packs from the two belts (five packs from each belt) lined up. The pressure from the last pack activated a switch, which in turn activated the plunger, pushing ten packs into a carton. The flaps of the carton were turned down by guides. When the carton emerged at the back of the boxer, it was sealed. At this point, an electronic inspector (operating on the basis of the metal in the foil) was used to detect missing tape or packs. The carton boxer's speed was determined by the speed of the packers, but generally it boxed 200 packs, or 20 cartons, per minute.

Next, the cartons proceeded up the elevator to the carton conveyor and down to the case packer. Usually at least five packers sent cartons to a single case packer; however, a single case packer could receive from as many as 20 packers. There were five case packers at the plant.

Flattened cases were stacked and fed down through one end of the machine, where guides opened them automatically. The cases had been preprinted with the brand name, but print was now applied to the cases to specify the date and the name of the plant. Cartons came down overhead slides from the carton collector and were conveyed into the back of the machine. The cartons were stacked in layers. As soon as ten rows of six cartons each had accumulated, a switch was activated to plunge the sixty cartons into one case. Thus each case contained 12,000 cigarettes. The filled case was then moved forward. Glue was applied from rollers to the end flaps. When the machine cycled again, these flaps were sealed down with pressure. The case stayed in this compartment until the glue was dried and sealed, which was less than a minute. Each caser had the capacity of packing approximately five cases per minute.

The sealed cases crossed an automatic scale before going up an elevator. This scale inspected for light cases; being underweight indicated that a pack or carton was missing. A heavy case was not rejected, because extra weight merely indicated the presence of collected moisture.

After reaching the top of the case elevator, the case traveled on a conveyor to the transfer room. Here all brands were assembled on pallets by brand. Each pallet had an identification number, which the computer married to the brand's code number to permit tracking these cases to the warehouse. After the cases had been palletized, elevators lifted the pallets to the conveyor to the shipping center. All of the shipping was done from the new, completely computerized central distribution center. The cigarettes were produced strictly to order. Everything produced during the day was shipped out at night so that there was virtually no work-in-process or finished goods inventory.

1. Diagram the process flow.

2. Speculate, as best you can, on the flows of information in the process.

3. Why might this operation be classed as a hybrid? What type of hybrid is it and how does it compare with the Stroh brewery?

4. What do you see as key challenges for management in this process?

5. What kinds of changes to the process would occur as new makers are purchased with speeds twice as great or more than those already in the plant?

A WORKER-PACED LINE FLOW PROCESS AND A SERVICE FACTORY
Burger King Restaurant, North Church Street, Burlington, North Carolina

The Burger King Restaurant on North Church Street in Burlington, North Carolina, was one of over 4000 fast food restaurants operated worldwide by Burger King Corporation, a wholly-owned subsidiary of the Pillsbury Company, and by the corporation's franchisees. The restaurant was open from 6 A.M. to 2 A.M. Monday through Thursday and from 6:30 A.M. to 4 A.M. Friday and Saturday. On Sundays it was open from 7 A.M. to 2 A.M. Breakfast was available from the opening until 10:30 A.M. and consisted of a choice of bacon, ham, sausage or steak biscuits and croissan'wiches, with or without eggs or cheese, French toast, hash browns, and a scrambled egg platter. The regular menu consisted of a wide selection of hamburger sandwiches (regular hamburger and cheeseburger; a special Whopper® sandwich with or without cheese; Whopper Jr.®, double burger, double cheeseburger and double Whopper; and a bacon double cheeseburger) as well as some specialty sandwiches (chicken, ham and cheese, fish), and a salad bar (platter or side salad). To accompany these selections, the restaurant offered various choices: french fries, onion rings, soft drinks, shakes, apple pie, and cherry pie.

The restaurant was located on North Church Street; the area was a busy one near an AT&T Technologies plant, a hospital, a large high school, and a residential area. The present restaurant had opened in September 1985. The Burger King Corporation had built this restaurant on the site of a former Burger King that had been smaller and less efficient.

The new restaurant was rectangular, freestanding on about an acre and a half, and was constructed mainly of wood planks, bricks, and glass. The building was situated toward the front of the lot, freeing the sides and rear for 54 parking spaces. A children's playground occupied the front portion of the lot. A "drive-thru" was operated on one side of the restaurant, with the order board at the rear and the pick-up window toward the front. Within the restaurant 85 seats (either benches or freestanding chairs) were arranged in groups. There were 11 tables of four, 16 tables of two, and 9 single places within the restaurant. The eating area was tastefully appointed in oak wood, with a handsome color scheme, an atrium off to the side of the main eating area, ceiling fans, and many hanging plants. In the eating areas there were service counters for napkins, straws, and so on, and several large trash cans for customer use. The restrooms were located next to the main door. The eating area occupied about half of the restaurant's square footage; the other half was occupied by the counter, the kitchen, and the storage areas.

The front counter, with registers on the right and pickup to the left. (*Courtesy of Burger King Corporation*)

PART ONE
PROCESS DESCRIPTION

RESTAURANT OPERATIONS

Order Taking (The Front Counter)

After entering the restaurant, customers walked between the railings of the queuing line (or, as Burger King calls it, the "customer guidance system"). While awaiting their turns to state their order at the counter, they could consult the brightly lit menu above the counter area. At the right-hand side of the counter were three cash registers. An order-taker greeted each customer there and took the order. As the customer spoke, the order-taker keyed the contents of the order on a point-of-sale device (for example, pressed the key for the Whopper—a large hamburger with lettuce, tomato, onions, pickles, ketchup, and mayonnaise), read the printed total for the order, took the customer's payment, and gave the customer change and a receipt that listed the order.

At the other end of the counter, one of two printers printed a duplicate copy of the order. Using this copy, an expediter proceeded to assemble the order. Assembling the order meant going to the counter and the chutes that lay between the front counter and the kitchen to gather the sandwiches, fries, or other items that flowed from the kitchen. When shakes were ordered, the expediter was responsible for drawing them from the nearby dispensing machines. After assembling the kitchen items of the order, the expediter presented them to the customer either on a tray (for inside use) or in a bag (to go). The expediter also gave cups to the customer so that he could fill them with the desired soft drinks, tea, or coffee. If the customer had ordered something from the salad bar, the expediter also gave the customer a plate or bowl, a knife and a fork, and a lid if the salad is to take out.

Several features of the front counter's operation were comparatively new and merit highlighting. The most important innovation was the split made in the duties of the order-takers and expediters. The system in use at the Church Street Burger King was known as the "multi-conventional" line-up. It was a throwback to the early years of Burger King when the "conventional" line-up was used. That system consisted of a single line of customers served by a single cash register where orders were taken. Expediters assembled the orders and presented them to the customers farther along the counter. The present system operated in much the same way, although up to three registers could be used simultaneously, and several expediters could handle the orders. The new, multiconventional system was thus far faster than the old system.

The multiconventional line-up was a more radical change from the "hospitality line-up" that had replaced the old conventional system. With the hospitality line-up, cash registers were evenly spaced across the entire front counter and customers had to choose which of several lines they wished to wait in. Cashiers both took orders and assembled them. The hospitality line-up, although somewhat more labor-intensive than the old conventional line-up, could handle peak hour demand more efficiently than the older system. With the advent of the multiconventional line-up, however, the labor-intensity of the hospitality line-up was reduced without sacrificing its peak period capacity advantages. Customers preferred the new line-up as well. With a single line, they did not risk becoming annoyed because some other line was moving faster than theirs. In addition, they were frequently better prepared to give their order to the order-taker, and this speeded up the process for everyone.

Another innovation involved the self-service drink dispensers. With their installation, customers could fix their drinks precisely the way they wanted (whether lots of ice or no ice). By moving the drink dispensers out of the kitchen, time and labor costs were also saved. Because free refills were possible, materials costs were somewhat higher, but not appreciably so.

The salad bar was still another comparatively recent innovation at Burger King. Americans were increasingly conscious of their diets, and the salad bar was one way diet-conscious customers could be better served.

Order Filling (The Kitchen)

Burger King differed from McDonald's and some other fast food restaurants in that comparatively little finished goods inventory was kept; sandwiches were assembled continuously. While certain orders might not have been delivered as quickly as when larger inventories were kept, this approach offered the distinct advantage of producing to order when appropriate. As an old Burger King slogan put it, you can "have it your way," say, by ordering a Whopper with double cheese and mustard but no pickle, or a hamburger with extra onions.

Providing this kind of customer order variation with minimum customer waiting de-

The self-service drink station. (*Courtesy of Burger King Corporation*)

manded a production system that was extraordinarily flexible. In fact, two kinds of flexibility were required: flexibility to meet special customer orders and flexibility to meet large surges in customer demand during lunch or dinner hours. Many aspects of the production system contributed to this flexibility.

The "Line": Layout and Job Descriptions

The process of making sandwiches and filling orders at Burger King was explicitly recognized as an assembly line. Production of the hamburger sandwiches (burgers, for short) followed a straight path from the back of the kitchen to the front counter. Along this path was a series of work stations. (See Figure F1.)

Any of the various burgers was begun either by taking a meat patty and bun out of an en-vironmentally controlled holding compartment called a "steamer" or by placing the appropriate patty (Whopper size or regular) and bun onto the chain drag at the feed end of a specially constructed, gas-fired broiler at the back of the kitchen. The meat patties were drawn from a freezer below the broiler. The broiler cooked the meat at approximately 800° F., allowing the grease to drip into a special compartment, and toasted the bun.

Next in the assembly line came the "board," where buns and meat were transformed into Whopper sandwiches, burgers, Whopper Jr. sandwiches with cheese, double cheeseburgers, and the like. This was the key portion of the line where the burger could be assembled "your way." The board itself was a long, stainless-steel table in the center of which were bins of con-

FIGURE F1   The kitchen layout of the Church St. Burger King. The circled numbers indicate the sequence of additions of workers to the kitchen as demand increases.

diments (cheese slices, bacon, pickles, onions, sliced tomatoes, shredded lettuce, mayonnaise) kept at room temperature. Below the table were racks for holding spare quantities of condi- ments and supplies and also places for waste disposal. There were two work areas, one on each side of the center inventory of condiments. Above each side were two microwave ovens that could be used for keeping assembled sandwiches hot, stacks of various boxes into which the sandwiches were placed, and a special series of touch controls that were part of the information flow system of the kitchen (more on this later). Beyond the board, on the pick-up counter, were chutes that held completed sandwiches ready for assembly into customer orders.

On one side of this main burger assembly line were the frying vats and the specialty sandwich board. The four frying vats were computer-controlled, two just for french fries and two for other products (such as onion rings, chicken sandwich portions, or fish portions). Near the frying vats were racks of thawed or thawing french fries (1 to 2 hour thaw times maximum), and above the vats were containers with blanched (half-cooked) onion rings and fish portions. Behind the frying vats was the specialty sandwich board, which had its own assortment of condiments, buns, and boxes. To one side of the specialty sandwich board was a warmer for items like cooked chicken patties and to the other side was a bun toaster.

On the other side of the main burger assembly line were the automatic drink machines for the drive-thru operation. A worker simply placed an ice-filled cup under the appropriate drink spout and pressed a button for small, regular, or large drinks; the machine then dispensed the proper quantity of soft drink, freeing the worker to do something else while the cup was being filled. The shake machine (for chocolate, vanilla, and strawberry) was located nearby, close to both the drive-thru window and the front counter.

Around the periphery of the kitchen were sinks and storage areas for food and supplies. There were also cooler and freezer rooms, an office, and an area in which workers could congregate and be trained.

The Drive-Thru Operation

Because the drive-thru at the Church Street Burger King accounted for approximately 55 percent of the restaurant's business, its smooth operation was critical. Work assignments at the drive-thru depended on how busy the restaurant was. In very slow times, a single worker (order-taker/expediter) handled the drive-thru alone. When business picked up, two people were assigned to the drive-thru—one as an order-taker and one as an expediter. At peak times, five workers were assigned to the drive-thru—three inside the restaurant and two outside. One of the two outside took orders while the other acted as a cashier. Of the three inside, one acted as an order-taker and two were expediters.

Peak versus Nonpeak Operation

Employees were allocated to the workstations at the restaurant according to the pace of demand. When demand was very slow, a skeleton crew operated the restaurant: an order-taker/expediter at the front counter, a drive-thru order taker/expediter, and a kitchen worker. As demands increased, another would be added to the kitchen: one worker would take the broiler and the burger board, while one worked at the fry station and the specialty board. At peak times, there were as many as 16 to 20 employees working in the restaurant plus two managers. Management knew from historical data exactly when the peak hours would be at the Church Street restaurant and so could plan worker arrivals.

Before the daily peaks in demand at lunch and dinner, considerable preparations were made, such as stocking the freezer under the broiler with hamburger patties, taking frozen fries out for thawing, and slicing tomatoes. If things worked as planned, minimal restocking would be needed during the peaks.

As demand picked up, more workers were added, and job assignments became more specialized. In slow times, for example, one worker split duties between the fry station and the specialty sandwich board; during peak periods there were separate workers for these two work areas. During slow periods, one worker handled the broiler and all burger sandwich preparation; during peak times, one worker "fed" the broiler, one "caught" patties and buns and monitored the steamer, and two workers assembled sandwiches at the burger board. At the Church Street Burger King, the burger board was divided during peak times into cheese and noncheese sides. (At other Burger Kings, this division might be Whopper-size sandwiches on one side and small sandwiches on the other. Such a split frequently depended on the composition of demand at the particular restaurant.) During peak periods as well, a worker would be assigned to the salad bar and would also help keep the dining area clean.

During very slow periods, much of the sandwich and drink production was triggered by the customer order itself. The burger given to the customer might actually be the one placed on the broiler chain in response to punching in the order. Some items could be held in inventory. An inventory of the most popular sandwiches (such as regular burgers and Whoppers) was usually kept in the chutes, but only for 10 minutes; if no customer requested them they were discarded. Each sandwich box was marked with a "time to discard." The system used the numbers pointed to by the minute hand on the clock. Thus, a Whopper boxed at 20 minutes after the hour (the 4 on the clockface) would have a 6 marked on the box, because at 30 minutes after the hour (the 6 on the clockface) its 10-minute hold time would have expired. French fries were handled in a special way. Fries took approximately 2 minutes and 10 seconds to cook—too long to have a customer wait. As a result, fries had to be waiting in finished goods inventory. Here, too, the restaurant kept track of the time fries were waiting. If no one claimed fries within 7 minutes, they were discarded. (The fry station computers helped by keeping track of the time between batches so that fries were not sitting out too long.)

As demand picked up, it became more and more likely that a finished goods inventory of the major burgers and specialty sandwiches would be kept and that the broiler feeder would be loading the broiler in response to the inventory situation rather than in response to the particular orders displayed on the video screens. To guide production and to maintain inventory levels as demand increased, the Church Street Burger King operated "stock level charts." There were five stock level charts—one each for the broiler-steamer, sandwich board, specialty sandwich board, specialty sandwich warmer, and drinks. The chart featured a stock level light indicator on which there were seven lights. Corresponding to each light was a volume of sales range to which were pegged inventory standards for the various items. Each change in the level (for example, from level 4 to level 5 or from level 6 to peak) was announced by a special bell and the light switched so that all workers could infer, for example, how many sandwiches of particular types should be in the finished goods chutes and how many patties and buns should be in the steamer. The workers at the board were constantly tracking how many sandwiches were in each chute as well as keeping an eye on the video screen for any special order variations entered by the cashiers. When a worker saw such an order, he or she pressed one of the special touch controls above the station (mentioned earlier), which removed the call for that sandwich from the video screen. The worker then began preparing that sandwich and marking the box to identify it to the expediters.

For the manager, the choice of a "level" represented a trade-off between meeting service standards with quick deliveries on the one hand, and keeping too much in inventory and risking waste on the other. The manager always wanted to raise the level just before a surge in demand and to lower it just before the surge evaporated.

Coping with Bottlenecks

Surges in demand or runs on particular items could strain the production system and cause it to miss its established service standards. Three service standards were routinely tracked: (1) door-to-door time—the time elapsed from the moment the customer entered a line to place an order until the customer was served, (2) drive-thru time—the time elapsed from the arrival of a car at the order station until the customer was served, and (3) drive-thru transaction time—the time elapsed between a car's arrival at the pick-up window and its receipt of the order. The Church Street Burger King restaurant tried to keep these service standards at company-mandated levels: three minutes average for the door-to-door and drive-thru times and 30 seconds average for the drive-thru transaction time.

To reach these goals consistently, the restaurant manager had to avoid bottlenecks in production. By providing both guidance to the crew and a set of spare hands, the manager could help ensure a smooth operation. During peak hours especially, it was not uncommon to see the manager stepping up to the board to assemble a sandwich or drawing a shake from the machine or bagging fries or replenishing materials. The manager also encouraged crew team work. For example, workers with some slack time helped those who were overloaded—a cheese sandwich worker might assemble some non-cheese burgers. In fact, the manager's mandate for each of the workers was (1) to be aware of which "level" was being operated and what was on the video screen, (2) to be aware of any materials that would soon be out of stock, (3) to keep the workstation clean, and (4) to help anyone needing help. This mandate to keep production smooth and efficient placed special demands on the manager. The manager's job was not only to break any current bottlenecks but also to anticipate any potential ones. The manager constantly sought information from the workers on where bottlenecks were, how many cars were in line, and which materials were running low, and encouraged the workers to handle as much of any surge in demand themselves without intervention.

Adequate prepeak period preparation also meant a great deal in coping with bottlenecks. If the shake machine was not completely filled with ingredients or if the cash register tape was close to running out, the operation was in danger of some bottlenecks that might affect service adversely. The restaurant manager had to check the status of items like these to be sure that incomplete preparation did not detract from the success of the operation.

PURCHASING AND MATERIALS MANAGEMENT

For any item, the quantity ordered was the amount needed to bring the restaurant's existing inventory up to a certain established level. This level was the quantity of the item the manager expected to be used between receipt of the order and receipt of the next order (three to five days at a maximum) plus a safety stock amount equal to 20 percent of the expected usage. This safety stock helped ensure that the entire menu was always available. The expected usage was calculated from the previous week's demand but was adjusted to reflect special trends or such conditions as holidays, school vacations, and newspaper promotions.

Orders were typically placed one day in advance of delivery. Materials were generally received in the early morning or in the evening. All materials were dated on receipt, and the oldest materials were always used first. However, usage levels were so high that the restaurant never needed to worry about spoilage, even for produce or dairy products.

Orders for meat, paper products, and certain other supplies were placed twice a week with the Greensboro regional office of Distron, Burger King's supply subsidiary. Fresh produce was ordered from either Distron or an independent supplier twice a week. Baked goods were ordered every other day and dairy products on a three-times-per-week cycle.

The Workforce

All 56 workers were part-time—with a typical worker putting in 20 to 35 hours each week, spread over five or six days. Most of the workforce was female and young, many just recently graduated from high school. Some were students who attended college at night. Almost all lived in the area of the restaurant. At night and on weekends, high school students and second job workers were often employed.

The crew for this Church Street Burger King was hand-picked by the manager. Almost none had worked at a Burger King before. Workers were paid for the hours worked, with overtime given after 40 hours each week. The average hourly wage was $3.45, with some workers receiving the minimum wage of $3.35 and the best-performing worker receiving $4.05. The fringe benefit package was modest. Labor turnover at the restaurant had run at 40 percent for its first three months of operation.

A worker's hours were likely to differ from day to day; for example, a worker might be scheduled to open the restaurant at 6 A.M. one day and to start at midmorning the next. The schedule for any week, however, was worked out about a week in advance. The schedule did try to reflect worker preferences about the amount and timing of their work. Work assignments were shuffled daily. The prime reason for shuffling assignments was to promote worker cross-training, which increased the operation's flexibility. A manager might also be forced to shuffle assignments because of worker scheduling or absentee problems. For these reasons, the order-taker knew how the kitchen operated, and the kitchen knew how to take orders. This cross-training also had the welcome benefit of heightening the tolerance any worker had for the momentary troubles of other workers.

The daily rise and fall of peak and off-peak demand required continual changes in crew size, so that neither too few nor too many workers worked at any one time. The flexibility needed in the schedule was achieved by using the part-time labor force and by scheduling their arrivals and departures at different times. Some, for example, reported to work just 15 minutes or so before the noon rush hour. The only restrictions were the various state regulations that the workers work at least a certain number of hours (typically three) in any day. A worker's departure from the restaurant was at the discretion of the manager. If sales were light, the manager could let some of the workers out early; if demand was heavy, it was understood that workers would be asked to stay past the scheduled departure time. The best crew, however, was generally scheduled for the peak times on Friday and Saturday.

The restaurant managers were responsible for training new workers. There were eight main stations on which to be trained (sandwich board, specialty sandwich board, fry station, drink station, broiler-steamer, order-taker/cashier, drive-thru, and salad bar). Training for any one of these stations took about three hours and consisted of reading some prepared material, watching a video tape on the station's work, doing a worksheet based on that video, reading a manual on procedures on the workstation, watching the manager demonstrate procedures at the workstation, performing on a trial basis from one to two hours, taking a written test, and then having performance evaluated by the manager. Usually, a new worker trained first on the broiler and steamer and then progressed to every station in the kitchen, finally winding up at the front counter and drive-thru operations. The fry station and the burger sandwich board were generally acknowledged to be the toughest tasks at the restaurant.

Quality

Periodically, about four to six times a year, a team from the corporation would visit the restaurant unannounced to perform a quality inspection. They used a form for rating the food, the service, the appearance of the restaurant, and some other factors. In addition, the district manager made twice monthly visits to the restaurant in order to audit quality. Twice a year, the district manager performed a three-day restaurant operations consultation during which every aspect of the restaurant's operation on every shift was analyzed. The results of such audits were taken very seriously.

In addition, much of the manager's time was spent in the dining room talking with customers and assessing how well the service was being delivered.

Management

The Church Street Burger King was a company-owned store. It was part of the company's Greensboro area and the Atlanta region. It was one of six stores in the Greensboro area that were under the same district manager. Supervising the Church Street Burger King was a manager and four assistant managers. One of these five was always at the restaurant. During peak times managers would overlap, so that two sets of extra hands and eyes were available for breaking bottlenecks. The four assistant managers worked five days a week, but on a rotating shift. On each 28-day cycle, each assistant manager would work seven day-shifts (opening to 2 P.M.) seven night-shifts (4 P.M. to closing), and 14 midshifts (noon to 8 P.M.). The restaurant manager generally worked the day shift from 6 A.M. to 4 or 5 P.M.

Any manager's primary responsibility was to ensure that a quality product was promptly served in a clean environment within company guidelines. Although a manager's ability to control costs was valued, meeting the corporation's service, quality, and cleanliness goals came first. Meeting these goals meant developing the capabilities of the production crew and maintaining its morale. Thus the manager was first and foremost a crew foreman, teaching new hires, guiding work assignments, checking quality, breaking bottlenecks, and providing an example for the crew.

Layered on these responsibilities were others—ordering materials, receiving deliveries, checking and posting standards of performance (such as the door-to-door or transaction times), checking on the preparations for the day and for the peak periods, and scheduling the part-time workforce.

Burger King headquarters provided restaurant managers with a number of aids. Chief among these aids for the week-by-week operation of the restaurant were the charts, formulas, and decision rules for scheduling the workforce, given the restaurant's particular configuration. The corporation had developed

Catching burgers as they come off the broiler. (*Courtesy of Burger King Corporation*)

aids that showed, for different sales levels and hours of operation, how much labor each restaurant should have and where that labor ought to be assigned. These charts, formulas, and decision rules greatly aided the managers in controlling labor costs, which was the second highest cost that could be controlled.

The restaurant's POS system (computer/cash register network) was also a useful management tool. From the computer, the manager could obtain information, by half-hour increments, on sales, product mix, and discounts. The POS system could also be used for inventory control by keeping track of waste and the level of inventory. This information helped the manager match crew sizes to the peak demands on the restaurant.

FACILITIES AND TECHNOLOGY

This Burger King was a design called BK50-long. According to Tom Faust, the restaurant's district manager and a five-year veteran of Burger King, the BK50-long was the most successful restaurant design the corporation had yet devised. The layout was very efficient, workers did not waste many steps in performing the tasks required of them, materials were readily available, and there was ample storage space. Workers at nonpeak times could easily cover more than one workstation.

In addition, the BK50-long in Burlington included several technological improvements that had been initiated by the corporation. For example, computerized frying vats had been

The burger board as seen from the kitchen. (*Courtesy of Burger King Corporation*)

installed with temperature probes that automatically adjusted the frying times so that french fries or other fried foods were cooked perfectly. Buzzers indicated when the fries should be shaken or removed from the vats. Baskets of fries or other foods were automatically lowered into the vats and raised when they were finished. The automatic drink machines were another advance; these permitted workers to engage in other tasks while soft drink cups were being filled automatically. The addition of TV screens to indicate variations on the standard sandwiches was another advance; these reduced the cacophony that could strike the kitchen during peak periods. The kitchen included a new breakfast grill and hood, a specially designed unit that could be set up for the breakfast business and then transformed into a work area the rest of the day. The heat chutes for finished sandwiches were enclosed at the Church Street Burger King to keep the sandwiches warmer. Perhaps the most recent addition was the drive-thru timer. This timer was linked to the computer in the manager's office and automatically printed out service standards and variances from that standard for any period of interest during the day.

PART TWO
DISCUSSION

The Burger King® Corporation is in no way responsible for the following views and presentation. They remain solely the responsibility of the author.

The Flow of the Process and of Information

In most service industries, the time delay between service provision and service consumption is necessarily very short. Put another way, one can rarely inventory a service, at least not for very long. Hotel room-nights cannot be inventoried, nor can timely tips on the stock market, nor can tasty hamburgers. Hence, a whole degree of freedom is removed from the service

manager, which heightens the importance of capacity choice in most service industries.

It is also frequently the case that services must be particularly flexible so that they can be customized to individual consumer needs. Think of the travel agent, the salesperson, the cab driver, and, yes, the fast food restaurant.

These two basic features of many service businesses place substantial demands on the process design and information systems of an enterprise like Burger King. Flexibility in both product and volume is paramount, and Burger King has adopted some classic policies for yielding such flexibility.

Figure F2 is a process flow diagram for assembling an order. It is simple, and that is one of its advantages. Responsibilities are clearly

FIGURE F2   A process flow diagram (nonpeak period) for the Church St. Burger King restaurant.

FIGURE F3   An information flow diagram (nonpeak period) for the Church St. Burger King restaurant.

the levels of the finished goods inventory and of the work-in-process inventory of broiled burgers and toasted buns. Instead of reacting to the order punched in, the broiler feeder reacts to the manager's posted list of burgers to be held as work-in-process, feeding the broiler so as to maintain the desired inventory level. Similarly, the board workers respond to the level of finished goods inventory, although these board workers must also respond to any special orders that are punched in. Special orders, of course, must take precedence over the maintenance of the finished goods inventory. The peak period changes in the process and information flow diagrams are pictured in Figure F4.

demarcated, and yet all of the key tasks for customizing the hamburger or specialty sandwich rest with the worker who actually assembles the sandwich at the board. This fact, in turn, simplifies the information flow so that only one worker need pay strict attention to the punch-in of a special order. (An information flow diagram is found in Figure F3.) In this way, with a clear delineation of tasks and direct information flows, rapid product changes can be facilitated.

Flexibility in changing production volumes is achieved by a continual rebalancing of the sandwich production line. The time pattern of demand is well known from past experience, and this knowledge has permitted the staggering of work hours for the part-time workforce so that varying numbers can be on hand at any one time. The workforce ebbs and flows from three during slack periods to 20 during peak periods. As more workers are added, the job contents narrow and, importantly, the flow of information changes. No longer is production keyed completely to the punch-in of the order. More and more, production is keyed by

Demands of the Process on the Workforce

The flexibility of the Burger King fast food operation demands flexibility from its workers. The job contents and the production pace vary markedly throughout any worker's shift during the day, requiring a special tolerance. Workers on a machine-paced assembly line get used to the rhythm of the conveyor. But, on a worker-paced line, and particularly one in a service industry, any rhythm may soon dissolve.

What is especially true of worker-paced lines is that the crew on the line views itself as a team, largely because they are so dependent on one another. This fact often permits worker-paced lines where the demand is steady (unlike at a fast food restaurant) to be paid according to a group incentive scheme. Some standard of production—X units per time period—is established and the crew on the line, if it can better the standard, is paid extra for doing so. This kind of group incentive pay scheme can tie a crew together as a team even more thoroughly than usual.

Process Flow Diagram for Burgers

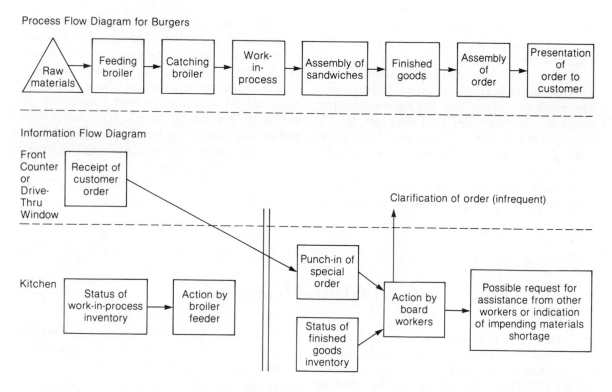

FIGURE F4   Process and information flow diagrams (peak period) for the Church St. Burger King restaurant.

Demands of the Process on Management

An operation like a Burger King restaurant places specific demands on management both because it is a service operation and because it is a worker-paced line flow process. As a line flow process, many of the issues that were discussed in Tour D with respect to C-P-C—Tarrytown surface:

- Balance of the line
- Materials management
- Technological advance
- Capacity planning
- Product design
- Workforce management

Managers of worker-paced lines should be sensitive to all these issues, since to fall down on any one could seriously jeopardize the entire operation.

The issue of technological advance is particularly acute, since such an advance may enable a smoother, more regular flow of the product. After all, a worker-paced line flow usually remains worker- rather than machine-paced because there is as yet no easy way to guard against a succession of overcycle conditions striking a worker all at once (such as a run on "Whoppers, hold the pickles"). If the mix of product options can somehow be smoothed out or if particular advances can be made in product or workstation design, a worker-paced line can easily be transformed into a machine-paced line. In other words, the worker-paced line is somewhat more vulnerable to radical, rather than incremental, change than is a machine-paced one.

The technological changes evident at the Church Street Burger King all contributed to a smoother flow of product. The automatic drink machines, the computerized frying vats, the TV monitors of information, and even the new BK50 layout all act to speed up and smooth the delivery process.

A Burger King's status as a service operation only heightens the importance of capacity planning, since service firms cannot ordinarily inventory their product. The new BK50 design is testament to the importance the corporation assigns to planning capacity. The importance of workforce management is also heightened, because the worker-customer interaction is part of the service. Ordinarily, one cannot hide the service process as readily as one can hide the manufacturing process. Keeping the workforce productive and interested in their jobs is a key challenge for managers in service operations.

QUESTIONS

1. Visit a fast food restaurant with a friend to perform an experiment. While one of you times the other's entry and exit and the time from the placing of the order to its receipt, the other should observe how many workers are actually involved with the order. Visit the fast food restaurant at a slack time and at a peak time, and compare the differences in time and number of workers.

2. Watch for bottlenecks the next time you are in a fast food restaurant (or any worker-paced service operation). Where do they arise and why? How might they be remedied?

3. Compare and contrast technological innovation and worker cohesiveness in a worker-paced operation.

4. Why is flexibility one of the key features for success in a worker-paced assembly line operation such as Burger King?

5. How would you define capacity at a Burger King? What factors influence the establishment of a limit to capacity?

6. Would you prefer to work on a machine-paced assembly line or a worker-paced one?

7. Visit a Burger King close to you. It is unlikely to be a brand new one with all the advances incorporated into the Church Street Burger King. Consider the ways by which the Burger King you visit could be modernized. Consider as well what could be done at the restaurant to increase capacity as sales increase. Prepare plans of action that specify which things ought to be done, and in what order, to modernize the restaurant and/or increase its capacity. Defend your choices.

8. Consider an alternative kitchen layout to the one at the Church Street Burger King. In what ways is your alternative better or worse than the one discussed in the chapter?

SITUATION FOR STUDY F-1
LEGACY HOMES

Tom Stoddard had been employed part-time as a "rough carpenter" by Legacy Homes while he completed his degree at Interstate Tech University. After his graduation, Legacy hired Tom as a construction superintendent; this job combined the duties of foreman, scheduler, and expediter.

By building only to order, Legacy took a conservative approach to the ups and downs typical of the home construction industry. Legacy offered a limited number of home designs; Tables F1 and F2 show the work involved on most of them—usually about 90 days' worth. When a buyer arranged a home loan from a lending institution, the local practice was to allow the construction company to receive the money in partial payments (cash draws) depending on the degree of completion of the home. Thus, for Legacy to receive the money, Tom needed to finish a home as fast as possible.

Legacy had a nucleus crew of highly skilled workers that it wanted to keep working most of the time. Other workers could be hired to supplement this crew when necessary. Table F3 shows this crew and the various tasks they were capable of performing. Each crew member knew well a primary function such as plumbing but could be counted on to help with other functions such as rough carpentry. The crew who installed the plumbing, for example, also installed the heating and electricity. This overlap of skills was possible for two reasons: (1) most of the work on a Legacy house was rather

TABLE F1   Crew size and times for various tasks (Legacy Homes)

TASK #	DESCRIPTION	TYPE OF WORK*	MINIMUM/MAXIMUM CREW SIZE	DAYS TO COMPLETE (with minimum crew)
1	Concrete footer	A	2–4	1.00
2	Foundation	F	Subcontract	1.00
3	Grading	A	2–4	0.50
4	Framing	B	5–8	2.60
5	Roofing	F	Subcontract	1.00
6	Concrete	A/B	3–5	1.50
7	Wiring	C	2–4	1.00
8	Furnace and ducts	C	2–4	2.25
9	Plumbing	C	2–3	2.50
10	Insulation	B	1–3	2.25
11	Dry wall	F	Subcontract	1.00
12	Siding	F	Subcontract	5.50
13	Sewer line	A	2–3	2.00
14	Painting	F	Subcontract	1.50
15	Finish carpentry	D	2–4	2.50
16	Tile	D	1–2	5.00
17	Electrical trim	C	1–2	1.50
18	Finish plumbing	C	1–2	3.50
19	Heating trim	C	1–3	2.50
20	Carpeting	F	Subcontract	2.00
21	Cleanup	E	1–3	2.00

*A = excavate; B = rough carpentry; C = plumbing, heating, electrical; D = finish carpentry; E = part-time clean-up; F = subcontract

TABLE F2   Precedence relationship
(Legacy Homes)

JOB #	PRECEDING OPERATION(S)
1	
2	1
3	2
4	3
5	4
6	2
7	4
8	5
9	5
10	7, 8, 9
11	10
12	10
13	9
14	11
15	14
16	14
17	14
18	15
19	14
20	6, 12, 13, 16, 17, 18, 19
21	20

pen that workers interfere with each other's work. Tom assumed that additional workers could work at the same rate as workers already on the job; he therefore scaled the number of workers up or down proportionately. For example, in task #1 if two workers can do the job in one day (that is, two labor days are required), three workers can do the job in two-thirds day (two labor days divided by three workers available), and four workers can do it in half a day.

All operations have been designed to require a low level of skill; thus, any worker can shift to another operation with only a negligible loss of efficiency. Usually one worker is used as parts chaser and relief. The supervisor can help with the parts chasing but is not expected to take part in operations except as a troubleshooter.

Although the products (houses) do not move, Tom feels that the principles of worker-paced lines can be applied with beneficial results.

straightforward and did not entail the total skill requirements of journeymen in any of the trades, and (2) Legacy hired nonunion workers.

Table F1 shows the minimum and maximum crew sizes for completing each task. For example, task #8 requires a minimum of two workers because one person working alone cannot position the furnace or handle the duct work; two people working on separate houses would take much longer to complete their work on both houses than if they worked together on one house at a time. At the maximum crew size, of course, it can hap-

1. Design a process flow for Tom.
2. What is the minimum time requirement to build a house? How many houses should be being built to keep the permanent crew busy? What is the maximum number of houses that should be under construction at one time?
3. Is the workforce balanced? If not, which crew sizes should be changed?
4. Design an information flow for Tom.
5. Set up a sequence for raw material flow for Tom.

TABLE F3   Labor force (Legacy Homes)

TYPE OF WORK	CURRENT LABOR AVAILABLE	TASKS PERFORMED*
A Excavate	3	1, 3, 6, 13
B Rough carpentry	5	4, 6, 10
C Plumbing, heating, electrical	4	7, 8, 9, 17, 18, 19
D Finish carpentry	2	15, 16
E Part-time cleanup	1	21
F Subcontract		2, 5, 11, 12, 14, 20

*See Table F1 for an explanation of these numbers.

SITUATION FOR STUDY F-2
SMALL CITY NEWSPAPER

Small City Newspaper (SCN) was a family-owned paper with a circulation of 43,000 in the morning and 22,000 in the evening. There were three editions of the morning paper and two editions of the afternoon paper; the earlier editions of each paper were for delivery further away.

Newspapers have two content inputs: news and advertising. For SCN, as with most daily newspapers, advertising determined the size of each issue, which in turn affected the length of the production run. To maintain an average of 43 percent news content and 57 percent advertising, the number of columns of news was allocated according to the number of columns of advertising sold for a particular issue. A minimum number of news columns (front page, sports, editorial, comics, and so on) was required for the morning paper (96 total columns) and for the evening paper (80 total columns). Information about the number of columns of advertising was communicated to the editors and the production manager by the advertising department.

Advertising was divided into three categories: display, classified, and national. Display was used primarily by local retailers and ad agencies, who often had camera-ready copy prepared for the paste-up department. On occasion, the advertising and art departments worked with the customer in preparing the advertisement. Three days' lead time was generally required of the client when placing a display ad; however, flexibility in this procedure allowed for changes to be made until press time. Classified ads had to be submitted by 5:00 P.M. the previous day and could be prepared for paste-up on the computer. National advertising copy was usually camera-ready and followed much

the same procedure as the display ads. To expedite the use of both display and national ad copy, an inventory of these ads was maintained.

The morning news department had a staff of 40: city desk, copy desk/AP wire service, sports, style, editorial, and cartoon. The afternoon paper had a staff of 22 (no cartoonist). The library kept microfilmed copies of newspapers, publicity brochures, and a master file of news clippings (filed alphabetically) on important individuals. A personal computer that was tied into the Associated Press news retrieval system was also located in the library.

The managing editor assigned reporters and photographers to cover newsworthy events. Editorials as well as style and feature articles had the earliest deadlines (5:00 P.M. for the morning paper and 9:00 A.M. for the afternoon paper) and so were often written the day before they were to be published. Front page stories and sports coverage demanded up-to-date reporting; the deadlines for these articles were 11:00 P.M. for the morning paper and 11:00 A.M. for the afternoon paper.

Flexibility in the entire operation was a must, to allow for reporting late-breaking news. Because these stories could significantly disrupt the process, reporters were encouraged to prepare as much of their other copy as far in advance of press time as possible. To facilitate this, the newspaper had adopted a flexible time schedule for its reporters, who were generally on the job from 3:00 P.M. to midnight (for the morning paper) and from 7:00 A.M. to 4:00 P.M. (for the afternoon paper). In spite of this effort, half of the newspaper was made up in the two hours before press time.

Generally, a reporter composed a story at a video display terminal (VDT). The story appeared on a screen (CRT) as it was typed. Errors could easily be corrected, and additions and deletions did not affect the rest of the story. Typewritten copy could enter the computer through the use of an optical character reader (OCR), which sensed typewritten copy if it was prepared in a compatible typeface. Once the reporter was satisfied with the story, a single key command put the story in line in the computer. If this was done close to the deadline and the reporter considered the story to be especially important, the reporter could supersede this queue by notifying the editor.

The editor had a list of all stories in the queue. He accessed the stories and made revisions using special keyboard commands. Once he was satisfied, the editor added the headline via the keyboard, specifying the type size of the heading (in points), and designated where the story should go in the paper. The story was then transferred by computer to page paste-up, where a hard copy was printed.

Syndicated features and wire service copy were transmitted to the paper in a form compatible with the VDT system, replacing the old teletypewriter and eliminating the need for re-keyboarding. At the copy desk these stories were reviewed and a determination was made concerning which stories to use; then the copy was forwarded by computer to page paste-up. The laser photo service was another external input. Photographs were beamed to the newspaper along with a subtitle and/or a short explanation. The photo came to the paper ready for paste-up.

Advertising copy, news stories, and photographs were pieced together on a page the size of a newspaper page. Reusable by-lines and photos of syndicated columnists were kept at the paste-up tables. Efforts were made to smooth the flow through paste-up by having advertising, feature articles, and as much of the news as possible to paste-up as early as possible.

The paste-up operation for the morning paper normally ran from 5:30 P.M. to 11:00 P.M. Paste-up for the afternoon paper generally ran from 8:00 A.M. to 11:30 A.M. The time difference for the papers was due to the latter's smaller size and the advance preparation the morning paper paste-up had to do for its Sunday edition. Changes for the final edition of each paper could be made after the presses began the earlier edition(s).

Once the pages had been laid out, they were photographed. An aluminum-backed, polymer-coated plate was placed in an exposure unit beneath the page negative. After a 45- to 70-second exposure, it was put through a wash unit, which used water and a small amount of biodegradable defoaming agent to remove the nonexposed polymer areas. After drying, the plate had a raised mirror image surface, which was curved to fit the rotary press cylinder. One page could pass through the engraving process in 22 minutes standard time, though several plates could pass through simultaneously. Once the plates had been prepared, a press room employee picked them up on the fourth floor and carried them to the press on the first floor.

The current printing process replaced several steps of the old letterpress system. It was compatible with both the rotary press and the offset press systems. An offset press, although it wasted as much as 4 percent newsprint per run, offered computerized printing capabilities, better quality of print, and flexibility with the use of color.

Press runs for the morning paper were approximately as follows: first edition (outlying counties) 12:10 to 12:40 A.M., second edition (adjacent county) 1:00 to 1:25 A.M., and final edition (city) 1:45 to 3:20 A.M. Press runs for the afternoon paper were approximately as follows: first edition (all counties, except the immediate one) 12:50 to 1:30 P.M., and final edition 2:15 to 3:15 P.M. The capacity of the press was

80 pages (16 per deck) per run. When full color was used, only 64 pages could be printed per run, because two half-decks had to be devoted to overlap the four colors necessary for full color. To circumvent this bottleneck, the Sunday feature section was printed on Saturday and many of the inserts were preprinted during slack time. The Sunday comics, for example, were printed externally and were delivered early in the week.

The press cylinders were on the first floor. Rolls of newsprint were loaded on the press in the basement, and the cutting and folding mechanism was on the second floor. The newly printed newspaper was carried by conveyor to the mailroom.

Maintenance could be performed by disconnecting the individual decks; however, all five were operated simultaneously by a central drive system. A problem with the electrically powered drive unit, which had happened recently, could prevent the press from operating. Fortunately, this situation was corrected in time to get the paper out, but it pointed up a weakness in the functioning of the entire operation.

In the mailroom, the sections and inserts were assembled. The papers were counted, bundled, labeled, and dropped through a chute to an alley where they were picked up by carriers or were trucked to drop points.

Timely delivery was very important. The evening newspaper had to reach the customer before the evening TV newscast, or it would not be read. The morning paper had to be to the carriers (who usually held day jobs) in time for them to make deliveries before they went to work. In meeting these objectives, the earlier editions of the morning paper were to leave the headquarters by 2:00 A.M. and the final edition was to be to the drop points by 4:00 A.M. The earlier afternoon edition was to be ready to go by 1:30 P.M., with the final edition due at the drop points by 3:30 P.M.

1. Diagram the process and information flows for this process.
2. In what ways is this a worker-paced line flow operation and in what ways, if any, is it not?
3. How do the concepts of line balance and rebalance apply to this situation?

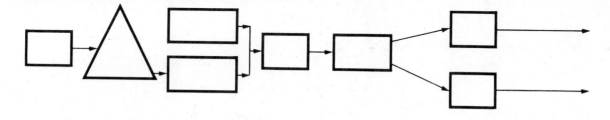

A SERVICE SHOP
Howard Ford-Isuzu-Peugeot
Auto Service and Repair
Durham, North Carolina

Howard Ford-Isuzu-Peugeot was located in Durham, North Carolina near the intersection of Interstate 40 and Duke Street. It was the second largest Ford dealership in the Southeast, occupying 11 acres and having 91,000 square feet under roof. The service department was correspondingly large, consisting of 64 service stalls available in the service area and 26 in the body shop, with 22,000 square feet dedicated to parts storage.

The dealership was owned by Dex Howard, who had grown up on the West Coast and had started his career as a salesperson for Ford. Howard rose through the ranks to sales manager and general sales manager before taking over his own dealership in Greensboro, North Carolina in 1956. He sold that dealership in 1969 and went on to Knoxville, Tennessee to become a Pontiac, AMC Jeep, and BMW dealer. In 1978 he retired but got bored and subsequently heard about a Ford dealership in Durham that had gone bankrupt. Howard purchased that dealership in June of 1980, after several months of negotiations, and moved to Durham. Within six months he had added the Peugeot and Isuzu lines to strengthen the dealership.

PART ONE
PROCESS DESCRIPTION

WRITING THE SERVICE ORDER

The service operation began at 7 A.M., Monday through Friday. At that time, the two service writers who were responsible for developing the service orders began greeting the customers who had lined up for service. The service writers' responsibilities were to detail (1) the symptoms of the problem experienced by the customer and/or (2) work the customer wanted to have performed. This called for skillful listening by the service writer and the knack for asking the right questions to glean the proper symptoms to explain to the mechanic assigned. The service writer was also responsible for suggesting additional services the customer might want

49878

HOWARD
FORD • ISUZU • PEUGEOT
600 Carr Street   P.O. Box 3577
DURHAM, N. C. 27702
Telephone 919/682-9171

PRELIMINARY ESTIMATE

THE FACTORY WARRANTY CONSTITUTES ALL OF THE WARRANTIES WITH RESPECT TO THE SALE OF THIS ITEM/ITEMS. THE SELLER HEREBY EXPRESSLY DISCLAIMS ALL WARRANTIES, EITHER EXPRESS OR IMPLIED, INCLUDING ANY IMPLIED WARRANTY OF MERCHANTABILITY OR FITNESS FOR A PARTICULAR PURPOSE, AND THE SELLER NEITHER ASSUMES NOR AUTHORIZES ANY OTHER PERSON TO ASSUME FOR IT ANY LIABILITY IN CONNECTION WITH THE SALE OF THIS ITEM/ITEMS.

I HEREBY AUTHORIZE THE BELOW REPAIR WORK TO BE DONE ALONG WITH THE NECESSARY MATERIALS. YOU AND YOUR EMPLOYEES MAY OPERATE BELOW VEHICLE FOR PURPOSES OF TESTING, INSPECTION OR DELIVERY AT MY RISK. AN EXPRESS MECHANIC'S LIEN IS ACKNOWLEDGED ON BELOW VEHICLE TO SECURE THE AMOUNT OF REPAIRS THERETO. YOU WILL NOT BE HELD RESPONSIBLE FOR LOSS OR DAMAGE TO VEHICLE OR ARTICLES LEFT IN VEHICLE IN CASE OF FIRE, THEFT, ACCIDENT OR ANY OTHER CAUSE BEYOND YOUR CONTROL.

TERMS: STRICTLY CASH UNLESS ARRANGEMENTS MADE

PARTS WILL BE DISCARDED UNLESS SPECIFIED OTHERWISE   SAVE □

CASH OR CREDIT CARD / VISA / MASTER CARD / AMERICAN EXPRESS / DINERS CLUB / CARTE BLANCHE

CUSTOMER LABOR CHARGES ARE BASED ON A RATE OF $ _____ PER HOUR ESTABLISHED BY FORD MOTOR CO. LABOR TIME GUIDE AND PUBLISHED MENU.

FOR YOUR SAFETY AND CONVENIENCE WE RECOMMEND THE FOLLOWING REPAIRS.

FIGURE G1   A sample customer ticket, as used at Howard Ford-Isuzu-Peugeot.

but had not thought of, such as oil changes, state inspections, or front-end alignments. The service writer was the operation's chief contact with the customer through the service process. If the customer needed to be informed about the progress on his car, or that additional work was needed, or that the car might not be ready in time, the service writer communicated that information.

Upon greeting the customer the service writer filled in necessary identification information and then began to complete the rest of the customer ticket (Figure G1). There were two different tickets that could be filled out from such a customer interaction; one involved warranty work (Figure G2) that was paid for by the manufacturer, and the other involved work for which the customer paid. (There was a third class of

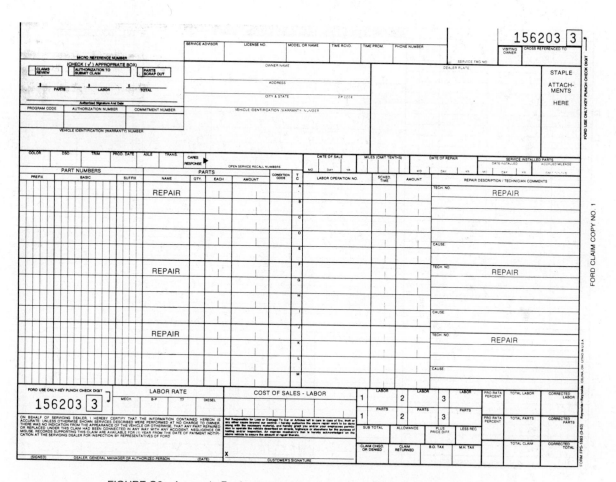

FIGURE G2   A sample Ford warranty ticket, as used at Howard Ford-Isuzu-Peugeot.

ticket (Figure G3) for "inside" work, that is, work done to prepare cars sold by the dealership for transfer to their new owners.) The service writer noted this distinction so that the tickets could be properly processed. When the customer finished detailing the work to be done on the car, he or she signed the ticket, giving the service operation authorization to work on the car. The service writer then assigned a control number to the job and placed a tag board sign with that number on the rear view mirror of the car and also attached a tag with the same number on the keys to the car. The service writer gave the customer a claim check with the control number to use in communicating with the service department. Reference to the control number helped the customer, for it speeded up the location of his car in the process.

The service writer then rolled up the ticket, placed it into a pneumatic air tube, and sent it into the dispatching tower, the nerve center for the service operation. Here the dispatcher logged

INTERNAL REPAIR INVOICE   ‹ SOURCE 310

W I	C	QTY.	PART NO. OR DESCRIPTION	SALE

REPAIR ORDER NUMBER

?REF **18385**

CUSTOMER NO. ?CTL

SERVICE WRITER NO. ?SWR

DATE _____

CUSTOMER'S NAME

MILEAGE ?MLG

ADDRESS

STOCK NO. ?CTL

CITY   STATE   ZIP CODE   YEAR-MAKE

TYPE OR MODEL   TRANS. NO.   MOTOR NO.   LICENSE NO.

SERIAL NO.   REPAIR LIMIT $ RES.

DELIVERY DATE   TIME PROMISED A.M. / P.M.   PHONE WHEN READY YES ☐ NO ☐   BUS.

OPR	√	OPERATION	LABOR
1		LUBRICATE	
2		CHANGE OIL	
3		CHANGE OIL FILTER CART.	
4		PACK FRONT WHL. BRGS.	
5		PACK U-JOINTS	
6		ROTATE TIRES	
7		BALANCE WHEELS	
8		ALIGN FRONT END	
9		MINOR TUNE-UP	
10		WASH	
11		6,000 MILE INSPECTION	
12		12,000 MILE INSPECTION	
13		18,000 MILE INSPECTION	
14		CARB. REPAIRS	
15			

OPR. NO.   INSTRUCTIONS

INTERNAL (watermark)

HOWARD FORD

TOTAL

P.O. NO. | SUBLET REPAIRS

ADDITIONAL REPAIRS

INTERNAL SALES

ACCOUNT	ACCT. NO.	AMOUNT	COST	ACCOUNT	ACCT. NO.	AMOUNT
REPAIR LABOR	# 3630 ⊟		%	NEW CAR INV.	# 1200 ⊞	
INTERNAL GROSS	# 9741 ⊟		%	NEW TRUCK INV.	# 1210 ⊞	
PARTS REPAIR	# 3470 ⊟		%	USED CAR INV.	# 1230 ⊞	
SUBLET TCTL	# 3650 ⊟		%	USED TRUCK INV.	# 1240 ⊞	
BODY SHOP MAT'L.	# 3660 ⊟		%	PRE-DELIVERY NEW VEHICLES	# 5020 ⊞	
GAS	# 3670 ⊟		%	FREE SERVICE NEW VEHICLES	# 5030 ⊞	
	⊟		%	MAINT./POLICY USED VEHICLES	# 6040 ⊞	
	⊟		%	DEMO.EXP.NEW	# 5160 ⊞	
STOCK NO. ?CTL	# 1200 ⊟			NEW CAR INV. SERVICE ADJ.	# 8040 ⊞	
STOCK NO. ?CTL	# 1210 ⊟			NEW TRK. INV. VEH. EXP.-SERV.	# 8070 ⊞	
STOCK NO. ?CTL	# 1230 ⊟			USED CAR INV.	⊞	
STOCK NO. ?CTL	# 1240 ⊟			USED TRK. INV.	⊞	
	TOTAL				TOTAL	

TOTAL SUBLET REPAIRS

GALS. GAS @
QTS. OIL @
LBS. GREASE @

TOTAL GAS, OIL, GREASE

FIGURE G3   A sample internal work ticket, as used at Howard Ford-Isuzu-Peugeot.

in the control number, the name of the customer, the type of car, the time it was written up, the time the service writer promised the car for delivery, and the work that was to be done. Figure G4 shows a sample dispatcher's log.

DISPATCHING

After jobs were logged in, they were placed into a "bucket" by categories. The categories included general repair, front-end work, rear-end work, transmission work, new car work, oil filter and lubrication, tune-ups, and heavy duty truck work. Within each of these categories, the orders were maintained on a first-come, first-served basis. It was the job of the dispatcher to match the mechanics (termed "technicians" at the dealership) to the work available. The dispatcher kept track of which of the 19 technicians did particular kinds of work well, which company-sponsored training programs they had

	NAME	YEAR AND MAKE	LOCATION NUMBER	TIME PROMISED		CONTROL NUMBER	WRITER	REPAIR ORDER NUMBER	TECHNICIAN	MAINTENANCE	TUNE-UP	AIR CONDITIONING	ELECTRICAL	FRONT END	BRAKES	REAR AXLE	EXHAUST	ENGINE HEAVY DUTY	TRANSMISSION	COOLING	SAFETY INSPECTION	PREPARATION	SUBLET	MISCELLANEOUS	REMARKS
				HOUR	WAIT																				
1																									
2																									
3																									
4																									
5																									
6																									
7																									
8																									
9																									
10																									
11																									
12																									
13																									
14																									
15																									
16																									
17																									
18																									
19																									
20																									
21																									

FIGURE G4   A sample dispatcher's log sheet, as used at Howard Ford-Isuzu-Peugeot.

attended, and what they liked to work on. It was his responsibility to assign work from a particular category to the next free technician. It was the policy of the service manager not to assign work to a technician who was not fully qualified to do the job. The service manager would rather take the heat from customers about not having their cars ready on time than risk doing jobs improperly.

When a technician became free he came over to the dispatch tower and was assigned a car to work on. When a job was given to the technician, his daily time card and the job ticket were punched (Figure G5), and when the job was returned completed from the technician, the job was again time punched. In this way, the dispatcher kept a record of which jobs had gone to each technician in the shop and at what times.

Routine items such as tune-ups and oil changes could be assigned to technicians without requiring a diagnosis about what was wrong. For a number of cars, however, some diagnostic work had to be done before the car could be fixed. Whether diagnostic work was needed was generally determined from the service writer's wording of the job ticket. Key words such as "hesitating sometimes," "occasionally stalling," and so on, were tip-offs. Either the service manager or the shop foreman examined the car and diagnosed what was wrong. This diagnostic work saved potential wasted motion for the technician. After either the service manager or shop foreman evaluated the car, he approached the technician with a suggested course of action to fix the problem. Occasionally, however, they assigned jobs to technicians without any sug-

FORM UAS 321-WHITE
FORM UAS 321-BUFF   PRINTED IN U S A

DAILY TIME AND
JOB TICKET

EMPLOYEE'S NAME		(JOB TICKETS)	NO.			DATE	
					OFF		12
STRAIGHT TIME(HRS.)	FLAT RATE PRICE	R. O. No.	TIME				
		EMP.NO. OPER. NO.					
					ON		
					OFF		11
STRAIGHT TIME(HRS.)	FLAT RATE PRICE	R. O. No.	TIME				
		EMP.NO. OPER. NO.					
					ON		
					OFF		10
STRAIGHT TIME(HRS.)	FLAT RATE PRICE	R. O. No.	TIME				
		EMP.NO. OPER. NO.					
					ON		
					OFF		9
STRAIGHT TIME(HRS.)	FLAT RATE PRICE	R. O. No.	TIME				
		EMP.NO. OPER. NO.					
					ON		
					OFF		8
STRAIGHT TIME(HRS.)	FLAT RATE PRICE	R. O. No.	TIME				
		EMP.NO. OPER. NO.					
					ON		
					OFF		7
STRAIGHT TIME(HRS.)	FLAT RATE PRICE	R. O. No.	TIME				
		EMP.NO. OPER. NO.					
					ON		
					OFF		6
STRAIGHT TIME(HRS.)	FLAT RATE PRICE	R. O. No.	TIME				
		EMP.NO. OPER. NO.					
					ON		
					OFF		5
STRAIGHT TIME(HRS.)	FLAT RATE PRICE	R. O. No.	TIME				
		EMP.NO. OPER. NO.					
					ON		
					OFF		4
STRAIGHT TIME(HRS.)	FLAT RATE PRICE	R. O. No.	TIME				
		EMP.NO. OPER. NO.					
					ON		
					OFF		3
STRAIGHT TIME(HRS.)	FLAT RATE PRICE	R. O. No.	TIME				
		EMP.NO. OPER. NO.					
					ON		
					OFF		2
STRAIGHT TIME(HRS.)	FLAT RATE PRICE	R. O. No.	TIME				
		EMP.NO. OPER. NO.					
					ON		
					OFF		1
STRAIGHT TIME(HRS.)	FLAT RATE PRICE	R. O. No.	TIME				
		EMP.NO. OPER. NO.					
					ON		

FIGURE G5 A sample technician's daily time and job ticket, as used at Howard Ford-Isuzu-Peugeot.

gestions, just to see what they would do. In this way they educated technicians to be better diagnosticians themselves. In such cases, the service manager or the shop foreman watched the technicians at work and, after a while, entered into a dialog about the car to test the technician's diagnostic ability, and, perhaps, to offer their own suggestions.

SHOP OPERATIONS AND THE WORKFORCE

The service floor had 64 stalls that were divided among the 19 technicians currently employed. Typically, there were three or four stalls assigned to each technician. The truck maintenance area had more stalls assigned to it because there tended to be more waiting for truck parts than for automobile parts.

In general, the shop's technicians (mechanics) had at most high school educations, but they frequently had a rich family heritage of working on mechanical things. The better-established mechanics could make $30,000 a year and carried $20,000 worth of their own tools. Established technicians earned a higher total income than younger technicians who did not have as many tools or as much knowledge. Younger technicians built up their collections of tools on a continual basis. Tool salespeople came to the shop every week to peddle their tools and collect payments from any technicians who were buying tools on credit.

The technicians were paid on a flat rate basis. A manual indicated what the time standard should be for every particular kind of job. The technician was paid according to the standard for the job and not according to the time spent on it. Thus, if he spent less time than that indicated in the manual, the technician could "beat the book" and earn increased wages. If he spent more time at the job than indicated, the technician would not earn as much. Any rework was directed back to the technician on an unpaid basis, and the shop's policy was that any rework had priority over other work. There were also some skill level differences incorporated into the wage structure. The most inexperi-

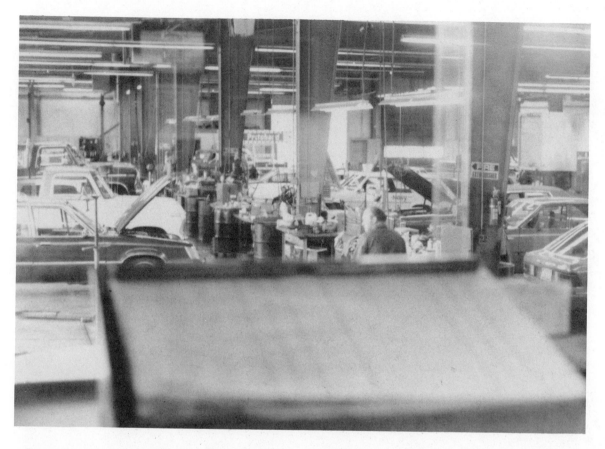

The service area at Howard Ford-Isuzu-Peugeot, as seen by the dispatcher. The dispatcher's log is in the foreground. (*Courtesy of Howard Ford-Isuzu-Peugeot, Durham, North Carolina*)

enced worker received $7.50 for every "flag hour" (standard hour), and the most experienced worker earned $13.00. Thus, a technician could earn more annually in two ways: (1) by improving his skill level or (2) by being more efficient. When technicians had to wait for a part, it was to their advantage to go to the dispatcher and get assigned some quick work, such as a tune-up, that they could perform while waiting. In this way technicians were able to convert more of the time they were in the shop into flag hours for which they earned income.

Generally speaking, newer technicians were assigned to easier work such as lubrications or oil changes, that they could perform readily and earn enough money on to build up their tool collections. The more prestigious jobs in the shop went to the technicians doing front-end work or foreign car work. The front-end work was done by a single man who was expert at conventional steering work, rack and pinion steering work, front-end alignments, and so on. Four of the 19 technicians were specialists on foreign cars, cross-trained to do both Peugeots

The island where the service writers began the repair process. (*Courtesy of Howard Ford-Isuzu-Peugeot, Durham, North Carolina*)

and Isuzus. These workers were likely to earn more each week than others, in part because they were in high demand by other repair shops.

After a mechanic finished working on a car, he road-tested it, and, if satisfied, returned the hard copy of the job ticket to the dispatch tower. All of the cars were also road tested by the service manager, the shop foreman, or, if they were busy, the service writer. One of them took a copy of the customer complaints about the car, as written on the job ticket, and determined whether, in fact, the proper service had been done. If something more had to be done, the car was returned to the technician involved. If, however, the car tested out fine, the hard copy of the job ticket went to the parts department, where it was matched up with any parts orders done for the car and then sent on to the cashier. Customers returning for their cars went to the cashier to pay, and there received a copy of the annotated job ticket and the keys to their car.

Cars typically arrived during the morning. On a busy day 75 to 100 cars might be worked on, and on a slow day only about 40. The day's chief period of stress came after 4 P.M., when most people came to pick up their cars. This was when customer complaints surfaced about cars not being ready or about the bill being too high. The service writers were pulled in many different directions during this time.

Inside the main service area at Howard Ford-Isuzu-Peugeot. (*Courtesy of Howard Ford-Isuzu-Peugeot, Durham, North Carolina*)

QUALITY CONTROL

Quality was enhanced in several ways. There were, of course, the road tests done on each car by both the technicians and the shop's management. And, because technicians had to do rework for no pay, there was an incentive to do things right the first time.

Shoddy workmanship was grounds for termination. If, in the opinion of the service manager, there were three instances in one month where poor workmanship was involved with no mitigating circumstances, then the technician was terminated. The technicians, of course, were alert to this policy, and each instance of shoddy workmanship was discussed between the service manager and the technician.

There was also scarcely a week that went by without at least one technician in one of the schools sponsored by Ford, Isuzu, or Peugeot. A week of schooling cost the dealership between $800 and $1000 per employee per week (a combination of average pay plus food, lodging, and transportation), but management felt that this had to be done both to meet the dictates of the auto companies and also to ensure that customers got the service to which they were entitled.

Every car owner dreads a situation where a mechanic does unnecessary work simply to be paid for it. There were two major controls in place to prevent this. One was management's road testing, with job ticket in hand. In addition, any special parts ordered from the parts department had to be signed for explicitly by the shop foreman. Technicians simply could not order a part without approval by management.

OPERATIONS CONTROL

By combining information on the actual time per job and its flat rate standard time, management kept control of productivity and cost. Every day information on each technician was accumulated by the payroll clerk. Every week this information was summarized in a productivity report (Figure G6). That report listed each technician, the total time that work was clocked out to him, the total manual-based standard time for that work, the percentage efficiency that he had accomplished (standard time divided by actual time), and also the pay of each technician for the week. Ford suggested that, on average, the efficiency measure should be 79 percent; Howard Ford, however, had been able to run percentages in the mid 80s or higher for its technicians. By looking at these weekly reports and by examining the efficiency rates for particular technicians, and any evident trends, the service manager could identify potential problems and seek explanations for them. For example:

- Was the technician sick?
- Was there an imbalance in the jobs that were assigned to various technicians so that some may have been overloaded and others underloaded?
- Was there a higher degree of warranty work than usual? (Because of increases in the technological sophistication of cars, warranty work could be very difficult to do, often taking more time than the book standard indicated):

- Was there an inordinate amount of major work done in the shop, for example, engine jobs? (Engine jobs tended not to have standards as loose as those adopted for more conventional work such as on brakes. Unlike some independent garages, Howard Ford could not turn away major work because its mechanics could not earn as much money on them.)

The productivity report was thus a key source of control for the shop. It highlighted variations from the norm and indicated to both the service manager and the dispatcher that there were problems needing their attention. The dispatcher, in particular, was pivotal in control of the shop, and because he was the one who assigned work, he was also a key person in keeping the shop happy.

The Parts Department

The parts department employed six people: a manager; two employees to work at the back counter, which served the shop; two to work at the front counter, which served wholesale and retail customers; and a shipping and receiving worker. The parts department was charged with purchasing all the parts used, maintaining that inventory, handling damaged parts, and filing claims and other returns. The department maintained an inventory of $300,000 worth of parts; that inventory turned 3.9 times a year. In a typical day perhaps 300 parts would be used to serve the needs of the technicians in the shop, but only two or three of those parts would be out of stock and have to be special ordered.

The parts department could place orders with six different categories of suppliers. For Ford products, the company could place orders with Ford itself, Motorcraft, (a Ford-owned parts supplier), Ford rebuilt parts, and outside jobbers. For Peugeot and Isuzu products, the parts de-

PRODUCTIVITY REPORT

Week of:

Technicians	Clock Time		Flat Rate Time	Salary for week Bonus

FIGURE G6   The service manager's productivity report used at Howard Ford-Isuzu-Peugeot.

partment could place orders with Peugeot and Isuzu only.

The parts department liked to turn a part around (sell it) every 30 days, but with an actual inventory turn ratio of around four they were only able to turn parts on the average every 90 days. Exactly which parts should be purchased at any time was determined jointly by the parts department and a computer program developed for the Texas Instruments computer system operated by the dealership. The TI system and its software were reasonably standard for the industry. This computer software used past sales histories to generate suggestions for which items

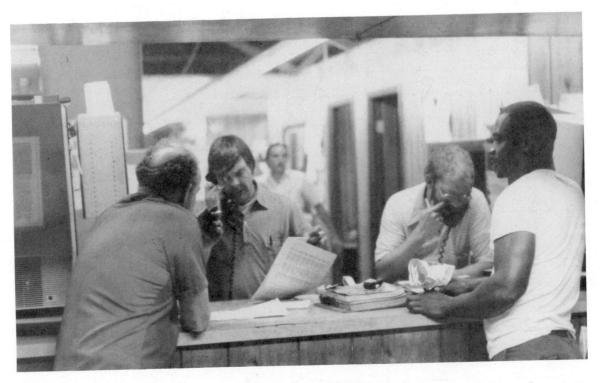

Technicians in front of the parts counter at Howard Ford-Isuzu-Peugeot. (*Courtesy of Howard Ford-Isuzu-Peugeot, Durham, North Carolina*)

should be purchased to replenish the inventory. Each day, the parts department manager made sure that parts that had been used or sold were removed from the perpetual inventory record kept by the computer. In this way the computer knew what was needed for replenishment, although the parts department manager could override the suggestions made by the computer to take into account special circumstances.

There were several ways by which parts were ordered:

1. *Stock Orders.* The stock order was the regular way to order parts. With Ford and Isuzu, parts were ordered every week at a set time. For example, parts orders for Ford were placed on Tuesdays. For Peugeot, parts were ordered twice a month.

Parts ordered by stock order through Ford Motor Company received a 5 percent discount and a 5 percent parts inventory protection plan credit. The parts inventory protection plan was useful because it permitted Howard Ford to return slow-moving parts at no cost thereby improving the way the dealership's inventory dollars were spent. Stock orders were issued for regularly used parts and for parts whose demands were known with considerable lead time.

The three other ways to order parts were more costly than stock orders, but involved faster service.

2. *Interim Orders.* Interim orders were handled faster than stock orders and, consequently no discounts or parts inventory protection plan benefits were given. For interim orders, Ford Motor Company checked the six closest depots in that region for parts. (The distribution channel for parts went through three types of depots. "A" type depots were local depots, the closest one to Durham being in Charlotte, North Carolina. "B" type depots were regional depots, the closest one being Atlanta. The "C" type depot was the National depot in Detroit.) With an interim order, six depots only would be checked, and if the part could be located, it was sent. If the part could not be located, then the dealership was so informed and would have to resort either to waiting for the part or giving it higher priority.

3. *Priority Orders.* Priority orders were taken off of the computer by Ford every hour. All depots in the country were checked for parts. The cost charged was dealer cost plus 10 percent.

4. *IVO.* This was the highest priority order a dealership in the Ford system could assign; it involved inoperable vehicles for which there were actual repair order numbers assigned. These vehicles were already in the shop needing a part in order to be finished. The cost was also dealer cost plus 10 percent.

5. *Hot Line.* If all else failed, Ford Motor Company itself could put the part on the "hot line." There had to be a formal customer complaint for this to be considered. With the hot line Ford tried to expedite the receipt of the part from its own suppliers. Hot line orders were done only if the part was not available anywhere within Ford.

6. *Other Dealers.* Howard Ford also bought parts from other dealers through informal relationships. The parts manager sometimes phoned other dealerships and asked whether they had specific parts that could be shipped by bus or some other means. Typically, the cost was dealer cost plus 18 percent.

In the parts department, parts for Ford were kept separate from parts for Isuzu and Peugeot. Within the first floor storage area designated for each product line there were both small bins and large bins. In the upstairs area, bulk materials such as sheetmetal parts were stored. Parts were stored in numerical order by the basic part number. Part numbers for Ford followed a special system. Basic numbers determined whether the part applied to brakes, exhaust systems, the transmission, or something else. In the Ford system, for example, 2000 numbers were for the brakes, 3000 numbers for front-end steering, 4000 numbers for rear axle parts, and so forth. Each part number consisted of the basic part number with both a prefix and a suffix. The prefix indicated the model of car for which it was a part. The suffix indicated some special features, such as whether it was for the left or right side of the car's body.

The workers at each counter were responsible for identifying the proper part for the job, tracking it down in the storage room, and then delivering it to the technician or the purchaser, with the proper paperwork done. At each counter, there were two microfiche machines. All of the information about a particular part was placed on microfiche so that no thick manuals were needed. All the counterman needed was to pull the proper microfiche and scan it for the information required. On the microfiche were diagrams of the parts and information about part numbers for particular years and models of cars. Also on the counter was the price book, which detailed the current prices for the parts, where they were stocked within Ford's distribution system, how they could be returned, and which discounts applied to them.

Also near the counter were racks that stored information about the parts used that day. At the end of the day the parts manager gathered this information and logged out those parts on the perpetual inventory records kept by the computer.

Body Shop

The body shop's major task was to repair cars that had been in accidents. These cars had smashed some sheet metal parts or even the car's frame itself. There were eight employees: a manager, four bodymen, a painter, a painter's helper, and a cleanup person. There were 12 stalls designated for the four bodymen, each taking three. The paint area was separate.

The body shop was a full-service body shop that could handle both ordinary sheet metal tasks and framework—the shop was equipped with the hydraulics, chains, and other equipment necessary to straighten automobile frames. The dealership provided benches, welding equipment, some special tools and the consumables such as sandpaper that were used in the course of the shop's work. Each bodyman, however, owned his own tools, which were valued between $15,000 and $20,000. The painter also owned his own equipment.

The availability of three stalls per bodyman permitted the body shop manager to schedule work more effectively. Typically, each set of three stalls was filled with one major job and two relatively simple jobs. Often the major job proceeded in fits and starts as parts became available. The smaller jobs thus served to keep him fully occupied. Each bodyman worked on between 2 and 3 cars per day on average, and the painter often did 10 a day.

Within the body shop, the bodymen continually helped one another with problems, such as opening smashed doors or attaching frame straightening equipment. Even though they were paid for their individual work, they recognized the need for assistance when one of them ran into trouble. Within the paint shop, the painter was aided by a helper who did much of the required sanding and the taping of those parts of the car that were not to receive paint. The painter was primarily responsible for "shooting" the paint and ordering supplies. The cleanup person was a general "gofer" for the shop who also cleaned the floor and the cars themselves as they were made ready for their owners.

The typical car spent one or two days in body repair and one to one and one-half days in paint. Some cars with major damage spent much longer in the shop. They required much more work and were sometimes delayed until parts were received. Typically the body shop did not begin work on an automobile until all the parts were received. Thus, if the owner could still drive the automobile, he or she continued to drive it until all the parts were received and an appointment was scheduled. However, if the car had sustained major damage and could not be driven, it remained outside the shop until all the parts were available. With major damage, however, there was always a substantial chance that hidden damage would be revealed as the car was worked on. Hidden damage took even more time to fix and often required the purchase of additional parts. This took time, especially if the car was a foreign make.

The body shop had two constituencies: car owners and their insurance companies. Almost all of the shop's work was paid for out of insurance claims, which meant that the shop had to agree with the insurance companies about how much a particular job was worth. The estimates by both the insurance companies and the shop itself were aided by reference to standard books that periodically updated prices and gave standards on the time it should take to remedy certain problems. The shop, in partic-

A technician works in the body shop at Howard Ford-Isuzu-Peugeot, Durham, North Carolina)

ular, followed the "Mitchell Crash Book" and had very few disputes with insurance company adjustors. Most of the disputes centered around which parts ought to be straightened versus replaced. (It was standard practice to replace a smashed part with a brand new one on new cars, whereas, on older cars, the existing parts were more often straightened or replaced with used parts of the same kind and quality as used on the car.) The shop contacted insurance adjustors either by telephone or when adjustors came by to check jobs in progress or to obtain estimates for potential jobs.

Adjustors could not insist that repairs be made by a particular body shop, but they could recommend shops. Thus, keeping the insurance adjustors happy was an important aspect of the body shop's efforts. The body shop manager kept the adjustors up to date on what was happening and indicated when hidden damage was found. (If any hidden damage was less than $75 and had been missed by the adjustor, the shop swallowed that cost. However, if the damage was more than that, the insurance adjustors were informed. They could check the damage themselves and then reach agreement with the shop on a supplement to the original estimate.) The shop tried to do its work quickly. Often the insurance company had to pay for rental cars for inconvenienced owners. Thus, the quicker work was done, the more likely the insurance company would not have to pay extended rental charges. To make life easier for the adjustors when they came to visit, the body shop maintained a small office and stocked it with supplies and a telephone.

The body shop manager also spent considerable time with car owners. Typically there were many occasions for such customer contact. The first occurred if an estimate of the damage was requested. An estimate was made by systematically examining the car, in the same fashion as an insurance company adjustor, and by using the pertinent information in the crash book. Once the owner received the estimate, the body shop manager typically followed up by phone to answer any questions about the estimate or about the insurance process itself. Often in these follow-up calls the shop was informed that it or some other shop had been selected to do the work. However, sometimes it took two or three follow-up calls before a determination was reached about what to do with the car.

After the car was brought in, the body shop manager went over with the owner what was going to happen and what the probable time for repair would be. The body shop manager instructed owners to call the shop before the car was due, in case there were any schedule problems, hidden damage, or the like. When the car was ready, he went over the car in detail with the owner, telling the owner what had been done and letting the owner check the quality. Once the car was back in the possession of the owner for a few days, the body shop manager placed another follow-up call, asking how everything was and making sure that the shop's interest in the customer extended past the delivery of the completed car.

The shop delivered cars to owners in as close to showroom condition as possible. Every car was road-tested, and some cars were sent out to a "detail shop" for cleaning, waxing, rug shampooing, and other clean-up work.

How Workers Were Paid

Workers were paid in different ways. As discussed previously, technicians were paid on the basis of a flat rate hour. The best technicians generally were the fast ones. They were the best at diagnosing problems, they did not squander time, and they knew exactly how to do each job. The bodymen and painter were paid in a similar way. If they were able to beat the standards set for their work, they were able to make more money. If they could not meet the standard then they made less. Some standards naturally were looser than others. In the body shop, for example, sheet metal standards were generally looser than other types of work: thus, sheet metal jobs were the most prized. The parts countermen were paid a salary, although they received a bonus if sales reached some target level. Service writers were paid commission. That is, they got a set percentage of the service business brought in. This was an incentive for them not only to do a good job so that people were satisfied, but it was also an incentive to suggest additional repairs that the owner may not have thought of.

The Duties of the Service Manager

The service manager was constantly on the move. In the early mornings and in the late afternoons his main interactions were with customers. He helped the service writers at the start of the day so that particularly concerned and/or aggressive customers could be handled individually by him. This saved time for the service writers and contributed to a routine flow of cars into the shop. In the late afternoon, the service manager spent time with customers who complained about work or registered dissatisfaction with the size of the bill. He listened to customers and then, typically, educated them as to the real problems with their cars and/or the reasons for the costs charged.

During the day the service manager made the rounds of the repair floor, the body shop, and the parts department. He checked the dispatching and the efficiency of technicians. He did diagnostic work and road tested completed cars. On heavy days the service manager was particularly stressed. The tasks were the same, but heavier days were more demanding on everyone, especially if the shop was short-handed.

Promotions and Specials

The flow of work into both the service area and the body shop was not even from day to day or month to month. People drove their cars more during the summer months and thus incurred more repair problems during that time. Periodically, in an effort to smooth the flow of work it received, the dealership publicized some service specials. These were typically cut-rate prices on services like oil changes and lubrications, cooling system winterizing, or total paint jobs. These specials were timed so they did not interfere with normally busy periods.

Another promotion that the dealership was proud of was its offer of a free loaner car to any patron whose car had to be held overnight and who had purchased his new or used car at Howard Ford-Isuzu-Peugeot and had come in for service prior to 10 A.M. The loaner fleet consisted of 28 current model cars. This policy helped to tie customers of the dealership to the service department.

PART TWO
DISCUSSION

Howard Ford-Isuzu-Peugeot is in no way responsible for the following views and presentation. They remain solely the responsibility of the author.

The Flow of the Process and Information

Figures G7 and G8 display process flow and information flow diagrams for a car in the course of its repair at Howard Ford-Isuzu-Peugeot. Similar diagrams could be drawn for the operation of the body shop or indeed for the operation of the parts department. (The development of those diagrams are left as exercises at the end of this tour.) Note that the customer's car may wait at almost any point in the process. The only wait shown in the diagram is between logging in the job and its diagnosis; it is but one of many such waits that could exist.

What is most striking about the flow of the process and of information at Howard Ford versus a service factory like Burger King is the extent to which there is communication between customer and management and between management and technicians. Because of the customization that is required in auto repair, the flow of information at Howard Ford is much more frequent and less structured than that at a Burger King. Management is very much an intermediary between the customer and the technician. At

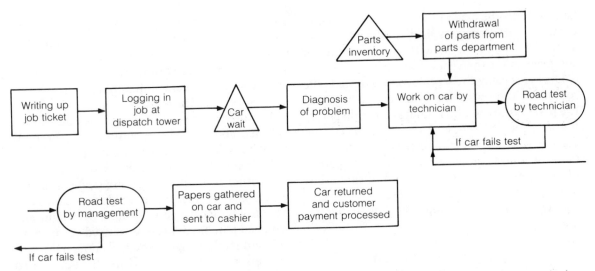

Note: The car may wait between any of the process steps shown and not simply between the log-in of the job and the diagnosis of any problem.

FIGURE G7   Process flow diagram that follows a car in the course of its repair at Howard Ford-Isuzu-Peugeot, Durham, North Carolina.

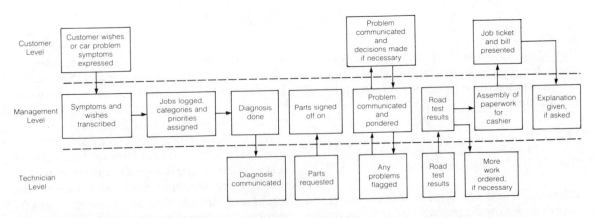

FIGURE G8   Information flow for a car in the course of its repair at Howard Ford-Isuzu-Peugeot.

the same time, management is also very much the source of control for the process.

One can see from this information flow diagram why peak days are so tough on manage-ment. There are no shortcuts in the informa-tion flows that must occur on busy days. The only source of help is to draw on others, such as calling on the service writers to do road tests or to give diagnostic work to technicians themselves.

Of interest is the fact that Howard Ford represents an example of a fixed position layout, where materials are brought to a particular location. Chapter 2 will have occasion to discuss this type of layout more and contrast it with other types.

DEMANDS OF THE PROCESS ON THE WORKFORCE

Most of the repair workers at Howard Ford-Isuzu-Peugeot are paid on an incentive basis. The technicians, bodymen, and painters all are paid according to the ratio of their performance relative to a time standard. The base wage against which that ratio is applied depends on their level of skill, which in turn depends on their willingness to learn and the experience they have accumulated. If a technician wants to get ahead and if he wants to be able to be promoted to more prestigious jobs in the shop, he must be willing to go to school. The increasing sophistication of cars demands this. The increasing sophistication of auto repair work is reflected in the fact that Howard Ford's mechanics are not called mechanics but *technicians*. The use of that term is a reflection on how the workforce and management alike consider the demands of the job.

Working hard as a technician means more than simply beating the standard as set in the book. Working hard also means being able to juggle several different jobs at once so that little time is spent waiting for parts or otherwise removed from the actual repair job. In this regard, the technician is responsible for the pace of his own work. That pace is not dictated by the dispatcher nor by the flow of work along a line. The pace is dictated solely by the technician and his level of skill and effort.

The high level of individual responsibility evident for the technician job carries over to the considerable inventory of tools that everyone is expected to carry. Indeed, the capital-to-labor ratio implied by this tool inventory nearly equals 1 (about $20,000 in tools and about $20,000 in annual wages, for an average technician) without counting any of the plant, equipment, or parts that are made available to the technicians by the dealership itself. As owners of their tools, technicians are almost like independent operators rather than employees of the company. They have considerable freedom to come and go on their own, for they are paid only for what they do and not for how many hours they spend in the shop per day. Nevertheless, being part of a dealership's service operation has its advantages. The work is steady, training is provided, and the technician does not have any of the headaches that would be involved in establishing and directing a business.

Howard Ford represents a significant contrast to a Burger King. The jobs involved in auto repair are more individual and varying, and, despite some specialization within the workforce, there are fewer job niches. Although some team work is required, the element of team work at the dealership is much less than that which has to apply in a service factory.

DEMANDS OF THE PROCESS ON MANAGEMENT

As the information flow diagram leads one to suspect, auto repair places some significant demands on management. Some of those demands deal with the control of the process, which essentially means control over the rather independent operators. The elements of control include dispatching, diagnosis, the periodic checking of efficiencies, and the quality checks made for both part ordering and road testing. Control over the workforce is a continual endeavor, and one that is fairly loosely defined.

In addition, management must deal with complaints from technicians about their pay or what has been assigned to them. Management must also keep track of the training possibilities for the technicians and who should be assigned to which school.

Monitoring technician training is just one aspect of keeping up-to-date. Other aspects deal with equipment and information. The use of computers is now standard in most auto dealerships, and computer facilities are steadily being improved. This permits more of the paperwork and information needs of the dealership to be put on computer. Keeping up-to-date with the increasing sophistication of cars requires added investments in plant and equipment and in manuals and documentation. It is important for management to have the right kind of equipment and enough of it so that workers are not cramped for space or equipment and thus do not impede the capacity of the shop. An important aspect of the capital

requirements of the dealership is the parts department. Dealers, of course, want to have enough of the right parts available so that they do not stock out too often, but they do not want to drown in inventory. The use of the computer helped to strike this balance, as did the discipline that was applied in keeping track of the parts on hand.

Another whole realm of management effort is devoted to dealing with customers. Managers were in repeated contact with customers—taking orders, handling complaints, and explaining the shop's actions. Senior managers, in particular, were safety valves for the service writers so that when all the service writers were occupied with customers, the flow of the process could continue unabated.

Management is also responsible for generating a steady flow of work into the shop. That means trying to perk up business in the off peak times of the year through promotions and specials. And, once a customer does come in, the service writer informs the customer about other services that his or her car could really use.

QUESTIONS

1. How does the payment scheme for the shop's technicians compare with other incentive pay schemes discussed in previous tours?

2. How does the Howard Ford dispatcher compare with the foreman at Norcen Industries?

3. Why was the time clock used by the dispatcher to log jobs in and out?

4. What might explain why Howard Ford's efficiencies, as measured by the productivity report, were higher than the Ford Motor average?

5. What kinds of parts orders suggested by the parts department's computer program would likely be overridden by the parts manager?

6. Why was the parts manager so dedicated to updating each day the perpetual inventory records kept of each part?

7. In what ways was managing the body shop similar to managing the service shop? In what ways were they different?

8. In what ways is the Howard Ford service manager's job like that of the Burlington Burger King's manager? In what ways is it different?

9. Develop process and information flow diagrams for the body shop.

10. Develop process and information flow diagrams for the parts department.

SITUATION FOR STUDY G-1
BIG CITY HOSPITAL EMERGENCY ROOM

The emergency room of the Big City Hospital served about 100 patients a day. Some patients' arrivals were unannounced. Others, however, were announced through communication with ambulance drivers or physicians. The pattern of admission was routine except for patients who were obviously in medical distress.

Each patient entering the emergency room was met by one of two clerks at the front desk. The clerk was the first to assess whether the patient needed immediate medical attention. The clerk would announce "patient here" over the loudspeaker and a triage nurse would take over, reviewing the paperwork that had been done, taking the patient's vital signs, and gathering additional information. The triage nurse then determined whether the patient had to be seen by a physician immediately or whether he or she could wait. If a patient arrived by ambulance, the communication from the ambulance would indicate an estimated time of arrival and some word of the patient's condition. If the patient could give some preliminary information on arrival to the clerk, that would be done; if not, the patient was wheeled directly into the emergency room treatment area.

There were several treatment areas to the emergency room. These included the acute trauma room; a large open area with seven bed slots with curtains to close off each of the slots; four other, separate holding slots; an ear, nose,

and throat room; an OB GYN room; a cast room; and a family room. The acute trauma room was kept always set up in anticipation of a patient with a severe problem. Up to 20 people could be mobilized to help stabilize a patient in acute trauma.

The open area with the seven bed slots was used for general admission patients. If the patient's condition warranted continual observation, he or she was placed near the nursing station. Patients not needing constant surveillance were placed at more of a distance. The ear, nose, and throat; the OB GYN; and the cast rooms were used for isolating patients with those conditions. The family room was used either for psychiatric patients or for the families of patients who were critically ill.

Once patients were seen by the triage nurse and then by the resident nurse, they were evaluated by a surgical or medical intern, and, if necessary, by an attending resident or physician. Upon examination, the patients were either treated and discharged or admitted to the main part of the hospital. The time goal for admitting, treating, and discharging a patient was four hours. Nurses handled any transfers to other areas of the hospital.

Each patient generated substantial amounts of paperwork: personal medical history, notes from physicians and nurses, diagnoses, orders and instructions, laboratory tests performed, and any supplies used. This paperwork was necessary for recording instructions to be used by other hospital personnel, or by departments for billing and for the creation of a permanent medical record. Given these various purposes, the record forms included space for personal data, the nature of the complaint, the physician's name, the type of insurance, notes from the physician, orders from the physician, diagnosis from the physician, and instructions for the discharge. Separate records were kept for nursing, the physicians, and insurance. Lab work was tracked using individual tickets that were kept grouped with the emergency room reports. After a specific time, these reports were entered in the hospital computer for storage.

1. Diagram the process flow.
2. Diagram the information flow.
3. How would you determine how the emergency room ought to be staffed with clerks, nurses, and physicians?

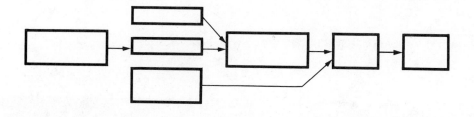

MASS SERVICE
Thalhimers—Cloverleaf Mall Store
Richmond, Virginia

The Cloverleaf Mall store of Thalhimers was one of 25 that the company operated in Virginia, North Carolina, South Carolina, and Tennessee. Thalhimers was a general department store chain, begun in Richmond in 1842, and the fifth generation of the Thalhimer family was presently in the senior management of the corporation. Through the years, Thalhimers grew both by acquiring stores and by building new ones. In 1978, the firm merged with the Carter-Hawley-Hale group of stores, headquartered in California.

By dollar volume, the firm's largest store was at Cloverleaf Mall, located in one of the fastest growing areas in the Richmond market, and situated in one of the 15 fastest growing counties in America. The store was built in 1972 and had been remodeled twice—extensively in 1978 when a second floor was added to the initial one-floor layout. It now occupied 130,000 square feet. As a general department store, Thalhimers carried a broad selection of merchandise for women, men, children and the home.

PART ONE
SERVICE PROCESS DESCRIPTION

LAYOUT

The store's layout was recognized as an important feature in attracting and generating sales. A good layout does several things. It catches the consumer's eye and brings excitement to the shopping experience. It flows in a logical pattern from one department to another, and it presents merchandise in an attractive and accessible manner. A good store layout is also dynamic, changing not only with the seasons but also with changes in consumer tastes, with changes in a department's sales potential, and with changes in what makes for dramatic presentations of the merchandise.

Years ago, department stores were designed with long central aisles that effectively divided the store into large quadrants. Over the years,

The cosmetics counter as seen from the Mall entrance to Thalhimers.
(*Courtesy of Thalhimers—Cloverleaf Mall Store*)

this kind of old-fashioned layout has been supplanted by more aesthetically pleasing ones. The Cloverleaf store, for example, did not have straight aisles. It was an open store with soft wall treatments to designate departments, and with a flow that was natural of the consumer. It incorporated shops—small, partially enclosed, well-identified areas that dramatized particularly important fashion statements. It did not follow the so-called "world" concept. (In that concept of department store design, the consumer enters a well-defined arena or "world" of a particular category of merchandise—such as a "Childrens World," a "Juniors World," and an "Electronic World." A world catches the consumers' eyes with dramatic wall treatments,

color schemes, and fixtures (racks, tables, and other furniture on or in which merchandise was displayed, and which is in keeping with all of the elements of design for the specific area).

The development of a layout for a new store began with space requests from the company's various merchandise managers. For example, the merchandise manager for ladies' accessories would present a request for a certain square footage based on a history of results from other stores. Similar requests would be submitted for men's furnishings, the home division, and other areas, each broken down to the level of detail of individual departments within each area. Management then examined the current sales trends for the various segments of the business and the sales per square foot that were generated in each area in the current stores. Decisions were then made concerning space allocation for the new store. Together with the Thalhimer in-house architects, management then decided on the character of the store's environment; a store in Charleston, South Carolina would likely be different aesthetically from one in Fayetteville, North Carolina. At this point, decisions were also made about which departments should be adjacent to one another, and what the proximity should be to the various store entrances. The different entrances generated different levels of traffic, and it was important to keep that in mind in developing the plan for the store. Plans and space allocations were changed from one store to the next, depending on the performance trends of the different areas of the business.

There were substantial differences in the sales per square foot generated by the different departments. For example, fragances enjoyed an annual sales volume per square foot that was 14 times the store's average. Men's ties produced sales per square foot of 7 times the store's average. Electronic sales were well above the average also. On the other hand, some areas such as infants' clothing or men's robes generated sales that were substantially less than the storewide average. Nevertheless, all elements of the store were important to the image of a department store with broad assortments of merchandise.

A tour of the store can help dramatize the importance of the layout. On the first floor, the Cloverleaf store had four entrances. The entrance with the most traffic was the north on mall entrance. The cosmetics department was centered in front of the mall entrance. Cosmetics generate high dollar volume per square foot. It is also an area that creates excitement and generates impulse purchasing. To capture the attention of the customer entering the store,

adjacent and to the right of cosmetics was a fashion shop featuring Liz Claiborne designer sportswear. Liz Claiborne was a very popular designer and a nice complement to the excitement generated at the cosmetics counters.

As demonstrated by both the cosmetics counters and the Liz Claiborne shop, the interior design of the store was dramatic, creative, and yet very pleasing to the eye. One could look at the presentations of the merchandise and sense a statement of fashion. The distinctiveness of these statements of taste and fashion were important aspects of the sales performance of the store.

Moving west from the cosmetics counters and the Liz Claiborne shop, a customer would find both fashion and fine jewelry, and on the right a large selection of famous label sportswear. In general, designer fashions and the more expensive labels were located nearer to the front of the store. As one continued moving west toward the west entrance (the third most important entrance) (see Figure H1), one could see the accessories department on the inside of the aisle and the women's petite sportswear and better dresses on the other side of the aisle. Each of these areas maintained its own fashion statements.

The men's area was located between the south and the east entrances. The south entrance was the second most important entrance, and the east entrance was the least trafficked entrance. As with the other areas on the first floor, the fashion statements were presented both on the aisle and with important wall treatments in the rear of the department, acting to draw the consumer's eye into that area of the store. The menswear area had its own brandname shops, (including Izod and Polo).

Several areas in the store served as "swing" areas. Some, for example, offered sweaters for the fall and winter seasons and bathing suits for the spring and summer seasons. Other areas

A. First floor layout.

FIGURE H1   Thalhimers—Cloverleaf Mall Store.

of the store were assigned even more temporary space, such as seasonal merchandise for Christmas. These trends and seasonal changes meant that the layout changed constantly.

The store's second floor was as fashion conscious as the first floor. On entering the second floor the customer viewed a broad assortment of the finest china, silver, and glass stemware from around the world in the tabletop area. To the right of this area was the gourmet housewares area, which dramatically presented a broad selection of both imported and domestic merchandise. Other areas on the second floor were the children's departments, gourmet foods, ladies' lingerie, the restaurant, television and electronics, and the linen and bedding shops.

B. Second floor layout.

FIGURE H1   *continued*

MANAGEMENT AND THE WORKFORCE

The organization chart for the Cloverleaf store is displayed in Figure H2. Reporting to the store manager were two assistant managers and the personnel manager. Reporting to the assistant managers were the supervisors for the various areas within the store. Reporting to the operations manager were the leased departments, the restaurant manager, the customer service supervisor and the supervisors for housekeeping and merchandise handling. Each department of the store was managed by a supervisor. The department's sales associates reported directly to the supervisor, as did the sales associate designated as the training coordinator.

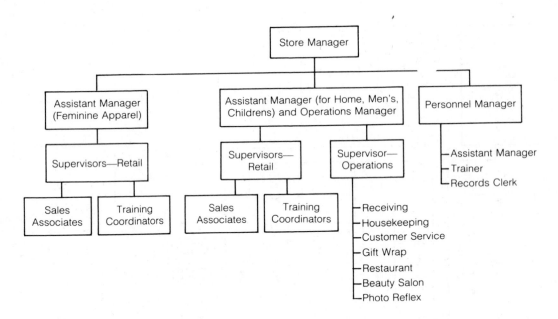

FIGURE H2   Organization chart for the Cloverleaf Mall Store of Thalhimers.

Also reporting to a supervisor could be an assistant supervisor or a selling supervisor (two intern-interim training positions for sales associates working their way through the ranks).

There were 275 employees in the Cloverleaf store, roughly half of whom worked full time and half part time. The store was open from 10:00 in the morning until 9:30 in the evening, Monday through Saturday; and from 12:30 to 5:30 on Sundays. With the store open so many hours during the week, employing part-time personnel was essential to providing maximum staffing. Full-time people were required to work two nights a week and to work every other Sunday. The part-time people worked a fixed schedule: mornings, evenings, and weekends.

During the Christmas season, additional, temporary employees were hired (180 for the 1985 Christmas season). This temporary workforce was hired in late September and early October, trained at the end of October, and began

work on the floor in early November. This hiring and training process ensured that every temporary employee had sufficient experience on the floor prior to Thanksgiving, the beginning of the strongest part of the Christmas buying season.

In addition to the store's part-time employees, there was an additional group of sales associates. This group was known as "flyers," and they formed the "flying squad." These substitute employees on the flying squad were called on short notice to work a particular day or period of time. Depending on their individual schedules, they would or would not be available to work. They were all fully trained to fill in in various departments throughout the store.

Sales associates and support personnel were paid between $3.35 and $7.00 an hour, based on experience and background, and the employee benefit package was in addition to these wages. Thalhimers was considering a program where

The Liz Claiborne shop. (*Courtesy of Thalhimers—Cloverleaf Mall Store*)

The young men's department. (*Courtesy of Thalhimers—Cloverleaf Mall Store*)

all sales associates would work on a commission arrangement. Presently sales associates in the shoes and television and electronics departments were paid on commission, while those in the cosmetics area were paid a combination of salary plus commission.

Turnover averaged about 65 percent each year. Although moves to higher paying jobs was responsible for some turnover, most of the turnover was caused by families moving out of town, by sales associates desiring to stay home, by scheduling problems, or simply by sales associates not enjoying sales work.

Both hiring and training were extremely important activities. The right sales associate for a particular department was critical to that department's sales performance. Different personalities were required for different departments. For example, cosmetics required sales associates who were aggressive and enthusias-

tic as well as highly knowledgeable about the product. China and silver, on the other hand, required sales associates of good taste and great patience, capable of serving the bride and the mother of the bride. Younger sales associates could interact more effectively with teenagers in the juniors' department. If "Miami Vice" clothes were selling well, then it was advantageous to have sales associates who could relate to the merchandise and enjoy wearing this style of fashion apparel.

For these reasons, the hiring decision was important and took on elements of theatrical casting. There were three required visits before a new employee could be hired, after which the employee was given 24 hours of training off the floor, two weeks of training on the floor, and then a 90-day period of evaluation. In addition, training sessions for sales associates (meetings and videotape viewings) were held every week.

The silver, china, and crystal departments on the second floor, just off the escalator.
(*Courtesy of Thalhimers—Cloverleaf Mall Store*)

Training was important not only for acquiring knowledge about the merchandise and the operation of the department, but also for learning selling skills: how to present the merchandise and how to close the sale. A trainer had recently been employed and showed great promise for increasing the productivity of the sales associates throughout the store.

The supervisors were essential to the successful operation of the store. They were responsible for a number of important activities, among which were:

1. Scheduling the sales associates in the department, both full and part-time, and determining when to use the flying squad.

2. Overseeing the training of sales associates.

3. Monitoring all sales transactions.

4. Receiving inventory, checking it against the paperwork, and reconciling any errors in its shipping or paperwork (explained later).

5. Adjusting prices and preparing the department for sales and promotions.

Some of the supervisors had worked their way up through the ranks from sales associates. Others were management trainees, employed out of college, who served in the store for two years before entering the merchandising arm of Thalhimers as assistant buyers.

The linens, located next to the silver and fine china. (*Courtesy of Thalhimers—Cloverleaf Mall Store*)

THE TRANSACTION—AND SUPPORTING IT

At the heart of the store's operation was the sales transaction itself, and the information it generated. Scattered throughout the store in the various departments were point-of-sale devices or registers. These registers were all tied into the store's computer, and via that computer, they were tied to the computer at Thalhimers in Richmond and the computers of Carter-Hawley-Hale in California. All transactions, once they were rung on the register, were immediately sent on to the computers in California and in the Richmond headquarters.

Each transaction consisted of the following items of information: the type of payment to be made (cash or charge), the personnel identification number for the sales associate (the "pin number"); the department's number, the class of merchandise being sold; the stock-keeping unit number for the item (the "SKU number"), and the price for the item (see Figure H3). Once these bits of information were entered into the register, the sale could be completed, the drawer opened, and if change was required, change would be returned to the customer. With these registers, immediate credit checks were possible. Credit card numbers could be traced immediately and information relayed to the register on whether or not to complete

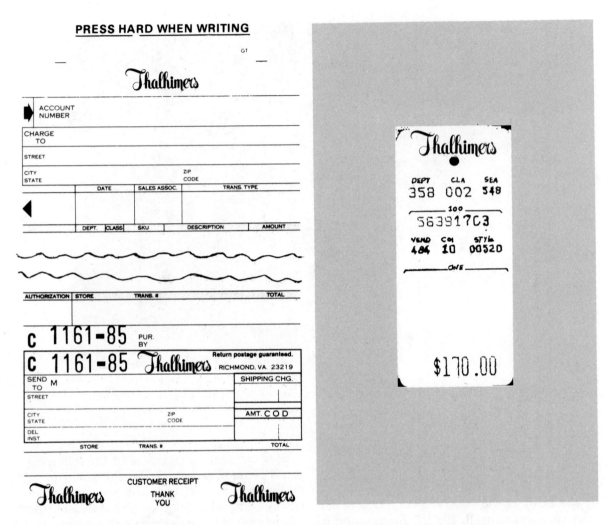

FIGURE H3   A price tag and sales ticket form used at the Cloverleaf Mall Store of Thalhimers.

the transaction. With the registers tied in to the company's computers, up-to-the-minute sales reports, or return reports, by department, could be generated at any time.

Supporting the store's transactions was a staff in the customer service area. The customer service department was responsible for opening up each register each day (including supplying it with $50 reserve change). Sales associates were required to log into the register upon arrival and to log out of the register when they had finished working for the day. At the end of the day the customer service staff was responsible for accounting for all cash and charges, and for checking any discrepancies. The money and the charge account media were taken to the registers by a sales associate and returned to the credit office in the evening by a sales associate. They were verified by the supervisors before being turned in to the customer service office.

The customer service department also ran the customer service window, through which it received payments, adjusted bills, sold tickets to various theater events, provided extra coins or cash to registers throughout the store, handled customer complaints about the store and its service, and cashed checks. Customer service was a vital center for the store's transactions.

MANAGING AND CONTROLLING THE INVENTORY

Providing the merchandise for the Cloverleaf store was the responsibility of Thalhimer's merchandising staff located at the Richmond headquarters. The buyers purchased the merchandise that would be sold at Cloverleaf and determined how much merchandise was to be purchased, when the merchandise was to be delivered, and for what price the merchandise would sell. Many of the items in Thalhimers were fashion-sensitive with lead times between ordering and receiving of 6 to 12 months. Thus, a buyer often had to gamble months in advance on what would sell during a particular season. If the buyer bought the wrong merchandise or ordered too much of the merchandise, the store's sales and profits suffered. If the buyer erred on the other side and did not order enough merchandise, the store suffered a loss of potential revenue. The buying decision was thus a very important one, but one that was essentially outside of the control of a branch store like Cloverleaf. Of course, the store could provide feedback to the buyers on what merchandise was selling well, the type of customer who seemed to be buying it, and how it could be effectively presented, but the merchandising

decision rested with those at the corporate headquarters.

Although there was little chance for significant replenishment of fashion-sensitive items, for basic merchandise replenishment was possible. Counts were made periodically of the inventory, and merchandise was ordered to maintain a minimum and maximum level that was preagreed upon by the buyer and the store manager.

Receiving

All items received at the store were sent from Thalhimer's service building in Richmond. At the service building items were checked, sorted, priced, and marked. Deliveries to the Cloverleaf store were made between 4 and 6 A.M. The receiving crew started work at 6 A.M. and delivered all of the merchandise that was received that morning to the floor by 10 A.M.

Several checks were made of the merchandise received to ensure that the merchandise received and accounted for was what was expected and had, in fact, arrived. Each truck was physically sealed and the number on the metal seal had to match the manifest that accompanied the shipment. (See Figure H4.) After the seal was broken, the crew grouped those boxes that were shipped together and checked their numbers against the manifest. Hanging garments in canvas rollers, termed "hampers," were similarly checked. Each group of boxes or "hampers" had been labeled with a movement tag (Figure H5). The movement tag indicated the store department to receive the merchandise, the purchase order number, the hamper number, and the seal number (which indicated the truck shipment). The movement tags came in triplicate; the white tags stayed with the hamper or box, yellow tags were kept by the receiving store, and pink tags were kept by the service building.

THALHIMERS RELAY TRANSFER MANIFEST 292101

DATE		TIME OUT	TIME IN		

DRIVER				SEAL No.
FROM		TO		TRUCK No.
DISPATCHER			RES. CLERK	

NO.	DEPT.	RECEIVING NO. OR ROSTN. NO.	HAMPER NO.	SEAL NO.	NO. OF CARTONS	NO. OF UNITS	Chk.
1							
2							
3							
4							
5							
6							
7							
8							
9							

FIGURE H4   A shipment manifest used in transporting merchandise at the Cloverleaf Mall Store of Thalhimers.

After the truck was unloaded, the merchandise was moved onto the selling floor. The merchandise handling group knew exactly where each department received its merchandise, usually near its register. The merchandise moved out to the floor was accompanied by the white movement tag and the paperwork on the purchase, typically the purchase order (see Figures H6 and H7 for examples of this paperwork).

Every morning the supervisor and the sales associates in each department checked the merchandise delivered against the accompanying paperwork to ensure that all of the items they expected to receive were, in fact, received. Each department checked the seals on their hampers and boxes, circled the counts to indicate agreement, stamped the paperwork "received," and then filed that paperwork appropriately. The stock was then displayed in the appropriate place in the department.

The records of the inventory received were kept in a "journal room." The journal room was also next to the office of the inventory controller, and the mailboxes for all of the supervisory personnel. It was the nerve center for processing the merchandise paperwork for inventory.

VARIATIONS ON THE STANDARD RECEIPT OF MATERIAL

While most of the merchandise received at the store followed the standard procedure, there

MERCHANDISE MOVEMENT TAG			SERVICE CENTER STOCK		
DEPT.	**RTW Pieces**		**22**		
			Wheeler Container NO.		
ATTENTION OF:			**Sent by**	**Location**	**Date**
		OF			

FIGURE H5   A movement tag that accompanies merchandise between the service center and the store.

were a number of errors and changes that had to be recorded. These errors and changes were kept in special books:

1. *Interstore transfers.* Often items of merchandise were transferred from one store to another. When this occurred, those stores involved made note of it so that the inventory records were accurate. Supervisors filled out the interstore transfer book (see Figure H8), and the inventory controller also checked the work.

2. *Errors in shipment.* If there were errors in a shipment received by the store (what was received did not match the paperwork), then these errors were noted in a special book,

again, so that possible errors could be identified (see Figure H9).

3. *Report of changes in retail price.* This book tracked changes that had occurred to the retail price, for example, missed markdowns, and month-end special sale liquidations of inventory (see Figure H10).

4. *Merchandise transfer.* If merchandise had been incorrectly charged to the store or had been incorrectly charged to another department, these errors were marked in the merchandise transfer book (see Figure H11).

Through the use of these books for changes and errors, the store kept excellent track of exactly what inventory it had and that with which

FIGURE H6 A purchase order sheet that is filled out by a buyer and that accompanies merchandise to the Cloverleaf Mall Store. Note that Cloverleaf is Store 19.

204

```
   11      99999      11      99999      •••••• MARKING AND TRANSFER ••••••     PRINTED 12/17/85  TIME 06:22      PAGE      1
  111     99 99      111     99 99
   11     99 99       11     99 99       MRKNG SEC/LOC _____ MRKNG LINE _____ MRKER ID ___ TKT PRT T3C@           OP ID TP00021
   11      99999      11      99999      RCV 12/16/85                   DOC : N        DOC TYPE P
   11         99      11         99
 1111         99    1111         99      VENDOR   878 . JOSIAH WEDGWOOD AND CO

DEPT    281 # OF STYLES    2  SKUS      2
RCVNG   281530               UNITS      2

PO  20155396

  MFG-STYLE STYLE CD COLOR     SIZE  RCVD  REA LINE  SSKU     DESCRIPTION         RTV  CLASS   RETAIL UM   EXT-RTL

       6 00006 00                        1   ___ 0601 56147314 OCEANSIDESANDWICHTRA   0     5    25.00 EA     25.00
       8 00008 00                        1   ___ 0801 55948658 OCEANSIDETANKARD      0     5    17.50 EA     17.50
```

FIGURE H7   A computer-generated marking and transfer sheet that performs the same function as the purchase order sheet. It, or the purchase order sheet, accompanies goods to the store. It is generated by a buyer and is store-specific. Note the 19 in the upper left corner.

☐ **BUS**

Thalhimers **INTER STORE TRANSFER**

ACCOUNTS PAYABLE COPY

REQ./INV. NO.   VENDOR   SEAL #

ACT. CD.	STORE NO. (FROM)	DEPT. NO.	STORE NO. (TO)	DEPT.	MO.	DA	YR.	NUMBER	CODE
62								**704999**	**2**

UNIT CLASS	VENDOR NO.	STYLE	COLOR CODE	SIZE OR DESCRIPTION							$ CLASS	QUANTITY	UNIT RETAIL	TOTAL RETAIL

SENDING STORE				TOTAL RETAIL	
AUTHORIZED BY	CHECKED BY	SEALED BY			
RECEIVING STORE				TOTAL COST	
RECEIVED BY	DATE	DEPT. MGR'S SIGNATURE		DISCOUNT	

FIGURE H8   An interstore transfer sheet that accompanies goods sent from one Thalhimers store to another.

FIGURE H9   An error-in-shipment report that is completed by a supervisor.

FIGURE H10   A change-in-retail-price report used at Thalhimers.

ACCOUNT PAYABLE

Thalhimers
MERCHANDISE TRANSFER

Act. Cd.	MO.	DA.	YR.	TRANSFER NO.	STORE NO. (FROM)	STORE NO. (TO)	CHARGE DEPT.	CREDIT DEPT.	CODE
60				439011					

UNIT CLASS	VENDOR	STYLE	COLOR	DESCRIPTION	CLASS FROM	TO	QUAN.	COST UNIT	TOTAL	RETAIL UNIT	TOTAL

OK BY RECEIVING DEPARTMENT

OK BY DELIVERING DEPARTMENT

TOTALS: $ $

AVERAGE DISCOUNT % $

REASON: ☐ Resale   ☐ Workroom Cost

☐ Other_____

A MARKDOWN MUST BE TAKEN BY DEPT. TRANSFERRING IF MERCHANDISE IS TRANSFERRED AT A LOWER RETAIL THAN MARKED.

FIGURE H11 A merchandise transfer sheet that a Thalhimers supervisor completes.

it should be credited. Price changes were also kept track of by the supervisors and the inventory controller. Figure H12 offers an example of a price change document.

Shipping Items Out of the Store

It was Thalhimer policy not to ship items between stores or back to the service building unless the dollar value of the transfer justified the expense. In general, unless a shipment was worth $1000 or more, no transfers were made. One day a month was allocated to transferring merchandise to other stores to balance inven-tories. There were some exceptions to this pol-icy: vendor returns, damaged goods, alterations, and monograms could be returned to the ser-vice center or moved between stores on a daily basis. Shipping of this merchandise invoked the same care and controls that were shown for the receipt of the merchandise.

EVALUATING THE STORE'S PERFORMANCE

The store was evaluated as a profit center. The profit plan for the store involved the determi-

Thalhimers   CORPORATE PRICE CHANGE   JUN 18 1984

TO STORES: (PLEASE CIRCLE STORE NO.)

	⑮_____	㉖_____	㉘_____	㉟_____
④_____	⑳_____	28_____	⑰_____	㊋_____
⑮_____	22_____	㉚_____	㊐_____	㊐_____
16_____	23_____	31_____	㊴_____	㊆_____
⑰_____	24_____	㊱_____	�_____	(75)_____
⑱_____	25_____	37_____	㊿_____	

CODE: 70 ◄—INDICATE ◄

MARK UP _____ by-CODE 70   REPORT OF ADDITIONAL
MARK UP CANCELLATION _____ by-CODE 71   MARK UP NO. _____
MARK DOWN _____ by-CODE 72
MARK DOWN CANCELLATION _____ by-CODE 73
MARK OUT OF STOCK _____ by-CODE 78

STORE 19   DEPT. 61   804707   DATE 6 /28/84

DO NOT PUT MORE THAN 5 CLASSES ON A FORM

VENDOR NO.	STYLE NO.	DESCRIPTION (Item, Color, Size, Etc.)	UNIT PRICE		Difference	MARKER'S QUANTITY	CLASS	AMOUNT OF CHANGE	
			Present Price	Price To Be Marked					
136755	Peacock	Vinyl Cloth 52:70	8 99	9 99	1 00	62	7	62	00
J. McCollete 6-28-84							TOTAL	62	00

MARKER'S SIGNATURE   DATE

☐ NOTICE ONLY   ☐ EMERGENCY   TO BE AUDITED ☐ _____ AUDITED BY _____ DATE

Please re-mark merchandise listed above for July Mailer _____ event or special promotion.

Effective date of price change is 6·28 . ☑ A.M. ☐ P.M.

COMMENTS _____

BUYER'S SIGNATURE   8479 6/11   MDSE. MGR'S. SIGNATURE   6/12 27
                     EXT.   DATE   DATE DIV. NO.

006-211   7020

FIGURE H12 Price changes to implement were noted every day on corporate price change sheets by Thalhimers supervisors and the inventory controller.

nation of sales for each department and a calculation of the proposed selling cost. (Selling cost was calculated as the wages paid divided by the sales in the department for the time period under consideration.) The sales for each department were forecast by the merchandising arm of the company. The merchandisers were responsible for analyzing the sales trend for the store as a whole and any trends for individual areas within the store. A sales plan was developed for each department of the store and stock levels were planned to vary seasonally.

Different "thrust" areas were also singled out for unusual attention; separate plans were developed for increased inventory, increased promotional activity, and additional personnel to achieve a substantially larger-than-normal increase in volume. There were daily, weekly, and monthly reports that monitored the progress of these departments and any variances from the projected sales and profit plan.

The store carefully monitored the "penetration" of particular departments. Penetration of a specific area was calculated by dividing the sales of the area by the total sales of the store. If this fraction for a particular area at Cloverleaf differed significantly from those of other Thalhimer stores, the store manager could then investigate reasons for that difference. In this manner, the store manager could move more aggressively to direct business opportunities.

The Cloverleaf store manager spent a great deal of time on the selling floor, observing the operation and communicating personally with the employees. His priorities for ensuring the store's profitability were clear: first, monitoring sales; second, selecting the proper personnel and the development of that personnel; third, presenting the merchandise; and fourth, monitoring expenses.

PART TWO
DISCUSSION

Thalhimers is in no way responsible for the following views or presentation. They remain solely the responsibility of the author.

THE FLOW OF THE PROCESS AND OF INFORMATION

During the course of a day the sales associates at Thalhimers do many things. The two chief processes in which they get involved are stocking, which occurs in the morning, and the sales transaction itself, which occurs all day long. Figure H13 diagrams both of those key processes. For the most part, these processes are fairly well structured. While there is interaction between customer and sales associate during the transaction, particularly in the presentation of the merchandise and the closing of the sale, for the most part the process is a fairly standard one, well known to both parties. Similarly the stocking process is something that is a routine occurrence, day in and day out.

Information flows are also fairly standardized, although there are many different kinds of information that can be passed down from management to the sales associate and up from the sales associate to management. Figure H14 indicates some of the key information flows that go both down and up in the organization.

A. Material Receipt

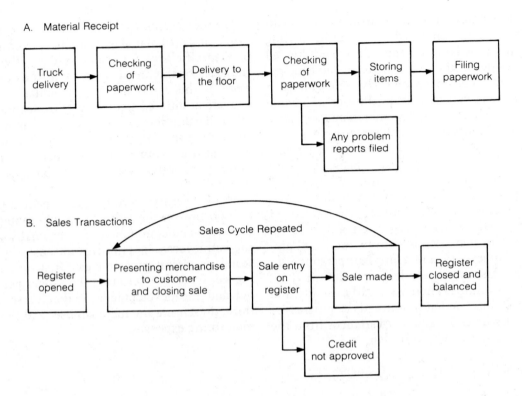

FIGURE H13   Rough process flows for material receipt and for sales transactions at the Cloverleaf Mall Store of Thalhimers.

For the most part, the information flowing downward relates to merchandising shifts, whereas the information flowing upward deals with irregularities in the routine of the inventory and sales transactions.

DEMANDS OF THE PROCESS ON THE WORKFORCE

Because Thalhimers is open so many hours, one key demand on the workforce relates to the scheduling of everybody's work hours. Evening and weekend work is sometimes required.

Another key demand relates to coping with the change that goes on around the employees all the time. Layouts are changing, inventory stock levels are changing, the character of the inventory is changing, and the workforce must cope with all of these changes. To help cope with these changes, there is considerable training. Workers are not only trained initially, but spend appreciable amounts of time week in and week out in training, both to improve their skills and to educate them about the merchandising changes in the store.

Another demand on the workforce is accuracy, both with respect to the transactions made and the inventory overseen. Such accuracy is crucial to the success of the store, and it is a routine to which they must apply themselves all the time.

A. **Information flowing down from management**
   Merchandising shifts
   - sales and promotions
   - changes to merchandise presentations
   - layout and space allocation changes
B. **Information flowing up from the sales associates and support staff**
   Irregularities
   - in transactions
   - in inventory status
   - in paperwork
   - in cash balances
   - other errors
   Inventory counts

FIGURE H14 Examples of information flows at the Cloverleaf
Mall Store of Thalhimers.

DEMANDS OF THE PROCESS ON MANAGEMENT

Like the sales associates and others of the workforce, management must also adhere to and foster the importance of controls on transactions and inventory. The customer service department and the journal room are the store's nerve centers for control, and they must be supported.

Personnel functions are also extremely important, as indicated by the personnel department's status within the organization chart. Hiring—perhaps better termed "casting"—training, and advancement all consume a lot of management time and care. Sales associates' skills are critical to the sales volume that the store generates, and thus hiring and training are key functions of management.

The other key elements to sales increases are the layout itself and the presentation of merchandise. Good layout and good merchandise presentation depended not only on the analysis of sales per square foot figures, but also on intuition and feel for the psychology of the sales situation. The worth of powerful fashion "statements" throughout the store is a clear indication of the art involved in a store's design and operation.

Because fashion can be so fickle and people's tastes can change so abruptly, it is important for the store to monitor sales and costs on a continual basis. Thus, not only are there controls on the transaction and inventory levels themselves, but also controls on sales and selling costs. Store management has to be ready to examine these costs and use them to make decisions about staffing levels and the responsibilities of sales associates and support personnel within the store.

QUESTIONS

1. Visit a department store near you. In what ways is its layout similar to that of Thalhimers? In what ways is it different?

2. One might suppose that theoretically, at least, departments ought to be given space in such proportions that the sales per square foot would be roughly the same anywhere in the store. Why is this point of view impractical?

3. Express some of the fashion statements you have observed at department stores. How

does the store's layout, fixtures, and decor contribute to those statements?

4. What kinds of questions would you ask of a prospective employee to work in the Liz Claiborne shop? What characteristics would you look for? How would those characteristics and questions differ for someone working in the jewelry department?

5. What is the argument for paying sales associates on a commission basis? What is the argument for paying them on an hourly basis?

6. Outline the various controls that exist on the store's inventory? Why are there so many controls?

7. What do you suppose a realistic selling cost would be for retail operations? Back up your estimate with some assumptions and analysis. Should there by any relationship between selling costs and commission rates?

SITUATION FOR STUDY H-1
ADAMS CONVENIENCE STORE

The Adams Convenience Store, located on a major state artery, was open from 6 A.M. until midnight every day and sold grocery items, fast food, and gasoline. Gasoline, dispensed through self-service pumps, represented about 50 percent of total sales. Customers paid first and pumped afterward. All of the gasoline pumps were multiproduct dispensers that handled both leaded and unleaded gasoline.

The store was laid out as in Figure H15. Seventy percent of the people who entered the store to do something other than to pay for gasoline, bought some sort of beverage. The fast food available at the rear of the store was the highest-margin item for sale; gasoline was the lowest-margin item. The Adams Convenience Store offered hot dogs, sandwiches, pastries, coffee, and other food items. There were two peaks for food item demand: breakfast and the four to six, after-work period. Sales slowed in mid-morning, early afternoon, and late at night.

The store operated two shifts. The store manager was there to open the store in the morning and stayed during the first shift; the store's assistant manager handled the second shift. During the busiest period of each shift there were a total of four working in the store: two to handle the fast food area and two to tend the registers. In addition to the manager and the assistant manager there were two full-time workers and the remaining were part-time employees. Pay averaged just above the minimum wage, and turnover rates often ran as high as 300 percent a year.

The manager and the assistant manager trained the others and determined which items met the company's definition for being short in supply and needed to be reordered. Orders were placed to a central Adams warehouse. The managers were also responsible for controls on cash and inventory so that everything was accounted for.

1. Why is the layout designed as it is? Give a rationale and explain what you think the typical traffic flow would be.

2. Why would the Adams Convenience Store invest in multiproduct gasoline pumps?

3. What do you see as the biggest challenges for the store's owners?

FIGURE H15   Adams Convenience Store Layout

TOUR I

A PROFESSIONAL SERVICE
Arthur Andersen & Company
Accounting and Auditing Services
Charlotte, North Carolina

Arthur Andersen & Co. was one of the world's leading accounting firms, with headquarters offices in Geneva, Switzerland, and in Chicago. As of 1984, the firm employed 26,380 people worldwide and operated 176 offices in 45 countries. In the United States, Arthur Andersen was the largest of the so-called "Big Eight" accounting firms. The firm was operated as a partnership, that is, the firm was owned and managed by a group of partners (in 1984 the partners totaled 1,528) who had been elected by other partners in the firm.

The Charlotte office was the administrative office that coordinated the practice for the two Carolinas, including Columbia, South Carolina; Greensboro, North Carolina; and Raleigh, North Carolina. These four offices combined employed about 300 people, of whom 260 were professionals and 40 were support personnel. Of the 300, 180 worked in the Charlotte office. The office served over 330 clients in a variety of industries.

PART ONE
PROCESS DESCRIPTION

LINES OF BUSINESS

Although Arthur Andersen & Co. was known as a Big Eight accounting firm, it did more than provide classic auditing attest services (described in detail later). Its practice also included tax, consulting, other accounting services, and a series of specialized services for small businesses. In fact,

the auditing and small business groups accounted for only half of revenues; the tax and consulting divisions accounted for the other half.

While this tour examines mainly the accounting and auditing practice of Arthur Andersen & Co.—Charlotte, the tax, consulting, and small business practices merit brief separate mention.

215

The Tax Practice

The tax practice in Charlotte employed 21 professionals. It was an important component of the office's business, and was well established in the firm at large. There were two major components to the tax practice. One dealt with client compliance issues—preparing returns for clients, representing clients at Internal Revenue Service reviews, and providing defense for any clients in legal matters involving taxation. The other component involved advice on business transactions that had significant tax implications, such as mergers, acquisitions, and syndications. This kind of work typically complemented that of investment bankers and lawyers.

Tax work consisted of many short-term jobs that often had to be done quickly but that typically did not involve substantial resources over extended periods of time; consulting or auditing services were longer term. Although there was considerable demand for tax services all through the year, the peak demands naturally occurred each February through April.

The Consulting Practice

The management information consulting practice for the Carolinas was concentrated in Charlotte: of the 75 professionals employed in the consulting practice, 70 worked in the Charlotte office. The mission of the practice was to help clients obtain the information they needed to plan and manage their organizations. The practice was broad-ranging and included the development and installation of computer systems for financial and operations control of both manufacturing and service businesses. Much of this work was customized for the client and thus called for skill in drawing together the disparate elements of each project.

Consulting revenues were evenly divided among banking, manufacturing/textiles, health care, government work, and some miscellaneous businesses. The projects performed by the consulting division varied widely in their scope and duration although many were accomplished for previous clients. Typical projects included the development of a new deposit system for bank customers and the installation of management information systems for a group of trucking companies.

Small Business Practice

The small business practice was technically a part of the audit practice of the firm; however, attest services only accounted for about half of the small business practice's revenues. The remaining revenues were generated by a diverse array of services: assistance in preparing financial forecasts and cash-flow projections, development of long- and short-range business plans, consultation in approaches to minimize taxes and maximize after-tax cash flow, evaluation of lease vs. buy decisions, breakeven analysis, capital budgeting, assistance with purchases, merger or divestiture plans, and an assortment of other services. The small business practice had been created nearly 40 years ago and had grown in Charlotte since the office opened in 1958. By 1985, there were 55 clients, and some of the original clients' businesses had grown so much that they were no longer served out of the small business practice.

For the professionals in the small business practice, the demands were quite diverse. While each professional had fine auditing skills, they also had to foster other skills so that the wide-ranging demands of small business could be met: use of the microcomputer, preparation of business plans, private placements for company stock, and so on. For these reasons, the small business practice was often difficult to schedule and manage—but it had been a significant source of growth over the years for all of Arthur Andersen & Co.

Report of Independent Public Accountants

To the Share Owners of International Paper Company:

We have examined the consolidated balance sheets of International Paper Company (a New York corporation) and consolidated subsidiaries as of December 31, 1985 and 1984 and the related consolidated statements of earnings, retained earnings and changes in financial position for each of the three years in the period ended December 31, 1985. Our examinations were made in accordance with generally accepted auditing standards and, accordingly, included such tests of the accounting records and such other auditing procedures as we considered necessary in the circumstances.

In our opinion, the consolidated financial statements referred to above present fairly the financial position of International Paper Company and consolidated subsidiaries as of December 31, 1985 and 1984, and the results of their operations and the changes in their financial position for each of the three years in the period ended December 31, 1985, in conformity with generally accepted accounting principles which, except for the changes in 1985, with which we concur, in the method of accounting for the cost of timber harvested and in the methods of determining pension costs, as described in Notes 8 and 16, respectively, to the consolidated financial statements, were applied on a consistent basis.

Arthur Andersen + Co.

New York, N.Y.
February 6, 1986

FIGURE I1   An opinion.

AUDITING ATTEST SERVICES

All publicly held companies (those regulated by the Securities and Exchange Commission) are required to have independent certified public accountants report whether their financial statements fairly represented their financial positions and results of operations. These reports were usually found in company annual reports.

(See Figure I1.) Usually, these opinions were unqualified, but occasionally, accounting firms had to qualify them to alert shareholders to particular risks or problems in the financial statements of the company. Thus, reports were important safeguards to company shareholders. The audit was the procedure by which Arthur Andersen & Co. developed and substantiated reports about the financial records of the client companies.

Arthur Andersen & Co.'s auditing methodology was designed to identify and concentrate on the risk areas of greatest exposure to a company's financial statements and the related key control elements put in place by management to mitigate the risks. It was a "top down" approach that addressed risks in two stages.

The first stage focused on the principal external and internal factors influencing the client company's operations, such as the industry in which it operated, the nature and complexity of its businesses and products, the operational and financial planning and control activities of management and management's attitudes toward risk control and financial reporting.

The second stage provided a systematic basis for evaluating individual internal controls over an organization's significant cycles of activity. Much as a manufacturer is concerned about the integrity and capabilities of the manufacturing process, so, too, an Arthur Andersen & Co. auditor is concerned about the integrity and capability of the internal controls in the client company for capturing accurately all of the accounts billed and collected, the invoices to be paid, the expenses authorized, the inventory, and other data.

The audit attest process could be broken into three major phases: the planning phase, the specific risk analysis phase, and the final phase. These different phases required different amounts of time and attention from the various members of the "engagement team" working on the audit.

The planning phase, for example, accounted for about 10 percent of the typical audit's effort, although much more than 10 percent of the time of the senior members of the engagement team. (The senior members of the team were the partner or partners in charge and the manager—the professional with rank just below partner, who had anywhere from 5 to 12 years of service—the manager was actually in charge of the day-to-day progress on the audit.) The planning phase was concerned with defining the scope of work to be done and its timing. It identified those risks that seemed to be important and those changes in the character of the business that ought to be scrutinized. Once the planning phase was over, the partners returned periodically to review progress, to help work through particular problems, and to monitor the quality of the work in progress.

The specific risk analysis phase was concerned with fact finding. In this phase, the junior members of the engagement team (that is, the staff accountants, and the "seniors") investigated the paperwork and controls of the client company. They checked to see that the controls actually worked. Sometimes, they identified substantive problems that had to be dealt with by the senior members of the engagement team. This phase could range from perhaps 30 percent of the time and effort in a small audit to 60 percent of the time and effort in a large audit.

The final audit phase led to the generation of the report. This phase updated the results of the specific risk analysis phase, involved substantiation of year-end balances, and included a review of the client company's financial statements and their accompanying footnotes. For large audits, this final phase might account for only 30 percent of Arthur Andersen & Co. time and effort, whereas for smaller audits it could account for fully 60 percent.

The total professional time devoted to an audit by the Charlotte office could vary dramatically, from 80 hours each year for the smallest audits to over 4000 hours each year for the largest. The median amount of time consumed for an audit was estimated at about 600 hours each year. The calendar for an audit varied somewhat. For the largest audits, Arthur Andersen & Co. professionals were in and out of the client company all the time; they were often part of quarterly reviews of the client's business. At more typical audits, however, the planning phase was done about six months into each fiscal year, the specific risk analysis work was accomplished in months 7 through 11, and the final work was done in the first 3 months after the close of the fiscal year.

Although two-thirds or more of the Charlotte office's audit work was repeat business, the office was always eager to attract new business. It secured this business by drafting a proposal to the target client company. This proposal discussed the key aspects of Arthur Andersen & Co. and what differentiated it from other accounting firms. It introduced the firm's other major clients in Charlotte and the services the entire office could provide a client company. It discussed in some detail the audit approach that Arthur Andersen & Co. planned to take. It profiled the personnel making up the engagement team, and it discussed how that personnel would be managed over time to provide the kind of continuity that was valued by clients. The proposal also established the fee schedule.

MANAGING THE PRACTICE

The Pyramid

Arthur Andersen & Co.'s auditing practice in the Carolinas totaled 121 professionals. Of this number, there were 8 partners, 19 managers, 33 seniors, and 61 staff accountants. These different classifications could be depicted as a pyramid, with the staff as the base and the partners at the top. Each engagement had its own pyramid, as well, with one or two partners at the top, one or more managers, and various seniors and staff accountants.

Staff, seniors, and managers were all salaried positions. The partners were not salaried; their compensation depended upon the profitability of the firm. If the partners were to make money, they had to use the salaried personnel of the firm effectively. This placed several demands on the partners: (1) effective scheduling of personnel so that everybody was working as much as possible, but without excessive overtime (scheduling will be discussed later) and (2) fostering as much responsibility in the lower ranks as possible. Firm profitability was enhanced to the degree that effort and responsibility were thrust to lower levels of the pyramid (this was termed having a broad-based pyramid). If the higher paid senior members of an engagement team were free to perform other duties, such as bringing in additional business, then everyone benefited and the firm as a whole would be profitable. If a job could be run with a broad-based pyramid, then it would likely be profitable. If, however, the pyramid were slender, it was likely not to be as profitable because the time of the senior members of the engagement team would not be as effectively levered as when the pyramid was broad.

Accounting firms like Arthur Andersen & Co. operated on an "up-or-out" basis; professionals within the firm were either promoted to the next higher rank or they left the firm. In a sense, the partners were the survivors, those who had proven themselves over the years by their performance and had demonstrated the qualities that made for effective partners. There was considerable turnover at the lower levels of the pyramid. If one followed the path of new recruits in the Charlotte office, for example, one typically found

that only 50 percent of each new cohort of college recruits was still with the firm after 3 years, and that only 25 percent of them were still with the firm after 6 years. After 10 years, the figure was 14 percent. Only about 9 percent reached partnership.

About three-quarters of the time, professionals left the firm of their own volition. More than half of those who left went for more attractive, higher-paying positions in other companies. Others left because of personal incompatibilities with the degree of overtime or travel, or because of other elements of life on the job. Some returned to school. The remaining quarter left at the suggestion of the firm itself; those were split between professionals who lacked the technical ability to do the job and those who lacked some other personal qualities that were required. While an up-or-out system might be viewed as harsh, Arthur Andersen & Co. was famed for its concern for the placement of its accountants in other jobs, often with valued clients.

The pyramid concept raised several issues. Broad pyramids meant lower costs, but because they encouraged the delegation of responsibilities to lower levels of the pyramid, there were quality control and cost-effectiveness issues associated with doing business that way. For example, staff might not have the capability or the training to do all that may be requested of them, or they might take a longer time than some more senior professionals in doing some job, thus raising the specter of cost effectiveness.

Another issue involved client perceptions. The accountants at client companies were knowledgeable about firm operations, since they were frequently former Big-Eight professionals themselves. Often they would prefer experienced personnel and staff continuity. The Charlotte office was careful about making its assignments and had to consider each client's perceptions on staffing.

The Cycle of Business Planning

Given the labor intensity of auditing, business planning for the Charlotte office was very much an exercise in determining labor needs. The business plan for the audit practice started with a forecast of chargeable hours for the Carolinas' four offices. The area had been growing and Arthur Andersen & Co. had been developing additional clients, so chargeable hours were growing at a healthy clip.

Once a defensible forecast of chargeable hours was developed, "productivity factors" (that is, average chargeable hours per person per year) were applied to determine how many people would be needed. In general, the Charlotte office averaged between 1400 and 1500 chargeable hours per person per year. That number differed by level within the pyramid: partners generally had the fewest and seniors the most. Nonchargeable hours were taken up in a variety of activities, including training, marketing and sales promotion, community service, administrative tasks, recruiting, and, of course, inefficiently used time. Given the application of the productivity factors to the forecasted chargeable hours, the office figured out how many people it needed. This, in turn, determined how many new recruits were needed to make up for any personnel shortfalls.

The business plan's forecast of profitability depended on the fee structure as well as the manpower plan. With the growth of business in the Carolinas, there was heavy competition for new business. The Charlotte office took this into account in developing its fee structure to match its chargeable hour plan and its staffing plan.

Scheduling

As mentioned previously, personnel scheduling was a key determinant of the office's profitability. The Charlotte office had responsibility for scheduling not only its own operation but coordinating those of Greensboro, Raleigh, and Columbia as well. One manager-level professional was assigned full time to the scheduling and other division administration functions.

The scheduling process began with the managers in charge of the office's engagements. For each engagement, the manager indicated how many hours of which levels of professional were required. (See Figure I2.) The manager was also permitted to request specific people to be part of the engagement. This planning could often be done far in advance, due to the recurring nature of much of the office's business. Each December and January, a rough-cut schedule for the following May through April period was devised.

The allocation of people to jobs was depicted on two different schedules: (1) the long-range schedule that planned people's assignments for an entire year, by week, and (2) the six-week schedule, which was a daily, more detailed and up-to-date version of the long-range schedule. Both of these schedules were known in the office as the "railroad," largely because the schedule itself looked like tracks on paper. (See Figures I3 and I4.)

The scheduling manager was responsible for pulling together the original schedule and then for adjusting it as time wore on and inevitable changes occurred. Naturally, the Charlotte office's profitability was greatest when everybody was fully scheduled and working effectively. The inexperienced staff accountants tended to have the most "open holes" in their schedules, and thus they were a constant concern for the scheduling manager. He reviewed the schedule continually to see whether all of the jobs being worked on were properly staffed. Was the pyramid broad enough for them? Were some projects in need of help? Were the Greensboro, Raleigh, and Columbia offices

CLIENT NAME AND # _COMPANY 555_
DESCRIPTION OF WORK _Audit_
CLIENT YEAR-END _12-31_
LOCATION OF WORK _CCT_
DATE SUBMITTED

MASTER JOB SCHEDULING SHEET

SUGGESTED STAFF PERSONS-
IN CHARGE _AA_
STAFF _BB_

THIS JOB CAN BE STAFF WITH ONE-
MID-YEAR OR INTERN ☐ TAX ASSISTANT ☐ MIC ASSISTANT ☐

	Staff Class	Total Hours	P	F	April				May				June				July				Aug.				Sept.				Oct.				Nov.				Dec.				Jan.				Feb.				March			
					1	8	15	22	29	6	13	20	27	3	10	17	24	1	8	15	22	29	5	12	19	26	2	9	16	23	30	7	14	21	28	4	11	18	25	2	9	16	23	30	6	13	20	27	3	10	17	24	3	10	17	24	30
PARTNER		20																						2				2																				
MANAGER		68																						4				8														8	8	40	
STAFF	SR	102																					16	-	X		X	16	X								16	16	40	
	EA	156																					16	-	X		X	40	X								40	10	40	
	IA	168																							X	40	X				8							40	40	40	
TOTAL STAFF HRS.		426																																											

Instructions:

1. Total hours shown should agree with the hours shown in the fee estimate or reconciled thereto. "Cushion" should not be scheduled.

2. Requirements for recurring type audits of Foundations, Pension Plans, etc., may be submitted separately or included as part of the time submitted for recurring audit of the Company financial statements. However, such time should be clearly identified as part of "Description of Work." If submitted on a combined basis, there should still be a clear indication of the pension, quarterly review, recurring registration statement, etc., time requirements.

3. Requirements for nonrecurring work including registration statements and major one-time projects should be submitted on a separate job scheduling sheet.

4. Requirements should be shown based on the ideal scheduling, however, where the time is absolutely not flexible, please so indicate in the "Comments" section. This is extremely important.

5. Known overtime requirements should be shown by merely showing Total Hours as 45 or 55 or whatever. In general, we would prefer to minimize overtime in all cases. When required, we should, in particular, attempt to avoid overtime at preliminary dates and for extended periods of time. Our office policy on overtime requires Partner/Manager approval of overtime.

6. In determining time requirements for each job, please consider the office need to achieve a balance of various experience levels on each job. Approximately 50% of our staff has one year or less experience.

7. Minimize situations where staff are assigned to a job for periods of time exceeding 400–500 hours or for extended periods on one job, particularly if out of town. Consider expanding the number of staff assigned.

Comments

Final is not flexible

FIGURE I2   A sample master job scheduling sheet, as used at Arthur Andersen & Co.—Charlotte.

```
CAROLINAS                           PERSONNEL SCHEDULING                    PAGE- 2        AS OF-20 NOV 85
DIVISION: CHARLOTTE AUDIT           PERSONNEL ASSIGNMENTS                                  PREP-20 NOV 85
TO: 450561                                                                                RPT-EC01000
FOR: CC, ASR, 206440
HOME ADDRESS:
                         LOC           SCHED
                         OFF  PTR MGR  HRS TO 11      12         01         02         03         04         05
JOB NUMBER/JOB YEAR END   DIV  SENIOR  STAT DATE 18 25 02 09 16 23 30 06 13 20 27 03 10 17 24 03 10 17 24 31 07 14 21 28 05 12
JOB NAME/DESCRIPTION
-----------------------  ---  -------  ----- ----- -- -- -- -- -- -- -- -- -- -- -- -- -- -- -- -- -- -- -- -- -- -- -- -- -- --
                              FGJ DLW   I    140:40  :    36:40 24:32   :    :50 50:50 50:50 50:      :         :         :
COMPANY 234              CC                        :      :         :         :         :         :         :         :
                                                  :      :         :         :         :         :         :         :
                              PAG RDG   I    240:      :      :         :         :         :10   :24  8:      :40 40>
COMPANY 345              CC                        :      :         :         :         :         :         :
                                                  :      :         :         :         :         :         :
                              FGJ JCH   I    260:      :      :         :         :         :         :40   :
COMPANY 456              CC                        :      :         :         :         :         :         :
                                                  :      :         :         :         :         :         :
4310000                  BRG                      :      : 3:      :         :         :         :         :
AUDIT DIV MEETING                                 :      :         :         :         :         :         :
                                                  :      :         :         :         :         :         :
555                                              :  2   :      :         :         :         :         :
P/M MEETING OR OFFICE MTG                         :      :         :         :         :         :         :
                                                  :      :         :         :         :         :         :
815                                              : 16:      :  16: 8   :         :         :         :
HOLIDAY                                           :      :         :         :         :         :         :
                                                 -- --  -- -- -- -- -- -- -- -- -- -- -- -- -- -- -- -- -- -- -- -- -- -- -- --
•TOTAL ASSIGNED HOURS          42 16    39 40 40 40       50 50 50 50 50 10    24  8       40       40 40
•TOTAL CHARGEABLE HOURS        40       36 40 24 32       50 50 50 50 50 10    24  8       40       40 40
•TOTAL NON-CHARGEABLE HOURS     2 16     3    16  8
•TOTAL OVERTIME HOURS
 TOTAL TENTATIVE HOURS          2                        50 50 50 50 50 10    24  8       40       40 40
 TOTAL UNASSIGNED HOURS              24 40  1       40 40 40          30 40 16 32 40 40    40
-----------------------------------------------------------------------------------------------------------
SCHEDULING CONSIDERATIONS:                                                       -----------------------------

•   INCLUDES TENTATIVE HOURS
•• STATUS - I = INCHARGE PERSON, R = REVISED SCHEDULE, T, X = TENTATIVE ASSIGNMENT,      •••••••••••••••••••
            C = STAFFING CONTINUITY, O = OUT OF TOWN                               • CC
                                                                                  • 18 NOV 85    WEEKS 1 - 26 •
                                                                                  •••••••••••••••••••
```

FIGURE I3   A long-range schedule, as used at Arthur Andersen & Co.—Charlotte.

AUDIT DIVISION PERSONNEL ASSIGNMENTS

11/22/85
Charlotte

Six Weeks Ending--January 4, 1985

Seniors	W/B 11/25 (M25 T26 W27 TH28 F29 S30)	W/B 12/2 (M2 T3 W4 TH5 F6 S7)	W/B 12/9 (M9 T10 W11 TH12 F13 S14)	W/B 12/16 (M16 T17 W18 TH19 F20 S21)	W/B 12/23 (M23 T24 W25 TH26 F27 S28)	W/B 12/30 (M30 T31 W1 TH2 F3 S4)
AA 7/82	987-------------HOL---	Company 987-----------	987------------------DM	Company 987-------------	987-HOL--------987-------	987--------HL----987 ----
BB 7/83	CHAR-S HOL---		Company 876--------DM	Company 678-----------	V----HOL--------VAC----	876 HOL
CC 7/83	REF HOL---	Company 123-----------	Company 123--------DM	Company 123-------------	123-HOL--------123------	123--------HL----123 ----
DD 12/82	NY OFCE------ HOL---	NY OFFICE -----------	NY OFFICE ----------DM	NY OFFICE ---------------	V----HOL -------	NY---------HL----NY -----
EE 6/85	753----------- HOL---	Company 684-----------	684--------------------DM	684------------------------	HOL -------	HOL
FF 6/83						
GG 7/82	357-------- HOL---	Company 555-----------	Company 444--------DM	555------------------------	HOL -------	444--------HOL
HH 8/83	45------------- HOL---	Company 776-----------	776--------------------DM	Company 884-------------	HOL -------	884--------HOL
II 7/82	56 HOL---	Company 86-----------	Company 933--------DM	Company 816-------------	23-HOL--------23 -------	23---------HL----23-------
JJ 9/83	740------------- HOL---		DM	740	V---HOL--------VAC-----	740--HOL
KK 12/84	517------------- HOL---	517 ------------------------	DM	REF 987 -------	HOL -------	517--------HL---517 -----

FIGURE 14   A six-week schedule, as used at Arthur Andersen & Co.—Charlotte.

busy? Could professionals be swapped between offices? The Charlotte scheduler acted as the central clearinghouse for the staffing needs of all of the Carolinas offices. In trying to fill the open holes in the schedule, he relied most on the six-week schedule, which was the one that was painstakingly updated with all the changes, and which was the office's controlling document for the next six weeks. That document was organized by individual and displayed the open holes for each professional in the Carolinas, as well as which engagements everyone was scheduled for. An associated document was generated automatically to show the converse, namely, which professionals in the office were available in each week. This document identified candidate professionals who could help with a new or existing engagement. (See Figure 15.)

As might be expected, there were continual inconsistencies in the schedule that had to be resolved. These inconsistencies resulted from many things—new work, changes in personnel, or changes in the scope of an existing engagement. Consider the following situation. The Greensboro office not only had been very busy but was short of seniors as well. The existing seniors there were working too much overtime and needed to be relieved in some way. As it happened, a new senior had been transferred to the Charlotte office from Dallas and was due soon. The scheduler's dilemma was how to help the Greensboro office without giving them the new senior for too long a time, because, after all, he had been transferred into Charlotte and not Greensboro. The scheduler knew that it would be toughest to adjust the schedule during the peak time of the year (February and March), so he concentrated on helping Greensboro during those two months. By consulting the schedule, he knew that the new senior could be used on the Company 792 engagement for the weeks of February 17, February 24, and March 3. That engagement also called for a senior's time dur-

```
CAROLINAS
DIVISION: CHARLOTTE AUDIT              PERSONNEL SCHEDULING                        PAGE-   1      AS OF-20 NOV 85
TO: 450561                                                                                       PREP-20 NOV 85
                                    PERSONNEL AVAILABILITY (CONDENSED)                            RPT-EC03100

            PERS                        AVAIL 11   12            01         02        03          04         05
CLASS GROUP NUMBER CLAS PERSONNEL NAME  TENT  18 25 02 09 16 23 30 06 13 20 27 03 10 17 24 03 10 17 24 31 07 14 21 28 05 12
----------  ------ ---- --------------  ----- -- -- -- -- -- -- -- -- -- -- -- -- -- -- -- -- -- -- -- -- -- -- -- -- -- --
SENIORS     115312 ASR  AA              AVAIL:    24:    :      :   40:      :   40:40 40:40 40:40 16:     :40 40:40 40:
            206440 ASR  CC              AVAIL:    24:40 1:    :   40:40 40:    :       :30 40:0 16 32:40 40:    40:      :
            295868 ASR  DD              AVAIL:38 24:40 37:40 24:32 40:24    :   :40 40:40 40:     :24 32:40 40:40 40:40 40:
            374725 ASR  EE              AVAIL:38 24:    1:   24:32 40:      :   :40    :   40:40 40:     :40 40:40 40:40 40:
            595772 ASR  HH              AVAIL:       :   1:   24:32 40:      :       :   :40 40:40 40:40 40:40 40:40 40:
            657221 ASR  JJ              AVAIL:    24:40 37:40  :16 40:      :       :   :   40:40 40:     :40 40:40 40:40 40:
            692981 ASR  KK              AVAIL:       :   37:40 24:32    :      :       :   40:  40:40 40:40 40:40 40:40 40:
            743739 ASR  LL              AVAIL:       :   37:40 24:24    :      :       :40 40:40 40:40 40:40 40:40 40:40 40:
            778001 ASR  MM              AVAIL: 6    :   1:40  :      :      :       :   40:40 40:    40:40 40:40 40:40 32:
            941701 ASR  NN              AVAIL:38 24:40 37:40 24:32 40:40 40:40 40:40 40:40 40:40 40:40 40:40 40:40 40:40 40:

            STANDARD WORKLOAD           40 24 40 40 40 24 32 40 40 40 40 40 40 40 40 40 40 40 40 40 40 40 40 40 40 40

                                                                        * 20 NOV 85   WEEKS 1-26  *
```

FIGURE 15   A personnel availability chart, as used at Arthur Andersen & Co.—Charlotte.

ing the week of December 2nd, which was fine, as the new senior was going to be in Charlotte at that time. In addition, Greensboro needed help on the Company 409 engagement for the weeks of February 3 and February 10. That also called for work in the week of December 23. This, too, fitted well into the new senior's schedule.

However, there were two other engagements, Company 642 and Company 322, that would need additional manpower and could not be assigned to the new senior. The scheduler looked to the six-week schedule for holes and then also looked at the personnel availability sheet for the time period greater than six weeks away. No one senior had time available in all of the time periods required for the jobs under consideration: thus, there were some incompatibilities that the scheduler had to check into and resolve. Upon investigation, two seniors' schedules showed some promise. In evaluating the jobs assigned to each of them during this period, it looked like one would be the more available. However, he would not be free for all of the three weeks slated for those jobs. He was available during the weeks of December 9 and December 16, but he was not available during the week of January 20, as he was sched-

uled on another job in the Greensboro office. The scheduler then had to do some horse trading. In order for him to assign the senior to the Greensboro office for the 642 and 322 jobs, he needed to take the senior off his other assignment at Greensboro. By calling around to the interested parties, it was agreed that the senior could be taken off the Greensboro job for the week of January 20 and thus assigned to the 642 and 322 jobs that were coming up immediately. The hope was that the Greensboro office could delay work on that job until sometime later, or, if that was not possible, perhaps use another senior for the week of January 20.

The scheduler continually made trade-offs in this way, for the most part following a hierarchy of preferences: (1) substitute a similar-level professional for the professional initially planned for (possible for preliminary audit work but not for final audit work), (2) substitute an available professional from a different level, if he or she were qualified, and (3) let the schedule slip so that the desired personnel could perform the job at a more convenient date. During the course of any week, there might be two or three problems that consumed up to four hours each to resolve. In addition, there were a host of smaller problems that might be resolved much more easily, say within an hour's time each.

The scheduler was in repeated contact with the managers who oversaw the office's engagements. Those managers informed the scheduler of changes in their needs, and they occasionally lobbied him for particular professionals to work their engagements. Sometimes, particularly with new clients, staff and seniors would also lobby the scheduler for those jobs. An important task for the scheduler was balancing the training and development needs of staff accountants and seniors against the practice's need for their services and the client company's desires for continuity in the personnel assigned to them.

PERSONNEL POLICY

While profitability was tied to the pyramid and to the efficient scheduling of people, the Charlotte office's managing partner believed that in the long run Arthur Andersen & Co. would be successful only if it served its clients well. His major concern was with the development of the professionals in the office and the culture in which they worked. Culture, of course, is an elusive concept, but a variety of indications of the Arthur Andersen & Co. culture could be cited:

- The Arthur Andersen motto: think straight, talk straight.
- No secrets were kept around the office.
- Team work and attention to detail were highly valued.
- Also valued was client service and the urgency in that. There was a "code red" program that called for some member of the engagement team to return a client's phone call within 60 minutes, no matter where the engagement's lead partner or manager might find themselves.
- The pride that Arthur Andersen had in having the widely acknowledged premier training program of any of the Big Eight.
- The desire that Charlotte's managing partner had for everyone to have fun doing their jobs. In support of this, the goal was to have every professional assigned to the industry of his preference at least half the time.
- All the office's professionals were reviewed each year. They filled out a form (Figure I6) and then met with a partner to discuss their performance and career development.

Training

One of the partners was responsible for monitoring the training of all of the audit professionals. Training at Arthur Andersen & Co. was done either within the local office or at the firm-wide level. To this end, the firm operated a training center in St. Charles, Illinois, and brought professionals from all over the world to it on a regular basis. Continuing professional education was required of all CPAs by the national and various states' accounting societies (120 hours over 3 years with no less than 20 hours per year in any year), so even partners and managers spent time in training. For the most part, partners and managers averaged at least 40 hours per year, while staff and seniors were likely to be more heavily involved in training. In the first year, for example, most staff accumulated between 150 and 200 hours of training, with 100 to 120 hours spent locally, and the balance at either the regional level or at the St. Charles campus. Seniors did not spend quite that much time, but they too spent a considerable amount of time in training.

Training was considered as important as a client assignment for the professionals in the

TO: _____
                          Reviewing Partner

FROM: _____

DATE: _____

SUBJECT: ANNUAL REVIEW _____

1. Am I satisfied with the assignments I have had? What particular assignments (industry, technical specialization, research, compliance, etc.) would I like in the next year?

    _____

    _____

2. What, if any, particular training would I like to receive during the next year?

    _____

    _____

3. Are the demands made upon me as a professional (overtime, travel, work pace, etc.) acceptable?

    _____

    _____

4. Am I progressing at a pace satisfactory to me?

    _____

    _____

5. Is my performance being evaluated currently and adequately?

    _____

    _____

6. My interests in professional and civic activities are:

    _____

    _____

7. Ideas or suggestions for the Firm:

    _____

    _____

8. Any concerns:

    _____

    _____

FIGURE I6 An annual review form used at Arthur Andersen & Co.—Charlotte.

office. The training plan was usually developed well in advance, and put out "on the railroad." Good attendance was viewed as important for career development. The slow period from April through August was the best time of year for training, although training programs were scheduled throughout the year.

The training program was considerably varied. Some of the programs were very basic for the first- and second-year professionals, but other programs were termed either intermediate or advanced. Some of these courses dealt with interpersonal relationships, marketing, effective presentations, and other aspects of management development. Still other courses had industry orientations, so that professionals could be better steeped in the nature and problems of the specific industries they served.

Recruiting

Recruiting was another important function that was overseen by a partner and that demanded considerable time from the senior professionals in the office. Recruiting concentrated on local schools, although all the recruiting was done for the firm at large and not just for the Charlotte office. Recruiting was done at both the undergraduate and the MBA levels.

The Manager's Life

Managers oversaw the day-to-day operations of each audit engagement. It was their job to see that the audit was done well and on time and that the fee level was appropriate. They were responsible for developing the staffing plan and budget for the engagement and for billing and collecting from the client. Managers wanted to avoid any surprises on an engagement, and thus it was in their interest to have seniors and staff that could be trusted and whose competence and capabilities would be unquestioned.

Managers spent a good deal of their time outside the office—perhaps 60 percent to 75 percent. Most of that time was spent at existing clients, attending to their needs and solving any problems that had cropped up. About 20 percent to 25 percent of the manager's time was spent with administrative chores. And, because managers were partners-in-training to a large degree, they spent some of their time developing new clients and new business for the firm.

In the main, managers were pleased with their lives at Arthur Andersen & Co. Their jobs were viewed as challenging, motivating, and educational, and the partners gave them a good deal of autonomy. The partners were also regarded as fair, and the up-or-out nature of the business was not unduly confining because the managers felt they could easily leave the firm for attractive jobs elsewhere.

The Partner's Life

Many duties fell on the partners in the Charlotte office. The typical partner incurred about 1000 hours each year that were charged to the engagements on which he was the senior member. Of that time, perhaps two-thirds was spent at the client, discussing the client's business and supervising the audit there. Other chargeable hours were spent in the planning phase and final report phases of the actual audit. As an accountant and auditor, the partner was responsible for solving problems, for analyzing risk, and for monitoring quality.

The other 1400 to 1500 hours of a partner's year were spent in many different activities: recruiting; training, including teaching the junior people; practice development, which was the marketing and sales function for generating new business; personnel matters, such as counseling junior professionals and reviewing their progress; and providing counsel to other Arthur Andersen & Co. professionals on matters of the partner's own expertise (for example, the Charlotte office was viewed as the firm's source of expertise for textiles).

The partners, as a group, were responsible for a multitude of functions. Not only did they have line responsibility for the audits being done, but they had to divide up the overhead functions necessary to further the practice: training, recruiting, expertise in special industry specializations (such as health care, manufacturing, closely held businesses), practice development, administration, and quality control.

Partners were well compensated. Their high incomes were a motivation for many of the junior people. Arthur Andersen & Co. partners were paid by splitting the worldwide profits of the company, according to how many "units" they held. Each unit was stated in U.S. dollars. All partners started with a fixed quantity of units, and over time, these units were added onto, based upon seniority and merit. In keeping with the no-secrets aspect of the firm, files were kept on all partners, and all partners knew what everyone else in the firm made.

A manager was not promoted to partner based solely on the evaluations of the office in which he or she served. There were uniform standards for the promotion to partner that were overseen by a firm-wide committee. Upon becoming partners, managers were required to contribute some capital to the firm, but this was a rather modest amount relative to the income the partner made.

PART TWO

DISCUSSION

Arthur Andersen & Co. is in no way responsible for the following views and presentation. They remain solely the responsibility of the author.

THE FLOW OF THE PROCESS AND OF INFORMATION

Figure I7 is a very rough process flow diagram of the audit process. It shows the degree of involvement by the various levels comprising the engagement team. This process flow also includes the proposal stage and the selection and scheduling stage for the development of the audit team. The diagram depicts only the major phases of the audit process. One could, of course, develop a more detailed schedule of the work for any engagement, but that detailed schedule would be very particular to the client, and complex as well. It would include many of the work elements of Arthur Andersen & Co.'s audit procedures; as such it is beyond the scope of this service tour.

Likewise, constructing a diagram of the information flow in a process like auditing is wellnigh impossible. The flows of information are so numerous and so idiosyncratic to the client and to the needs of the engagement team itself, that it is not worth characterizing here. A Big Eight accounting organization simply lives on information, and that information flow must be swift, it must involve all layers of the company, and it must carry differing quantities of information.

There are no real distinctions in either the process or information flows during peak versus nonpeak times. During peak times, of course, lots of overtime is put in, and people

	Proposal Writing	Engagement Team Selection and Scheduling	Planning Phase	Specific Risk Analysis Phase	Final Audit Phase
Senior Members of the Engagement Team (Partners and Managers)	High involvement with client and among themselves	High involvement, especially by managers. Scheduler is very much involved	High involvement	Little involvement by partner(s), except for periodic troubleshooting and for quality reviews Day-to-day involvement by manager	High involvement
Junior Members of the Engagement Team (Seniors and Staff)	Little or no involvement	Some preferences for work are stated	Little involvement	High involvement. Much work done at client	Limited involvement

FIGURE I7   Rough process flow diagram for auditing services at Arthur Andersen & Co.—Charlotte.

are perhaps more charged-up about the work, but all of the steps must still be done, and all of the information must still flow as it does at nonpeak times.

DEMANDS OF THE PROCESS ON THE WORKFORCE

The workforce at Arthur Andersen & Co. is composed of the salaried professionals (managers, seniors, staff) and the less numerous support people. The process demands on them are essentially a high degree of training and a tremendous amount of flexibility. The firm's accountants have to move from job to job, to put in long hours when called upon, and to be out in the field for, perhaps, long stretches of time. Some of the work is tedious, although much of the work can be challenging and rewarding.

The firm's accountants, at all levels, must make decisions all the time. Even in the preliminary phase of an audit, there are decisions to be made and many issues that need to be resolved. Thus, the members of an engagement team have to be constantly on the lookout for problems or opportunities (for example, add-on

business) that they should surface to the senior members of the engagement team for resolution. This is one reason why so much continual training is required to keep everyone fresh and knowledgeable as times and clients change.

Accountants must also face the up or out nature of advancement within the firm. Happily, the alternatives to employment are generally good. Arthur Andersen & Co. accountants are typically in high demand by client companies and others. The care with which advancement decisions are made and the counsel given accountants through this process helps to ease any stress that this kind of advancement places on the accountants proceeding through the ranks.

THE PYRAMID [1]

Let us simplify the organizational structure of Arthur Andersen & Co. a bit to examine in more detail the nature of the professional pyramid (Figure I8). Consider only three ranks of professionals: partner, manager, and junior. The partner is chiefly responsible for client relations and the running of the firm itself. The

FIGURE 18   The professional pyramid.

the professionals were used on audits to the following degree:

AUDITORS	TYPICAL TIME COMMITMENT	UTILIZATION RATE
Partner	60 hours	50%
Manager	140 hours	70%
Junior	400 hours	85%
	600 hours	

Note: These are meant to be illustrative and do not reflect figures for Arthur Andersen & Co.

The utilization rates reflect the facts that other things take up professionals' time (training, recruiting, scheduling, counseling, soliciting new business) and that these other activities are relatively more demanding of the senior professionals in the firm.

Given a planning figure of 2000 hours of work per individual per year, one partner could sustain supervision of 16.67 average audits (calculated as 1000 hours of partner time available for audits divided by 60 hours of time per typical audit, or 16.67 audits per year). A manager, on the other hand, could sustain direction of 10 audits (1400 hours available and 140 hours average for each audit.) Thus, for every partner, there has to be 1.67 managers in order for the firm to be balanced. Similarly, a junior can work on 4.25 audits each year (1700 hours available and 400 hours for each audit). In this way, the pyramid's shape is determined: Every partner supports 1.67 managers and 3.92 juniors.

The shape of the pyramid, in turn, largely determines the rate at which professionals can be advanced and how selective that advancement has to be. Assume, for example, that juniors are 6 years in rank and that managers are 4 years in rank. If there are 10 partners, then the pyramid would look as in Figure 19. Suppose that every year a partner has to be added, either to sustain the growth of the firm or to replace a partner who retires or otherwise leaves the

manager is the one who controls the day-to-day activities of the project (engagement)—what there is to do, how it is to be done, and whether it is being done properly, on schedule, and within budget. The junior professional is assigned many of the tasks that constitute the "legwork" of the project. This dispersion of responsibility among partners, managers, and juniors has led some wags to term this hierarchy one of "finders, minders, and grinders."

What determines the shape of the pyramid—whether it is broad or narrow? There are two major determinants of the pyramid's shape:

1. The composition of work on the projects undertaken, and

2. The utilization rates of the firm's professionals.

Let's explore these factors in greater detail.

Assume, for example, that the typical audit of 600 hours required the following time commitments from the firm's professionals and that

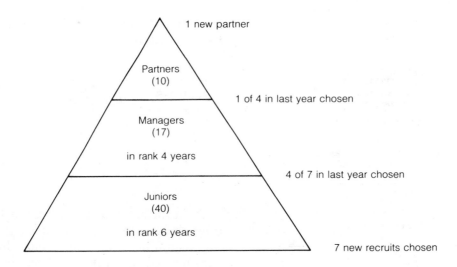

FIGURE 19   The pyramid and advancement.

firm. Every year, then, a manager has to be made a partner in order for the pyramid to be in balance. If, on average each year, 4 of the 17 managers are in the fourth year, then the advancement rate has to be 1 in 4. Similarly, if during any year, 4 new managers are required and there are 7 juniors in their final sixth year, then roughly half of the juniors can be promoted to manager status. In this way, the pyramid sustains itself. Of the 11 juniors and managers in their last year, 1 becomes a partner, 4 become managers, and 6 leave the firm. Of the 7 new recruits, only 1 can expect to make partner after 10 years.

DEMANDS OF THE PROCESS ON MANAGEMENT

The partners in a professional firm like Arthur Andersen & Co. have a number of responsibilities that they alone must shoulder. Many of these responsibilities relate to the workforce. Managing the pyramid well, as discussed earlier, is an absolute requirement. Partners must take the lead in recruiting new accountants, in training them, and in managing their advancement through the firm. These activities take up tremendous chunks of partner time.

Partners must also use that pyramid well in order to make money. Thus, the assignment of accountants to engagements and the scheduling of those accountants are important areas of partner concern. Even though the actual schedule itself is accomplished by a manager-level professional, the partners must develop the strategy underlying the schedules developed.

Partners are also responsible for procuring new business. They are the ones who must contact the clients, develop proposals, and establish fees.

And, of course, the partners must be, in themselves, excellent accountants. They must be intimately involved in the general risk analysis and the final phase of each audit. They are called on to troubleshoot and to review the quality of the audit through all of its phases, particularly the preliminary phase. In addition to this line management authority, they are also called on by others in the firm as experts in certain areas (for example, industries and certain accounting practices). Thus, partners must wear many hats, and are pulled in many different directions.

QUESTIONS

1. What advantages do you see to the hierarchical structure of an accounting firm like Arthur Andersen & Co.? Do you see any disadvantages?

2. What kinds of factors do you suppose would affect the fee schedule advanced in a proposal to a client?

3. In a partner-manager-junior type organization, as described in the discussion to this service tour, suppose the time commitments were changed from a 60–140–400 breakdown to one of 100–200–300. Assuming the same utilization rates, how would the pyramid change, if it were to remain perfectly balanced?

4. What benefits and costs are involved in increasing the average chargeable hours in the office from its current level of 1400–1500 hours per year?

5. What kinds of trade-offs are the hardest for the office's scheduler? What kinds are the easiest?

6. What are the characteristics you would look for in the typical recruit for a staff accountant position?

REFERENCE

1. Much of the discussion is based upon David Maister, "Balancing the Professional Service Firm," *Sloan Management Review*, Fall 1982, pp. 15–29.

SITUATION FOR STUDY I-1
JOHNSON AND TROTTER ADVERTISING

The Johnson and Trotter Advertising Agency was a large, New York based agency with a wide variety of clients. J&T was organized into six functional departments: account management, research, creativity, production, media, and legal. The account management department was charged with client relations and was responsible for coordinating the efforts of all of the other departments on the client's behalf. The research department was responsible for uncovering useful facts about the products and services advertised that may be of use in developing new ads, and they were also charged with substantiating the advertising claims made by the ads. The creativity department was the lead department in developing new ideas and the means by which the client's products and services could be advertised. The production department was responsible for making the print, radio, and TV ads that had been conceived by the creativity department. The media department interacted with all of the media in which the agency's clients advertised, while the legal department handled any legal issues raised by the agency's efforts.

The agency accomplished its work in teams. Members of the various departments generally worked on more than one account at the same time except for the account executive, who was charged with keeping all members of the product team informed about such things as the client's situation, research findings, creative ideas, production status, and any other information on the account. The account executive was also charged with keeping the entire effort on the established timetable and within budget. Members of each product team could expect to spend several years working for a client, before being rotated off.

Any differences of opinion were generally dealt with by compromise within the product team. Account executives did not have the authority to overrule a specialist on a question involving that specialist's realm of expertise. If a difference of opinion persisted, the team could take its dispute to its superiors within each department, where it was usually resolved.

There were three quality control mechanisms at J&T: a strategy review board, a creative review board, and a media review board. At key stages of the firm's process, these quality control mechanisms could be invoked.

Promotion for the professionals of the agency came from within each department. For example, within account management, one typically started as an assistant account executive, moved up to account executive, then, on to account supervisor, management supervisor, and then executive vice-president for client services. A general manager oversaw all of the six functional groups.

1. What strengths do you see in the organization of Johnson and Trotter?

2. What potential disadvantages exist with this operation?

CHAPTER 1

A COMPARISON OF PRODUCTION AND SERVICE PROCESSES

In the Section I tours, nine different production and service processes were introduced and their key features described. There were threads in common among some of them as well as some sharp differences. The purpose of this chapter is to tie together the common threads and expose the sharp differences by comparing the processes described. Part One of the chapter deals with manufacturing while Part Two deals with services.

PART ONE
MANUFACTURING

TRENDS

First we should recognize that there are some clearly discernible trends among the six manufacturing processes introduced. The trends become evident when the processes are arrayed in the following order, a sort of "spectrum" of production processes:

- Job shop (example: Norcen Industries)
- Batch flow (example: Jos. A. Bank)
- Worker-paced line flow (example: Burger King Restaurant—Burlington, North Carolina)*
- Machine-paced line flow (example: GM C-P-C group—Tarrytown, New York)
- Continuous flow (example: International Paper Company, Androscoggin Mill)

The hybrid process represented by the Stroh brewery at Winston-Salem, which displayed aspects of both a batch flow and a continuous flow process, is somewhat more difficult to place since it is not as pure an example as the others.

*The Burger King restaurant can be viewed usefully as both a manufacturing process (a burger factory) and a service process (a fast food restaurant). For this reason, it is included in both parts of this chapter.

233

ANALYZING THE TRENDS

In order to provide some cohesion and organization, this discussion of process trends is divided into six parts, each part devoted to a comparison and analysis of some specific features: (1) product features, (2) general process features, (3) materials-oriented features, (4) information-oriented features, (5) labor-oriented features, and (6) management features. These six features will be addressed in turn.

Product Features

Arrayed as they have been here, the different processes introduced demonstrate some distinct trends involving the types of products manufactured and how those products compete against others. Specifically, the more one goes from a job shop toward a continuous flow process, the more it is generally the case that:

1. The number of different kinds of products made declines.
2. Product volumes increase to the point where the continuous flow process is essentially producing a commodity for the mass market.
3. Product customization declines and product standardization increases.
4. New product introductions become less frequent and are more costly.
5. Competition is more likely to center on price.
6. Competition, at least in the middle ranges of the array, is more likely to emphasize aspects like workmanship, product performance, and product reliability; but as the process becomes more and more a continuous flow, these differences between rival products become narrower and narrower.

General Process Features

There are complementary trends in some general process features as well. For example, as one progresses down the array of processes from job shop to continuous flow, it is generally true that:

1. The pattern of the process becomes more rigid, and the routing of products through their various process steps becomes less individual, less unprescribed, and better defined.
2. Process segments become more tightly linked together.
3. Equipment becomes more specialized.
4. The operation becomes huge, and economies of scale are possible.
5. More, and generally larger, equipment is part of the process.
6. Equipment is less likely to be idle. Pieces of equipment become better balanced in size and speed to one another.
7. Equipment setups are fewer and run lengths are longer.
8. The pace of the process is determined largely by machine capabilities or regulated by machines or conveyors.
9. The pace of production keeps increasing.
10. The notion of capacity becomes less ambiguous and more measurable in physical, rather than dollar, units.
11. Additions to capacity come in large chunks, and incremental additions to capacity become less viable.
12. Bottlenecks become less and less movable and thus better understood.
13. Incremental change to the nature of the process itself becomes relatively more frequent and routine, but the impact of radical

change to the process is likely to be more sweeping and thus scarier to contemplate.

14. Process layouts, with like machines grouped together, give way to line flow layouts.

Materials-Oriented Features

Again, keeping the array of different processes ordered from job shop through continuous flow process, some general trends in materials-oriented features can be observed. For example, as the process becomes more and more a continuous flow, it becomes more and more the case that:

1. The span of the process (vertical integration) becomes broader. A plant is more and more likely to start with "very raw" raw materials and transform them into products that may need little or no "finishing" before consumers purchase them.

2. Most processes take uniform materials and make differentiated products from them. Norcen Industries takes uniform blocks, bars, or rods of steel and machines a multitude of different parts from them. Jos. A. Bank uses the same materials to produce suits in different styles and sizes. The parts going into a Buick Century are much the same as go into a Pontiac 6000; moreover, General Motors goes to great lengths to make sure that cars that are supposed to be exactly alike contain exactly the same components. Such is not the case with many continuous flow processes. Often these processes take differentiated raw materials and make uniform products from them. One log of timber may not be the same as the next log, and so pulp and paper mills are constantly monitoring their raw materials and adjusting them so that the finished product, be it publication gloss or newsprint, looks exactly the same at the end of the roll as it does at the start. Similarly, steel plant blast furnaces make constant changes to their raw materials input mix.

3. As the time of actual production draws closer, materials requirements are generally known with more certainty.

4. Raw materials requirements are large, but their purchase and delivery can be made steady.

5. Supplier ties are long term, with frequent deliveries.

6. Because of large production volumes and steady purchases, control over suppliers for price, delivery, quality, design, and the like is great.

7. Control over the delivery time of the finished product becomes greater.

8. Work-in-process inventories, because of process design, become scant. Queues of work cease to exist.

9. Finished goods inventories are larger (relative to other inventories).

10. Finished goods are sold through formal distribution channels and can sometimes be forced down those channels for the sake of keeping production running smoothly.

Importantly, however, the batch/continuous flow hybrid process does not follow all of these trends. There is a definite work-in-process inventory situated between the batch flow portion of the process and the continuous flow portion. At least some of the raw materials are inventoried as a buffer stock to be drawn down in perhaps unexpected or haphazard fashion, while other raw materials are purchased to coincide with the production plan.

Information-Oriented Features

A number of trends are evident as well for many information-oriented features of the various production processes. As the process changes from job shop to continuous flow, generally it is more and more likely that:

1. Production has not been instigated by a bidding procedure.
2. Longer-term sales forecasts are used, and orders are "frozen" long before production is scheduled to start.
3. The corporation outside the plant is an integral part of the plant's scheduling and materials movement tracking.
4. Order scheduling is done on a very sophisticated basis.
5. A finished goods inventory is managed.
6. The flow of information and paperwork between management and workers is less.
7. Quality control measures become formal.
8. Inventory adjustments become important in responding to seasonal or business cycle changes in demand.
9. The process is less flexible in making swift adjustments to demand changes, and so production must be carefully planned in advance.

Labor-Oriented Features

Again, trends are evident across the spectrum of production processes explored, this time concerning labor issues. Progressing from job shop to continuous flow process, it is more likely that:

1. The labor content of the product becomes smaller and smaller, relative to the product's value.

2. Job contents diminish, although "art" is more likely to be found at either end of the process spectrum.
3. Labor is paid by the hour rather than by some incentive system. In fact, the progression of wage payment schemes tends to go from hourly or individual incentive rates for the job shop, through individual and then group incentive schemes, and then on to hourly rates.
4. The importance of setting standards for labor remains high. The mechanization of the continuous flow process, however, means that such standards are useful less to define the process and its capacity than to assign the workforce to the equipment.
5. As production moves more and more to mechanical or technological pacing, the scramble to complete a lot of production to meet monthly goals or billings becomes less and less prevalent.
6. The path of worker advancement becomes more well-defined and even formal.

Management Features

Finally, some trends can be identified as well for several aspects of the management of these diverse production processes. Progressing from job shop to continuous flow process, it is more and more the case that:

1. Staff operations concerning such topics as materials movement, scheduling, capacity planning, new technology planning, and quality control become more important relative to line operations.
2. The size of the plant's management (line and staff) is often larger relative to the size of the workforce both because the capital intensity of the operation is greater and because staff operations are more important.

TABLE 1-1   Ratio of management staff to total employment

COMPANY	PROCESS	MANAGEMENT STAFF/ TOTAL EMPLOYMENT
Norcen Industries	Job shop	7/41 = 0.171
Jos. A. Bank	Bath flow	28/362 = 0.077
Burger King, Burlington	Worker-paced line flow	5/61 = 0.082
C-P-C—Tarrytown	Machine-paced line flow	475/4475 = 0.106
Stroh, Winston-Salem	Batch/continuous flow hybrid	80/670 = 0.119
International Paper, Androscoggin Mill	Continuous flow	175/1200 = 0.146

Table 1-1 uses statistics from the processes we have discussed to show the ratio of management staff to total employees.

3. Given that the plant involved is part of a multiplant company, the involvement of managers situated at the corporate offices (rather than at the plant itself) becomes greater. The corporation's influence may extend to operations as well as to capital planning and spending.

4. The operation is controlled more as a cost center, as opposed to a profit center.

5. The major challenges that management faces are significantly altered, largely shifting from day-to-day operational considerations to very long-term, high-expense items.

THE PROCESS SPECTRUM

By comparing these trends it is fairly plain that entire lists of characteristics hang together to describe particular processes. Table 1-2 is an effort to compile just such lists for the range of production processes that have been introduced. Note that the batch/continuous flow hybrid, exemplified by the Stroh brewery, has been segregated from the others so that the process spectrum stretching from job shop through to continuous flow process remains as pure as we can reasonably expect.

Table 1-2 offers some generalizations about particular types of production processes, drawing mainly from the processes discussed in the plant tours. Not all of the generalizations may ring true for all of the production processes one may conceivably classify in each category from job shop to continuous flow process. Most of the generalizations, however, are representative of a typical production process in each category.

THE PRODUCT-PROCESS MATRIX

Another useful way to visualize some of the similarities and differences among different types of production processes is to array the processes within what has been called the product-process matrix.[1] This matrix is nothing fancier than a box, one side of which describes the varieties of product mixes that are possible and another side of which describes the process patterns (the ease of flow of product through the process) that are possible. Figure 1-1 portrays this.

As we can see in Figure 1-1, the mix of products handled by the plant may range from a one-of-a-kind item (such as a work of art or a custom-designed house) to a very standard product that is produced and consumed in high volumes (such as sugar). In between, a company can produce many different products, each at relatively

TABLE 1-2 Comparing processes of different types

FEATURES	(1) JOB SHOP (example: Norcen Industries)	(2) BATCH FLOW (example: Jos. A. Bank)	(3) WORKER-PACED ASSEMBLY LINE (example: Burger King® Restaurant, Burlington)	(4) MACHINE-PACED ASSEMBLY LINE (example: C-P-C Group, Tarrytown)	(5) CONTINUOUS FLOW (example: International Paper, Androscoggin Mill)	BATCH/ CONTINUOUS FLOW HYBRID (example: Stroh Brewery, Winston-Salem)
			PRODUCT FEATURES			
Product mix	Generally custom products	Lots of generally own designed products	Mostly standard products; some opportunities for selected options	Same as for 3	Standard products with little or no customization possible; not produced in discrete units, so has to be measured in tons, barrels, and so on	Same as for 3 and 4
Products compete largely on:	Speed of delivery, product customization, new product introduction	Product performance, product reliability and workmanship, delivery reliability, new product introduction, flexibility to produce either low or high volumes	Product performance, price, product reliability and workmanship, delivery reliability	Product performance, price, product reliability and workmanship, delivery reliability	Price	Product reliability and workmanship, price
Products unlikely to compete on:	Price				New product introduction, product customization	
New product introduction	All the time; easy	Frequent; routine	Sometimes	Sometimes; generally expensive	Hardly at all; very costly	Infrequent; expensive
			PROCESS FEATURES			
Process pattern	No rigid pattern; product can be routed anywhere; sometimes a dominant flow	Not all procedures performed on all products; product can be routed many ways; often a dominant flow	Clear pattern, though special treatment of some products sometimes permitted	Clear, rigid pattern, though some off-line work possible	Clear, very rigid pattern	Same as for 5

TABLE 1-2 Comparing processes of different types (*continued*)

FEATURES	(1) JOB SHOP (example: Norcen Industries)	(2) BATCH FLOW (example: Jos. A. Bank)	(3) WORKER-PACED ASSEMBLY LINE (example: Burger King® Restaurant, Burlington)	(4) MACHINE-PACED ASSEMBLY LINE (example: C-P-C Group, Tarrytown)	(5) CONTINUOUS FLOW (example: International Paper, Androscoggin Mill)	BATCH/CONTINUOUS FLOW HYBRID (example: Stroh Brewery, Winston-Salem)
PROCESS FEATURES (continued)						
Linking of process segments	Very loose	Loose	Between tight and loose	Tight	Very tight	Loose link between different process types
Type of equipment	General purpose	Mostly general purpose	Specialized	Same as for 3	Same as for 3	Same as for 3, 4, and 5
Balance of equipment	Balance of speed and time done in only the grossest, long-run terms. At any one time, an imbalance is likely to exist	Balance likely to be imperfect between segments of process but better coordinated than typical job shop	Machinery speed and size in good balance with peak needs	Speed and size of equipment very well balanced. Capable of being adjusted together over small changes in line speed	Good balance of speed and size. Any excess capacity often placed in latter portion of process to provide insurance against breakdowns or unusual order requests	Same as for 5
Type of layout	Process layout; similar machines grouped together	Process layout; similar tasks and equipment grouped together	Line flow layout; distinct for product produced	Same as for 3	Same as for 3	Two distinct layouts, one for batch and one for the continuous flow
Capital use	Labor intensive; machines frequently idle	Labor intensive, although less machine idleness	Although equipment is specialized, it is fairly cheap; labor still a big item	Capital intensive	Very capital intensive; machines nearly always used	Same as for 5
Typical size of operation	Generally small	Generally medium-size	Variable	Large	Mammoth	Same as for 4
Economies of scale	None	Few, if any	Same as for 2	Some, perhaps	Yes	Same as for 5
Yields	Often dependent on setup and product complexity	Often dependent on workers; yields usually high	Same as for 2	Often dependent on both workers and equipment function; yields usually high	Often dependent on raw materials; yields can be variable	Can vary depending on type of hybrid

239

TABLE 1-2 Comparing processes of different types (continued)

FEATURES	(1) JOB SHOP (example: Norcen Industries)	(2) BATCH FLOW (example: Jos. A. Bank)	(3) WORKER-PACED ASSEMBLY LINE (example: Burger King® Restaurant, Burlington)	(4) MACHINE-PACED ASSEMBLY LINE (example: C-P-C Group, Tarrytown)	(5) CONTINUOUS FLOW (example: International Paper, Androscoggin Mill)	BATCH/CONTINUOUS FLOW HYBRID (example: Stroh Brewery, Winston-Salem)
			PROCESS FEATURES (continued)			
Notion of capacity	Very fuzzy; definable vaguely in dollar terms; useful only in long run	Fuzzy; product mix implies a dollar definition only	Increasingly clear; some physical unit measures possible	Clear; physical unit measures	Same as for 4	Same as for 4 and 5
Additions to capacity	Incremental over full range of possible capacity	Larger increments possible, but over full range of possible capacity	Same as for 2	Changes can be made, but costly to do so because capacity comes in large chunks; otherwise, mild fluctuations possible within relatively narrow limits (such as line rebalance)	Only modest range for incremental change; otherwise, huge chunks of capacity required	Comparatively modest range for incremental change; then huge chunks of capacity required
Speed of process (dollars of output/unit of time or dollars of output/dollars of input/unit of time)	Slow	Reasonably slow	Increasingly fast	Fast	Fast, sometimes astounding	Same as for 5
Pacing	Worker discretion key	Worker-paced	Worker-paced but set within some bounds by management action (such as line balance)	Machine-paced, but can be a management goal as well (such as line balance)	Determined technologically; built into equipment	Generally determined technologically but some leeway available
Bottlenecks	Movable; frequent	Movable, but often predictable	Occasionally movable, but often predictable	Generally known and stationary	Known, stationary	Same as for 5

240

TABLE 1-2 Comparing processes of different types (continued)

FEATURES	(1) JOB SHOP (example: Norcen Industries)	(2) BATCH FLOW (example: Jos. A. Bank)	(3) WORKER-PACED ASSEMBLY LINE (example: Burger King® Restaurant, Burlington)	(4) MACHINE-PACED ASSEMBLY LINE (example: C-P-C Group, Tarrytown)	(5) CONTINUOUS FLOW (example: International Paper, Androscoggin Mill)	BATCH/ CONTINUOUS FLOW HYBRID (example: Stroh Brewery, Winston-Salem)
			PROCESS FEATURES (continued)			
Nature of process change	Incremental	Mostly incremental; some significant radical changes possible	Mostly routine (rebalance); sometimes radical (equipment)	Same as for 3	Most change incremental but radical change possible; means big bucks and sweeping conversions	Sometimes radical; sometimes incremental
Place of technological change in process itself	Little impact; unlikely to be revolutionary	Important once in a while; usually incremental	Increasingly important; embodied in equipment	Important; embodied in equipment	Far-reaching; surprisingly regular	Same as for 4
Setups	Many; varied expense	Some setups needed, but generally easy to do	Same as for 2	No setup required; line already set up	Few and expensive, if any; process organized to simplify most kinds of setups	Little or no setup required; process simplifies need for most kinds of setups
Run lengths	Short	Medium	Some long, some short	Long	Very long	Same as for 5
			MATERIALS-ORIENTED FEATURES			
Materials requirements	Uncertain	Can often be placed statistically within reasonably narrow bounds	Known statistically within fairly close limits	Certain once production plan established	Same as for 4	Some aspects certain, others known statistically
Character of materials	Set bill of materials; uniform quality; can adapt to nonstandard types	Set bill of materials; uniform quality; often many types possible	Set bill of materials; uniform quality; can adapt to nonstandard types	Same as for 3	Sometimes variable bill of materials; variable quality, since often processes are agricultural/ mining extracts	Sometimes variable quality, sometimes uniform quality
Vertical integration	None	Sometimes backward, sometimes forward	Same as for 2	Sometimes backward, often forward	Often backward and forward	Same as for 2 and 3

241

TABLE 1-2 Comparing processes of different types (continued)

FEATURES	(1) JOB SHOP (example: Norcen Industries)	(2) BATCH FLOW (example: Jos. A. Bank)	(3) WORKER-PACED ASSEMBLY LINE (example: Burger King® Restaurant, Burlington)	(4) MACHINE-PACED ASSEMBLY LINE (example: C-P-C Group, Tarrytown)	(5) CONTINUOUS FLOW (example: International Paper, Androscoggin Mill)	BATCH/ CONTINUOUS FLOW HYBRID (example: Stroh Brewery, Winston-Salem)
MATERIALS ORIENTED FEATURES (continued)						
Inventories Raw materials	Small; most raw materials purchased to coincide with orders	Moderate; some purchased to coincide with orders and some purchased to provide buffer stock	Varies; often steadily purchased since material needs are generally known within reasonably narrow bounds	Varies; often steadily purchased to coincide with production plan	Often large, but can vary and be steadily purchased to coincide with production plan	Varies; some purchased for buffer stock and some purchased to coincide with production plan
Work-in-process	Large	Moderate	Little	Same as for 3	Very little	Inventory placed between batch and continuous flow segments of process; moderate batch WIP, little continuous flow WIP
Finished goods	Low, if any	Varies	Same as for 2	Can vary; often thrust down distribution channels	Varies; often thrust down distribution channels; safety stocks often required	Same as for 5
Control over suppliers	Low	Moderate	Great	Same as for 3	Same as for 3	Same as for 3, 4, and 5
Control over customers	Little or none	Same as for 1	Same as for 1	Same, as to delivery	Same as for 4	Same as for 4 and 5
Supplier ties	Informal; spot buys	Some spot buys, some longer term contracts	Contracts increasingly long term	Formal; long term	Formal; generally long term	Same as for 5
Customer ties	Informal; repeat business encouraged, however	Some informal, some formal distribution	Can be informal or formal	Formal distribution channels	Same as for 4	Same as for 4 and 5

TABLE 1-2 Comparing processes of different types (continued)

FEATURES	(1) JOB SHOP (example: Norcen Industries)	(2) BATCH FLOW (example: Jos. A. Bank)	(3) WORKER-PACED ASSEMBLY LINE (example: Burger King® Restaurant, Burlington)	(4) MACHINE-PACED ASSEMBLY LINE (example: C-P-C Group, Tarrytown)	(5) CONTINUOUS FLOW (example: International Paper, Androscoggin Mill)	BATCH/CONTINUOUS FLOW HYBRID (example: Stroh Brewery, Winston-Salem)
INFORMATION-ORIENTED FEATURES						
Order handling and sales	Often bid for; sales are to order	Varies; some to order, and some from stock with lagged adjustments to that stock	Same as for 2	Sales well established ahead of time or from finished goods inventory; lagged adjustments to stock	Sales well established ahead of time or from finished goods inventory	Same as for 5
Degree of information coordination outside factory	Needed only for bids, receipt of any supplied materials, and to initiate supplies	Needed only to monitor sales and to initiate supplies	Needed to monitor sales and to place orders for supplies; sometimes for order scheduling	Elaborate order scheduling, materials tracking; various levels of forecasts; great deal of corporate communication	Elaborate order scheduling, materials tracking, forecasting; great deal of corporate communication	Monitoring sales, placing supply order; little corporate communication on day-to-day operations
Information systems within factory	Elaborate, viewed as central; lots of flow between factory workers and management; lots of paperwork	Less elaborate, but still considerable; less feedback required; considerable paperwork	Little information needed, basically just to communicate order; flow from management to workers. Opposite flow used primarily to signal breakdowns; more informal; little paperwork	Same as for 3	Little information needed, basically just to communicate product change; flow from management to workers. Opposite flow used primarily to signal breakdowns; generally more informal	Same as for 5
Trigger for production	Order itself; expediting common	Could be order or level of finished goods inventory; some expediting	Level of finished goods inventory, longer term forecasts, or "frozen" orders; little expediting	Level of finished goods inventory, longer term forecasts, or "frozen" orders; no expediting possible	Same as for 4	First portion of process triggered by forecasts; second portion triggered by "frozen" orders

243

TABLE 1-2 Comparing processes of different types (continued)

FEATURES	(1) JOB SHOP (example: Norcen Industries)	(2) BATCH FLOW (example: Jos. A. Bank)	(3) WORKER-PACED ASSEMBLY LINE (example: Burger King® Restaurant, Burlington)	(4) MACHINE-PACED ASSEMBLY LINE (example: C-P-C Group, Tarrytown)	(5) CONTINUOUS FLOW (example: International Paper, Androscoggin Mill)	BATCH/CONTINUOUS FLOW HYBRID (example: Stroh Brewery, Winston-Salem)
INFORMATION-ORIENTED FEATURES (continued)						
Scheduling	Uncertain, flexible; always subject to change	Flexible, but not as uncertain; less subject to change	Process designed around fixed schedule	Same as for 3	Easy to group similar jobs or orders; fixed schedule often set technologically and well in advance	Similar jobs or orders grouped together; fixed schedule set in advance, at least for second portion of process
Quality control	Informal, by each worker; spot checks; machine capabilities can be determined	Can be more formal, though often is not	Some on-line checks, some postassembly checks; process capability can be monitored	Same as for 3	Essentially done by process control people; designed into process; periodic sampling often done and process capability monitored	Much of quality designed into process; periodic sampling often done and process capability monitored
Response to cyclicality in demand	Overtime, shift work, some subcontract, hire/fire	Overtime; adjustments can be made by building and depleting inventory, shift work, and hire/fire	Overtime work or closing line early; some adjustments can be made by building and depleting inventory, rebalance, and close down shift or plant	Same as for 3	Inventory adjustments; otherwise, shift or plant is shut down	Same as for 5
End-of-month syndrome (more produced at end of month for billing than at beginning)	Inevitable	Often happens	Close to nonexistent	Same as for 3	Nonexistent	Same as for 5

TABLE 1-2 Comparing processes of different types (continued)

FEATURES	(1) JOB SHOP (example: Norcen Industries)	(2) BATCH FLOW (example: Jos. A. Bank)	(3) WORKER-PACED ASSEMBLY LINE (example: Burger King® Restaurant, Burlington)	(4) MACHINE-PACED ASSEMBLY LINE (example: C-P-C Group, Tarrytown)	(5) CONTINUOUS FLOW (example: International Paper, Androscoggin Mill)	BATCH/ CONTINUOUS FLOW HYBRID (example: Stroh Brewery, Winston-Salem)
			LABOR-ORIENTED FEATURES (continued)			
Advancement for worker	Knowledge of more and more machinery and machine capabilities. With more skills and/or seniority acquired, greater pay and responsibilities given, such as "lead worker." Seniority can lead to change in shift assignment	Knowledge of more and more machinery and machine capabilities. With more skills and/or seniority acquired, greater responsibilities given, such as "lead worker." Seniority can lead to change in shift assignment or department	With more skills and/or seniority acquired, greater responsibilities given, such as "lead worker" or "group leader." Seniority can lead to change in department or shift assignment	Seniority can lead to change in department or shift assignment	Seniority can lead to change in shift or, sometimes, department assignment	Same as for 5
Worker payment	Hourly; piece rate or other incentive wage	Often piece rate or other incentive wage	Hourly base; sometimes also tied to percentage of standard that crew achieves	Hourly	Same as for 4	Same as for 4 and 5
Labor content per $1 of product value	Very high	High	Medium	Low	Very low	Same as for 4
Job content	Large	Medium	Small	Same as for 3	Often small "push button" stuff; but can be "art" as well	Same as for 5
Importance and development of standards for labor	Key for scheduling and planning growth; big purpose of information system; sometimes key for wage payment	Often key for wage payment; needed also for scheduling product mix	Crucial for process design	Same as for 3	Important largely for assigning workforce to equipment	Same as for 5

245

TABLE 1-2 Comparing processes of different types (*continued*)

FEATURES	(1) JOB SHOP (example: Norcen Industries)	(2) BATCH FLOW (example: Jos. A. Bank)	(3) WORKER-PACED ASSEMBLY LINE (example: Burger King® Restaurant, Burlington)	(4) MACHINE-PACED ASSEMBLY LINE (example: C-P-C Group, Tarrytown)	(5) CONTINUOUS FLOW (example: International Paper, Androscoggin Mill)	BATCH/CONTINUOUS FLOW HYBRID (example: Stroh Brewery, Winston-Salem)
MANAGEMENT FEATURES						
Staff-line needs	Small staff (information, quotes, and new product development). Much line supervision needed	Small staff (generally methods related). Line supervision more critical	Large staff for process redesign, methods, forecasting, capacity planning, and scheduling. Line supervision and troubleshooting still critical	Same as for 3	Large staff for technology and capacity planning, and scheduling. Line supervision less crucial; maintenance key	Same as for 5
Degree of corporate influence on operations, if plant within a multiplant company	Modest	Same as for 1	Same as for 1	Great, for both operations and capital expenditures	Same as for 4	Variable; more likely that corporate influence is with capital expenditures than with day-to-day operations
Means of control	Usually a profit center	Can be either a profit center or a cost center	Same as for 2	Usually a cost center	Same as for 4	Same as for 4 and 5
Challenges to management	Scheduling, bidding, information flows, expediting, product innovation, shifting bottlenecks	Order processing, labor issues and pay, handling cyclicality	Balance (process design), product design, managing workforce, technological advances, capacity planning, materials management	Same as for 3	Capital needs, maintenance, site, technological change, vertical integration, raw materials sourcing	Same as for 5

Product Mix

Process Pattern	One of a kind or few	Low volumes; many products	High volumes; several major products	Very high volumes; standard product (commodity)	Challenges for Management
Very jumbled flow; process segments loosely linked					Scheduling; materials handling; shifting bottlenecks
Jumbled flow, but a dominant flow exists					
Line flow Worker paced					Worker motivation; balance; maintaining enough flexibility
Machine paced					
Continuous, automated, and rigid flow; process segments tightly linked					Capital expenses for big chunk capacity; technological change; materials management; vertical integration
Challenges for Management	Bidding; delivery; product design flexibility	Quality (product differentiation); flexibility in output volumes		Price	

FIGURE 1-1   A product-process matrix.

low volumes, or it can cut down on the number of different products offered but produce higher volumes of each.

As we might expect, management faces different sets of challenges in bringing each of these different product mixes to market. For example, a commodity item undoubtedly has to compete on price. While there may be a limited number of grades of the commodity, the ability to offer the item at low cost is absolutely critical to company success, whether the company produces paper clips or paper.

At the other end of this product mix spectrum, the one-of-a-kind item is frequently purchased with scarcely a thought about price. Since it is a custom item, the buyer is likely to have contracted for it beforehand. Thereafter, the buyer typically becomes concerned about whether the product meets specifications and whether it can be delivered on time. These concerns place a different set of demands on the manufacturer. Instead of paying near-exclusive attention to product cost, the manufacturer must pay particular attention to product design flexibility and delivery, since the manufacturer's success depends more on these features of the production system. Because most work is contracted for, management must be accomplished at developing bids for each, which entails thorough knowledge of costs within the factory.

In between these two extremes, management confronts somewhat different challenges. When many different products—each with low production volumes—are made or when fewer products—each with substantial production volumes—are made, product features such as quality or the ability to gear up (or down) rapidly in production become relatively more important than before. Product quality is a key element in differentiating one's product from others available, and is a chief reason why some products command price premiums. Flexibility in production volumes, while less evident to the marketplace than quality, is often a reason why some companies have been so successful—either beating their competitors to the market with seasonal, cyclical, or faddish products (for example, building supplies or fashions) or turning off production when the market for a product appears to have dried up. Depending on the situation, product design flexibility, price, and delivery can still be very important to the manufacturer; but it is likely that as product design flexibility or quality rises in importance, price falls in importance.

These then are the chief challenges that various product mixes pose for their managers. A corresponding set of management challenges derive from the process patterns depicted in Figure 1-1. As the matrix reveals, the process pat-tern varies from a very jumbled flow to a continuous, automated, and rigid production flow. The linking of segments of the production process varies from loose to tight. The process patterns in between exhibit varying degrees of rigidity, pacing, and process segment linking.

For the jumbled process pattern, the challenges to management include scheduling, routing materials efficiently, and coping with shifting production bottlenecks. At the other end of the process pattern spectrum, the continuous, automated, and rigid process flow demands increased attention to such items as capital expenses for large-scale capacity increases, technological change in the process, materials management, and vertical integration. Between the process poles, factors like worker motivation, balance of capacities for different process segments, and process flexibility become relatively more important.

The arrays of product mix, process patterns, and their respective challenges to management line the outside of the product-process matrix. Now to fill in the inside. As our survey of production processes has revealed, different process types follow different process patterns and are also better suited to particular product mixes. It is easy, then, to match process types to the appropriate position within the matrix, as Figure 1-2 does.

As is readily apparent from the chart, process types should fill out the diagonal of the product-process matrix, from projects and job shops in the upper left corner down to continuous flow processes in the lower right corner. Only by being on the diagonal do processes match properly the process pattern to the prevailing product mix. Consider what it means to be off the diagonal. Suppose, for example, that a company tries to manufacture low volumes of many different products by using a continuous, automated, and rigid flow process that is typically capital intensive and vertically integrated. The

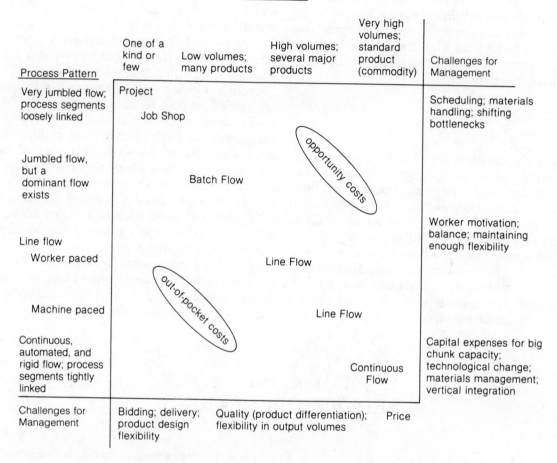

Process Pattern	One of a kind or few	Low volumes; many products	High volumes; several major products	Very high volumes; standard product (commodity)	Challenges for Management
Very jumbled flow; process segments loosely linked	Project Job Shop				Scheduling; materials handling; shifting bottlenecks
Jumbled flow, but a dominant flow exists		Batch Flow			
Line flow Worker paced			Line Flow		Worker motivation; balance; maintaining enough flexibility
Machine paced			Line Flow		
Continuous, automated, and rigid flow; process segments tightly linked				Continuous Flow	Capital expenses for big chunk capacity; technological change; materials management; vertical integration
Challenges for Management	Bidding; delivery; product design flexibility	Quality (product differentiation); flexibility in output volumes	Price		

FIGURE 1-2   The product-process matrix, filled in.

match is clearly inappropriate since the process would have to be interrupted constantly and retooled often to permit the kind of product flexibility needed to produce low numbers of lots of products. Not only is the match inappropriate, but it is expensive. The purchase prices of the automated machines and the cost of product changeovers would be staggering, involving a great deal of out-of-pocket expenses.

Being above the diagonal brings on costs of a different kind. In this case, suppose a very standard product consumed in great quantity were manufactured in a jumbled flow process pattern. Here again the match is clearly inappropriate, though not because too many dollars go out-of-pocket to buy expensive machinery. Rather, operating costs (mainly, labor costs) are much higher than they could be, which means that the profit margin on each unit of the product made is much lower than it should be. By not substituting specific, special purpose machinery for high labor input and general purpose equipment, the company forgoes profits that it would otherwise earn.

OPPORTUNITY COST

This phenomenon goes by the name of "opportunity cost," since by not investing in more equipment and a more rigid production flow, the company is forgoing the *opportunity* to earn increased profits. These costs are every bit as real as the payment of dollars out-of-pocket.

This notion of opportunity cost can be reinforced by a famous saying of Benjamin Franklin, no slouch himself at operations management. To make the point, however, we must make a brief excursion into logic. One truth of logic is the validity of the so-called contrapositive, which says simply that if the statement "If A, then B" is true, then it is also true that "If not B, then not A." That is to say, if every time A occurs B follows, then we can be sure that if B does not occur, then A did not occur as well.

Enough of logic then, and back to Ben Franklin. One of his Poor Richard sayings is that "A penny saved is a penny earned." We have all recognized the truth of that since childhood, but I assert that by this saying Ben showed us he knows everything about opportunity cost. After all, what is the contrapositive of "A penny saved is a penny earned"? A penny *not* earned is a penny *not* saved (that is, a penny spent). All we are saying by this notion of opportunity cost is that "a penny not earned (an opportunity forgone) is a penny spent." We shall often have occasion to consider opportunity costs, as well as out-of-pocket costs, in analyzing and deciding various operations issues.

PART TWO
SERVICE OPERATIONS

DISTINGUISHING SERVICE OPERATIONS FROM MANUFACTURING OPERATIONS

Five of the nine tours described in the preceding section deal strictly with manufacturing operations. The other four, however, reveal significant distinctions between service and manufacturing. Some of the management challenges for service operations parallel those in manufacturing, but others are unique.

What is a service operation anyway? The answer to this question is surprisingly ambiguous. We may know service operations when we see them but have difficulty describing them in general. Perhaps the term can be better understood as what it isn't rather than what it is. Some have tried to define service employment as nonfarming and nonmanufacturing employment; others have also excluded government employment. This approach includes operations such as hotels, restaurants, repairs, amusements, health, education, real estate, wholesale and retail trade, transportation, and professional services like law, engineering, architecture, finance, and advertising. Although these selections may be intuitively clear, there are still some definitional problems. For example, what about public utilities? Some public utilities companies have service in their name (such as Public Service of New Hampshire), yet in many ways power generation is more manufacturing than service. And is a company like IBM a manufacturing company or a service company? As in the old story of the blind men and the elephant, the answer may depend on what part of the beast you are touching. Surely there are aspects of IBM that are strictly manufacturing, but there are other aspects that are service (examples are field repair and the IBM subsidiary that published this textbook).

This ambiguity is growing. As technology advances, more and more labor will be driven out of manufactured products; that is, there will be less direct labor involved in manufacturing companies and more indirect labor—the kind of labor that is oriented to support services. Even now, some high technology companies have overhead rates that are six to ten times the direct labor component, mainly because of the substantial indirect labor in these companies. The traditional management focus on direct labor is becoming less and less relevant. Service operations management affects more than just service companies per se. Furthermore, the service sector will continue to grow. About two-thirds of America's Gross National Product is now accounted for by services; the same fraction applies to the percentage of the workforce employed in service jobs. These fractions can only rise. Similar trends are observed in other developed countries.

Characteristics of Service Operations

Most services share certain characteristics to a greater or lesser extent. It is helpful to understand these characteristics and how they separate manufacturing from service.

1. The service provided is often something that the consumer cannot touch or feel. It may be associated with something physical (such as the food we eat, the airplane we fly in, the life insurance policy), but what is valued about the service and may be the focus of management typically involves intangibles, such as ambiance, information, or peace of mind.

2. The service is often created and delivered on the spot, in many cases with significant involvement of the customer in the service process (consider salad bars in restaurants). Because the process is often more on display in service operations than in manufacturing, whether it functions well is critical. The process cannot be saved by a quality control check at the end; it has to live with its defects. Therefore, training, process design, and employee relations are especially important to service industries.

3. Because of the visibility of the service process in many instances and the intangibility of many services, operations management and marketing are more interdependent than in manufacturing. Marketing and operations have to work together in service companies; they cannot afford to be antagonists.

4. Frequently, the consumption of a service is nearly simultaneous with its production. Services cannot be inventoried for use later on. This fact has some serious implications for capacity choice and capacity management in a service business. The site, size, and layout choices for service industries are critical. The wrong site, a size either too large to too small, or a poor layout can dramatically affect the performance of a service unit. This concern for capacity is heightened by the irregularities in the pattern of demand over time (whether a day, week, or season). Demand irregularities place a tremendous

burden on a service operation to be flexible. They also force services to manage their demand via prices or the kinds of services offered.

5. Many service operations, although by no means all, require little in the way of capital investment, multiple locations, or proprietary technology. For these services, barriers to the entry of competing firms are rather low. Service companies are generally very sensitive to the real—or even potential—entry of others and must react quickly to the competition's actions and threats. Many service operations also possess rather low barriers to exit; that is, the assets of a service organization can be sold easily (such as planes or trucks). Because firms can get in and out of the service business quickly, some service strategies can play for the "hit and run."

Analyzing Service Operations

In analyzing a service operation, it is useful to distinguish three notions: the service concept, the service level, and the service delivery system. The *service concept* refers to what a business provides the consumer; it defines the fundamental nature of the business. To get at the service concept for a particular operation, we can ask, What is it about the service that the consumer values? With so much of service being intangible, the answer to this question must be clear to both management and the workforce. As was said before, in a service business, marketing and operations must cooperate. Operations cannot ignore marketing's insight into why the consumer values the service.

A *service level* is any measure that can be applied to the process to indicate its quality. The time standards at Burger King are examples of these measures. The service level is the guardian of quality for the service firm. Because, in most cases, a service cannot be inspected before it is provided, there must be clear checks on whether the process itself is working well.

The *service delivery system* is concerned with producing and delivering the service to the consumer. The service tours discussed are, at root, descriptions of the key elements of service delivery systems. How orders are taken, how the service is provided, how any materials are controlled are all aspects of the service delivery system. The challenge of service operations management is to devise a service delivery system that supports the service concept and maintains designated service levels.

Comparison of Services

The characterization of services as service factories, service shops, mass service, and professional service can be used as well for comparing service processes in much the same way that Table 1-2 compared manufacturing processes. This is accomplished in Table 1-3. The various features compared there are placed into various groups: service, process, customer-orientation, labor, and management. These features undergird the challenges for management that were introduced earlier.

Much as we have thought of manufacturing enterprises in terms of different kinds of production processes, we can think of service operations in terms of distinct "processes." It is helpful to view these different service processes in terms of a matrix that contrasts the labor intensity of the process on the one hand, and the degree of interaction with and customization of the service for the consumer on the other.[2] This matrix is shown in Figure 1-3. The quadrants of the matrix roughly define four reasonably distinct service processes.

TABLE 1-3   A service comparison

	SERVICE FACTORY (Example: Burger King® Restaurant)	SERVICE SHOP (Example: Howard Ford)	MASS SERVICE (Example: Thalhimers-Cloverleaf)	PROFESSIONAL SERVICE (Example: Arthur Andersen & Co.)
SERVICE FEATURES				
Mix of services:	Limited	Diverse	Limited	Diverse
Products compete largely on:	Price, speed, perceived "warmth" or "excitement"	Wide choice, competence	Price, Choice, Perceived "warmth" or "excitement"	Competence, range of expertise
New or unique services introduced or performed	Infrequent	Routine	Limited experimentation	Routine
PROCESS FEATURES				
Capital intensity	High	High	Low	Low
Pattern of process	Rigid	Adaptable	Rigid	Very loose
Ties to equipment	Integral part of process, little choice applies	Equipment important to process, but usually several options exist for its use	Limited ties to equipment, more tied to plant and layout	No close ties to plant or equipment
Importance of balance of tasks and any equipment to smooth process functioning	Balance critical	Balance often not critical	Balance not critical,	Balance can be critical
Tolerance for excess capacity	Excess capacity abhorred	Excess capacity often not a problem	Excess capacity implies workforce adjustment that is fairly easily made	Excess capacity abhorred
Ease of scheduling	Sometimes tough to schedule, peak demand can be difficult	Scheduling more easily done	Scheduling easily done	Sometimes tough to schedule, peak demand can be difficult
Economies of scale	Some	Some—permits better equpiment use and thus justification	Few, if any, except those related to any inventories	Few, if any, although some specialization can occur
Notion of capacity	Fairly clearcut, sometimes definable in physical terms	Fuzzy, very dependent on mix of demands. Only definable in dollar terms	Not as fuzzy as with service shop. Limits are often due to plant, not processing time	Fuzzy

TABLE 1-3 A service comparison (continued)

	SERVICE FACTORY (Example: Burger King® Restaurant)	SERVICE SHOP (Example: Howard Ford)	MASS SERVICE (Example: Thalhimers-Cloverleaf)	PROFESSIONAL SERVICE (Example: Arthur Andersen & Co.)
PROCESS FEATURES (continued)				
Layout	Line flow-like preferred	Job-shop or fixed position	Typically fixed position although layout may change frequently, customers move through layout	Job-shop frequently
Additions to capacity	Can be in variable increments, requires balance of capital and labor	Can be in variable increments, aspects of balance more murky	Often takes big changes to plant to enact. Processing can sometimes be sped up by adding some labor	Means adding primarily to labor in incremental fashion
Bottlenecks	Occasionally movable, but often predictable	Movable, frequent	Typically well known, predictable	Can sometimes be forecast, but otherwise are uncertain
Nature of process change	Sometimes routine (rebalance), sometimes radical (new equipment)	Occasionally radical (new equipment and procedures)	Process change seldom occurs, although it can be radical (such as big change to plant)	Mostly incremental
Importance of material flow to service provision	Both inventories and flow are important	Inventories important but not so much the flow	Inventories are often important and must be controlled	Incidental to most services
CUSTOMER-ORIENTED FEATURES				
Importance of attractive physical surroundings to marketing of service	Can be critical	Often insignificant	Critical	Often insignificant
Interaction of customer with process	Little, brief	Can be great	Some	Typically, very great
Customization of service	Scant	Significant	Scant	Significant
Ease of managing demand for peaks and nonpeaks	Can be done through price	Some promotion of off-peak times can be done, but often difficult	Same as for service shop	Often very difficult to manage demand, may not be responsive to price

TABLE 1-3   A service comparison (*continued*)

	SERVICE FACTORY (Example: Burger King® Restaurant)	SERVICE SHOP (Example: Howard Ford)	MASS SERVICE (Example: Thalhimers-Cloverleaf)	PROFESSIONAL SERVICE (Example: Arthur Andersen & Co.)
CUSTOMER-ORIENTED FEATURES (continued)				
Process quality control	Can be formal, amenable to standard methods (such as control charts)	Can be formal. Checkpoints can easily be established. Training can be critical to quality	Mainly informal. Training critical to quality	Mainly informal. Training critical to quality
LABOR-RELATED FEATURES				
Pay	Typically hourly	Varies, could include individual incentive or commission schemes	Same as for service shop	Salary, often with bonus of some type
Skill levels	Generally lower skills	High skills	Variable, but most often lower skills	Very high skills
Job content	Small	Large	Often medium, but variable	Very large
Advancement	With more skills and/or seniority acquired, greater responsibility given. Seniority can lead to change in department or shift assignment	Often, worker is an independent operator of sorts and can exert some control on what he gives and gets from job; limited hierarchical progression	Often a hierarchy to progress upward through	Often a pyramid, up or out. Top of pyramid exerts leverage over bottom of pyramid
MANAGEMENT FEATURES				
Staff-line needs	Large staff for process redesign, methods, forecasting, capacity planning, and scheduling. Line supervision and troubleshooting still critical	Limited staff, mostly line operation	Some staff, often focused on personal issues	Limited staff, many line managers wear multiple hats
Means of control	Variable. Can be cost or profit center	Usually a profit center	Usually a profit center	Usually a profit center

Degree of Contact with, and Customization
for, the Consumer

		Low	High	Challenges for Management
Degree of Labor Intensity	Low	**The Service Factory** Airlines, trucking, hotels, resorts, and recreation	**The Service Shop** Hospitals, auto, and other repair services	Capital decisions, technological advances, managing demand to avoid peaks and to promote off-peaks, scheduling delivery of service
	High	**Mass Service** Retailing, wholesaling, schools	**Professional Service** Physicians, lawyers, accountants, architects	Hiring, training, methods development and control, employee welfare, scheduling workforces, control of often geographically spread locations, start-up of new units, managing growth
Challenges for Management		Marketing, making service "warm," attention to physical surroundings, managing fairly rigid hierarchy with need for standard operating procedures	Fighting cost increases, maintaining quality, reacting to customer intervention in process, managing advancement of people delivering service, managing flat hierarchy with loose subordinate-superior relationships, binding workers to the firm	

FIGURE 1-3   A matrix of service processes.

The Service Factory

Some service processes have relatively low labor intensity (and thus a greater fraction of service costs associated with the facility and its equipment) and also a low degree of customer interaction and customization. These can be characterized as *service factories*. Much of the transportation industry, hotels, and resorts, for example, are service factories, as are "back-of-the-house" operations for banking and financial services companies. The Burger King Restaurant in Burlington, North Carolina (Tour F) is an example of a service factory.

The Service Shop

As the degree of interaction with—or customization for—the consumer increases, the service factory gives way to the *service shop*, much as a line flow operation gives way to a job shop operation when customization is required in manufacturing. Hospitals and repair services of all types are prime examples of service shops. Tour G of Howard Ford's auto repair operation is an example of a service shop.

Mass Service

Mass service processes have a high degree of labor intensity, but a rather low degree of interaction with or customization for the consumer. Retail operations, retail banking, schools, and wholesaling are examples of mass services. The Thalhimer department store at the Cloverleaf Mall, characterized in Tour H, is an example of mass service.

Professional Service

If the degree of interaction increases and/or customization becomes the watchword, mass service gives way to *professional service*, as provided by doctors, lawyers, consultants, architects, and the like. Arthur Andersen & Co.'s audit services in Charlotte (Tour I) provide an example of professional service.

Challenges to Management

Let us look at the challenges to management that are implied by labor intensity and interaction/customization differences.[3] The service operation that is more highly capital intensive has to look carefully at (1) its capital decisions regarding land, facilities, and equipment; and (2) technological advances that may affect them. Capital intentive processes often cannot easily augment capacity, so demand must be managed to smooth any demand peaks and to promote the offpeak times. The inflexibility of capacity also implies the scheduling service delivery is relatively more important for these process types.

For process types with high labor intensity, managing and controlling the workforce become paramount. Hiring, training, methods development and control, employee welfare, scheduling the workforce, and controlling what may be far-flung locations are critical. If new units of operations are contemplated, their start-up may become a problem; managing the group of such new units can be difficult.

What about the challenges to management implied by differences in the interaction with and customization for the consumer? Those service processes that have a low degree of interaction and customization face a stiffer marketing challenge. They must try to make the service "warm" and "exciting" even though they may not give the personal attention that a customer might want. Attention to the physical surroundings and the layout become more important. With a low degree of interaction and with little customization, standard operating procedures can safely be instituted. The hierarchy of the service organization itself tends to be the classic pyramid, with fairly rigid relationships between levels.

As the service takes on a higher degree of interaction and customization, management must deal with higher costs and more talented labor. Keeping costs down and yet maintaining quality becomes a challenge. Talented employees want attention given to how they may advance in the organization. The hierarchy of control tends to be flat, with much less rigid relationships between superiors and subordinates. Keeping workers bound to the firm rather than hopping from job to job becomes a challenge as well. Service firms with a high degree of consumer interaction also must react to frequent consumer intervention in the process.

Naturally, there are some gray areas as one passes from low to high on either dimension of this matrix. For example, while fast food restaurants are probably best seen as service factories, the traditional restaurant is more problematic. Traditional restaurants offer a higher degree of interaction and customization for the consumer, and they are more labor intensive than fast food restaurants. While they may be best characterized as service shops, they are fairly low in that quadrant, with at least some gourmet restaurants arguably characterized as professional services.

QUESTIONS

1. The Stroh brewery discussed in Tour E is an example of a batch/continuous flow hybrid. However, other kinds of hybrids are possible (such as batch/assembly line or job shop/batch). Give some examples of other hybrids. How would one of these other hybrids differ from the Stroh hybrid? How would they be similar?

2. Compare and contrast a "service shop" and a job shop. Compare and contrast a "service factory" and an assembly line.

3. Discuss some of the main challenges management faces in bringing different product mixes to market. What other management challenges can you think of for a product mix that have not been included in the product-process matrix?

4. Examine some of the implications of the concept of opportunity cost for a company and its attitude toward profit. From your own experience, give some examples of the notion of opportunity cost.

5. The dimensions used for the product/process matrix were process pattern and product mix while the dimensions of the service matrix were degree of labor intensity and interaction with, and customization for, the consumer. How are these dimensions related to each other? How are they different from each other?

SITUATION FOR STUDY 1-1
DAVIS FARM—SPECIALTY VEAL OPERATION

There are three types of veal:

- *Bob veal.* This type of veal comes from calves less than one week old. The meat is pale, immature, tasteless, gelatinous, of little nutritional value, and completely unacceptable to all but the most uncultured of palates.

- *Grain-fed veal.* A more accurate description is puny beef. The calves are raised on a combination of milk, silage, and grass, and slaughtered at about 4 to 6 months. Though called veal, the meat is red and has a distinctive "beefy" flavor.

- *Specialty veal.* This type of veal is from calves raised on a strict all-milk or milk-replacer diet. It is distinguished by its light pink color, firm texture, consistent fat mar-

bling, fitness for a wide variety of cooking techniques and recipes, and digestibility.

The Davis farm operated out of three barns: a 56-stall indoor barn, a 68-stall indoor barn, and a 116-stall outdoor enclosure (summers only).

Roughly, raising veal calves is a four-step process:

1. The barns are prepared for the arrival of the calves.
2. A batch of one- to two-week-old bull calves is purchased and placed in pens in the barns.
3. The calves are fed, cleaned, and medicated twice daily for 12 to 16 weeks.
4. The calves are shipped to slaughter, and the process repeats.

Because young calves are highly susceptible to disease, the barns had to be as clean as possible when they arrived. Pens, floors, walls, and buckets were steam-cleaned with an antiseptic solution, and the feeding equipment was scrubbed and sterilized. To assure good ventilation, the dust filters and air screens on the vents were brushed clean and the fans were carefully checked.

Bull calves, the raw material of the veal industry, are a by-product of the dairy industry. Dairy cows must be freshened (that is, must give birth to a calf) once a year to maintain milk production. Ideally, the cow gives birth to a heifer, which the farmer could raise to be another milk-producing cow. Half the time, however, the cow gives birth to a bull calf, which, except for the gain upon immediate sale, is useless to most dairy farmers. At an age of one to two weeks, these bull calves are taken to a regional commission sales barn and sold at auction to vealers and slaughterhouses. The ideal veal calf is healthy, and larger (weighing 90 to 120 pounds) than the average calf.

The calves purchased by Davis were trucked to the farm and penned. For the next 12 to 16 weeks, the calves would be fed, cleaned, and medicated every day at 5 A.M. and 5 P.M. The twice-daily feeding was the heart of the veal-raising process. The feed had a very high conversion ratio: on average, 1.4 pounds of the nonperishable powdered feed yielded 1 pound of growth. The feed was mostly dried milk and milk products, fortified with vitamins, antibiotics, and butterfat; the feed had a higher fat content than whole milk. It was shipped in 50-pound bags in loads of several tons, and stored on wooden pallets in the mixing room until needed. Generally, a batch of calves consumed 22 to 24 tons of the powdered feed during their 12- to 16-week stay.

The milk was prepared by adding the powder to hot water and agitating the mix with an electric motor. After it has thoroughly dissolved, enough cold water was added to bring the temperature of the mix to between 100° and 105° F. The amount, type, and proportion of feed depended on the age of the batch of calves, the condition of the individual calves, and their willingness to drink. The feed was mixed in a 300-gallon bulk-tank, into which water flowed from two 120-gallon drums suspended above it. A major problem with such a bulk feeding system was keeping it clean. Because calves are so susceptible to disease, it was vital that the tank, pump, and hoses be kept as clean as possible. These parts were sterilized by rinsing with hot water and hypochlorite bleach.

The normal mortality rate for bull calves (for all purposes, not just vealing) was 15 to 20 percent. This high figure was the result of both the calf's natural susceptibility and mistreatment at birth. After giving birth and before the milk comes in, a cow (or any other mammal) lactates colostrum that contains various antibodies and other enzymes that greatly improve the newborn's chances of survival. Unfortunately, many bull calves did not get colostrum because the suckling might damage the mother's teat. In addition, the calves were poorly handled at the auction house and shipped long distances to their final destinations. Usually, they got nothing to eat for several days. Davis could avoid the high mortality rate somewhat by buying only the larger, healthier calves. However, calves were always dehydrated and suffering from stress when they arrived at the barn. For most batches, 4 or 5 percent died within the first 48 hours.

The most common disease of these young calves was scours. A scouring calf has very loose feces with a distinctive odor and mottling. The cause of the disease can be either intestinal bacteria or a virus, augmented by stress. If untreated, scours led to dehydration and death within 24 hours. Treatment consisted of massive amounts of intravenous fluids, electrolytes, and an oral antibiotic. To survive, scouring calves needed fluids three or four times daily. The most serious problem with scours, as with most other disease, was that it is highly contagious. Thus, tremendous emphasis was placed on cleanliness and observation, particularly during the first few days.

Respiratory diseases, especially pneumonia, were of particular concern at about the fourth week but could occur at any time. The animal with such a disease breathes rapidly and has a runny nose and fever. (A calf's normal temperature is 101.5° F. One gets concerned when it rises about 103° F. and panics when it goes over 104° F.) The treatment for this was an injectable antibiotic, normally a compound based on penicillin, streptomycin, or tetracycline. The veal farmer had hundreds of different drugs at his disposal and based his choice on the seriousness of the symptoms. For example, a high fever might require a tetracycline-based compound that was good for bringing down temperature. If the fever was only low grade, a penicillin compound with good long-term results could be used.

During the later days of a batch, a serious medical problem was bloat. Because of the complexity of their stomachs, calves cannot belch; any gas generated during digestion is either passed out through the intestines or absorbed. If gas generation occurs faster than the calf's natural ability to eliminate the gas, pressure builds up and slowly suffocates the animal. This condition is known as bloat. Treatment consisted of inserting a flexible tube about five feet down the calf's throat to permit the air to escape. If this did not work, a trocar had to be inserted into the calf's abdomen, and a tube into the rumen. Of course, the calf had to be given antibloat medication. In the case of a trocar insertion, the calf was given antibiotics as well to prevent peritonitis. A mortality rate of under 10 percent was considered good.

After feeding, all the feed buckets were hosed clean and suspended above the pens to dry. After that, the floors were washed to clean up the day's urine. Every two days or so, the pens were cleaned more thoroughly. Manure was scraped from under the pens and washed down a four-inch pipe at the end of every gutter. This pipe carried the manure underground to a man-made manure lagoon (pond), where it decomposed naturally.

One hour after feeding, the calves had to be checked for bloat. At this time, any animal beginning to bloat could be easily recognized and fairly easily treated. In addition to the twice-daily bloat check, the calves were checked at lunchtime, mid-afternoon, and midnight. At the very beginning and very end of a batch, they were checked more often. Most of the time, these checks yielded no problems, or nothing more serious than a leaky faucet. Sometimes, though, a problem with a calf appeared—bloat, a broken stall, the beginnings of pneumonia maybe. Such a problem had to be solved immediately, or watched closely, or else it would be much more serious by the next feeding.

Calves could be shipped to market any time between the twelfth and sixteenth weeks. At this point, the cost of the feed began to exceed the benefit of resultant weight gain. This three-week period allowed some leeway for finding the best price. A contract negotiated with a slaughterhouse specified the price (per pound of carcass) and the delivery date.

1. As described, this is a batch flow process. What would it take to transform it into a line flow process?

2. What advantages or disadvantages to such a transformation can you identify? Be specific.

REFERENCE NOTES

1. The concept of the product-process matrix owes much to Robert H. Hayes and Steven C. Wheelwright. See the two articles by Hayes and Wheelwright in the January–February and March–April 1979 issues of the *Harvard Business Review* entitled "Link Manufacturing Process and Product Life Cycles" and "The Dynamics of Process-Product Life Cycles," respectively.

2. My thinking about a matrix of service processes was stimulated by David Maister's working paper entitled "Balancing the Professional Service Firm" (Harvard Business School, working paper 82–01).

3. Additional information on the management of service operations can be found in the following:

Levitt, Theodore "The Industrialization of Service," *Harvard Business Review* 48, no. 5 (September–October 1970), pp. 63–74.

Chase, Richard B. "Where Does the Customer Fit in a Service Operation?" *Harvard Business Review* 56, no. 6 (November–December 1978), pp. 13, 42.

Chase, Richard B. "The Customer Contact Approach to Services." *Operations Research* 29 (1981) pp. 698–706.

Sasser, W. Earl, R. Paul Olsen, and D. Daryl Wyckoff. *Management of Service Operations* (Boston: Allyn & Bacon, 1978).

Thomas, Dan. "Strategy Is Different in Service Businesses." *Harvard Business Review* 56, no. 4 (July–August 1978), pp. 158–65.

Lovelock, Christopher, and Robert Young, "Look to Consumers to Increase Production", *Harvard Business Review* 57, no. 3 (May–June 1979), pp. 168–79.

Shostack, G. Lynn "Designing Services That Deliver", *Harvard Business Review* 62, no. 1 (January–February 1984), pp. 133–39.

Maister, David H., and Christopher Lovelock, "Managing Facilitator Services", *Sloan Management Review* (Summer 1982), pp. 19–31.

Maister, David H. "Balancing the Professional Service Firm", *Sloan Management Review* (Fall 1982), pp. 15–29.

Fitzsimmons, James A., and Robert S. Sullivan, *Service Operations Management* (New York: McGraw-Hill, 1982).

Collier, David A., *Service Management: The Automation of Services*, (Reston Wash.: Reston Publishing), 1985.

II

IMPROVING EXISTING OPERATIONS

This segment of the text discusses the problems and concerns that surface repeatedly in the day-to-day operations of a business. As the previous segment has demonstrated, production processes can differ markedly and, as a consequence, so too can the problems and concerns of the managers who run them. Throughout this segment, the relationship between problem and process should be clear.

Five areas of day-to-day management concern are the foci for the chapters in this segment:

1. *Bottlenecks.* Having enough capacity in the short run is a constant headache in any process. Identifying where bottlenecks are or might occur, understanding why they occur, and taking measures to overcome them are always on an operation manager's agenda. They are the subject of Chapter 2.

2. *Workforce.* A good workforce is a company's most prized asset. Building up a team of skilled workers who truly care about what they are doing takes a lot of care from a company's managers. Workforce management is a rich topic and can be as diverse as individual company situations. Chapter 3 concentrates on the important and universal concerns of job design, worker motivation, and wage schemes.

3. *Planning and controlling production.* Even as most operations managers are wrestling with today's problems, they must keep an eye out for the problems sneaking up over the horizon. Trying to meet future sales demands in a timely and inexpensive way is both a worthy goal and one that requires much planning. Keeping the process functioning smoothly requires a good deal of control. The planning, scheduling, and control of production are the concerns of Chapter 4.

4. *Materials.* The movement of materials from a "raw" to a "finished" state is what a production process is all about. Managers justly worry about having either not enough or too much material at various times during the production cycle, since it often costs significant amounts of money to purchase and to hold materials. Managing materials and inventories of all types takes thought and is the topic of Chapter 5.

5. *Quality.* What does it mean to put quality into a product? And what can be done to realize the goal of quality production? Chapter 6 deals with quality—its definition operationally and the tools and attitudes managers can use to make it happen.

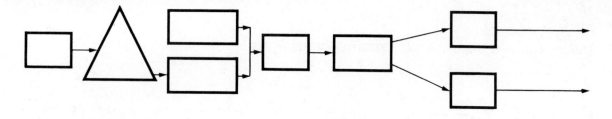

CHAPTER 2

BREAKING BOTTLENECKS

Production bottlenecks are generally considered to be temporary blockades to increased output; they can be thrown up anywhere along the course of a production process. Some are easy to identify and to remedy, while others are devilish.

The bottleneck that is easy to cope with is stationary. Work-in-process inventory piles up quickly behind it; clearly, little is getting through. Its cause is usually also clear—a machine has broken down or key workers are absent or demand has simply outstripped the clear, rated capacity of a machine—and the remedy follows easily. Such bottlenecks often occur in service operations, causing customer waits.

More subtle are bottlenecks that shift from one part of the process to another or that have no clear cause. Inventories build up in different places and at different times. Such bottlenecks creep up on management and demand more thorough investigation. Perhaps they were detected as flaws in a product's quality caused inadvertently by one or more workers trying to keep pace with production demands that should not have been placed on them. Or, they may be caused by missing parts. They may be caused by new product start-up or changes in the mix of products through the factory. In such cases

the remedies are less clear-cut, and some analysis is called for.

ANALYZING BOTTLENECKS

In analyzing bottlenecks, it is always helpful to trace the production process by using a process flow diagram and to assign what capacity numbers are available to each stage of the process. Simply being systematic in this way and being as precise as possible with capacity measures can uncover primary and secondary bottlenecks straightaway. Such an analysis is naturally easier with well-delineated processes and ones where capacity is unambiguous. The process flow diagram, in that case, becomes a planning aid for breaking significant, stationary bottlenecks. It is also an aid in the design of processes themselves, as it clearly shows how the capacities of process segments can be balanced against one another.

As an example, consider the steel industry. The process is largely continuous flow; capacity, in tons, is well known and dependent primarily on equipment capabilities. A process flow diagram for a steel mill, with associated capacity measures, might well look like the one

265

FIGURE 2-1   A process flow diagram for a steel mill.

shown in Figure 2-1. The diagram makes it clear that the bottleneck at this steel mill is the blast furnace; in order to increase the mill's capacity, blast furnace capacity must be enlarged. The secondary bottleneck resides in the casting and semifinishing operation; that is, once the blast furnace is expanded past 4.7 million tons per year, casting and semifinishing will be the bottleneck.

The most slack element of the process flow shown in Figure 2-1 appears to be the finishing mills. In most steel mills, however, the nominal capacity of the finishing mills is purposely greater than the other elements of the process to ensure capacity under all kinds of product mixes. Thus, even in steel mills the notion of capacity becomes somewhat blurred and ambiguous. A process flow diagram must be modified somewhat and interpreted if it is to be useful for analyzing bottlenecks.

Even more modification and interpretation of process flow diagrams is needed when less rigid production processes (such as batch flow or job shop) are involved. In such processes, not only are capacity figures potentially very volatile, but the process flow itself may be indeterminate. Identifying bottlenecks in these processes becomes a formidable task. Typically, ranges of capacity must be used and different arrangements of the process flow must be tried. Still, judicious and systematic use of a process flow diagram can be a valuable tool in identifying the process elements *and conditions* that account for bottlenecks.

Service operations are particularly ripe for such analysis. Their process and information flows are only seldom analyzed systematically, and seemingly minor adjustments in the service delivery process can frequently yield significant improvements.

Another useful tool in analyzing bottlenecks is an inventory buildup graph, a pictorial way of accounting for the rates at which inventories are either piled up or depleted. These graphs are particularly useful when the demand on an element of the process is especially erratic, such as occurs routinely in the processing of many raw agricultural commodities but can occur in other industries. To illustrate the use of an inventory buildup graph and to provide a groundings in some classic problems of capacity and bottlenecks, consider Situation 2-1.

Discussion of Devine Nuts

In analyzing the situation Frank Coyne finds himself in at Devine Nuts, it is helpful to picture what is going on—how peanuts build up in inventory after delivery and how the inventories are drawn down by completed drying. What is of concern to Frank are the peak days, when 300 tons of soggy peanuts arrive during a 10-hour period and have to be dried for 36 hours. Figure 2-2 pictures how inventories build up at Devine Nuts during a succession of peak days, assuming an even distribution of truck arrivals.

SITUATION 2-1

DEVINE NUTS, INC.

It was autumn and the peanut harvesting season was winding to a close. Frank Coyne, the proprietor of Devine Nuts, was reflecting on the past season and speculating whether he would have enough peanut drying capacity for next year, especially if the local crop increased by 10 percent, as many of the peanut farmers were saying.

Frank Coyne was a peanut broker. Devine Nuts purchased peanuts from farmers in the area (Devine, Texas, is situated about 30 miles southwest of San Antonio) and sold them to peanut processing companies and cooperatives, which used them for making peanut oil, peanut butter, candy, and a host of other items.

Devine Nuts' principal operating functions were straightforward. During the peanut harvesting season, farmers delivered loads of so-called "green" peanuts to Devine Nuts. The trucks, with their loads, were weighed and records kept by the issuance of scale tickets. After weighing, a moisture sample was taken. This inspection step was critical, since the peanut processing companies would not accept any peanuts without the government's grading certificate on them, and a grading certificate would not be issued unless the moisture content of the peanuts was 10.5 percent by weight or lower. If a delivered load of peanuts met this moisture standard and was thereby granted a certificate, another sample of peanuts would be drawn, weighed, and shelled so that the kernels could be classified into four size categories (large, regular, medium, and small). Kernel weight and size determined the price the farmer would be paid, typically about 30 cents per pound. Once the price was determined, the peanuts were loaded into railcars or trucks and shipped to a shelling plant. Sometimes immediate transportation could not be arranged, and the graded peanuts would have to be stored in Devine Nuts' bulk warehouse, which had room for 5500 tons.

More often than not, the delivered loads of peanuts would not meet the moisture standard and would have to be dried and then reweighed and graded. Devine Nuts owned a number of dryers of various sizes: 38 6-ton capacity dryers, 10 11-ton capacity dryers, and 14 14-ton capacity dryers. How long a load of peanuts would have to remain in a dryer depended on its moisture content. Peanuts with a moisture content of only 10 to 15 percent could be dried in about 12 hours, but peanuts with a moisture content of 15 to 25 percent could take anywhere from 24 to 36 hours to dry. Devine Nuts did not have any storage for wet green peanuts; they were dumped directly from the farmers' trucks into the dryers. If dryer space was not available, trucks had no recourse but to wait until it became available.

The drying operation was critical because harvested peanuts that were wet began growing a fungus about 12 hours after harvesting. To avoid spoilage, it was essential that drying start within 12 hours after harvesting. A day's harvesting began after the morning dew had dried and continued until dusk. Deliveries to Devine Nuts began about noon and lasted until about 10 P.M. in a more or less steady stream.

Frank Coyne's success as a broker rested on his ability to meet the needs of the farmers who brought their crops to him each year. If Frank could not dry a farmer's peanuts on time, he stood an excellent chance of losing that customer forever to another broker. In addition, if Frank left too many trucks waiting too long for available dryer space, he risked souring his customer relations, since the farmers needed those trucks out in the field for the next day's harvest.

On most days, Devine Nuts' drying capacity was more than enough to handle the demand. A typical day's delivery would be about 120 tons; roughly half would have a moisture content between 10 and 15 percent, and half between 15 and 25 percent. What grayed Frank Coyne's hair were the peak days that would occur right after a rainstorm. Storms usually kept the farmers from harvesting, and so loads that ordinarily might be stretched over several days would be bunched together in just a few. On such days, 300 tons of green peanuts might be delivered. What made matters much worse was that the peanuts were soaking wet from the rain and had moisture contents that required a full 36 hours of drying.

Devine Nuts had been able to handle the past season's peak days without turning away a customer, although some trucks had to wait at times to unload. Frank Coyne's immediate concern was calculating whether a 10 percent increase in the local crop (which he translated into a 10 percent increase in peak day activity) would overload his drying capacity and (1) force trucks away, (2) cause them to wait longer than dawn (6 A.M.) of the day following their delivery, or (3) cause them to wait longer than 12 hours to unload.

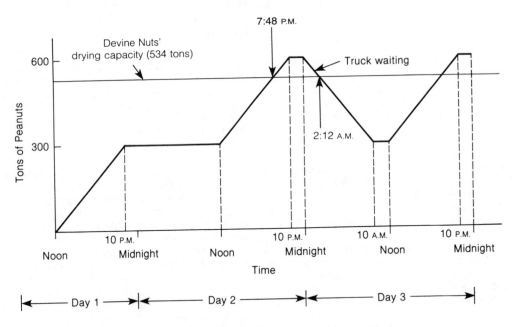

FIGURE 2-2   Inventory buildup at Devine Nuts after several peak days.

Figure 2-2 assumes that at noon on day 1 all the dryers are empty. As loads of peanuts arrive from then on, at an average rate of 30 tons per hour, dryers are successively filled up. By 10 P.M. when the farmers' shipments cease for the day, 300 tons of peanuts are in the dryers. Because they are so wet, these peanuts will not be removed from the dryers until after midnight on day 2. In the meantime, another day's worth of soggy peanuts will have arrived. Most of these can be transferred directly to waiting dryers, but some will have to wait until day 1's peanuts are removed.

How many tons of peanuts will have to wait for dryers, and how many hours will they have to wait in their trucks? Devine Nuts' total drying capacity is 534 tons, figured as $[(38 \cdot 6) + (10 \cdot 11) + (14 \cdot 14)]$. Thus, 66 tons of peanuts $(600 - 534)$ cannot be transferred immediately from trucks to dryers. Since peanuts are arriving at a rate of 30 tons per hour, dryer capacity can be expected to run out at 2.2 hours $(66/30)$ before 10 P.M. on day 2. The dryers will not be available until midnight, but at that time dryer space will be released at the rate of 30 tons per hour, the same rate that peanuts entered the dryers. The first truck that cannot dump its load immediately into a dryer will have to wait until midnight to be unloaded, a wait of 4.2 hours. Because the withdrawal rate of peanuts from the dryers exactly matches the arrival rate of peanuts to Devine Nuts, all of the trucks will wait an average of 4.2 hours. The last truck will be free to return to its farm at 2.2 hours after midnight. Thus, Figure 2-2 confirms Devine Nuts' record over the past sea-

FIGURE 2-3   Inventory buildup at Devine Nuts when peak day tonnage has increased by 10 percent.

son: trucks did have to wait, but none had to be turned away or came close to spoiling the peanuts or not getting back on time.

How does a 10 percent increase in peak day deliveries affect operations? Figure 2-3 deals with that situation. The slightly steeper slopes pictured in this inventory buildup graph reflect the increased average arrival rate of 33 tons per hour. Since drying still must take 36 hours, Devine Nuts runs out of capacity sooner than in Figure 2-2. Specifically, Devine Nuts' capacity falls 126 tons short (660 − 534) and the dryers begin overflowing at 3.82 hours (126/33) before 10 P.M. Since the dryers will not be available until midnight, each truck will have to wait an average of 5.82 hours before unloading. The latest arriving truck will still be free to return to service at 3.82 hours past midnight, well before dawn. Thus, even with an increase of 10 percent

in peak day tonnage, Devine Nuts can expect not to have to turn away customers for lack of capacity.

Frank Coyne may also be interested in knowing how much the current peak day demand (30 tons per hour) would have to grow before Devine Nuts' present capacity would be insufficient to free up the delivery trucks by dawn. To find the answer to this question, we need to calculate how short of the peak Devine Nuts' capacity would have to be before six hours (midnight to dawn) would be too little time to work down the excess.

Let x represent the factor by which we would have to multiply present demand to yield the peak day demand that strains capacity. Thus, the total tonnage of peanuts accumulating in dryers and in trucks at 10 P.M. on day 2 would be the present 600 times x. In the six hours after midnight, x times the present rate of 30 tons per hour would be freed from the dryers each hour. Thus, we can write out the following relationship:

$$6 \cdot 30x = 600x - 534$$

$$\begin{pmatrix} \text{drying capacity} \\ \text{freed up in 6 hours} \end{pmatrix} = \begin{pmatrix} \text{wet peanuts} \\ \text{waiting for dryers} \end{pmatrix}$$

Solving for x, we get

$$180x = 600x - 534$$

$$534 = 420x$$

$$1.27 = x$$

Thus, peak demand will have to rise by 27 percent over the present level before Devine Nuts' present capacity will be insufficient. Frank Coyne should be reassured.

This type of calculation, where the general question is asked "At which point does one alternative begin to dominate another?" is often called an *indifference* calculation. Here we asked "At what level of demand would Devine Nuts' capacity begin to be insufficient?" and the indifference point was a demand 27 percent greater than the present. As one might expect, the indifference calculation can be exceedingly useful and flexible, and we shall be using it in several guises throughout this text. It is particularly useful in gauging the sensitivity of a decision to variations in a particular variable. In fact, the indifference calculation computed here is a form of sensitivity analysis. How sensitive is Devine Nuts' capacity needs to an increase in peak demand?

With the background of these tools of analysis for finding bottlenecks—the process flow diagram, the inventory buildup graph, and indifference calculations—we turn now to outlining the causes of bottlenecks of various types.

THE CAUSES OF BOTTLENECKS

At this point, it makes sense to discuss why bottlenecks typically occur. Such a discussion helps put several concepts in perspective. Of course, we cannot hope to cover all the remedies to the problems that cause bottlenecks in this section; indeed, avoiding and/or remedying bottlenecks of different kinds is a key concern of much of the remainder of the book. Nevertheless, outlining the most common causes of bottlenecks helps build appreciation for some of the topics to follow.

Bottlenecks can be divided into two types: chronic, recurring ones; and ones more episodic in character. Of course, individual bottleneck episodes can easily develop into chronic problems. Episodic bottlenecks call on the "fire fighting" skills of the workers and managers involved, while chronic bottlenecks demand more planning or design changes.

Episodic Bottlenecks

Episodic bottlenecks can be classed into three major categories: (1) machine breakdowns, (2) materials shortages, and (3) labor shortages. Let's consider these in more detail.

1. *Machine breakdowns.* Perhaps the biggest of the fires to fight in a factory involve machines, tooling, or fixtures that break. When this happens, lots of scurrying around occurs to fix the broken machine and to reroute, if possible, the job it was performing. Often the best maintenance tradespeople in a factory are assigned the firefighting role of repairing broken equipment. Plant managers can also be dragged in, if their technical skills are appropriate.

Some machine breakdowns represent unavoidable accidents. On the other hand, many breakdowns can be avoided with some planning and preventive action. Preventive maintenance is a too frequently neglected activity; there is never enough time for it when business is booming (so it is claimed), and it is a low priority item when business is faltering. Breakdown time often exceeds the planned downtime of preventive maintenance, and planned downtime is naturally easier to cope with and does not risk the quality problems that surround breakdowns. Putting the factory's best maintenance tradespeople on the task of preventing breakdowns is increasingly being recognized as the most cost-effective policy.

In a similar vein, attention to tooling and fixturing can eliminate unplanned downtime. Tooling or fixturing that was meant to be temporary too frequently winds up as permanent, and that can create problems. More effort and expense up front often saves frustration and cost down the road.

2. *Material shortages.* If unplanned machine downtime is the biggest of the fires fought in the factory, materials shortage is the most common. The typical factory always seems to be short some part or material. Sometimes it is traceable to a vendor; sometimes it is another department within the factory that is responsible. Chapters 4 and 5 tackle materials management and the kinds of policies and procedures that can be used to avoid material shortages and the "work around" that the factory is forced into to cope with them.

3. *Labor shortages.* Unexpected absences, retirements, and terminations are all examples of how an operation can be temporarily short of workers. This is more of a problem for some types of processes, of course, but it has an impact for all.

Allied with this problem is the job bumping that is endemic to operations when there are many labor grades and when the most senior workers can bid for job openings in the next higher grade. The cascade of job openings created by workers moving up to the next grade can be many times the number of jobs initially vacated. The residual problem is that lots of workers require training for their new positions and initially are not as productive as they will become. It is as if there was a labor shortage when significant job bumping occurs.

Workforce issues are treated in Chapter 3.

Chronic Bottlenecks

Chronic bottlenecks, much like episodic ones, can be categorized. Chronic bottlenecks can be thought of in terms of materials problems and process problems.

Materials Problems

1. *Ordering the wrong materials or not enough materials.* This potentially recurring problem suggests deficiencies in production planning or in purchasing. Not all vendor shortages are caused by the vendor; some can be traced to late or incorrect purchase orders, poor forecasting of needs, incorrect and/or obsolete bills of material, inappropriate inventory policies, myopic production planning, unwillingness to release the funds, and the like. Chapters 4 and 5, which focus on materials management, deal with these issues.

2. *Constantly changing product mix.* Even if the production planning and purchasing departments are on their toes, there could be bottlenecks simply because a constantly

changing product mix places irregular demands on the capacity of individual departments within the factory. (Situation 2-2 is an example of this.) That is, in aggregate the factory might have enough capacity, but the character of that capacity does not fit the product mix being pushed through. This phenomenon emphasizes the importance of capacity planning, a topic discussed in Chapter 4.

Process Problems

1. *Insufficient capacity.* Frequently it is not merely a problem of the product mix being inappropriate in the short term for the capacity in place. Rather, the demand, in the aggregate, may well exceed capacity. In this case, if the bottleneck is to be broken, capacity must be increased with more equipment, people, and perhaps, "bricks and mortar." This is the focus of discussion in Chapter 7.

2. *Quality problems.* Quality problems may, of course, lead to episodes such as those associated with machine breakdowns. If the fundamental causes of quality problems are not remedied, however, the problems become chronic. Quality management is a rich subject, and Chapter 6 deals with it.

3. *Poor layout.* One of the key aspects of a process is its layout. Poor layouts—those with convoluted routings, crowded conditions, difficult and costly materials handling, and the like—can be terrible drain on a plant's productivity. Later in this chapter we discuss some key aspects of plant layouts.

4. *Inflexible process.* Some bottlenecks turn out to be chronic because of the process design. In these cases, a bottleneck gets designed into the process or is exposed by some shift in the pattern of demand. A classic reason for inflexibility is the purchase of a large, general-purpose piece of equipment that is supposed to do a series of automatic operations. If the equipment delivers as expected, all is well. However, often such process designs run amok because the equipment does not deliver, is not properly tooled up, takes too long to set up, or is very temperamental. Because so much is routed to it, when the equipment fails or has to be shut down for long periods of maintenance or setup, the rest of the process becomes crippled. Better, in many people's eyes, to design a process with smaller scale, easier to set up, and more special-purpose equipment that does not leave production so vulnerable. As Situation 2-2 reveals, a series of small-scale equipment can be more flexible and timely than an expensive piece of allegedly general-purpose equipment.

Discussion of Wyoming Valley Furniture Company

Wyoming Valley Furniture knows that a bottleneck is coming, a definite advantage, but it is disadvantaged because its normal means of dealing with bottlenecks (namely, to schedule around them) appears inadequate. If the company could routinely expect such heavy demands on the lathe department, George Sowerby might feel free to expand its equipment and workforce. However, the lathe demands made by this particular piece of furniture are unusual and, as yet, it is not a steady order. Only three or four orders for the buffet are likely in any year. Wyoming Valley Furniture seems to occupy some no-man's land between capacity expansion and the status quo.

As it stands, the company can plan for lots of overtime when the entire order is scheduled for production and hope that no disruption will occur to the finish mill. Or, the company can try to stock up early on the problem buffet leg.

SITUATION 2-2

WYOMING VALLEY FURNITURE COMPANY

It was the first part of July, time for another monthly planning meeting on the production schedule for the upcoming 16-week period. George Sowerby, owner and president of Wyoming Valley Furniture, normally relished this opportunity to grapple with what he viewed as the most important management activity in the furniture business. Today, however, he was a bit apprehensive because the newly arrived order from Pennsylvania House threatened another bottleneck in the lathe department, just like the one the company had suffered through only last month.

The Wyoming Valley Furniture Company was a small manufacturer of casegoods furniture (that is, all-wood furniture as opposed to upholstered furniture), situated in the Wyoming Valley of Pennsylvania, near Wilkes-Barre. It was one of thousands of small firms in the furniture industry. The company did not produce its own brand; it was a subcontractor to several of the large furniture retailers such as Pennsylvania House and Ethan Allen. A retailer like Pennsylvania House authorized Wyoming Valley Furniture to manufacture a variety of pieces (such as hutches, tables, bureaus) and each month ordered so many thousand dollars of furniture, specifying a particular mix of the items authorized. It was up to a company like Wyoming Valley Furniture to deliver the ordered pieces within its 16-week planning period and to have them pass the retailer's quality standards.

The Threatened Bottleneck

About four months ago, Pennsylvania House placed an order for 150 of a newly authorized piece, a rather elaborate dining room buffet table. Last month was the first time Wyoming Valley Furniture manufactured the buffet; the time and trouble it took to make it were greater than expected. The buffet's legs, in particular, demanded more time and care in lathe work than Wyoming Valley Furniture had allocated. (Machine setups, for example, took 15 minutes for each lot rather than the planned 8 minutes, and run times per leg were 20 minutes rather than the planned 15 minutes. In addition, considerably more rework was required than expected.) As this became evident, the company began scheduling overtime in the lathe department. Still, the buffets were delivered late. What is more, the slowdown the order caused in the lathe department spilled over into the finish mill, and 10 workers in the finish mill were without work for about 8 percent of their time over the two-week period the buffet order was scheduled through their shop. Management had been caught with no work suitable to give those workers, as orders got bottled up in the lathe department. This failure in production scheduling was not only embarrassing but also expensive. (Wages averaged $6 per hour, and workers generally worked 40 hours per week.)

The Furniture Making Process and Coping with Bottlenecks

Wyoming Valley Furniture's production process was similar to that employed by most other casegoods manufacturers. It started with the purchase and storage of rough-cut lumber of various species and grades. This lumber was then dried on racks for two weeks in the predrying shed (a large enclosure in which moderately heated air was circulated) and for two weeks in the kiln, where higher heat was applied. From the kiln the lumber was sent to the rough mill, as it was called, where an assortment of power saws (for lengthwise ripping, mitering, and end cutting), planers, tenoners, lathes, gluing machines and presses, and other tools formed the basic parts out of which the piece of furniture was assembled. Typically an order spent three weeks in the rough mill.

From the rough mill the order traveled to the finish mill, which was responsible for boring, routing, and sanding the rough milled parts and for a modest amount of subassembly. Three weeks in the finish mill was standard for an order. All of the parts needed for the assembly of a piece of casegoods furniture were gathered at the finish mill before being sent to the assembly and finishing departments. The assembly department put together each piece of furniture, and the finishing department applied the stain and lacquer to each. Inspection and packing for shipment completed the process. The typical order spent two weeks in assembly and finishing. Thus, the entire process took about 12 weeks. By adding a month, the planning period of 16 weeks was determined.

Ordinarily, Wyoming Valley Furniture was thoroughly familiar with the particular demands that the various authorized pieces of furniture it manufactured placed on machines and workers. These demands could be accommodated in the development of the production schedule so that the entire factory ran as close to perfect balance as possible. Of course, perfect balance was an ever-elusive and only momentarily achieved goal. In striving for this balance, however, the company employed a variety of rules of thumb that helped determine which orders would be grouped together in the same week and which ones shifted into other weeks. For example, only one model of dining room suite would be scheduled in one week, and only one model of hutch. In essence, bottlenecks were scheduling around whenever possible.

Most of the bottlenecks that struck the factory could not be anticipated. New products and their start-ups (such as the buffet) were a persistent cause of bottlenecks. New wood species also caused occasional problems (for example, a recent switch to oak in a particular model had caused problems). Machine breakdowns, especially of one-of-a-kind machines, always created a stir in the factory. If demand was particularly high, bottlenecks might occur simply because more orders were released to the factory than the factory could realistically be expected to work through.

Most bottlenecks were overcome by throwing more labor-hours at them—usually through calling for overtime, but sometimes by hiring or transferring workers to the bottleneck task. Other bottlenecks, usually the chronic ones, were broken by buying new equipment.

Dealing with the Threatened Bottleneck

What was particularly disheartening to George Sowerby and his production scheduler, Vic Baiz, was that there seemed to be no way that the current order of 300 buffets could be scheduled through the lathe department without incurring overtime; the demand on the lathe department was unavoidably constant. Of the 400 labor-hours estimated now for the entire order (300 pieces · 4 legs per piece · 20 minutes per leg), only 250 could safely be scheduled during regular hours. The remaining 150 hours appeared headed for overtime and a pay rate of 1.5 times the regular rate.

George and Vic were eager to avoid the problem that occurred last month, when overtime in the lathe department created scheduling problems in the finish mill that could not be resolved easily by working on orders further back in the queue. To some extent, they would rely on better scheduling now to permit smoother functioning of the finish mill, but exactly how much smoother operations would be was unknown.

An alternative to this strategy of running lots of overtime during the order and hoping for the best was a strategy of working a modest amount of overtime beginning immediately and inventorying quantities of the troublesome buffet leg. This, of course, meant incurring some inventory carrying expenses. Vic Baiz estimated the inventory expense at an average of 25 cents for every buffet leg that had to be produced in overtime.

Here were two ways of coping with the upcoming bottleneck, and George Sowerby wondered which he ought to authorize. One involved some certain extra costs (inventory expenses); the other involved an uncertain, but possibly lower, cost—the disruption that significant amounts of overtime in the lathe department might have on the finish department. George wondered how little the disruption would have to be before the latter option dominated the inventory one.

In this case, the same number of overtime hours will have to be scheduled, although they would be stretched over a longer period of time. In fact, stretching out production will almost surely increase the setup times involved on the lathe, implying even more overtime.

How costly would a disruption be if it occurred again in the finish mill? The previous order of 150 pieces, half the current order, disrupted 10 workers for 8 percent of their time over 2 weeks. Thus, 64 worker hours (10 workers · .08 · 2 weeks · 40 hours/week) were lost at a cost of $6 each, for a total cost of $384. If twice the number of pieces causes twice the level of disruption, $768 would be sacrificed. Unfortunately, we do not know whether this level of disruption in the finish mill will be maintained or whether better production planning will leave enough slack so that the finish mill workers can work around any stalled buffet legs. This uncertainty suggests some of the same sort of sensitivity analysis that we did in the Devine Nuts situation.

How costly is the inventory building alternative? The estimated overtime is 150 hours, implying that 450 legs (150/400 · 1200 legs) will be completed using overtime. At an average inventory expense of 25 cents per leg, $112.50 would be spent for the inventory itself.

This $112.50 inventory expense is considerably below the $768 estimate for the "grin and bear it" alternative. Yet both figures are "soft" and require some interpreting. The inventory expense figure, for example, is almost surely too low, because it omits the extra setup time for the lathes to run the numerous small lots. We can make some estimate of how much setup time and expense would be required. Suppose the overtime on the legs takes 10 hours per week for 15 weeks, and that the 10 hours each week consists of one lathe operator working 1 hour longer on each weekday and 5 hours on Saturday. Thus, 6 setups of 15 minutes each would be required each week, for a total of 90 setups (6 · 15) over the next 15 weeks. At 15 minutes per setup and $6 per hour, the 90 setups would cost an additional $135. A better estimate of the cost of the inventory building alternative would be $247.50 ($112.50 + $135.00).

The cost is still considerably below the $768 estimate for the "grin and bear it" alternative. This $768 figure, too, may need to be revised. If, for example, the order does not create any of the disruptions in the finish mill that prevailed last time, the $768 figure vanishes to nothing. The $768 figure assumes the same kind of disruption of worker time (8 percent) that occurred with the previous order. With the company on the alert now, it is likely that something less than an 8 percent disruption in the finish mill will actually occur. How much less of a disruption would be needed before the "grin and bear it" option dominates the inventory buildup one? The same kind of indifference calculation that we introduced with Devine Nuts can be employed here.

Let x be the fraction of the 8 percent disruption needed to equalize the costs of the two options. Then,

$$x \cdot \$768 = \$247.50$$
$$x = .32$$

This calculation suggests that if Wyoming Valley Furniture feels that it can lower the finish mill disruption to less than a third of its previous level, it should treat the order like any other. If, on the other hand, the company feels that more than that level of disruption would occur, the inventory buildup option should be followed. While these calculations do not make George Sowerby's decision for him, they serve to focus the issue.

*Lessons from Wyoming Valley
Furniture Company*

Wyoming Valley Furniture, unfortunately, was caught in a very uncomfortable position. The company did not have sufficient capacity so that the rescheduling of the order could alleviate the impending bottleneck, nor was the extra demand on the lathe department steady enough to warrant an expansion of its equipment and workforce. The company was limited in its options: it could try to head off its problems by building up an inventory of parts or it could try to "gut" it out. The assessment of such nebulous bottleneck situations is one of the chronic management dilemmas of job shops and batch flow processes. In this case, a new product introduction, which changed the product mix considerably, placed excessive demands on a single department and threatened to clog up the flexibility in scheduling that keeps a job shop or batch flow process from grinding to a halt every time a problem like this is encountered. The threat to the factory's flexibility could just as easily have come from engineering changes or quality problems demanding rework or missing parts from a supplier or something similar.

Coming to a decision on how to remedy the bottleneck called for an analysis of the costs associated with each of the options. Specifically, the analysis involved comparing the *extra* costs incurred by each alternative, since those were the only costs that differed between the options being considered.

The importance of this type of analysis and the role of demand as well as supply considerations in confronting bottlenecks is pursued in Situation 2-3.

SITUATION 2-3

CITRUS AIRLINES

Larry Klock had to confess that he hadn't thought of it, but his operations manager, Dave Dove, had proposed an intriguing, possible solution to Citrus Airlines' present shortage of seats. Larry was the president of Citrus Airlines, a small intrastate carrier serving Miami, Jacksonville, Orlando, Fort Lauderdale, Tampa, Tallahassee, and a host of smaller Florida cities. Recently, business had been booming, largely, Larry thought, because of an upturn in the economy. Citrus Airlines was using much of its equipment to the hilt and faced the prospect of having to purchase more in order to provide more seats. Larry was leery of this option, both because of the tenuousness of the current economic recovery and the comparatively recent financial good health of the airline. Dave Dove's proposal struck an imaginative middle ground.

Dove had proposed that Citrus abolish first-class seating on all of the Boeing 727s that Citrus owned.

(The 727s operated primarily between the major Florida cities, averaging 91 flights each day.) By abolishing first class, space would be provided for more seats. According to the cabin configuration of seats that Citrus had always maintained, 20 of the plane's total of 125 seats were provided for first-class passengers. If the first-class cabin were reconfigured to conform to the coach cabin, an additional eight seats could be provided. These seats could be added because coach sat five across in each row of the airplane as against four across in each first-class row and because the distance between rows in coach was slightly less (less legroom) than in first class. Dove estimated that it would cost $15,000 to alter each of the fifteen 727s in Citrus' fleet.

Of course, abolishing first class meant abolishing first-class fares as well. At present, the average first-class fare in the Citrus system was $71 as opposed to the average coach fare of $56. On the other hand, first class was a little more costly to serve, an average of $3.28 versus $1.77, because first-class food and beverage service was more elaborate.

Larry was concerned that the abolition of first-class service would adversely affect the patronage of Citrus' first-class travelers, even though Larry knew that the availability of more seats could mean substantially more revenue. To investigate these matters, Larry had called upon Sarah Hammans, the airline's marketing manager. Hammans' report is shown in Figure 2-4.

Dave Dove's suggestion about eliminating first-class service would surely help cut down on the number of flights that leave standbys behind, but Larry Klock couldn't help but wonder whether that benefit would offset the costs of reconfiguring the first-class cabins and of losing loyal first-class passengers.

Memorandum

To: Larry Klock
From: Sarah Hammans
Subject: Abolition of First-Class Seating on 727s

You asked for analysis of two points related to the abolition of our "sun-kissed" (first-class) service. Let me address them in turn.

1. Retention of "sun-kissed" travelers. Although our retention rates will vary by city-pair depending on our competition and the prevailing flight schedules, I think we would be hard-pressed to retain more than 60 percent after abolition, if these travelers can go with another airline. If the loads continue high or if other airlines abolish first class as well, we may retain them all. It's a tough call.

2. Current loads in first class and coach. Over the past two months (61 days) on our 727s, we have averaged a first-class load factor of 61.2 percent and a coach load factor of 82.9 percent.* The distribution of flights by load factor over the same period is shown in the table below:

Incidence of Load Factors (Percent of 727 Flights)

	LESS THAN 50%	50-60%	60-70%	70-80%	80-90%	90-100%	1-5 STANDBYS LEFT	MORE THAN 5 STANDBYS LEFT
Sun-kissed Service	42.3%	11.6%	12.7%	13.8%	10.9%	7.7%	1.0%	—
Coach	16.4%	10.4%	10.7%	11.3%	20.9%	18.3%	7.4%	4.6%

FIGURE 2-4   The report on abolishing first class on Citrus Airlines' 727s.

*The load factor (i.e., occupied seats as a percentage of all available seats) is a useful capacity measure, not only for airlines but for many other types of service businesses.

Discussion of Citrus Airlines

Citrus Airlines is experiencing a bottleneck. Given the heavy loads it has been carrying recently, an increasing number of standbys have been left at the airport. The heavy loads and the high number of completely booked flights have no doubt caused a number of customers to switch flight times or even airlines. If such a strong demand continues, Citrus may be well advised to add equipment and offer more flights.

As a way around the current bottleneck, Dave Dove has suggested that Citrus can fly eight more seats on every flight if first-class service is abolished. This change has some real appeal. Not only does it solve the present oversubscription of some flights, but Citrus could conceivably make more money by flying an all-coach airplane.

How is this true? For every first-class passenger under the present scheme, the airline receives $71, on the average, and expends only $3.28 on services. The company thus stands to gain $67.72 for every first-class passenger. This is money it can use to pay back its debt on the planes and other facilities and the overhead it buys. This money is also the source of its prof-

its. The figure ($67.72) is an important one; it is known as the *contribution* per first-class passenger.

Back to Citrus Airlines

At present, the contribution per first-class passenger is $67.72. The similarly calculated contribution per coach passenger is $54.23 ($56 − $1.77). Given both an empty first-class seat and an empty coach one, Citrus Airlines would naturally prefer to have a first-class passenger. The issue, however, is not which type of passenger

---

* ASIDE *

Contribution and Variable Cost

Technically, *contribution* is the difference between a company's revenue and its so-called variable costs. *Variable costs*, as the name suggests, are the costs that vary directly with production activity. Drinks and dinners served on airlines are variable costs, since they are only expenses to the airline when passengers are in their seats to drink and eat them. The lumber used in making furniture and the labor used to transform it are variable costs; they vary directly with the quantity of furniture produced. Similarly, the natural gas for drying peanuts and the casual labor used to run Devine Nuts are examples of variable costs.

These variable costs are easy to see, largely because they can be readily assigned to the units of output that people pay for—airplane tickets, pieces of furniture, tons of dry graded peanuts. The "variableness" of other costs may not be quite so neat. For example, are flight attendants' salaries a variable cost? Salaries are certainly variable when it comes to devising the schedule of flights; more flights mean more flight crews. But once the flight schedule is set, the salaries paid flight attendants do not vary with the number of passengers. In terms of our situation at Citrus Airlines, the revamping of airplanes to eliminate the first-class cabin does not alter the flight schedule or

the number of flight crews. Crew salaries then are fixed and only materials expenses are variable in this instance. This example serves to illustrate that one must be careful to think through which costs are fixed and which are variable with the particular production activity under consideration.

The $67.72 contribution per first-class passenger goes to pay crew salaries as well as to pay off airplane costs, ticketing, and a host of other costs that, for this decision, are fixed. Every additional passenger to first class who can be accommodated will contribute $67.72 to pay off these fixed charges and to secure a profit for Citrus Airlines.

Note that we can speak of contribution in a variety of forms. Total contribution is measured in dollars, as revenues less all variable costs. Contribution per unit is total contribution per unit of output and is measured in dollars per unit. In using this notion of contribution, both total contribution and contribution per unit supply the same information, but it is sometimes easier to think in terms of one rather than the other. What is esential, however, is that the costs that are considered variable be consistent with the nature of the decision for which the contribution figures are being used.

---

*

the airline prefers, but whether Citrus Airlines should abolish its first-class seating.

At present, a full cabin of 20 "sun-kissed" travelers contributes $1354.40 (20 seats · $67.72 contribution per passenger). If these 20 seats were eliminated and replaced by 28 coach seats, the total contribution would be $1518.44 (28 seats · $54.23 contribution per passenger). Thus, if Citrus Airlines can be assured of filling its converted first-class cabin with coach travelers, the company will make more money than it currently does—$164.04 ($1518.44 − $1354.40) per flight more.

By performing the same kind of calculation that was introduced with Devine Nuts and Wyoming Valley Furniture, we can easily see that the $15,000 cost of cabin conversion can be paid off in just 92 flights. To wit:

$$\$15,000 \text{ cost} = \$164.04 \text{ contribution/flight} \cdot x \text{ flights}$$

$$x = 92 \text{ flights}$$

If each Citrus Airline plane flies one completely booked flight every four days, the cabin conversion cost would be paid off in a year.

This analysis suggests that Dave Dove's recommendation to convert the first-class cabin should be followed. Yet, on closer examination, this entire analysis hinges on the assumption that the *additional* eight seats placed in the converted first-class cabin will be occupied. It is not enough to state that the *average* load factor for coach is higher than the average load factor for first class or that, if the plane were full, more contribution would ensue if all seats were coach. The decision rests with what Citrus Airlines can expect will actually happen with the additional seats in the former first-class cabin. This mode of thinking about decisions concentrates on the incremental (often called marginal) change involved; the use of such marginal analysis is absolutely fundamental to management decision making.

---

* ASIDE *

Marginal Analysis and Sunk Costs

The concept of marginal (incremental) analysis for decision making is not fancy. It's just common sense that finds application in one business situation after another. In basic terms, *marginal analysis* states that the decision to do something should depend only on how that decision would change the situation and on nothing else. The question to ask is not whether a company will be profitable after some investment or policy change has been implemented, but whether the company will be *more* profitable for having made the choice than it would otherwise have been. Everything that has gone on before is irrelevant to the decision at hand.

This kind of situation is all too common: a project is almost finished when it is recognized as a turkey. Because the finish is so close, someone argues that "for

just a little more money the project could be completed and the investment outlays to date will not be wasted." Marginal analysis says that what has gone before is irrelevant; the costs incurred are "sunk" and have no bearing on the decision. If the *additional* investment it takes to complete the project does not return *additional* revenues that are greater, the investment should be junked. As the old saying goes, "Don't throw good money after bad." The saying is absolutely right; the "bad" money represents sunk costs, and they have no bearing on the decision whether or not to continue with a project.

We shall have occasion many times to employ the concept of marginal analysis in this text. In fact, the analysis already completed on Wyoming Valley Furniture was couched implicitly in marginal (incremental) terms. The decision there rested on whether the additional costs from one option (build an inventory of legs) were likely to be lower than the additional costs from the other option (grin and bear it). In both cases, the additional revenues to be earned from the order were the same.

✳

Back Again to Citrus Airlines

Can Citrus Airlines fill enough of the additional eight seats so that the total contribution of an all-coach plane exceeds that of the present airplane configuration? We have some information from the marketing report memorandum.

In the first place, we know about the standbys that have been left behind. Assuming an average of two left behind in the "one to five" category and six left behind in the "more than five" category, we can calculate the number of passengers that we could have been sure to seat on the 91 daily flights over the past 61 days. To wit:

$$\frac{61 \text{ days} \cdot 91 \text{ flights}}{\cdot 1\% \cdot 2 \text{ standbys/flight}} = 111.02$$

$$\frac{61 \text{ days} \cdot 91 \text{ flights}}{\cdot 7.4\% \cdot 2 \text{ standbys/flight}} = 821.55$$

$$\frac{61 \text{ days} \cdot 91 \text{ flights}}{\cdot 4.6\% \cdot 6 \text{ standbys/flight}} = 1532.08$$

$$111.02 + 821.55 + 1532.08 = 2464.65 \text{ people}$$

At a contribution per coach passenger of $54.23, these stranded passengers could have provided a total contribution of $133,660 in those two months if the first-class cabin had been remodeled.

This is not the full story, of course, since the previous first-class passengers must be accounted for. At best, Citrus Airlines will forgo the increased contribution that the first-class passengers made on all of the 727 flights. This "opportunity cost" is every bit as real a cost as the $15,000 per plane conversion change. The difference in contribution is $13.49 ($67.72 − $54.23) per first-class passenger. Over the past two months the total added contribution forgone (the opportunity cost of remodeling the cabin) would have been $916,568 (61 days · 91 flights · 20 seats · 61.2% load factor · $13.49).

This figure is naturally much larger than the gain in contribution from seating standbys in the eight additional seats provided by remodeling. The vast contribution gained by having first-class passengers on the flights that are not completely booked far outweighs the opportunity costs represented by standbys who could not get on existing flights. This comparison is all the more unfavorable to remodeling the first-class cabin if in fact customers begin deserting the airline.

Given these considerations, Dave Dove's ingenious plan for increasing capacity and breaking a bottleneck does not appear to be attractive enough to implement.

Lessons from Citrus Airlines

The Citrus Airlines situation brings together three of the basic concepts that guide good decision making at all levels of a company.

1. Opportunity cost (revenue forgone)
2. Contribution, and its companion concept, variable cost
3. Marginal analysis, and its companion concept, sunk cost

A useful analysis of Citrus Airlines' decision on "sun-kissed" service demands that these concepts be melded together. By the conclusion of this text these concepts should be second nature to every reader.

Let us review how each concept fits into the analysis of Citrus Airlines' situation:

1. *Opportunity cost.* By eliminating first class the airline was forgoing the difference in contribution between "sun-kissed" service and coach service. This loss would be every bit as much a cost to the airline as the cabin conversion expense of $15,000 per plane.

2. *Contribution.* For an already scheduled flight the cost of adding more passengers is small, since all the expenses of flying are fixed except for the drinks and food the airline serves. Thus, variable costs are very low, and the contribution each passenger makes to pay off the fixed investment in equipment and salaries is high. Contribution (revenue less variable costs) is the key statistic used in deciding the issue in this situation.

3. *Marginal analysis.* The decision about eliminating first-class service rested on the use of the additional eight seats put into the first-class cabin. Could the change they represented, including the opportunity cost incurred, be expected to generate enough contribution to pay off the added expense of converting that cabin?

PLANT LAYOUTS AND BOTTLENECKS

Earlier, this chapter discussed the use of process flow diagrams and inventory buildup graphs as tools for identifying and analyzing bottlenecks. Those tools look essentially at process elements, their capacities, and the time involved (capacity per unit of time or inventories accumulated per unit of time). What those tools ignore is the spatial aspects of production—how materials and product move from point to point in the factory. This "geography" is too important to ignore. As noted previously, bottlenecks can be created from poor plant layouts. Poor layouts can

- interrupt the physical flow of materials
- add direct labor time to the product
- introduce excessive handling with the risk of damage and loss
- cause queues of work-in-process inventory to proliferate throughout the factory
- keep workers and/or managers at a distance from one another when in fact they should be close
- increase the time it takes to manufacture the product
- increase setup time unduly
- add to overhead
- crowd departments into too little space
- contribute to poor housekeeping
- make any plant expansion more difficult to accomplish
- and otherwise add costs to the operation

Some poor layouts are born, but most are made. That is, some poor layouts are bad designs from the beginning, but most poor layouts develop bit by bit over time, as one change after another is made. New products get introduced, and the space they need is hurriedly assigned. New equipment is purchased, and a place is quickly found for it so that the rest of the process is not disturbed while it is debugged. The plant is expanded, but to avoid disruption, it is not completely re-laid out; only a few areas are. In these ways, over time, bottlenecks are built into the process and its layout.

Types of Layouts

The plant and service tours of Segment I described a number of different layouts. Generally those layouts can be classed into three major categories—job shop, time flow, and fixed position—although several offshoots are possible.

The Job Shop (or Process) Layout

The *job shop layout,* as exemplified by Norcen Industries, groups similar machines together. Such a layout makes sense if jobs are routed all over the place, there is no clear dominant flow to the process, and tooling and fixturing need to be shared. For example, if the process sheet calls next for grinding, in a job shop layout, it is clear where the job is to be routed. The job can then enter the queue of work for the next available grinder in the group. If, on the other hand, grinding machines were scattered throughout the factory, there would be chaos. The job of production control and materials handling would be difficult; priorities and machine availabilities would be very tough to track and to execute well.

There are some other benefits to grouping like machines together, as well. For example, maintenance and setup equipment can be stored nearby. And, operators can run two or more pieces of equipment without thorough cross-training to enjoy the productivity gains inherent in such a scheme.

The job shop (or process) layout is attractive when routings are unique to each job, a situation that would create chaos in a more line flow layout.

The Line Flow (or Product-Specific) Layout

If there is a discernible, dominant flow to the process, then a *line flow layout* has tremendous advantages over a job shop layout. Materials handling can be greatly simplified, and the space necessary for production can be reduced. Production control is easier; the paperwork trail to each job in the job shop can be largely abandoned. In effect, the layout itself acts to control priorities. Work-in-process inventories can be shrunk to a fraction of what they would be in a job shop layout. Production cycle times can be similarly reduced, making the feedback of quality information that much quicker and more effective, as well.

There are a variety of line flow (or product-specific) layouts. At one extreme are the continuous flow process layouts, with their very high capital intensity (for example, International Paper's Androscoggin Mill). For these processes, it is very true that the process is the layout and the layout is the process. Changing one means changing the other, and any changes involve tremendous expense, and, for that reason, are accomplished only occasionally.

At the other extreme are worker-paced line flow processes that do not involve much plant and equipment (such as Burger King). Rather, they are more labor and materials intensive. These processes are very flexible; they can be rebalanced, turned, lengthened, chopped up, etc. with comparative ease. Lying in between the extremes are machine-paced lines (as those in General Motors-Tarrytown) that are more flexible than continuous flow process but not as flexible as worker-paced lines.

The worker-paced lines can typically produce a number of different product "models" at the same time. This is often also true of some machine-paced lines. These mixed-model lines are equipped and their workers trained to do quick setups, where needed, and to choose (or adapt) the proper materials to the model indicated. In these mixed-model lines, similar models are typically interspersed among the other models assembled. Often, this helps balance the line by not tossing a succession of over-cycle* tasks at key workers. (Recall the discussion of GM-Tarrytown, which practiced mixed-model assembly.)

The Fixed Position Layout

A layout in which materials are brought to a stationary product is termed a *fixed position layout*. It is common when the product itself is so massive and/or awkward that transporting it through the process is unreasonable. Construction and shipbuilding are readily recognizable examples of fixed position layouts. So, too, is the auto repair operation of Howard Ford (Tour G).

Fixed position layouts are typically chosen by default. There are several crippling aspects of fixed position layouts that do not recommend them for a wide variety of products. First, they make materials handling more difficult because a "kit" of similar parts has to be broken up and distributed at the proper time to a variety of products-in-process rather than delivered to a single point along the line. Second, workers of different types and skills have to move from product to product, or else a single set of workers has to remain with the entire job. In the former case, scheduling worker movements becomes a chore, while in the latter case training workers to do the entire job takes time and resources. Third, quality control becomes more problematic in fixed position layouts. Inspectors often have to roam, and that may waste operators' time. Moreover, one does not have the luxury of evaluating the process capabilities of just one machine or one station along the line; there are many stations to eval-

uate, as many stations as there are stalls filled with work-in-process.

In the past 20 years, there have been some attempts by automotive companies (notably Volvo) to employ a fixed position, "stall build" layout. The argument for it was enhanced responsibilities and motivation for the workers involved. Despite their best efforts, however, the stall build experiments were never as successful as the conventional assembly line. In sum, fixed position layouts are usually not the most efficient layouts, but for the products or services to which they apply, there is no good substitute.

These, then, are the three major categories of operations layouts. As we noted in Segment I, many processes are hybrids, and often these hybrids exhibit hybrid plant layouts. The most common hybrid is the job shop/assembly line hybrid process with a job shop/line flow layout.

The Power of the Line Flow Layout—Recent Trends

As described previously, the one layout that is not in some way a default is the line flow (product-specific) layout. The job shop layout works best only when there is no dominant flow to the process, and the fixed position layout applies to products and services where moving the product is just too troublesome. There is real power in the line flow layout: efficient use of labor, sure and effective materials handling, little buildup of work-in-process inventory, specialization of tooling and methods, and quick feedback of quality problems.

The spread of a concept termed "group technology" is testament to this power.** In es-

*For a definition of *over-cycle*, see Tour D.

**See N. L. Hyer and V. Wemmerlov, "Group Technology and Productivity," *Harvard Business Review*, (July–August 1984), pp. 140–49; N. L. Hyer, "The Potential of Group Technology for U.S. Manufacturing," *Journal of Operations Management* 4, no. 3 (May 1984), pp 183–202.

sence, group technology is the conversion of a job shop layout into a line flow layout. Instead of grouping similar machines together, group technology may call for grouping dissimilar machines together into a line flow process all its own. In the new arrangement, a part can travel from one machine to another without waiting between operations, as would be customary in the job shop. Work-in-process queues of material are thus reduced; individual parts move more quickly through the process.

Group technology takes a hard look at the products or parts manufactured in a job shop layout and identifies those that are similar enough to share the same dominant flow. These products/parts are then grouped together and routed through a series of machines that are placed in close proximity to one another. These machine "cells," typically U-shaped, may be manned by one or by several individuals. (See Figure 2-5.)

Grouping the products or parts that require the same sequence of operations may demand a special, sophisticated part numbering scheme that helps to isolate the key common characteristics. Product/part characteristics that may differentiate product/part families from one another include the diameter of the part, whether the external surface is smooth, whether the internal surface is smooth, whether flat milling has to be done, and whether there are any holes to be drilled. By developing a numbering scheme to highlight these characteristics, routings and production plans can be concocted without undue difficulty.

Many group technology layouts have been adopted by plants that have not required elaborate part numbering schemes. These plants have been clear from the start about which parts are compatible with group technology; thus, they do not need much sophistication in scheduling parts to particular cells.

Closely related to group technology is the U-line. In its most common application, the U-line is a spur off of a main assembly line that feeds the main assembly line with precisely the parts required to synchronize with the main assembly line's schedule of production. (See Figure 2-6.) With a U-line, parts fabrication that traditionally was accomplished elsewhere in the factory and in big batches is done adjacent to the main assembly line and in just the quantities needed by that line. The U-line is generally responsible for several different models or options of parts, so it must maintain considerable flexibility with the ability to make quick setups of the machines along its line. One of the advantages of the U-shape is that one, or just a few, workers can tend the line without having to take too many steps. There are also some materials handling advantages to the U-line layout, as well as quick feedback about quality problems. However, the most persuasive argument for U-lines is their ability to feed the main line precisely, without the buildup of any inventory and without interrupting the smooth flow of the process. U-lines were popularized in Japan, and more discussion of them, in the context of Japanese manufacturing techniques, is found in Chapter 10.

It is worth repeating: The attractiveness of both group technology and U-lines is the conversion they make possible from the job shop layout to the line flow layout. They help turn a hybrid process into a process that is line flow in character from stem to stern.

Other Trends in Plant Layouts

Although two of the most interesting trends, group technology and U-lines, have already been discussed, there are some other trends to note as well, many inspired by the Japanese. For example, in recent years, layouts are incorporat-

A. A conventional job shop layout.

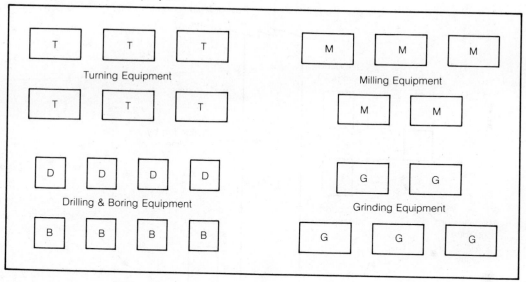

B. A group technology layout.

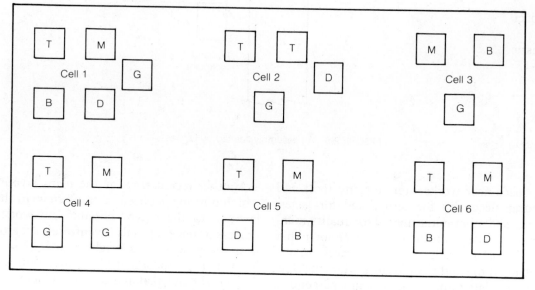

FIGURE 2-5   What group technology does to the layout.

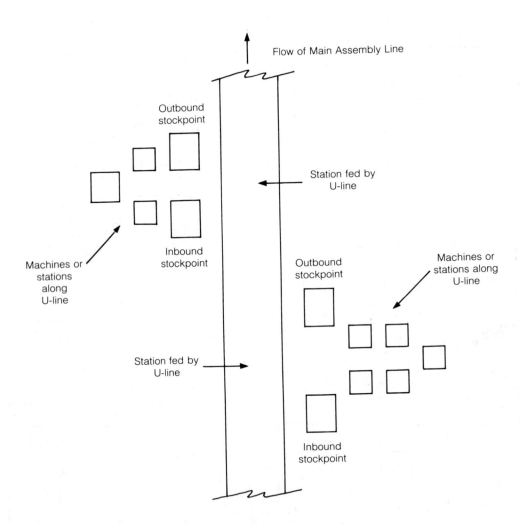

FIGURE 2-6 An assembly line fed by U-lines.

ing space near workcenters for any tools and fixtures necessary for setup, and for gages, charts, and other items needed for quality management. Often, the new layout is such that the flow of materials can progress easily in one direction through the workcenter while the flow of setup-related items can flow in a perpendicular direction through the workcenter.

Another recent trend is the plant layout in which nothing is obscured from view. In these layouts, to the extent possible, no work-in-process or raw materials inventories, are stored near the process at a height greater than eye level. This protocol helps keep inventories under control and also makes any problems with the process more visible for both workers and managers. Often, the stockpoints are carefully labeled with paint or tape on the floor to indicate material storage locations. Such spatial discipline can assist production control; see Chapter 4's discussion of "kanban squares."

There has been some rethinking, as well, about materials handling. Many conventional layouts have significant investments in conveyors of various types. Besides being an expense, conveyors sometimes encourage more room between workcenters and more work-in-process inventory than is necessary. Instead, rethinking argues for simpler materials handling—gravity feeds, push-along carts—and workcenters positioned close together. Counter to this trend in one sense but consistent with it in another is the trend in some companies to use automatic guided vehicles. These riderless carts travel along guide paths either embedded or grooved into the floor. The carts carry loads of materials to specific points in the factory. They are an expense and a complication to materials handling, and some managers do not favor them for just that reason, but they do not use labor, and, in that sense, are consistent with the other moves to simplify materials handling.

Devising New Layouts

The industrial engineering of layout design is both art and science. It is beyond the scope of this book to explain in any depth the techniques used to develop new layouts or to improve existing ones. We will merely indicate some key steps one can take in devising layouts for factories or services:

1. *Examining the process flow.* Is there a dominant flow? What is it? What constraints to layout exist because of the process itself?

2. *Gaging the extent and importance of the flows.* How much material and information travels from one element of the process to another? Which flows are so important that close proximity is absolutely required?

3. *Determining area space needs.* How much space do particular operations or departments require? Are there special constraints to be aware of, such as with any existing structures? Has enough space been allocated for tooling, fixtures, and work-in-process?

4. *Arranging the layout.* What kinds of layouts satisfy the nature and extent of the flows within the process and do so within the space constraints specified? Which ones may be more flexible, or perhaps more streamlined, than others?

5. *Determining traffic flows.* What are the prevailing traffic patterns around and within the process? Do they cross or otherwise threaten congestion or safety? How will materials, tools, and fixtures be moved?

WAITING LINES AND BOTTLENECKS

Let's look again at Devine Nuts and some other concerns Frank Coyne has about his operation.

THE GENERAL ANATOMY OF WAITING LINE PROBLEMS

The situation at Devine Nuts is but one variant of an entire family of waiting line problems. The tremendous variety of waiting line problems is due to the many combinations of the following types of characteristics they can exhibit:

1. The arrival (or input) process
   - What kind of distribution do the arrivals follow? A popular, and useful, distribution to employ is the Poisson (discussed later), although others can be used.
   - Do the arrivals come singly, or do they sometimes also come in bulk? (Think of customers waiting to be seated at a restaurant in parties of one, two, three, four, and more.)
   - Does the length of any line serve as a deterrent to arrivals, or will the arrivals all simply take their chances?

2. Queue discipline (the order in which arrivals are served)
   - First come, first served? Last come, first served? Random?
   - Are arrivals permitted to leave the waiting line? If so, what characterizes their leaving ("reneging")?

3. The service process
   - What type of probability distribution describes how arrivals are served by the process? Is the rate of service a constant, or is it also a stochastic event, like the arrival rate? Clearly, in many types of service situations the amount of time a service employee must spend with a customer can vary markedly; we have all kicked ourselves for choosing the wrong line at the bank, or ticket counter, or supermarket.
   - Is there more than one line? How many?
   - Must arrivals go from service person/station to service person/station, or can one handle all of an arrival's needs?
   - A *mixed system* includes more than one line (sometimes called a *channel*) and more than one person/station (some-

SITUATION 2-4

DEVINE NUTS (REPRISE)

Although Frank Coyne's major concerns were with the massive truck waits that were possible when too many wet peanuts arrived for drying, he was also concerned about the level of service that Devine Nuts provided farmers even when there was plenty of drying capacity. Even on good days, trucks generally had to wait in line for a while, especially during the early evening peak period. Frank was concerned how a 10 percent to 15 percent expected increase in next year's harvest might affect this routine waiting, and naturally whether any additional waiting might deter farmers from contracting with Devine Nuts.

During a typical day, 120 tons of peanuts were delivered between noon and 10 P.M., 40 tons of that total within the 5 to 7 P.M. time period. Trucks averaged 8 tons per delivery. Devine Nuts' unloading crew could dump only one truck's contents at a time, averaging 15 minutes per unloading.

times called a *phase*). What kinds of paths through any mixed system are there?

With so many possibilities for the arrival and service processes and the queue discipline, it is easy to appreciate that most queuing problems are tackled either by (1) simplifying the problem so that mathematically tractable means can be applied, or by (2) using computer simulation techniques to ape what we think the true behavior is and draw out its implications.

ROUTINE WAIT AT DEVINE NUTS

It has been discovered that many ordinarily occurring phenomena—radioactive decay, calls coming into a telephone switchboard, as well as people or trucks entering lines—come close to obeying a particular kind of probability distribution called the Poisson distribution, named for the French mathematician who first studied it in 1837.

According to the Poisson distribution, the probability that exactly k events (e.g., phone calls, people entering a line) occur in a time period of length t is equal to

$$\frac{e^{-\lambda t}(\lambda t)^k}{k!}$$

Where e is the base of the natural logarithms $(e \approx 2.71828)$ and $k!$ (k factorial) means $k \cdot (k-1) \cdot (k-2) \cdot \ldots \cdot 1$. As it turns out, this distribution has a mean (arithmetic average) of (λt) and a variance of (λt) as well.* We can think of λ (the Greek letter lambda) as indicating the arrival rate, the number of events that occur per unit

---

*The variance of a distribution, $f( )$, of a random variable, x, is a measure of how dispersed the distribution is. It is obtained by squaring each deviation of x from the mean, $\bar{x}$, and weighting the squared deviations by their corresponding probabilities. Symbolically for a discrete distribution of N values, the variance (var x) can be written as

$$\text{var } x = \sum_{i=1}^{N} P_i(x_i - \bar{x})^2$$

where P_i is the probability that x_i occurs. Alternatively, it may be written as

TABLE 2-1 Formulas describing the performance of a single channel, single phase waiting line with Poisson arrival and service rates

λ = arrival rate (such as units entering the line per hour)

μ = service rate (such as units processed from the line per hour)

1. Average Utilization = $\dfrac{\lambda}{\mu}$

2. Mean Number in the Waiting Line = $\dfrac{\lambda^2}{\mu\,(\mu\text{-}\lambda)}$

3. Mean Number in the Entire System = $\dfrac{\lambda}{(\mu\text{-}\lambda)}$

4. Mean Time in the Waiting Line = $\dfrac{\lambda}{\mu(\mu\text{-}\lambda)}$

5. Mean Time in the Entire System = $\dfrac{1}{\mu\text{-}\lambda}$

Let us see how these waiting line formulas can come to Frank Coyne's aid. There are four situations we can examine:

1. A routine day with no peak period
2. The peak two-hour period of a routine day
3. A routine day with no peak period, but with 10 percent to 15 percent more delivered
4. The peak two-hour period of a routine day, but with 10 percent to 15 percent more delivered

Let us calculate the performance of Devine Nuts in each of these situations.

of time t. This arrival rate, λ, is a key component of the various waiting line formulas that can be applied.

The Poisson distribution anchors the simplest formulas for examining waiting lines and their performance. The performance of the simplest waiting line case, where there is one line (or channel) and one station (or phase), can be described by the formulas in Table 2-1. These formulas depend on λ (the arrival rate) and μ (the service rate, which is defined in exactly analogous fashion to λ). Naturally, μ must be greater than λ; otherwise, the service could never catch up with the arrival rate, and an ever-growing waiting line would result.

Routine Day, No Peak Period

The arrival rate of trucks (λ) is 1.5 per hour, calculated as

$$\frac{120 \text{ tons/10-hour day}}{8 \text{ tons/truck}} = 15 \text{ trucks per 10-hour day}$$

or 1.5 trucks per hour.

The service rate (μ) is 4 trucks per hour (15 minutes for unloading each truck)

1. Average utilization is $\dfrac{\lambda}{\mu} = \dfrac{1.5}{4} = 37.5\%$.

2. Mean number in line is
$$\frac{\lambda^2}{\mu(\mu-\lambda)} = \frac{(1.5)^2}{4(4-1.5)} = 0.225 \text{ trucks.}$$

$$\text{var } x = \sum_{i=1}^{N} P_i(x_i^2) - \bar{x}^2$$

The standard deviation is another way to express the dispersion of a distribution. It is merely

$$\text{standard deviation, } s_x = \sqrt{\text{var } x}$$

The standard deviation has the advantage that it is measured in the same units as the random variable x itself.

3. Mean number in system is
$$\frac{\lambda}{(\mu - \lambda)} = \frac{1.5}{(4 - 1.5)} = 0.60 \text{ trucks.}$$

4. Mean time in line:
$$\frac{\lambda}{\mu(\mu - \lambda)} = \frac{1.5}{4(4 - 1.5)}$$
$$= 0.15 \text{ hours or 9 minutes.}$$

5. Mean time in system is
$$\frac{1}{(\mu - \lambda)} = \frac{1}{(4 - 1.5)} = 0.40 \text{ hours or 24 minutes.}$$

Note that even though the unloading crew is idle most of the time, there is a small average wait of 9 minutes per truck. Because it takes an average of 15 minutes to unload each truck, it is no surprise that the mean time in the system is 15 minutes more than the mean wait time.

Let's now examine the peak period to see how much worse it can be expected to be.

Peak Period, Routine Day

While the service rate, μ, is the same, the arrival rate, λ, has increased to 2.5 trucks per hour. That is calculated as

$$\frac{40 \text{ tons/peak period}}{8 \text{ tons/truck}}$$
$$= 5 \text{ trucks per 2-hour peak period}$$
$$= 2.5 \text{ trucks/hour}$$

1. Average utilization is up to
$$\frac{\lambda}{\mu} = \frac{2.5}{4} = 62.5\%.$$

2. Mean number in line is
$$\frac{\lambda^2}{\mu(\mu - \lambda)} = \frac{(2.5)^2}{4(4 - 2.5)} = 1.04 \text{ trucks.}$$

3. Mean number in system is
$$\frac{\lambda}{(\mu - \lambda)} = \frac{2.5}{(4 - 2.5)} = 1.67 \text{ trucks.}$$

4. Mean time in line is
$$\frac{\lambda}{\mu(\mu - \lambda)} = \frac{2.5}{4(4 - 2.5)}$$
$$= 0.417 \text{ hours or 25 minutes.}$$

5. Mean time in system is
$$\frac{1}{(\mu - \lambda)} = \frac{1}{(4 - 2.5)}$$
$$= 0.667 \text{ hours or 40 minutes.}$$

Observe that a 67 percent increase in the arrival rate—from 1.5 to 2.5 trucks per hour—leads to a 178 percent increase in waiting time.

We can turn now to Frank Coyne's concern about a prospective increase in the harvest.

Routine Day, No Peak Period, 10 Percent to 15 Percent Increase in Deliveries

For convenience, assume that the number of deliveries increases from 15 per day to 17 per day, a 13.3 percent increase. Thus, $\lambda = 1.7$ per hour and μ remains the same at 4 per hour.

1. Average utilization is $\frac{\lambda}{\mu} = 42.5\%$.

2. Mean number in line is
$$\frac{\lambda^2}{\mu(\mu - \lambda)} = \frac{(1.7)^2}{4(4 - 1.7)} = 0.31 \text{ trucks.}$$

3. Mean number in system is
$$\frac{\lambda}{(\mu - \lambda)} = \frac{1.7}{(4 - 1.7)} = 0.74 \text{ trucks.}$$

4. Mean time in line is
$$\frac{\lambda}{\mu(\mu - \lambda)} = \frac{1.7}{4(4 - 1.7)}$$
$$= 0.185 \text{ hours or 11.1 minutes.}$$

5. Mean time in system is
$$\frac{1}{(\mu - \lambda)} = \frac{1}{(4 - 1.7)}$$
$$= 0.435 \text{ hours or 26.1 minutes.}$$

In this case, deliveries have increased by 13.3 percent, but the waiting time has increased by 23 percent.

Peak Period, Routine Day, 10 Percent to 15 Percent Increase in Deliveries

Again, assume 17 trucks per day, with a third of them arriving within the 5 to 7 P.M. peak period. Thus, λ grows to 17/3 = 5.67 trucks in 2 hours or 2.833 trucks per hour.

1. Average utilization is
$$\frac{\lambda}{\mu} = 70.8\%.$$

2. Mean number in line is
$$\frac{\lambda^2}{\mu(\mu - \lambda)} = \frac{(2.833)^2}{4(4 - 2.833)} = 1.72 \text{ trucks.}$$

3. Mean number in system is
$$\frac{\lambda}{(\mu - \lambda)} = \frac{2.833}{(4 - 2.833)} = 2.43 \text{ trucks.}$$

4. Mean time in line is
$$\frac{\lambda}{\mu(\mu - \lambda)} = \frac{2.833}{4(4 - 2.833)}$$
$$= 0.607 \text{ hours or } 36.4 \text{ minutes.}$$

5. Mean time in system is
$$\frac{1}{(\mu - \lambda)} = \frac{1}{(4 - 2.833)}$$
$$= 0.857 \text{ hours or } 51.4 \text{ minutes.}$$

Compared with the peak period of a routine day now, deliveries have increased by 13.3 percent (5.67 trucks versus 5 trucks), but the waiting time has increased by 46 percent. Observe that this peak period increase in waiting time, given the 13.3 percent increase in deliveries, is even greater than the 23 percent increase in waiting time for the no-peak-period case, given the same 13.3 percent increase in deliveries. This is an important point about waiting lines.

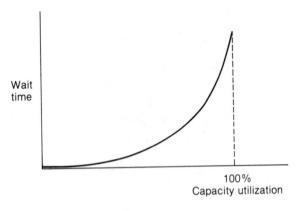

FIGURE 2-7   Wait time versus capacity utilization in queuing situations.

The length of any wait can rise dramatically as capacity approaches full utilization.

For many businesses the plot of waiting time versus percent capacity utilization looks like the curve in Figure 2-7. This truism about waiting lines suggests that capacity choice for operations like Devine Nuts or Burger King or others is absolutely critical; a capacity use that is too high can have disastrous effects on customer waits and customer satisfaction.

This phenomenon reinforces the need to manage capacity effectively. In a service operation, not only is having some spare capacity essential to avoiding lengthy waits, but that capacity must be available when needed. This typically means that labor must be scheduled to match peaks in demand and any equipment or supplies must be thoroughly prepared in advance.

More Discussion of Devine Nuts: Some Further Refinements

The previous analysis treated Devine Nuts's situation on routine days when there were no

FIGURE 2-8   Inventory buildup at Devine Nuts when day's supply of peanuts arrives early.

large deliveries of especially soggy peanuts. Of special concern to Frank Coyne are days when 300 tons of wet peanuts arrive. The analysis of this situation earlier in the chapter assumed that trucks arrived at an even pace of 30 tons per hour. In reality, of course, truck arrival is likely to be a much more random occurrence (sometimes referred to as a "stochastic event"). For example, there might be an early rush on the dryers that would put 300 tons of peanuts before the dryers within 2 or 3 hours after noon. In that case, Figure 2-2 might be altered to look like Figure 2-8. Here, on day 2, 300 tons of peanuts arrive for drying by 2 P.M. We already know that, once all Devine Nuts' dryers are filled, it will be midnight before any of the first dryers to be used will be free again. In fact, our calculations showed that it would be 2.2 hours after midnight before the last truck could unload into the dryers and head home. If we have trucks waiting from near 2 P.M. in the afternoon until after 2 A.M. the following morning, those trucks will have been waiting over 12 hours,

and their peanuts may be ruined. Such a situation is exactly what Frank Coyne wishes to avoid.

How likely is such an occurrence? Should Frank be worried?

It can be shown that if events occur in accordance with a Poisson probability distribution, the time spent waiting for the rth event (say, the tenth truckload of peanuts) follows a probability distribution of

$$(1) \qquad f(t) = \frac{\lambda}{(r-1)!}(\lambda t)^{r-1}e^{-\lambda t}$$

where $f(t)$ is the probability that the rth event occurs in time period t. This expression is called *a gamma distribution* with parameters r and λ.

This gamma distribution implies in turn that the probability that the number of events occurring in the time from 0 to t is at least r is equal to

$$(2) \qquad 1 - \sum_{k=0}^{r-1} \frac{1}{k!}(\lambda t)^k e^{-\lambda t}$$

where Σ indicates a summation of different terms and k takes on integer values from 0 to $r-1$ in successive terms.

While awkward, expression 2 is a tool we can use to soothe a potentially worried Frank Coyne. How so? Well, first we can assume that the arrival of truckloads of peanuts follows a Poisson distribution. The next step is to come up with a plausible value for λ, the rate at which arrivals occur per unit of time. On a peak day we know that 300 tons of peanuts arrive in 10 hours, and so it is fairly natural to assign the value of 30 tons per hour to λ.

We are ready now to define our problem in terms of expression 2. What we want to find out is the probability that 300 tons of peanuts arrive in the space of two hours. The values to plug into expression 2 are

$$\lambda = 30 \text{ tons per hour}$$
$$t = 2 \text{ hours}$$
$$r = 300 \text{ tons}$$

Expression 2 can be rewritten as

$$(3) \qquad 1 - \sum_{k=0}^{300-1} \frac{1}{k!}(30 \cdot 2)^k e^{-30 \cdot 2}$$

The first term of the summation is thus

$$(4) \qquad \frac{1}{0!}(60)^0 e^{-60} = 1 \cdot 1 \cdot e^{-60} = 8.75 \cdot 10^{-27}$$

and the last term is

$$(5) \qquad \frac{1}{299!}(60)^{299} e^{-60}$$

which, unfortunately, is very tedious to evaluate, since 60^{299} and $299!$ are such huge numbers that they blow up even the most sophisticated calculators.

Fortunately, we can scale down our problem to manageable size and lose little in the process. Instead of setting λ at 30 tons per hour, let us set it at one truckload per hour, implicitly assuming that one gargantuan truck arives, on the

TABLE 2-2   Evaluating expression 6

k	Value of $\frac{1}{k!}(2)^k e^{-2}$
0	.1353
1	.2707
2	.2707
3	.1804
4	.0902
5	.0361
6	.0120
7	.0034
8	.0009
9	.0002
Total	.9999

average, each hour with 30 tons of peanuts. Thus, r becomes 10 truckloads instead of 300 tons. Expression 2 can be rewritten as

$$(6) \qquad 1 - \sum_{k=0}^{10-1} \frac{1}{k!}(1 \cdot 2)^k e^{-1 \cdot 2}$$

Table 2-2 evaluates expression 6 to determine the probability that ten 30-ton truckloads of peanuts will descend on Devine Nuts in the space of two hours. Using these data, then

$$\text{value of } 1 - \sum_{k=0}^{9} \frac{1}{k!}(2)^k e^{-2} = 1 - .9999 = .0001$$

The result, of course, is that Frank Coyne need not fret at all, if indeed peanuts arrive at Devine Nuts in the way we have assumed. There is next to no chance that Devine Nuts would be inundated with peanuts so quickly. Even if the time were extended to three hours, the probability would rise to only .0012.

We can use the Poisson distribution to answer still another question surrounding the situation at Devine Nuts. Recall that a crop increase of 10 percent was expected in the next year and that Frank Coyne had translated that figure into a corresponding rise of 10 percent in his expected peak day. Was Frank justified in doing that? Will the peak day's harvest increase in direct proportion to the increase in the total year's harvest?

Let us assume again that the Poisson distribution does an adequate job of describing the arrival of peanuts at Devine Nuts. An increase in the year's harvest will raise the daily mean harvest, since the days of harvesting cannot be expected to change. A 10 percent increase in the year's harvest can thus be expected to raise the daily mean harvest by 10 percent as well. But what about the peak day?

Suppose we class a peak day as any day that is at least two standard deviations (2σ) greater than the mean (λ). What we want to know is what happens to the positioning of the peak day $(\lambda + 2\sigma)$ when λ is increased. Remember that in a Poisson distribution the mean and the variance are the same. Thus, one standard deviation is equal to $\sqrt{\lambda}$. An increase of 10 percent in the mean, say, from 1.00 to 1.10 will only increase the peak day's harvest, as we have defined it, from

$$1.00 + 2(1.00) = 3.00$$

to

$$1.10 + 2(\sqrt{1.10}) = 3.20$$

which is an increase of only 6.6 percent. Under a Poisson distribution, the size of the peak day's harvest rises at a rate that is less than proportional to the increase in the average daily harvest.

This result should be even more comforting to Frank Coyne. Not only is it unlikely that he will be swamped by a too rapid delivery of soggy peanuts on a peak day, but his estimate of how much greater the peak day's arrivals will be as a consequence of the farmers' increased planting is high.

There are, of course, more refined and complex formulas available for describing the performance of more complicated queuing problems. However, most of the queuing problems one finds in actual production and service operations quickly become more complicated than mathematical techniques can solve. One then confronts the choice of using mathematical techniques to approximate a solution or of investing time and effort in simulating the waiting line and thereby discovering its properties. Frequently, a queuing problem that may be complex can be broken apart into smaller problems that resemble simpler queuing phenomena. A multichannel system, such as a drive-in bank with three lanes, might be approximated as three separate single-channel systems, each with a third the demand of the full operation. For many applications, however—especially if the waiting line problem is an important one to the operation—simulation is the best way to find a solution.

✳ ASIDE ✳

Simulation

The ever-increasing size and speed of computers have made simulation an ever more attractive means of obtaining some acceptable solutions to large-scale and/or complex problems, such as many queuing problems. In many ways simulation substitutes brute force (raw computer power) for the elegance (but lack of realism) of the mathematical model. Although often more realistic, simulation is much more art than science; mathematical models can often be characterized as right or wrong, whereas simulation models tend to be either good or bad. The typical simulation model is a kind of mathematical "black box" that takes some initial inputs, processes them, usually over a number of periods of time, and spits out some outputs.

The first step in constructing such a model is to identify the variables of interest. Variables, quite naturally, refer to those values within the simulation that are permitted to vary over time. The choice of variables for a simulation takes judgment, since only variables that are important to the result should be included and they should be defined in units of measure that are appropriate. A simulation of truck arrivals at Devine Nuts, for example, would surely define arriving peanuts (measured in, say, tons per hour), truck wait (hours), and peanuts processed as variables. One might also include the moisture content of the peanuts as a variable as well, freeing the analysis from the assumption that all the arriving peanuts are uniformly soggy and thus need a full 36 hours in the dryer. On the other hand, the unloading time per truck may not matter much and thus not be worth including. Once identified, the variable should be set with some initial values (subject to change, of course) in different model runs.

Initial conditions apply not only to variables but also to some of the parameters of the simulation. Parameters, in contrast to variables, are those simulation values that remain fixed during any single run of a simulation. Often, successive runs of a simulation will modify one or more parameters intentionally, but during any one run all parameter values remain fixed. For example, the *mean* rate of arrival of peanuts to Devine Nuts and the company's total drying capacity are likely parameters for a simulation of Devine Nuts' operations.

A crucial stage in developing any simulation model is detailing the relationships among the variables and parameters and how they will vary, if at all, with the march of time. A number of these relationships will almost always be of an accounting nature, but many will serve to "drive" the model. The kinds of relationships that alter variable values in important and often systematic ways are frequently termed *decision rules*. They specify under which conditions variables of all kinds will be changed and how. In a simulation of Devine Nuts' situation, for example, one decision rule might check to see whether the drying capacity has been reached and then allocate arriving peanuts either to dryers or to the truck wait. Accounting relationships would then keep track of the peanuts dried and drying, and the trucks waiting.

Simulation models can be either deterministic or probabilistic. That is, the simulation can be built to yield exactly the same outputs, given the same sets of initial conditions and parameters (a deterministic model); or some elements of chance can be introduced so that the same initial conditions and parameters would yield different, although probably similar, outputs (a probabilistic model). The most useful simulation of Devine Nuts' situation would be a probabilistic one (also called a *Monte Carlo simulation* after the casino in Monaco), which would draw at random a value for the arriving peanuts variable from a probability distribution like the Poisson. The choice of probability distribution for such purposes is thus another important feature of building a simulation model.

Once a simulation model has been constructed—variables, parameters, initial conditions, accounting relationships, decision rules, probability distributions—it is put through its paces. Usually a lot of tinkering goes on—more or fewer periods are run, parameters changed, initial conditions revised, relationships altered, variables added. All of this tinkering occurs to check on the simulation model's behavior. Are the results plausible? Do changes in parameters, initial conditions, or relationships yield the expected results?

After the model has been debugged and is functioning smoothly, its outputs can be used directly for decision making or (as is common for probabilistic models) can be accumulated in a data bank and investigated with statistical tools and hypothesis testing.

---
*

Simulation Models

To understand more clearly how a simple simulation model might be developed, consider Situation 2-5.

Discussion of Burger Queen Steamer Inventory Decision

Determining the level of cooked burger pattie inventory that should be kept in the steamer is

SITUATION 2-5

BURGER QUEEN—STEAMER INVENTORY DECISION

The Burger Queen restaurant in Gastonville, North Carolina, operated much like a Burger King. It offered regular hamburgers and a large hamburger sandwich called "The Big One." Burger patties were broiled at a high temperature on a continuous chain broiler; they had to be placed on the chain broiler no oftener than one pattie every 5 seconds. Meat patties of both sizes were completely cooked during their 30-second ride through the continuous chain broiler. After the broiler was a "burger board" where workers assembled regular burgers and Big Ones. A regular burger could be assembled, packaged, and placed in the finished goods chutes within 20 seconds; a Big One took 30 seconds.

Between the chain broiler and the burger board was a steamer that could keep cooked meat patties warm for 10 to 15 minutes without any deterioration in their taste and freshness. Burger Queen's management was interested in determining how many cooked meat patties of each type should be kept in the steamer at different times. The success of the inventory level for the steamer would be judged by whether a transaction time standard of 1 minute or less for any order could be maintained.

A typical stream of orders during a reasonably busy time of day was as follows:

	Order Number	Order
Start	1	2 burgers
	2	1 Big One
	3	1 burger, 1 Big One
	4	2 Big Ones
	5	3 burgers
1 minute elapsed time		
	6	2 burgers
	7	3 Big Ones
	8	1 burger
	9	2 burgers, 1 Big One
	10	1 Big One
	11	4 burgers
2 minutes elapsed time		
	12	2 burgers
	13	1 burger
	14	1 burger, 2 Big Ones
	15	3 Big Ones
3 minutes elapsed time		
	16	1 burger, 1 Big One
	17	3 burgers
	18	1 Big One
	19	2 burgers, 2 Big Ones
	20	1 burger
4 minutes elapsed time		

a problem ideally suited to simulation. Let us work through how such a problem could be simulated.

The parameters of this simulation—those values that stay unchanged during the simulation—include the ride time through the broiler (30 seconds), burger assembly time (20 seconds), Big One assembly time (30 seconds), waiting time interval between patties on the broiler (5 seconds), the number of patties that can be cooked per minute (12 patties), and the level of inventory in the steamer (maximum chosen for each run).

The key variable of interest is the *transaction time*—the time between the placement of the order and its presentation to the customer. The goal is to have that time be 1 minute or less. In this somewhat simplified situation, the transaction time for any order will equal the longest time to complete any burger or Big One in the order. We are assuming that on orders of more than one burger or Big One, assembly of the multiple items is simultaneous and that board capacity is great enough that sandwich assembly is not delayed for any sandwich. We are also assuming that all Big Ones in any order

TABLE 2-3   Completion times and transaction times
(assuming no inventory is kept in the steamer)

ORDER NUMBER	COMPLETION TIMES (seconds) SANDWICHES				TRANSACTION TIME (seconds)
	#1	#2	#3	#4	
1	50	55			55
2	60				60
3	60	55			60
4	60	65			65
5	50	55	60		60
6	50	55			55
7	60	65	70		70
8	50				50
9	60	55	60		60
10	60				60
11	50	55	60	65	65
12	50*	55*			55
13	50				50
14	60	65	60		65
15	60	65	70		70
16	60	55			60
17	50	55	60		60
18	60				60
19	60	65	60	65	65
20	50				50

*Order #11 calls for the thirteenth and fourteenth meat patties in the previous minute's time. Thus, if order #12 is called for within the first 10 seconds of its time period (between minutes 2 and 3), its transaction time will be later than 55 seconds because the broiler can cook only 12 patties in a minute. Its transaction time could be as high as 65 seconds. To be accurate, the simulation should keep track of capacity demands on the broiler.

are worked on first, because they have the longer assembly time. The variables that make up the computation of transaction time include the number of burgers in the order, the number of Big Ones in the order, the cooking time for each pattie, and the extent of any wait in placing patties on the chain broiler.

To calculate the longest time to complete any burger or Big One in an order, one must compare the completion times for all the sandwiches in the order. A sandwich's completion time depends on whether the pattie was drawn from the steamer or had to be broiled. If the former, the completion time equals the time it takes to assemble the sandwich. If the latter, the completion time is the sum of both the assembly time and the cooking time (which is the ride time through the broiler plus any waiting because the broiler can take only one pattie every 5 seconds). This wait can be calculated by multiplying 5 seconds times the number of patties preceding a particular one in an order through the broiler.

The simulation of transaction times is driven by the sequence of orders. One such sequence is given in the situation description, but others are possible and, indeed, desirable for computing an effective level of inventory for the steamer. Suffice it here to use the stream of orders given above.

Table 2-3 displays the completion times for each sandwich in the order (Big Ones first) and the transaction times for that order, assuming that no inventory is kept in the steamer. These simulation results show that the transaction time standard is exceeded 6 times in the 20 orders simulated, or almost one-third of the time. This finding suggests that keeping an inventory of cooked meat patties in the steamer is indeed desirable. Hence, the next trial of the simulation model could attempt to keep one meat pattie of each size in the steamer to see how transaction times are affected. (The calculation of transaction times for this stream of orders, assuming steamer inventory levels of one or two patties, is part of Problem 13 at the end of the chapter.)

How should the simulation keep track of the steamer inventory? This monitoring is clearly needed. The steamer inventory has to be constantly replenished, and it cannot be if more than 12 meat patties are ordered in a minute. (How the steamer inventory can be monitored and replenished is part of Problem 13 at the end of the chapter.)

Now, in broad terms, we give a description of the simulation model that the Burger King Corporation developed.

Burger King Revisited: The Restaurant Simulation Model

The Burger King Corporation's restaurant simulation model (actually there were several models, because each type of restaurant configuration required a different model) was one of the tools that the corporation used in 1982 to keep it a technological leader in the fast food business. That a simulation model would be useful for helping to make many different decisions was not immediately apparent to Burger King management; the realization crept up on them gradually.

In the late 1970s Burger King experimented with a number of innovations, the most prominent of which was the introduction of several specialty sandwiches. Market research had shown an encouraging consumer response to specialty sandwiches, but it was not known how they would affect service delivery at existing restaurants. As mentioned in the tour F discussion of Burger King, a key measure of a restaurant's operation was its speed of service; the faster people can be served a quality product, the happier they will be and the more customers a restaurant will serve, particularly during peak periods. Burger King in the late 1970s had no easy way to assess the impact of specialty sandwiches or other innovations on a restaurant's speed of service. Before something like a new specialty sandwich could be rolled out to the thousands of Burger Kings worldwide, the company had to experiment in an actual restaurant to see what its effect on operations would be. Generally speaking, several restaurants were used for each experiment. Typically, two weeks' worth of data were collected so that there would be enough data for different days of high and low sales volumes. A typical experiment cost between $6,000 and $8,000 and required a good deal of time to analyze the results.

It occurred to some farseeing Burger King managers that a mathematical description of a restaurant might be able to perform the same kind of service as a field experiment but at much lower cost. At first, a linear programming model was used to isolate particular bottlenecks in a restaurant's operations, but it was soon realized that a linear program could not adequately capture the dynamics of restaurant operations, where the most interesting problems occurred. Given this insight, it was decided to embark on building simulation models for Burger King restaurants.

The Structure of the Simulation Model

As initially conceived, the simulation model, like an actual restaurant, consisted of three broad, interrelated areas: (1) customer arrivals and orders, (2) food preparation, and (3) the delivery of orders to customers. Within each of these areas, the simulation model had various modules that described particular aspects.

- *Customer arrivals and orders.* Of course, Burger King has little or no influence on arrival and order process. Thus, the simulation model simply attempted to mimic accurately what occurred in the typical restaurant on various days of the week and during various hours of the day. Particular modules isolated the behavior of in-store versus drive-thru arrivals as well as in-store versus drive-thru order generation.

  These modules were based on observed facts. It had been observed, for example, that the arrival pattern of customers followed an exponential function (that is, the plot of the cumulative percentage of arrivals versus the time between those arrivals traced out an exponential curve). It had also been observed that a relatively small number of order types account for most orders received at the restaurant (the five most common combinations of choices—such as burger, fries, and drink as opposed to specialty sandwich and shake—accounted for 45 percent of all the orders placed).

  In sum, the customer arrival and order segment of the model was designed to reflect, on a day-by-day and an hour-by-hour basis, the specific orders that were typically placed at a Burger King.

- *Food preparation.* Of the three areas, Burger King had the most control over food preparation. The company had considerable discretion in changing equipment, procedures, layout, and staffing. The production system was thus modeled in considerable detail. Elements of this modeling included descriptions of all the operating procedures for mak-

ing anything that could be requested of the kitchen. There were, thus, modules that detailed how regular Whoppers were made, how regular chicken sandwiches were made, how french fries were prepared, and how shakes were drawn. The model's descriptions of these activities, in turn, depended upon (1) the labor times for each task (such as the time it took to dress a bun crown for the Whopper Sandwich); (2) the kitchen layout that determined the distances workers had to walk between tasks; and (3) the equipment configuration, since processing times depended in part on the choice of equipment for the kitchen. Other elements of the production system included the number of workers who worked at any time and their positions and responsibilities within the kitchen, the inventory rules (for example, 10-minute maximum hold time for all sandwiches). Typical simulation modules for the production system included such things as regular Whopper preparation, special Whopper preparation, regular burger preparation, shake preparation, broiler and steamer operation, and in-process and final inventory levels.

- *The order delivery system.* This area of the simulation model dealt with how orders were taken, assembled, and presented to the customer. Tasks in this delivery system were divided between in-store and drive-thru tasks. The times for customers to state orders and for cashiers to punch them in, make change, and assemble orders were determined separately for different order configurations and staffing assignments of the cash registers. Representative simulation modules included in-store order assembly and delivery, and drive-thru order assembly and delivery.

The Burger King simulation models are written with a special simulation computer language called *GPSS*. The GPSS simulation style is to simulate activities by orienting discrete events in time. A GPSS model begins its simulation at time period 0 and inquires about which activities are to begin then or are to be continuing at that time. When the model is stepped ahead to time period 1, it keeps track of those activities that are to be continued, those that will end in that period, and those that will start then. The simulation is analogous to constructing a movie by taking a series of snapshots at numerous points in time. In 1982, a typical Burger King simulation model application required 3,000 lines of GPSS code and took about one minute of processing time on an IBM 3033 computer to execute.

The construction of the simulation model required an enormous amount of data. Time and motion studies specific to Burger King were used along with methods time measurement (MTM) data to develop time standards for the many operations performed by workers in the kitchen or at the counter. Information was also gathered from a sampling of 40 restaurants nationwide. These restaurants offered a diversity of characteristics such as sales volumes, ownership (franchise versus company), and facilities (drive-thru versus non-drive-thru). The information gathered from these restaurants was incorporated into the model to ensure that its operation matched operations at typical Burger King restaurants.

Before the corporation was willing to use the simulation model to run low-cost "experiments" of proposed innovations, the model underwent a "live test." The company took some space in a warehouse and set up an actual restaurant kitchen and service area. Actual orders from cash register tapes, representing both high and low sales volumes, were read to the service counter people. This live test ran an entire week, during which all aspects of the operation were measured and videotaped. The same streams of orders were fed into the simulation model, and its results were compared with those from the live test. The simulation model was adjusted until the differences between the two according to measures such as service times, lengths of queues, and locations of bottlenecks turned out to be very slight. This success convinced upper management of the worth of simulation for analyzing their type of operation.

The Burger King simulation model is modular in that any of the many restaurant configurations operating at any given manning level can be represented relatively easily by joining the appropriate modules together. These individual models undergo constant revision, because each innovation that the company would like to test requires reprogramming at least certain aspects of the model.

Uses of the Simulation Model

The Burger King simulation model has been used for a variety of purposes. Its first major use came in the development of the Burger King Productivity Improvement Program. For this program, manuals were developed that indicated the potential service bottlenecks and their remedies for each level of restaurant sales. Thus, a franchisee could examine a manual to discover how to break those bottlenecks and so maintain service standards as restaurant sales grew. The manual also indicated the rates of return for expenditures on remedying any of the potential bottlenecks. These studies took between six and eight months to complete, with about 300 runs of the model each month.

From this success, the corporation's industrial engineering and operations research department, responsible for the development and maintenance of the simulation model, moved on to develop labor staffing standards for each restaurant configuration. About a year was spent exploring the issue and developing the standards. Two key needs were addressed:

- The minimum number of employees needed for any sales level and their duties so as to be able to satisfy corporate speed-of-service goals.
- A means for management to control the labor needs (a "labor" formula).

By repeated use of the simulation model for different store configurations, given different levels of sales and different positioning of the workforce, a set of manning tables was derived. For example, before the use of the simulation model, it was not known definitely how best the tenth worker could be positioned as sales climbed. Was that worker best added to the burger board or added as a cashier? The output of the model showed that more customers could be served and the average speed of service could be kept within the three-minute standard by shifting that worker to the cashier position. In fact, the model's results showed that five more customers per hour (150 versus 145) could be served in this way and that the average speed of service could be maintained at 176 seconds per customer as opposed to 188 seconds. Results of this type resulted in savings, for each restaurant, of 1 to 2 percent of sales.

To address the management control needs, equations were estimated by regression analysis to predict the aggregate level of labor needed, given an optimum schedule for that labor. The equations, defined for different restaurant configurations, used real weekly sales and the number of hours open as explanatory variables.

The simulation model was instrumental in the design of the BK50 restaurant configuration, which was described in Tour F. The model permitted "experiments" that shifted equipment around the kitchen, seeing how these changes would affect service times and staffing

levels. Burger King's use of a two-window drive-thru lane, rather than a multilane drive-thru as is often seen in drive-thru-banks, is another example of the use of the model. The simulation model predicted that this innovation would increase capacity by 15 percent during peak hours; this estimate has been borne out with actual increases of 14 percent.

In a drive-thru, what is the optimum stack size (number of car lengths) between the order board and the pick-up window? This was another question that Burger King wanted addressed. If that distance was too short, a car would have to wait at the pick-up window because the food was not ready; if the distance was too long, the food would be cold by the time the car got there to pick it up.

Analyzing this question through the use of the simulation model was straightforward. The model's customer arrival and order system generated cars for the drive-thru lane. The model also specified the distance between the street and the order box and between the order box and the drive-thru window. Naturally, if the drive-thru lane between the order box and the window was filled, no other car could reach the order box to place an order.

A longer stack size was simulated simply by altering the capacity of the drive-thru lane between the order box and the window. By varying this parameter from one to 11 or 12 car lengths, the company was able to see which stack sizes were most conducive to reducing the transaction time at the drive-thru window and thus to increasing the number of cars served per hour. The graph in Figure 2-9 shows that a stack size of six to eight seemed optimal.

A more challenging problem was whether to add small specialty sandwiches to the Burger King menu to complement the large specialty sandwiches that were Burger King staples. It was known, for example, that if small specialty sandwiches were introduced, they would some-

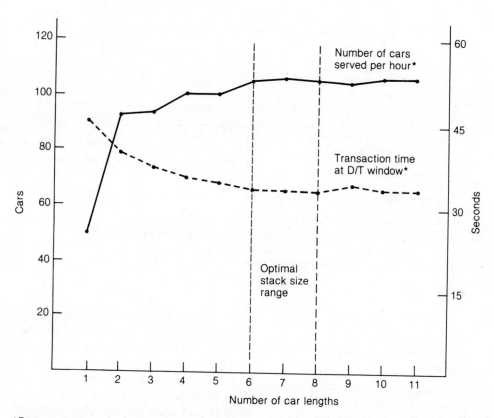

*Does not include car at window or at order box.

Based on (1) December 1979 Miami prices, (2) average company order configurations and product mix, (3) a capacity for 20 cars from pick-up window to drive-thru entrance, and (4) K-700 kitchen layout.

FIGURE 2-9 Stack size between order box and pick-up window (in car lengths).

times be ordered instead of large specialty sandwiches and sometimes instead of other Burger King menu items (particularly burgers). Specialty sandwiches take somewhat longer to prepare than burgers, and small specialty sandwich patties would have to be cooked separately from large ones because the frying times are different. At issue then was how the introduction of small specialty sandwiches would affect service times, given a different pattern of orders and some additional constraints on the kitchen.

Studying such a problem involved changes to five modules in the simulation model:

1. *Order generation.* To obtain data for changing this module, a marketing test on small specialty sandwiches was performed in Wilkes-Barre, Pennsylvania.

2. *Preparation of regular specialty sandwiches.* MTM analysis was used to obtain data for adapting the module on preparation of specialty sandwiches to the smaller sandwiches.

TABLE 2-4   Operational effects of adding small specialty sandwiches

EFFECT TYPE	POSITION/EQUIPMENT/ATTRIBUTE	UTILIZATION		
		BEFORE SMALL SPECIALTY SANDWICH	WITH SMALL SPECIALTY SANDWICH	
			CURRENT FRYER CAPACITY	WITH EXTRA FRYER
Equipment and Manpower Utilization	Fry operator (% of time busy)	52.8	54.2	57.4
	Specialty board (% of time busy)	58.5	70.2	68.7
	Multipot 1 (times down/hour)*	23	26	25
	Multipot 2 (times down/hour)†	—	—	3
Customer Service	Average number of customers behind customer being served	1.14	.95	.93
	Average transaction time (seconds)	109	121	119

Note: The data are based on a product mix of 72% Whoppers and burgers, 19% specialty, and 9% small specialty.

*The frying vat that was used for cooking chicken.

†The frying vat that was added to break the potential bottleneck at multipot 1.

3. *Preparation of special specialty sandwiches.* Again, MTM analysis was used to study the changes in labor standards implied by the smaller sandwiches.

4. *Fry station operations.* This module had to be changed because the patties for these small specialty sandwiches would be cooked by the fry station operator. Moreover, at low volumes, the fry operator would also take on the responsibility of preparing the sandwich and not simply frying the pattie.

5. *Stocking rules.* The introduction of small specialty sandwiches modified some of the stocking rules for work-in-process inventory and finished goods inventory in the chute. For example, the introduction of a small chicken sandwich might change the stocking rules for the large chicken sandwich, given some substitution away from the large chicken sandwich to the smaller one.

Table 2-4 reports the simulation results for small specialty sandwiches—what effect they can be expected to have on the utilization of equipment and manpower and on customer service. As can be seen in the figure, the introduction of small specialty sandwiches, even with the addition of an extra fryer, increased average transaction times by at least 10 seconds. This deterioration of service was even more pronounced at lower sales levels. There were two reasons for this deterioration:

• Preparation times for the small specialty sandwiches remained longer than the preparation times for the burger and Whopper sandwiches that they sometimes replaced; thus they made the entire kitchen operation more labor-intensive.

• The demand for small specialty sandwiches was rather low to begin with, and effective stocking was difficult, implying a high risk of waste. Consequently, an order for a small specialty sandwich was similar to an order for a special on any of the sandwiches, and these specials always took longer to prepare.

Based on these results and insights, Burger King withdrew its plans for the introduction of small specialty sandwiches.

QUEUING THEORY AND DECISION MAKING

The raison d'être for both the mathematical and simulation techniques for analyzing queuing problems, of course, is to provide insights for management action on the queues themselves. Typically, queues can be managed in a host of ways. Earlier, in discussing the anatomy of waiting line problems, elements of the arrival process, queue discipline, and the service process were noted. Many of these elements can be affected by particular management actions. Indeed, in service industries, where customer happiness while waiting in line is crucial, significant management attention is focused on managing the queue properly and with techniques to make the wait feel shorter (diversions).

To illustrate the importance of waiting line management to a company and the types of management actions available to it, recall the Burger King restaurant description in Tour F. It was noted there that two major shifts had occurred in the way Burger King managed customer wait. The company had switched from a single-line system that was multistation (a single channel, multiphase system in the jargon) to the so-called hospitality line-up, which is multiple line but single station (a multichannel, single-phase system in the jargon). No longer did people place their orders with one hostess and receive their order from another; one hostess took care of all tasks. Furthermore, a single, sometimes long line was replaced by shorter, multiple lines. Although somewhat more labor-intensive, the hospitality line-up apparently could serve more people, cutting down on customer wait.

For the new Church St. Burger King, the company has changed to a multichannel, multiphase system that is at once less labor-intensive and still able to meet the demands of the peak period rush.

In an operation like Burger King's, attention to customer wait stands behind the careful modulation of capacity (line rebalancing) that occurs both in the kitchen and at the front counter. The decision on when each day to add another checkout stand and hostess is an important one and a direct application of waiting line analysis and the Burger King restaurant simulation model.

QUESTIONS

1. What do you understand by the term *bottleneck?* Describe one method of analyzing bottlenecks.

2. What is an indifference calculation and why is it used? Formulate your own example to show how the indifference calculation is used.

3. What is contribution?

4. Explain opportunity cost.

5. Explain marginal analysis.

6. Define the three important decision-making concepts embodied in the problem-solving process undertaken by Citrus Airlines. Taking an example of your own, show how these concepts can be applied.

7. Waiting line problems have similar general characteristics. What are these? Give an example of each from the situations presented in this chapter.

PROBLEMS

1. How can bottlenecks arise in a multistage production system?
2. How can bottlenecks be remedied? Be specific.
3. What was the fundamental decision faced by Wyoming Valley Furniture? Why was the company's initial problem characterized as a bottleneck problem? Could the company have arrived at the same decision by any other management method?
4. Hope Hospital currently has 80 rooms and is able to charge $75 per day for occupancy of each room. Because Hope has had to turn away patients several times during the last two months, the administrator is considering expansion of the facilities to 100 rooms at a cost of $500,000. Assuming that variable costs per day average $60 per room and that all rooms will be filled, how long will it take the expansion to pay for itself?
5. If Hope Hospital expands to 120 rooms, it can do so by spending $600,000 rather than the $500,000 in problem 4. In addition, however, variable costs will increase to $65 per room per day, and it is expected that the average occupancy rate will be only about 90 percent.

   a. How does this change your analysis from problem 4?
   b. Which alternative is better?
   c. If revenue per day could be changed for the second alternative, at what revenue per day would the two alternatives break even?

6. Flowers' Gourmet Food Store has come into vogue; sales are up by 20 percent over last year. On an increasing number of occasions, however, the wait for checkout has been uncomfortably long. The store is served by only two cash registers, which are located near the exit. The store's management realizes that an additional cash register or two must be installed, but where? One option, of course, is to install the register(s) near the other two, although this would necessitate some rearrangement of the exit area. Another option, requiring less rearrangement, would be to put a cash register in a particularly busy department or two (such as deli, wine bins, butcher shop). Many customers come in for one or two items only and could use these cash registers.

   a. How should Flowers' Gourmet make such a decision?
   b. What data should be collected?
   c. What factors would tip the decision toward one option or the other?
   d. Would a simulation model (as discussed in the chapter appendix) be helpful for such a decision, and, if so, what should its structure be?

7. Refer back to Situation 2-4. Suppose to unloading crew at Devine Nuts can reduce the unloading time of a truck to 10 minutes instead of 15. Recalculate the queuing performance formulas for this change.
8. Refer back to Situation 2-4. Suppose the unloading crew at Devine Nuts can only unload a truck in 20 minutes rather than 15. Recalculate the queuing performance formulas for this change.
9. The Thunder Bank was a regional processor of VISA and Mastercard transactions for merchants. For transactions over a certain dollar limit, merchants were required to phone in for an authorization before the sale could be completed. The Thunder Bank handled an average of 2000 authorization calls per hour during most of the year and 4000 calls per hour during the Christmas buying season. The receptionists at the bank could handle 45 calls per hour on average.

The bank wanted to maintain a service standard of 60 seconds average wait per call.

a. How many receptionists do you estimate the bank needs to employ during the non-peak period of the year in order to meet its service standard? What assumptions have you made to come up with this estimate?

b. How many receptionists does it need for the Christmas season?

10. Suppose the Thunder Bank purchased the credit card business of another bank which had itself a substantial volume of transactions (1000 per hour average during the off-peak season and 2000 calls per hour on average during the Christmas peak). How would the additional volume of calls affect the authorization process? Would you expect the number of receptionists to have to increase in the same proportion as the increase in calls (50 percent more), less than proportionately, or more than proportionately? Why?

11. Sal's Pizza operates a delivery service that promises delivery within 40 minutes of a call-in order or the customer gets $2 off the price. Sal's operation can make a pizza every 3 minutes, on average. Pizzas take 12 minutes to bake, leaving Sal's delivery team 25 minutes to deliver the hot pizza. The travel area around the pizza shop was 10 minutes maximum. Assuming that calls for pizza came in at a rate of one every 5 minutes, and that both pizza demand and supply are Poisson distributed, what do you think of Sal's policy? Support your answer as best you can.

12. How would the advice we gave to Frank Coyne in the chapter appendix (see "More Discussion of Devine Nuts") change if he were concerned about 250 tons of peanuts arriving within a space of three hours, when the normal arrival rate (Poisson distributed) is 50 tons per hour?

13. Using the order sequence provided in Situation 2-5 in the chapter appendix, how would the simulation of the Burger Queen restaurant's operations change if one meat pattie of each size were kept in steamer inventory? if two meat patties of each size were kept in steamer inventory? How must you monitor and replenish the steamer inventory to get the best results you can?

14. Suppose that in Situation 2-5 in the chapter appendix we cannot assume that sandwich assembly is simultaneous and that board capacity is always great enough not to cause delays. Suppose there were only four workers assembling sandwiches. How would that affect transaction times in the simulation? Suppose there were five workers. What would change?

SITUATION FOR STUDY 2-1
BEACON GLASS WORKS REVISITED

Jose Torrez, production manager at Beacon Glass Works, Marysville, West Virginia (see Situation for Study A1), recently decided that the packaging department of his plant should package all finished goods and place the goods in stock rather than wait for customer orders.

The packaging department had four sections: finished goods storage, package breakdown,

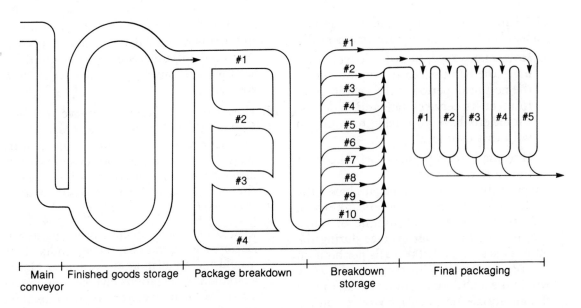

FIGURE 2-10   The flow of goods through the packaging department at Beacon Glass Works.

breakdown storage, and final packaging. Figure 2-10 is a diagram of the packaging area. The finished goods storage consisted of a circular conveyor that held trays of 1000 pieces of each product. This conveyor could hold up to 5000 trays of products, depending upon the mix of lengths and diameters of the products. The production process could feed up to 3000 trays of tubing per day into the storage area. The package breakdown area was necessary because different customers wanted different numbers of pieces for each order—normally, anywhere from 100 to 500 pieces per container. The breakdown area consisted of four long conveyors, each of which could handle a maximum of 400 trays per day. The foreman in charge of the breakdown area, Jesse Brown, normally scheduled breakdown by looking in the storage area to see what product had the largest quantity in storage.

Once the trays were broken down into individual containers, they were passed to a breakdown storage area with 10 gravity-feed conveyors that could store the equivalent of 5000 trays at any one time. The final packaging area had five packaging stations, fed by a conveyor belt that went from the breakdown storage into the packaging area. Here packaging could be done at a rate of 500 trays per day per station. Final packaging originally had been done to customer order, but because of storage problems at the finished goods storage area, Jose had decided to package to stock.

After three months of trying the new packaging procedure, Jose noticed that (1) finished goods storage was continuing to pile up, (2) package breakdown was almost always running at full capacity, (3) breakdown storage was full, and (4) final packaging was still being done basically to customer order, with "expeditors" running around the packaging area looking for products to fill customer orders.

1. What is the information flow in the packaging area? How should information be processed in this area? Why?

2. What suggestions do you have for Jose to "break the bottlenecks" in the packaging area? How would your suggestions help?

3. What other information would you like to have to make the "best" economic decision about how to break the bottlenecks? Explain how you would use this information.

SITUATION FOR STUDY 2-2
UNIVERSITY VENDING

University Vending President Ted May had to decide soon what to do about the request from his operations chief, Dwight Bradley. One of the company's five routemen was retiring, and Bradley wanted to train a new person.

May had not approved Bradley's request for a new person yet because of his concern about the company's already-high labor costs. University Vending's labor costs for the routes averaged 20 percent of total costs, while the industry average was only 16 percent. (University Vending's total costs and its average salary and benefit package of $14,500 per worker were close to the industry average.)

Ted suspected that the route structure was inefficient. The system currently had five routes, as shown in Table 2-5. Three of the routes were "product" routes (i.e., they serviced particular kinds of drink or food machines such as candy, sandwiches, and soft drinks), and the other two were "geographic" routes (that is, they serviced all types of food and drink machines within a particular geographic area). Many locations were serviced by two product routes, and some were serviced by all three product routes. The product routes had originally been set up to minimize the costs of holding inventory; with fewer people handling any one type of product, the amount of buffer stock was kept to a minimum.

The number of machines to be serviced had expanded dramatically in the last several years. As new locations and new machines were added to the system, their service requirements had simply been tacked on to the existing routes.

The routemen received a daily schedule of the machines they had to service, which they followed exactly. Because of the add-on process of scheduling new machines and the lack of strong supervision of the route schedules, the daily schedules would typically take the routemen back and forth across University Vending's service territory several times a day.

The five routes covered all the vending machines at Eusden University and Woodruff College. The vending machines were spread uniformly throughout 63 different buildings on the Eusden and Woodruff campuses. The two campuses were located four miles from each other. University Vending had the exclusive contract

TABLE 2-5   Routes currently serviced by university vending

ROUTE	PRODUCT	GEOGRAPHIC COVERAGE	TIME
1	Soda, candy, snacks	Hospital	Day
2	Soda, candy, snacks	Hospital	Night
3	Candy, snacks	Both campuses	Day
4	Candy, snacks	Both campuses	Day
5	Drinks	Both campuses	Day

TABLE 2-6   Time standards at university vending

MACHINE TYPE AND NUMBER OF EACH	STANDARD SERVICE TIME/MACHINE (minutes)	NUMBER OF SERVICINGS	TOTAL STANDARD SERVICE TIME* (minutes)
Showcase (26)†	29	189	5481
Small candy (37)	16	88	1408
Small snack (15)	16	46	736
Soda (57)	19	156	2964
Hot drink (23)	15	61	915
Milk (5)	20	28	560

*Weighted average standard time 19 minutes per machine.

†Showcases (with big glass fronts) handle candy, chips, and snacks.

to service all the vending machines on both campuses, including Eusden's large, on-campus medical facility, in which University Vending's two geographic routes were located.

Each of the routes followed a two-week cycle, during which every machine was serviced between one and six times, depending on the machine's sales volume; most machines were serviced two or four times during each two weeks. There were 163 machines on the two campuses, each of which was serviced an average of 3.5 times every two weeks. Almost all the buildings had two or more machines.

The hospital routes were unusual because they required no driving between machine locations. University Vending kept a separate vending warehouse within the hospital, from which the routemen walked to the machines they had to service.

Servicing the machines entailed not only refilling the product levels and collecting the revenues, but also cleaning the machines and making sure they were working properly. As shown in Table 2-6, time standards had been established for the service of different types of machines; these standards were found to match the actual service times closely.

Each routeman had six hours a day available to service the machines; the other two hours were spent on lunch, breaks, inventory stocking, and other nonservice activities. A recent study showed there was a wide discrepancy in the amount of time each routeman actually spent servicing the machines. (See Table 2-7.)

The study also indicated that even though the workers on the hospital routes had the best service ratio, some of the time they spent walking to the machines was actually aimless wandering. The workers on routes 3, 4, and 5, however, were hard pressed to finish their routes in the time allotted. The study pointed out that the nonhospital routes averaged 19 minutes of driving between locations, and four minutes of walking to each machine. The hospital routes currently took five minutes to walk to each machine.

According to the study, a switch to the more efficient geographic routes would reduce the driving time on the nonhospital routes to an average of four minutes; it also pointed out that the walking time to any machine in the five routes should be only four minutes. These new estimates would result in substantial time savings. For instance, a building that had a drink and a food machine currently took 38 minutes to drive to (two routemen at 19 minutes each), while under a completely geographic system, one person could service both machines with only four minutes of driving.

The current service schedule required 351 separate stops in a two-week period, which could be reduced to a minimum of 202 stops by getting rid of all multiple route stops, that is, by switching to geographic routes. Ted felt

TABLE 2-7   Time study results for university vending

ROUTE	PERCENTAGE OF 6 HOURS SPENT SERVICING	PERCENTAGE OF 6 HOURS SPENT DRIVING OR WALKING	MACHINES SERVICED PER DAY	LOCATIONS SERVICED PER DAY
1	79%	21%	15	5
2	79%	21%	15	5
3	55%	45%	9	8
4	56%	44%	9	8
5	55%	45%	9	8

that the company should stop using product routes and should put in a complete system of geographic routes.

The main argument against that type of route structure was that inventory levels would have to be increased 25 to 33 percent to provide a suitable buffer stock for the additional routemen using each product. The current inventory levels are shown in Table 2-8. All inventories were replenished weekly, with ending inventories kept as low as possible. The company's cost of carrying inventory was 15 percent of the value of the inventory, and its opportunity cost on the money tied up in inventory was estimated at 12 percent.

Ted did not foresee any further expansion for his company in the next several months. He decided to take a detailed look at the possible savings of switching to geographic routes.

1. If University Vending switches to geographic routes, how much time would it take to service, drive to, and walk to the vending machines?

TABLE 2-8   Current inventory levels at university vending

PRODUCT*	AVERAGE NUMBER OF CASES IN INVENTORY	AVERAGE COST PER CASE
Chips	100	$ 7.38
Candy bars	90	31.49
Gum	6	67.50
Soda	40	17.00
Cigarettes	10	346.80
Hot drinks	5	45.00

*Excess milk products were picked up daily by the dairy.

2. How many routemen would be necessary to service geographic routes?

3. How much extra cost is involved in increasing the buffer stocks of inventory?

4. Based on the answers to questions 2 and 3, what would your recommendation to Ted be?

REFERENCE NOTE

Suggested readings for queuing phenomena include Harvey M. Wagner, *Principles of Operations Research*, 2d ed. (Englewood Cliffs, N.J.: Prentice-Hall, Inc., 1975) and James A. Fitzsimmons and Robert S. Sullivan, *Service Operations Management* (New York: McGraw-Hill Book Co., 1982). Wagner's book includes a discussion of simulation.

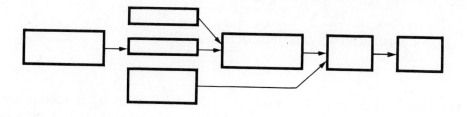

MANAGING THE WORKFORCE

What makes a workforce supervisor truly effective? The answer to this question will be sought as long as there are workers and supervisors. No text can pretend to teach all the subtleties involved in successfully managing workers, and this text certainly does not. It can aspire only to introducing some of the issues involved in understanding work performance and behavior in the workplace. To this limited end, this chapter deals with methods and time study; standards, incentives, and wage schemes; and aspects of job design and worker relations.

While this chapter concentrates on the worker, we should not lose sight of the fact that workforce performance is greatly affected by product design, materials, process design, plant and work station layout, tooling, maintenance, and setup. Workforce policies cannot be divorced from an appreciation for how these factors interact with the workers themselves.

METHODS IMPROVEMENT[1]

From taking our various plant tours we already know that companies spend a great deal of time and effort to improve the methods used by their workers. This was particularly true of the more labor-intensive operations—Norcen Industries, Jos. A. Bank, General Motors, Burger King, and Howard Ford. While methods engineering is not ignored at places like Stroh's and International Paper, their capital-intensive operations are much more dependent on the choice, layout, and functioning of equipment; in many such plants, the workforce methods are determined largely by the equipment choice and the flow characteristics of the process. In contrast, at places like Norcen, Bank, General Motors, and Burger King, considerable supervisor and industrial engineer time is devoted to the study and improvement of particular operations.

The range of such change is instructive.

- At Norcen Industries, the sequencing of operations for particular orders could be changed, or markedly different equipment and techniques could be applied, to improve either the time spent on manufacture or the quality of the part or both.

- At Jos. A. Bank, the supervisor's main responsibilities were to check quality and instruct workers in proper methods. The industrial engineer spent much time establishing standards and, in the process, improving the methods used so that quality could be maintained but with less worker effort and time.

- General Motors' methods improvements were constrained by the balance requirement of the moving assembly line. Not only were there the usual pressures to keep quality up and total manufacturing time down, but methods improvements might have to be made in order to keep one task on the line balanced against other tasks, particularly if flexibility in production was to be encouraged. Industrial engineers and workers in this situation spent a great deal of time developing worker aids and thinking about methods changes that would put tasks into balance with one another.

- At Burger King and Howard Ford, methods were studied to meet the quality and service standards set by the corporation. As with General Motors, methods improvements often came with the introduction of new equipment and worker aids and in layout of workstations to improve the movement of materials and people within the process.

I reiterate these features of the tours we have already taken to illustrate the pervasiveness of methods improvement in smooth-running operations. Methods improvement is an important *daily* consideration in such operations.

Methods improvement and engineering is too little appreciated in many companies, especially those in the service sector. As we have seen from our plant and service tours, it is frequently detailed, nitty-gritty work but it can pay off. Methods improvement basically requires an open, inquisitive mind, an eye for detail, and a passion for keeping things simple. There are no pat solutions to apply in most instances; thus, methods improvements usually involve a systematic study of the current methods, an appreciation of what the job really calls for, and a disdain for any explanation that is not thoroughly persuasive.

Over time, many dos and don'ts have evolved about good methods practice, especially as regards the actions of individual workers. Good methods practice is always concerned with what tasks can be eliminated, simplified, combined with other tasks, or changed in sequence. While these kinds of change can frequently be accomplished with little or no investment in new tools, worker aids, or equipment, often methods study will lead to suggestions for capital investments of both large and small scale. Table 3-1 presents a list of suggestions for improving methods. This list provides a glimpse into the commonsense mind of the methods engineer.

A whole study of the human body's advantages and limitations in the workplace has developed. This study, called *ergonomics*, has helped make manufacturers aware that methods changes and workplace redesign can decrease worker fatigue and improve worker satisfaction and productivity. However, ergonomics can go too far. Sometimes the changes considered are costly and have only marginal significance. The good methods engineer must constantly assess which improvements are necessary and cost effective and which suggestions (or demands) for workplace or tool change are not worthy of implementation. Calls by employees or unions for better workplace design are sometimes bones of contention between management and the workforce.

Studying Methods

As with most jobs, when one attacks a task systematically, one's productivity is likely to improve. Systematic methods improvement calls for systematic methods study. Formal study of work methods—including concern for raw materials, product design, process design, tooling, plant layout, and the workers' interaction with all of these features—is sometimes referred to as *motion study*. While attention to methods has always existed, the formal study

TABLE 3-1   Some principles of methods improvement for workers
Basic principles

A. Reduce total steps to a minimum.
B. Arrange in best order.
C. Combine steps where feasible.
D. Make each step as easy as possible.
E. Balance the work of the hands.
F. Avoid the use of the hands for holding.
G. The workplace should fit human dimensions[1]:
1. Can a suboperation be eliminated?
   a. As unnecessary?
   b. By a change in the order of work?
   c. By a change of tools or equipment?
   d. By a change of layout of the workplace?
   e. By combining tools?
   f. By a slight change of material?
   g. By a slight change in product?
   h. By a quick-acting clamp on jig, if jigs are used?
2. Can a movement be eliminated?
   a. As unnecessary?
   b. By a change in the order of work?
   c. By combining tools?
   d. By a change of tools or equipment?
   e. By a drop disposal of finished material?
      (The less exact the release requirements, the faster the release.)
3. Can a hold be eliminated? (Holding is extremely fatiguing.)
   a. As unnecessary?
   b. By a simple holding device or fixture?
4. Can a delay be eliminated or shortened?
   a. As unnecessary?
   b. By a change in the work that each body member does?
   c. By balancing the work between the body members?
   d. By working simultaneously on two items?
      (Slightly less than double production is possible with the typical person.)
   e. By alternating the work, each hand doing the same job, but out of phase?
5. Can a suboperation be made easier?
   a. By better tools?
      (Handles should allow maximum flesh contact without sharp corners for power; easy spin, small diameter for speed on light work.)
   b. By changing leverages?
   c. By changing positions of controls or tools?
   d. By better material containers?
      (Bins that permit a slide grasp of small parts are preferable to bins that must be dipped into.)
   e. By using inertia where possible?
   f. By lessening visual requirements?
   g. By better workplace heights?
      (Keep workplace height below the elbow.)
6. Can a movement be made easier?
   a. By a change of layout, shortening distances?
      (Place tools and equipment as near place of use and as nearly in position of use as possible.)
   b. By changing direction of movements?
      (Optimum angle of workplace for light knobs, key switches, and handwheels is probably 30° and certainly between 0° to 45° to plane perpendicular to plane of front of operator's body.)
   c. By using different muscles?
      (Use the first muscle group in this list that is strong enough for the task.)
      (1) Finger? (Not desirable for steady load or highly repetitive motions.)
      (2) Wrist?
      (3) Forearm?
      (4) Upper arm?
      (5) Trunk? (For heavy loads, shift to large leg muscles.)
   d. By making movements continuous rather than jerky?
7. Can a hold be made easier?
   a. By shortening its duration?
   b. By using stronger muscle groups, such as the legs, with foot-operated vises?

Source: Marvin E. Mundel, *Motion and Time Study: Improving Productivity* 5th ed. (Englewood Cliffs, N.J.: Prentice-Hall, 1973), pp. 230–31.

of work methods in operations is generally associated with the Gilbreths (Frank and Lillian), who in the late 1800s and early 1900s developed many of the charting techniques and early filming techniques that have done much to improve worker productivity. The Gilbreths had a passion for describing methods precisely through the isolation, identification, and subsequent improvement of the elements of a task.

Today, motion study of repetitive tasks can involve a number of techniques, most involving charts of one variety or another. Methods engineers have found that by charting methods and the process, they can be more effective in thinking creatively and exhaustively about potential methods changes. Four forms of these charts are worth mentioning:

- *Process flow charts for materials* typically focus on what happens to products as they move through the process—where they get caught in bottlenecks, how materials are handled, and what has to come together before a product can proceed. A simplified form of these charts was introduced in Segment I, where it was called a process flow diagram. Vastly more detailed diagrams—involving maybe even floor plans—are often helpful in tracking materials movement and in documenting how long it takes to perform particular operations.

  Process flow charts such as the one in Figure 3-1 are sometimes used to document what occurs with materials used by a particular worker. Charting such a task forces the methods engineer to break down the elements of the job thoroughly and to question which elements can be improved—as by adding a worker aid, laying out the workstation differently, resequencing the operations, eliminating needless movement of workers or materials, or perhaps redesigning the product or the materials going into it. The objective of such systematic study is to simplify the operation so that the worker can do it quickly and well.

- *Process flow charts for workers* focus solely on what the worker does. Whereas it is usually more advantageous for methods study to track materials and what happens to them, worker-oriented flow charts can sometimes be more effective, particularly when the worker's job forces him or her to travel around the operation, interrupting contact with the product or service. A chart like that in Figure 3-1 can be used to detail such a worker's efforts, just as it can be used to detail the flow of materials and what workers do with them. In this case, however, movement would refer to the movement of the worker and not the materials, and temporary storage or delay would refer to the delay of the worker, not the materials.

- *Worker-machine charts* are typically time-specific bar charts that track a worker together with his machine(s). This tracking can be in general terms or it can be as specific as the hand, feet, and body movements necessary to perform a given task. One popular analysis is to chart a machine's cycle time against the cycle time of the machine operator, so that any conflicts between the two can be isolated and resolved. Figure 3-2 is an example. In this analysis, the worker is seen as a "machine," with a cycle time of his own. Like the machine, the worker can be either functioning or idle. Such a worker-machine chart helps to coordinate the two so that their idle times are minimized and their outputs are maximized.

- *Worker-worker charts* investigate the potential interference and room for coordination of one worker with others. Such charts are the simple extension of the worker-machine charts in Figure 3-2. They are particularly

Quantity Processed	Distance Involved	Task	Explanation
1	8 feet	◯ ☐ ⇨ D ▽	Procure headlight from bin
1		◯ ☐ ⇨ D ▽	Inspect headlight for damage
	8 feet	◯ ☐ ⇨ D ▽	Move headlight to line
2		◯ ☐ ⇨ D ▽	Procure two mounting screws from bin at line
		◯ ☐ ⇨ D ▽	Wait for next car to reach work station
1		◯ ☐ ⇨ D ▽	Mount headlight and tighten screws
1		◯ ☐ ⇨ D ▽	Inspect positioning of headlight
1		◯ ☐ ⇨ D ▽	Make any needed adjustments

◯ Operation performed

☐ Inspection made of quality or quantity

⇨ Movement of material

D Temporary storage or delay experienced by materials

▽ Controlled storage of materials (requisition required for withdrawal)

FIGURE 3-1   A sample detailed process flow for materials: a hypothetical description of headlight mounting on an assembly line.

effective in service operations, which tend to be more labor-intensive than many manufacturing operations.

The data for these charts can come from several sources. The most widely used, quite naturally, is in-person observation of the task in question by the methods engineer. This is often the quickest, easiest, and least costly means of studying the job. Given some preliminary observation to determine what the important aspects of the job are, the methods engineer can then devise the most appropriate chart(s).

For tasks that are either very complex or of long duration, methods engineers have often found that filming or videotaping is useful. Films and videotapes have a number of advantages: (1) they catch everything in the field of view of the camera; they do not inadvertently miss seeing something; (2) they can be viewed over and over again; and (3) they are accurate. For these reasons, films and videotapes are especially helpful for methods study involving great detail or many workers. And, if the film is taken at unusually slow speeds, long or complex tasks can be reviewed

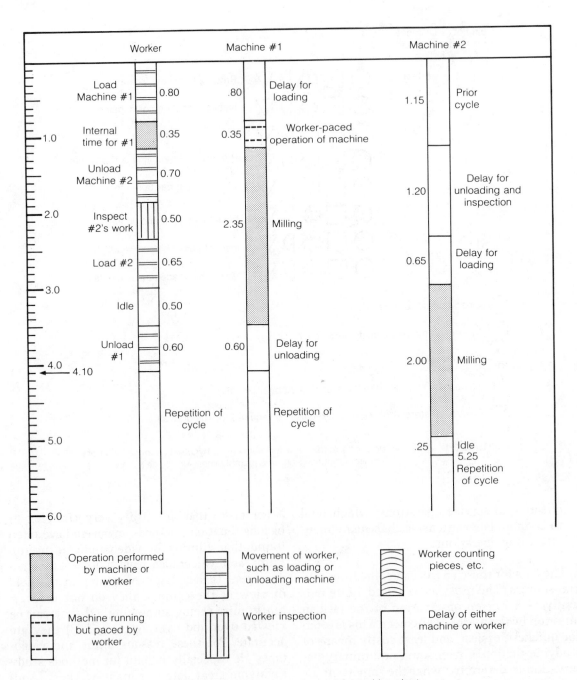

FIGURE 3-2   An example of a worker-machine chart.

quickly. (This is termed *memomotion analysis*.)

The analysis of great detail—generally for small-scale tasks—for which filming or videotaping is useful is termed *micromotion analysis*. This technique was pioneered by the Gilbreths, who divided movements into 17 distinct categories, which they named "therbligs" (their name spelled backwards). These therbligs (grasp, position, pre-position, use, assemble, disassemble, release load, transport empty, transport loaded, search, select, hold, unavoidable delay, avoidable delay, rest, plan, and inspect) provide a convenient and clear framework for analyzing small-scale manual tasks and suggesting ways to improve or eliminate elements of them through the use of tools, fixtures, equipment, workplace layout, or just a different sequence of motions.

Other Ways to Improve Methods

The discussion so far has concentrated on the study of worker methods when repetitive motions in standard settings are the rule. Many jobs, particularly those in support roles or in the service sector, are not repetitive, however. Memomotion analysis can be of use in such situations. Frequently, two other techniques are employed: work activity analysis and work sampling.

Work activity analysis simply calls on the worker to list chronologically the work he performs, indicating the type of task, the time spent on it, and the number of actions completed (forms processed, memos written). Because work activity analysis can be time-consuming for the worker (especially when many short tasks are performed), this analysis is generally not extended over a long period. It is more appropriate for jobs with an irregular daily pattern of work but fairly stable day-to-day and week-to-week content. It can indicate the need for change in a job and point up aspects of the job that require further study.

Work sampling is the random observation of a worker and the ensuing calculation of the relative amounts of time spent performing specific tasks or tied up in avoidable or unavoidable delays (for example, 10 percent of the time making phone calls, 20 percent of the time writing reports, 5 percent of the time waiting for materials). As such, it is a good means of analyzing jobs whose pattern of work is irregular over long periods of time. While less disruptive than work activity analysis, work sampling can entail much travel throughout the operation by the analyst or supervisor involved and much time to gather enough observations. In its favor, work sampling enjoys some advantages over stopwatch or film/tape studies. For example, a single industrial engineer can study a number of tasks simultaneously; if the tasks involve a considerable amount of machine time, as opposed to operator time, work sampling can be more efficient. For nonstandard jobs, notably in support functions (such as engineering) or in service industries, work sampling is often the preferred means of studying the job and suggesting revisions to the responsibilities assigned or suggesting further study of particular aspects of the job.

The implementation of work sampling requires:

- Categorizing what the studied worker does so that the relative frequencies of each task or type of delay as computed by the study can have real application to methods improvement.

- Using an irregular pattern of observation of the worker; ideally, it should be random.

- Making a suitable number of observations must be made.

TABLE 3-2 Representative observation sample sizes

ACCURACY AND RELATIVE FREQUENCIES	PROBABILITY PREFERENCE (LEVEL OF CONFIDENCE)		
	90% ($a = 1.645$)	95% ($a = 1.96$)	99% ($a = 2.576$)
Accuracy of 10% ($x = 0.10$)			
$p = .10$	24	35	60
$p = .25$	51	72	124
Accuracy of 5% ($x = 0.05$)			
$p = .10$	97	138	239
$p = .25$	203	288	498

One approach to gauging how many observations are required is to make a certain number of observations and then calculate the relative frequency of each task or type of delay. Then another set of observations is made and added to the first set. The relative frequencies for specific tasks, as calculated for the first set of observations and the enlarged second set, are compared. If the computed relative frequencies are nearly identical, further sampling need not be done. However, if the relative frequencies differ by much, another set of observations should be taken and added to the other observations, relative frequencies should be computed, and comparisons should be made. When the calculated relative frequencies are judged to be stable, further sampling can cease.

Another approach to the determination of observation sample size is to use statistics. In this approach, the methods engineer states a preference for the probability that a given relative frequency is within X percent of the true relative frequency for the entire population (say, a 95 percent probability that the relative frequency is within 10 percent of the true frequency). Assuming that the relative frequencies are distributed according to a binomial distribution, the sample size can be computed by the following formula:

$$N = \left(\frac{a}{x}\right)^2 [p(1 - p)]$$

where N is the number of observations required for the study, p is the relative frequency of interest (task or type of delay), a is the number of standard deviations associated with a given probability preference (such as 2 if the preference is a 95 percent chance), and x is the accuracy desired for the frequency (such as 0.10 for an accuracy within 10 percent of the true frequency).

As is clear from Table 3-2, the higher the level of confidence that the computed relative frequency is within tolerance, or the greater the accuracy sought, the more observations that must be made. The higher the relative frequency of the task or delay studied, the more observations that are needed as well.

Value Engineering

Value engineering generally refers to a systematic investigation of the product manufactured to see how the design or materials can be changed to improve the product's performance and/or lower its cost. Value engineering (sometimes also called value analysis) looks at a product from the standpoint of the end user and asks what changes in design or materials are possible, what those changes would be worth to the user, and how such changes can be made economically. Value engineering is a useful complement to much of methods engineering, which focuses more on the process and the worker's contribution to it. Productivity gains can occur in many ways, and value engineering helps guard against "overengineering" a product.

Value engineering can be accomplished in several ways. Most commonly, a panel of managers and engineers questions aspects of the product's design and manufacture (Does this feature of the product provide value for the consumer? What other features or designs could be substituted at lower cost that could do the same thing? Can components of the product be standardized? Or eliminated? Can materials be changed? Which tolerances are truly the ones that must be held to tightly? How reliable is the product or its components? Is it too strong or in some other way over engineered? Does it have excess capacity or excess weight?) The panel asking these questions sometimes involves the staff of design engineers initially responsible for the product.

Another useful value engineering approach is to study all of the parts or products of the company that might be considered similar, with the object of identifying useful simplifications, design changes, or materials substitutions. Still another means of value engineering is to query suppliers about the changes or improvements they see can be made.

Value engineering is very much a "habit of mind," but it is one that can pay tremendous dividends.

Balancing Methods Improvements against Other Considerations

Often, improvements in methods can be made that are relatively easy to do, save much more money than they cost, and greatly aid product quality and/or worker safety. These are the methods improvements that are easy to adopt. Sometimes, however, a more efficient way of accomplishing a task must be balanced against other considerations—an acknowledged, or even potential, drop in the product's performance characteristics or the maintenance of a particular service standard. Consider Situation 3-1.

SITUATION 3-1

EASTERN BELL TELEPHONE COMPANY

The more Charlie Harris thought about it, the more attractive it became, but it still meant a significant change in the telephone company's repair practices. Charlie was a young district manager with responsibility for installation and repair of telephone equipment in a 200-square-mile area north of the city. In response to some higher level pronouncements about the importance of measured installation and repair productivity, Charlie conceived the idea of changing the way telephone repair technicians were assigned to residence repair jobs.

In the prevailing system, each repair technician reporting to the garage in the morning would be assigned to the repair of a subscriber's telephone that had been reported and checked out at the central office as out-of-service. After repairing that phone, the repair technician would call in to the dispatcher, who would assign the next repair task. Over three-quarters of the repair tasks involved telephones out-of-service, but the rest involved trouble not severe enough to cut off service (for example, an extension phone out of order, a worn cord, a sagging wire from the telephone pole to the house). The repair technician would not know, starting the day, how many jobs he or she would have to do or where any of them would be. The person was at the mercy of the dispatcher.

Because the Bell System's standards for responding to trouble calls were so demanding (respond to out-of-service calls within 24 hours), a considerable portion of the repair technician's day was spent in transit, chasing the urgent calls for service by the telephone company's customers. If the repair technician could be routed better, less time would be spent in transit, and more service calls could be made. Better routing, however, meant bunching up more service calls geographically, which could be done only by waiting longer and collecting more trouble calls. Charlie recognized that improving work productivity almost always implied a lowering of existing service standards. Charlie knew that he could never wait to accumulate out-of-service trouble calls; they would always require immediate action. However, the less severe trouble, involving calls where the home still had telephone service on at least one phone, was a candidate for delayed service with better routing of the repair technicians.

Charlie wondered how best such a delayed response system could be implemented. Several questions still plagued him:

1. How much delay would the customer accept? Should the customer be granted the right to insist upon immediate service like before?

2. How could a program of bunched orders and better routing be designed to promote worker productivity in the best way? Should the dispatching system remain the same as before, with the repair technicians calling in for their next assignment, or should they be given a full day's load from the start? Should the same person be assigned to this bunched order work, or should the work be rotated among all repair technicians? If rotated, how long should a person be assigned to such work?

3. Would the benefits in increased productivity outweigh the diminishing level of service that the proposed system necessarily implied?

Discussion of Eastern Bell Telephone Company

It is clear that Charlie Harris's idea to accumulate the noncritical repair calls and bunch them up to provide better routing and thus higher productivity will reduce the company's ability to meet its established service standard on repairs. The issue is whether the service standard itself is worth keeping. The notion of having customers indicate how perturbed they are without service is probably a good one. Particularly irate customers can then be put in with the out-of-service trouble calls for immediate attention. A simple question asked of customers (such as "We can fix it the day after tomorrow. Is that all right with you?") when they phone in their complaints may placate them and yet accumulate enough calls to ease the routing problem.

Bunching orders in this way to facilitate routing may not only improve productivity in the repair of noncritical service calls, but also provide a demonstration whose effects could be broad-ranging if in fact productivity rises markedly, say from 8 calls to 12 calls per day. This improvement could make the entire repair fleet more conscious of productivity. This argument for a demonstration effect suggests that the noncritical calls be rotated among the repair technicians so that the productivity gains are experienced first-hand by everyone. The duration of the assignment should be long enough to make an impact but short enough so that everyone can get into the act during the year. Perhaps two weeks to a month on this assignment would do. The likely impact of the demonstration argues further that the repair technician be given a full day's load in the morning. Counting orders then will probably make more of an impression than counting up the day's accomplishments on the way home from work.

Time Study and Time Standards[2]

Paralleling the motion study pioneered by the Gilbreths was the time study of individual worker tasks. The pioneer in this study was Frederick Taylor, who worked during the same period as the Gilbreths. Much of the work of Taylor and his followers had a similar intent to that of the Gilbreths—to improve productivity by looking closely at what workers did. However, rather than focus on the motions involved, Taylor broke down the job into elements and timed them. As in motion study, each element was studied to determine what should be kept and what should be discarded, but the stopwatch was the chief aid to the engineer rather than the movie camera or the process chart.

Use of Time Standards

The time standards developed by Taylor have at least four broad applications:

1. They can be used for planning and budgeting. As we discovered in the plant tour of Norcen Industries, Joe Gehret could not bid properly for jobs, plan how much labor to have at any time (how much overtime to schedule), and determine how many of the various types of operators were needed unless he knew how long a particular job would take. Standards in an operation like a job shop are critical for planning production and scheduling workforce, materials, machines, and orders.

2. They can be used to improve performance. As we saw in Tour D, the work of the industrial engineering department at GM C-P-C—Tarrytown to improve the operation of that plant's assembly line required time studies to be done to evaluate technique and equipment changes. Burger King has improved its process by using time standards for service and seeing what changes in the operation could be made without jeopardizing those service standards.

3. They can be used to evaluate individual workers and to serve as a basis for wage payments. As we saw in Tour C on Jos. A. Bank, time study can be used as a basis for incentive wages. Time standards, once they are accepted as fair by the workers, can be used to evaluate worker performance: workers who match or beat the standard can be rewarded, and workers who fail to reach the standard can be disciplined or even removed from the job. Use of time standards is discussed more later in the chapter.

4. They can be used to define a measure of labor productivity. The popular "efficiency" measure of labor productivity is conventionally defined as

$$\text{Efficiency} = \frac{\text{Standard Hours}}{\text{Actual Hours}} \times 100\%$$

Thus, efficiencies of over 100 percent represent situations where the direct labor (that is, those workers for whom standards have been set) has beaten the standard. This efficiency measure is sometimes combined with a measure of utilization (the fraction of time the work place was available to do work with all equipment "up" and all materials there) to yield an "effectiveness" index.

$$\text{Effectiveness} = \text{Efficiency} \times \text{Utilization}$$

If utilization is less than one (and it always is), then effectiveness is always less than efficiency, in percentage terms.

Development of Time Standards

Time standards can be developed in a variety of ways, as we saw in the plant tours of Segment I: history (Norcen Industries), time study (Jos. A. Bank), predetermined motion time systems (Burger King), and standard data systems (GM C-P-C—Tarrytown).

History

The time standards that Norcen Industries used in its planning were generally based on having worked on the same or similar parts before. Considering the diversity involved in a job shop like Norcen Industries, using history is a very economical way by which to establish useful standards. The workers at Norcen were not paid or evaluated according to these standards and thus great precision was not required. History provided enough rough but useful standards so that planning could be done effectively.

Time Study

Time study typically involves dividing a job into distinct "elements" that have unambiguous starts and stops and recording the time spent performing each of those elements. At Jos. A. Bank, the timing was accomplished by an electronic stopwatch that automatically time different elements of the job. Alternative techniques include (1) the "snap-back" method (where three different stopwatches mounted on a special clipboard are started, stopped and reset by a lever that is punched at the beginning of every job element), and (2) the continuous reading method (where a single stopwatch is used and elements are timed by reading off the running times).

Time study recognizes that the measured actual times of workers may not be appropriate for use as standards. Two major types of corrections are usually made: performance rating and allowances.

A worker, when timed, might purposely "dog it" so that the standard is set at an easily attainable level. To counter this possibility, methods engineers typically try to "rate" the worker's efficiency in doing the job. This performance rating serves to convert the measured actual time to so-called normal time, as follows:

$$\text{Normal time} = \text{Measured actual time} \times \text{Performance rating}$$

A performance rating less than 1 implies that the methods engineer thought the worker was underproducing. A rating greater than 1 implies that the methods engineer did not think an average worker could sustain the pace.

Performance ratings can be made of the entire job studied, but accuracy is enhanced if individual ratings are made of each element of the job. Normal times are then computed for each element. Establishing a performance rating is a tricky endeavor. Before a job can be rated, the methods engineer must appreciate the difficulty of the job and the conditions under which it is done. The engineer must then gauge what a normal tempo would be under such circumstances and assess how the worker's efforts match up against the normal tempo. Films or videotapes are often employed to give methods engineers a sense of what the normal tempo should be; they also provide methods engineers with opportunities to practice rating workers.

Allowances, the other major correction to measured actual times, relate to delays in performing a job that are unavoidable for the worker or are irregular but that can nevertheless be expected as routine occurrences. Typically included as such delays are waits due to materials shortages, special instructions, machine adjustment or repair, quality problems, workplace housekeeping, and the like. Personal time taken to get a drink or to go to the bathroom are also generally counted as allowances. If fatigue was not taken into consideration in rating the job, it can be added as an allowance.

These allowances modify the normal time so that it can be used as a standard:

$$\text{Standard time} = \text{Normal time for the job} \times \text{Allowance factor for the job}$$

where

$$\text{Allowance factor} = 1 + \frac{\text{Allowed minutes}}{\text{Normal minutes}}$$

The allowance factor is always greater than 1, often between 1.1 and 1.3. The methods engineer can arrive at the specific factor by studying the job to identify the delays inherent in it and the frequency of their occurrence. Such study can be made by continuous observation of the job for a reasonably long time (such as several hours) or by work sampling techniques.

Time study is a fairly accurate way to establish time standards for tasks for which the methods are well known. In practice, however, time study has two drawbacks: (1) it cannot be used effectively for jobs that have not been well defined and are only being contemplated, and (2) time study depends critically on the "rating" of the worker. The subjective determination of what the standard pace of the operation should be is often tricky and can become a bone of contention between industrial engineers and the workforce.

Predetermined Motion-Time Systems

The two difficulties encountered with time study techniques are to some extent remedied by predetermined motion-time systems. These systems build on the notion that any task can be decomposed into a series of basic motions. The original task, then, can be seen as the sum of its basic motions. Extensive libraries of basic motion information indicate, for example, the time it takes to move one's hands various distances to perform tasks of varying complexity, with or without tools or materials of various weights. Using this information, an analyst can develop time estimates for tasks that are contemplated; such computations can be more objective than those computed by engineers rating actual operators. Standards set by good analysts are consistently shown to be accurate, although many companies periodically use direct time studies to check their use of predetermined motion-time systems.

The most widely known of these predetermined motion-time systems is MTM (method

time measurement), developed by H. B. Maynard in the late 1940s. Several versions of the MTM system (MTM-1, MTM-2, MTM-3) have been developed. The original system, MTM-1, uses very short and well-defined movements to build up a particular task. Although MTM-1 can be used successfully for even short-cycle jobs (that is, jobs that are accomplished within a short period of time) that are repeated over long periods, its application requires great skill. The industrial engineer must be very precise in decomposing a task into all its component motions and must carefully identify which of the multitude of choices from the MTM-1 data base best characterizes each motion. Many of the problems encountered with MTM analysis are caused by engineer errors in its application rather than by inaccuracies in the time values.

Some of these applications problems are remedied in a new predetermined motion-time system from the H. B. Maynard Company, which pioneered MTM. The MOST (Maynard Operation Sequence Technique) system was developed in the late 1960s and early 1970s. It was built on the observation that most worker tasks can be decomposed into three basic *sequences* of motions:

- A "general move" sequence for the movement of objects freely through the air. This sequence is represented by the series of letters ABGABPA where

  A = Action distance—the movement through space of one part of the body or the entire body

  B = Body motion—the up and down movement of the body or an action of the body to eliminate some obstruction to movement (e.g., opening a door)

  G = Gain control—typically, the manual dexterity needed to gain control over an object

  P = Place—the alignment of an object with one or more other objects before control is relinquished

TABLE 3-3   General move sequence with index numbers

INDEX	A ACTION DISTANCE	B BODY MOTION	G GAIN CONTROL	P PLACE
0	≤2 inches			Hold or toss
1	Within reach		Move light object, or move light objects using simultaneous motions	Lay aside or loosely fit
3	1–2 steps	Bend and arise, 50% occurrence	Use nonsimultaneous motions; move heavy or bulky objects; move where vision is obstructed or not possible; disengage, interlock, or collect objects together	Make adjustments, use light pressure, or make two placements
6	3–4 steps	Bend and arise		Use care or precision, use heavy pressure, move where vision is obstructed or not possible, or make intermediate moves
10	5–7 steps	Sit or stand		
16	8–10 steps	Through door, climb on or off		

- A "controlled move" sequence for the movement of objects that remain in contact with a surface or attached to another object during the movement. This sequence is represented by the series of letters ABGMXIA where A, B, and G are defined as before and

  M = Move controlled—the manual control of the object through its path
  X = Process time—the work done by machine and not by the worker
  I = Align—worker actions needed to align objects after the controlled move itself or after the machine's work on the object

- A "tool use" sequence for the use of common hand tools. This sequence is represented by the series of letters ABGABP ABPA where the A, B, G, and P are defined as before and the blank space can be filled with an activity specific to the tool being used. Typical tool-related activities are fastening, loosening, cutting, treating an object's surface (painting, sanding), measuring, and recording.

Using the MOST system, the analyst follows these steps:

1. Determine the appropriate sequence from the task under study.
2. Index the movements that comprise the sequence. (Each sequence has its own index definitions. Table 3-3 presents those for the general move sequence.)
3. Add these index numbers together.
4. Multiply by 10 to compute the time standard in time measurement units (TMUs), each of which is equal to 0.00001 hour (0.036 second).

Figure 3-3 illustrates, in general terms, the MOST system for a routine task such as might

Movement Fetching a bin of sliced tomatoes from under a counter and placing the bin into its slot

General move sequence ABGABPA

		Appropriate Index from Table 3-2
1. Walking a step or two	Action distance	3
2. Bending down	Body motion	6
3. Picking the bin up	Gain control	3
4. Walking back a step or two	Action distance	3
5. Dropping the bin into its slot	Body motion, Place	0,1
6. Staying in the same place to resume other work	Action distance	0

Indexed sequence $A_3B_6G_3A_3B_0P_1A_0$

Time measurement units $(3 + 6 + 3 + 3 + 0 + 1 + 0) \times 10 = 160$ TMUs, or 5.76 seconds

FIGURE 3-3 Using MOST to compute the standard time for a sample movement.

occur at a fast food restaurant. (Recall that the Burger King simulation model used MTM analysis to develop data on the making of Whoppers, drawing of drinks, and other tasks.)

By investigating sequences of motions rather than the motions themselves, the MOST system reaps some statistical benefits that help ensure the accuracy of its computed times if long enough sequences of movements are analyzed. Thus, the MOST system can be both accurate and intuitive as well as easier and faster. For many applications the MOST system is now preferred. It can operate manually or, as with other predetermined systems, in a series of computer programs, which can expedite the updating of time standards and process descriptions.

Standard Data Systems

The MOST system represents an aggregation of the small movements that made up the original MTM system. Likewise, standard data systems can be viewed as aggregations of smaller, more specialized tasks for use by plants that have a number of routine jobs. Standard data systems are generally based on a wealth of data derived from many time studies of similar jobs. To apply them to a new or redefined job requires the breakdown of the contemplated job into not only those elements that have direct counterparts in the standard data base but also those elements that may not have precise counterparts but are related to tasks previously done and for which there is considerable data. By judiciously combining both types of elements, standards can be derived easily and with reasonable accuracy.

As well one might expect, standard data systems were used at C-P-C—Tarrytown more than any of the other methods for determining time standards.

Choosing among Systems

As we have seen, each of the methods for establishing time standards has advantages and disadvantages. Some (such as time study and MTM-1) are costly; some are detailed; and some are useful for particular purposes. Although the choices are not clear-cut, direct time study and very detailed MTM analysis are generally preferred when very accurate standards are required for relatively short-cycle jobs that may be repeated often and for which worker evaluation is important. Intensive time study may also be required in processes that pay incentive wages. For tasks that may not be repeated exactly over long periods of time, more aggregated predetermined motion time systems (such as the MOST system) are useful for developing standards; such systems are suitable when there is considerable worker discretion involved in each task. Standard data systems are particularly attractive for routine work that has a rich history of time study data. Purely historical data provide a very low-cost way to establish standards if great accuracy is not required and if the tasks studied are not routine.

Standards, Incentives, and Wage Payments[3]

As noted previously, time standards can be used by companies in four major ways: (1) to estimate capacities and costs, (2) to improve performance, (3) to evaluate workers and to form a basis for wage payments, and (4) to measure labor productivity. The use of time standards for estimation, methods improvement and productivity measurement is widespread; in fact, almost all companies use standards for these purposes. In somewhat less than half of all manufacturing companies, time standards are used as well in the development of incentive wage schemes for at least a fraction of the workforce.[4] Thus, while hourly wage payment (sometimes referred to as *daywork*) is more prevalent, incentive wage schemes are fairly common and widely discussed.

Incentive schemes are logically divided into two groups: individual incentives and group incentives.

Individual Incentives

The plant tour at Jos. A. Bank introduced both key variants of individual wage incentives—the piecerate system and the standard-hour system. The appeal of these incentive wage systems is readily understandable. The worker is paid according to how much he produces, not how long he works. It is generally accepted that workers on incentive wages work harder than those who are paid by the hour, other things being equal.

In the piecerate system, every unit of output has its own "price," or wage reward. Workers are paid strictly according to how much they produce. Typically, there are no wage floors or ceilings, although the piece rate itself must be set so that the federally mandated minimum wage is easily met. Piece rates are generally inviolate over time except for well-recognized changes in methods, materials, equipment, or product specifications. About a third of the companies with wage incentives use a piecerate system. At Jos. A. Bank we saw it used in the coat shop and the pants shop. Also, as we saw at Bank, it is typical practice in a piecerate system for most workers to earn a premium above any standard. It is hoped, however, that these standards are not so "loose" that wage costs escalate with little control.

In the standard-hour system, there are no wage "price tags" on every unit. Rather, a certain rate of output per hour is set as the standard, and pay varies according to what percentage of the standard is actually achieved. At Jos. A. Bank, the standard-hour system applied in the cutting room. There are many variations of this system. Some pay proportionally (for example, a 115 percent average performance for the week will earn 115 percent of the standard wage); others use formulas based on a tally of "points" earned. Many variations place a floor on earnings (a base rate, as applied in the cutting room at Jos. Bank), with the standard set so that a typical worker can expect to better it consistently (110 or 120 percent of the standard); other systems have no wage floor. These standard-hour systems are the most popular wage incentive scheme, prevailing in about three-fifths of the companies with wage incentive programs. While they function much as piecerate systems, their advantage is that pay increases can be made simply by adjusting the base rate, which is much easier to do than adjusting the many piece rates involved so that a given percentage increase for the workforce as a whole is proportioned equitably among all piecerate workers. (Recall the discussion of piece rates in the plant tour of Jos. A. Bank.)

The attractiveness of individual incentive wages is, of course, to spur worker effort. But are there unattractive features as well? Consider Situation 3-2.

SITUATION 3-2

TOWER MANUFACTURING COMPANY

"Boy, did I just get ambushed. I haven't been dressed down like that since I forgot my wife's birthday a few years back. Those guys are steaming and we better do something about it." Bruce Hillman, foreman of the machine shop, was addressing his supervisor, Clint Oster, the manager of machining operations at Tower Manufacturing Company. Tower Manufacturing, a supplier of chassis components for heavy, customized, off-highway trucks and construction equipment, had recently added a second computer-controlled milling machine to the machine shop. It was the worker response to this second machine and its implications for worker compensation that had Bruce Hillman agitated.

Bruce continued. "I don't know how we're going to fix things. All I know is that this current arrangement simply has to go. We can't continue to pay Bestmann for piece work on both machines. His pay is way out of line. The others in the shop like him all right but pulling in almost half again the pay of the others is plain ridiculous. Everyone is clamoring for an increase in the rates or an override in the standard pay."

Clint Oster was kicking himself for not anticipating this confrontation. The machine shop at Tower Manufacturing had traditionally been a highly skilled shop, stocked with general-purpose machine tools, with workers compensated through a piecerate incentive wage system. Times had been changing, though, and the increasing stability of Tower's major contracts had made possible the introduction of computer numerically controlled (CNC) machines into the shop. Management had agonized over the decision, since even one such machine was an investment of hundreds of thousands of dollars. But Clint was convinced that Tower had to purchase such equipment if it was going to stay competitive. Compared with what even a first-class machinist could do using conventional equipment, the computer-controlled machine was far superior. It took much longer to set up for a job, but once it was set up, its speed and quality of output were extraordinary. All the operator had to do was feed the machine with material and remove the completed, machined output. For longer production runs, which was the situation now at Tower, the new machine was ideal.

When Tower purchased its first computer-controlled machine, Clint and Bruce assigned one of the shop's best workers, Jay Bestmann, to it. It had taken quite a while for Tower's industrial engineers and Bestmann to get the bugs out of the new machine, but, once accomplished, everyone was satisfied with the machine's capabilities. During this start-up period, Bestmann had agreed to be taken off incentive pay. Instead he was paid an hourly rate equivalent to his last two months' average hourly pay. When the new machine was proven out, Bestmann agreed to a piece rate that was two-thirds of the rate for equivalent output from conventional machines. This rate worked out to be slightly higher than the rate of pay he was earning just prior to the introduction of the new machine, but Clint Oster had agreed to it since none of the shop's machinists wanted to work on this less-skilled job. Setups for both the new computer-controlled machine and conventional machines were paid at the same rate.

It had been planned from the beginning that one operator would be responsible for two of the new machines, since otherwise the operator would be idle much of the time, watching the machine do the job. Therefore, when the second computer-controlled machine was installed, Bestmann was assigned to it. Once again, the piece rate had to be adjusted. The engineers felt it was unlikely that both machines would always be perfectly syncopated (so that Bestmann never had to be at both machines at once); the piece rate therefore was not cut in half (to one-third from two-thirds of the rate applicable to conventional machines), but rather was set at 40 percent of the rate other workers were given—also as sort of a bribe to get Bestmann to accept the assignment to the two machines.

Since this rate was agreed on, however, two things had happened to increase Bestmann's pay considerably. One was that Bestmann began setting up one machine while the other was working. This procedure entailed a lot of movement between machines so that the working one was always fed with material, but it meant that Bestmann was carrying piece-rate pay even when setting up one of the machines, something the company's industrial engineers had not planned for. The other occurrence was an increase in the lot size with which the CNC machine was loaded. This increase meant fewer setups and a lengthened time for the fast output rate of the machine. Both of these factors combined to push Bestmann's pay to levels far in excess of the pay levels for other workers.

This fact, of course, was apparent to the other workers—hence their confrontation with Bruce Hillman. If Bestmann was going to be paid so much more, they wanted a more equitable arrangement for everybody in the shop.

Clint Oster was in a quandary. He could reset the already agreed-to piece rate for the new machine and risk antagonizing Bestmann or anyone else who might be assigned to the machine. Or, he could take the machine off incentive pay and put it on hourly pay, risking not only Bestmann's displeasure but the suspicion of the other workers in the shop about the future abandonment of piece work, a wage scheme that had widespread approval among them. Or, he could place a much lower-skilled worker on each of the new machines, put Bestmann back on conventional machines, and risk even more suspicion from the workforce about job trends in the shop.

Lessons from Tower
Manufacturing Company

This situation uncovers a number of the problems associated with incentive wage schemes, the most important of which is the gradual erosion of the time standards on which the incentive wage is based. The erosion of standards is to be expected in many cases because workers are clever and knowledgeable about what they do and can often find ways to beat the standard. At Tower Manufacturing, for example, Bestmann found a way to beat the standards set for the new CNC machines and his pay jumped appreciably. The resulting inequities in the factory have to be dealt with.

Dealing with these inequities, however, is no easy task. Tightening up on the standards can sometimes be done, but naturally does not make management popular with the workforce. In most union contracts involving incentive pay, after a given period of time the standards cannot be changed without first changing the product, materials, methods, or machinery; any such change is subject to the union-management established grievance procedure.

Of course, changing a standard is far from a costless endeavor. The task must be studied, often by stopwatch, and that takes time. This fact tends to make wage incentives less popular in companies that undertake a lot of product or product mix changes or that are subject to repeated innovation in the production process itself. Wage incentives, and piece rates in particular, are more likely to flourish in processes where (1) the output of every worker is easily measured; (2) the jobs are standard, clear-cut, and unlikely to be altered much through technological changes; (3) the flow of the process is regular and thus every worker has a backlog of work to do; and (4) workmanship is either easy to judge or not critical to the product. It is no accident then that piece rates predominate in the needle trades.

The situation at Tower Manufacturing is delicate because it would be difficult, if not impossible, to change the standard now that it has been established. If the job were switched to an hourly paid one, suspicion would likely grow in the factory that all jobs in the department would be switched to hourly pay or that CNC equipment would gradually take over. These changes might mean a switch in pay schemes and a deskilling of the operation, both fearsome developments for the workforce. Some reas-

surances about pay policy and the direction the department is taking are definitely called for. Perhaps even the formation of a distinct new department for the CNC equipment would help allay some fears and still enable the company to continue with a program of modernization.

This predicament at Tower Manufacturing brings up another aspect of wage incentives—their effect on supervisors. Often supervisors let the wage incentives themselves manage the workforce. That is, given wages as an effective prod for production, some supervisors step back from taking an active role in discovering productivity gains or in monitoring the pace of production. Under an hourly pay scheme, the supervisor is much more directly responsible for the pace and quality of the work.

A different kind of problem with wage incentives and productivity is illustrated in Situation 3-3.

SITUATION 3-3

BALDRIDGE CHAIN SAW

The numbers on the page he was staring at said so, but Dave MacDonald still couldn't believe it. Productivity on the new lightweight chain saw assembly line had declined for the second consecutive week. There was no way now that the company could meet its commitment to a large national retailing organization. That entire account, not to mention MacDonald's own job, appeared to him to be in serious jeopardy.

Dave, a recent M.B.A., was in his first year at Baldridge Chain Saw. The company was a small, family-owned manufacturer of chain saws used primarily by professional loggers. Baldridge marketed these professional chain saws under its own name. Recently, however, the growing demand for small, lightweight chain saws by what the company regulars termed "weekend woodsmen" had triggered the current project to design and manufacture a lightweight chain saw to compete with McCulloch, Homelite, and

others. On the basis of its reputation, Baldridge had won a substantial trial contract from a large mass merchandiser. If quality and delivery expectations were met, Baldridge could anticipate regular orders. Dave MacDonald was the so-called project manager, responsible for shepherding the project through the company. The job was a mix of marketing, engineering, production, sales, and finance.

The new lightweight chain saw that Baldridge's engineers had developed was not very complex—at least not as complex as the company's other models. The saw had fewer parts and used many standardized parts that were readily procured either from other operations at Baldridge or from outside suppliers.

The company's industrial engineers had designed a 14-station assembly line for the new saw. This line was staffed half with assemblers pulled from other models' assembly lines and half with new employees. The new employees were paid at a fixed hourly rate for the first month (the start-up) and then they went on incentive pay. During the same start-up period, the experienced workers were paid at the average of their last month's wages; then they too went on incentive. The incentive, similar to the one that prevailed in Baldridge's other assembly lines, depended on the output of the entire line. If the line operated at 110 percent of standard, all of its assemblers would receive a given percentage increase in their base pay. Production at 120 percent of standard would yield a higher pay increase. The engineer-rated speed of the line was such that the average expected wage for all assembly workers was set at 110 percent of standard. Production below 100 percent of standard was paid at the start-up wages. The trial contract could just be met, if the workers averaged 110 percent of standard for the 12-week life of the trial contract.

Because the workers could be expected to continue learning how to assemble more efficiently, the standard inched up higher each week after week 4 and then leveled off after week 8. The company's industrial engineers had developed this new, ever-tightening standard based on the company's past performance with other chain saws.

It was now six weeks into the contract's life. Productivity, relative to standard, had traced this pattern (with standards higher in weeks 5 and 6):

Week	Percent of Standard
1	70%
2	90
3	101
4	111
5	107
6	98

When production slipped in the fifth week, Dave MacDonald had called in the industrial engineers to check whether the line had been properly set up. Dave was concerned lest the line be unbalanced. In that situation, one or more workers might be constituting a bottleneck for the whole line. Dave's concern was heightened by a report from Vic Elgin, the line's foreman, that several of the experienced workers had been complaining about the standards. After studying the matter, however, the industrial engineers reported back that they saw no reason to alter any of the stations along the line. Dave had to wonder then what was holding up production.

Lessons from Baldridge Chain Saw

The situation at Baldridge Chain Saw is suspicious, but probably not as perplexing as Dave MacDonald senses it to be. After all, the productivity drop coincides with the tightening of the group incentive wage scheme. The complaints about the standards registered by the older workers to Vic Elgin are other indications that the fall-off in productivity results from a deliberate slowdown in worker pace, as a veiled protest against what the workers would insist are too tight standards. This slowdown may also be a protest against MacDonald himself or the new lightweight saw product line. In any event, the probabilities are that the workers are "pegging their production."

What to do about it? It may already be too late to save the trial order for the mass merchandiser. If it is, the company may want to maintain the standards as they are, deliver late, accept its fate, but make a point about the company's resolve in establishing production standards. If, on the other hand, it is not too late to save the order, the tightening of the standards may have to be postponed and perhaps some overtime scheduled in order to catch up. This approach, of course, would increase costs. Neither of these alternatives is very attractive, but then the situation the company finds itself in does not leave much room for maneuvering.

Group Incentives

As the Baldridge Chain Saw situation suggests, group incentive programs try to encourage cooperation among workers by rewarding each worker according to how the group performs. Many such programs are initiated in work situations where it is difficult to calculate what each individual produces, apart from what the individuals ahead or behind him produce. It is well known that the group working together can greatly advance productivity.

There are a variety of group incentive programs, but they can be divided into two major groups:

- Those group incentives that apply to small groups of workers within a single plant consider the work group as an individual. Each worker receives a rate of pay that depends on the productivity of the group as a whole. Under such a group incentive, all the group members are encouraged to work together to improve the group's productivity. Peer pressure can be great under such a system. As with individual piece rates, good time studies are essential to the smooth functioning of such group incentives. Although not widespread, small work group incentive schemes are most likely to be found in worker-paced line flow jobs.

- Those group incentives that apply plantwide or even companywide can be grouped under the heading "productivity gain-sharing plans." These plans are devised in such a way that changes in the production process suggested by either workers or managers, as well as changes caused by increased worker effort, result in bonus payments for the workforce. Such plans are designed to increase the cooperation between all those in the plant, both direct and indirect labor, and to have everyone work smarter, not just harder.

The best established of these productivity gain-sharing plans is the so-called *Scanlon plan*, devised by Joseph Scanlon in the late 1930s to save the Empire Steel and Tinplate Company in Ohio. (Scanlon was the president of the steel-workers union local and had training in cost accounting.) In essence, the Scanlon plan calls for sharing, on a monthly basis, the productivity gains made that month as compared with an accepted historical standard. The "pot" of money to share is determined by multiplying a historical base ratio and the sales value of production (loosely defined as sales adjusted for any increases or decreases in inventory, with that inventory generally valued at the sales price) that month. The "base ratio," in the simplest instance, is defined as labor costs divided by the sales value of production. The labor costs are for both direct and indirect labor; they include wages, most fringe benefits, and overtime payments. Generally excluded from labor costs are such things as social security contributions, state and federal unemployment insurance, and the pension plan. In many companies the base ratio is between 10 and 30 percent. Multiplying this base ratio by the month's sales value of production produces an "allowed labor cost" for the month. If actual monthly labor costs are less than that allowed by the formula, a bonus pool is created that is divided between the company and the employees. In a typical division of the bonus pool, half goes to all employees (including management) in proportion to their earnings for the month, a quarter to the company, and a quarter to a reserve pool for those times when there is no bonus pool because actual labor costs have exceeded those allowed.

More formally, the bonus pool in a Scanlon plan is computed as follows:

$$BP_t = ALC_t - AMLC_t$$

where BP_t is the bonus pool for the month in question, ALC_t is the allowed labor cost for the month, and $AMLC_t$ is the actual monthly labor cost. The allowed labor cost, in turn, is computed as

$$ALC_t = BR * SVP_t = \frac{LC_b}{SVP_b} * SVP_t$$

where *BR* is the base ratio (computed as base period or representative labor costs, LC_b, divided by base period or representative sales value of production, SVP_b) and SVP_t is the actual sales value of production for one month.

A Scanlon plan encourages workers and managers alike to propose suggestions for the improvement of productivity. If the sales value of production increases for a given level of labor costs, the bonus pool increases, and both workers and managers benefit. The administration of a Scanlon plan thus requires a mechanism by which to evaluate and implement the suggestions offered. Some of these suggestions involve significant capital expenditures. A well-respected bipartisan group of managers and employees is needed to decide on the proposals. The implementation of a Scanlon plan also requires some sophisticated cost accounting so that the formula and any proposed variations can be straightforwardly calculated and communicated to all involved. Merely installing a Scanlon plan calls for a great deal of trust and communication; workers have to believe that they will not be manipulated by the numbers in the formula, and management must be prepared to cede some of its authority to the workforce and to communicate more thoroughly than in the past.

While there have been some notable successes with the Scanlon plan, there have been some failures as well and some criticisms of its workings. Many of these criticisms relate to the base ratio. For a Scanlon plan to work well with a simple base ratio involving labor costs, the ratio of labor costs to the sales value of production must be fairly stable over time. To the extent that it is not stable, and to the extent that it is influenced by outside factors such as energy or materials price escalation or product mix changes, the size of any bonus pool will be seriously affected by forces outside the control of the workforce. When this happens, questions about the fairness of the plan arise, and often its success is threatened.

There are, of course, ways to improve the formula. For example, costs other than labor can be made part of the base ratio calculation, or individual product lines can be isolated with their own ratios to minimize the effect of product mix changes. Or, the calculation of the sales value of production can be adjusted so that it is a value-added measure, with outside purchases of material and supplies being netted out from the sales value of production. Such formula changes make the Scanlon plan more adaptable to inflation, product mix change, and other environmental considerations, although with the risk of complicating the administration of the plan and losing the understanding and thus the backing of the workforce. While some companies have been able to keep their Scanlon plans flexible and popular with the workforce, other companies have been forced to abandon them because of problems with formula calculation or plan administration.

A recently devised productivity gain-sharing plan that resembles the Scanlon plan is Improshare, meaning "improved productivity through sharing." Improshare can be simpler than the Scanlon plan. It relies less on employee involvement and administration, thus making it easier to install. Under Improshare, the bonus is calculated from the difference between the actual hours worked to produce the plant's output and some standard hours allowed, the so-called Improshare hours. The Improshare hours are calculated using "work-hour standards," based on plant history and defined as total production hours divided by the units produced. The value of the hours saved is thus greater when more units are produced with the same or fewer worker hours. As with Scanlon plans, the success of Improshare depends on the choice of a representative and equitable base period for the calculation of the work-hour standard and on a reasonable amount of trust and communication between management and the workforce.

Other Bonus and Profit-Sharing Plans

There are many other bonus and/or profit-sharing plans that various companies have instituted. Some involve only pension benefits for profit sharing while others pay cash bonuses that come from company profits. Some of these plans encourage worker suggestions and initiative; others do not.

Two bonus plans have received some comment in the press and are worth discussing briefly as interesting examples of what can be done. The Lincoln Electric Company in Cleveland uses a series of incentives and bonuses. Base rates are developed for each of the jobs, typically the average for the industry around the Cleveland area. In addition, there are some extensive individual piece-work incentives, a large profit-sharing type of bonus, and peer review. The company also guarantees employment for a certain number of hours per week. In practice, employee bonuses are sometimes equal to annual wages. Employees own a sizable fraction of the company.

Another interesting example is that of Nucor, a steel joist and specialty steel product manufacturer that also operates many steel mini-mills (mini-mills use scrap as input to electric furnaces); these mini-mills make the angles, rounds, and other very specialized shapes that go into the products manufactured by the company. Nucor uses an ingenious series of bonuses to ensure communication and the transfer of technology across the company's geographically dispersed operating units. Every production worker is in a group and earns a given percentage bonus for every percentage increase over standard that his or her group makes. These bonuses are sometimes as large as 100 or 200

percent of the base wage. Department manager bonuses depend on whether plant goals (not department goals) are attained. Similarly, plant manager bonuses depend on whether company (not plant) goals are attained.

JOB DESIGN AND QUALITY OF WORK LIFE[5]

Methods improvement, as discussed earlier in this chapter, could be characterized as "job dissection study," since it focuses on simplifying jobs and improving methods by breaking jobs apart and sometimes deskilling them, perhaps by adding more equipment. Many of the productivity advances since the beginning of the Industrial Revolution have involved this type of systematic analysis. But how do workers feel about doing jobs that have been simplified, deskilled? How do they feel about tending machines that do what they used to do?

Similarly, the section on wage payments earlier in this chapter stressed the link between worker effort or insight and worker compensation. But do workers work only for money? Do they really consider other forms of compensation to be much less important?

Recent evidence has raised more and more questions about job dissection and money compensation. Many processes that have relied on these notions have inadvertently created situations in which workers feel that the job is not worth doing, certainly not worth doing well. In these instances, quality has declined—waste, absenteeism, and labor turnover have increased. This phenomenon has made some people wonder whether companies should shift from selecting people for particular jobs to fitting the jobs to the workers.

Many companies have tried to counter worker disaffection with innovations that make work more meaningful to people and thus more likely to receive their full attention and care. These innovations still have as a goal high company profits, but they are attentive to worker needs, especially as the character of the workforce has changed. A number of factors have emerged as important dimensions of satisfaction with one's job and workplace, and each demands some attention from managers concerned about workforce wellbeing and productivity. In no particular order:[6]

- *Adequate and fair compensation.* Still an important consideration for all workers. Is the pay sufficient, and is it in line with expectations and demands of other, perhaps similar, jobs?

- *Safe and healthy working conditions.* Is the plant structurally sound and is the machinery safe to operate? Is the workplace attractive and comfortable? Are the hours long? Is there flexibility in the time workers can start or stop work?

- *Immediate opportunity to use and develop human capacities.* Does the job give the worker a sense of identity? Does it call for any substantial autonomy? Is the job self-contained or merely a small piece of a task with no real identity itself? Does the job call for planning as well as execution? Does it call for multiple skills? Is the job tied into the larger flow of information about the process and the control of that process?

- *Future opportunity for continued growth and security.* What opportunities exist for advancement on the job? How secure is the employment? Will the job provide the training and development needed to tackle still larger jobs?

- *Social integration into the workplace.* To what degree is the workplace open and supportive of each worker? To what degree is the workplace free of prejudice and status symbols? How upwardly mobile are workers?

- *Rights in the workplace.* To what extent does the rule of law and due process characterize an individual's rights in the workplace? Are privacy, free speech, and equity fully respected?

- *Work in perspective.* Are the demands of the job in balance with family and leisure dimensions of the worker's life?

- *Company vis-a-vis society.* Is the company perceived as socially responsible and socially accepted?

With these kinds of considerations in mind to deal with worker dissatisfaction, a host of work restructure policies have been tested by companies like General Foods, Procter and Gamble, General Motors, TRW, Ford Motor, Goodyear, Cummins Engine, Eaton Corporation, and Mars, Inc., among others. The work restructuring that has been tested in these and other companies tends to be very idiosyncratic; no two programs are alike. Goals are held to only loosely and timetables are extraordinarily flexible. The goals are dual; the intended benefits are to be reaped by both management and the workforce. The adopted programs work by altering the "culture" of the workplace. Walton summarizes the process in a diagram (see Figure 3-4).[7]

As quality of work life innovations have taken hold, there have been some clear distinctions that have emerged for workers between the old and new modes of management:[8] Jobs have become broader in scope for workers, workers have voiced more of their own concerns about the nature and direction of the workplace, labor relations have mellowed, employment security has become a higher priority, and the wage system has been altered to reward learning and/or group achievement.

There have been distinctions important for management as well: layers of management have been reduced in number, traditional work

Level I **Design techniques** ⟶	Level II **Work culture ideals** ⟶	Level III **Intended results** ⟶
Job design	High skill levels and flexibility in using them	*For business:*
Pay	Identification with product, process, and total business viewpoint	Low cost
Supervisor's role		Quick delivery
Training	Problem solving instead of finger pointing	High-quality products
Performance feedback	Influence by information and expertise instead of by position	Low turnover
Goal setting		Low absenteeism
Communication	Mutual influence	Equipment utilization
Employment stability policies	Openness	*For quality of work life:*
Status symbols	Responsiveness	Self-esteem
Leadership patterns	Trust	Economic well-being
	Egalitarian climate	Security
	Equity	

Note: The design techniques, culture ideals, and intended results listed above are presented as illustrative, not as comprehensive nor even as universally applicable. Also, the items in the three columns are not horizontally lined up to relate to each other. The arrows indicate influence.

FIGURE 3-4   Three-level conception of work improvement.

standard expectations have been replaced with more ambitious and flexible expectations, and overhead has been removed. In Walton's view, quality-of-work-life (QWL) initiatives have shifted management away from exercising control over the workforce towards seeking worker commitment to the company, its goals, and its constituencies.

There are sometimes some casualties in this process, however—notably first-level supervisors. Supervisors are often caught in the middle, forced to jettison their former attitudes, strengths, and training. While some supervisors have adjusted very well to change, others have been left floundering. They no longer have the control they once enjoyed, and the skills demanded of them by QWL initiatives are often foreign and of seemingly low esteem.

The movement to restructure work has taken several broad tacks and the variations on them have been almost as diverse as the companies involved. Broadly, however, one can divide work restructuring into job redesign on the one hand and QWL innovations on the other. The chief distinction here is that job redesign looks at altering the character of the job itself to make it inherently more interesting for the worker and thus more apt to draw his attention, care, and effort, so that both worker satisfaction and productivity are enhanced. QWL innovations, on the other hand, can be seen largely as a process that may or may not involve job redesign but that tries to engage workers actively in solving problems of concern in the workplace. Let us consider job redesign first.

Job Redesign

Job redesign can be divided into two major areas: job enlargement and job enrichment. Job enlargement typically involves combining what may have been separate workplace activities, done by different people, into one enlarged job. In an enlarged job a worker may be required not only to run a machine but also to perform routine maintenance on it. To that may be added machine setup, or quality checking, or a number of other tasks. While job enlargement risks performing the job more inefficiently than when individual tasks were assigned to different, specialized workers, proponents of job enlargement argue that its savings in improved quality, lower absenteeism, lower turnover, and the like more than make up for any efficiency losses implied by combining job elements.

Job enrichment takes a different approach to restructuring each individual job: it seeks to provide workers with more opportunities for planning and controlling their jobs and the surrounding environment. Job enrichment typically gives workers more autonomy and responsibility, not just more things to do.

In some companies, there has been a move toward autonomous work groups or worker teams that combine job enlargement and job enrichment. The teams generally have charge of something that they can "own" (such as a particular subassembly or a well-defined portion of the process such as packaging). Individual team members may be trained to do more than they used to do; the new, restructured jobs may have more elements in them or workers are rotated through different jobs more frequently. Often such job enlargement is combined with job enrichment; a team may be charged with tasks like production scheduling, performing its own maintenance, setting up its own equipment, tracking its own quality, calling in engineering support for equipment modifications, working on inventory control with other teams elsewhere in the process, or monitoring materials quality.

Quality-of-Work-Life Innovations

Quality of work life has been conceptually defined as the *process* of increased worker involvement in the workplace rather than a specific program such as job enlargement or job enrichment. Nevertheless QWL innovations have often resulted in job enlargement and/or job enrichment programs. Thus, it is often hard to disentangle the QWL process from its effects on job designs.

Although the distinction between QWL innovations and job redesign should not be pushed too strenuously, it does exist. For example, many of the real advances at C-P-C—Tarrytown have come about not so much because of job enrichment or job enlargement. Cars at Tarrytown are assembled pretty much like cars at other plants; the cycle time is still a minute, and a moving assembly line is still used. Nevertheless, at Tarrytown (and other places), the quality of work life has been greatly enhanced by increasing the communication between management and the workforce and sincerely soliciting worker ideas to solve problems that are everybody's concern.

What does it take to have a QWL innovation succeed? Nobody knows for sure. These efforts are still in their infancy and, in many cases, are wrought of fragile stuff. Nevertheless, some useful observations have appeared in the burgeoning literature on the subject. Successful QWL innovations, it seems, generally entail sincere commitment by both management and the workforce (and any unions involved), patience on the part of all parties, and a measure of risk taking and faith about what might be accomplished. Quality of work life should, in these instances, be regarded as an end in itself, even though other benefits, such as improved productivity, can also be realized. Successful QWL innovations have been very flexible and open to change as conditions warrant, because the means of worker involvement are just as important as the results of any problem solving. A union cannot be sidestepped; QWL innovations have to be viewed as supplements, not as replacements, to the collective bargaining process.

Most strong QWL innovations were hatched from small select groups of workers and supervisors that found themselves successfully solving some problems. They then spread, as a sort of "healthy infection," into other work groups in the plant. Typically, the QWL process cannot be forced on workers; they must embrace it in their own time. Management must make a lasting commitment to the QWL process, through rough economic times as well as smooth.

Quality of work life typically involves changing much or all of the culture of the workplace—worker attitudes toward the job, toward the product, toward fellow workers, toward management. As one might expect, new social systems sometimes step on toes. There has been some low-level management backlash to quality of work life as well as upper-level management indifference: some supervisors see the QWL process as a deskilling of their own roles that, at the same time, demands from them a lot of work and communication. Many supervisory personnel, especially in operations that have incorporated worker teams, have difficulty viewing quality of work life as a supplement to their jobs, not as a replacement for them. Supervisors and overhead function personnel (such as engineers) often have to recast the way they look at their jobs. No longer are they working for management; instead they are working for the worker teams. Rather than directing the work, they are brought in as consultants or teachers, and this change of emphasis and role is sometimes difficult for lower-level managers to accept.

Moreover, pressures on the new plant social system have to be overcome. Demands for high-volume production or for production innovations tend to lengthen hours, reduce time for team meetings, introduce rivalries, and slow personnel development. Decisions about pay and worker advancement sometimes have to be sidestepped or compromised because of the touchiness of peer evaluation or the vagaries of the business cycle and foreign competition.

On balance, however, work restructuring and the QWL process have proved to be a modest success, and much more experimentation and development of the concept can be expected. Work restructuring and quality of work life must be carefully evaluated since they have not been, nor are they likely to be, embraced wholeheartedly by all company workforces. There are still many instances where workforces resist change and do not want to assume any managerial roles. Often workers would rather have more time off than more responsibility. Any work restructuring must be carefully tuned to the situation at hand.

In this regard, it is interesting to follow one of the most recent management crazes, that of introducing *quality circles* (sometimes called *quality control circles*) into the operation. These quality circles are a much heralded aspect of Japanese management and are prevalent in many of the most successful Japanese companies. Many U.S. companies have tried to emulate the Japanese. Quality circles share much with other QWL innovations in that they are problem-solving groups involving members of the same department, both workers and supervisors. (Other QWL innovations have joined workers and supervisors from different departments; quality circles deal strictly with one department's workers and supervision.) Each quality circle receives some training in problem identification, data gathering, and data analysis. After this training, the quality circle chooses a particular problem to work on. The problem may involve quality, but it may also involve production speeds, worker safety, or something else. Once the problem has been chosen, it is analyzed by gathering data to see what its causes are. Various solutions are then proposed and tested. Quality circle meetings generally take about an hour a week, typically on company time.

The success of quality circles in the United States has been mixed. For some companies the time devoted to quality circle meetings is more than made up for by the savings that have resulted. In other cases, the costs of the quality circles have been greater than the savings, but worker morale is much higher, and for that reason the companies maintain them. In other situations, however, neither savings nor morale has been high enough to merit the continued use of quality circles. It is said that in Japan, quality circles are seen much more as one of the last resorts to improve quality and the flow of the process, not as one of the first things to do. It seems that quality circles, just as other QWL innovations, must be implemented with care and with real understanding of their potential problems as well as their potential advantages.

OTHER ASPECTS OF WORKFORCE RELATIONS

Discipline

One of the most difficult and vexing of any supervisor's tasks is that of disciplining a worker, for whatever cause. While some employee actions are automatic causes for dismissal (theft of company property, deliberate destruction of equipment, or blatant insubordination), there are seemingly countless infractions that merit less severe action. But exactly what action should be taken is often not clear.

To help matters out, companies typically have a well-defined series of steps to follow in worker infraction cases. As we saw in the plant tour of Jos. A. Bank, these steps may range from an initial reprimand to formal warning letters and on to a forced suspension and finally dismissal. Such formality serves to guard worker rights and forces the company to document, as well

as it can, the instances of worker infractions of company rules and regulations.

As an example of the gray areas of management in these matters, consider Situation 3-4 and how you would handle the matter.

SOME COMMENTS ON LABOR RELATIONS[9]

The trade union movement in the United States is about a hundred years old, spawned as a reaction against some sorrowful management exploitation of labor that must stand as one of the lowest points in business history. Seen against this backdrop, the accomplishments of the union movement are dramatic and heartwarming, won as they were against fierce opposition, although with too much violence from both sides.

Since World War II, however, while the union membership rolls have generally continued to increase (19.8 million in 1982),[10] the percentage of the employment of nonagricultural establishments which is unionized has steadily dropped. In 1982, only 22.1 percent of the employees of nonagricultural establishments were union members, down from 33.2 percent in 1958 and from a high of about 35 percent in 1945.[11]

The unionization of production workers in manufacturing is considerably higher than this, as might be expected. Still, the extent of unionism in manufacturing has declined somewhat over the last generation. Nevertheless, unions remain an important influence on managers. Wage rates in many companies are set to be comparable with union-bargained rates in other companies in the same industry or in the same geographic area. The same can be said of benefits packages. Business decisions (plant locations, for example) are often made with unions, or their avoidance, in mind.

SITUATION 3-4

CENTRAL LOUISIANA OIL

Charlie Clotfelter had been on his job as production manager at Central Louisiana's holdings in the Lucile field for about six months. Before that time he had held a staff position in the company's headquarters. The Lucile field had been producing for decades. Central Louisiana Oil operated numerous leases in this oil field, which was owned by scores of local established families. Being an old field, it suffered from a number of disadvantages relative to new oil fields, where the most advanced recovery techniques could be used. For example, the natural gas dome that rides on the top of an oil field had been blown early in the career of the Lucile field, thus reducing the pressure that could be used to help bring the oil to the surface. Vacuum pumping had also been used at this field, which meant that pumps in the field were attracting oil to each well. This action essentially forced all of the operators in the field to use vacuum pumping to attract their fair share of oil. Central Louisiana Oil was the major operator in the field, but there were two dozen smaller operators pumping from hundreds of wells.

One result of the pumping was the unavoidable collection of a light condensate, especially in winter. This condensate was highly volatile and was typically run off in small-diameter buried pipes to an open pit near each pumping station, where it evaporated. This condensate is compatible with refined gasoline and, when mixed with leaded gasoline in a ratio of 50:50, makes a fuel that can be burned in any car. Understandably, it is termed "drip" gasoline. For years, workers in the Lucile field had tapped into the buried pipes and diverted the condensate from the pits into 55-gallon drums buried in the dense foliage that covered nearly all of the Lucile field. Each drum usually collected between 25 and 30 gallons of drip gasoline a week. In the evening, workers came along the dirt roads that criss-crossed the field to uncover their 55-gallon drums, pump out the contents, and transport it back to their homes or barns. Naturally, this drip gasoline was dangerous to handle, and the area suffered more than its share of barn fires.

The workers felt they were simply being frugal, because the drip gasoline would be vented by an operator like Central Louisiana Oil. Of course, the pipes used to divert the drip gasoline and the drums used to store it were generally taken from the operators. In the eyes of the workers, however, this was merely petty theft of company scrap pipe and drums.

Although the gathering of drip gasoline was a long-standing practice for workers of many producers, it was not known to Charlie Clotfelter when he first arrived. Nor was it known to Clotfelter's predecessor. In fact, Charlie would not have known of it at all if a disgruntled construction contractor had not tipped him off. Upon hearing of the possibility of this drip gasoline operation on Central Louisiana Oil's property, he alerted the corporation's security people to come out and check. After several weeks of sleuthing, the security people reported back to him that nearly all of Central Louisiana's 35 employees in the Lucile field had, at one time or another, been engaged in the sale of drip gasoline. Two of the three supervisors were ignorant of the practice, but one, who had risen to the supervisor level from being a field worker, knew of the operation because, as a worker, he had engaged in the practice. To make matters worse, the security people uncovered the fact that the largest dealer in drip gasoline was the president of the local union representing Central Louisiana workers, who served as the chief bargaining agent for the union in contract negotiations with the company.

This was the dilemma that Charlie Clotfelter faced. The drip gasoline operation was clearly illegal, although the workers apparently regarded it as a fringe benefit that did not harm the company since the drip gasoline would only be evaporated. What should he do about the situation? Should he fire all of his workers? Should he fire just a few? Should he make an example of the union local president, who was the biggest dealer? Should he fire the supervisor who failed to inform him of this illegal operation? If he didn't fire the workers, should he engage in some other form of discipline? What actions should he take?

TABLE 3-4   Two views of trade unionism

	UNION EFFECTS ON ECONOMIC EFFICIENCY	UNION EFFECTS ON DISTRIBUTION OF INCOME	SOCIAL NATURE OF UNION ORGANIZATION
Anti-Union Arguments	Unions raise wages above competitive levels; hence there is too little labor relative to capital in unionized firms. Union work rules decrease productivity. Unions lower society's output through frequent strikes.	Unions increase income inequality by raising the wages of highly skilled workers. Unions create horizontal inequalities by creating differentials among comparable workers.	Unions discriminate in rationing positions. Unions (individually or collectively) fight for their own interests in the political arena. Union monopoly power breeds corrupt and nondemocratic elements.
Pro-Union Arguments	Unions reduce quit rates, induce management to alter methods of production and adopt more efficient policies, and improve morale and cooperation among workers. Unions collect information about the preferences of all workers; hence the firm can choose a "better" mix of employee compensation and a "better" set of personnel policies. Unions improve the communication between workers and management, leading to better decision making.	Unions' standard-rate policies reduce inequality among organized workers in a given company or a given industry. Union rules limit the scope for arbitrary actions concerning the promotion, layoff, recall, and the like of individuals. Unionism fundamentally alters the distribution of power between marginal (typically junior) and inframarginal (generally senior) employees, causing union firms to select different compensation packages and personnel practices than nonunion firms.	Unions are political institutions that represent the will of their members. Unions represent the political interests of lower-income and disadvantaged persons.

SOURCE: Richard B. Freeman and James L. Medoff, "The Two Faces of Unionism," *The Public Interest*, no. 57 (Fall 1979), p. 75.

The apoplexy with which unionism is greeted by many companies, however, is caused less by the additional wages or benefits that companies must pay because of unions. Most managers would agree that keeping unions out of a company is as expensive or even more so than having them in, at least in terms of wages and benefits. The major management complaint rests more with the inflexibility that can creep into a plant as a result of unionism. This complaint is mainly against so-called "work rules," which are largely rules and procedures governing the manning of a plant. Frequently, the work rule agreed to years ago and insignificant then comes back to haunt a manager who for a reason like technological change wants to alter the way things are done. It often takes great management foresight to avoid future pitfalls with work rules; with a union, bad management decisions, many think, are more difficult to remedy. Moreover, the importance of work rules has gradually increased as more and more issues are bargained over by labor and management at contract time.

Despite these arguments against unionism, there are still some strong arguments in its favor. Table 3-4 summarizes the major arguments for and against unionism.

QUESTIONS

1. Having read the chapter, how would you answer the question posed in the chapter's first sentence: "What makes a workforce supervisor truly effective?"

2. What examples of ergonomics have you observed? What benefits do you see from such ergonomics designs or practices? What costs?

3. In what ways is motion study a substitute for time study? a complement to time study?

4. Using some easily available products, consider how a company might undertake some value engineering of them. Be as specific as you can.

5. Discuss the means by which individual incentive schemes, like piece rates, become eroded over time. Given such erosion, why are they as prevalent as they are?

6. In what situations do you think a Scanlon plan would be inappropriate or likely to fail?

7. Tower Manufacturing Company and Baldridge Chain Saw have problems. In what ways are their problems similar? In what ways are they different?

8. React to the statement "Quality of work life is a giveaway to the workers."

PROBLEMS

1. Detail how the role of the supervisor varies from one type of process to another.

2. Using a chart such as found in Figure 3-1, chart a worker's task in some process (manufacturing or service) with which you are familiar or which you can observe firsthand.

3. A worker is charged with operating two machines simultaneously. The jobs assigned by the foreman call for the worker to engage in some loading and unloading (termed external time) of each machine and some observation and machine operation while the machines are running (termed internal time). Some machine running time requires no worker intervention. Using a device such as found in Figure 3-2, determine how many of each part the worker can make at 100 percent of standard during an eight-hour workday.

STANDARD TIMES PER PIECE	MACHINE 1	MACHINE 2
External time	0.55 minutes	0.68 minutes
Internal time	0.40 minutes	0.52 minutes
Total machine running time (including internal time)	1.90 minutes	1.65 minutes

4. The worker in the previous problem can earn incentive pay by performing the external time for each job more quickly (neither the internal times nor the running times can be altered without re-engineering both jobs). How much better than standard (as a percentage) for each machine must the worker perform in order to earn 115 percent of the standard pay? to earn 130 percent of the standard pay?

5. The engineering department has just devised some jigs that improve the external time

TABLE 3-5   Times and ratings (problem 8)

ELEMENT	OBSERVATION TIMES (seconds)						AVERAGE PERFORMANCE RATING
	1	2	3	4	5	6	
Examine front	7.6	7.3	8.2	7.8	8.0	8.1	115%
Press front	15.5	15.9	17.0	16.5	16.2	17.5	100
Examine lapel	6.0	5.9	7.0	5.9	6.4	7.5	95
Press lapel	20.5	17.8	19.2	18.6	20.2	18.0	105
Inspect lining	8.7	7.7	7.4	8.2	6.8	9.6	90
Hang up coat and pick up new one	4.3	4.0	4.6	5.6	5.6	4.8	110

standards for the worker in problem 3 from 0.55 minutes to 0.40 minutes for machine 1 and from 0.68 to 0.48 minutes for machine 2. The foreman is considering adding to the worker's tasks a third machine nearby. For the job contemplated, that machine's external time is 0.35 minutes, its internal time is 0.27 minutes, and total machine running time is 0.95 minutes. Given these additional responsibilities, how many of each part can the worker now make at 100 percent of standard during an eight-hour workday?

6. Suppose, as in problem 4, the worker wanted to earn 115 percent or 130 percent of the standard pay. At what percentages of the standard external times would he have to perform in order to satisfy his desires?

7. How are therbligs and the MOST system alike? How are they different?

8. An apparel firm's industrial engineer has observed a worker in the pressing and inspection department of a men's coat shop. Six observations have been made, with average performance ratings on each element for the six observations. The times and ratings for each element and observation are shown in Table 3-5.

To ascertain the extent of allowances for the job, a work sampling study was done. The job was divided into normal time working, unavoidable delay (machine downtime, talks with foreman, out of materials), and allowance time (breaks and rests). Fifty random observations were made with the following results:

	OBSERVATIONS
Normal time working	35
Unavoidable delay	6
Allowance time	9
Total	50

Given this information, what should be the standard time for the job?

9. Using the MOST system as spelled out in Figure 3-3 and some reasonable assumptions of your own, estimate a time standard for:

a. making a Burger King hamburger

b. boxing that hamburger

c. dumping fries from vat to bin and salting them

10. Develop a piece-rate system of your own using, say, ten different piece rates. Alter that system so that all workers receive a 10 percent wage increase. Compare what you have to do to effect such a change with a similar set of ten jobs on a standard-hour incentive system.

11. Calculate the size of the Scanlon plan bonus percentage under the following conditions:

   a. The sales value of all production is $2 million. The allowed payroll costs are 20 percent and actual payroll runs $330,000. The company share is 25 percent; of the employee share, a reserve of 25 percent is kept. What is the average worker's bonus percentage?

   b. How does the calculation change when different allowed payroll cost percentages are introduced? Suppose that Product A now accounts for 60 percent of sales (up from 50 percent) and Product B accounts for 40 percent. A's allowed costs are now 25 percent, and B's are 15 percent. Actual payroll costs of $330,000 are split 50–50 between the products. What is the bonus per worker?

   c. Why might such a split between product lines be advantageous?

12. In your opinion, under what conditions does the institution of quality circles make sense, and under what conditions does their institution *not* make sense?

13. As Charlie Clotfelter of Central Louisiana Oil, what would you do?

SITUATION FOR STUDY 3-1
COUNTRY GELATIN COMPANY REVISITED

Thomas Brewer, plant manager for Country Gelatin Company (see Tour E), noticed that every time he went into the break room, at least one of the process control technicians was drinking a cup of coffee, reading a book, or generally being nonproductive. He concluded that the technicians did not have enough work to fill their eight-hour shifts, and he asked Connie Darvin, the personnel manager, to look into the situation. Connie proceeded as follows:

1. A preliminary work sampling study was done to find out what the technicians were doing.
2. Some changes were implemented based upon the preliminary study.
3. A second work sampling study was done to determine the effects of the study.

The preliminary work sampling study was done over a ten-week period; of the 1200 working hours for the three types of technicians, about 15 percent (or 180 hours) were observed. The results of the study are shown in Table 3-6 for the three technician types. The figures represent the average percentage of an eight-hour shift that was spent performing the duties listed. The technicians spent approximately 20 to 25 percent of the time preparing for testing (such as cleaning glassware) and doing paperwork and calculations: 25 to 34 percent of the time, the technicians were idle.

Several points need to be raised about Country at the time of the study: (1) the plant was running at about three-fourths of capacity, (2) the job procedures were not clearly defined, (3) technicians were performing menial tasks and, therefore, had a low concept of job worth, and (4) technicians had serious communication problems with production foremen and others who should be using their information.

As a result of the preliminary study, the powder technician's duties were consolidated into

TABLE 3-6   Results of preliminary work sampling (Country Gelatin Company)

DUTIES	SOLUTIONS TECHNICIANS	PERCENTAGE OF SHIFT POWDER TECHNICIANS	LINE TECHNICIANS
Prepare	10%	6%	0%
Check floor samples	18	22	26
Run tests (in lab)	17	18	15
Do paperwork and calculations	11	17	29
Consult with supervisors	2	4	2
Run extra tests and retests	8	7	3
Idle time	34	26	25

TABLE 3-7   Line technicians' duties after changes
(Country Gelatin Company)

| DUTIES | PERCENTAGE OF SHIFT | | | |
	4/10	4/11	4/16	4/17
Retrain*	7%	4%	0%	0%
Take measurements and readings†	19	27	21	31
Obtain samples†	9	12	15	13
Run tests (in lab)	6	2	10	4
Do paperwork and calculations	29	38	31	36
Consult with supervisors	4	1	4	1
Run extra tests and retests	11	6	6	5
Idle time	15	10	13	10

*The line technicians had to be retrained when they took over some of the duties of the powder technicians. Preparation became a duty of the solutions technicians only.
†These two categories are very much the same as the category "check floor samples" in Table 3-6.

the duties of the line technician and solutions technician; the powder technician's job was eliminated.

After these changes, Connie observed the work of the line technicians on four different dates. The percentage of eight-hour shifts was recorded, and these results are shown in Table 3-7. Connie noticed that some changes had occurred other than just the change in work duties. For example, before the changes, the technicians would complete whatever work they were doing before taking breaks (albeit long ones); however, after the changes, the technicians took their breaks by the clock regardless of whether the particular test they were working on was completed. Also, several technicians were observed to be making the data "fit" rather than completing long tests.

These results led Connie to question (1) whether the work sampling studies were done properly and (2) whether the changes in job were proper. What suggestions do you have for Connie?

SITUATION FOR STUDY 3-2
AUTOMOTIVE TRIM PLANT

The Trim Plant of Mayflower Motors, one of Detroit's Big Three automakers, manufactured seat covers. These seat covers joined various upholstery fabrics (e.g., cloth, vinyl, velour) to polyurethane padding. Completed seat covers were shipped to Mayflower's assembly plants, where they were attached to seat frames of various types for installation in Mayflower Motors' cars.

The Trim Plant was located along an interstate highway in a major city. It was over 40 years old and employed 700 workers, mostly in sewing operations. The plant was organized by the United Auto Workers (UAW).

The plant's reputation for quality was excellent. However, given the sorry state of the automobile industry during the prevailing recession and Mayflower Motors' own perilous standing, the plant had to be cost effective as well as quality conscious in order to survive. A recent study by the corporation compared the cost of a model year's output as manufactured by the Trim Plant ($51.5 million in cost to Mayflower Motors) with that of outside vendors who used non-UAW labor ($30.8 million for the same level of output). This was a devastating comparison; other Mayflower Motors plants had been closed because of similarly poor economic comparisons. Of course, if the plant were to close, the corporation would still incur some ongoing costs (e.g., pension), estimated at $9.3 million. And if the corporation went to outside vendors, it might meet with some delivery and quality problems, the value of which was estimated at roughly $5 million per year. Still, there was an unfavorable difference of $6.4 million per year that argued powerfully for closing the plant.

The United Auto Workers' local recognized the implications of such a comparison. Moreover, the union admitted to itself that the plant was too "fat" with workers, because many sewing machine operators were finishing their daily quotas of work with an hour or more to spare. In order to keep jobs for its members, the union was willing to discuss changes in manning, work rules, quotas, etc., if the company was willing to consider keeping the plant open. About the only thing the UAW would stand firm on was wages; no cut in wages would be considered, because that would set a bad precedent at other company plants.

This was the situation facing John Gwynne, the plant manager. The UAW was apparently willing to concede some jobs, work rules, breaks, etc., and abide by tougher standards (that is, quotas) in order to keep the plant running. The time was fast approaching (another two months) when the corporation had to know whether the plant could be "rehabilitated" or whether it should place orders with some outside vendors. Gwynne needed to know how much cost could realistically be saved and by which means.

1. What should he do to find out the true weaknesses in the plant?

2. What new standards, manning levels, and the like should be established?

3. What principles should be adopted for any future managing of the plant?

4. What "give" should management evidence, and how much of any job reduction should management share with the hourly workforce?

REFERENCE NOTES

1. Additional information on methods improvement can be found in the following:

Barnes, Ralph M. *Motion and Time Study: Design and Measurement of Work.* 7th ed. New York: John Wiley & Sons, 1980.
Mundel, Marvin E. *Motion and Time Study.* 5th ed. Englewood Cliffs, N.J.: Prentice-Hall, 1978.
Niebel, Benjamin W. *Motion and Time Study.* 7th ed. Homewood, Ill.: Richard D. Irwin, 1982.

2. For additional information on time standards, see the following:

Barnes, Ralph M. *Motion and Time Study: Design and Measurement of Work.* 7th ed. New York: John Wiley & Sons, 1980.
Hornbruch, Frederick, Jr. *Raising Productivity: Ten Case Histories and Their Lessons.* New York: McGraw-Hill, 1977.
Katzell, Raymond A., Penny Bienstock, and Paul Faerstein. *A Guide to Worker Productivity Experiments in the United States, 1971–75.* New York: New York University Press, 1977.
Kendrick, John W. *Understanding Productivity.* Baltimore: Johns Hopkins, 1977.
Mundel, Marvin E. *Motion and Time Study.* 5th ed. Englewood Cliffs, N.J.: Prentice-Hall, 1978.
Niebel, Benjamin W. *Motion and Time Study.* 7th ed. Homewood, Ill.: Richard D. Irwin, 1982.
Zandin, Kjell B. *MOST Work Measurement Systems.* New York: Marcel Dekker, Inc., 1980.

3. For additional information on incentives and wage schemes, see:

Dearden, John. "How to Make Incentive Plans Work." *Harvard Business Review* 50, no. 4 (July–August 1972): 117–24.
Dunn, J. D., and F. M. Rachel. *Wage and Salary Administration.* New York: McGraw-Hill, 1971.
Geare, A. J. "Productivity from Scanlon-Type Plans." *Academy of Management Review* 1, no. 3 (July 1976): 99–108.
Moore, Brian E. and Timothy L. Ross. *The Scanlon Way to Improved Productivity: A Practical Guide.* New York: John Wiley & Sons, 1978.
National Commission on Productivity and Work Quality. *A Plantwide Productivity Plan in Action: Three Years of Experience with the Scanlon Plan.* May 1975.

4. See Robert S. Rice. "Survey of Work Measurement and Wage Incentives." *Industrial Engineering* (July 1977), pp. 18–31.

5. The literature on job design, job enrichment, and quality of work life is large and growing. For some additional information, see:

Cooper, Michael R., et al. "Changing Employee Values: Deepening Discontent?" *Harvard Business Review* 57, no. 1 (January–February 1979): 117–25.
Davis, Louis E. and Albert B. Cherns. *Quality of Working Life: Problems, Prospects, and State of the Art.* Glencoe, Ill.: Free Press, 1975.
Dickson, Paul. *The Future of the Workplace.* New York: Weybright and Talley, 1975.
Drucker, Peter F. *Management: Tasks, Responsibilities, Practices.* New York: Harper & Row, 1973.
Drucker, Peter F. *The Practice of Management.* New York: Harper & Row, 1954.
Fein, Mitchell. "Job Enrichment: A Reevaluation." *Sloan Management Review* 15, no. 2 (Winter 1974): 69–88.
Foy, Nancy, and Herman Gadon. "Worker Participation: Contrasts in Three Countries." *Harvard Business Review* 54, no. 3 (May–June 1976): 71–83.
Goodman, P. S. "Realities of Improving the Quality of Work Life—Quality of Work Life Projects in the 1980s." *Labor Law Journal.* August 1980: 487–94.
Guest, Robert H. *Innovative Work Practices.* Work in America Institute Studies in Productivity: No. 21. New York: Pergamon Press, 1982.
Guest, Robert H. "Quality of Work Life—Learning from Tarrytown." *Harvard Business Review* 57, no. 4 (July–August 1979): 76–87.
Gyllenhammar, Pehr G. "How Volvo Adapts Work to People." *Harvard Business Review* 55, no. 4 (July–August 1977): 102.
Hackman, J. Richard. "Is Job Enrichment Just a Fad?" *Harvard Business Review* 53, no. 5 (September–October 1975): 129–38.
Hackman, J. Richard, and Greg R. Oldham. "Development of the Job Diagnostic Survey." *Journal of Applied Psychology* 60 (1975): 159–70.
Hackman, J. Richard, and Greg R. Oldham. *Work Redesign.* Reading, Mass.: Addison-Wesley, 1980.

Hulin, C. C., and M. R. Blood. "Job Enlargement, Individual Differences, and Worker Responses." *Psychological Bulletin* 69 (1968): 41–55.

Kanter, R. "Dilemmas of Managing Participation." *Organizational Dynamics.* Summer 1982.

Lawler, Edward E., III, and J. A. Drexler, Jr. "Dynamics of Establishing Cooperative Quality-of-Worklife Projects." *Monthly Labor Review.* March 1978: 23–28.

Moore, Brian E., and Timothy L. Ross. *The Scanlon Way to Improved Productivity, A Practical Guide.* New York: John Wiley, 1978.

Nadler, D. A., and E. E. Lawler. "Quality of Work Life: Perspectives and Directions." *Organizational Dynamics.* Winter 1983: 20–30.

Robison, D. "General Motors Business Teams Advance QWL at Fisher Body Plant." *World of Work Report.* July 1977: 73, 80–81.

Rosenberg, R. D., and E. Rosenstein. "Participation and Productivity: An Empirical Study." *Industrial and Labor Relations Review.* April 1980: 355–67.

Rosow, Jerome, ed. *The Worker and the Job.* Englewood Cliffs, N.J.: Prentice-Hall, 1974.

Rubinstein, S. P. "Participative Problem Solving: How to Increase Organizational Effectiveness." *Personnel.* January–February 1977: 30–39.

Scobel, Donald N. "Doing Away with the Factory Blues." *Harvard Business Review* 53, no. 6 (November–December 1975): 132.

Stein, B. A., and R. M. Kanter, "Building the Parallel Organization: Creating Mechanisms for Permanent Quality of Work Life." *Journal of Applied Behavioral Science.* July–August–September 1980: 371–88.

Taylor, Frederick Winslow. *Scientific Management.* New York: Harper, 1911.

Trist, E. L., et al. *Organization Choice.* London: Tavistock Institute, 1963.

Upjohn Institute for Employment Research. *Work in America.* Cambridge, Mass.: MIT Press, 1973.

Walton, Richard E. "How to Counter Alienation in the Plant." *Harvard Business Review* 50, no. 6 (November–December 1972): 70–81.

Walton, Richard E. "Improving the Quality of Work Life." *Harvard Business Review* 52, no. 3 (May–June 1974).

Walton, Richard E. "Successful Strategies for Diffusing Work Innovations." *Journal of Contemporary Business* (Spring 1977).

Walton, Richard E. "Work Innovations in the United States." *Harvard Business Review* 57, no. 4 (July–August 1979): 88–98.

6. The following list is drawn from Richard E. Walton. "QWL Indicators—Prospects and Problems," *Studies in Personnel Psychology* 6, no. 1 (Spring 1974), pp. 7–18.

7. See Richard E. Walton. "Work Innovations in the United States," *Harvard Business Review* 57, no. 4 (July–August 1979), pp. 88–98.

8. For a discussion of these points, see Richard E. Walton, "From Control to Commitment: Transforming Work Force Management in the United States," Division of Research, Harvard Business School, March 1984.

9. For more information on unions and company management, see the following:

Brett, J. "Why Do Employees Join Unions?" *Organizational Dynamics.* Spring 1980: 47–59.

Freedman, A., and W. E. Fulmer, "Last Rites for Pattern Bargaining." *Harvard Business Review* 60, no. 2 (March–April 1982): 30–37.

Fulmer, W. E. "Step by Step Through a Union Campaign." *Harvard Business Review* 59, no. 4 (July–August 1981): 94–102.

Halley, William H., Jr. and Kenneth M. Jennings, *The Labor Relations Process, Second Edition.* Hinsdale, IL: The Dryden Press, 1984.

Kochan, T. A. "How American Workers View Labor Unions." *Monthly Labor Review.* April 1979: 23–31.

Sloane, Arthur A. and Fred Whitney, *Labor Relations, Fifth Edition.* Englewood Cliffs, NJ: Prentice Hall, 1985.

10. *Handbook of Labor Statistics,* U.S. Department of Labor, Bureau of Labor Statistics, The Statistical Abstract of the U.S., and the Directory of U.S. Labor Associations.

11. Ibid.

PLANNING AND CONTROLLING PRODUCTION

The goals of production planning are straightforward: figuring out which products to produce, when to produce them, and how much of each. Nevertheless, accomplishing this task effectively (at low cost and with all obligations met on time) can be devilishly difficult. There are wide variations in the means by which such decisions are made. A quick review of key planning features of the plants toured in the first segment of this text can give us some hints about that diversity. See Table 4-1.

As the brief review in the table clearly reveals, these six examples share several common features, but differ in several others. Part One of this chapter is devoted to a more detailed discussion of the ideas and techniques of production planning and how they can be used to answer effectively the issues of which products to produce at what time, and in what quantities.

Part Two deals with controlling the process so that the production plan is achieved.

TABLE 4-1   Production planning across process types

ITEM	JOB SHOP (NORCEN INDUSTRIES)	BATCH FLOW (JOS. A. BANK)
Which Products	Products planned for production are strictly those for which there are firm orders.	The mix of products to be produced is geared to merchandising's forecast of a desired finished goods inventory. Some special orders are also permitted.
When	When these products enter production depends on (1) whether the materials for the job are on-hand (an order is not released to the shop floor unless materials are on-hand). and (2) how the foreman schedules them. The schedule is heavily influenced by due dates. To be able to meet due dates, the foreman must monitor machine capacities and availabilities as well as worker availabilities and the possibility of overtime. Complications and bottlenecks are encountered continually, requiring quick rescheduling.	Each week's production is largely determined by the expected demand for the entire season. The process is flexible enough to respond in a matter of hours to identified problems (such as recutting).

351

TABLE 4-1　Production planning across process types (*continued*)

ITEM	JOB SHOP (NORCEN INDUSTRIES)	BATCH FLOW (JOS. A. BANK)
How much of each	How much is produced depends primarily on the quantity ordered. There may be some slight modifications made to that quantity depending on yields, materials availability, and other factors.	How much is produced depends largely on the target finished goods inventory levels. Hot-selling items may be constrained by materials availability.

ITEM	WORKER-PACED LINE FLOW (BURGER KING)	MACHINE-PACED LINE FLOW (GENERAL MOTORS—TARRYTOWN)
Which Products	Products produced are typically firm orders. Some products, such as french fries, are routinely produced to maintain a certain level of finished goods. When demand is high, a number of products are produced to maintain a finished goods inventory target. The general pattern of demand is known statistically in advance and preparation is geared to that forecast.	Firm orders only are produced.
When	Nothing can be inventoried for long, so that all production occurs either minutes prior to the receipt of an order or seconds after an order has been placed.	The process is only somewhat elastic and cannot stretch to fill all orders with the same lead times. Long-term demands can be estimated and used to set the speed of the line and to guide suppliers. Once line speed is set, only overtime or an extra shift can increase production.
How much of each	The amounts filled out of finished goods inventories or from production itself are precisely the quantities ordered. What may get produced slightly ahead of time are quantities determined from a statistical analysis of demand.	How much is determined precisely by what is ordered.

ITEM	CONTINUOUS FLOW (INTERNATIONAL PAPER'S ANDROSCOGGIN MILL)	HYBRID PROCESS (BATCH/CONTINUOUS FLOW—STROH BREWERY, WINSTON-SALEM)
Which Products	Products produced are those paper grades and colors that have been ordered and those that marketing has decided will sell in the marketplace. During any planning cycle, some production will be geared to customer orders, while other production will augment the finished goods inventories.	The products brewed are indicated by a forecast, but the amounts canned or bottled are set by specific wholesaler order.
When	There is a rigid four-week planning cycle. Capacity can be a severe constraint, so great care is taken in matching specific products to machines and in scheduling production to leave little or no waste and to avoid additional handling of rolls of paper. Long runs are sought. Expediting is anathema. Orders are carefully fit into a patterned use of capacity. Each schedule is frozen at least five days prior to its run.	Most production is accomplished to match wholesalers' initial due date requests, although modest adjustments may have to be made. Lead time is generally two to six weeks. The extent of shift work varies with the level of demand and its seasonality. The schedule is fixed for labor one week in advance, but for packaging only one day in advance. Brewing is done in anticipation of packaging demands. These batches are held in inventory until called for use by the packaging schedule.
How much of each	The quantities of output depend on order sizes and the requirements of the finished goods inventory.	The size of each batch brewed is determined by the forecast. Wholesaler orders determine the quantities packaged.

PART ONE
PLANNING A PRODUCTION SCHEDULE[1]

FACTORS IN THE DESIGN OF PRODUCTION PLANS

As mentioned previously, an effective production plan meets its demand obligations on time and at low cost. Being on time with production requires management to know what the process capacity is and not to promise deliveries it does not have the capacity for. Keeping costs low requires a match of resources (workforce, equipment, materials) to obligations that neither unduly stretches those resources nor leaves too much excess capacity. As was noted in the discussion of process types, short-term capacity can be augmented in several ways—adding extra workers, scheduling overtime or extra shifts, and placing auxiliary equipment into service. Sometimes, companies can subcontract with others for extra production. All of these options, however, raise costs. Extra workers are frequently more costly to secure and less productive than regular workers. Overtime and extra shifts add costs to direct labor bills, maintenance, and overhead. Auxiliary equipment is typically less efficient and more expensive to operate and maintain. The production planner is justifiably loath to force short-term capacity increases by these means. However, the production planner also inflicts extra costs on the company if too much excess capacity is held. These costs are opportunity costs, the revenues forgone by failing to produce output that could have been sold. Striking a balance between resources and demand obligations is what production planning is all about.

Let us explore in greater detail how various kinds of processes can meet their delivery obligations at low cost.

Meeting Delivery

In all of the factory processes described in Segment I, there was a sincere desire to produce to exact customer specifications and to ship precisely when the customer indicated. This goal was not fully achievable in all of the processes because of some inherent constraints. In those that did achieve this goal, various policies were adopted.

A match of production to customer orders and timely delivery were best achieved at Burger King, Jos. A. Bank, and Norcen Industries. It is not surprising that these processes were the best performers on this criterion, since they all lie toward the job shop end of the process spectrum and are more apt to view their strengths as lying in customer service. Yet, their customer service was outstanding because of three different policies of production planning:

- *Modulating Capacity.* At the Burger King, timely delivery of the customer's precise order is ensured by continually varying the restaurant's labor and materials resources so that it is not swamped during the lunch and dinner peak hours. While the restaurant's physical size limits capacity, within that constraint output is adjusted by altering the size of the workforce and by continually rebalancing the restaurant's "assembly line." Modulating capacity is a common production planning policy in service industries because many services cannot be inventoried; thus, demands must be met primarily by adjusting capacity.

  Jos. A. Bank and Norcen Industries also modulated capacity to meet their delivery demands by scheduling overtime for their workers.

- *Inventory Buffers.* Jos. A. Bank filled its orders out of the finished goods inventory it held in its warehouse. Individual products were not generally customized, but the demands that the company handled could be vastly different. Jos. A. Bank maintained its high level of customer service by adopting a production planning policy that geared production to the maintenance of a finished goods inventory large enough to buffer the company against erratic demand patterns.

- *Managing demand.* In trying to ensure the timely delivery of its customized products, Norcen Industries could act both directly and indirectly. Scheduling overtime was a direct action it could take to expand its capacity. Alternatively, by adjusting the level of its bid on any order, Norcen Industries could indirectly, and more imperfectly, control the load on the shop and thus the shop's ability to deliver on time. In effect, Norcen Industries could manage demand. In times of high demand on capacity, its bids for business could be on the high side to help choke off the business it would have trouble delivering on time; similarly, in times of excess capacity, it could lower its bids and hope to draw in more business.

The other processes described—International Paper's Androscoggin Mill, General Motors' Tarrytown plant, and Stroh's Winston-Salem's brewery—all did a superb job of meeting their customer orders, but their inflexibilities sometimes constrained delivery. For example, Stroh and GM-Tarrytown sometimes had to defer production for a particular order until room appeared in the schedule. The time deferred was never particularly long—usually a week or two—but these delivery dislocations were an inevitable consequence of the rigidity within the process itself.

To cite another example, if the demand for paper were particularly strong, delivery simply could not be made. Carrying spare pulp and paper capacity is an increasingly expensive undertaking, and so the capacity utilization of pulp and paper mills is generally high to begin with. A peak demand situation, such as described in Tour A, is likely, then, to imply a rationing of paper to customers.

The hybrid process—Stroh's Winston-Salem brewery—offers an example of another means by which deliveries can be met effectively. This type of a process is intriguing precisely because it mixes production planning systems. The brewing portion of the process, on the one hand, is triggered by a sales forecast; the packaging portion, on the other hand, is triggered by actual orders.

What permits the brewery the luxury of planning production and managing materials in two different ways is the existence of an inventory of beer that separates the brewing process from the packaging process. This inventory "decouples" one from the other. Without an inventory that functions in this manner, the packaging portion of the process would probably have to be geared to the sales forecast, not to actual orders, and the brewery would probably have to store more beer in finished goods inventory, at higher cost, than it does now. Alternatively, incentives would have to be introduced to lock wholesalers into longer lead time orders than is now the case, so that brewing and packaging could both be done to order.

The key advantage of such a decoupling inventory is that it breaks up the information and materials management needs of the entire process into pieces that can be managed more easily on their own. There is a cost, of course, because the inventory must be financed, but the cost can often be substantially less than the introduction of process-wide computer systems or the financing of increased finished goods inventories.

The peak demand period at the Burger King restaurant offers another example of a decoupling inventory. There, as demand builds up, the information that triggers the meat patty broiling operation shifts from the punch-in of orders to the maintenance of a forecasted work-in-process inventory of broiled meat and toasted buns. This intermediate inventory is a decoupling one that is very effective in speeding up service and in keeping all of Burger King's sandwiches freshly made.

Keeping Costs Low

Identifying the Scarce Resource

In almost all cases, the mix of resources capable of meeting the prevailing demand obligations is not perfectly balanced between the workforce and the available equipment. Either the workforce will be the scarce resource and idle equipment will exist, or equipment will be the scarce resource and idle workers will exist. What the scarce resource is has a critical impact on how production is planned. Is the production plan designed to keep the equipment loaded (long production runs), or is it designed to keep the workforce busy (perhaps through many set-ups and shorter production runs)?

Because more workers can generally be added to any process, low-cost production plan design is essentially concerned with the economics of the process. Is equipment relatively cheaper to hold idle than labor, or is the reverse true? The question is easy to state, but in practice it may be very difficult to answer. On the one hand, it is easy to see why a company like International Paper devotes its talent to a careful scheduling of all the paper machines that it owns; an unnecessarily idle paper machine costs the company a bundle in foregone revenues. On the other hand, it stands to reason that a job shop like Norcen Industries would house a number of machine tools that would lie idle a good deal of the time. Some machines have specialized uses and remain idle for that reason, while others can pay for themselves by being used strictly for sporadic in-tandem jobs with another machine or for addressing chronic bottlenecks. At Norcen Industries, at least, holding equipment idle is cheaper than holding labor idle; production planning could call for a schedule of short runs if they would lead to on-time delivery and fewer bottlenecks.

These two examples are polar cases; in between is a sea of gray. For processes that are mostly batch and line flow, it is not always clear whether it is cheaper to hold idle some equipment or some labor, and thus whether the long production run is to be valued above a series of smaller runs. The decision depends on factors such as the costs of equipment, labor, inventory carrying, and inventory stockouts, and on production speeds, prices, and quality levels. We shall return to this point later.

Identifying the Valued Aspect of the Product or Service

If the full range of a company's product mix cannot be produced on time, which of the product mix ought to be produced? The production plan should be sensitive to those products or services that earn more contribution per unit of time or per unit of some other scarce resource. Production plans—particularly at the end of a month, quarter, or year—are often weighted heavily toward high contribution items or toward those that can easily be completed and billed. In many companies, the great end-of-month scramble to push product out the door is a scramble to push out the "winners," leaving poorer selling or poorer earning products until the next month. This kind of scheduling, of course, is more prevalent in job shop and batch flow processes; the more inflexible processes follow more rigid production plans.

An important management task is identifying how planning and scheduling can help gain or sustain high levels of contribution. The airline industry is a good case in point. Prior to the deregulation of the airlines in the late 1970s and the subsequent boom in air travel, airline load factors were not as high. The schedule of flights was used as a weapon to attract travelers; the prevailing wisdom was to schedule flights to be as convenient as possible, even if it meant cutting back on the time airplanes were scheduled to be in the air. Given the prevailing modes of competition, the valued aspect of the service was convenient time slots in the major city markets each airline served. The airlines that could provide the most convenient departure and arrival times were seen as the most successful.

With deregulation and the significant price declines that ensued, the mode of competition shifted from convenience to price. Load factors shot up, and the valued aspect of the service became airplane seats at low prices, not convenient times. There were travelers who demanded plane travel at every hour of the day, not merely at convenient hours. Airline planning and scheduling adjusted. Schedules were revised to lengthen the time airplanes were in the air, even if it meant some modestly inconvenient departure or arrival times for passengers. Many airlines adopted "hub and spoke" systems, where big city hubs (Dallas-Ft. Worth for American Airlines, Atlanta for Delta Airlines) were established and fed by numerous flights from other cities in a kind of pulsating pattern of arrivals and departures. With the scheduling adjustments, airline profits (contri-

bution per unit of scarce resource) shot up dramatically, other things equal.

Developing a Good Match Between Resources and Demands

The development of a lost-cost production plan depends not only on the identification of the most valued resource and how that scarce resource should be scheduled, but also on the specific techniques that can be brought to bear on the match between resources and demands. The remainder of this part of the chapter is devoted to a discussion on those techniques that have proven helpful in matching up resources with demands. A discussion of how demands are forecast is reserved for Appendix A. Suffice it here to assume that the forecast is a given (say, from the marketing or sales department) and that the operations managers must live within its confines.

CAPACITY PLANNING AND THE DEVELOPMENT OF THE MASTER PRODUCTION SCHEDULE

An effective production schedule is the heart—or at least the pacemaker—of many operations. Constructing one is an important but involved task, and the discussion of scheduling in this section is necessarily long and involved as well. With this in mind, it is appropriate to outline here the organization for this discussion of the schedule.

First we outline the evolutionary stages of production scheduling over time. This gives some perspective for the scheduling tools that are introduced throughout the remainder of the discussion. The first of the tools deals with assessing how much capacity exists for the process at any period of time (see Capacity Planning). Knowing capacity is a prerequisite for accepting orders and/or for scheduling production.

The discussion continues with coverage of the ways the schedule (either the master schedule, or the more general, aggregate plan) can be filled. This discussion begins in broad terms—see Master Scheduling and Aggregate Planning—but gets more precise and mathematical with the material under Scheduling Techniques. The scheduling techniques introduced involve both flow processes, where capacities are known with some certainty, and job shops, which are more ambiguous about capacity.

Stages in the Development of a Production Schedule

As a review of the plant tours reveals, the final production schedule for a plant is developed bit by bit, in stages, as more definite information on demands, materials, and capacities becomes available. Figure 4-1 depicts these stages. The first-cut planning of production is generally concerned only with broad aggregates—entire product lines, gross materials needs, rough estimates of labor and machine availabilities—for time periods that can stretch 12 to 18 months into the future, long enough that all materials needs can be planned for but not so long that production cannot be regarded as significantly constrained by the present facility and any changes already in the works for it. Because it deals with broad aggregates of resources, this stage of production scheduling is frequently termed *aggregate planning.*

The aggregate plan serves as the first alert for marshaling resources—getting initial commitments from suppliers, checking whether more (or less) labor is needed, ensuring the inventories on hand are adequate to meet demands, determining whether machine capacity is adequate. Given this alert, the managers responsible can go about securing the resources needed

to meet the plan. Decisions can be made as well about how production is going to vary to cover the expected pattern of demand. Should production remain "level," building up inventories to cover anticipated peaks of demand? Or, should production try to "chase" demand, with little or no accumulation of inventory? Or, should some mixed, in-between strategy prevail? It is in assessing the aggregate plan that decisions of this type are generally first made.

Since the aggregate plan is associated with marshaling resources, it inevitably becomes entwined with the budgeting process for the plant and the company division it reports to and, for that reason, often follows the same 12-month timetable. It also becomes a prime battleground between marketing—with its forecast of sales and any plans for product changes or new products—and manufacturing. If the planning is done well, general management will rule explicitly on the conflicts exposed by this process of schedule development. General management should resolve any differences between the desires of marketing/sales and those of manufacturing, so that both functions can be committed to meeting the schedule, as planned.

As demand firms up, the broad outlines of the production schedule, as determined by the aggregate plan, can be filled in with greater detail. Broad product line demand forecasts are replaced with more detailed forecasts of specific products and eventually, with specific product variations. Material supply capabilities and lead times are known with more certainty. More specifics are known about actual labor and machine availabilities. The aggregate planning stage gives away to successive stages of more detailed scheduling, generally termed *master production scheduling (MPS).*

The production schedule starts to reflect orders actually booked as well as those expected. The schedule begins to become firm, but it generally cannot be completely set until days or

FIGURE 4-1   Stages in the development of a production schedule.

weeks before actual production. Thus, some day-to-day or week-to-week leeway is permitted in the schedule; it is the job of the production scheduler to use this leeway in devising a detailed production schedule (sometimes termed a final assembly schedule) that places as balanced a demand on the process as possible. This means that the scheduler must be thoroughly aware of the capacities of each segment of the process and where any bottlenecks are likely to show up. This kind of knowledge often leads a scheduler to concoct rules of thumb that help develop a schedule that is feasible, balanced, and reasonably low cost.

The MPS must also reflect material availability. In the interest of clarity and order on the factory floor itself, it is often unwise to release an order whose component parts have not yet arrived or to release an order just to "get it moving" through the process. In both of these situations, work-in-process inventories build up; excessive work-in-process is too often disruptive and time-consuming to manage. Often companies are better off if they risk some idling workers temporarily because of no work than they would be purposely littering the floor with work-in-process. The hidden costs of work-in-process induced inefficiencies are frequently greater than the highly visible costs of idle labor. Yet, of course, many plants feel compelled to get something going in order to accommodate sales pressures, even if it means provoking inefficiencies in the process.

As the foregoing discussion has made clear, the scheduling process requires increasing refinement about capacities, demand, and material availability. The rest of this chapter examines capacities, demands, and their match. Material availability and management is the central topic of Chapter 5; the remainder of this chapter will largely ignore problems with material availability. Instead, what follows implicitly assumes that there will be material enough when needed to avoid rescheduling. This assumption will be relaxed in Chapter 5.

Capacity Planning

The goal of capacity planning is to estimate how much process capacity will be taken up by any proposed level and mix of product demands. Effective capacity planning can indicate whether a proposed production schedule is feasible; thus, it is an important tool for the scheduling process. There are several useful capacity planning techniques. These techniques vary in their sophistication, specificity, and data requirements.[2]

Capacity Planning Using Overall Factors

The roughest cut means of assessing capacity, so called "capacity planning using overall factors," uses three readily available bits of data: (1) the output demanded for each product (or aggregation of products, such as an entire product line), (2) the labor and/or machine standards for that product (such as the hours required per unit), and (3) the historical data on average usage by each workcenter.

The first step in the calculation is to determine the expected total hours required to produce what is demanded. If the demands are as follows:

PRODUCT	TIME PERIOD		
	1	2	3
X	10	15	5
Y	20	20	25

and the labor standards for the two products are

	LABOR STANDARD (AT 100%)
Product X	0.60 hours per unit
Product Y	0.40 hours per unit

then the expected total hours required for period 1's demands are:

Product X total hours
= 10 units · 0.60 hours/unit = 6 hours
Product Y total hours
= 20 units · 0.40 hours/unit = 8 hours
Total = 14 hours

The second step in the calculation uses the historical average utilizations by each work center (or department) to apportion the total capacity required to the various work centers. For example, if the work center utilizations, determined from accounting records, were as follows:

WORKCENTER	UTILIZATION
10	50%
11	30%
12	20%
	100%

Then the expected loads on each work center implied by the product mix demanded in each time period are:

WORKCENTER	TIME PERIOD 1	TIME PERIOD 2	TIME PERIOD 3	TOTALS
10	7	8.5	6.5	22.0
11	4.2	5.1	3.9	13.2
12	2.8	3.4	2.6	8.8
	14.0	17.0	13.0	44.0

These expected loads can be compared with actual capacities at the workcenters to suggest possible managerial adjustments (such as rescheduling some orders or working overtime). For simple, stable operations, this rough-cut technique is frequently good enough.

Capacity Bills

This technique gets more specific about the demands of each product on each of the workcenters; thus, shifts in the product mix will result, by this method, in shifts in demands on particular workcenters. Such a result is not possible in the overall factors technique because of its use of historical averages. This capacity bills technique, of course, requires more data—in particular, labor and/or machine hour standards for each product and its components, and knowledge of how the product is routed through the shop (that is, which workcenters come into play in producing it). By using this information, a "bill of capacity" can be constructed. Such a capacity bill is an estimate of the labor and/or machine time required by each workcenter to make a unit of the product(s) in question.

Suppose that the following represents the capacity bill for products X and Y, from the previous example:

WORKCENTER	PRODUCT X	PRODUCT Y
10	0.25 hrs/unit	0.10 hrs/unit
11	0.15	0.15
12	0.20	0.15
Totals	0.60 hrs/unit	0.40 hrs/unit

Note that the labor standard totals for each product (0.60 hr/unit and 0.40 hr/unit, respectively) are the same as those given in the overall factors example given previously.

The next step in the technique involves the application of each capacity bill to its respective product demand (its proposed master schedule) and summing the time estimates across products. Using the same demands as before results in expected workcenter loads as follows:

WORK-CENTER	TIME PERIOD 1	TIME PERIOD 2	TIME PERIOD 3	TOTALS	UTILIZA-TION
10	4.5	5.75	3.75	14	32%
11	4.5	5.25	4.5	14.25	32%
12	5.0	6.0	4.75	15.75	36%
Totals	14.0	17.0	13.00	44.00	100%

where workcenter 10's estimate of 4.5 hours for time period 1 is the sum of 2.5 for Product X ($0.25 \cdot 10$) and 2.0 for Product Y ($0.10 \cdot 20$). The other capacity estimates are calculated in similar fashion.

Note that the total labor hours required in each time period match those calculated by the overall factors technique, but the expected demands on each workcenter are vastly different from those calculated via historical usage. The usage rates of the workcenters implied by the product mix proposed differ markedly from the historical averages.

Resource Profiles

In the *resource profile* technique, production lead times for each product and its components are melded with bills of capacity to compute a time pattern projection of the capacity demands for individual workcenters. For complex products whose time in the production cycle is many weeks and whose components must be worked on well in advance of final assembly, making such a time pattern adjustment is an important correction.

Capacity Requirements Planning

Capacity requirements planning (CRP) is the most sophisticated technique available to estimate period-by-period demand for each workcenter. This technique takes into consideration not only the time pattern of demand on the workcenter (as well as the product structure, routings, and labor and/or machine standards required to develop capacity bills) but also any lot sizing decisions for components, inventory already on-hand or expected to be received, work-in-process status (remaining work on any shop orders already opened), service parts demand, and any recent production planner changes. Thus, capacity requirements planning provides a very detailed estimate of the workloads implied by the master production schedule and by the current status of individual workcenters. For complex and unstable operations, this technique can be well worth its significant computational expense and data needs. Capacity requirements planning is often an available module in computerized *materials requirements planning (MRP)* systems. More will be mentioned about CRP when MRP systems are described in Chapter 5.

Whichever technique is used—overall factors, capacity bills, resource profiles, or capacity requirements planning (or some other rough-cut technique)—the goal of capacity planning should be clear. That goal is namely to estimate, for any given period, how much capacity will be used up by any proposed production schedule. Without capacity planning of some sort, production planners would not know if a schedule stood a good chance of being infeasible. They would not be able to head off, in effective fashion, the resulting poor delivery performance, stranded work-in-process inventories, frustrated vendors, confused supervisors, and other ramifications of escalating chaos.

Without effective capacity planning, production planners would also not know "how much money they had left on the table" during any planning period by failing to schedule what the factory could have produced and for which they had sufficient demand in hand to justify.

Master Scheduling

Master scheduling is a process—an on-going activity—that melds forecasts, booked orders, and knowledge of the effective capacity of the factory. It is a process that periodically and systematically "publishes" a document—the master production schedule—that indicates how many of each product the factory will produce for a specified time period or succession of time periods. The master production schedule is stated in physical units for every end item for which there is a bill of materials, or more often, for a readily recognizable aggregation of end items that could be termed a model, style, series, product line, or something similar.

If an aggregation of end items constitutes the MPS, then a more precise schedule must be developed for the specific end item variations that will actually be produced. Often, this more precise schedule is termed the *final assembly schedule (FAS)*. The final assembly schedule paces the flow of products and materials through the process. It acts as both a planning tool and as a control document against which actual performance can be measured.

In the case where the MPS is not the most specific schedule, the MPS acts primarily as a planning tool. However, because it relates to an aggregation of specific products, it does not have a bill of materials, in conventional terms, that makes sense. A bill of materials is a precise list of all product components in exactly the quantities used. Usually, there is a different bill of materials for every model or type of the product made. In order for it to coordinate specific materials and parts effectively, then, the end item aggregation in the MPS must have its own "phantom" bill of materials that indicates, on average, how many of particular parts and how much of particular materials will be consumed in the construction of the "average" product. These bills of materials are called *planning bills* (or sometimes *super bills*). Unlike conventional bills of material, they can indicate fractional levels of usage and can change if the mix of specific end items shifts the composition of the "average" product.

The MPS is a key bridge between manufacturing and marketing/sales because it is with the MPS that manufacturing commits to making what marketing/sales has either forecast or actually booked as orders. Typically, manufacturing's commitment takes the form of a due date for the completion and shipping of the product in some agreed-upon quantity. In order for this order promising to proceed smoothly over time, manufacturing has to keep track of the production quantities that are available or could be expected to be available, and also how much of any of those quantities could actually be committed for shipment.

There are two principal techniques for such tracking: graphical and tabular. Let us explore them in turn.

A Graphical Master Production Schedule

The graphical technique typically tracks cumulative sales and production of a particular product or product line over time. It can easily show the build-up or depletion of inventory and the extent of any buffer or safety stock. Figure 4-2 is an example. Three lines have relevance in the figure: the cumulative sales forecast and two distinct cumulative MPS's that are possible, one a "level" production strategy and the other a "chase" strategy. The chase strategy matches the sales forecast week for week so that the buffer stock remains at a constant 40 units. The level strategy, on the other hand, produces a constant quantity of output in every week (160/12 = 13.33 units)—just enough so that at the end of the planning horizon, 12 weeks, the planned buffer stock of 40 units is maintained. However, during the course of the 12 weeks, sometimes the buffer stock is temporarily eroded (Area A in the figure) and sometimes it is padded with excess inventory (Area B in the figure).

Figure 4-3 presents a different MPS—one that incorporates batch runs of the product in lot sizes of 40. In contrast to Figure 4-2, where there was production in every period, here production is scheduled to occur only in weeks 1, 5, 8, 10, and 12. The shaded areas in Figure 4-3 represent the so-called "cycle" inventories, those created to tide the plant over until the next batch of the product is run.

Over time, one can expect that sales forecasts and orders actually booked will change. Often, such changes will necessitate changes to the MPS. Thus, as the schedule "rolls through time," there will be continued adjustments made to the position and shape of the MPS graph.

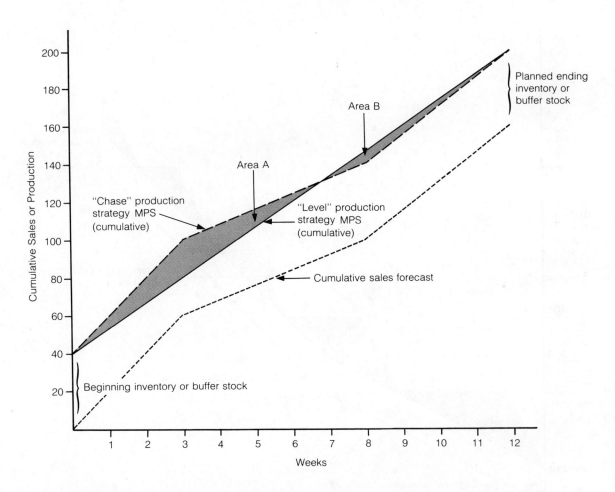

FIGURE 4-2 A graphical master production schedule, showing level and chase production strategies.

One can also use this graphical technique to track actual sales (or shipments) and the orders booked. Figure 4-4 depicts the same sales forecast and MPS as in Figure 4-3, but with the order backlogs per each of the first two weeks also shown. The order backlog for Week 2 reflects the additional orders booked during Week 1. As the figure indicates, actual sales in Week 1 exceeded the forecast. As of the start of Week 2, booked orders have not fully "consumed" the forecast quantity, but are very close to it. At the start of Week 1, there were no booked orders past Week 3, and there are no booked orders past Week 4 at the beginning of Week 2. The difference between the MPS and the order backlogs gives an indication of what is "available to promise" customers. For example, in Week 4 there are 30 units available to be promised (60 − 30), and in Week 5 there are 70 units available to promise (100 − 30).

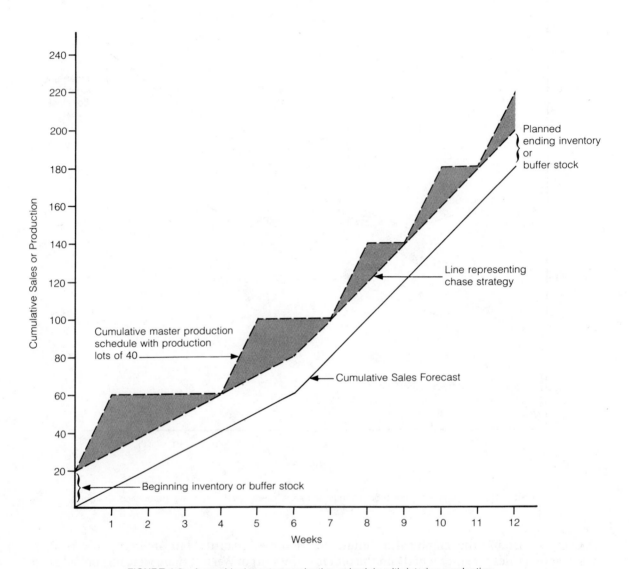

FIGURE 4-3 A graphical master production schedule with lot size production.

A Tabular Master Production Schedule

Another technique used to depict the MPS, and one that can easily be kept by computer, employs a tabular, time-phased record, such as that shown in Figure 4-5. The information in the figure mirrors exactly the data in the graphical presentation of Figure 4-3. While we lose the power and simplicity of the graphical approach by using a table, we do gain real precision in what is available (that is, what the expected ending inventory is) and what is available to promise. This tabular time-phased record is also easy to update from one time period to another.

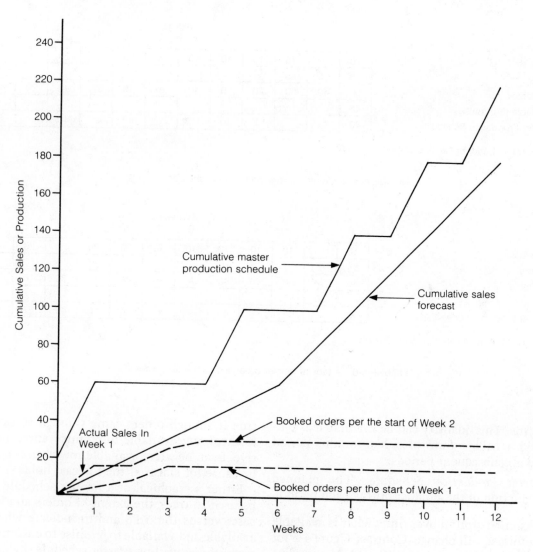

FIGURE 4-4   A master production schedule with booked orders shown.

Some definitions are helpful in understanding the figure:

Forecast.   The quantity forecasted to be sold during each period

Orders.   The orders actually received for delivery in the period indicated

Available.   The expected ending inventory each period computed as on-hand at the start of the period + MPS for that period − Forecast that period, or, if the orders exceed the forecast then the quantity available is on-hand + MPS − Orders.

Available to Promise.   The quantity for which there are no pending orders that can act as

| | Weeks | | | | | | | | | | | |
	1	2	3	4	5	6	7	8	9	10	11	12
Forecast	10	10	10	10	10	10	20	20	20	20	20	20
Orders	5	5	5									
Available	50	40	30	20	50	40	20	40	20	40	20	40
Available to Promise	45											
Master Production Schedule	40				40			40		40		40

On-hand as buffer at the start of Week 1 = 20

FIGURE 4-5   A tabular master production schedule, week 1.

| | Weeks | | | | | | | | | | | |
	1	2	3	4	5	6	7	8	9	10	11	12
Forecast	10	10	10	10	10	10	20	20	20	20	20	20
Orders	14	5	7	4								
Available	46	36	26	16	46	36	16	36	16	36	16	36
Available to Promise		30										
Master Production Schedule	40				40			40		40		40

Total on-hand at the start of Week 2 = 46

FIGURE 4-6   A tabular master production schedule, week 2.

claims. This quantity can be calculated as On-hand + MPS − Sum of orders for this period and all subsequent periods.

Master Production Schedule. The planned production of the product during each period.

As orders roll in over time, what is available to promise will change. Contrast Figure 4-5 for Week 1 with Figure 4-6 for Week 2. More orders have been taken, and thus the available-to-promise row has changed. (Note that we could have constructed the table with a rolling forecast of 12 weeks, but for convenience we have kept the time horizon at the 12th week.) Of course, if orders remain strong, marketing may want to revise the forecast upward and, correspondingly, manufacturing may want to revise the MPS upward. This would be particularly

true if enough orders came through to turn a forthcoming available-to-promise entry negative. Even negative available row entries could be cause for alarm, if the forecast holds.

Either a graphical or a tabular schedule can be used to track the extent of orders and forecasts versus the MPS and to indicate what is available and available to promise to customers, given the prevailing master schedule. By using this technique, manufacturing management can be alert for prospective deficiencies or surpluses in production and can act to remedy the situation, either by cranking up capacity (and increasing the MPS) or by shutting down capacity (and decreasing the MPS).

The MPS lies at the heart of how the factory gets loaded. It gives the process direction and drive. A master production schedule that is feasible and low cost, but yet satisfies customer demands, can do much to remove chaos from the factory floor, enhance productivity, and flow dollars to the bottom line.

Aggregate Planning Revisited

There are typically many master production schedules for a plant, and each of them marches through time. In the best of all possible worlds, of course, they are all expected to march in step with one another. However, if actual occurrences vary too much from the expected, there simply may not be enough resources for some of the master schedules to be met. One can see, then, the usefulness of some overarching planning of resources that can govern the trade-offs that may occur between one MPS and another. Without such a planning mechanism, one can expect to be short of some products, carrying extra inventory on others, wasting capacity somewhere, or scrambling for capacity somewhere else. This overarching plan is termed the *aggregate plan* or the *production plan*. As it was introduced earlier, the plan deals with aggregates of resources (materials, capacity, workers) and outputs; it extends over a time period of from 6 to 18 months. Planning that far in advance encourages discipline and enforces consistency among the various master schedules as they are concocted and refined. The plan is typically stated in dollars, labor-hours of output, or, for some commodity or near-commodity products, a physical measurement as units or tons of product. It can act as both an aid in establishing MPS's for the end products and as a control document against which the MPS's can be assessed.

A variety of aggregate plans can be chosen and followed. Just as we noted chase and level strategies with MPS's, so too can those notions be applied to aggregate production plans. A level strategy, for example, would maintain a stable workforce and build up and draw down on inventories as needed. Exactly which inventories to build up, of course, would depend on the particular MPS's adopted to be consistent with this level aggregate plan. A chase strategy, on the other hand, would try to eliminate any build-up of inventories, but permit the workforce to fluctuate. Such aggregate plans, and any modifications lying in-between these extremes, can be depicted either graphically or tabularly. Graphs and tables can be very effective ways to track (1) the conformity of specific MPS's to the aggregate plan, and (2) actual performance against the aggregate plan. In this way managers can see when and where things are going out of control, and they can then adjust schedules and production in the most fitting ways.

SCHEDULING TECHNIQUES

There are several techniques that can be used effectively to help develop both MPS's and aggregate plans. Before discussing them, however, it is important to distinguish between scheduling a flow process (continuous, line, or batch), where capacities are clearly defined, and scheduling a job shop, where capacities are muddled. Continuous flow and machine-paced line flow processes enjoy an inherent scheduling advantage because of their rigid production cycle times. Knowing that cars can come off the assembly line at the rate of one per minute—no more, no less—or that paper of a certain weight and grade can be made at a set rate is a tremendous advantage to scheduling. The capacities are known as close to certainty as possible. Even some batch flow processes with fairly standard products can be described with clear capacity measures (475 suits per week) that facilitate efficient scheduling. Once capacities are known, the task of matching production to demand is greatly simplified.

The task is made even simpler if the process is permitted to build up some finished goods inventory. Although there is, of course, a cost to carrying inventory, such processes can keep the flow of work balanced across products and/or time periods more easily than processes that do not enjoy such freedom.

The job shop is clearly the worst to schedule because its capacity is so ambiguous and it can- not build up finished goods inventory. We will address job shop scheduling later in the chapter.

Scheduling Techniques for Flow Processes When Capacities Are Clear-Cut

To focus this discussion, consider the aggregate planning problem of Situation 4-1.

SITUATION 4-1

RIDGELY SPORTING GOODS COMPANY, LEATHER GOODS DEPARTMENT

The leather goods department of the Ridgely Sporting Goods Company manufactured two ma- jor products: baseball gloves and hockey gloves. By far the larger selling item was baseball gloves. The market for them was fairly stable, tending to follow population growth trends. Recently, the modest drop in the birth rate had been compen- sated for by a rise in sales to girls. Sales of hockey gloves were localized predominantly in the North- east, the upper Midwest, and Canada. The market for these gloves was only about a fifth the size of the baseball market but was growing at about 5 percent a year.

Sales of each type of glove paralleled the sport's season, with sales greater just before and just after the start of each season. For baseball gloves in particular, the Christmas season was also a strong sales period. The forecast for the nine months be- ginning in July is given in Table 4-2. The factory had to ensure that the company's distributors were fully stocked with gloves about two months before the season's official start in April for baseball and in November for hockey. This timetable meant that a third of the department's forecast sales for this nine-month period had to be produced by the first week in February (baseball) and September (hockey).

The baseball gloves were easier to manufacture, requiring roughly 45 minutes of labor per glove. The hockey gloves took about two hours per pair. The average factory variable costs of the gloves were $17 (baseball) and $40 (hockey).

The department liked to keep the production rate steady over the course of the year because hiring and then laying off workers was disturbing and ex- pensive. Layoffs cost the company $400 per worker in severance pay and hiring cost, $50 per worker in out-of-pocket expenses, and two weeks of inef- ficient productivity (an average of 50 percent of standard) while the new hire was trained. Recalls of previously laid-off workers cost only half of the new hire expense. Worker pay plus fringes aver- aged $8 per hour. Adding a second shift to the factory was possible, but it meant an additional 15 percent wage hike per worker to institute, in addition to the new hires such an action would generate.

There were no readily identifiable costs in chang- ing over from the production of one type of glove to another. However, given the many variations in the basic styles of each type of glove, it was con- sidered too confusing to make both baseball and hockey gloves at the same time. Thus, separate days were generally allotted to each kind of glove. A finished goods inventory was used to smooth out the demand on the factory. The inventory carrying cost rate was determined to be 20 percent.

The leather goods department was in the process of planning production for the next nine months to meet forecasted demand. Maintaining at all times an inventory equal to 100 percent of current monthly demand was considered prudent. To facilitate planning, the work weeks were grouped into fours and labeled with the months in which most of the production occurred. The inventories of gloves were 6500 (baseball) and 700 (hockey). At present, also, there were 26 workers in the department.

TABLE 4-2   Forecast of sales by product line, July–March
(Ridgely Sporting Goods Company, Leather Goods Department)

PRODUCT LINE	JULY	AUG.	SEPT.	OCT.	NOV.	DEC.	JAN.	FEB.	MARCH	TOTAL
Baseball gloves (units)	4000	3000	2500	1000	500	5000	2000	4000	7000	29,000
Hockey gloves (pairs)	100	100	700	1600	2000	1900	1450	1200	1400	10,450

Note: Each month has four weeks of production.

Ridgely Sporting Goods—General Discussion

As we can tell from the situation at Ridgely Sporting Goods, developing the MPS means deciding how much capacity the factory should gear up for over the short term and how that capacity should be realized. At some point, the factory must commit itself to meeting the sales forecast or some other agreed-to pattern of shipments. But, generally speaking, it can accomplish this task in several ways.

1. *Chasing Demand.* The factory can raise and lower its production rate so that it produces only as much of each item as it expects to ship that month. If forecasted sales vary greatly, such a "demand chase" strategy will generally entail a good deal of (a) overtime and/or (b) layoffs and recalls or new hiring.

2. *Leveling Production.* Under this alternative, no changes in the workforce size or overtime policy are planned over the planning period. All variations in shipments are absorbed by a finished goods inventory. Thus, over the planning period, inventory is built up and depleted on a regular, planned basis.

3. *A Combination Approach.* A pure chase strategy and a pure level strategy are extreme, polar cases. In between lies a whole range of cases where some chasing of demand and some leveling of production occur.

No matter what the strategy, developing an MPS involves decisions on a number of important issues and collecting data from a variety of sources. Among them:

- Decisions
  a. Desired inventory levels by production period (such as a month)
  b. Desired workforce levels by production period
  c. Desired levels of overtime by production period
  d. Desired mix and pattern of production, by product and by production period
- Data
  a. Reliability of the short-term forecast of sales in each product line
  b. Current capacity of the operation, by product line
  c. Cost and productivity of overtime
  d. Cost and productivity of second or third shift operation
  e. Cost of layoff, hiring, and recall of the workforce
  f. Cost of carrying finished goods inventory
  g. A sense of how rapidly adjustments can be made in the product mix produced,

which has an impact on the size of any buffer stocks

h. Costs and difficulties of shifting work among different products

The process of developing the production schedules that the factory follows and by which it tries to control operations takes several stages. The transition through these stages occurs as sales become more and more certain and as details are learned about the quantities to be manufactured of product lines, products, models, and variations like color and extras. The scheduling process begins with rough approximations; generally, months later firmer and firmer numbers take hold. As mentioned earlier, the initial approximation is termed the "aggregate plan" because the plant, at that stage, deals only in aggregates of workers, product models, and even products themselves. Over time, as sales forecasts become firmer, the aggregate plan can be refined and detail added to yield a "master schedule" that deals typically with the major products to be made, although perhaps not with all the models or variations on those major products. The master schedule treats end items that in turn trigger materials flows through the process for all component parts or materials. The master schedule is an important document because it triggers actions such as specific workforce assignments, personnel actions, and more detailed materials flows. Even more detailed production schedules, which can sequence and synchronize the work of the factory are derived (again with even firmer information) from the master schedule.

Attacking the Master Schedule at Ridgely Sporting Goods

We need to determine how many baseball and hockey gloves the company ought to produce each month and the corresponding size of the workforce, inventory levels, and overtime levels, given that the forecast of Table 4-2 must

be met. A more detailed schedule would indicate the precise mix of catcher's mitts, first base gloves, and fielding gloves in which style, model (for example, Dale Murphy, autograph), and variation (right- or left-handed) to be produced, and on which days. Our present task, of course, is not so detailed, but it involves the same type of thinking.

The first task is to decide whether a chase or a level strategy should guide our thinking. If holding inventory is cheaper than the costs of overtime, laying off, recalling, and/or hiring, then a level production strategy is recommended. If, on the other hand, inventory cannot be held or is more costly than such personnel actions, a chase demand strategy becomes attractive. How costly then is inventory holding and the various personnel actions?

- Holding inventory
  1. At a carrying cost rate of 20 percent, a baseball glove costs $3.40 per year, on the average, to hold in inventory (0.20 × $17 variable cost), or about 28¢ per month.
  2. Carrying a hockey glove is more expensive—$8 per glove per year or about 67¢ per month.

- Personnel actions
  1. Layoffs cost $400.
  2. New hires cost $50 out-of-pocket plus the equivalent of one week's wages, which amounts to $320. The total new hire cost is $370. Recalls cost only $185.
  3. A second shift's labor bill would cost 115 percent of the first shift.
  4. Overtime costs are 150 percent of first shift labor costs.

With these data as background, it is useful to ask questions like the following in gauging the extent to which a chase or a level strategy should be followed.

- How long would you be willing to keep a worker on the job (thus producing units of

TABLE 4-3 Inventory cccumulation over time
(Ridgely Sporting Goods Company, Leather Goods Department)

	MONTH 1	MONTH 2	MONTH 3	MONTH 4
Worker production	80	80	80	80
Inventory built up	80	160	240	320
Inventory costs at 67¢/month/unit	$53.60	$107.20	$160.80	$214.40

Total cost − 4 Months = $536.00

output that have to be carried for some time) rather than lay off the worker now and recall him or her later?

• At what point would the cost of having the existing workers work overtime give way to hiring another worker or, indeed, hiring an entire second shift?

Questions such as these are difficult to answer definitively because they often involve many hidden contingencies. For example, the perceived need for 300 more units of output six months from now may be met by having one worker work for six months, by having two workers work for three months each, by having three workers work for two months each, or some similar choice. It is difficult to analyze all of the situations conceivable, and each has its own cost.

Nevertheless, some reasonably straightforward calculations can provide some insight into the relative attractiveness of chase and level strategies. In trying to answer the first question alone, we can calculate a point of indifference where the inventory carrying costs incurred by keeping a worker on the job just equal the hire and recall costs. Suppose a worker can produce 80 hockey gloves in a month that are sold. Over time the inventory grows as Table 4-3 indicates. Inventory is built up according to an arithmetic progression whereby 80 gloves are added each month. The accumulated inventory is simply the sum of this arithmetic progression, which fortunately has an easy formula:

$$\text{Inventory} = \frac{n}{2}(a + 1) = \frac{n}{2}[+ n(80)]$$

where n is the number of months, a is the first inventory value, and 1 is the last inventory value.

We can use this formula to solve for the value of n that equates inventory carrying costs with the layoff and recall costs involving a single worker.

$$(.67) \cdot \left\{ \frac{n}{2}[80 + n(80)] \right\} = 400 + 185$$

(Inventory · (Sum of = (Layoff + (Recall
carrying   inventory   expense)   expense)
cost per   months
month)   to finance)

Working out this value involves solving a quadratic equation for a positive root by using the quadratic formula,

$$\frac{-b \pm \sqrt{b^2 - 4ac}}{2a}$$

In this instance, the solution yields a value of n of 4.2 months. Thus, it takes 4.2 months of inventory accumulation before the costs of carrying that inventory outweigh the expenses of laying off and then recalling a worker. This calculation is helpful in that it confirms the view that the company should not lay off workers at the first seasonal downturn in hockey glove sales. Only if the sales drop is persistent would it be less costly to lay off some workers. What is more, if demand is high once it turns up, having accumulated so much inventory would

TABLE 4-4   Trial master production schedule
(Ridgely Sporting Goods Company, Leather Goods Department)

PRODUCT LINE	JULY	AUG.	SEPT.	OCT.	NOV.	DEC.	JAN.	FEB.	MARCH	APRIL
Baseball Gloves										
Sales target	4000	3000	2500	1000	500	5000	2000	4000	7000	
Production	4800	0	3200	3200	0	6400	4800	3200	4800	
Starting inventory	6500	7300	4300	5000	7200	6700	8100	10,900	10,100	7900
Hockey Gloves										
Sales target	100	100	700	1600	2000	1900	1450	1200	1400	
Production	600	2400	1200	1200	2400	0	640	1280	680	
Starting inventory	700	1200	3500	4000	3600	4000	2100	1290	1370	650
Workforce	30	30	30	30	30	30	30.5	31	31	

Total cost of this schedule = $383,737

Production rates: Baseball gloves—Given 30 workers, 6400 per month.
Hockey gloves—Given 30 workers, 2400 per month
These rates, as well as the trial schedule, ignore the start-up inefficiencies of the four newly hired workers.
However, these amount only to a total of 213.33 baseball gloves or 80 pairs of hockey gloves.

Inventory goals: Baseball gloves—9667 in February
Hockey gloves—3483 in September

---

be advantageous, since many workers would have to be hired to produce a lot in a short time.

It should be emphasized that this calculation is meant only to suggest the relative advantages of a chase versus a level production strategy. The calculation ignores the costs of carrying inventory past the point of indifference as well as the extra costs involved in hiring many new workers to build up production in a hurry to the level of the inventory being carried.

With similar logic, however, some crude trade-offs between various other personnel actions (overtime, second shift) and inventory holding can be evaluated as well.

The Trial and Error of Master Schedule Development

Having established, in rough fashion, the relative attractiveness of a level production strategy for Ridgely Sporting Goods, we need to develop a MPS that satisfies the sales forecast and

the other suggested constraints such as (1) inventories a third of the total nine-month sales in the relevant months (September for hockey, February for baseball), and (2) inventories at the beginning of the month large enough to cover all of that month's demand.

Table 4-4 is a first trial at matching production to these requirements. It is based in part on the workforce needs implied by the sales forecast of Table 4-2 (as depicted in Table 4-5). The trial master schedule begins by hiring four more workers immediately to bring the workforce to 30 workers; one more hockey glove worker is hired midway through January to bring ending inventory for hockey gloves to within 50 of July's starting level. In most months, both baseball and hockey gloves are produced, and no overtime is employed. The inventory goals— 9667 baseball gloves by February 1 and 3483 pairs of hockey gloves by September 1—are met easily, as is the goal of having starting inventory greater than the month's expected sales.

TABLE 4-5 Workforce levels implied by the sales forecast
(Ridgely Sporting Goods Company, Leather Goods Deparment)

PRODUCT LINE	JULY	AUG.	SEPT.	OCT.	NOV.	DEC.	JAN.	FEB.	MARCH	TOTAL
Baseball gloves (units)	18.75	14.06	11.72	4.69	2.34	23.44	9.38	18.75	32.81	135.94
Hockey gloves (pairs)	1.25	1.25	8.75	20.00	25.00	23.75	18.13	15.00	17.50	130.63
Total	20.00	15.31	20.47	24.69	27.34	47.19	27.51	33.75	50.31	266.57
Average workforce level implied for all previous months	20.00	17.66	18.59	20.12	21.56	25.83	26.07	27.03	29.62	

The cost of this MPS is $383,737, broken down as follows:

Worker wages: 30 workers × 9 months × $1280/month + 1 worker × 2.5 months × $1280/month = $348,800

Hiring costs: 5 workers × $370 = 1,850

Inventory carrying: $.28 × 66,100 inventory unit-months (baseball) = 18,508
$.67 × 21,760 inventory unit-months (hockey) = 14,579
$383,737

No doubt some dollars can be whittled off this cost figure by investigating alternative hiring patterns and production patterns by product and by month. Successive trial-and-error schedules would consider such alternatives and compare them with this first trial effort. Many actual master production schedules are derived by just such trial-and-error means. Stability of the product mix and/or sales levels over time is naturally helpful in this search for better and better MPS's.

"Optimal" and "Near-Optimal" Aggregate Plans and Master Schedules

To this point, we have used common sense and trial-and-error to devise aggregate plans and more detailed master schedules. As with almost any trial-and-error approach to problem solving, one always suspects that "a better way" must exist, or a way that guarantees some "optimal" solution. In the case of the Ridgely Sporting Goods Company, we cannot help but think that a lower cost means of meeting all the shipping and inventory requirements exists.

In the schedule development for Ridgely Sporting Goods, what costs should be minimized and what constraints must be satisfied? We have already talked about them, but it is helpful to state them more formally. In essence, the costs of the plan that we want to minimize include wage costs, inventory carrying costs, and costs of hiring and laying off workers; the constraints that we want to satisfy include the inventory targets for each month, some reasonable expectations on how much overtime can be worked, and some more prosaic requirements such as how many units of which product line can be produced in any month and how inventory and the workforce can be supplemented or reduced. To be even more formal about the Ridgely Sporting Goods situation, we seek to minimize

$(1280W_1 + 1280W_2 + \ldots + 1280W_9$ (Regular shift wage costs, since W_t is the level of the month's workforce and

$+ 1920OT_1 + 1920OT_2$
$+ \ldots + 1920OT_9$

(Overtime wage costs, since OT_t is the level of overtime worked on a monthly basis and $1920 is the cost of a month's worth of overtime)

$+ .28BI_1 + .28BI_2$
$+ \ldots + .28BI_9$

(Inventory carrying costs for baseball gloves, since 28¢ is the carrying cost per month for baseball gloves and BI_t is the stock of baseball gloves carried each month)

$+ .67HI_1 + .67HI_2$
$+ \ldots + .67HI_9$

(Inventory carrying costs for hockey gloves, since 67¢ is the monthly carrying cost and HI_t is the stock of hockey gloves carried each month)

$+ 370WFI_1 + 370WFI_2$
$+ \ldots + 370WFI_9$

(Costs of increasing the workforce, since it costs $370 for each new hire. WFI_t is the size of the workforce increase in each month.)

$+ 400WFD_1 + 400WFD_2$
$+ \ldots + 400WFD_9)$

(Costs of laying off workers since each layoff costs $400. WFD_t is the size of the workforce decrease in each month.)

subject to the following constraints:

1. The following variables must all be greater than or equal to zero for all months t where t can range from 1 to 9

W_t, OT_t, BI_t, HI_t, WFI_t, WFD_t, BP_t, and $HP_t \geqslant 0$

where

$W_t =$ workforce in month t

$OT_t =$ overtime in month t

$BI_t =$ baseball glove inventory in month t

$HI_t =$ hockey glove inventory in month t

$WFI_t =$ workforce increase in month t

$WFD_t =$ workforce decrease in month t

$BP_t =$ baseball glove production in month t

$HP_t =$ hockey glove production in month t

2. Regular workforce hours and overtime hours are composed of those devoted to baseball glove production and those devoted to hockey glove production:

$$W_t = WB_t + WH_t$$

$$OT_t = OTB_t + OTH_t$$

where

WB_t is regular time, in worker months, devoted to baseball glove production in month t

WH_t is regular time, in worker months, devoted to hockey glove production in month t

OTB_t is overtime, in worker months, devoted to baseball glove production in month t

OTH_t is overtime, in worker months, devoted to hockey glove production in month t

3. Production is governed by the following relationships:

$$BP_t = 213.33WB_t + 213.33OTB_t$$

$$HP_t = 80WH_t + 80OTH_t$$

The figure 213.33 is derived by noting that, in four weeks of 40 hours per week, 213.33 baseball gloves can be produced at an average of 45 minutes per glove; the figure 80 is derived by noting that during the same 160-hour period only 80 pairs of hockey gloves can be produced since an average of two hours are required for each pair.

4. Overtime, however, has a practical ceiling, which we might peg at a quarter of the hours spent on regular shift work. Thus,

$$OTB_t \leqslant .25WB_t$$

$$OTH_t \leqslant .25WH_t$$

5. Inventory for the period must be accounted for by the following:

$$BI_t = BI_{t-1} + BP_t - BS_t$$

$$HI_t = HI_{t-1} + HP_t - HS_t$$

where BP_t and HP_t represent production of baseball and hockey gloves, respectively, and BS_t and HS_t represent sales or shipments of baseball gloves and hockey gloves, respectively. BI_{t-1} and HI_{t-1}, of course, refer to inventories in the prior period.

6. The size of the workforce in any period must also be accounted for by the following:

$$W_t = W_{t-1} + WFI_t - WFD_t$$

Remember, both WFI_t (workforce increase) and WFD_t (workforce decrease) are defined to be nonnegative numbers.

7. Shipments must be equal to the forecasted figures of Table 4-2; inventory levels in any month must be greater than or equal to the forecasted sales in the next month; and the special inventory goals of $BI_7 \geq 9667$ and $HI_2 \geq 3483$ must also be met.

8. To be compatible with the trial master schedule of Table 4-4, some initial and closing conditions must be specified:

(Initial conditions) $BI_0 = 6500$, $HI_0 = 700$, $W_0 = 26$

(Closing conditions) $BI_9 = 7900$, $HI_9 = 650$

Fortunately, there exists a mathematical linear programming technique that can solve this minimization problem subject to the constraints we have specified, largely because all of the relationships specified are linear ones. (Consult Appendix B for a discussion of linear programming.) Observe that all the relationships involve variables multiplied by constants and added together (geo-metrically, straight lines or planes) with no squared terms, trigonometric functions, inverse terms, logarithmic functions, or anything even fancier. Thus, variable values rise and fall in proportion to one another and this permits the use of linear programming to aid in this scheduling.

We can state Ridgely Sporting Goods' linear program, using symbol Σ (sigma) to indicate the summation of terms.

Objective function

minimize

$$\sum_{t=1}^{9} (1280W_t + 1920OTB_t + 1920OTH_t + .28BI_t$$

$$+ .67HI_t + 370WFI_t + 400WFD_t)$$

subject to

Nonnegativity conditions

$$W_t, WB_t, WH_t, OT_t, OTB_t, OTH_t, BI_t, HI_t, WFI_t,$$
$$WFD_t, BP_t, \text{ and } HP_t \geq 0$$

and structural constraints

$$W_t - WB_t - WH_t = 0$$

$$OT_t - OTB_t - OTH_t = 0$$

$$PB_t - 213.33WB_t - 213.33OTB_t = 0$$

$$PH_t - 80WH_t - 80OTH_t = 0$$

$$.25WB_t - OTB_t \geq 0$$

$$.25WH_t - OTH_t \geq 0$$

$$BI_t - BI_{t-1} BP_t + BS_t = 0$$

$$HI_t - HI_{t-1} - HP_t + HS_t = 0$$

$$W_t - W_{t-1} - WFI_t + WFD_t = 0$$

$BS_1 = 4000$	$HS_1 = 100$
$BS_2 = 3000$	$HS_2 = 100$
$BS_3 = 2500$	$HS_3 = 700$
$BS_4 = 1000$	$HS_4 = 1600$

TABLE 4-6   Optimal master production schedule as determined by linear programming
(Ridgely Sporting Goods Company, Leather Goods Department)

PRODUCT LINE	JULY	AUG.	SEPT.	OCT.	NOV.	DEC.	JAN.	FEB.	MARCH	APRIL
Baseball Gloves										
Sales target	4000	3000	2500	1000	500	5000	2000	4000	7000	
Starting inventory	6500	3000	2500	1000	500	5000	4317	9667	7550	7900
Production	500	2500	1000	500	5000	4317	7350	1883	7350	
Hockey Gloves										
Sales target	100	100	700	1600	2000	1900	1450	1200	1400	
Starting inventory	700	2493	3535	4540	4832	3413	2650	1200	2050	650
Production	1893	1142	1705	1892	58.1	1137	0	2050	0	
Workforce	26.0	26.0	26.0	26.0	30.7	34.5	34.5	34.5	34.5	

Total cost of this schedule = $380,525

$$BS_5 = 500 \qquad HS_5 = 2000$$
$$BS_6 = 5000 \qquad HS_6 = 1900$$
$$BS_7 = 2000 \qquad HS_7 = 1450$$
$$BS_8 = 4000 \qquad HS_8 = 1200$$
$$BS_9 = 7000 \qquad HS_9 = 1400$$

$$BI_0 = 6500 \qquad HI_0 = 700$$
$$BI_1 \geq 3000 \qquad HI_1 \geq 100$$
$$BI_2 \geq 2500 \qquad HI_2 \geq 3483$$
$$BI_3 \geq 1000 \qquad HI_3 \geq 1600$$
$$BI_4 \geq 500 \qquad HI_4 \geq 2000$$
$$BI_5 \geq 5000 \qquad HI_5 \geq 1900$$
$$BI_6 \geq 2000 \qquad HI_6 \geq 1450$$
$$BI_7 \geq 9667 \qquad HI_7 \geq 1200$$
$$BI_8 \geq 7000 \qquad HI_8 \geq 1400$$
$$BI_9 \geq 7900 \qquad HI_9 \geq 650$$

$$W_0 = 26$$

When this formulation of the linear program to minimize the cost of the master schedule at Ridgely Sporting Goods is entered on a computer and run, a solution like that found in Table 4-6 results. (The entries in this table are to the nearest integer.) Several things about the optimal master schedule are worth noting:

1. The workforce is not increased right away but later on and to necessarily higher levels than the level strategy adopted in Table 4-4.

2. Inventory levels are lower than in Table 4-4. Lower inventory carrying expenses are in-

curred in this schedule, more than balancing off the higher hiring costs incurred.

3. Somewhat remarkably, though, the cost of the linear program's optimal solution is only a few thousand dollars less than the trial-and-error schedule developed earlier.

The last observation is important. Although linear programming is immensely attractive for developing optimal solutions to sophisticated problems, there is no guarantee that the optimal solution will be much different from a solution arrived at through common sense and trial and error. In this case, going through the pain, suffering, and expense of developing a linear program to capture Ridgely Sporting Goods' needs and of solving it seems scarcely worth the effort. Nevertheless, in other instances, such linear programming would more than pay for itself.

Furthermore, although linear programming (or its cousins like integer or mixed integer programming) can help lower the cost of a master schedule, qualitative features of production planning can override cost considerations. One instance of a huge payoff from using linear programming for schedule development, however, is International Paper Company (see Situation 4-2).

SITUATION 4-2

INTERNATIONAL PAPER COMPANY REVISITED, PRODUCTION PLANNING, SUMMER 1982

As we learned in the Tour A discussion of the operation of the Androscoggin Mill, the capabilities and costs associated with paper machines can vary dramatically from one machine to another. Generally speaking, new machines are wider and faster than older ones and use fewer workers and less energy per ton of output. It makes sense then to be careful about which orders for paper are assigned to which machines. The total contribution earned from one assignment of orders to machines may be very different from the total contribution earned from another assignment. Moreover, because both International Paper's mills and its customers are widely scattered and because paper companies typically absorb the costs of transporting completed orders to customer locations and because several paper machines companywide may be set up to run a particular type and grade of paper, it can be difficult to make the most cost-effective assignment of a specific order.

In response to this problem of allocating "paper machine products" destined for particular customer locations, International Paper Company (among others in the forest products industry) developed a linear programming model. The general outline of this model was straightforward although, as will be apparent, the program was very large and complex. The company wanted to assign particular orders (demands defined by the choice of paper machine product and customer location) to specific paper machines in such a way that the contribution to the company was maximized. Contribution, in turn, was defined as revenue less variable costs. Revenue was arrived at by multiplying price per ton times tons for each paper machine product made, while variable costs encompassed the costs of production as well as the costs of distribution. Variable production costs per ton included pulp and other materials, energy, direct labor, scrap, and any variable overhead expenses. The distribution cost was specific to each paper machine/customer location pair considered.

Suppose that there are a total of L customer locations, P paper machine products, and M paper machines. The revenue from each paper machine product for each customer location had to be considered as well as the cost of making each paper machine product (PMP) on each machine and transporting it to each customer location. The linear program's objective function, the contribution to be maximized, can be expressed more formally in words as shown by Figure 4-7.

In algebraic terms, the objective function can be more easily written as total contribution to be maximized equals

$$\sum_{m=1}^{M} \sum_{p=1}^{P} \sum_{\ell=1}^{L} (Q_{\ell pm} \times (P_p - (PC_{pm} + TC_{\ell m})))$$

where p indexes paper machine products, ℓ indexes customer locations, and m indexes paper machines, and where P_p is the price per ton of product p, $Q_{\ell pm}$ is the output in tons of product p for customer location ℓ from machine m, PC_{pm} is the variable cost of producing a ton product p on machine m, and $TC_{\ell m}$ is the cost of transporting a ton of output from machine m to customer location ℓ.

In the simplest case, there were two structural constraints on the objective function:

1. The sum of the specific outputs from each machine must not exceed the demands. That is, for each ℓp combination,

$$\sum_{m=1}^{M} Q_{\ell pm} \leq D_{\ell p}$$

where $D_{\ell p}$ is the demand in tons for paper machine product p for customer location ℓ.

2. The capacity of each paper machine during the planning time period (such as one month) cannot be exceeded. That is, for each m,

$$\sum_{p=1}^{P} \sum_{l=1}^{\leq} (Q_{\ell pm} \times HPT_{pm}) \leq H_m$$

where HPT_{pm} is the hours per ton for product p on machine m and H_m is the hours available during the time period for machine m.

Total contribution = Revenue for each order—Variable cost of filling each order

or

Total contribution = (Tons for customer location #1 of PMP #1 × Price of PMP #1 per ton)
+ (Tons for customer location #2 of PMP #1 × Price of PMP #1 per ton) + · · ·
+ (Tons for customer location L of PMP #1 × Price of PMP #1 per ton)
+ (Tons for customer location #1 of PMP #2 × Price of PMP #2 per ton) + · · ·
+ (Tons for customer location L of PMP #2 × Price of PMP #2 per ton) + · · ·
+ (Tons for customer location #1 of PMP #P × Price of PMP #P per ton) + · · ·
+ (Tons for customer location L of PMP #P × Price of PMP #P per ton)
− (Tons for customer location #1 of PMP #1 on machine #1 × Cost of making a ton of PMP #1 on machine #1 plus transport cost from machine #1 to customer location #1) − · · ·
− (Tons for customer location L of PMP #1 on machine #1 × Cost of making a ton of PMP #1 on machine #1 plus transport cost from machine #1 to customer location L) − · · ·
− (Tons for customer location #1 of PMP #P on machine #1 × Cost of PMP #P on machine #1 plus transport cost from machine #1 to customer location #1) − · · ·
− (Tons for customer location L of PMP #P on machine #1 × Cost of PMP #P on machine #1 plus transport cost from machine #1 to customer location L) − · · ·
− (Tons for customer location #1 of PMP #1 on machine #M × Cost of PMP #1 on machine #M plus transport cost from machine #M to customer location #1) − · · ·
− (Tons for customer location L of PMP #1 on machine #M × Cost of PMP #1 on machine #M plus transport cost from machine #M to customer location L) − · · ·
− (Tons for customer location #1 of PMP #P on machine #M × Cost of PMP #P on machine #M plus transport cost from machine #M to customer location #1) − · · ·
− (Tons for customer location L of PMP #P on machine #M × Cost of PMP #P on machine #M plus transport cost from machine #M to customer location L)

FIGURE 4-7   The linear program's objective function.

There were, of course, the standard nonnegativity constraints as well that had to be met.

The scope of this allocation problem at International Paper was staggering. In the White Papers Division, of which the Androscoggin Mill was a part, the allocation involved 600 to 700 paper machine products for between 16,000 and 20,000 customer locations assigned to 26 paper machines in seven different mills. Of course, not all machines were capable of making every product and the linear program was written to reflect this. The linear program to make the allocation was run on a large IBM 3033 computer, but it took so much time (over an hour of CPU time per run) that it could be run only at night.

The program used a time horizon for the plan of one month, although the plan generally consisted of allocating products for four "cycles" each month.

Thus, there was only one week between times when the most popular paper products were produced. The data for this linear program were continually updated. The latest demand forecasts and lists of orders received were used along with the latest price quotes from the order entry file. The program used transportation costs between mills and customers that were updated each month, and the production costs used the then prevailing standard costs for each machine. These standard costs were updated at least twice a year, and variances from actual costs were tracked carefully. If variances were too great, the standard cost was immediately updated.

The output from the linear program included its solution—the assignment of orders to machines and the contribution calculation associated with each order assignment—as well as a number of summary reports. For example, there was a report listing tons of paper in each product line produced by specific machine. Other reports listed what each machine was assigned by product, by grade, and by basis weight. Still other reports listed any orders that the program's solution had left unallocated, by grade or by region.

The discussion so far has been limited to the most basic aspects of International Paper's allocation program. There were several refinements worth describing:

1. The solution to this linear program was strictly "by the numbers," listing what maximized contribution for the company during the next month. The model ignored any longer time frame as well as the maintenance of particular customers' business.

   The linear program could be modified, however, to take into account marketing considerations of the type where customers, for one reason or another, might insist that their order come from a particular paper machine. In that case, an additional constraint specified that the output of a particular machine be directed to a certain customer location and that it be exactly X tons; that is, the constraint specified that, for specific values of ℓ, p, and m, $Q_{\ell pm}$ exactly equal X.

2. When initially constructed, the model allocated orders just to paper machines. As was mentioned in Tour A, however, the bottleneck in a paper mill can lie elsewhere, particularly in finishing, where logs of paper are rewound and slit or where sheets of paper are cut from logs. International Paper's allocation model was augmented to include the allocation of orders to finishing lines (perhaps in different mills), as well as paper machines.

3. International Paper's linear program could be used to assess what should be done if demand fluctuated. For instance, if demand far outstripped International Paper's capacity, some

decisions had to be reached about which orders would be filled and which would go unfilled (unallocated). The solution to the linear program provided information on which orders yielded the lowest contributions and thus were prime candidates for not being filled. If, on the other hand, demand was weak, the linear program could be used to determine which paper machines had negative contributions and thus ought to be closed.

In regard to the third refinement, consider this chapter's earlier discussion on identifying the scarce resource. Typically, demand for International Paper's products exceeded the company's capacity. In such a case, the scarce resource was time on the mills' paper machines, and the linear program was constructed to maximize the total contribution per unit of time (the planning month). This need not have been the case. The linear program's solution during periods of weak demand could be interpreted so as to maximize contribution per ton of output rather than contribution per unit of time. In such periods, the scarce resource was not time on a paper machine but working capital for the purchase of materials, labor, and other inputs to the process. International Paper's managers recognized this feature and used their linear programming model with an eye to the maximization of either contribution per machine hour or contribution per ton of output depending on the strength or weakness of the demand for paper.

By company estimate, the use of this linear program to help plan production resulted in a 12 percent reduction in delivered costs for one of International Paper's product lines. Linear programming can be a powerful tool.

It should be noted that the linear program at International Paper typically allocated paper machine products to individual weeks within the month. This is a "rough cut" schedule. A more precise schedule had to be devised, usually by the mill itself, to assign products to particular days and shifts within the week.

Cautions about the Use of Linear Programming

In addition to this concern for the cost effectiveness of applying linear programming techniques to situations like master schedule development, there are several fundamental cautions that any manager contemplating the use of linear programming should be aware of. Among them:

1. *Meeting the Linearity Assumptions.* As we have observed previously, the objective function and the structural constraints must all be linear for a programming problem to be capable of solution by a technique like the simplex method. In particular, the production relations defined in the constraints must exhibit constant returns to scale, and all prices and costs must be fixed and invariant with quantity (no price discounts can be allowed). In many cases, of course, constant returns to scale production, especially in the short term, is a very reasonable assumption, as is the absence of any significant price or cost discounts. In fact, the applicability of these assumptions has largely facilitated the already existing use of linear programming techniques in production planning. Yet, companies should be acutely sensitive to those times when such linearity assumptions stretch reality too much to be useful.

2. *The Time Horizon.* The solution to most linear programming problems is sensitive to the time horizon chosen. In the case of Ridgely Sporting Goods, a time horizon of nine months was chosen, and ending inventories of certain sizes were specified. If the time horizon were extended to, say, 12 months or shortened to, say, 6 months, the specifics of the solution might vary significantly. This is, of course, a general caution about planning horizons, but it is especially relevant to techniques like linear program-

ming since their solutions tend to be very volatile, with no presentiments that a future beyond the problem's time horizon even exists.

3. *Problem Size.* Our problem at Ridgely Sporting Goods spanned only two products and nine months. Yet, the size of the linear program developed was substantial. For more products and more months to be included, ever larger computers must be called on, and expenses can increase dramatically.

Other Applications of Linear Programming

As we have seen, linear programming has a natural application in the development of aggregate production plans and schedules. There are other operations problems, however, for which linear programming has been used with success.

Product Mix Decisions. Companies are constantly bumping up against capacity constraints and must make decisions about which of their products they should produce during any span of time. Some products, of course, are relatively more profitable than others. All products are likely to make different demands on a company's scarce resources. Given these scarcities, then, and the profitability of each product, what mix of products should be produced? This question is somewhat different from the one we faced in aggregate production planning. There we asked for the lowest cost way of meeting a particular schedule, given some constraints. Here we ask for the most profitable mix of products, given other constraints. This formulation of linear programming has found application in many continuous flow operations (such as oil refineries) when there is little question that all of their output can be sold on the open market with no modification to price. It is a feature of linear programming solutions that the number of products that ought to be produced will not exceed the number of structural constraints in the problem. This fact implies often that the breadth of a product line to be run at a refinery should be reduced if maximum profits are to be earned.

Product Specification Decisions. A variant of the foregoing application of linear programming is to use the technique to determine the lowest cost mix of inputs for a given product, given that certain requirements (for example, product performance) must be met. Animal feeds, paints, gasolines, and similar products are classic examples where certain inputs can be substituted for others and where cost and performance characteristics can be balanced off against one another. Linear programming can thus be used as a purchasing tool, or even as a make-buy decision tool.

Transportation and Distribution Decisions. How should a company supply its warehouses from its plants so that its transportation costs are as low as possible? This problem is so well known that it has been termed "the transportation problem," and there are special solution algorithms that can cut down on the expense of solving problems of this type. The mathematical description of the transportation problem is:

minimize

$$\sum_{i=1}^{m} \sum_{j=1}^{n} c_{ij} X_{ij}$$

subject to

$$\sum_{j=1}^{n} X_{ij} \leq S_i \text{ for } i = 1, 2, \ldots, m$$

(a supply constraint)

$$\sum_{i=1}^{m} X_{ij} \geq D_j \text{ for } j = 1, 2, \ldots, n$$

(a demand constraint)

$X_{ij} \geq 0$ for all i and j (the nonnegativity condition)

The X_{ij}'s are quantities shipped from plant i to warehouse j during a given time period. The cost of shipping between i and j is represented by c_{ij}. Each plant i is limited to shipping S_i of the good, and each warehouse must have at least D_j of it. There are m plants and n warehouses.

Plant Location Decisions. Some companies, particularly those in the food industry, that incur significant transportation expenses in taking their products to market use linear programming as an aid in their new plant location decisions. This application is an extension of the transportation problem. Proposed new plants are added to the existing network of plants, and the minimum costs of transport for the expected levels of sales to each geographic market are calculated. Various location trials are made and the lowest cost locations for fulfilling the expected level and pattern of demand are seriously scrutinized for new plant start-ups.

Alternatives and Refinements to the Linear Programming Approach

It is worth mentioning, if only in passing, that there exist some alternatives and refinements to the linear programming approach to aggregate plan and master schedule development.[3] Some (like dynamic programming and the linear decision rule approach of Holt, Modigliani, and Simon) yield optimal results although at the expense of some restrictive assumptions.[4] Often, too, these techniques, for computational reasons, are simply unworkable for problems of any more than a very small size.

A refinement to the linear programming approach, the hierarchical system concept, shows some promise.[5] This approach tries to enlarge the size of problem that linear programming can tackle by breaking it up into separate but manageable pieces (hierarchies). Naturally, something is lost by such disaggregation; but if the problem is broken apart cleverly, that "something" may be small. Different products placing demands on different equipment, for example, might be broken apart for separate analysis. Or, different levels of decisions might be separated from one another (such as the assignment of products to plants, aggregate plans within plants for broad product lines, or specific items within a product line) and analyzed separately, given the results of the next highest step in the hierarchy.

Other Approaches to Production Scheduling

So far we have discussed a couple of different approaches to the problem of developing increasingly detailed production schedules over time, notably the commonly used method of trial and error and the potentially cost-minimizing linear programming approach. We noted that linear programming has several offshoots that either refine its mathematical potential (integer programming, dynamic programming) or improve its applicability to broad, complex schedules (such as hierarchical planning).

Several other techniques, though infrequently used, can improve on the trial-and-error approach; these are not optimizing techniques like linear programming, but they can be used when the problem size or structure does not lend itself to linear programming or its offshoots. Of these approaches, two bear some mention: search techniques (the search decision rule of Taubert[6]) and simulation. Both of these approaches try to retain the detail of the scheduling problem as desired by the managers involved, by keeping the cost relationships true-to-life. They are useful because they can systematically inform management of the costs of various trial schedules.

Search techniques try to isolate good schedules by systematically probing the multidimensional surface that describes how costs differ with changes in the key elements of the production plan (such as overtime, workforce levels, inventory). If the search procedures used are effective, the techniques can yield optimal or near-optimal schedules. Simulation techniques do not search systematically for good production schedules but, rather, simply provide a means by which production planners and schedulers can test modifications to the established schedule. Simulation can be seen as a way to make trial and error easy.

Scheduling Techniques for the Job Shop

By all accounts the most difficult scheduling task is to schedule a job shop, be it a machine shop, a print shop, a plastics fabricator, or whatever. Fine minds have spent years trying to devise priority rules and scheduling procedures that job shops could successfully adopt.

The job shop and, to a lesser extent, the batch flow process are devilish to schedule because the work centers or departments within them are so disjointed and independent and because the products manufactured there place such diverse demands on machine and/or worker capacity. What determines how quickly a job can proceed through a job shop depends fundamentally on the priorities assigned to it. Jobs with rush priorities can sail through the shop, but at the risk of stalling those jobs with low priorities. Thus, scheduling a job shop is very much an exercise in sequencing the many jobs awaiting work by the various workcenters. This task of sequencing particular jobs is sometimes termed *dispatching* and, depending on one's scheme of things, may be classified as one element of what is called *shop floor control*.

Dozens of priority setting rules for determining job sequence have been tested over the years, both in actual shops and in computer simulations. Consider the following additional priority rules:

- Work first on the job with the closest due date.
- Work first on the oldest job (first come, first served).
- Work first on the job with the shortest processing time to completion.
- Work first on the job with the longest processing time to completion.
- Work first on the job with the most successor operations.
- Work first on the job with the least "slack," that is, the least difference between the time remaining until the job is due and the time it is expected to take to do the job.

These rules could be termed "pure," or simple, priority rules. There are other "mixed" or compound, rules that have been considered as well:

- Work first on the job with the lowest critical ratio as defined by

$$\text{Critical ratio} = \frac{\text{Due date} - \text{Current date}}{\begin{array}{l}\text{Standard processing time} \\ + \text{ Standard queue time} \\ \text{remaining}\end{array}}$$

(The rationale is that jobs with low critical ratios are most likely to be late and thus deserve the most attention.)

- When there is slack in the shop, work first on the job with the closest due date; but when there is no slack in the shop, work first on the job with the shortest processing time to completion.

What is apparent from all the testing done on these various rules is simply the intuitively appealing notion that no one priority setting rule—simple or compound—can simultaneously meet all order due dates and spend the least amount of shop time working on those orders.

To see some of the difficulties inherent in job shop scheduling by using priority rules, consider Situation 4-3.

SITUATION 4-3

MORRIS MACHINE SHOP

The Morris Machine Shop in Bristol, Connecticut, specialized in machining brass parts as a subcontractor to larger firms in the brass industry of western Connecticut. David Lee, the shop's foreman, had always tried to schedule jobs by assigning highest priorities to those jobs with the closest due dates. Glenn Morris, the shop's owner and founder had recently visited some other shops that used different priority rules. Curious, Glenn asked David to work out the implications of three other priority rules on the last five jobs that had been released to the shop: (1) first come, first served; (2) work first on the job with the shortest processing time to completion; and (3) work first on the job with the longest processing time to completion.

David was curious himself. The sequences and times for the last five jobs released were as shown in Table 4-7. The total time for each machine (drill, lathe, grinder, and mill) was eight hours. A perfect schedule would use all four machines and finish all five jobs in eight hours.

The jobs' due dates were such that job 1 had the closest due date followed in order by jobs 5, 3, 2, and 4. David wondered which priority rule would work best and whether any of them would yield an absolutely perfect schedule.

TABLE 4-7 Sequence and times (in hours) for last five jobs (*Morris Machine Shop*)

JOB 1		JOB 2		JOB 3		JOB 4		JOB 5	
Drill	1	Lathe	2	Grind	2	Drill	1	Mill	2
Lathe	2	Mill	2	Drill	2	Grind	2	Drill	2
Grind	1	Grind	1	Mill	2	Lathe	2	Lathe	1
Mill	2	Drill	2	Grind	1			Grind	1
				Lathe	1				
Total	6		7		8		5		6

Discussion of Morris Machine Shop

Tracing the implications of each priority rule is easy enough using a chart of operations by hours and filling in the boxes with the appropriate job number. For the traditional, closest-due-date priority rule, the priority sequence is jobs 1, 5, 3, 2, 4. As shown in Figure 4-8, under this rule both jobs 2 and 3 take more than eight hours to perform, with job 2 not finishing until the thirteenth hour. Job 2's lathe setup was broken by job 1's higher priority, as was job 4's grinding setup. The machine utilization implied by this priority rule is not good.

For the priority rule of "first come, first served," the sequence of jobs is 1, 2, 3, 4, 5. As shown in Figure 4-9, the performance of this priority rule is as bad, or worse, than the closest-due-date rule. Three of the five jobs exceed eight hours, and the grinding setup for job 4 is interrupted by job 1.

For the priority rule of "work on the job with the shortest processing time to completion," the sequence of jobs is 4, 1, 5, 2, 3, with jobs 1 and 5 both having six hours of processing time

required. As shown in Figure 4-10 two jobs are slow, with job 3 completed only in hour 13. Several setups are broken as well.

The final priority rule to be tried, "work first on the job with the longest processing time to completion," yields a schedule of jobs 3, 2, 1, 5, 4. Its performance is shown in Figure 4-11. Of the priority rules for this test of five jobs, this one performs the best. Only one job is late. Still, it is not a perfect schedule, and in another test of five jobs, its performance could be as poor as the others tested here.

Approaching the Job Shop Scheduling Problem from a Different Angle

As we have seen, traditional priority rules for scheduling job shops do not seem to work. No one rule seems to dominate any other.

Most managers, when confronted with the task of scheduling jobs for expensive machine tools, try to make sure that those machines are fully loaded with work. This typically means that these managers will tolerate substantial queues of jobs awaiting work by those ma-

FIGURE 4-8 Chart of tasks versus hours—closest due date. (1, 5, 3, 2, 4) Path for job 1 is traced.

Hours

	1	2	3	4	5	6	7	8	9	10	11	12
Lathe	2	1	1	2		4	4	5				3
Mill	5	5			1	1	2	2	3	3		
Grind	3	3	4	1	4				2	5	3	
Drill	1	4	3	3	5	5				2	2	

FIGURE 4-9   Chart of tasks versus hours—first come, first served. (1, 2, 3, 4, 5)

Hours

	1	2	3	4	5	6	7	8	9	10	11	12	13
Lathe	2	2	1	4	4	1	5						3
Mill	5	5	2	2				1	1	3	3		
Grind	3	4	4	3	2		1	5				3	
Drill	4	1	5	5	3	2	2	3					

FIGURE 4-10   Chart of tasks versus hours—shortest processing time. (4, 1, 5, 2, 3)

Hours

	1	2	3	4	5	6	7	8	9	10	11	12
Lathe	2	2	1	1	4	4		3	5			
Mill	5	5	2	2	3	3	1	1				
Grind	3	3	4	4	2	1	3			5		
Drill	1	4	3	3	5	2	2	5				

FIGURE 4-11   Chart of tasks versus hours—longest processing time. (3, 2, 1, 5, 4)

chines. In many job shops, 95 percent of a job's time on the shop floor is spent in one queue or another; only 5 percent of the time is it actually being worked on.

This fact has led some observers to concentrate on reducing queues. The potential advantages of reduced job queues are seductive. For one thing, massive queues represent substantial investments in work-in-process inventory. Reduce queues and capital is freed for other uses. The many choices to work on in any queue invite expediting and rescheduling, with the result that machine setups are broken and total processing time increases. With reduced queues there is less time devoted to placing work in queues and retrieving it later. Reduced queues also mean that bottleneck operations in the shop are more visible and thus more likely to receive management attention—more rerouting around the bottleneck, more switching of labor from underutilized operations to bottleneck operations, more of the most effective overtime, more helpful subcontracting.

But how can one reduce queues in a job shop? Two major ways have proved effective: (1) using simulation techniques to plan the life of each job in the shop as well as to plan the life of each workcenter and (2) turning the job shop into a line flow process. A third way, the repetitive lots concept, shows promise.

Simulation Techniques

Priority rules act only to plan the life of each machine or work center in the shop, with the result that queues themselves go unmanaged. Through simulation techniques (Q-Control®, OPT) it is now possible to plan the position of every job in the shop so that jobs can be assigned to successive workcenters with little or no buildup of queues.[7] These techniques can control, as opposed to merely keeping track of, the jobs in the shop. They can regulate the amount and sequencing of work so that workcenters neither get starved for work (underutilization) nor swamped with work (excessive queuing). Although it is not ensured, a simulation approach may well have happened upon the perfect schedule for the Morris Machine Shop, namely the sequence of jobs 3, 5, 2, 4, 1. (See Figure 4-12.)

Both OPT and Q-Control® are proprietary software packages, so not much is known about their inner workings. OPT, which stands for Optimized Production Technology, has received more media and business attention, and

Hours

	1	2	3	4	5	6	7	8
Lathe	2	2	1	1	4	4	5	3
Mill	5	5	2	2	3	3	1	1
Grind	3	3	4	4	2	1	3	5
Drill	4	1	3	3	5	5	2	2

FIGURE 4-12   Chart of tasks versus hours—perfect schedule. (3, 5, 2, 4, 1)

somewhat more is known about how it operates. The key insight of OPT is that if the shop is to produce more, it has to schedule jobs efficiently through the bottleneck operations. The known bottlenecks constrain capacity so it is important to schedule them for maximum output, namely to run large lots through them and have few setups. For the nonbottleneck operations, on the other hand, it doesn't matter whether there are few or many setups; all that matters is that the bottleneck operations are fed work in time. OPT thus often splits lots into different sizes and keeps some buffer stocks in front of the bottleneck operations.

Q-Control® apparently applies a different notion, although it, too, is simulation-based. It employs what is called *dual-balance scheduling*. The simulation works to schedule both capacity usage over time and the utilization of orders, and it tries to match the two. Its vision is to devise the schedule so that the job shop looks like a line flow process; jobs are planned so that they never have to stop for long.

Both OPT and Q-Control® require nightly computer runs to yield a schedule for the next day that indicates the exact sequence of jobs for each workcenter. The data needed to run the simulation are considerable. Accurate data on setups, run times, and routings for all products and capacities for each workcenter are required. Neither technique can guarantee perfect schedules, and, of course, machine breakdowns, faulty materials, and the like can ruin any schedule. These techniques, however, can point out the bottlenecks and plan the flows, and this information can lead to capacity adjustments (overtime of the right kind, switching of labor to the bottleneck operation), workload adjustments (subcontracting), or job mix adjustments (split order, reroutings) that can increase throughout in the shop. What these techniques do not permit is expediting.

Rearrangement

The attractiveness of simulation scheduling is that conceptually it plans out what has to happen for the job shop to act like a line flow process. Line flow processes use minimal work-in-process inventories because they are designed that way; simulation scheduling, in conceptual terms, rearranges the job shop into a line flow process to achieve the same result.

Suppose that instead of using a schedule to yield the "line flow effect" in a job shop, one physically rearranged the job shop into a line or series of lines. The physical layout of the factory would be altered so that queues of work could not build up. Workcenter capacities along each "line" would be balanced. Extensive work-in-process inventories would be designed out of the process. Some of the flexibility of the job shop would be lost but the increases in factory throughput could be significant.

Of course, not all job shops could be rearranged in this way. Norcen Industries certainly could not; its jobs are too varied. There are, however, job shops—many of which are part of a hybrid process—that need not be managed as job shops. Demands, in these instances, are not so variable that with some modest investments in equipment, a re-layout of the plant, and attention to easy machine changeovers, a "line

flow" process could not be devised. Group technology, discussed in Chapter 2, seeks just this kind of change from job shop to line flow.

This insistence on defining the process to limit the buildup of work-in-process inventory smacks of the Japanese approach to manufacturing. The process, and the production control within it, are geared to the "just-in-time arrival" of materials at workstations. The process is defined to remove queuing problems; with attention to quick changeovers, remarkable flexibility can be maintained and scheduling can be simplified. (More on the Japanese will be presented later in this chapter and in Chapter 10.)

The Repetitive Lots Concept

Recently, Jacobs and Bragg have introduced a concept they call "repetitive lots"; it shows good promise for improved job shop scheduling.[8] The repetitive lots method combines the advantages of small batches (lower inventories, shorter queues, quicker throughput times through the process) with the advantages of limited setups (less downtime devoted to setup, greater workcenter capacity per unit of time). Jacobs and Bragg distinguish among three different kinds of batches: (1) "order batch" (the batch released to the shop that often matches the customer order), (2) "transfer batch" (the batch, usually smaller than the work order, that is actually moved from one workcenter to another), and (3) "operation batch" (the batch that is actually worked on at a given time at a workcenter). Splitting an order into several batches is an old trick for expediting things in a job shop (sometimes known as *overlapping production*); it is effective because it permits work to be done on units of the order in parallel rather than series. What repetitive lots do is to provide some discipline to this traditional practice.

With repetitive lots, the order batch is split into an integer number of smaller, independent "transfer" batches. At any workcenter, the next job to be worked on is determined by:

1. A traditional priority rule such as first-come, first-served or earliest due date worked on first, unless
2. In the queue of jobs awaiting work there is a transfer batch that matches what is already set up for the workcenter. In this case, that

transfer batch is pulled in, and thus the "operation" batch size can be greater than the transfer batch size. The logic here is that, by so doing, setup time is reduced.

Although there are still a number of questions to be asked of this approach (such as what the size of transfer batches is and which priority rules to use), its initial results are encouraging. While repetitive lots may not improve on simulation, it certainly is easier to implement.

PART TWO
CONTROLLING THE PROCESS

Production control, unfortunately, is one of those terms that has a slightly different meaning to each manager. Sometimes the differences are of function and sometimes only of emphasis. This text takes a broad perspective on the topic, outlining here the major aspects of production control, and then devoting the remainder of this chapter to a more thorough discussion of them. There are four main functions that are reasonably identified with production control:

1. *The specific, sequential assignment of jobs to each workcenter.* This is the finest detail of production scheduling, the most nitty gritty aspect of that function. It is what many mean when they talk of shop floor control or dispatching. We have already discussed several of its facets in the discussion of job shop scheduling. More will be said of it later.

2. *Monitoring the performance of actual production versus the schedule and informing management of the status of orders (for example, on-time, behind schedule, ahead of schedule).* This function has production

control as the nerve center of day-to-day operations, the hub of information flow such as which orders are open and where they are in the factory, which have been closed, what materials are behind schedule and how that will affect the orders opened, what the actual capacities of work centers are and whether there are any impending impediments to planned capacity (maintenance problems, excessive setups or changeovers), and what the steps remaining are for all outstanding open orders. Production control is a key consumer of the factory's paperwork, as well as a generator of it (in forms such as the daily dispatch list).

3. *Taking action to remedy the unacceptable status of some jobs.* In this role, production control is more than a monitor of job order status; it is an expediter (or de-expediter) of selected jobs. This is an active function that requires production control not only to revise the detail of scheduling but to prepare the way for those selected jobs with managers and workers at downstream workcenters.

TABLE 4-8   Worker information requirements in different processes

PROCESS	WHAT SHOULD BE WORKED ON	HOW IT SHOULD BE DONE	HOW LONG IT SHOULD TAKE	WHERE PRODUCT IS TO BE DIRECTED NEXT
Job shop	Told by foreman	Written on process sheet attached to order	Written on job sheet attached to order	Written on a routing slip attached to order
Batch flow	Told by foreman or implied by a priority numbering scheme for batch	Either known from training or written on process sheet attached to batch	Implied by piece rate or written on process sheet accompanying batch	Written on a routing slip
Line flow	Determined by sequencing of line	Basically known from training, though options may be indicated on a process sheet	Implied by known worker standards or mechanical pacing of line	Known from the layout of the line
Continuous flow	Determined by process layout	Known from training; few options available indicated by independent information from management	Determined by process layout	Determined by process layout

4. *An architect of information flow in the process.* This is the long-term role for production control, the role where it can simplify its own job and further the interests of the company at the same time.

All of these functions, of course, are related. One cannot devise an appropriate dispatch list without monitoring the schedule, and one cannot expedite orders without constant attention to the dispatch list. Nevertheless, it is instructive to focus on these individual functions, and particularly the first two. Before we do, however, it is helpful to be grounded again on the information requirements of various processes. What is sometimes forgotten in the rush to satisfy orders and bird-dog materials is that some of the wealth of information that can help guide and control the process relates to the work-

force. Workers need to know several things before they can plunge comfortably into doing their work: what they should work on, how they should do it, how long it should take, and where their output ought to be directed. As should be clear from the various tours, sometimes this information must be transmitted to the workers repeatedly; other times they already know what is required of them. Table 4-8 summarizes the worker information requirements that are typical of various processes.

MONITORING A PRODUCTION
SCHEDULE

One of the key tasks mentioned here, that of monitoring the status of job orders, is information-intensive. Vast amounts of paperwork must be consumed by an effective production control staff. Consider the following kinds of information and paperwork that production control must keep abreast of:

- Orders opened, closed, or worked on, by workcenter or department, with quantities tracked
- Routings for each order. (Sometimes routing information can be combined with order status to show the status of orders at workcenters or departments immediately preceeding or following a job's current location. This helps give visibility to foremen and workers, so that they will more often work on exactly what is needed)
- Stock status lists for inputs, including material shortage lists
- Bills of material (the link between inputs and outputs)
- Workcenter capacities, and efficiencies
- Standards for run time, setup time, queue time, and move time, by part or item
- Master production schedules and/or final assembly schedules
- Dispatch lists (that production control may generate itself) indicating the most recent assignment of jobs to workcenters, and thus, the availability of workcenters for additional work.

All these pieces of information are requested by the production control function in order to know:

1. what the schedule is;
2. which orders are where in the process and, thus, how they stack up to the schedule (whether they are on time or behind schedule);
3. where orders are due next in the process;
4. which of those orders have material enough to be completed and which do not;
5. how much of each type of operation remains to be done to the order;
6. whether the workcenters stand a chance of completing the order per schedule, given the other work assigned to them.

Integrating this information in a way that makes sense for the process is an important undertaking. Usually, monitoring schedules is helped greatly by using some visual aids. Schedule—monitoring aids can be laid out in many ways. One common way is a column tracking scheduling chart.

Figure 4-13 is an example of a schedule monitoring device that tracks progress down a column indicating the present day or week of production. The figure illustrates job/batches that were scheduled to begin on different production days and whose expected durations varied. Expected durations are indicated by the box outline itself while completed production is indicated by the shaded portion of the box outline. Those job/batches whose shaded-in portions fall left of the panel indicating the present production day are behind schedule; those whose shaded-in portions are right of the panel are ahead of schedule.

Tasks with scheduled starts and stops that differ can be readily portrayed. Also, job/batches that take up unscheduled time can be depicted (for example, Job/Batch 2 and the lighter shaded portion of the line.) Because the chart is laid out for production days rather than tasks, different tasks can be represented by the same production day. Of course, the capacities and capacity utilizations of various tasks or machines must be accounted for separately so that too much is not asked of any task or machine.

Such visual aids lend themselves to a variety of graphic conventions. For example, different

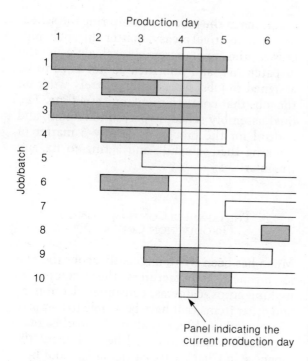

FIGURE 4-13 A column tracking schedule monitor.

symbols or colors can distinguish wait time or maintenance time from actual production. Different symbols or colors can indicate the task or factory department in which the job/batch is, was, or will be. This choice of convention depends solely on what information is useful and what is available; and various charts like these can be bought commercially for scheduling up to a year ahead.

DISPATCHING

The prior section on job shop scheduling already discussed some aspects of dispatching—that element of shop floor control devoted to the precise sequencing of jobs to particular workcenters. We saw two major ways job shops (or batch flow processes) can be scheduled: (1) with priority rules to guide the selection of which job to pull into the workcenter, or (2) with simulation to plan how each job should move from workcenter to workcenter.

Those are two characteristically different approaches to dispatching, and they carry different general labels: *vertical loading* and *horizontal loading*. Vertical loading views the problem from the standpoint of the workcenter and asks which job (or succession of jobs) should be assigned to it. Horizontal loading, on the other hand, views the problem from the standpoint of the job itself and asks how and when the job will be sequenced through all the workcenters. Vertical loading leads one to consider priority rules for the selection process, an essentially static procedure. Horizontal loading is more dynamic because it forces the dispatcher to consider what happens to orders and workcenters over time. As noted in the section on job shop scheduling, while it is an appealing notion, horizontal loading is difficult to accomplish well, even with computers. Nevertheless, many think it holds more promise than the static, simpler approach represented by vertical loading.

The oldest, and least sophisticated, form of horizontal loading technique is the Gantt chart, which is essentially a bar chart visual aid to the scheduler named after Henry Gantt who popularized them in the early 1900s. Despite their simplicity, Gantt charts can be very useful tools.

To construct a Gantt chart we need to know when the item is due and how long each required operation (including setup time, run time, and move time to the next operation) can be expected to take. Starting with the due date, one can then follow operations backwards, figuring out when the start date has to be. One has the choice of including queue time in these calculations or not. Queue time can often be

75 percent to 95 percent of the time an item spends on the shop floor. Naturally, the better the schedule, the lower the amount of unproductive queue time.

The charts used in the section on job shop scheduling (Figures 4-8 to 4-12) are Gantt charts. Their use forces the scheduler to think of the dynamics of the situation, the germ idea for the simulation sophistication of OPT or Q-Control.® In fact, the simulation of a workcenter over time so that jobs are chosen not to exceed its capacity has been given the special term of *finite loading*. The contrast, of course, is called *infinite loading*, which permits an assignment of jobs past rated capacity, necessarily triggering action such as overtime to take up the excess. (Priority rules are compatible with infinite loading because their use does not recognize explicitly the capacity of the workcenter). Finite loading essentially shaves off any more-than-capacity loads on workcenters and distributes that excess into later time periods, invariably delaying the expected completion of some jobs. While often more realistic than infinite loading, finite loading can confuse workers and foremen, because they may not be so easily accepting of the logic that may keep a workcenter idle in anticipation of a job to come. In fact, if they are measured by standard efficiency measures (standard hours/actual hours), they may strenuously resist finite loading for the equipment under their control.

This discussion of dispatching focuses on job shops and batch flow processes. Line flow and continuous flow processes, of course, require the same functions of sequential assignment of jobs for the process and of monitoring the performance to the schedule. However, with the rigidness of routing, the relative certainty of capacity, and the attention to balance in the flow, what gets started in a line or continuous flow process is generally what gets finished, and in the same order. And, unless there are malfunctions in the process, monitoring the schedule is a relatively easy matter. In such processes, the final assembly schedule is the dispatch list, and priorities do not have to be assigned to jobs, workcenters merely work on the jobs that come to them, one at a time. The final assembly schedule paces production, and control for the process is largely a matter of tracking that schedule and acting to fix any irregularities.

THE JAPANESE CONTRIBUTION TO PRODUCTION CONTROL[9]

Much has been written recently about the major Japanese manufacturers, those companies making autos, cameras, consumer electronics, and other items that have been able to compete to tremendous effect in all of the world's marketplaces. Much more will be said about the Japanese in Chapter 10, particularly about how various Japanese manufacturing techniques can be integrated into a manufacturing philosophy that merits careful study by all students of production. Nevertheless, it is worthwhile introducing here several concepts about Japanese-style production control, for it contrasts sharply with the traditional practice of many Western companies.

Much of the discussion in this chapter and the previous one has been about coordination, how materials ought to be managed so that they are coordinated effectively with the production schedule, no matter how that production schedule is derived. Implicit in that point of view is the notion that materials ought to be ready and waiting for the delivery of materials. To avoid such idle worker and machinery time, however, the traditional Western outlook is to make sure that there are queues of work ahead of each machine and that there are banks of parts awaiting work or assembly by the workforce. This attitude toward production scheduling and control could be characterized as a "push," where materials are to be pushed out of material stockrooms or out of particular manufacturing departments according to a set schedule that is influenced heavily by demand. In such a system, considerable time and effort are spent making sure that particular problems can be expedited efficiently if changes to the schedule have to be made on short notice. Extensive coordination is needed to be certain that the materials are made available according to the dictates of the often changing production schedule. Buffer stocks, safety lead times, and other tactics are often used to make sure that the materials are there "just in case" they may be needed.

Some of the finest Japanese companies have a very different perspective on production scheduling and control. As Chapter 10 relates, the foundations for this perspective lay more with company attitudes toward quality improvement than with schedule flexibility. Suffice it, at this point, to note that the Japanese view is to have production be "just in time" rather than "just in case." The just-in-time notion is to have as little inventory in the process as possible, yet for the process to flow smoothly. Raw materials, fabricated parts, subassemblies, and the like are to be delivered to the respective segments of the process just before they are required by the workers there, much as in the continuous flow process. Indeed, much of Japanese manufacturing can be seen as a movement to try to change batch flow operations into as close a facsimile of a continuous flow process as possible. In contrast, the traditional Western view is to develop information-intensive schemes such as MRP to salvage the flexibility of batch flow processes.

If this kind of batch-to-continuous flow transformation is to occur, then one cannot expect to "push" materials out into the factory without risking a buildup of inventory. After all, if the process cannot handle the production as scheduled, inventory will accumulate. For this reason, the Japanese do not value as highly the philosophy of coordination underlying an information-intensive MRP system. Using an MRP system to release orders to the factory floor risks increasing inventories and abandoning the concept of just-in-time production.

The implications of just-in-time production are far-reaching: low inventory levels, better product quality, smoother production flow, and increased worker involvement. Just-in-time production is indicative of a point of view different from that implicit in MRP systems as they are commonly adopted.

If materials are not to be "pushed" out of the materials stockroom or out of one manufacturing department and into another, what kind of production control is consistent, then, with the just-in-time production perspective? The answer is to adopt a system that "pulls" materials through the factory. The authority to draw materials out of the stockroom or to begin production in a department is given only when it is called for by an operation downstream. Production is thus triggered not so much by the production schedule as by the needs of operations that follow.

The most celebrated of the Japanese "pull" production control systems is the kanban system developed over many years by the Toyota Motor Company. *Kanban* is Japanese for card, and the Toyota system uses a plasticized card for indicating what upstream operations should be doing to keep the downstream operations functioning. The Toyota system uses two kanban cards: (1) a "production" kanban, which triggers production in the manufacturing department upstream, and (2) a "move" kanban, which indicates use by the downstream department. Figure 4-14 displays the contents of a move and a production kanban card. The move

A. Typical move card

FROM SUPPLYING WORK CENTER #52 PAINT	PART NO. A575 GAS TANK MOUNT	TO USING WORK CENTER #2 ASSEMBLY
OUTBOUND STOCKPOINT NO. 52-6	CONTAINER: TYPE 2 (RED) NO. IN EACH CONTAINER: 20 CARD NO. 3 NO. CARDS ISSUED: 5	INBOUND STOCKPOINT NO. 2-1

B. Typical production card

WORK CENTER #52 PAINT
PART NO. A575 GAS TANK MOUNT
PLACE AT STOCKPOINT NO. 52-6
MATERIAL REQUIRED: PAINT #5 ST. BLACK
                   PY 372 STAMPING
FOUND AT: WORK CTR. 31 PRESS SHOP
          STOCKPOINT NO. 31-18

C. Move card used by Hino Motors Ltd. to pick up parts from a supplier

Supplier and pick up location   Customer and delivery location

Note the bar code. Only move cards sent to suppliers are imprinted with the bar. Upon receipt, the bar code is read, and a cumulative total is kept on-line by computer. Hino uses it only for development of receipts to pay the supplier's invoice, an accounting function not related to control of the part for production. However, the cumulative counts can be used by production control to keep a cumulative count of parts received.

The times posted at the upper left refer to delivery times, twice daily for this part. Sometimes the times posted refer, more precisely, to the times the move cards must be picked up to give to the truck driver bringing a new delivery of parts.

Source: Robert W. Hall, *Zero Inventories*, Dow Jones-Irwin, 1983, pp. 44–45.

FIGURE 4-14 Kanban cards.

Using only two work centers, the paths of the cards can be shown in more detail:

■ Move card   ——— Move card path

□ Production card   ——— Production card path

Source: Robert W. Hall, *Zero Inventories*, Dow Jones-Irwin, 1983, p. 44.

FIGURE 4-15   The operation of a two-card kanban system.

card includes the following information: part number, capacity of the standard container the part is held in, the card number (such as 2 of 3), the supplying workcenter (its outbound stockpoint number), and the using workcenter (its inbound stockpoint number). The production card includes this information: the part number to be produced, the standard container's capacity, the supplying workcenter number, the card number (such as 2 of 3), the materials required by the workcenter and where

these materials can be found, and often useful information like tooling or fixturing needed.

The use of these kanban cards is illustrated by reference to Figure 4-15 and the following discussion.* Note that workcenter 1 feeds workcenter 2.

1. A container of parts is selected for use at workcenter 2's inbound stockpoint. The container's move card is removed and stored in a hold box.

---

*This discussion follows Robert W. Hall. *Zero Inventories*, Dow Jones-Irwin. (Homewood, Ill., 1983).

2. Later, the move card is picked up from its hold box and taken to workcenter 1's outbound stockpoint, where several full containers of parts are located. The production card in a container there is removed and replaced by the move card, and the container is transported from workcenter 1's outbound stockpoint to workcenter 2's inbound stockpoint.

3. The production card that was removed at workcenter 1's outbound stockpoint is stored in a hold box. From time to time, when the workcenter is ready to perform more work, the production hold box is checked. Each production card is authorized to produce a standard container of parts. A worker merely goes over to the workcenter's inbound stockpoint, removes the move card from a container (as in point 1), substitutes the production card, and proceeds with the work.

There are several rules to follow as workers use the kanban cards:

1. Either a move card or a production card must be attached to any container full of parts.

2. Containers of parts are never moved from a supplying workcenter's outbound stockpoint to a using workcenter's inbound stockpoint without a move card attached.

3. Standard containers are always used and filled only to their indicated capacity.

4. Work is accomplished at a workcenter only when there is an unattached production card to authorize it.

This Toyota-type kanban system is appropriate for those just-in-time production processes that make relatively high-volume parts under demand conditions that do not fluctuate se-verely. Such a kanban system, therefore, is not advised for all types of production.

There is another type of kanban system that is also used in Japanese companies: a single-card kanban system. This system uses only the move card that serves to regulate deliveries to user workcenters. Parts are produced or bought according to a schedule, but delivery is controlled by a kanban. This single-card kanban system has much in common with the well-known two-bin system that is employed in many companies to control the stock of parts flowing to the process. In a two-bin system, orders of parts are triggered when the last container (the "second bin") is opened and parts are withdrawn from it. The single-card kanban system works much like the two-bin system in that it triggers replenishment only when available parts have been depleted to a fixed level. The single-card kanban system, however, is somewhat more disciplined than the typical two-bin system. Only standard containers are used, and the quantity per container is kept exact. The number of full containers is severely limited, and the quantity in any container is generally small so that at least one container is used up daily.

The single-card kanban system does not exercise as much control over production as does the Toyota two-card kanban system, but it still can act to keep inventories lower than they might otherwise be. They help orient production control more toward pull rather than push.

A variation on the single-card kanban system that has been popularized by Hewlett-Packard and others is the *kanban square*. In this variation, colored tape is placed on the floor at and between various workcenters. Workers are instructed not to work on anything unless there is free space in the kanban square between their workcenter and the next, and not to bring in any work that cannot fit into their work area.

The kanban squares thus work like a limited number of standard containers to restrict the amount of work-in-process permitted on the factory floor. By making the squares either smaller or larger, management can adjust the quantity of work-in-process on the floor.

The success of these just-in-time production control techniques has been, at times, spectacular. Work-in-process inventory levels and space requirements typically drop sharply and throughput typically increases, sometimes substantially. The use of kanban cards, of course, is not wholly responsible; there are many other elements of manufacturing in this environment, as Chapter 10 notes. Nevertheless, kanban cards are an indication of the potential that good production control has for improving operations.

A

FORECASTING DEMAND

Of the six plant tours, only Norcen Industries—the job shop that bid on all orders—knew with certainty beforehand exactly what it was to produce. In each of the other processes, there was some uncertainty about the demands to be placed on it; forecasts had to be made to guide production. In a sense, these forecasts could be said to "drive" those processes.

In the typical company, production managers are not responsible for the forecast used to drive production schedules. The marketing department is more often the source of these forecasts. This is not to say that production managers should not be interested in the assumptions and methods used to build these forecasts. In many circles, marketers are notorious for their optimism and are resented when manufacturing gets stuck with unsold inventory. A second-guessed forecast that is actually used by manufacturing, instead of the "official" forecast, is often a sore point between marketing and manufacturing. Forecasting is one of the most important interfaces between marketing and operations, and it often helps for operations managers to be well versed in forecasting, if only for defensive purposes.

Several types of forecasts are needed to guide production. Long-term forecasting of demand is required (even in a job shop) to help decide capacity and technology choices. Medium-term (6–18 months) forecasts of demand for broad families of products are needed to help marshal production resources, and short-term (less than six months) forecasts are needed to specify demands for particular products and product variations (models, sizes, colors, and so on) Table 4-9 summarizes some of these requirements.

As one might expect, there are different kinds of forecasting techniques that can be used to satisfy different forecasting needs. Figure 4-16 divides the various forecasting techniques available into broad categories and distinguishes those that are appropriate for long-term forecasting from those that are appropriate for short-term forecasting. The next sections briefly describe each of the forecasting techniques introduced in Figure 4-16.

QUANTITATIVE TECHNIQUES USING TIME SERIES DATA

The simplest quantitative techniques use only the past history of the demand itself. These techniques try to isolate patterns that could be expected to repeat in the future. Their strength

TABLE 4-9   Forecasting requirements for different time periods

	SHORT TERM (≤6 months)	MEDIUM TERM (6–18 months)	LONG TERM (≥18 months)
Uses	Production schedules Staffing manpower plans	Aggregate production plans Levels of employment and inventory	Capacity or process changes
Needs	High accuracy	Reasonable accuracy	"Ballpark" accuracy
	Detailed, disaggregated by product, model, style	Some detail, some aggregation of products	Not detailed, high aggregation into product lines
	Forecast often by week or even day	Forecast often by month	Forecast often by either month or quarter
	Turning points less important	Turning points of modest interest	Turning points important
	Low cost, quickly done	Modest cost and speed	High cost, takes time
	Used by lower-level management	Used by middle-level management	Used by top-level management

*Appropriate for short-term uses
†Appropriate for long-term uses

FIGURE 4-16   A classification of forecasting techniques.

lies in identifying these patterns easily and translating them into predictions.

Simple rules are the least sophisticated quantitative forecasts. They involve rules such as "this period's demand equals last period's demand," or "this period's demand equals last period's demand plus 5 percent." Although simple, such rules do not yield consistently, reliable predictions.

Both trend identification and decomposition techniques are more sophisticated than simple rules because they break down the history into variations that may be cyclical or seasonal or that show a specific linear trend. These techniques, in a sense, massage the data (1) to remove seasonality or business cycle fluctuations and expose what may be general trends and (2) to isolate the extent to which variations and past demands have been random.

The usefulness of this data decomposition and trend identification is evident from the following situation.

SITUATION 4A-1

THE YOUNG FOREVER BOUTIQUE

The Young Forever Boutique was started five years ago in space in an old, renovated factory in suburban Chicago. Kathy Wilkerson, its owner, had been a buyer with a department store chain in the area, but had always wanted to satisfy an itch to run her own store. The boutique concentrated on casual and sports clothes for "baby boom generation" women, although both younger and older women felt comfortable shopping there as well.

Kathy had been pleased with the store's progress. Sales each year had grown, and the store had been turning a nice profit. In late July of the boutique's third year, Kathy had been able to relocate the store to a modern mall, not too far from the renovated factory. The rent was more expensive, but Kathy saw the opportunity to attract more customers in the mall environment.

Recently, Kathy had sensed that sales were more erratic than they had been, and she was concerned that her sales forecasts were increasingly inadequate. She also wondered about how much of a boost to sales the move to the mall had been. Kathy hoped that more sophisticated forecasting techniques would help. Monthly sales since the shop's start-up are found in Table 4-10.

Discussion of the Young Forever Boutique

Kathy Wilkerson's situation at the Young Forever Boutique presents a fine opportunity for contrasting some of the more important techniques of forecasting using time series data.

One simple forecasting rule that Kathy could have used rests on the premise that next year's sales will follow the same growth and pattern as this year's sales. The implications of such a rule are left as exercises at the end of the chapter.

Although simple rules can often generate perfectly acceptable forecasts, they can, just as often, be wildly incorrect. Two of the most popular alternatives to the use of simple rules are the moving average and exponential smoothing. Both of these forecasting methods rely exclusively on the historical pattern of demand, under the assumption that the future will look like the past. In contrast to the simple rule, however, moving average and exponential smoothing estimates can be designed to adapt very quickly to abrupt changes in the historical pattern.

Let us consider the *moving average* first. It is simply an average of past data and, each period, the data used in the average are updated to reflect, at least in part, what the most recent actual demand was. Moving averages can be simple in construction, with each period's value evenly weighted, or they can be more complex, with different weights applied to different time periods. When weights are used, they are typically defined so that they always sum to 1. In Kathy Wilkerson's case, for example, we could base the forecast on the past three months, but give the most weight (0.5) to the most recent month, less weight to the next to the last month (0.3), and the least weight to the month furthest back (0.2). This weighted moving average can be represented mathematically as,

$$F_t = 0.5\,D_{t-1} + 0.3\,D_{t-2} + 0.2\,D_{t-3}$$

Where F_t is the forecast for this time period (month), D_{t-1} is the actual demand last period. D_{t-2} and D_{t-3} the actual demand two and three periods ago, respectively. Table 4-11 displays the forecast for Year 3 for the Young Forever Boutique using this weighting scheme.

TABLE 4-10   Young Forever Boutique sales volumes by month

	YEAR 1	YEAR 2	YEAR 3	YEAR 4	YEAR 5
January	—	$ 6,381.07	$ 11,016.55	$ 11,965.68	$ 10,580.74
February	—	4,405.83	8,264.14	12,761.98	13,420.87
March	$ 4,566.40	9,126.95	6,843.95	18.126.70	34,476.27
April	6,941.89	10,970.45	20,109.68	19,092.90	19,108.79
May	7,047.23	10,189.28	11,148.64	15,384.01	18,109.54
June	6,784.37	7,043.85	8,365.40	12,237.00	13,743.60
July	5,814.23	6,717.37	9,469.08	13,252.53	18,339.25
August	6,906.38	9,139.72	10,221.00	13,819,77	—
September	8,075.13	11,315.19	15,161.41	21,755.64	—
October	7,913.56	10,838.40	17,713.08	24,838.10	—
November	9,054.18	11,150.94	17,508.99	15,955.60	—
December	14,114.58	17,592.20	27,566.89	19,370.70	
Annual Totals	$77,217.95 for 10 months	$114,871.25	$163,388.72	$198,560.61	$127,779.06 for 7 months

TABLE 4-11   Young Forever Boutique moving average estimates

	FORECAST YEAR 3	ACTUAL YEAR 3
January	$ 14,309.06	$ 11,016.55
February	13,016.12	8,264.14
March	10,955.48	6,843.95
April	8,104.53	20,109.68
May	13,760.85	11,148.64
June	12,976.01	8,365.40
July	11,549.23	9,469.08
August	9,473.89	10,221.00
September	9,624.30	15,161.41
October	12,540.82	17,713.08
November	15,449,16	17,508.99
December	17,100.70	27,566.80
	$148,860.15	$163,388.72

Observations:

1. Because the sales in Year 3 are a dramatic increase over those for Year 2, the moving average estimates lag behind the year's actual sales.

2. The weighting scheme insures that the forecast does not dip as low or reach as high as actual sales do.

We could, of course, introduce more past data into the moving average calculation, or vary the weights applied, or specify particular time periods for use or exclusion (for example, forecast first quarter data using only values from first quarters in the past, or exclude period $t-1$ from the calculation). The more weight applied to recent history, the more responsive the forecast is to changes in the pattern of demand. The less weight applied to recent history—perhaps by the inclusion of many past actual demands— the more stable the forecast and the less apt it is to be swayed by aberrations in the data. The choice of weights and data points to use should reflect the forecaster's desires for stability versus responsiveness in the forecast.

Exponential smoothing is allied to the moving average. It represents a special weighting scheme that has the advantage of being particularly easy to compute, requiring only the most recent forecast and the most recent actual value. The forecast for period t takes the following form:

$$F_t = F_{t-1} + \alpha(A_{t-1} - F_{t-1})$$

which is built on the very logical assumption that the next period's forecast (F_t) equals the last period's forecast (F_{t-1}) plus the error in that forecast $(A_{t-1} - F_{t-1})$ adjusted by a correction factor (α).

Algebraic manipulation of this equation yields the following alternative formulation, which is often preferred for doing computations:

$$F_t = \alpha A_{t-1} + (1 - \alpha) F_{t-1}$$

where F_t is the forecast value for the time t, A_{t-1} is the actual value for the last period, and F_{t-1} is the forecasted value for the last period. The factor α can vary between 0 and 1, although in practice it is frequently limited to less than 0.5. The higher α is, the quicker the forecast follows past actual demand. If high values of α work well (i.e., lower errors than others), there is a good case that a significant trend exists in the data. That is why values greater than 0.5 are not frequently used for α.

This smoothing technique is termed exponential because by substitution with past value, the weights of prior periods decline exponentially from the most recent period on back in time as shown:

$$F_t = \alpha A_{t-1} + (1 - \alpha) \alpha A_{t-2} + (1 - \alpha)^2 \alpha A_{t-3}$$
$$+ (1 - \alpha)^3 \alpha A_{t-4} + \cdots$$
$$+ (1 - \alpha)^{t-2} A_1 + (1 - \alpha)^{t-1} F_1$$

The forecast for the Young Forever Boutique's Year 3 using exponential smoothing $(\alpha = 0.3)$ is found in Table 4-12.

Evaluating Forecasts

A forecast's performance can be judged after the fact by its errors. Errors, however, can be assessed in various ways. Three commonly used errors are displayed in Table 4-13: the simple difference between actual and forecast needs or sales (sometimes called *bias*), the mean absolute deviation (that is, the mean at the absolute value of the differences between actual and forecast), and the mean squared error (the square of the differences). Table 4-13 compares the Year 3 forecasts and actuals for the moving average and exponential smoothing techniques. The table reveals how the three different measures of error react in this situation. The results indicate that while the exponential smoothing estimates offer less bias than the moving average

TABLE 4-12   Young Forever Boutique exponential smoothing with $\alpha = 0.3$

	FORECAST YEAR 3	ACTUAL YEAR 3
January	$ 17,592.20	$ 11,016.55
February	15,619.51	8,264.14
March	13,412.90	6,843.95
April	11,442.21	20,109.68
May	14,642.45	11,148.64
June	13,174.31	8,365.40
July	11,731.64	9,469.08
August	11,052.87	10,221.00
September	10,803.31	15,161.41
October	12,110.74	17,713.09
November	13,791.44	17,508.99
December	14,906.71	27,566.80
	$160,280.29	$163,388.72

Observations:

1. The exponential smoothing technique, in this instance, yields forecasts that sum more nearly to the actual sales in Year 3.

2. The sales estimates are really "smoothed," in the sense that they do not vary dramatically from one month to another. They are much smoother than the moving average estimates.

estimates, they differ more wildly on a month-to-month basis from the actuals, having a higher mean absolute deviation and a higher mean squared error.

Note that when the mean difference (or bias) is computed, errors that are positive and negative cancel one another out to some degree. This is eliminated by taking the absolute values of the errors in calculating the mean absolute deviation. Squared errors penalize forecasts that are far off much more heavily than forecasts that are only a little off; mean squared errors are much more sensitive to outlying observations than are mean absolute errors.

The *mean absolute deviation (MAD)* can be a handy number, for it can be used to approximate the standard deviation of a sample of observations. If a sample is drawn from a normally distributed population, then the standard deviation (σ) is related to the MAD as follows:

$$\sigma \approx 1.25 \text{ MAD}$$

TABLE 4-13a   Young Forever Boutique error analysis
A.   Moving average estimates

	FORECAST	ACTUAL YEAR 3	DIFFERENCE (BIAS)	ABSOLUTE DEVIATION	SQUARED ERROR (MILLIONS)
January	$14,309.06	$11,016.55	−$3,292.51	$3,292.51	10.84
February	13,016.12	8,264.14	−4,751.98	4,751.98	22.58
March	10,955,48	6,843.95	−4,111.53	4,111.53	16.90
April	8,104.53	20,109.68	12,005.15	12,005.15	144.12
May	13,760.85	11,148.64	−2,612.21	2,612.21	6.82
June	12,976.01	8,365.40	−4,610.61	4,610.61	21.26
July	11,549.23	9,469.08	−2,080.15	2,080.15	4.33
August	9,473.89	10,221.00	747.11	747.11	0.56
September	9,624.30	15,161.41	5,537.11	5,537.11	30.66
October	12,540.82	17,713.08	5,172.26	5,172.26	26.75
November	15,449.16	17,508.99	2,059.83	2,059.83	4.24
December	17,100.70	27,566.80	10,466.10	10,466.10	109.54
	$148,860.15	$163,388.72			
Sum of errors			$14,528.57	$57,446.55	$398.90
Mean difference (bias)			$1,210.71		
Mean absolute deviation (MAD)				$4,787.21	
Mean squared error (in millions)					33.24

TABLE 4-13b   Young Forever Boutique
B.   Exponential smoothing with $\alpha = 0.3$

	FORECAST YEAR 3	ACTUAL YEAR 3	DIFFERENCE (BIAS)	ABSOLUTE DEVIATION	SQUARED ERROR (MILLIONS)
January	$ 17,592.20	$11,016.55	−$6,575.65	$6,575.65	43.24
February	15,619.51	8,264.14	−7,355.37	7,355.37	54.10
March	13,412.90	6,843.95	−6,568.95	6,568.95	43.15
April	11,442.21	20,109.68	8,667.47	8,667.47	75.13
May	14,642.45	11,148.64	−3,493.81	3,493.81	12.21
June	13,174.31	8,365.40	−4,808.91	4,808.91	23.13
July	11,731.64	9,469.08	−2,262.56	2,262.56	5.12
August	11,052.87	10,221.00	−831.87	831.87	0.69
September	10,803.31	15,161.41	4,358.10	4,358.10	18.99
October	12,110.74	17,713.08	5,602.35	5,602.35	31.39
November	13,791.44	17,508.99	3,717.55	3,717.55	13.82
December	14,906.71	27,566.80	12,660.09	12,660.09	160.28
	$160,280.29	$163,388.72			
Sum of errors			$3,108.43	$66,902.68	481.25
Mean difference (bias)			$ 259.04		
Mean absolute deviation (MAD)				$ 5,575.22	
Mean squared error (in millions)					40.10

This relationship is sometimes employed in calculating safety stocks or in calculating control limits for quality control charts, topics discussed more in succeeding chapters.

Dealing with Seasonality

The previous forecasts that use moving averages and exponential smoothing are flawed because they do not deal with the obvious seasonality of sales at the Forever Young Boutique. If adequate forecasts are to be made, this seasonality must be accounted for. There are several ways to deal with seasonality. Already mentioned is the technique of basing, say, a quarterly forecast on past data from similar quarters. In Kathy Wilkerson's case, however, when monthly forecasts are needed and only a few years of history are available, another technique is probably preferable.

This technique employs the observation that demand can be decomposed into several components: a trend term, a seasonality term, and a randomness term.* Thus,

Demand = Trend · Seasonality factor
· Randomness component

If moving averages or exponential smoothing or some other technique is to work well, then the data should be purged of their seasonality so that the trend can be identified and exploited for making the forecast. To purge seasonality, we can develop some seasonal indices (monthly, in this case) that can be used to deflate actual sales, leaving only the trend and the random-

ness components. These seasonal indices are typically ratios: average demand for the season (or month) divided by an average of demand for the 12 months surrounding it (or some time period not susceptible to the seasonality which you are trying to control).

There are several steps to follow to deseasonalize data in this way. Consider them for the Young Forever case.

1. Calculate a 12-month moving average of demand (where there is no seasonality, by definition) where that demand is centered on the month in question. For proper centering, we need an odd number of observations, so that developing centered moving average of demand for 12 months is itself a three-step procedure:
   a. Calculate a 12-month mean, using months 1–12. This will be centered on month 6 ½.
   b. Advance the calculation by a month and calculate the new 12-month mean that is centered on month 7 ½. This calculation uses months 2–13.
   c. Average the two 12-month means to get a value centered on month 7.
   Table 4-14 displays uncentered moving averages and then centered moving averages for the Young Forever data. Note that the first 6 months of data and the last 6 months are "lost" in the calculations.

2. Develop seasonal indices (or, in this case, monthly indices) by dividing the sales figures of Table 4-10 by the centered moving averages of Table 4-14. See Table 4-15.

*One could also include a cyclicality term to account for business cycle fluctuations. This discussion omits consideration of cyclicality, in part because cyclicality could have been expected to play little or no role in explaining the Young Forever Boutique's steady growth. More complete discussion of forecasting demonstrates how cyclicality can be removed from an identified, underlying trend.

TABLE 4-14   Moving averages for 12 months' demand, centered and not centered

Moving averages (not centered, value placed into month 7)

	YEAR 1	YEAR 2	YEAR 3	YEAR 4	YEAR 5
January	—	$8,332.96	$11,041.85	$15,600.72	$18,202.68
February	—	8,408.22	11,271.16	15,916.01	18,626.57
March	—	8,594.33	11,361.26	16,215.90	
April	—	8,864.34	11,681.78	16,765.42	
May	—	9,108.07	12,254.67	17,359.18	
June	—	9,282.80	12,784.51	17,229.73	
July	—	9,572.60	13,615.73	16,546.72	
August	—	9,958.89	13,694.82	16,431.31	
September	$7,333.74	10,280.42	14,069.64	16,486.21	
October	7,713.78	10,090.17	15,009.87	17,848.68	
November	8,049.50	10,851.77	14,925.14	17,850.00	
December	8,311.33	10,931.72	15,278.09	18.077.13	

Moving averages (centered)

January	—	$ 8,370.59	$11,156.51	$15,758.37	$18,414.63
February	—	8,501.28	11,316.21	16,065.96	
March	—	8,729.34	11,521.52	16,490.66	
April	—	8,986.21	11,968.23	17,062.30	
May	—	9,195.44	12,519.59	17,294.46	
June	—	9,427.70	13,200.12	16,888.23	
July	—	9,765.75	13,655.28	16,489.02	
August	—	10,119.66	13,882.23	16,458.76	
September	$7,523.76	10,185.30	14,539.76	17,167.45	
October	7,881.64	10,470.97	14,967.51	17,849.34	
November	8,180.42	10,891.75	15,101.62	17,963.57	
December	8,322.15	10,986.79	15,439.41	18,139.91	

3. Average these seasonal indices over the years for which they were developed. That is, average all the January indices, average all the February indices, and so on. (Table 4-15, Panel B, column 1).

4. Sum these average indices and scale them up or down appropriately. In this case, the sum of the monthly indices is 1180.33. If sales were the same in every month, however, the monthly indices would total exactly 1200. Thus, the indices as originally calculated can be scaled up by 1.0167 (= 1200/1180.33). (Table 4-15, Panel B, column 2).

5. Divide the monthly sales figures of Table 4-10 by the seasonal (monthly) indices to purge the seasonality from those raw sales figures. Table 4-16 displays the deseasonalized sales figures.

Identifying Trends

Once the data have been purged of seasonality, what remains are the trend and randomness factors. Normally, we choose to think about the trend as a linear function of time (sales change by $X each time period), although, just as easily, we could think of the trend as exponential, logarithmic, or something else. For the sake of simplicity, let us think of the trend as linear. Thus, mathematically, we view the sales data as exhibiting the following form.

(4-1) $$D_t = a + b P_t$$

TABLE 4-15   Seasonal indices Young Forever Boutique
Panel A. Data transformed to seasonal indices (raw sales divided by centered moving averages)

	YEAR 1	YEAR 2	YEAR 3	YEAR 4	YEAR 5
January	—	76.96	98.75	75.93	57.46
February	—	51.23	73.03	79.43	
March	—	104.55	59.40	109.92	
April	—	122.08	168.03	111.90	
May	—	110.81	89.05	88.95	
June	—	74.71	63.37	72.46	
July	—	68.78	69.34	80.37	
August	—	90.32	73.63	83.97	
September	107.33	111.09	104.28	126.73	
October	100.40	103.51	118.34	139.15	
November	110.68	102.38	115.94	88.82	
December	169.60	160.12	178.55	106.78	
		1,184.41	1,211.71	1,164.41	

Panel B. Average of seasonal indices

	UNCORRECTED	CORRECTED
January	77.09	78.37
February	68.10	69.23
March	91.29	92.81
April	134.00	136.23
May	96.27	97.87
June	70.18	71.35
July	72.83	74.04
August	82.64	84.02
September	112.36	114.23
October	115.35	117.27
November	104.46	106.20
December	155.76	158.36
	1,180.33	

TABLE 4-16   Deseasonalized sales for the Young Forever Boutique

	YEAR 1	YEAR 2	YEAR 3	YEAR 4	YEAR 5
January	—	$ 8,142.24	$14,057.10	15,268.19	$13,501.01
February	—	6,364.05	11,937.22	18,434.18	19,385.92
March	$4,920.16	9,834.02	7,374.15	19,530.98	37,147.15
April	5,095.71	8,052.89	14,761.57	14,015.19	14,026.86
May	7,200.60	10,411.04	11,391.27	15,718.82	18,503.67
June	9,508.58	9,872.25	11,724.46	17,150.67	19,262.23
July	7,852.82	9,072.62	12,789.14	17,899.15	24,769.38
August	8,219.92	10,878.03	12,164.96	16,448.19	
September	7,069.18	9,905.62	13,272.70	19,045.47	
October	6,748.15	9,242.26	15,104.93	21,180.27	
November	8,525.59	10,499.94	15,486.81	15,024.11	
December	8,912.97	11,108.99	17,407.68	12,232.07	

where D_t is the actual sales for period t, P_t is the time period applicable, a is a constant, and b describes the trend.

The constant term a and the trend coefficient b can be estimated statistically through a technique termed linear regression.

✳ ASIDE ✳

Linear Regression

Standard linear regression uses the principle of least squares to select the straight line that best fits a scatter of data in two dimensions. Look at Figure 4-17, which displays a scatter of points in the xy plane. Point (x_i, y_i) lies above the line $a + bx$ by the amount e_i. That is,

$$e_1 = y_i - \hat{y}_i = y_i - (a + bx_i)$$

The principle of least squares states that a and b—which determine the positioning and slope of the estimating line—should be chosen so that

$$\sum_{i=1}^{n} e_i^2$$

is as small as possible.

This minimization of the sum of the e_i^2's over all n data points is accomplished when

$$\hat{b} = \frac{\sum_{i=1}^{n}(x_i - \bar{x})(y_i - \bar{y})}{\sum_{i=1}^{n}(x_i - \bar{x})^2}$$

The value of a is found as a residual,

$$\hat{a} = \bar{y} - \hat{b}\bar{x}$$

where $\bar{x}$ and $\bar{y}$ are the arithmetic means of the x's and y's in the scatter. It turns out that $\hat{a}$ and $\hat{b}$ share some desirable properties, which are best explored by consulting applied statistics or econometrics texts.

A common measure of the goodness of fit of a regression line to the data is the R^2 statistic. It is an estimate of the fraction of the variation in the data that is "explained" by the regression line itself. Values for R^2 vary from 0 to 1. A value of 0 indicates that the regression line has uncovered no relationship of independent and dependent variables, while a value of 1 indicates that all of the data points lie on the regression line. Naturally, high values of R^2 are sought, when other factors are equal.

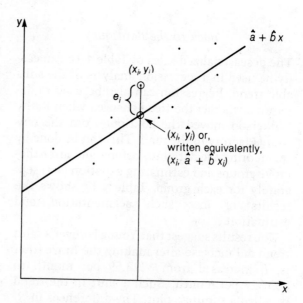

FIGURE 4-17   Scatter of data and principle of least squares.

✳

TABLE 4-17   Trend identification regression results for the Young Forever Boutique

Results for before-move data	
Estimates of *a*:	$6,007.23
b:	$ 223.59 per month
$R^2 = 0.62$	

Results for after-move data	
Estimates of *a*:	$13,783.32
b:	$ 307.27 per month
$R^2 = 0.18$	

Back to the Boutique

The deseasonalized sales of Table 4-16 can easily be used in a regression analysis of the suitable trend. Regression can also be used to determine whether the trend changed when Kathy Wilkerson moved the boutique from the renovated factory to the mall. This can be done by segmenting the data into before- and after-the-move groups and estimating equation (4-1) separately for each group. Table 4-17 shows the results of just such segmentation and estimation.

The results suggest that Young Forever's sales trend did increase after making the move (that is, *b* increased from $223.59 per month to $307.27 per month). Such a shift in the trend is called a turning point. The differences in R^2 statistics also suggest that Kathy was right to sense that sales were more erratic in the mall; the trend explains less of the variation for the after-move data than it does for the before-move data.*

By using the estimated trend to predict a deseasonalized forecast and then by applying the relevant seasonal (monthly) index, forecasts can be made of the Young Forever Boutique's sales.

Five months of forecasts are shown in Table 4-18.

There are other, more sophisticated techniques for forecasting.[10] They are too elaborate for full explanation in a text on production/operations management, but some brief comments on them are in order.

- *Adaptive Filtering.* This technique often gives better results than exponential smoothing or moving averages. It uses weighted averages of past actual demands but allows the weights to vary from period to period in such a way that the forecast error is substantially lowered. Each weight in the adaptive filtering scheme is adjusted by an equation that uses the error in the previous forecast period.

- *Box-Jenkins.* Even more sophisticated than the adaptive filtering technique is the technique devised by George Box and Gwilym Jenkins. The Box-Jenkins method is particularly appropriate for complex time periods in which one suspects that a variety of patterns exists in the data. The technique is too complex to describe briefly, and it can be expensive to run, requiring considerable past histories of observations.

Causal Models

The other major type of quantitative forecasting model uses not only time series data on the demand itself but also time series data on other variables that could be expected to influence demand in a cause and effect way. A model that can accurately capture the cause and effect relationship among the other variables and the demand can be very useful, especially in pick-

---

*There are also tests to determine whether the two regressions could reasonably be expected to be truly different from one another. Refer to statistical or econometrics texts for an explanation.

TABLE 4-18   Predicting sales for the next five periods
Young Forever Boutique

	DESEASONALIZED ON TREND	SEASONAL ADJUSTMENT MADE
August	$21,465.07	$18,034.95
September	21,772.34	24,870.54
October	22,079.61	25,892.76
November	22,386.88	23,774.87
December	22,694.15	35,938.46

ing turning points in the demand pattern. However, these models tend to be expensive to run and the analysis required to define them properly takes more time; thus they are much more appropriate for long-term forecasting than for short-term forecasting. The two major classes of causal models are single equation regression models and multiple equation regression analysis, sometimes termed *econometric modelling*. In single equation regression analysis, the item forecast, or dependent variable, is postulated to vary systematically with one or more "independent variables." These independent variables can be constructed in a variety of ways, including the use of time series data (GNP, industrial production), past values of the dependent variable, and dummy variables (for example, 1 if the month is May and 0 otherwise). Regression analysis fits the specified independent variables to the dependent variable by using historical data; this is termed estimating the coefficients of the model's specified independent variables. Predictions can then be made by assigning expected future values to the independent variables and solving the estimated equation for the dependent variable's value. Econometric modelling is a step up from simple regression analysis in that it looks at collections of regression equations where some of the dependent variables in one equation turn up as independent variables in the other equations. Econometric modelling, in particular, can be very expensive and time consuming, since the data demands are voracious and the estimation tricky.

Qualitative Techniques

The techniques previously explored make use of quantitative data, developed from history. However, if one thinks that the future is likely not to depend much on history—because of vast disruptions in the economy or the industry, or simply because what is to be forecast is new and uncharted—one may then want to rely on the expertise of specific people. Qualitative forecasting is often applied to new technology, trying to forecast the kinds of changes to expect. The Delphi method is perhaps the most common qualitative approach. This method uses a panel of experts who are asked particular questions. Their answers are collected and summarized (with means, ranges, standard deviations, and so on), and this information is passed out to the panel. The panel then deliberates for another round of forecasting using the information provided. Their responses are again collected, summarized, and disseminated. Numerous rounds of prediction and summary can occur. In some cases, consensus is reached after several rounds; this is particularly true if outlying responses are not held with much conviction. On the other hand, consensus is not guaranteed if outliers are stubborn about their views.

Choosing a Forecasting Technique

As was mentioned at the start of this section, particular forecasting techniques are associated, in the main, with different forecasting needs. The simple time series techniques are easy to use and are generally applied to very short-term forecasts of individual product models and variations. In those cases, history is likely to be a good guide to the immediate future. The more sophisticated of the time series techniques are more useful when the historical pattern appears to be more confused and when varied trends in the data are likely to exist. The causal and qualitative techniques are more satisfactory for longer-term needs, with the qualitative techniques being at an advantage only when history is deemed to be of little significance for prediction.

B

BASIC CONCEPTS OF LINEAR PROGRAMMING

The statement of the production planning problem (see Situation 4-1, Ridgely Sporting Goods) can be broken down into pieces. First, there is the mathematical expression for schedule cost, which we wish to minimize. This expression is often termed the "objective function," since minimizing that function is our objective. Second, there are the numerous constraints or restrictions that we have placed on the solution. These constraints, in turn, can be broken down into "structural constraints" and "nonnegativity conditions." Together, the structural constraints and the nonnegativity conditions define the so-called "feasible region."

The notion of a feasible region is important since it is only within the feasible region that all of the constraints are met. Thus, our cost minimum, given the constraints, must also be found within the feasible region. Our example of the Ridgely Sporting Goods Company is too complex to represent in two-dimensional graphic terms; let us scale down the problem to consider only two structural constraints and two nonnegativity conditions. Arbitrarily, let us choose the following:

Structural constraints:

$$1.5X + Y \leq 12$$
$$-X + Y \leq 5$$

Nonnegativity conditions:

$$X \geq 0, \ Y \geq 0$$

What is the feasible region defined by these constraints? Figure 4-18 offers a picture of the implied feasible region. Note that the feasible region is bounded by straight lines. That is what is meant by a *linear* program; lines (in two dimensions) or planes (in three or more dimensions) always serve as boundaries of the feasible region. In turn, this linearity means that the feasible region has very definite corners, the importance of which we will soon explore. Only in the feasible region are all of the inequalities of the constraints met, and it is in this region that our solution will be found.

Let us turn now to consider the objective function to be minimized (or to be maximized—linear programming can do either). Arbitrarily again, let us define the following as the objective function to be minimized: $-X + 2Y$. We can interpret this objective function as a cost function that we want to minimize. If we introduce cost, then, as a third dimension, we see that the objective function is a plane that cuts through our feasible region, as demonstrated in Figure 4-19. Again, the *linear* nature of our problem ensures that the objective function will be a plane, and not some curved shape.

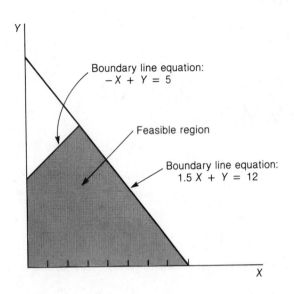

FIGURE 4-18   The feasible region defined by structural constraints and nonnegativity conditions.

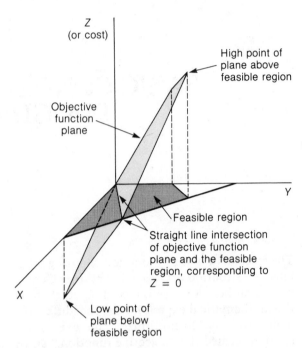

FIGURE 4-19   Objective function plane depicted with feasible region.

Solving our minimization problem then becomes a matter of choosing the point in the feasible region over which the objective function plane is lowest. Although this task may sound difficult, the linearity of the geometry involved ensures that the minimum cost point will occur *not only on the feasible region's boundary but at a corner as well.* This is an extraordinarily convenient result: in solving a linear problem we need evaluate only the corners of the feasible region to determine those values of the variables that either maximize or minimize the given objective function. This statement is one form of the basic theorem of linear programming.

We may be able to see this result geometrically, but what does this really mean in terms of our cost minimizing example? The logic is this. If by pursuing an activity (X or Y) we can cut costs, we should pursue that activity as long as we can. Because of the linearities involved, costs always remain proportional to changes in X or Y. No economies or diseconomies of scale are encountered; production is always at constant returns to scale. If pursuing an activity like X or Y cut costs, then we should use up as much X or Y as we can. We cannot be penalized for using too much. In our example, using Y always adds to costs; thus we should use as little Y as possible—in fact, we can get away with using none. Using X, on the other hand, always cuts costs; so we should use up as much

*Unless, of course, the slope of the isocost lines is the same as that of a boundary line, in which case the entire boundary as well as its two corner endpoints will be optimal.

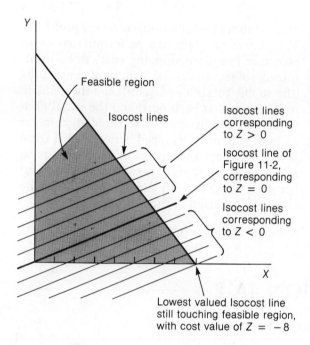

Feasible region

Isocost lines

Isocost lines corresponding to Z > 0

Isocost line of Figure 11-2, corresponding to Z = 0

Isocost lines corresponding to Z < 0

Lowest valued Isocost line still touching feasible region, with cost value of $Z = -8$

FIGURE 4-20 Isocost lines and the feasible region.

X as we can—namely, 8 units, as determined by our feasible region. This logic forces us to the corner solution of X = 8, Y = 0, and a cost minimum of −8.

This fundamental result that objective function minimums or maximums always occur at corners can be seen another way, by using isocost lines. We can think of cutting the objective function plane with another plane that is parallel to the feasible region's XY plane but that takes on different values of Z (cost). The intersection of these two planes is a straight line such as is shown in Figure 4-19. Such lines are isocost lines: any combination of X and Y that lies along such lines shares the same cost. The projection of these isocost lines onto the XY plane (the feasible region's plane) is a family of parallel lines. In our particular example, the isocost lines all have a slope of $+\frac{1}{2}$. Figure 4-20

depicts this family of isocost lines superimposed on the feasible region.

As a study of Figure 4-20 should make clear, the lowest valued (or the highest valued) isocost line that intersects the feasible region will always intersect that region at a corner. Thus, solving for the optimum value of the objective function of a linear program need only entail an evaluation of the corners of the feasible region.

LINEAR PROGRAMMING IN PRACTICE

That linear programs can be solved by evaluating just the corners of the feasible region is comforting, but the fact that there were only four corners to the feasible region in our small example should not fool anybody into believing that solving linear programs is necessarily easy. In our situation with the Ridgely Sporting Goods Company and the 99 variables and 153 constraints we must define in order to state its linear program for schedule cost minimization, the number of corners to the feasible region is well over 10^{24}. Hardly a reassuring number.

It is of some importance then to note that several techniques can be programmed on computers to search systematically through the astronomical numbers of possible corner positions for the optimal solutions to linear programs. The most notable of these techniques is called the *simplex method*. It does not evaluate all the corners of the feasible region but rather selects, in a very systematic way, those areas of the feasible region that best improve upon the value of the objective function. With each selection, the method gets closer and closer to the optimum; after so many of them we are guaranteed a solution, if in fact one exists.

Since it is highly unlikely that future business managers will be called on to solve linear programs by hand using the simplex method—after all, that is what computers are for—this book does not attempt to describe the workings of the simplex method.[11] However, it is important to know how to set up a problem like an aggregate plan or master schedule development so that a "canned" computer program can solve it.

As an introduction to the formulation of linear programs see Situation 4A-2.

Discussion of Bailey Steel
Products Company

The current circumstances of Bailey Steel Products can be modelled easily as a linear program.

(It is often termed *the transportation problem*.) That linear program can be formulated as an objective function (shipping costs to be minimized) subject to several structural constraints (the supply totals for each mill and the demand requirements at each port) and the usual nonnegativity conditions. To accomplish this, let X_{ij} be the quantity shipped between mill i and port j. Number the mills and the ports as in tables above, so that X_{13} is the quantity shipped between the Ohio mill and San Francisco. The objective function is thus

$$\text{Minimize Shipping Cost} = 25\ X_{11} + 40\ X_{12} + 75\ X_{13} + 50\ X_{21} + 10\ X_{22} + 60\ X_{23}$$

SITUATION 4A-2

BAILEY STEEL PRODUCTS COMPANY

The Bailey Steel Products Company manufactured specialized steel tube products used primarily in the construction of off-shore oil drilling rigs. The company operated two mills, one in Ohio and one in Texas. Steel tube from those mills was used in oil rigs all over the world, but the company shipped nearly all of its output to one of three ports: Baltimore, Houston, and San Francisco. The shipments to Baltimore serviced accounts in Europe (such as the North Sea). The shipments to Houston serviced

domestic accounts (for example, the Gulf of Mexico) and the shipments to San Francisco serviced some domestic accounts in the Pacific but also some in the Far East. The shipping costs to these various ports differed, naturally, depending upon which mill made the shipment. A summary of the shipping costs per ton and the weekly quantities of steel tube supplied from each mill and required by each port for the company's established accounts follows:

SUPPLY OF STEEL TUBE PER WEEK		REQUIRED AT EACH PORT	
From Mill #1 (Ohio)	600 Tons	1. Baltimore	300 Tons
From Mill #2 (Texas)	400 Tons	2. Houston	500 Tons
		3. San Francisco	200 Tons

SHIPPING COSTS FROM EACH MILL			
From Mill #1 (Ohio) to:		From Mill #2 (Texas) to:	
1. Baltimore	$25 per ton	1. Baltimore	$50 per ton
2. Houston	$40 per ton	2. Houston	$10 per ton
3. San Francisco	$75 per ton	3. San Francisco	$60 per ton

The issue to be resolved was how much steel tube ought to be shipped from each of the two mills to each of the three ports.

Subject to

$$X_{11} + X_{12} + X_{13} = 600$$
$$X_{21} + X_{22} + X_{23} = 400$$
$$X_{11} + X_{21} = 300$$
$$X_{12} + X_{22} = 500$$
$$X_{13} + X_{23} = 200$$

and X_{11}, X_{12}, X_{13}, X_{21}, X_{22}, and X_{23} all ≥ 0.

This is an easy problem for a linear programming computer software package to solve, and the solution makes a lot of sense and can even be demonstrated by hand. The solution has a shipping cost of $30,500, and calls for Mill 1 (Ohio) to ship 300 tons to Baltimore, 100 tons to Houston, and 200 tons to San Francisco. The Texas mill feeds all of its output to Houston. Thus,

$X_{11} = 300$	$X_{21} = 0$
$X_{12} = 100$	$X_{22} = 400$
$X_{13} = 200$	$X_{23} = 0$

DUALITY AND THE ECONOMIC INTERPRETATION OF LINEAR PROGRAMMING

Linear programming can be used either to minimize or to maximize an objective function. As it happens, however, any linear program designed to minimize an objective function can be restated as a completely equivalent linear program to maximize a different, although related, objective function. This complementary linear program is termed the *dual*. All linear programs, therefore, come in pairs—a primal program and its dual. It does not matter which is designated the primal program and which the dual, since the dual of the dual is the original primal program.

How are the dual and primal programs related? Suppose the primal program, like the production schedule development at Ridgely Sporting Goods, involves cost minimization and can be characterized abstractly as follows:

minimize

$$C_1 N_2 + \ldots + C_m N_m$$

subject to

$$a_{11} N_1 + \ldots + a_{1m} N_m \geq P_1$$
$$\cdot \qquad \cdot \qquad \cdot$$
$$\cdot \qquad \cdot \qquad \cdot$$
$$\cdot \qquad \cdot \qquad \cdot$$
$$a_{n1} N_1 + \ldots + a_{nm} N_m \geq P_n$$

and

$$N_1 \geq 0, \ldots, N_m \geq 0$$

Then the dual program can be written as:

maximize

$$P_1 Q_1 + \ldots + P_n Q_n$$

subject to

$$a_{11} Q_1 + \ldots + a_{n1} Q_n \leq C_1$$
$$\cdot \qquad \cdot \qquad \cdot$$
$$\cdot \qquad \cdot \qquad \cdot$$
$$\cdot \qquad \cdot \qquad \cdot$$
$$a_{1m} Q_1 + \ldots + a_{nm} Q_n \leq C_m$$

and

$$Q_1 \geq 0, \ldots, Q_n \geq 0$$

It is worth noting some of the transpositions and changes involved in setting up the dual:

1. The goal of minimizing the primal's objective function becomes the maximization of the dual's own objective function.

2. The coefficients on the primal program's objective function variables become the right-hand-side constraints in the dual program, and the right-hand-side constraints in the primal become the objective function variable coefficients in the dual.

3. The m variables of the primal's objective function and the n constraints of that program are rearranged into n variables of the dual's objective function and m constraints in the dual.

4. The matrix of coefficients of the constraints in the primal program are transposed around the main diagonal to yield the corresponding dual matrix. Thus, if there are n constraints involving m variables in the primal program, there will be m constraints involving n variables in the dual program. The a_{ij}th coefficient in the primal program is transposed to be the a_{ji}th coefficient in the dual.

5. Inequalities reading "$\geq$" in the primal program read "$\leq$" in the dual.

6. The variables denoted by N in the primal program are replaced by variables denoted by Q. Further, if the N variables could be interpreted as physical quantities in the primal program, the Q variables of the dual can be interpreted as dollar values.

What does all this mean? Let us consider once again our problem of developing a master schedule for the Ridgely Sporting Goods Company. In that problem we wanted to minimize schedule costs and the variables we were interested in were physical quantities like inventories, production rates, and workforce levels. The dual of this problem, although yielding the same solution, carries with it a different interpretation. The dual, rather than seeking to minimize costs, seeks instead to maximize profit. The variables we are interested in are the dollar-valued portions of the profit we can impute to each item such as inventories, workforce, and production level. In purely economic terms, these contrasts between primal and dual programs make sense. Minimizing costs is likely also to lead to maximizing profits, and the optimal quantities of several variables are likely also to lead to an optimal apportionment of the profit among the rival variables.

Let us push this evaluation of the meaning of the dual and its solution even further. In seeking to maximize profits, the dual program's solution for the Q's tells us what would be added to the company's profits if somehow any input Q_i could be increased past its constraint of C_i. But what is this telling us? Merely what the *marginal* value of Q_i is to us in increasing company profits. When profits are maximized, any other imputation of the profits among the variables will not yield higher profits. That is, the *opportunity costs* of a different apportionment are negative or zero. Thus, lurking in the background (the dual) of all programming problems are these fundamental concepts of marginal value and opportunity cost. Solutions to the basic problems facing businesses, those involving the allocation of their scarce resources, simply cannot avoid the fundamental concepts of marginal value and opportunity cost.

C

PROJECT MANAGEMENT AND SCHEDULING

A project—constructing the World Trade Center or sending a man to the moon—shares many characteristics with other types of production processes. We can picture a project with the same kind of precedence relationship with which we pictured the line flow process. Certain activities must be completed before others begin, and each activity can be expected to take a given period of time, just as in other process types. But our concern for balance in the factory, so prominent in our thinking about production processes, does not trouble us in thinking about a project since a project is, by definition, a one-time endeavor and workers can generally expect to work only so long on it and then move on to something else. It is typical for a project to employ wildly fluctuating numbers of people, many with different skills. We do not worry about idleness—construction workers move on to the next project as do space scientists and engineers.

What does trouble us in a project is getting it done on time, for projects often have important deadlines to meet. Scheduling is thus absolutely critical to the management of a project. Several techniques have been developed to highlight the project activities that must be accomplished on time (or else risk delaying the entire project) and the activities that can be delayed somewhat. One such scheduling technique is called the critical path method; what follows is a brief description of its rationale and workings.

THE CRITICAL PATH CONCEPT

As an illustration, let us consider the simplified example of a project many companies face—the start-up of a new plant. The major tasks involved in a plant start-up are arrayed and described in Table 4-19. The table makes clear that some tasks cannot be started until other tasks (predecessors) have been completed.

The precedence relationships of the start-up can be depicted in a graph or network, as shown in Figure 4-21. This network follows a particular convention known as *activity-on-node*. This convention is intuitively appealing and somewhat less confusing than the alternative convention, known as *activity-on-arrow*.

The key principle of the critical path concept is that a project cannot be completed any faster than the longest time path between the project's start and its finish. In Figure 4-21 the longest path from the start (project approval) to the

TABLE 4-19   A plant start-up project

JOB NAME	JOB DESCRIPTION	IMMEDIATE PREDECESSORS	TIME (MONTHS)
A	Selection of plant manager and management personnel	—	3
B	Site survey soil test	—	1
C	Extension of roads, water, utilities, sewer	—	6
D	Selection and purchase of equipment	A	2
E	Final engineering plans for construction	B	3
F	Employment interviews and hiring	A	3
G	Equipment delivery	D	9
H	Construction of facility	E	11
I	Precise layout of plant	D, E	1
J	Institution of management systems for control of production, inventory, purchasing, accounting	A	4
K	Worker training	F, G, H	2
L	Equipment and system installation	G, H, I, J	1

finish (plant start-up) involves the following activities—B, E, H, and K; they take a total of 17 months. The longest path between project approval and plant start-up is termed the *critical path*, primarily because any delay along this path of activities sets back the entire project. It is this critical path that merits the most management attention.

All the other paths from start to finish enjoy at least a month's slack time, and so they can experience delays of varying lengths and still not harm the 17-month completion schedule. For example, the next two longest paths after the critical path involve the following activities:

1. B-E-H-L ——— 16 months
2. A-D-G-K ——— 16 months

There can be delays of up to a month on these two paths without setting back the entire project. However, note that the first path is very much like the critical path itself; it differs only

in that activity L is substituted for activity K. The slack in this path then can be taken only on activity L (equipment and system installation). If a delay occurred on any other activity, say H (construction of the facility), the critical path would also be affected, and the entire project would be delayed.

The second path is much more flexible about where its slack can be used up. Only one of its activities, K (worker training), is shared with the critical path. Thus, its month of slack can be used up on activities A, D or G without affecting the critical path in any way.

Other paths, of course, have considerably more slack and can be accomplished at a more leisurely pace, if need be. For example, the uppermost path in the diagram (A-F-K) is expected to take eight months, with only activity K on the critical path. Activity F could be delayed as much as nine months without making the project late. However, activity A could not be de-

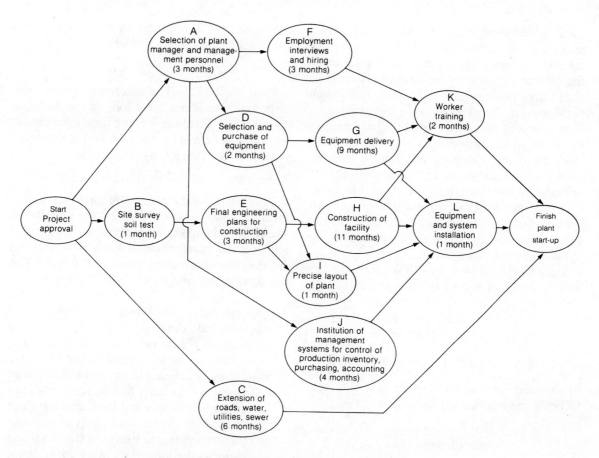

FIGURE 4-21   Precedence diagram for a plant start-up project.

layed that long, since it is on one of the second longest paths and can be delayed only a month before it would affect the project's completion time.

This example raises an important point about critical paths and project scheduling. As time wears on in a project's life, delays and even some speed-ups can be expected. What may look like the critical path at a project's start (such as B-E-H-K) may not remain the critical path if many delays (or speed-ups) strike the project. This means that the project manager should periodically recalculate the critical path to check that he or she is focusing on the activities that really matter to finishing a project in the least time.

Calculating the Critical Path[12]

To this point we have calculated the critical path solely by inspecting all the paths and choosing the one with the longest duration. In simple cases, such as this generalized plant start-up, inspection is a perfectly feasible and reasonable way of selecting the critical path. When projects get more complicated, with many more activities, inspection as a means of computing the critical path bogs down. Happily there is an alternative procedure or algorithm, which can cut down the speed of solution markedly.

In essence, the critical path algorithm is a procedure to identify which activities have some slack time and which do not. Those with no slack time, of course, make up the critical path or paths. Before describing the algorithm, however, it is helpful to define some terms:

Early Start (ES)—the earliest time a job can begin, which is the latest time that any of the job's predecessors are finished.

Early Finish (EF)—the earliest time a job can finish, which is the early start time plus the time it takes to do the job.

For any job i, the early start and early finish can be represented symbolically.

$$ES(i) = max [EF \text{ (all of } i\text{'s predecessors)]},$$

or the start time of the project if we are considering the beginning jobs.

$$EF(i) = ES(i) + t(i)$$
$$\text{where } t(i) \text{ is the time}$$

to perform job i.

Late Start (LS)—The latest a job can start without causing the entire project to be completed any later, which is the late finish time less the time for the job.

Late Finish (LF)—The latest time a job can finish, which is the earliest time that any of the job's successors have to be started. These can be represented symbolically, as well, for any job i.

$$LF(i) = min [LS \text{ (all of } i\text{'s successors)]}$$

or the earliest finish time for the project if we are considering the ending jobs.

$$LS(i) = LF(i) - t(i)$$

Total Slack (TS)—The difference between the early and late starts for a job, or the early or late finishes. Total slack is the time a particular job could be delayed without delaying the completion of the project. Symbolically,

$$TS(i) = LS(i) - ES(i) = LF(i) - EF(i)$$

The critical path algorithm involves calculating ES, EF, LS, and LF for all the jobs in the network and then comparing them to discover which nodes have zero total slack.* These nodes are the ones comprising the critical path(s). The calculation and comparison involve three steps:

1. *Forward Pass.* The forward pass through the network calculates the early start *(ES)* and early finish *(EF)* times. It does so by moving from start to finish, figuring first the early start time and then adding the job's duration to it to figure the early finish. The early start for any job is calculated by scanning all of its immediate predecessor activities (those with arrows pointing into it in the path) and choosing as the job's early start the latest of all the predecessors' early finish times. The *ES* and *EF* times for our plant start-up example are noted in Figure 4-22.

2. *Backward Pass.* The backward pass through the network calculates the late start *(LS)* and late finish *(LF)* times. It does this by moving from the finish back to the start, figuring first the late finish times and then deriving the late start times by subtracting the job's duration from the late finish time. The late finish for any job is calculated by scanning

---

*Or a minimum total slack if there is some discretion about the completion time possible for the project. Note the appendix's later discussion of windows of time.

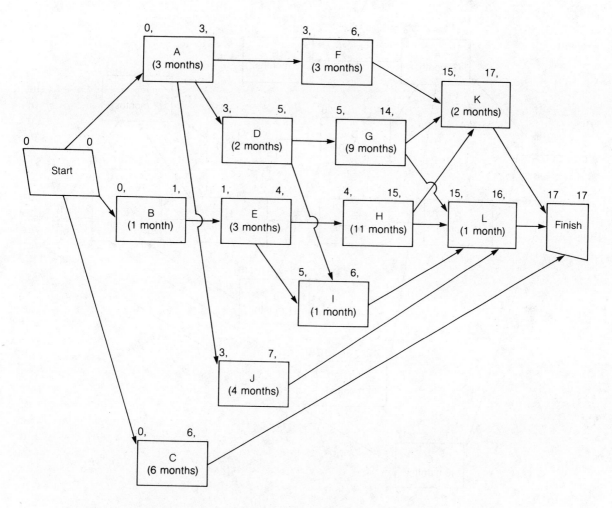

FIGURE 4-22 Early start (number at upper left of box) and early finish (number at upper right of box) months for the plant startup project depicted in Figure 4-21.

all of its immediate successor activities (those with arrows leading away from it on the path) and choosing as the job's late finish the earliest of all the successors' late start times. The LF and LS times for our plant start-up example are noted in Figure 4-23.

3. *Comparison.* The comparison of either early start with early finish or late start with late finish is the way to figure whether the job has any total slack (TS) associated with it. If the $LS(i) - ES(i)$ or $LF(i) - EF(i)$ calculations are zero, then the job has no total slack and is on the critical path. Figure 4-24 combines all the times in one diagram and displays the critical path.

For very large projects, of course, and ones that go into significant detail, even following

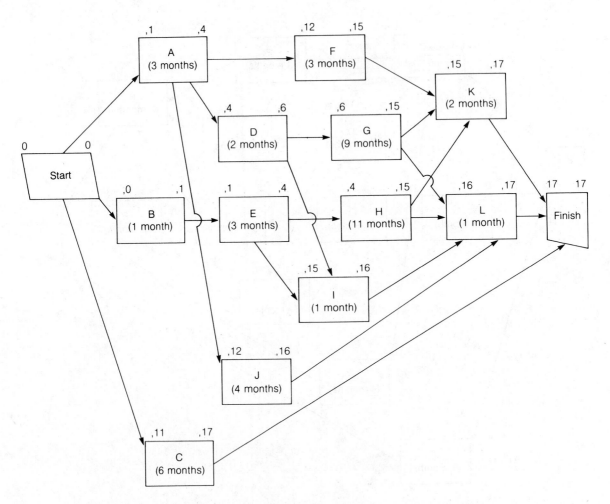

FIGURE 4-23   Late start (number at upper left of box) and late finish (number at upper right of box) months for the plant startup project depicted in Figure 4-21.

the critical path method can become tedious. To aid in the analysis, there are computer programs that calculate the critical path. These can be used with ease to determine how differences in expected completion times for various activities (and even the introduction of variations in the network of activities itself) affect the critical path(s). Because so many things can go awry in a project, it is advanta-geous to compute the critical path on a regular basis so as not to be caught napping.

Project Costs and Timing and the Critical Path

Frequently, actual projects (such as the new plant start-up outlined in Figure 4-22) need not be finished in the least time possible but, rather,

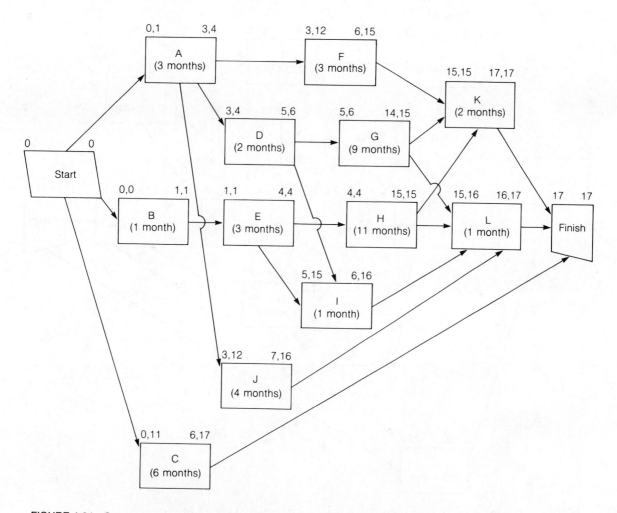

FIGURE 4-24 Composite of starting and finishing months given in Figures 4-22 and 4-23 for the plant startup project.

can be finished during any portion of a "window" of time. When during the acceptable window of time the project's finish ought to be targeted depends largely on the project's managers. Often they are influenced by cost considerations, because it is not uncommon for a project's contract to stipulate rewards for an early finish and penalties for a late finish. These rewards and penalties must be weighted against

the costs that hurrying up any of the project's activities could impose on the project's budget.

Windows of Time and the Critical Path

Windows of time can be easily incorporated into the calculation of the critical path; in fact, the terminology is already in place to handle them. The acceptable window of time can be denoted as the difference between the early finish and

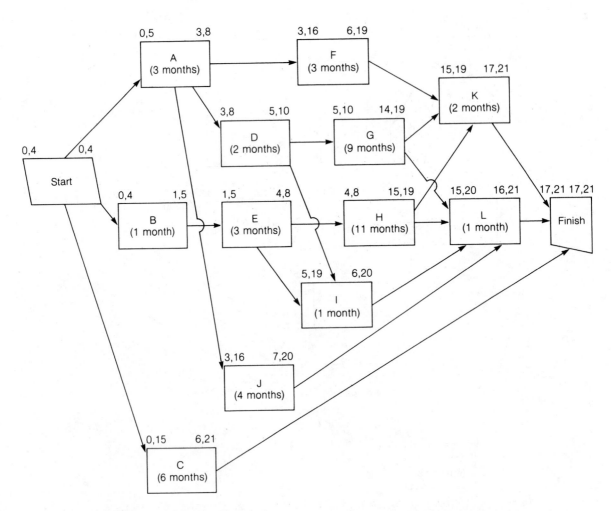

FIGURE 4-25 The addition of four months (a window of time) to the plant startup project.

the late finish (or between the early start and the late start). To return to our example, if the plant start-up could be completed between 17 and 21 months from the start, the values for Figure 4-24 would be recast as in Figure 4-25.

Building a window of time in the critical path computation makes it important to distinguish between two different kinds of slack time during the project: total slack and free slack. *Total*

slack, as discussed previously, is the difference between the early and late finishes (or early and late starts) for any activity. An activity's total slack time is the maximum time that activity may be delayed beyond its early start without forcing the delay of the entire project. As previously noted, this notion of total slack can be used to define the critical path; the critical path is composed of those activities that have the lowest total slack (the smallest differences—possibly zero—between early and late starts or finishes).

Free slack, on the other hand, is the time by which an activity can be delayed without delaying the early start of any other activity. *Free slack* is defined as the difference between an activity's early finish time and the earliest of the early start times for all its immediate successor activities. Symbolically, the free slack (FS) for any job *i* can be defined as

$$FS(i) = min \, [ES \, (all \, of \, i's \, immediate \, successors)] - EF(i)$$

Consider the path A-J-L in Figure 4-25. Activity L can be delayed at most a month without risking the delay of the entire project; as it is, its early finish time (16 months) is but 1 month shy of the project completion's early start month (17 months). Its free slack is 1 month. Activity J, on the other hand, has more free slack. Its early finish time of 7 months is 8 months shy of its only successor activity's (K's) early start time of 15 months; its free slack is thus 8 months. Activity A, the predecessor to activity, has no free slack because its early finish time (3 months) is equal to the early start time of activities D, F, and J.

This lack of any free slack does not mean, however, that if activity A were inadvertently delayed, the entire project would be delayed. Activity A, after all, does not lie on the critical path. It has a positive total slack and thus could be delayed by one month without necessarily delaying the project.

It is often useful to employ a network-based Gantt chart as an aid in tracking and scheduling noncritical activities (see Figure 4-26). Such charts usually display two panels, one depicting all activities at their earliest starts and the other depicting all activities at their latest starts. Network-based Gantt charts can also include data on manpower schedules per time period

and cost incurred per time period. Figure 4-26 refers back to Figure 4-24's network where there is no window of time for the completion of the project. Note how the activities on the critical path coordinate with one another on the chart.

Trading Off Time against Cost

Suppose up to two months could be shaved off both the time it took to construct the new plant and the time it took to deliver the necessary equipment, although at a cost. The costs that would have to be incurred to "crash" each of these activities are shown in Table 4-20. Suppose also that having the new plant on stream a month or two early was estimated to be worth $70,000 per month, since the new plant promised capacity that was unobtainable any other way. Should these activities be "crashed" by one or two months? How can the critical path aid in the analysis?

As should be increasingly evident by this point in the text, this decision is one for which marginal analysis is appropriate. That is, it pays to speed up the project if the additional benefits enjoyed are greater than the additional costs incurred. If the costs outweigh the benefits, it is best to keep the project on its original schedule.

This use of marginal analysis to decide which activities are to be "crashed", and how, is a central element of the *critical path method (CPM)*, which is one of the key tools for project management. It is particularly popular with construction companies, although it has a wide following elsewhere.

The use of the critical path is important for this kind of analysis, for it indicates, for any project length chosen, exactly which activities have to be speeded up and which can be left on the original schedule. Ideally, of course, we would like to leave slack all that can be left slack and speed up only what must be speeded up (and, if a choice exists, to speed up the least

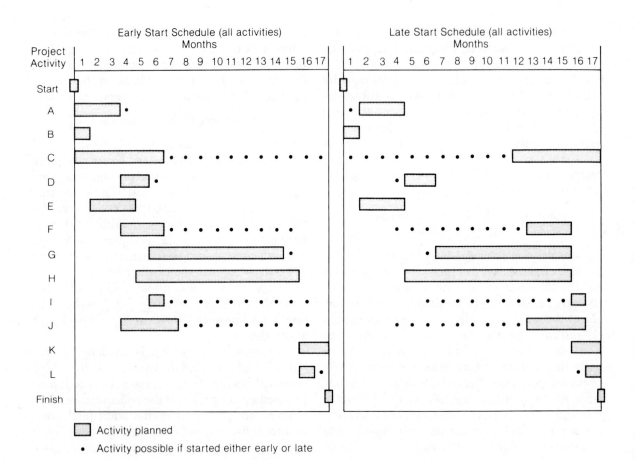

FIGURE 4-26   A network-based Gantt chart for the plant startup project.

TABLE 4-20   Costs to "crash" three activities in the plant start-up project

ACTIVITY	COST TO CRASH FIRST MONTH	COST TO CRASH SECOND MONTH
Construction of facility (H)	$50,000	$75,000
Equipment delivery (G)	20,000	40,000
Selection of plant manager and management personnel (A)	5,000	Impossible

costly activities). Put another way, to the extent possible, we would like every path to be a critical path because in so doing, the least expenditure for project speed-up will be incurred.

What does this mean for our example? To complete the plant start-up in 16 months rather than 17, activity H (plant construction) must be crashed since it (not activity G, equipment delivery) lies on the critical path. Activity G can be left as originally scheduled. The costs incurred for speeding up the project to 16 months are thus only $50,000 and the expected benefit from the early completion is $70,000. It is clear that the project ought to be speeded up by at least one month. Note that there are now two critical paths: B-E-H-K and A-D-G-K.

What about speeding up the project from 16 months to 15 months? To complete the plant start-up in only 15 months would require that plant construction (activity H) be speeded up an additional month (for critical path B-E-H-K) and that either equipment delivery (activity G) or personnel selection (activity A) be speeded up by one month (for critical path A-D-G-K). The additional cost would be at least $80,000 ($75,000 for crashing activity H again and $5000 for crashing activity A), which exceeds the benefits of $70,000 for being another month early. Speeding up the project from 16 to 15 months is thus not advised. Note that the critical path and marginal analysis are both called for in analyzing trade-offs of time and cost in project scheduling.

AN ALTERNATIVE PROGRAM: EVALUATION AND REVIEW TECHNIQUE (PERT)

At about the same time as the CPM was developed in the late 1950s, a similar technique called PERT (program evaluation and review technique) was also developed. Both CPM and PERT require the construction of a network diagram, and they both share the concept of the critical path as determining the least time for project completion. In contrast to our discussion so far, PERT offers a different graphical technique and an added wrinkle.

Graphing PERT

Where the networks we prepared previously place activities to be performed at the nodes of the network diagram and use arrows only to indicate which activities follow others, PERT uses a different convention. Activities are placed on arrows and the nodes of the network serve as events—the starts and completions of various activities. In order to preserve the proper precedence relationships when using this graphical convention, dummy activities and events must sometimes be introduced. Figure 4-27 illustrates this with a portion of the precedence relationships from the plant start-up example. As Figure 4-27 implies, PERT is more cumbersome to graph than the activity-on-node networks.

Time Estimate Variations

PERT can be used to provide some insight into likely variations in the completion time of the project. Individual estimates (an optimistic one, a pessimistic one, and a most likely one) of the variance in performing each activity are made. This is accomplished by assuming a certain distribution for these variances—the *beta distribution* (a skewed distribution that permits the possibility of occasional *very* late events, but no *very* early events)—and by insisting on the independence of each activity from others. An estimate of the time variance in accomplishing the entire project (and thus the probability of completing it by various dates) can be made by summing the variances along the critical paths. The assumptions ensure that the distribution of the summed variances will be normal.

The expected value of the time for each activity is

$$T = \frac{oe + 4ml + pe}{6}$$

where *oe* is the optimistic estimate, *pe* is the pessimistic estimate, and *ml* is the most likely estimate. The variance of the time for each activity is

$$\sigma_T^2 = \left(\frac{pe - oe}{6}\right)^2$$

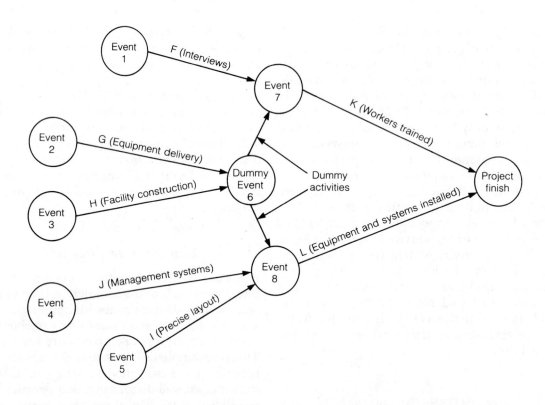

FIGURE 4-27 A sample PERT network using a portion of the plant startup example. The dummy event and activities are used only to clarify that both activity G and activity H must precede activities K and L.

It is the sum of these variances along any path in the network that is normally distributed. By using the summed variance for the path (for example, the critical path) and the fact that the summed variance is distributed normally, a probability of completion of any event can be computed.

As may be surmised, using PERT in this way to calculate a project completion time variance and probabilities of completion by specified dates can be a bit concocted. The variance for the entire project can be only as good as the variance estimates for individual activities, and often there is little information on which to base such variance estimates. Using PERT in

this way can be more trouble than it is worth. Nevertheless, PERT does make explicit a concern for time variations and the fact that the critical path itself cannot be known with certainty. These insights are useful reminders to any project manager.

SOME PRINCIPLES FOR PROJECT MANAGERS

Although critical paths, the critical path method, and PERT have been exceedingly useful to managers in scheduling projects, effective project management means more than the adept use of these techniques. Drawing on his own vast experience in project management, Herbert Spirer has arrived at a dozen principles that serve as a useful checklist for project managers:[13]

1. A project has to have a clear objective or set of objectives, and these objectives ought to be stated in terms of specific items (tangible or intangible) to be delivered to the project's sponsor.

2. The project manager ought to be able to structure the project clearly, detailing which bundles of major activities (work packages) are required and how they comprise the deliverable items that meet the project's objectives. Spirer calls this a "work breakdown structure," and he sees it as a hierarchical representation of the project.

3. The work packages making up the work breakdown structure are composed of individual activities. These activities have to be listed and organized into groups that can be overseen by specific people. The specific activities for a major project can number in the thousands. Spirer recommends, however, that no one manager have direct responsibility for more than 50 specific activities. Top level management itself should not be responsible for more than 30 to 50 aggregations of these activities, a precept that highlights the need for an effective work breakdown structure.

4. These activities should then be placed in a precedence diagram or network, and a critical path developed with the concomitant early and late start and finish times and slack calculations. The development of the precedence diagram or network is an important task in itself; analyzing such a network can lead to various suggestions or to resequencing activities. Calculations of the critical path need to be done periodically as the project proceeds.

5. The calendar of activities and times that comes out of the network creation and the critical path analysis must be combined with some knowledge of resource constraints to produce a schedule that tells management when activities *will* be done, not simply when they *must* be done.

6. Managing the resources needed to meet the schedule is eased by making use of Gantt charts and plots of cumulative resource use such as are applied in manufacturing situations.

7. Activity times can be estimated often by analyzing similar activities and modifying their times by using common sense. Sometimes more analytic methods (regressions, cross tabulation) can also be used. The estimation of activity time is often helped by referring explicitly to the network and the critical or near-critical paths that are implied by the first-round estimates.

8. Use pessimistic, optimistic, and most likely estimates for as many activities as possible. It is always helpful to recognize the uncertainty inherent in projects.

9. Tracking the progress of a project is helped by establishing milestones, which are easily grouped events. Such milestones can help serve as motivation for the project as well as checkpoints for the project's progress.

10. Assign one and only one person to be accountable for every activity.

11. Use the plan to control the project. This is done by keeping the plan current and monitoring the actual performance in timely fashion. Determine how the actual performance measures up to the plan and what variances are implied by that contrast. Take

any corrective action that is necessary, assessing the likely consequences of any corrective action and adjusting the plan accordingly.

12. Assess the status of the project by using various "earned value concepts" such as the budgeted cost of work scheduled, the budgeted cost of work performed, and the actual cost of work performed. By comparing the budgeted cost of work scheduled against the budgeted cost of work performed, one can come up with a general measure of the on-schedule performance of the project. Similarly, by comparing the budgeted cost of the work performed with the actual cost of the work performed, a measure of the cost variance of the project can be ascertained.

QUESTIONS

1. What are the main differences in the key planning and control features of each of the following pairs of production processes?

   a. Job shop and continuous flow
   b. Worker-paced line flow and machine-paced line flow
   c. Job shop and a hybrid process

2. What are the factors that should govern a manager's choice of forecasting?

3. What is the purpose of establishing a production schedule?

4. The development of a master production schedule requires serious decision making, certain types of data, and a strategy for meeting the production goals set. List the main elements in each of these that must be considered. How do these elements influence the preparation of a master schedule at Ridgely Sporting Goods?

5. The text makes a distinction between scheduling processes whose capacities are clear-cut and those whose capacities are muddled. Where do hybrid processes fit into this scheme of things? What types of problems are likely to be encountered when scheduling hybrid processes?

6. Compare optimization and nonoptimization techniques for deriving production schedules.

7. Define and/or give the mathematical expression for the following:

   a. objective function
   b. structural constraints
   c. nonnegativity conditions
   d. feasible region
   e. boundary line
   f. isocost lines

8. The linear programming method has numerous applications in operations problems; it also has several limitations. Discuss each of these in turn.

9. What is the concept of duality as it relates to linear programming? How is it useful in understanding production planning?

10. Compare and contrast the worker information requirements in the batch flow and line flow processes.

11. Briefly describe the critical path method and discuss its relation to project costs and timing. How does PERT differ from CPM?

12. What are the advantages of a decoupled inventory?

13. Discuss briefly how scarce resources can affect production planning.

14. What criteria should be used in determining whether long-term, medium-term, or short-term forecasting techniques are appropriate for a given production process?

15. What is capacity planning? Why is it important?

16. What are some key considerations in deciding between a "chase" strategy and a "level" strategy for a master production schedule?

17. How is linear programming useful in making product specification decisions? in plant location decisions?

18. Why are job shops difficult to schedule? How are job priorities determined?

19. What is an alternative to scheduling by priority rules?

20. Discuss the concepts of vertical and horizontal loading. How do they differ from one another?

21. What is the "just-in-time" philosophy? How is it different from the "just-in-case" philosophy? What determines the flow of production in each philosophy?

22. According to the critical path concept, what is the shortest amount of time in which a product may be completed?

23. Why is it important for managers to continually recalculate the critical path?

24. How is marginal analysis used in the critical path concept?

PROBLEMS

1. Can a material requirements planning system be implemented successfully in a process that operates with a decoupling inventory? Support your answer.

2. As the demand on a factory falls, should its managers adopt different rules concerning the number of setups and/or the run lengths desired? Why or why not?

3. It has been observed that large-tract builders do *more* subcontracting than do smaller builders. This runs against the typical view that large size fosters more vertical integration. How can you explain this phenomenon?

4. Owens, Inc., has been awarded a blanket one-year contract for the requirements for the bracket in Tour B. (Situations for Study B1). Fred wants to start and end the year

with 500 units in inventory for safety stock. The contract is for 6000 brackets (average usage 500 per month) with the following estimated demand:

July	500
August	500
September	350
October	400
November	450
December	450
January	650
February	700
March	500
April	550
May	400
June	550

Fred has made the following estimates of production and inventory carrying costs information: start-up costs to produce 1–500 on a sin-

TABLE 4-21   Time and money considerations (problem 6)

ACTIVITY	FOLLOWS	TIME TO COMPLETE (weeks)	LENGTH ACTIVITY CAN BE SHORTENED (weeks)	EXTRA COST FOR OVERTIME (per week)
A		$2\frac{1}{3}$	1	$300
B		4	1	$250
C	A	$1\frac{1}{6}$	none	
D	A	$4\frac{5}{6}$	1	$275
E	B	$1\frac{1}{6}$	none	
F	C	10	3	$250
G	D	7	1	$400
H	F,G	$4\frac{5}{6}$	1	$300
I	E	$6\frac{5}{6}$	2	$325
J	H	$3\frac{2}{3}$	none	
K	I	$3\frac{1}{6}$	none	
L	J,K	6	2	$350

gle shift are $200; to run a second shift, startup costs are $250; to shut down either shift is $150. Storage will cost approximately 50¢ per unit per month, with maximum storage space for 1500 units.

a. What is Fred's best production schedule for the year?
b. Could you set up this problem for the linear programming technique? Support your answer.
c. Fred has just learned that the second shift operator will return to college in January, and Fred does not want to replace him. How will this affect your production plan?

5. "Maintenance should be viewed as a machine that must be scheduled like any other." Comment on this statement.

6. Christopher Carson has investigated a future project and has determined the sequence of activities, their duration (both normal and if speeded up), and the cost of overtime (Table 4-21). Mr. Carson has found that for each week over 25 that it takes to finish the project, his firm will have to pay a penalty cost of $325.

a. What is the critical path, and how long is it?
b. Where should Mr. Carson use the overtime, if at all?
c. After the project had been started, Mr. Carson found that a vital piece of equipment had broken down, causing activity F to be delayed an extra two weeks. What, if any, action should he take?

7. The Pork & Rind firm manufactures "Tater Chips" and "Cheezy Crackers." The firm has combined some old and some new techniques that have caused these two products to have a high sales volume. It can run 9000 ounces of chips or 16,000 ounces of crackers through the oil spray unit per day; 15,000 ounces of chips or 13,000 ounces of crackers can be baked in the oven daily. What's more, the basic dough is the same for both products, and the firm can mix enough for 12,000 ounces of crackers or 15,000 ounces of chips per day. Pork & Rind can purchase enough potato extract for 6000 ounces of chips and enough cheese for 14,000 ounces of crackers. Pork & Rind anticipates a profit of 14¢ per ounce of crackers and 11¢ per ounce of chips.

TABLE 4-22   Actual and forecasted monthly sales (in millions of dollars) for a certain retail product (problem 9)

MONTH	YEAR 1		YEAR 2		YEAR 3		YEAR 4	
	ACTUAL	FORECAST	ACTUAL	FORECAST	ACTUAL	FORECAST	ACTUAL	FORECAST
Jan.	$ 3.934	3.9	$ 2.639	$ 3.4	$ 4.016	$ 3.1	$ 3.633	$ 3.4
Feb.	3.162	3.3	2.899	2.9	3.957	3.2	4.292	3.6
March	4.286	3.9	3.370	3.2	4.510	3.7	4.154	3.8
April	4.676	4.5	3.740	4.0	4.276	4.3	4.121	4.4
May	5.010	5.3	2.927	3.1	4.986	4.5	4.647	4.8
June	4.874	5.1	3.986	3.9	4.677	5.0	4.753	5.0
July	4.633	4.6	4.217	4.3	3.523	4.4	3.965	4.5
Aug.	1.659	1.8	1.738	1.6	1.821	1.7	1.723	1.8
Sept.	5.951	6.0	5.221	5.3	5.222	5.7	5.048	5.8
Oct.	6.981	6.8	6.424	6.6	6.872	6.9	6.922	6.9
Nov.	9.851	10.0	9.842	10.0	10.803	10.2	9.858	10.1
Dec.	12.670	13.1	13.076	12.9	13.916	13.4	11.331	13.0

a. Prepare a linear program for the daily production schedule that will generate the most profit.

b. If Pork & Rind were to try to generate more capacity, on which constraint should it exert the most effort?

c. The firm develops a new product, "Puffy Cheezies," which requires the same inputs as the crackers plus a gun from which to "shoot" them. This gun can produce 8000 ounces per day. The Puffy Cheezies would generate a profit of 8¢ per ounce. Generate a new production schedule that will maximize profit.

8. The Wyoming Valley Furniture Company (see Situation 2-2) periodically had significant pulses in demand that were difficult to meet without delays in the delivery schedule. In particular, the finish shop would often be pinpointed as the production bottleneck. It was alleged that too much time there was being spent on rush orders and short runs and not enough time on long runs of finished parts.

A number of potential solutions had been tossed out for consideration, among them (1) the introduction of a computerized material requirements planning system and (2) a decoupling inventory.

How would you expect each recommendation to work in solving the bottleneck in the finishing department? What kinds of considerations would argue for one solution over the other?

9. Using several of the techniques of forecasting described in the text (moving average, exponential smoothing, decomposition) and the data in Table 4-22, make a forecast for the next year. Do not hesitate to play with the data. How do these various techniques differ in the forecasts they make? What explains the differences?

10. How good have the past forecasts in problem 9 been? How would you measure the quality of those forecasts? Was one year's forecast better than the others?

11. Return to the Morris Machine Shop (Situation 4-3) and consider another set of jobs to be released to the shop as shown in Table 4-23. The total times for each machine are: lathe (8 hours), mill (10 hours), drill (3 hours), grinder (9 hours).

TABLE 4-23   Sequences and times (in hours) for five jobs (Morris Machine Shop—problem 11)

JOB 1		JOB 2		JOB 3		JOB 4		JOB 5	
Lathe	2	Drill	1	Drill	1	Mill	2	Lathe	2
Mill	3	Lathe	1	Mill	2	Drill	1	Mill	2
Grind	2	Mill	1	Grind	2	Lathe	3	Grind	2
		Grind	1			Grind	2		
Total	7		4		5		8		6

What is the best schedule for the jobs? How do the various priority rules perform: first-come, first-served; work first on shortest processing time; work first on longest processing time; work on earliest due date (the order of which is 1, 3, 5, 4, 2)?

12. The sales forecast for product number A107 is 50 units a week for the next 8 weeks. There are 65 units of A107 on hand; the master schedule calls for delivery of 75 units next week (week 2) and 60 more in week 3. The booked customer orders are 73 for week 1 (past due included), 68 for week 2, and 52 for week 3. An order of 12 has just been received. Which week is it scheduled for? Fill out the form (Figure 4-5 is an example) for this situation.

13. Consider Situation 4-2 (Bailey Steel Products Company) again. Suppose the cost of transporting steel tube from Mill 2 (Texas) to San Francisco declined from $60 per ton to $40 per ton. How do you suspect that the solution might differ? Prove your intuition by evaluating the objective function again. (Hint: The new minimum cost is $29,500.)

14. Calculate the expected loads for three work centers, given the following information. Expected total hours required to produce what is demanded:

Product	Time Period		
	1	2	3
X	5	10	15
Y	15	25	30

Labor Standards:

Product X	.75 hours/unit
Product Y	.25 hours/unit

Historical average utilization by each work center:

Work Center	Utilization
1	60%
2	25%
3	15%

15. Calculate the forecast of sales (broken down by month) for Year 3, given the following information.

Sales of textbooks:

Year 2	$/month	% of total
Jan.	71,025	7.3
Feb.	63,429	6.5
Mar.	82,630	8.8
Apr.	51,345	5.1
May	74,350	7.7
Jun.	82,964	8.4
Jul.	94,899	9.8
Aug.	108,465	11.2
Sep.	97,048	10.1
Oct.	63,748	6.7
Nov.	83,971	8.6
Dec.	95,437	9.8
	969,374	100.0

Calculate the forecast first using the following simple rule, which uses these three assumptions:

- Year 3's total sales will grow at the same rate that this year's sales grew by.
- The monthly breakdown of sales for Year 3 will match this year's breakdown.

- Year 2's sales were 17.3 percent greater than Year 1's sales.

16. Using the same data, predict monthly sales for Year 3 using the moving average technique.

17. Assume that you found a trend in the data. What would be your next step in dealing with the data?

SITUATION FOR STUDY 4-1

STAINLESS TANK COMPANY, INC.

Jack Black, the president and chief salesperson of the Stainless Tank Company, Inc., has been having difficulty keeping his company "in the black." For several months, Stainless Tank had been showing a loss, even though Mr. Black and the other two salespeople were working hard on generating new sales. Mr. Black had some ideas he wanted to use to increase sales volume and thus offset this loss; but being a cautious person, he though he would first ask an outside expert to look at his operation. Mr. Black asked Dr. Hanna Hendricks, professor of operations management at the local university, to visit Stainless Tank and provide some insight into the problem.

Mr. Black had purchased the Stainless Tank Company and moved it to its present location. At that time the firm manufactured stainless steel tanks and mounted the tanks and ancillary equipment on modified truck and trailer chassis. These tank trucks were used to transport milk for the dairy industry. This portion of the business had remained stable, both in product design and demand, for the last several years. In addition, the firm contracted with insurance companies for the repair of tanks that had been damaged in accidents.

In recent years the government environmental agency had decided that sewage plants could

no longer dump their effluent into the local waterways. This regulation opened up a new market for Stainless Tank. Among the current methods of disposing of the liquid and semi-liquid output from sewage plants was to haul it to a farmer's field and spread it over or plow it under the field. The sewage tank trucks used the same basic manufacturing technology as the milk tank trucks, with only moderate differences.

The manufacturing process started with the delivery of the truck or trailer from a local dealer. First the truck was modified with extra wide fenders and tires that could be fitted before the tank was mounted. The tank fabrication entailed shearing, rolling, and welding. The rounded tank ends, the pumps, and various other parts were purchased. The tank support brackets were fabricated and mounted, after which the tank was mounted. After tank mounting, the piping was done. Some difficulty was usually encountered in getting all the components to fit as they had been designed; thus, that portion of the assembly needed some "cut-to-fit" work.

The workers in the shop were all welders; however, they were expected to do any of the other work necessary to "build" a unit. The shop foreman was the official "expert" on deal-

FIGURE 4-28   Partial organization chart for Stainless Tank Company.

Job #		Name
	in	Time clock punch
	out	

FIGURE 4-29   Time card used by Stainless Tank Company.

ing with problems encountered in the construction of a unit. Although Mr. Black knew that this informal delegation of duties and responsibilities would not work well in a large organization, he thought it had worked well for Stainless Tank. See Figure 4-28 for a partial organization chart of the company.

After careful scrutiny of the firm and its records, Dr. Hendricks concluded that the major problem was caused by the larger volume of sales. The larger volume had created information needs that could not be handled in an informal manner. The time card for a job (Figure 4-29) recorded that Tom, Dick, or Harry had worked on a particular job for a particular length of time. These cards were the basis for calculating the cost of production both for each unit and for the plant. The total cost of production for each tank was compared with its contracted sales price to determine its profit or loss.

Dr. Hendricks thought the first thing Mr. Black should do to get Stainless Tank back on the road to profitability was to establish a method of scheduling the production of tanks. She thought that this scheduling method would not only provide the shop foreman with the proper sequence of operations and estimated times but also provide management with a comparison of actual progress and planned progress. The analysis of the information and the reconstruction of events from this proposed method should provide insight into where and why the firm was losing money.

1. If you were Dr. Hendricks, what part of the process would you start with to establish a scheduling method? Set up a plan for your proposed investigation.

2. What information or data would you search for? What data would you want the shop to collect and to whom should this information go?

3. How should the materials be controlled in this situation?

4. What do you think of Mr. Black's desire for more volume? How would you discuss this aspect with him?

5. What method of master production scheduling would you use in this case? Support your answer with your reasons.

6. Do you think linear programming would help Mr. Black? If so, how would you set it up?

7. Mr. Black particularly likes the critical path method of scheduling and thinks he understands it. How would you counsel him on its use in his tank shop?

SITUATION FOR STUDY 4-2
WHITE LAWN & GARDEN EQUIPMENT

White Lawn & Garden Equipment manufactured rakes, hoes, shovels, and assorted other lawn and garden tools. Planning was done every quarter for the next 6 months, and Bill White, a member of the founding family, was charged with overseeing the production planning process.

The latest sales forecast, just for the three lines of rakes, is shown below.

Rake Sales Forecast (next 6 months in units)

PRODUCT LINES (rakes)	MONTHS					
	APRIL	MAY	JUNE	JULY	AUG.	SEPT.
A models	10,000	9,000	4,000	5,000	7,500	7,000
D models	5,500	4,000	3,000	3,000	2,500	1,000
L models	1,500	2,500	2,000	2,000	3,000	4,000

Policy was to keep one-half of average monthly sales in ending inventory at the end of any quarter. The current inventory positions were: A models, 4,500 units; D models, 3,500 units; and L models, 1,500 units.

The rake department was responsible for fabricating and assembling all three product lines. All aspects of fabrication, assembling, inspection, and packing took 1/2 hour of direct labor for the A and D models and 45 minutes of direct labor for the L models. There were 45 direct labor workers in the department who worked an average of 160 hours a month at an average wage of $9.00 per hour. Overtime was paid at the standard of time and a half. The task of making rakes was accomplished by small groups of employees working together, so changeovers were of little consequence. All three types of rakes could be made at the same time.

The standard cost of the A models was $10, that of the D models was $12, and that of the L models, $15. Inventory costs were at 25 percent of the standard cost, on a yearly basis.

1. Develop a master production schedule for the next 6 months.

2. Formulate this as a linear program.

CASE FOR STUDY
SPIRIT BOTTLING COMPANY

In early June 1983, Miles Seabrook, president of Spirit Bottling Company, called in his newly appointed vice-president and manager of the Soft Drink Division, Donald Whitcomb. He wanted to discuss several inventory problems.

Seabrook: Don, I am concerned about inventory levels throughout the company. Finished goods inventory levels reached $4 million in May, and May was just an average month for the company in terms of production, sales volume, and the accompanying inventory levels.

Whitcomb: I agree, Miles, our inventory levels do appear excessive. Besides, they are increasingly expensive to hold and are taking up valuable space.* The Rochester plant is a good example. Finished product occupies most of the storage space inside the plant, while empty returnable bottles are stored outside in an open yard.

Seabrook: I have two questions about our inventory situation. Are our finished goods inventory levels where they should be throughout the company? If not, is it possible to cut these levels, solve our problems in Rochester, and keep the 15 distribution centers supplied with production?

Whitcomb: I've already done some work to determine whether the company has a problem with excess inventory. I began an analysis of inventory and sales figures for the Mankato distribution center. [See Table 4-24.] I chose this center because the number of days' supply for each product and package in Mankato was representative of companywide in-ventory-to-sales levels. So I was able to get a quick idea of the company's inventory situation. It appears we have been operating with excess inventory.

Seabrook: I thought so. I have repeatedly asked our production plant managers to reduce inventory.

Whitcomb: Miles, in my opinion, the only way to solve the inventory problem is by changing the way we schedule production and transportation. The amount of goods the three plants produce and ship to the 15 distribution centers determines product inventory levels. I think the solution lies there.

Seabrook: Have at it then, but I want some results soon.

To answer the questions that Seabrook had raised, Whitcomb knew he had to analyze company inventory levels and scheduling methods in the production plants in Rochester, Minneapolis, and St. Cloud. If the decision was made to reduce inventory levels in these plants substantially, production management would experience the pressures of operating with low inventory levels and could no longer afford low efficiency runs or equipment breakdowns because stockouts would result.

Brief History of Spirit Bottling Company

Spirit Bottling Company bottled and marketed soft drinks in a franchise territory covering the

---

Copyright © Roger W. Schmenner, 1983.

*In determining the carrying cost of inventory, the company used a carrying cost percentage of 15 percent. This percentage consisted of two elements:

Opportunity cost − Finance charges = 12.5%
Physical costs − Handling, storage, obsolescence = 2.5%

TABLE 4-24   Inventory and sales analysis, May 1983 (Spirit Bottling Company, Mankato Plant)

PRODUCT AND PACKAGE	INVENTORY (cases)	SALES (cases)*	INVENTORY/ SALES	DAYS' SUPPLY† (days)
Returnable Bottles				
Spirit 6½ oz.	280	2,454	.11	3.5
Spirit 6½ oz. 6-pack	65	1,107	.06	1.8
Spirit 10 oz.	155	2,895	.05	1.6
Spirit 10 oz. 6-pack	100	320	.30	10
Spirit 16 oz.	284	1,418	.20	6.2
Spirit 1 liter	1,208	856	1.41	43
11-Up 10 oz.	138	294	.47	15.3
11-Up 16 oz.	40	10	4.0	125
11-Up 1 liter	50	19	2.63	83
Pep 10 oz.	234	1,168	.20	6.1
Pep 16 oz.	126	178	.70	21
Pep 1 liter	78	68	1.15	35.4
Brite 10 oz.	86	923	.09	2.8
Brite 16 oz.	130	44	2.95	92.8
Brite 1 liter	63	79	.79	25.2
Dr. Spice 10 oz.	98	448	.22	6.8
Dr. Spice 1 liter	33	12	2.75	82.5
Dr. Spice SF 10 oz.	102	100	1.02	31.8
Jazz 10 oz.	67	303	.22	6.8
One-way bottles (nonreturnable)				
Spirit 10 oz.	248	644	.39	11.9
Spirit 16 oz.	3,206	2,872	1.11	34.6
Spirit 28 oz.	64	97	.66	20.6
Spirit 2 liters Plastic	2,115	4,205	.50	15.59
11-Up 10 oz.	59	36	1.6	49.2
11-Up 16 oz.	75	239	.31	9.7
11-Up 28 oz.	28	22	1.27	40
11-Up 2 liters Plastic	70	170	.41	12.7
11-Up SF 2 liters	101	63	1.6	50.5
Plastic	48	69	.70	21.8
Pep 10 oz.	377	447	.84	26.1
Pep 16 oz.	24	11	2.18	68.5
Pep 28 oz.	188	338	.56	17.24
Pep 2 liters Plastic	74	64	1.16	35.2
Brite 10 oz.	315	619	.51	15.75
Brite 16 oz.	105	286	.37	11.4
Brite 2 liters Plastic	61	43	1.42	43.5
Viva GA/CS 28 oz.	37	106	.35	10.8
Viva 2 liters Plastic	25	14	1.79	55.5
Viva T.Water 28 oz.	51	16	3.19	102
Dr. Spice 10 oz.	119	680	.17	5.4
Dr. Spice 16 oz.	92	53	1.74	54
Dr. Spice 2 liters Plastic	127	50	2.54	79.3
Jazz 10 oz.				
Cans				
Spirit	2,542	7,879	.32	10
11-Up	660	862	.77	23.7
11-Up SF	235	216	1.08	34
Pep	574	1,803	.32	11.2
Lean Green	85	15	5.66	177

TABLE 4-24 Inventory and sales analysis, May 1983 (Spirit Bottling Company, Mankato Plant) (*continued*)

PRODUCT AND PACKAGE	INVENTORY (cases)	SALES (cases)*	INVENTORY/ SALES	DAYS' SUPPLY† (days)
Cans (continued)				
Brite	862	2,043	.42	13
Viva	70	125	.56	17.5
Dr. Spice	185	941	.19	6.1
Dr. Spice SF	104	117	.89	28
Jazz	807	2,115	.38	11.8
Premix (for commercial sales)				
Spirit	147	2,188	.07	2.1
11-Up	27	56	.48	15
Pep	84	176	.48	15
Dr. Spice	13	28	.46	14.4
Syrup (for commercial sales)				
Spirit	270	600	.45	13.9
Pep	105	35	3	95.4
Dr. Spice	70	60	1.16	35
Others	95	150	.63	19.7

*Total case sales for returnables, one-way bottles, and cans amount to 39,906.

†Calculated as inventory divided by average daily sales. Average daily sales were determined by the previous four weeks' sales. This calculation was specific to each product and package combination.

Note: SF = sugar-free; GA/CS = ginger ale/club soda; T.Water = tonic water.

southern half of Minnesota and portions of Wisconsin. In 1902 the first bottle of Spirit Cola was sold in Minnesota by a bottling plant in Rochester, which was the predecessor of Spirit's plant in Rochester. Through the years other bottling plants were built or acquired by Spirit and in May 1983, the company consisted of 15 distribution centers and three bottling plants. In 1983, the company bottled and sold 20 national brands for five companies: Spirit, Viva, Action Ade, Blink, Dr. Spice. Total sales in 1981 were 22.3 million cases, consisting of 20 different packages.

Since 1972 the company's stock had been listed on the New York Stock Exchange. During the last two years the stock price ranged from a low of 11¼ to a current high of 25½. The financial condition of the company had remained healthy.

The company was organized into three operating divisions. Individual plants reported to division managers who in turn reported to corporate.

The Production Plants

The three production plants (located in Rochester, Minneapolis, and St. Cloud) produced and shipped the company's products to 15 distribution centers, which marketed and sold them in Spirit's franchise territory. Table 4-25 shows which plants produced and shipped the various products. Table 4-26 gives data for the cases produced at each of the three plants.

The St. Cloud and Minneapolis plants were similar in size—112,000 square feet and 95,000 square feet, respectively—whereas the newer Rochester plant (built and equipped in 1973 for $9 million) covered 280,000 square feet.

St. Cloud had two operating lines but used only one at a time, depending on the size required. Minneapolis had only one operating line.

TABLE 4-25   Production assignments by facility, May 1983 (Spirit Bottling Company)

PACKAGE AND PRODUCT	HUTCHINSON	MANKATO	RED WING	LITTLE FALLS	MINNEAPOLIS	NEW ULM	MAPLE GROVE	RUSH CITY	ST. CLOUD	ST. BONIFACIUS	SAUK CENTER	PRINCETON	ARKANSAW, WIS.	ROCHESTER	COON RAPIDS
Returnable Bottles															
6½ oz. Spirit	R	M	M	R	M	S	M	M	S	R	R	R	S	R	M
10 oz. Spirit	R	M	M	R	M	S		M	S	R	R	R	S	R	M
10 oz. 11-Up	R	M	M	R	M	S		M	S	R	R	R	S	R	M
10 oz. Pep	R	M	M	R	M	S		M	S	R	R	R	S	R	M
10 oz. Brite	R	M	M	R	M	S		M	S	R	R	R	S	R	M
10 oz. Action Ade	R	M	M	R	M	S		M	S	R	R	R	S	R	M
10 oz. Orange Orange	R	S	S	R		S			S		R			R	
10 oz. Dr. Spice		M			M			M		M		M	M		
10 oz. SF Orange Orange		S	S		M	S			S						M
16 oz. Spirit	R	R	M	R	M	S	M	R	S	R	R	R	M	R	R
16 oz. Brite	R	M	M	R	M	S	M	M	S	R	R	R	M	R	M
16 oz. 11-Up		M			M		M	M				M	S		M
16 oz. Pep		M	M		M		M	M		M		M	M		M
16 oz. Dr. Spice		M			M		M	M		M			M		M
1 liter All products	R	R	R	R	R	R	R	R	R	R	R	R	R	R	R
One-Way Bottles (nonreturnable)															
10 oz. All products	R	R	R	R	R	R	R	R	R	R	R	R	R	R	R
10 oz. Viva	S	S	S	S	S	S	S	S	S	S	S	S	S	S	S
16 oz. All products	R	R	R	R	R	R	R	R	R	R	R	R	R	R	R
28 oz. All products	R	R	R	R	R	R	R	R	R	R	R	R	R	R	R
2 liters All products	R	R	R	R	R	R	R	R	R	R	R	R	R	R	R
Cans															
12 oz. All products	R	R	R	R	R	R	R	R	R	R	R	R	R	R	R
Premix															
All products	R	R	R	R	R	R			R	S	R	R	R	S	R	R

Note: R = Rochester; M = Minneapolis; S = St. Cloud.

However, each plant operated with one crew consisting of eight workers—one 10-hour shift, four days a week. In contrast, the Rochester plant operated four bottling lines and two canning lines. Bottling line 1 operated two 10-hour shifts per day four days a week. Lines 2 through 6 operated one 10-hour shift four days a week. Each line was operated by an eight-worker crew. At all three plants, production runs were made Monday through Thursday; Fridays were spent on maintenance and repairs. The capacities and sizes produced by each line at the three plants are shown in Table 4-27.

The Rochester operation, although generally well managed, had one obvious problem. There was not enough warehouse space for raw materials and finished goods. During May, for example, the plant held 452,785 cases of finished product. Lack of space within the plant cost the company in several ways:

1. The company was forced to store 86,334 cases of used returnable glass in cartons and cases outside in an open yard. The cases covered 24,500 square feet. When it rained the cardboard cartons in a case were ruined. There

TABLE 4-26   Case production by facility, May 1983 (Spirit Bottling Company)

PLANT	CURRENT	BUDGET	CHANGE	PERCENT CHANGE	PRIOR YEAR	CHANGE	PERCENT CHANGE
St. Cloud							
Returnable bottles	125,353	131,500	(6,147)	(4.7)%	135,353	(10,000)	(7.4)%
One-way bottles	8,527		8,527		42,948	(34,421)	(80.1)
Total	133,880	131,500	2,380	1.8	178,301	(44,421)	(21.9)
Minneapolis							
Returnable bottles	164,764	121,300	43,464	35.8	200,226	(35,462)	(17.7)
One-way bottles	9,064		9,064			9,064	
Total	173,828	121,300	52,528	43.3	200,226	(26,398)	(13.2)
Rochester							
Returnable bottles	185,963	255,300	(69,337)	(27.2)	214,206	(28,243)	(13.2)
One-way bottles	518,707	501,000	17,707	3.5	355,782	162,925	45.8
Cans	381,871	400,400	(18,529)	(4.6)	458,053	(76,182)	(16.6)
Total	1,086,541	1,156,700	(70,159)	8.2	1,028,041	58,500	5.7
Division Total	1,394,249	1,409,500	(15,251)	(1.4)	1,406,568	(12,319)	(0.9)

TABLE 4-27   Line capacities of production plants
(Spirit Bottling Company)

PLANT	LINE NUMBER	PACKAGE	LINE CAPACITY (cases/hour)
Minneapolis	2	6½ oz. R, 10 oz. R	1,000
Minneapolis	2	16 oz. R	1,000
Minneapolis	1	32 oz. R	600
Minneapolis	1	16 oz. R	670
St. Cloud	1	6½ oz. R, 10 oz. R	700
St. Cloud	1	16 oz. R	609
St. Cloud	2	1 liter R	562
St. Cloud	2	10 oz. OWB	500
Rochester	1	2 liters Plastic	960
Rochester	2	1 liter R	1,149
Rochester	2	28 oz. OWB	1,149
Rochester	3	10 oz. OWB	1,463
Rochester	3	16 oz. OWB	1,463
Rochester	4	6½ oz. R, 10 oz. R	1,000
Rochester	4	16 oz. R	938
Rochester	5	Cans	1,875
Rochester	6	Cans	2,000

Note: R = returnable bottles; OWB = one-way bottles

were four cartons in a case, each costing 5 cents.

2. During the winter (December, January, and February), approximately 20 percent of the bottles that had been stored outside would break when they were soaked in the hot caustic solution in the bottle washer. The replacement cost for returnable bottles was $4.30 per case of 24.

3. The space problem forced the Rochester plant to operate an additional 28,000-square-foot warehouse 15 miles from the production

plant. The warehouse stored 30,000 cases of finished product in May 1983. Transport drivers were paid $10 per hour to drive a trailer load to the warehouse, unload, and drive back to the Rochester plant. The round trip took an hour and a half. During May, the Rochester transportation department made 33 trips to this warehouse.

The Production Process

The production process began after several pallets of empty bottles were moved by forklift to the back of the bottling line. At this point, an employee loaded the inclined conveyor with cases of empty bottles, which were gravity fed to the decaser. The decaser lifted 24 bottles from a case every 2.4 seconds and placed them on an automatic steel conveyor, which fed the bottles into the bottle washer. The washer cleaned and sanitized every bottle by means of a 3.8 percent caustic solution, heated to 140° F. After the bottles rotated through the hot caustic bath, fresh water jets sprayed and rinsed each bottle. The washer then placed each row of 28 bottles onto the bottling line every 3.5 seconds. The steel conveyor carried the clean bottles through two inspection stations. Chipped or cracked bottles were removed by an empty-bottle inspector, and an electronic eye rejected bottles containing foreign particles.

Before the filling process, fresh water was mixed with Spirit Cola syrup or other concentrates in the proper proportions. (A $6\frac{1}{2}$-ounce bottle of Spirit contained 1 ounce of syrup and 5.5 ounces of carbonated water.) The syrup and water mixture flowed through a "carbo cooler," where it was cooled to 34°F., carbonated, and released to the filler.

The washed bottles were engaged, one by one, in the rotating filler, which filled them as they moved through 360 degrees. The fillers contained 60 filling valves and were capable of speeds up to 2000 cases per hour depending on package type and size. After being filled, the bottles were sealed by the adjacent crowner, which stamped the bottle caps in place. The full bottles then went to the case packer, which dropped the bottles into an empty case every 2.8 seconds. The finished goods traveled along an overhead conveyor to the palletizer, which stacked each pallet. Forklift operators took the full pallets to transports or warehouse storage. The time required for a bottle to flow through the production process was 35 minutes.

The Production Scheduling System

During Donald Whitcomb's first week as vice-president, he visited the three production plants and discussed production and transportation schedules with the plant managers. After asking these managers a number of questions about their scheduling procedures, Donald believed he had a good idea of what was going on. As a first step in scheduling, each production plant tabulated the previous week's sales and average daily sales by product and by package for their distribution centers. The inventory figures divided by average daily sales gave the number of days' supply "on the floor" for each product and package. Days' supply was the key factor in determining what and when to produce. A product with two days' supply would normally be produced before an item with four days' supply.

Whitcomb recalled a production scheduling meeting where he questioned the production manager from St. Cloud, John Wolfe, and the production manager from Rochester, Marcia Fox, on the issue of which product to produce first.

Donald: If you had a three-day supply of 10-ounce returnable Spirit and a two-day supply of 10-ounce returnable 11-Up, which would you produce first?

Fixed Costs	St. Cloud	Minneapolis	Rochester
Operating expenses	$30,583	$18,107	$191,185
Indirect labor	16,846	20,960	134,036
Payroll	2,200	2,864	21,553
Depreciation	6,429	3,538	47,640
Total fixed costs	$56,058	$45,469	$394,414

Product Changeover Cost

Washdown expense
24 oz. syrup @ $3.92/gallon = 72 ¢
Carbon dioxide and water = 6 ¢
Total = 78 ¢

Labor cost for mixing concentrate
1 man @ $8/hour
Time required = 15 minutes
Labor cost = $2.00
Total cost = $2.78

Package Changeover Cost

Labor cost for resetting machine
2 men @ $8/hour
Time required = 35 minutes
Total cost = $9.34

Notes: In May 1983 there were 30 product and 15 package changeovers during producing hours in the three production plants.

There was an unwritten policy of guaranteeing production workers 40 hours per week, even though actual production hours were usually fewer than 40.

A 10-hour shift in each producing plant included two 15-minute breaks and a half-hour for lunch.

FIGURE 4-30 Production cost information for Spirit Bottling Company.

Marcia: I would play it safe and produce 10-ounce returnable Spirit first. Spirit is a high-volume product and I would hate to lose the contribution dollars resulting from a possible stockout.

John: Well, I could stick to the days' supply calculations and produce 10-ounce returnable 11-Up. I know we have three days of inventory on 10-ounce Spirit. What is there to worry about?

In determining the order of production, the managers also looked at minimizing downtime due to changeovers. There were two kinds of changeovers: product changeovers (such as from Spirit to 11-Up) and package changeovers (such as from 10-ounce to 16-ounce bottles). A product changeover during producing hours cost the bottler 15 minutes of downtime. A package changeover required approximately 35 minutes. The actual costs involved in these two types of changeovers are shown in Figure 4-30, along with data on fixed costs.

Donald recalled that the changeover issue had surfaced in his conversation with Marcia and John.

Donald: Suppose the line just finished producing 16-ounce returnable Spirit. There was a two-day supply of 10-ounce returnable Spirit and a three-day supply of 16-ounce returnable Brite on the floor. Which product should be produced first?

John: 16-ounce returnable Brite. Package changeovers require 35 minutes of downtime. That is valuable production time. I believe in maximizing production volume because it reduces case cost.

Marcia: I disagree. The 10-ounce returnable Spirit should be produced first because (1) 10-ounce Spirit has fewer days' supply on the floor; (2) changeover costs are inexpensive; and (3) large-volume production runs can also mean large inventories.

In deciding how much of each item to produce, the managers studied the following: raw materials inventory, production time required for other products, safety stock levels, warehouse space, sales promotions, product age, and inventory costs. Sales forecasts were occasionally observed but not relied on because they were routinely off by at least 10 percent.

The production manager knew he or she should not run greater than a 90-day supply of any product and package because of quality control requirements concerning product age. The low-volume items, such as 10-ounce returnable Action Ade, were produced every two and one-half to three months. Faster selling items, like 2-liter Spirit, were produced almost daily. A safety stock of two to four days was added to each production run to allow for uncertainties in demand.

Because of present inventory levels, warehouse space was at a premium in all three production plants. This, in addition to the demand for other products to be produced, limited the length of a production run. The actual length of a run really became a judgment call. This was evident to Donald at the scheduling meeting he attended at the Rochester plant. These meetings were held every Thursday to decide the next week's production schedule. The schedule shown in Figure 4-31 was to be followed the next week.

In the meeting Donald questioned production manager Marcia Fox:

Donald: Why are we going to produce a five-month supply of Lean Green cans?

Marcia: The five-month supply requires only a three-hour production run. A run length of less than three hours is not cost justified.

Donald: Long runs are great—volume is spread over the same fixed costs. But a five-month supply is expensive to hold and product age could be a problem.

The Transportation System

The company's transport fleet consisted of 17 tractors and 60 trailers. Three tractors and eight trailers were located in St. Cloud. Five tractors and eleven trailers were in Minneapolis, and the remainder were in Rochester.

During Donald Whitcomb's first visits to the production plants, he discussed transportation schedules with each transportation manager. Donald discovered that in setting up a weekly transportation schedule, each manager began by observing a day's supply figure for each product and package in each plant to which they shipped. Products with the lowest days' supply were shipped first.

Each plant had warehouse space assigned for every product and package. For example, in the

SPIRIT BOTTLING CO.—ROCHESTER PLANT
PRODUCTION SCHEDULE

Week of 5/9 -13/83

Date	Line 1			Line 2			Line 3			Line 4			Canning		
	Item	Hrs.	Cases to produce	Item	Hrs.	Cases to produce	Item	Hrs.	Cases to produce	Item	Hrs	Cases to produce	Item	Hrs	Cases to produce
Monday 5/9	2 liter OWB Spirit	18½	16225	1 Liter RET Spirit	9	8055	16 oz. OWB SF orange orange Spirit	5 / 3½	4408 / 3063	6½ oz. RET Spirit	9	1500 6-Pack 5250 regular carton	Spirit	9	2534
Tuesday 5/10	2 liter OWB Pep Spirit	9 / 9	7854 / 7893	1 Liter RET Spirit	9	8055	16 oz OWB Pep	9	7812	10 oz. RET Spirit	9	2550 6-Pack 4200 regular carton	SF Dr. Spice	8½	4469
Wednesday 5/11	2 liter OWB Viva Spirit	9 / 9	8052 / 7893	1 Liter RET Spirit	9	8055	16 oz. OWB Brite	9	7040	10 oz. RET Spirit	9	2550 6-Pack 4200 regular carton	Lean Green Spirit	3 / 5½	8460 / 1554
Thursday 5/12	2 liter OWB SF 11-up Spirit	9 / 9	7875 / 7893	28 oz. OWB Viva Spirit	4 / 4½	3605 / 4095	10 oz. OWB Pep 11-Up	4½ / 4	3806 / 3264	16 oz. RET Spirit	9	7155	Brite	9	2538
Friday 5/13															

Note: OWB = one-way bottle; RET = returnable.

FIGURE 4-31   Production schedule for the Rochester plant of Spirit Bottling Company.

St. Cloud warehouse, there were three rows of 2-liter plastic Spirit capable of holding 90 pallets of product. Maximum inventory levels for retail promotional packages shipped from the Rochester plant are shown in Table 4-28. The actual amount shipped to a distribution plant is sufficient to bring the plant's inventory level to the maximum level for the shipped products. For example, if there were 1000 cases of Pep cans on inventory in a distribution plant and the maximum inventory level for Pep cans was 2500 cases, then 1500 cases would be shipped to the distribution plant.

Conclusion

Donald Whitcomb knew that Miles Seabrook would soon hold a follow-up meeting to the

TABLE 4-28 Inventory analysis for retail promotional packages of spirit shipped from Rochester plant (Spirit Bottling Company)

DISTRIBUTION CENTER	CURRENT INVENTORY (cases)	DAYS' SUPPLY (days)	MAXIMUM INVENTORY (cases)	DAYS' SUPPLY (days)
St. Cloud				
16 oz. OWB	2,355	6.9	2,520	7.4
2 liters OWB	5,918	6.2	3,600	3.7
Cans	6,635	4.3	6,480	4.2
Coon Rapids				
16 oz. OWB	728	3.4	1,176	5.2
2 liters OWB	5,628	5.2	6,000	5.6
Cans	6,336	7.6	7,128	8.5
Minneapolis				
16 oz. OWB	2,107	7.0	924	3.2
2 liters OWB	2,103	4.1	2,960	5.7
Cans	4,421	4.8	3,888	4.2
Rochester				
16 oz. OWB	2,596	5.0	2,772	5.3
2 liters OWB	3,356	3.1	4,320	4.0
Cans	4,166	2.0	6,480	3.1
Little Falls				
16 oz. OWB	3,199	17.1	4,704	25.2
2 liters OWB	6,602	19.2	8,640	24.8
Cans	2,955	6.2	4,032	8.5
Princeton				
16 oz. OWB	571	7.6	420	5.6
2 liters OWB	1,164	2.3	2,320	5.8
Cans	2,564	10.8	2,880	12.1
St. Bonifacius				
16 oz. OWB	1,724	13.0	2,520	19.0
2 liters OWB	4,169	9.2	6,000	13.2
Cans	2,208	7.8	4,320	15.3
New Ulm				
16 oz. OWB	2,056	7.2	4,700	16.4
2 liters OWB	2,833	8.8	4,000	12.4
Cans	3,209	9.1	6,048	17.2
Red Wing				
16 oz. OWB	798	5.0	1,008	6.3
2 liters OWB	480	1.8	1,360	7.1
Cans	2,160	6.2	2,448	7.1
Arkansaw, Wis.				
16 oz. OWB	1,191	7.3	1,344	8.3
2 liters OWB	1,830	13.6	2,080	15.4
Cans	2,650	11.9	3,240	14.5

TABLE 4-28   Inventory analysis for retail promotional packages of spirit shipped from Rochester plant (Spirit Bottling Company) (continued)

DISTRIBUTION CENTER	CURRENT INVENTORY (cases)	DAYS' SUPPLY (days)	MAXIMUM INVENTORY (cases)	DAYS' SUPPLY (days)
Hutchinson				
16 oz. OWB	723	8.4	1,344	15.5
2 liters OWB	614	1.8	2,640	8.0
Cans	2,620	10.8	2,736	11.2
Mankato				
16 oz. OWB	1,623	16.1	3,136	31.2
2 liters OWB	1,998	10.6	4,160	22.1
Cans	2,348	5.8	3,168	7.8
Rush City				
16 oz. OWB	320	11.5	420	15.1
2 liters OWB	870	15.3	1,200	21.1
Cans	1,751	14.0	4,320	34.4
Maple Grove				
16 oz. OWB	221	3.0	252	3.4
2 liters OWB	2,933	2.6	2,880	2.5
Cans	1,621	10.6	1,728	11.3
Sauk Center				
16 oz. OWB	378	2.1	1,008	5.7
2 liters OWB	2,800	5.2	4,520	8.4
Cans	3,384	11.9	4,536	15.9

Note: Company transportation costs are $1.10 per mile. OWB = one-way bottle

June meeting. Seabrook expected Whitcomb to analyze company inventory levels. If there were problems, Whitcomb would be expected to correct them. Possibly a new scheduling method, which would reduce inventory levels and overall costs, would have to be developed. Donald had compiled company sales and inventory figures for May 1983. (See Tables 4-29 and 4-30.) This information, along with the other information he had collected, would enable him to construct a sample production schedule for each production plant for the first week of June. (See Figure 4-31.)

It appeared that the Rochester plant had outgrown itself. Marcia Fox was convinced the plant should be expanded, at a cost of $21 per square foot. Donald wondered what he should recommend.

TABLE 4-29 Sales, May 1983 (Spirit Bottling Company)

PACKAGE AND PRODUCT	COON RAPIDS	ROCHESTER	ARKANSAW, WIS.	PRINCETON	SAUK CENTER	ST. BONIFACIUS	ST. CLOUD	RUSH CITY	NEW ULM	MINNEAPOLIS	LITTLE FALLS	RED WING	MANKATO	HUTCHINSON
Returnable Bottles														
6½ oz. Spirit	7,862	12,070	4,422	3,311	4,910	4,700	13,959	2,690	5,700	6,510	3,669	5,072	3,561	3,030
10 oz. Spirit	3,610	12,861	2,231	1,948	4,150	4,688	16,491	829	5,892	8,087	3,922	3,255	3,215	2,870
10 oz. 11-Up	562	1,815	277	215	448	451	1,187	98	557	781	302	1,133	1,168	168
10 oz. Pep	1,202	3,572	678	415	1,370	1,162	4,360	400	1,484	2,536	1,082	748	923	688
10 oz. Brite	1,157	3,500	569	840	1,363	663	4,038	529	877	2,213	888	1,582		543
10 oz. Action Ade														481
10 oz. Orange Orange							4,800		550	756	321	839	405	
10 oz. Dr. Spice													448	
10 oz. SF Orange Orange	466	1,770	143	65	578	87	2,341	124	82			100	100	
16 oz. Spirit	26,035	5,486	14,829	3,853	6,539	6,241	10,842	9,539	3,358	32,838	2,894	6,041	1,418	1,026
16 oz. Brite	1,525	287	2,003	97	468	280	1,107	1,005	926	2,343	1,370	639	44	104
16 oz. 11-Up				28		177		305		1,798		363	10	
16 oz. Pep	1,228			158		208		1,156				771	178	
16 oz. Dr. Spice	3,196		1,836	2		19		160		4,611			3	
1 liter All products	3,747	25,341	354	6,078	4,680	8,207	25,300	640	5,151	10,865	1,111	4,728	1,034	2,615
One-Way Bottles (nonreturnable)														
10 oz. All products	2,340	14,685	1,188	547	336	272	2,458	1,183	1,031		2,281	394	854	567
10 oz. Viva	225	811	149	4	8	24	677	87	51	231	6	40	19	4
16 oz. All products	8,071	33,275	9,347	2,611	7,358	2,968	19,282	1,521	11,220	5,624	2,201	9,562	4,857	1,383
28 oz. All products			745	311	439	340	3,187		687	1,889	393	959	187	87
2 liters All products	855	7,993	3,821	6,417		2,255	9,210	1,521	10,569	8,105	11,689	6,201	1,031	1,948
Cans														
12 oz. All products	19,641	21,952	3,821	6,417	13,112		56,957		13,887	59,070	16,947	17,863	2,960	9,755
Premix	3,396	32,280	1,008	468	2,064	4,096	5,972	260	1,784	7,804	656	1,948	1,948	1,268
All products	39,613	118,456	9,557	12,307	14,956	16,020		7,027					16,116	

449

TABLE 4-30 Inventory, May 1983 (Spirit Bottling Company)

PACKAGE AND PRODUCT	COON RAPIDS	ROCHESTER	ARKANSAW, WIS.	PRINCETON	SAUK CENTER	ST. BONIFACIUS	ST. CLOUD	RUSH CITY	NEW ULM	MINNEAPOLIS	LITTLE FALLS	RED WING	MANKATO	HUTCHINSON
Returnable Bottles														
6½ oz. Spirit	1,951	3,064	2,076	2,136	1,480	2,356	2,551	995	2,561	7,140	2,024	731	345	870
10 oz. Spirit	603	2,197	1,568	968	1,111	1,159	2,574	383	2,355	3,521	2,072	924	255	1,328
10 oz. 11-Up	48	374	127	194	190	346	321	137	90	204	168	138	138	70
10 oz. Pep	429	968	378	226	916	164	3,165	140	437	298	606	254	234	398
10 oz. Brite	196	868	281	569	401	87	4,282	164	618	265	343	180	86	492
10 oz. Action Ade	276	186	224	132	19	58	384	110	233	133	97	91	67	97
10 oz. Orange Orange		645	78	4	140		2,686		218	295	121	206	168	259
10 oz. Dr. Spice	97					157	939	98	211			425	98	
10 oz. SF Orange Orange													102	
16 oz. Spirit	4,047	663	1,492	608	1,509	2,264	3,353	913	1,302	3,571	1,013	1,285	284	525
16 oz. Brite	190	157	488	97	168	140	1,180	88	333	1,317	362	62	130	56
16 oz. 11-Up	204		370	44		44		110		416			40	
16 oz. Pep	299		104	209		94		131		833		201	126	126
16 oz. Dr. Spice	132			88		110		65		517			53	53
1 liter All products	2,229	4,474		2,163	2,191	5,613	8,898	646	1,908	9,178	1,453	1,842	1,479	1,703
One-Way Bottles (nonreturnable)														
10 oz. All products	156	5,743	683	147	1,372	821	500	180	448	2,497	660	405	646	623
10 oz. Viva		598	327	131	35	89	89		112	619	108	49	148	109
16 oz. All products	3,357	8,267	4,252	1,295	2,623	3,203	3,203	1,105	8,910	4,123	6,283	4,188	4,558	2,773
28 oz. All products	910	3,054	797	580	550	899	899	452	569	1,820	548	1,176	433	609
2-liters All products	10,439	12,015	4,057	4,408	5,259	6,283	6,283	2,911	5,864	13,401	10,068	3,475	2,831	3,092
Cans														
12 oz. All products	19,573	25,887	8,443	6,116	6,470	7,629	22,748	5,877	9,968	15,801	8,004	6,863	7,040	4,885
Premix	498	838	108	111	180	414	2,070	109	213	439	114	159	358	200
All products														

450

REFERENCE NOTES

1. For additional information on production scheduling, see:

Berry, W. L., et al. *Master Scheduling*. Washington, D.C.: American Production and Inventory Control Society, 1979.

Bowman, E. H. "Consistency and Optimality in Managerial Decision Making." *Management Science* 9, no. 2 (January 1963): 310–21.

Bowman, E. H. "Production Scheduling by the Transportation Method of Linear Programming." *Operations Research* 4, no. 1 (February 1956): 100–103.

Buffa, Elwood S., and Jeffrey G. Miller. *Production-Inventory Systems: Planning and Control*. 3d ed. Homewood, Ill.: Richard D. Irwin, 1979.

Conway, R. W., et al. *Theory of Scheduling*. Reading, Mass.: Addison-Wesley, 1967.

Eilon, Samuel. "Five Approaches to Aggregate Production Planning." *AIIE Transactions* 7, no. 2 (June 1975): 118–31.

Holt, C. C., et al. *Planning Production, Inventories, and Work Force*. Englewood Cliffs, N.J.: Prentice-Hall, 1960.

Plossl, George W., and Oliver W. Wight. *Production and Inventory Control: Principles and Techniques.* Englewood Cliffs, N.J.: Prentice-Hall, 1967.

Sandman, W. E., with J. P. Hayes. *How to Win Productivity in Manufacturing*. Dresher, Pa.: Yellow Book of Pennsylvania, 1980.

Vollman, T. E., Berry, W. L., and Whybark, D. Clay. *Manufacturing Planning and Control Systems*. Homewood, IL: Dow Jones-Irwin, 1984.

2. See William L. Berry, Thomas G. Schmitt, and Thomas E. Vollmann, "Capacity Planning Techniques for Manufacturing Control Systems: Information Requirements and Operational Features." *Journal of Operations Management* 3, no. 1 (November 1982), pp. 13–25.

3. For information on alternatives and refinements to the linear programming approach, see Buffa and Miller, *Production-Inventory Systems*, Chapter 6.

4. C. C. Holt F. Modigliani, and H. A. Simon, *Planning Production, Inventories, and Work Force* (Englewood Cliffs, N.J.: Prentice-Hall, 1960). Also, Holt, Modigliani, and Simon, "A Linear Decision Rule for Production and Employment Scheduling." *Management Science* 2, no. 2 (October 1955), pp. 10–30.

5. See particularly "Hierarchical Integration of Production Planning and Scheduling" by Arnaldo Hax and Harlan Meal in M. A. Geisler, ed., *Studies in the Management Sciences: Logistics*, Vol. 1 (New York: North-Holland, 1975); and "On the Design of Hierarchical Production Planning Systems" by G. R. Bitran and Arnaldo Hax in *Decision Sciences* 8, no. 1 (January 1977), pp. 28–55.

6. See W. H. Taubert, "A Search Decision Rule for the Aggregate Scheduling Problem," *Management Science* 14, no. 6 (February 1968), pp. 342–59.

7. For Q-CONTROL, see William E. Sandman and John P. Hayes, *How to Win Productivity in Manufacturing* (Dresher, Pa.: Yellow Book of Pennsylvania, 1980); for OPT, see Gene Bylinsky, "An Efficiency Guru with a Brown Box," *Fortune* (September 5, 1983): 120–32.

8. F. Robert Jacobs and Daniel J. Bragg, "Repetitive Lots: Job Flow Considerations in Production Dispatching, Sequencing, and Batch Sizing," working paper, School of Business, Indiana University, December 1985.

9. See Richard Schonberger, *Japanese Manufacturing Techniques: Nine Hidden Lessons in Simplicity* (New York: The Free Press, 1982) and Robert W. Hall, *Zero Inventories,* (Homewood IL: Dow Jones-Irwin, 1983); Richard Schonberger, *World Class Manufacturing: The Lessons of Simplicity Applied.* New York: The Free Press, 1986; and Robert W. Hall, *Attaining Manufacturing Excellence*, Homewood, IL: Dow Jones–Irwin, 1987.

10. For additional information on forecasting, see:

Box, George E.P., and Gwilym M. Jenkins. *Time Series Analysis: Forecasting and Control*. San Francisco: Holden-Day 1976.

Brown, Robert G. *Decision Rules for Inventory Management*. New York, Holt, Rinehart and Winston, 1967.
———. *Smoothing, Forecasting and Prediction of Discrete Time Series*. Englewood Cliffs, N.J.: Prentice-Hall, 1963.
Chambers, John C. et al. "How to Choose the Right Forecasting Technique." *Harvard Business Review* 49, no. 4 (July–August 1971): 45, 74.
Wheelwright, Steven C. and Spyros Makridakis, *Forecasting Methods for Management*. New York: John Wiley and Sons, Inc., 1985.

11. For the intellectually curious, a good description of the simplex method is found in W. J. Baumol, *Economic Theory and Operations Analysis*. 4th ed. (Englewood Cliffs, N.J.: Prentice-Hall, 1977). Harvey Wagner, *Principles of Operations Research: With Applications to Managerial Decisions*. 2d ed. (Englewood Cliffs, N.J.: Prentice-Hall, 1975) is also a useful source.

12. For information on critical paths and PERT, consult:

Kelley, J. R. "Critical path Planning and Scheduling: Mathematical Basis." *Operations Research* 9, no. 3 (1961).
Levy, F. K. et al. "The ABCs of the Critical Path Method." *Harvard Business Review* 41, no. 5 (September–October 1963): 98–108.
Malcolm, D. G., et al. "Application of a Technique for Research and Development Program Evaluation." *Operations Research* 7 (September-October 1959): 646-69. Reprinted as Chapter 29 in *Readings in Production and Operations Management*, E.S. Buffa, ed. (New York: John Wiley & Sons, 1966).
Smith, Larry A., and Joan Mills. "Projection Management Network Programs." *Project Management Quarterly* (June 1982): 18–29.
Wiest, Jerome D., and Ferdinand K. Levy. *A Management Guide to PERT/CPM: With Gert-PDM, DCPM, and Other Networks*. 2d ed. Englewood Cliffs, N.J.: Prentice-Hall, 1977.
Wiest, Jerome D., "Precedence Diagramming Method: Some Unusual Characteristics and Their Implications for Project Managers." *Journal of Operations Management* 1, no. 3 (February 1981): 121–130.

13. See Herbert F. Spirer, "The Basic Principles of Project Management," *Operations Management Review* 1, no. 1 (Fall 1982), pp. 7–8ff.

CHAPTER 5

MANAGING MATERIALS

As was evident from both the plant and the service tours of Segment I, considerable management attention is focused on ensuring that the proper materials are directed to the right places in timely fashion and at low cost. Managing materials well is not easy. A surprisingly large fraction of many operations' overhead personnel are devoted to the task, often a quarter or more.

It is useful to break the topic into three broad, interrelated areas:

- *Procurement.* This includes purchasing, materials receipt and inspection, storage, and any preparation and grouping of materials for the factory floor.

- *Materials Planning and Control.* This includes production planning, production control, and inventory control.

- *Logistics.* This includes transportation of inputs and outputs, and maintenance of customer service throughout the channels of distribution.

Chapter 4 dealt with production planning (aggregate planning, master scheduling) and production control (schedule monitoring, dispatching, and the elements of shop floor control). This chapter tackles what remains on the list: materials management. Let us consider procurement first.

PART ONE
PROCUREMENT

Procurement for most companies deliberately means more than simply purchasing.[1] It also involves all the steps it takes to prepare those materials to be used. In many plants, the materials organization "owns" all the materials until such time as they are released to the factory floor with specific orders, and the mainline manufacturing supervisors actually take charge of making the product. In addition to purchasing, then, procurement involves the receiving operation, any inspection done of incoming materials, their storage in a stockroom, and the withdrawal and preparation of those materials for the factory floor—for example, the assembly of kits of parts for release to the floor. In keeping with this division of responsibilities, let us explore the purchasing function first and then move on to a discussion of receiving, inspection, and storage.

Purchasing

The common duties of a purchasing department include all those discussed here.

Understanding Material Needs for Engineering and Manufacturing

One of the purchasing group's rights, too frequently overlooked, is to question the materials specifications established by design engineering (perhaps in consultation with manufacturing engineering). Sometimes purchasing can suggest substitute materials or product redesigns that use standard materials, thus lowering the costs implied by engineering's initial specifications. Purchasing should be actively engaged in any value engineering that occurs. (Recall Chapter 3's discussion of value engineering.)

How can purchasing perform this role effectively? Often, in the course of meeting with vendor (supplier) salespeople and in keeping abreast of developments in the industry, purchasing departments can uncover materials and products that may have been overlooked by design engineering. More and more, too, purchasing departments are asking their vendor base to be more innovative in what they do for the company. Often this means not defining the specifications so rigidly for the product and actively seeking the vendor's ideas for improving quality or costs.

Selecting and Evaluating Vendors

Many production and operations people believe that purchasing's chief obligation is to obtain materials at the lowest cost. This, however, is a narrow view of purchasing. Low cost is only one of the aspects of a vendor's performance that a purchasing department needs to monitor and foster. Exactly what constitutes a good vendor varies, of course, with the situation, but among the characteristics that purchasing departments should seek in addition to low cost are

- Quality (conformance to the established specifications)
- Delivery reliability
- Ability to deliver frequently, and/or speed of delivery
- Trustworthy and timely communication on any problem encountered
- Initiative in product design or materials; suggestions

Taking a lesson from Japanese companies, many U.S. companies (such as the auto companies) have recently undergone a massive reorientation of purchasing, shifting the emphasis from price to quality, special performance characteristics, and delivery. Many companies like to have at least two vendors supplying each raw material: they feel that competition for their business encourages lower prices and better service and that reliance on a single vendor can be risky in case of strikes, natural disasters, and other uncommon causes of delay. Other companies, particularly Japanese ones, feel that dealing with a single vendor can be more advantageous, especially if the customer can exercise clout with that vendor by being a significant customer. By employing a sole supplier, a company can often foster the quality and delivery performance that meshes best with its own operations; in a very real sense the vendor can act as an extension of the company's operations. The current trend among American companies is to reduce the vendor base. In some cases, this reduction has been dramatic.

No matter what the company decides about single versus multiple vendors, the purchasing department has to act as the company's eyes and ears in the raw materials marketplace. Vendors have to be sought for new materials or products, and the quality level of vendors has to be assessed before orders can be placed. Thereafter, purchasing must continue to evaluate the vendors it uses and help them to improve their performance.

Increasingly, companies are establishing formal vendor qualification or certification programs. This has been inspired mainly by increased devotion to quality conformance and the desire to move the vendor's product right into production (or storage) without having to inspect it. As one might expect, the stringency of the various programs varies markedly from company to company. In some companies a vendor can be "qualified" or "certified" merely by shipping two consecutive orders that have no detected defects. In other companies, the vendors must surmount a number of hurdles that may take years: inspection of their processes, filing process quality documents (control charts), developing histories of on-time shipments with no quality problems. For companies serious about quality and willing to use single source for their purchases, such stringent programs can lead to situations in which both customer and supplier win.

Negotiating Price, Delivery, and Quality

Purchasing typically must decide whether it wants a long-term (multiyear) contract with the vendor or a short-term or even spot (single-transaction) contract. Frequently, a long-term contract is required even to interest a vendor

in providing a specific item, particularly if the item is nonstandard. Otherwise, price expectations and views of supply risk usually play a major role in choosing between long- and short-term contracts. On many long-term contracts the specific price may not be settled ahead of time but instead may be negotiated at regular intervals.

Many companies (for example, General Motors) are using fewer suppliers and longer-term contracts. Many of these contracts are "blanket orders," which cover a variety of items, or "open-end orders," which permit items to be added and/or time to be extended. Customer companies using such tactics are flexible about prices and often are willing to share their demand forecast and order backlog information, but they demand consistent quality and frequent deliveries in return. As we saw in the plant tours, the huge demands of operations like GM—Tarrytown and Stroh—Winston-Salem permit those companies to seek—and be accorded—regular deliveries, thereby cutting down on inventory storage and carrying costs.

In large multiplant companies, purchasing can proceed at different levels. The corporate staff, for example, may negotiate and monitor the large supply contracts that feed a number of plants. By centralizing this activity, the company often can exert more clout over price and delivery terms than could plants each acting on their own. In addition, centralizing such purchasing may aid plant-to-plant coordination of materials. Smaller supply contracts may be left to individual plant negotiations. In some other companies, individual plants' purchasing departments may take the lead in keeping abreast of new developments in particular industries and negotiating company-wide contracts with vendors in those industries.

Quality checking varies from contract to contract. Many companies inspect incoming supplies (100 percent or a sampling). Some vendor contracts allow the posting of inspection teams within the vendor's plant to monitor quality and delivery and to aid that plant in meeting the requirements specified by the customer; both vendor and customer can reduce costs and overhead if incoming inspection in the customer plant can be avoided through a joint quality effort.

Placing Purchase Orders with Vendors

Traditionally, vendors did not deliver orders unless they had received purchase orders from the customers. This traditional mode of operation is still prevalent. However, with longer contracts and use of fewer suppliers, the actual release of the vendor's products to the customer is becoming more flexible. With closer customer/vendor ties and innovations like blanket or open-end long-term contracts, vendor deliveries can be released more informally, through telephone calls or plant paperwork that is less formal. In many instances, the contracts have been negotiated by a centralized purchasing function in the company that may have a more talented and savvy staff than any plant could hope to have. Nevertheless, the delivery of needed parts may be triggered by the plant itself and not by the centralized purchasing group.

Working Out Vendor Problems and Monitoring Orders

Here is where the procurement function, particularly at the plant level, wins its reputation, for good or for ill. Rarely does all go smoothly with orders and deliveries. The typical purchasing department must spend much time dealing with vendor quality or delivery problems—going to the vendor's plant, arranging meetings between engineering staffs, or tracing and expediting orders that are needed before the vendor's quoted lead time or for which ship-

ment has been delayed. The purchasing department can thus act as an early warning alarm system for materials shortage or quality problems that can affect the organization's schedule and quality performance.

Just-in-Time Production and Purchasing

Some of the elements of just-in-time production were discussed in Chapter 4, and more will be addressed in subsequent chapters, particularly Chapter 10. Several elements of just-in-time production relate to the purchasing function. Among them:

- Quality conformance viewed as more important than price
- Long-term relationships with suppliers
- Many single-source contracts
- Frequent deliveries of small quantities with the aim of being able to deliver directly to the factory floor, with no incoming inspection
- More stable production schedules for vendors to meet; visibility given to vendors about the customer's true needs

More and more companies are adopting aspects of just-in-time production and finding out how effective it can be. For some companies, however, just-in-time production does not mean implementing fundamental change on the factory floor. Rather, it constitutes an excuse to take advantage of vendors, forcing them to hold the inventory the customer does not want to hold, under the guise that the customer should receive it "just in time." This attitude does not really reflect the just-in-time concept. Companies adopting true just-in-time production typically work first on cleaning up their own operations before they try to work with vendors on theirs. The idea is to lower inventories throughout the pipeline and not just at the customer's plant.

The ABC Classification

Many companies have organized their purchasing staffs to mesh with the *ABC classification* of parts and materials. It has long been observed that in most companies a small fraction of the number of parts accounts for a disproportionately large fraction of purchasing expenditures. This small group of high-value items is typically classified as A items. The A items might account for 5 to 10 percent of the number of parts but 75 percent of the value of all parts. At the other extreme are the C items: 80 percent of the number of parts that account for only 10 percent or so of their value. The B group falls between the extremes—perhaps 10 to 15 percent of the number of parts and 10 to 15 percent of their value. Such an ABC classification provides a means of breaking down the tasks of dealing with vendors and tracking the materials needed by the operation. Specific staff members can be assigned to deal with A items only, B items only, or C items only; in this way, purchasing department resources can be matched well to the importance particular parts have to purchasing expenditures. The ABC classification can be used by the production and inventory control groups to assign responsibilities for tracking materials and orders.

The benefits a company derives from a well-functioning purchasing department have often been overlooked. In the typical manufacturing company, purchasing materials account for about half of the cost of goods sold. Securing good prices for these materials can have a substantial impact on the company's profit. The smooth coordination between materials and individual plants is also important so that production schedules are not impeded by the purchasing department's failures. Consistent vendor quality is a third essential aspect of the purchasing function. Recently many companies have elevated the status of the materials function, both formally in the company's organization chart and informally in the attention, prestige, and talent devoted to it.

RECEIVING, INSPECTION, AND STORAGE

The functions of receiving and inspecting incoming materials and then storing them are sometimes overlooked. Nonetheless, they can be very important for the smooth functioning of the operation. Processing incoming orders is becoming increasingly automated and linked better to the rest of the process. Several issues surface when we examine these functions, and these issues are helpful in suggesting some of the alternatives available.

Receiving and Inspection

1. Did the vendor ship the proper items and in the quantities requested? Was the order received on time?
2. Is the receipt properly reported in the plant's materials system so that its status can be tracked accurately?

   For most plants, now, this information is computerized. Terminals in the receiving area log in this information and reconcile it with purchasing and production control information.
3. Are the incoming materials packaged in convenient ways for use by the factory floor? Less popular today are the old practices of shipping bulk quantities of material that a factory's receiving operation has to break down into more convenient quantities. Instead, shipments are not only being made in

smaller quantities, as already noted, but also in containers and packaging that facilitates their use in the process.

4. What kind of inspection is appropriate for incoming materials?

- What orders require 100 percent inspection, where every piece is inspected and sorted into good or bad categories?
- What orders receive acceptance sampling, where a sample from every lot of material shipped is inspected and inferences are then drawn about the disposition of the entire lot?
- When can purchases receive no inspection at all on a routine basis; perhaps, only some occasional auditing done at random?

There will be considerably more discussion of quality matters in Chapter 6. Suffice it here to note that acceptance sampling is currently overwhelmingly the most popular means of doing incoming inspection. As Chapter 6 will discuss, however, doing no inspection may make more sense, and current trends are moving toward reduced inspection of incoming materials.

5. What is done with any rejected material?

The discipline with which plants return rejected material to vendors varies considerably. Some plants are rigid and prompt with returns. Others hang on to rejected material just in case it might turn out to be needed.

Storage

1. How many storage areas are there, and is access to them controlled?

2. How automated are the storeroom's operations?

3. How is control kept?

Most manufacturing plants have a single, restricted access storeroom and a stringent routine for checking material in or out. Other plants have multiple storerooms. Traditionally, storage operations have used standard racks, bins, boxes, and pallets to store and to stage materials either for the factory floor or for shipment. Such systems are fairly labor-intensive in both materials handling (fork-lift truck operators, workers to break down bulk lots) and materials control functions. There are two conventional types of layouts for storerooms. The first keeps all the material of a particular kind together in a unique location in the storeroom. When an order has to be filled (either for the factory floor or for shipment), storeroom personnel travel the aisles and pick the required materials from their many locations. A second alternative saves labor by diminishing the travel from bin to bin; however, it requires more space and racks. This alternative adds some staging area storage so that some racks are used for bulk storage and others strictly as intermediate storage. Thus, when orders are filled, they are filled from the intermediate, staging area racks only. From time to time, as the material in the staging area dwindles, it is replenished from the bulk racks. The appropriateness of one alternative versus the other depends, naturally, on the balance of storage space and rack costs versus personnel costs. The higher a company's personnel costs are relative to space and rack costs, the more attractive is the intermediate, staging area layout. Conventional storage systems have some endemic problems, however. They often use space ineffectively, suffer from inaccurate counts of material, and misdirect materials.

There have been some recent developments that have improved on the traditional systems, however. Bar-coding and automated storage and retrieval systems merit mention.

Bar-coding involves the use of codes, like the universal product codes now found on grocery items, to identify particular lots of material. Storeroom workers can pass light scanning wands over these codes easily and ensure that accurate information on the status of material is placed into material management's computerized records. Bar-codes are also used to direct boxes, trays, and pallets along a plant's (or distribution center's) conveyor system. Stations along the conveyor automatically read the bar-coding and route the material to the proper area.

Automated storage and retrieval systems (AS/RS) use specially constructed aisles, stacks, and bins with computer controlled cranes to store and retrieve automatically what conventional systems do with operators riding fork-lift trucks or manually picking items. The AS/RS system's computer keeps track of where all the material is, when it was stored, and the remaining quantity. The computer can also route the crane's movement along the aisle and up and down the stacks most efficiently, so that the crane does not become a bottleneck. AS/RS systems can be very expensive, but they offer labor and space savings, increased accuracy, and the capability of always using the oldest material first.

There are, of course, some less-automated options that still improve on the conventional stacks. These semiautomated options may involve man-aboard cranes and routings that are not controlled by computer. They can still offer substantial improvements for the storeroom, however.

With the advent of computer systems, control over what is in the storeroom has become easier. The computer can easily track the transactions (in, out, inspected or not, returned, scrap) entered by the storeroom's personnel.

What remains critical is the discipline of the storeroom's personnel and systems. Are discrepancies identified quickly and reconciled immediately and completely? If the personnel are permitted to be sloppy about handling transactions, the control of the storeroom will suffer. Although most plant auditors still require annual physical inventories to count parts, some plants are maintaining control so effectively with *cycle counts* (counts of one item at a time at periodic intervals) that physical inventories are no longer required.

THE MAKE-BUY DECISION

Although typically not the responsibility of the purchasing department, the decision as to what the factory should make for itself and what it should purchase on the outside is one for which the purchasing department is a key source of information. The make-buy decision is a common one, especially in companies that have purposely split their supply needs between in-house operations and outside vendors.

What does a make-buy decision entail? Consider Situation 5-1.

Discussion of Dulaney Toy Company

The decision Rick Jerauld faces, that of pulling in some subcontracted parts, is one that companies in cyclical industries face regularly. The five criteria that Jerauld considers appropriate are all issues that a manager should consider for a make-buy decision. A part should not be pulled back to the injection molding department unless (1) it would make a significant dent in the excess labor the company is experiencing, (2) it costs less to do it inside (more com-

SITUATION 5-1

DULANEY TOY COMPANY

He knew that the business was sometimes boom or bust, but that still didn't mean he liked the "bust" part. Rick Jerauld, the manager of the injection molding department at the Dulaney Toy Company, was on the horns of a dilemma. After several years of record sales and growth, Dulaney Toy appeared to be in for a slow year. Sales for Dulaney's two latest entries in the fickle toy market—the incredible Smiling Monster and the Cynical Santa—simply did not appear to be taking off as the company's marketing people had claimed. Given the sales declines of some of Dulaney's older toys, which was characteristic of product life cycles in the industry, many of Dulaney's manufacturing departments had spare capacity. The injection molding department, which was responsible for all the plastic injection-molded parts of Dulaney's toys, was among them.

Rick was loath to lay off any of the workers in his department, particularly given the company's often stated goal of lifetime employment for its loyal and productive workforce. What this left was for Rick to start pulling back to his department the manufacture of plastic parts that Dulaney had subcontracted to other firms. Fortunately, Dulaney had a battery of such plastic injection-molded parts, but this abundance did not lessen Rick Jerauld's concern about which of the parts now produced by vendors (suppliers) he should pull back to his own department.

As Jerauld thought about it, several criteria appeared to be appropriate to deciding the issue:

1. Whether the part demanded many labor-hours because of its complexity or because it was produced in large quantities.

2. Whether the part could be manufactured as cheaply at Dulaney Toy as at the vendor's. At

TABLE 5-1   Candidate parts for pulling back to the factory (Dulaney Toy Company)

PART	AVERAGE VOLUME PER MONTH	CURRENT STATUS	VENDER PRICE (includes adjustment)	INTERNAL COST—ACTUAL OR ESTIMATE				COMMENTS
				MATERIALS	LABOR	OVERHEAD	TOTAL	
Caboose under-carriage	6000	Long-term contract; made in shop before	11.97¢	3.20¢	1.37¢	5.20¢	9.77¢	Vendor problems with quality and delivery
Caboose roof	6000	Long-term contract	9.60	2.77	3.93	12.57	19.27	
Caboose railings	12,000	Short-term contract	3.79	0.88	3.03	5.75	9.66	Same vendor as caboose roof
Crib gym bar	2000	Long-term contract; made in shop before	22.39	5.91	6.70	9.53	22.14	
Crib gym flower	8000	Long-term contract; always made outside	18.26	3.58	4.43	11.66	19.67	$1500 in tooling needed

present, Dulaney Toy's formula for such cost comparisons called for comparing the vendor's price for the part (adjusted upward for the expected costs Dulaney Toy would incur in purchasing the part and in having it transported and inspected) against the calculated, internal factory cost for the part, which included all materials, labor, and overhead.

3. What effect pulling the part back would have on the vendor and on Dulaney Toy's expected future use of the vendor in boom times when Dulaney Toy was short of capacity. Rick was naturally leery of doing anything to antagonize his vendor base to the point where many vendors would be reluctant to bid for Dulaney Toy's business in the future.

4. What risk the part carried for becoming obsolete in the near future.

5. What impact the part would make on shop operations, given the prevailing conditions on the shop. That is, would the part need special tooling or require setup times that would make its coordination with other parts running through the shop difficult?

One of Rick's assistants had developed a sheet of candidate parts for pulling back to the factory (Table 5-1). Some were made exclusively by vendors, while others were made both by the injection molding department and by vendors. The candidate parts identified to date derived from two of the company's more successful toys, Walter the Caboose and the Little Monkey Crib Gym.

Rick needed to decide which of the parts should be pulled back inside his department and which should be left with the vendors. Also, Rick wanted to develop a system whereby he could put priorities on parts that should be brought back first and ones that could be allowed to wait.

ment on this later), (3) the vendor would not be so adversely affected that it could not be counted on for future contracts, (4) the part is not in danger of becoming obsolete in the near future, and (5) the part could be fitted into the shop fairly smoothly.

Judgment is required in assessing many of these. The cost comparison is more mechanical, but it should be noted that Dulaney Toy's present method for comparing costs is plainly incorrect. The present cost comparison ignores the fact that the make-buy decision is a marginal one, just like the Citrus Airlines situation examined in Chapter 2. That is to say, although the vendor's price, as adjusted, is a variable cost to Dulaney Toy, not all of the internal factory costs vary with the factory's level of production. Overhead expenses, for example, would have to be covered no matter what the level of factory output. And, if Dulaney Toy is serious

about lifetime employment for its workers, it can be argued that, for the short run at least, the factory's labor costs are fixed as well.

Thus, by bringing in-house any product for which the materials-plus-labor factory cost is less than the vendor quote-plus-adjustment, Dulaney Toy's contribution (see Chapter 2) would be enhanced. Table 5-2 computes the contribution for each of the candidate parts listed in Table 5-2.

Table 5-2 suggests that under no circumstances should the caboose railings be pulled back to the factory. In fact, the vendor producing both the caboose railings and the caboose roof looks like it should be encouraged to produce even more than it is, since its prices look very good indeed. Perhaps, the short-term contract for railings should be extended to long-term. The possibility remains, however, that the vendor price is not low, but that the fac-

TABLE 5-2　Contribution figures for candidate parts (Dulaney Toy Company)

PART	VENDOR PRICE PER UNIT (includes adjustment)	INTERNAL VARIABLE COST (materials and labor)	CONTRIBUTION PER UNIT (if pulled back to factory)	CONTRIBUTION PER MONTH
Caboose undercarriage	11.97¢	4.57¢	7.40¢	$444.00
Caboose roof	9.60	6.70	2.90	174.00
Caboose railings	3.79	3.91	−0.12	−14.40
Crib gym bar	22.39	12.61	9.78	195.60
Crib gym flower	18.26	8.01	10.25	820.00

TABLE 5-3　Index of contribution per penny of labor cost (Dulaney Toy Company)

PART	CONTRIBUTION PER UNIT (if pulled back to factory)	LABOR COST PER UNIT	CONTRIBUTION PER PENNY OF LABOR COST
Caboose undercarriage	7.40¢	1.37¢	5.40¢
Caboose roof	2.90	3.93	0.74
Caboose railings	−0.12	3.03	−0.04
Crib gym bar	9.78	6.70	1.46
Crib gym flower	10.25	4.43	2.31

tory's estimated cost is high. This should be investigated.

Dulaney Toy would earn additional contribution by pulling in any of the parts except the caboose railings. Even the $1500 tooling expense for the crib gym flower would be paid for out of added contribution within two months. The issue remains, however, in what order the various parts should be pulled back to the factory, at least according to the prevailing economics. In a sense, what we are looking for is to pull back the parts with the most "bang for the buck." Here this translates into the most contribution per some unit of scarce resource, which might be something like factory time or labor cost. In fact, time and labor costs are likely to be highly correlated. This means that an index constructed as contribution per unit/labor cost per unit should give us a fair picture of which parts can add the most contribution quickly. Table 5-3 displays the values for this index of contribution per penny of labor cost.

It is clear from Table 5-3 that the company is best served by pulling in-house the caboose undercarriage first, then the crib gym flower, followed by the crib gym bar, and the caboose roof. From the comments in Table 5-1 this priority appears consistent with some of the other criteria mentioned for the make-buy decision. We must be sure, however, to include in the evaluation whether the crib gym flower, with the tooling required, will be pulled back for a long enough time to justify pulling it back.

A sensitivity analysis can help here. Let x be months. We want to calculate the number of months it would take before the crib gym flower would contribute as much as the crib gym bar, knowing that we would rather pull in the flower because its contribution per penny of labor cost is higher. Drawing from the contribution per month figures in Table 5-2,

$$contribution\ from\ bar = contribution\ from\ flower$$

$$\$195.60x = \$820.00x - \$1500$$

$$x = 2.40\ months$$

If we plan to produce crib gym flowers for 2.4 months or more, we can expect to gain more contribution than by producing the crib gym bar, in addition to a higher contribution per penny of labor cost.

PART TWO
MANAGING INVENTORIES

Our investigation of the different production processes of Segment I has already uncovered a number of places within the typical process where inventories come in handy. In broad terms, we saw inventories of raw materials, work-in-process, and finished goods.

Other things being equal, of course, a company would like not to hold any inventories, because they mean tying up its cash in goods that cannot improve the company's earnings like a new piece of machinery can, or even like putting cash in the bank.* In other words, inventories represent some very real opportunity costs to the company since, by financing inventories, the company forgoes the opportunity to earn a better return by using its cash in some other, income-generating way.

As we also saw in Segment I, some processes are organized in certain ways expressly for the purpose of reducing inventories of one kind or another. The job shop, for example, typically produces only to order—eliminating any concern for managing a finished goods inventory. Because many orders require very specialized raw materials either supplied by the customer or placed on special order, the job shop's need to manage raw materials inventories is very modest. It is in the realm of work-in-process inventories that the job shop is truly challenged with the control of inventories.

The inventory concerns of the continuous flow process are almost exactly the reverse of those of the job shop. The entire design of the continuous flow process revolves around speeding the manufacture of a very standard product, which implies a rock-bottom level of work-in-process inventory. Because the process's appetite for raw materials is so steady and predictable, raw materials inventories can usually be held down by insisting on long-term supply contracts with a steady flow of materials. It is only at the finished goods end where inventories can mushroom and where their control presents real management challenges.

Process types in between the poles of job shop and continuous flow generally strike some middle ground in the importance of raw materials, work-in-process, and finished goods inventory control.

THE OBJECTIVES OF INVENTORY MANAGEMENT

Raw materials inventories, work-in-process inventories, and finished goods inventories all play different roles in the operation. As we have seen, the importance of those roles depends on the process. Managers should be clear about the major functions of these types of inventory for their particular processes.[2]

The major functions of raw materials inventory are:

- To protect (as a buffer) against the unreliable delivery of needed raw materials
- To hold costs down if possible by buying large quantities or by buying at propitious times

*Other things are not always equal, however. Sometimes holding large inventories can make sense; the seasonality of logging, for example, is one reason why International Paper's Androscoggin Mill has a significant raw materials inventory. Also some raw materials purchases may be unusually large for speculative reasons—to avoid an expected increase in price.

The major functions of work-in-process inventory are:

- To protect (as a buffer) against the unreliable delivery of materials from elsewhere in the production process
- To permit one segment of the process to operate under a different production plan and schedule from another segment of the process (a decoupling inventory)
- To permit individual workstations or machine centers to produce parts/assemblies/materials in sizable batches, rather than individually or in smaller batches. Such "cycle" inventories act to tide the process over until the next setup.

The major functions of finished goods inventory are:

- To supply the product quickly to the consumer
- To protect (as a buffer) against the uncertainties of consumer demand
- To smooth (through the accumulation of finished goods inventory) the demands on the process even while demand is erratic or temporarily depressed

The tools that production managers can wield in dealing with work-in-process inventories are frequently very different from the tools they can use to control raw materials or finished goods. As we shall soon see, the available techniques for controlling either raw materials inventories or finished goods inventories are relatively well developed and widely known. Because of this, it is often taken for granted that these inventories are managed adequately; when many production managers think about managing inventories, they think about work-in-process inventories. Here the management tools are more ill-defined, since reducing work-in-process inventory generally means grappling with the production process itself and/or with the flow of information through it.

To control work-in-process inventory levels, the manager might contemplate ways to shorten production cycle times (such as shortening process steps or coupling operations more closely) or ways to break existing production bottlenecks or ways to improve the flow of information around the process. Some situations already discussed (2-1 and 2-2) have dealt with such means of managing work-in-process inventories and more situations to come will deal with it, since this kind of inventory management is intimately involved with the planning of production, with capacity changes, and with the organization of operations.

So far, we have classified inventory solely according to its place within the process (raw materials, work-in-process, finished goods). There are other classifications possible; one useful one was developed by Joseph Orlicky, who distinguishes between inventories of dependent demand items and independent demand items. *Independently demanded items* are those finished goods or other items whose demands are unrelated to anything else produced or sold by the company. *Dependently demanded items*, on the other hand, are those that can be directly linked to a specific product—typically, they are components and subassemblies that can be linked to an end item by a bill of materials. In such a case, demand for the end item automatically triggers demand for known quantities of the parts and materials that go into the product.

This distinction is useful because dependent demands fall out naturally from knowledge of their end items—there are no uncertainties—whereas independent demands are full of uncertainties as to both quantities required and timing desired. The inventory policies applicable to independently demanded items can be very different from the inventory policies applicable to dependently demanded items. For the most part, the management of finished goods inventories and, to a lesser extent, raw materials inventories is management of independently demanded items.

It is not too far off the mark to visualize the problem of managing either raw materials inventory or finished goods inventory as one of managing piles of "stuff" that either the process itself or consumers in the marketplace draw down. The objective of good inventory management in this case is to offer good service to either the process or the market at reasonably low cost. This objective, in turn, means deciding how many items should be in each pile, when orders to replenish the piles ought to be placed, and how much each of those orders should contain. Managing such inventory stocks (as opposed to managing work-in-process) essentially means deciding these three questions of pile size, order time, and order size.

Because the timing of independent demands is often so uncertain, the techniques typically used for managing inventories of such demands are themselves independent of time. These techniques are sometimes called *non-time-phased inventory systems*, meaning simply that they do not attempt to be so precise about timing orders to expected use.[3] Their purpose is the same, however: to replenish a pile of items in timely fashion and at reasonably low cost. Retailing and distribution activities easily lend themselves to such techniques; consumer demands are frequently variable and uncertain.

The two major non-time-phased techniques have these differing philosophies:

1. Replenish the pile on a regular basis (daily, weekly, monthly) and bring it back up to the size you want (we will talk shortly about the desired size of the pile). The amount by which you replenish the pile may vary from one time to another, but you always replenish the pile. This basic strategy is often called a *periodic reorder system*.

2. Keep a constant watch over the pile. When its size dips to a predetermined level (we will talk shortly about this level), replenish the pile enough to bring it back up to the size you desire. Under this philosophy, the amount by which you replenish the pile stays the same, but the time spans between replenishments may vary. This basic strategy is frequently termed a *reorder point system*, the "reorder point" being the predetermined level that, once reached, triggers the replenishment of the pile by the same amount.

More will be said about periodic reorder and reorder point systems and their application to independent demand inventories. These same systems can also be applied to dependent demands inventories, as well, although frankly, with much less success. There is another approach to managing inventories that merits immediate introduction, namely an anticipatory approach. Such an approach has its most powerful application with dependent demand, but it can apply as well to independent demand.

By this approach, a company manages its inventories by anticipating their use and planning order size and timing accordingly to keep the stocks at some desired, low level. One ideal for such an anticipatory approach to inventory is to have no finished goods inventory over and above that expressly planned for, and little or no raw materials inventory. Work-in-process inventories then would account for by far the greatest chunk of total inventory costs. What is needed to accomplish this anticipatory approach to inventory is a firm fix on exactly what products are to be produced and when, what materials go into making each product, when in the production cycle each part or material is used, and how long it takes suppliers to deliver these parts or materials. This is a lot of information, but every bit is needed if in fact inventories are going to be matched to a company's output. In more formal phrasing, such an approach to inventory management demands the following pieces of information:

1. Master production schedule (MPS)—when each product is scheduled to be manufactured. Usually the MPS is developed for a month or a week. The firmness by which the schedule is held to can vary markedly from company to company and from time to time.

2. Bills of materials for each product—exactly which parts or materials are required to make each product.

3. Production cycle times and materials needs at each stage of the production cycle—how long it takes to manufacture each product and at what points along the way different parts and materials are needed. For many products the production cycle time is so short that all of the product's "ingredients" must arrive at essentially the same time. For more complex products, the manufacturing time is considerable; if all parts were delivered at the same time, a portion of them would be lying around for months before being incorporated into the product. Here, then, the staggering of parts delivery makes good sense.

4. Supplier lead times—how long it takes each supplier to deliver each part purchased from it.

These four pieces of information work together to determine what should be ordered and when. The MPS, together with the bill of materials, determines what should be ordered; the MPS, the production cycle times, and the supplier lead times jointly determine when the order should be placed.

These elements form an anticipatory approach to inventory management, which lies at the heart of material requirements planning (MRP). MRP can become quite a bit more involved than this in actual practice (as we shall see later in the chapter), but at its roots lies this relatively simple notion of managing raw materials stocks by anticipating their use.

Before continuing the discussion of each of these inventory management philosophies—material requirements planning, periodic reorder systems, and reorder point systems—a glance at Figure 5-1 may help to summarize the fundamental differences in their approaches to inventory management.

The Workings of Non-Time-Phased Inventory Systems

Relevant Costs and Concepts

The decisions that have to be reached in non-time-phased inventory systems—those of pile size, when to replenish the pile, and how much should be in a replenishment—involve balancing a variety of costs. Several kinds of costs are relevant, as described here.

Costs of Holding the Inventory

Inventory is not costless to stock. There are a number of costs to consider, the major one being *opportunity cost of capital*. This is the cost incurred by having the company's capital devoted to financing the inventory rather than invested in some other, income-producing endeavor (machines, personnel, a bank account). Often the company's cost of capital is used to estimate the magnitude of this opportunity cost.

FIGURE 5-1 Different philosophies of inventory management.

Other, lesser costs of holding inventory include:

1. Storage and handling: the costs of warehousing, handling, counting, and keeping track of the inventory.
2. Insurance and taxes: standard, out-of-pocket costs mandated for inventories of all types.
3. Obsolescence and shrinkage: costs that should be imputed to inventories because, typically, not all of the items placed into inventory can be pulled back out and used when needed. Some items become obsolete because of engineering changes. Other items deteriorate or break or, in some other way, become unusable. This represents a cost of holding inventory.

Costs of Securing More Inventory

There are several kinds of costs incurred in securing one more replenishment for a pile of inventory. Moreover, it is important to recognize that these costs ought to be marginal (incremental) costs and not average costs. For example, consider preparing a purchase order for

an outside vendor. The average costs of that order might include the time of the buyer and clerk involved, as well as the cost of the paperwork and phone calls to place and keep track of the order itself. If, as is nearly always the case, the buyer and the clerk would be employed anyway, then their costs are not relevant to the calculation of the cost of the order and thus should be excluded.

The kinds of costs incurred to secure more inventory can include:

1. Order costs: costs associated with placing orders for materials from outside vendors. The marginal costs of ordering are generally very low, consisting for the most part of some telephone charges and some paperwork.
2. Production changeover costs: if the inventory to be secured is from within the plant, then the replenishment will likely impose some costs over and above the costs of the inventory units themselves. A new setup takes time, imposing an opportunity cost on the factory because that setup time might have been spent producing output. Some-

times the opportunity cost is zero (that is, no output would be foregone by using the time for setup), but it is a point well worth considering. The setup itself may involve costs—fresh tooling, cleaning, new production materials, generated scrap. The replenishment may also cause the factory to increase capacity through overtime, new hires, subcontracting, or the like, and these means of enhancing capacity can be costly in incremental terms.

3. Tracking costs: costs involved in determining when an order or production changeover should happen. Stashes of inventory have to be monitored, which takes people, systems, and paperwork. Frequently, inventory levels cannot be accurately determined easily, so real economies exist in tracking inventory items in bunches and in placing purchase or production orders in groups, rather than one at a time.

    This is particularly true for items for which perpetual inventory records (records of the current quantities for each item, updated constantly through transactions of receipt and disbursement of the item from the stockroom) are not kept, or, at least, not kept very accurately.

4. Volume discounts: the considerable savings that often can be enjoyed by buying (or manufacturing) items in quantity. Many vendors publish price lists with discounts given for bulk purchases.

Costs of Not Having Enough Inventory

When a company cannot meet demand out of finished goods inventory, it can incur several (sometimes significant) costs. If the customer is willing to wait for the item—the item is then said to be *backordered*—there are likely to be additional costs for tracking the order: expediting it, shipping it specially, and invoicing. If

the customer is not willing to wait for the item and presumably goes elsewhere to purchase it or its substitute, the company forgoes a sale and, thereby, the contribution to fixed costs and profits that sale could have made. Indeed, by stocking out, the company may forgo all future sales by that consumer, thus losing the contribution possible from future purchases. Backorders are cheap compared to this kind of loss. However, determining the cost of a stockout, or even of a backorder, is fraught with problems, because so many different assumptions can be made about the consumer's present and future actions. Sometimes a backorder is regarded as appropriate, whereas other times the penalty is stiffer: no future sales. A typical cost assigned to a stockout is the one-time loss of contribution from the item, but such an estimate could be high or low without the company knowing for sure.

Also relevant to inventory management are lead time for the item (the time it takes to receive an ordered shipment) and safety stocks held. Safety stock levels will be discussed later; for the present we will simply acknowledge their usefulness. Lead times are important to calculations of the expected demand for the item between ordering a supply of it and receiving the order.

Exactly how the costs of inventory interact among themselves and interact as well with lead times and safety stocks—to determine inventory levels, timing, and replenishment quantities—depends upon which approach is taken. The periodic reorder technique balances these costs differently from the reorder point technique. In general, though, the higher the costs of holding inventory, the less inventory we want to have on hand at any time, the more frequently we want it to be replenished, and the smaller we want any replenishment quantity to be. The higher the costs of securing more inventory or of not having enough, the more

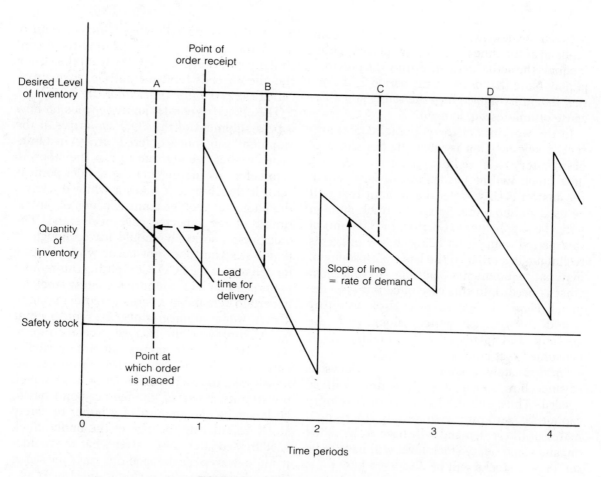

FIGURE 5-2 The periodic reorder system.

inventory we are willing to have on hand, the less frequent the replenishment, and the larger the replenishment quantity. These costs thus pull in opposing directions and must be balanced against one another. The next sections examine how those balances are made.

The Periodic Reorder System

The periodic reorder system is governed by the simple decision rule of "order enough each period (day, week, month, or whatever) to bring the pile of items inventoried back up to its desired size." This is similar to filling the car's gasoline tank every Friday. The workings of the system can be clarified by reference to Figure 5-2. The solid line traces the actual level of inventory held. The replenishments arrived at equally spaced times (1, 2, 3, 4), but their amounts differed each time. The replenishments were also ordered at equally spaced intervals (A, B, C, D), separated from the arrival times by a consistent delivery lead time. The amount ordered each time was the difference between the desired level and the actual amount on-hand at the time the order was placed. Thus, it equals the actual demand during the previous period. Note that during time period 2, the actual inventory dipped into the safety stock because of unforeseen demand.

In the workings of the periodic reorder system, a key question is what the desired level of inventory is. If we know in advance exactly how much will be needed during any period, the answer is easy: order the amount that will be used and no more. So, as the truck pulls in with the supply for next period, the last unit of this period's supply is being drawn off. This technique is similar to the basic philosophy of material requirements planning—to order just what is needed. In this case of certainty of demand, Figure 5-2's desired level of inventory would change each period, along with the amounts anticipated (always correctly) to be consumed that period.

Unfortunately, a company rarely knows in advance how much of a given item will be needed. Thus, the desired level of inventory cannot be determined so readily. Mere estimates of likely demand will have to be relied on, and some safety stock level will have to be set. (Safety stocks will be discussed later.)

The Reorder Point System

The reorder point inventory system follows the decision rule of "watch withdrawals from the pile of inventory until the designated reorder point is struck and then order the fixed amount needed to build the pile back up to its desired size." This is similar to filling the gasoline tank whenever the gauge reads 1/4 full. But, again, the question is, What is the desired size? Consult Figure 5-3.

The desired size in this case is not determined, as in the periodic reorder system, by the expected usage over the period, since there is no regular period following which inventory needs are checked. The pile is monitored continually, not every so often. Instead, the size of the pile depends fundamentally on a quantity called the *economic order quantity* or *EOQ*.

The choice of reorder point depends on how soon a shipment of the EOQ can arrive. If the shipment can, once ordered, arrive instantaneously, then we are safe to run the stock to zero before reordering and the reorder point is zero. If the shipment takes a while to arrive, the choice of reorder point depends on an estimate of the expected pace of demand. The order point normally should leave enough so that a stockout does not occur while waiting for delivery of the EOQ. Computing this reorder point is much like computing a safety stock for uncertain demand in a periodic reorder system. If there were no uncertainty, the reorder point would simply be the average expected rate of withdrawal from inventory per time period (x parts per day) times the number of time periods it will take to receive the order of EOQ. Given uncertainty, however, the reorder point has to be larger by the amount of a buffer or safety stock (calculating the size of the buffer stock is addressed later). No matter what the reorder point, however, the decision rule stays the same: When the reorder point is struck, order the EOQ.

How does the company determine how much the EOQ should be? The key to this order quantity and the reason it can be claimed as economic is the process by which it is found. The EOQ is chosen as the order quantity that minimizes the "total variable costs associated with changing order quantities." Every word of this phrase is meaningful. There are a variety of EOQ formulas, but what is important is the *process* by which the EOQ is found, not any formula that might seem to apply.

Let us consider a very simple, conventional, but suggestive case where we can discover a minimum for the total variable costs. In this

Notice that the reorders are not done at periodic times but at irregular times that are a function of the demand rate at that point.

FIGURE 5-3 The reorder point system.

case, there are only two variable costs that are in any way associated with any changing of order quantities.

1. *Inventory carrying costs.* These carrying costs vary directly with the order quantity, since the larger the order quantity, the larger is the average inventory held and thus the larger the carrying costs incurred. To illustrate this point in greater detail, let us make the common—and convenient—assumption that the demand on the inventory is absolutely steady, as is represented in Figure 5-4. Given this constant rate of draw upon the inventory, the average number of units in inventory is half of the order size. So if Q is the order size (see Figure 5-4), the average inventory is $Q/2$. As we shall discuss later,

this is an important simplification in this computation of minimum total costs.

2. *Order costs.* The order cost for any single order is a constant. The costs of actually placing or setting up the orders for the inventory thus vary inversely with the order quantity. The larger the size of the order (for a fixed annual demand), the fewer the orders that have to be processed, and thus the lower the order costs are. These order costs can be the costs incurred in dealing with vendors or the costs incurred in setting up the order in a manufacturing department of the company. For this case, assume that (1) the time from order to receipt is a constant and (2) no stockouts are deliberately permitted. (In Figure 5-3 stockouts are deliberately permitted.)

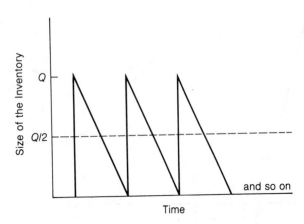

FIGURE 5-4 Graph depicting the assumption of steady demand on an inventory.

we can define the total variable costs in symbols as follows:

Total variable costs = order costs + carrying costs

= (cost per order)(number of orders) + (period carrying cost as a percentage)(value of average inventory)

$$= (S)\left(\frac{D}{Q}\right) + [i]\left[C\left(\frac{Q}{2}\right)\right]$$

where

S = cost per order

D = period demand, usually annual demand

Q = order quantity

i = period carrying cost as a percentage (includes opportunity cost, physical costs of handling and storage, obsolescence)

C = *variable* cost per unit inventory

$\dfrac{Q}{2}$ = average number of units in inventory, assuming a steady and constant demand

It is important to note what is not included as a variable cost associated with changing order quantities. For example, the cost of the inventory itself is not included because, for a fixed annual demand and a fixed price per unit, the cost of the inventory does not vary with changes in the order quantity. However, if a supplier were willing to give discounts on orders above a certain size, for example, the cost of the items in inventory would become a cost that varies with different order quantities and should be included in the total cost calculation. Transportation costs are also assumed not to vary with changes in the order size, nor are any production or other related costs.

Given the assumptions spelled out above, and with the knowledge that the only variable costs we can associate with different order quantities in this case are carrying costs and order costs,

We want to solve for the order quantity (Q) for which the total cost is a minimum. Given the particular expressions for carrying cost and order cost, one way to solve for this minimum is to set the order cost equal to the carrying cost, since the intersection of these two lines falls directly below the low point of the graph of total cost. (see Figure 5-5).*

---

*In general, of course, one cannot rely on friendly mathematical functions to solve for the minimum of an expression like that for total costs. One must rely on calculus to develop an expression for the slope and solve for Q, the order

FIGURE 5-5 Costs versus order quantities for the simple case of carrying costs and order costs only.

Setting order cost equal to carrying cost and solving for Q yields

$$S\left(\frac{D}{Q}\right) = iC\frac{Q}{2}$$

$$2SD = iCQ^2$$

$$Q = \sqrt{2SD/iC}$$

What does this solution mean for this simple example? It has the intuitively appealing properties that the cost-minimizing order quantity, the EOQ, rises with increases in period demand and cost per order and declines with increases in the inventory carrying-cost rate and in the

variable cost of the inventoried item. Importantly, the EOQ varies by the square root in this simple case. That is, an increase in company sales does not require a proportional increase in inventory to service it, but merely an increase according to the square root. In other terms, a doubling of demand does not require a doubling of inventories, but merely an increase of 41 percent, all other things held constant.

To reiterate, the key thing about the determination of an EOQ within a reorder point inventory system is not the formulas themselves, but the method by which an EOQ is found—namely, by use of the framework of total variable costs associated with changing order quantities. To see this point more clearly, consider some variations on the simple case just analyzed. The EOQ calculated earlier was simple because of the numerous assumptions that were made. Some of these assumptions can be relaxed easily and a new, modified EOQ can be calculated.

Variation: Simultaneous Production and Consumption

For example, consider a case where the inventory to fill an order is not received all at once but is instead allowed to trickle in. (This is sometimes the situation when the "order" is placed on another department or plant within the company.) The units produced at rate P are

---

quantity, at the lowest point, where the slope is zero. Differentiating total cost (TC) with respect to Q and setting the resultant expression equal to zero yields

$$TC = S\left(\frac{D}{Q}\right) + iC\left(\frac{Q}{2}\right)$$

$$\frac{\partial TC}{\partial Q} = -\frac{SD}{Q^2} + \frac{iC}{2} = 0$$

$$Q = \sqrt{\frac{2SD}{iC}}$$

FIGURE 5-6   The case when inventory
is permitted to trickle in.

withdrawn (consumed) from inventory at a rate W with $P > W$. Instead of resembling the sawtooth graph in Figure 5-4, the graph of simultaneous production and consumption looks more like the inventory buildup graphs in Chapter 2.

Under this revised assumption, the average level of inventory will be lower because for at least some part of the time period, both production and consumption are proceeding. In fact, the average inventory will be lower by the factor $(P - W)/P$. To see this, consult Figure 5-6. As shown in the figure, the quantity Q is produced only for the period of time T. Thus,

$$Q = PT$$

where Q is the total amount of inventory produced and shipped, P is the production rate, and T is the time during which there is production. The maximum quantity ever on hand, X, can be expressed as

$$X = (P - W)T$$

At time T, the quantity of inventory held is at its peak of X and the inventory accumulates at the rate of $(P - W)$. The average inventory held is $X/2$. Thus, average inventory in this variation is lower by

$$\frac{X/2}{Q/2} = \frac{X}{Q} = \frac{(P - W)\,T}{PT} = \frac{P - W}{P}$$

We can substitute this result for the average inventory held into the expression for total cost.

$$TC = (S)\frac{D}{Q} + (i)\,(C)\,\frac{Q}{2} \cdot \frac{P - W}{P}$$

When calculus is used to minimize total cost with respect to Q, we obtain a revised expression for an optimal order quantity.

$$Q = \sqrt{\frac{2SD}{iC} \cdot \frac{P}{(P - W)}}$$

Variation: Stockouts Permitted

Now let us change the stockout assumption. As mentioned earlier, the basic EOQ calculation does not permit any deliberate stockouts; it implicitly assumes that the stockout costs are infinite. Figure 5-3, however, suggests that there may be times when stockouts ought to be tolerated. Indeed, many stockouts can be handled by backordering (shipping an order late once the EOQ replenishment has arrived) that is not too expensive. If backorders are possible without too high a penalty, it is worthwhile recalculating the economic order quantity by introducing backorder costs to the total variable costs associated with the changing of order quantities. (See problem 16 at the end of the chapter for some hints on how the basic EOQ formula could be changed to accommodate back orders.)

Variation: Price Discounts

Another factor that the simple EOQ model does not allow for is price discounts with volume orders. It is common practice for vendors to quote reduced prices for orders of a certain size.

SITUATION 5-2

GONDER-ODELL MANUFACTURING COMPANY

The Gonder-Odell Manufacturing Company placed a number of orders each year with local job shops. A typical order was for some machining of small castings provided by the company. In assembling its own products, Gonder-Odell drew upon an inventory of these parts at a more or less steady rate. At issue was how large an order the company should place each time and thus how much inventory to hold. Some relevant information is as follows:

- Usage expected: 5000 units per year
- Order cost: $10. This figure constituted only costs that the company viewed as varying with each order, such as mailing and phone fees, transporting the castings to the job shops, and some necessary computer time. It did not include any clerical time, as that was regarded as a fixed cost.

- Inventory carrying cost percentage: 20%
- Volume discounts on machining:

  $25 per unit if less than 100 ordered each time
  $22.50 per unit if 100 to 499 ordered each time
  $22 per unit if 500 or more ordered each time

- Transport costs: $20 for each pallet of 100 units; 30¢ for any unit not part of a 100-unit pallet. (The castings could be packaged and shipped on standard pallets in quantities of 100. This factor greatly helped transportation and unloading.)
- Handing cost: $5 for each pallet of 100 units; 10¢ for any unit not handled in 100-unit-pallets.

Thus, after certain order size threshholds, the variable cost of a unit of inventory declines. The lower costs for successive ranges of order volumes naturally change the computed value of the EOQ. The conventional technique uses the following steps:

1. Compute EOQs for each different unit cost. Compare each with the range of volumes for which it applies to see if the EOQ is feasible (the EOQ calculated with a given price lies within the quantity range for that price). Start with the lowest cost per unit range; if its EOQ is feasible, it will be the minimum-cost one.

2. Compute the total cost for each price-break quantity and for each feasible EOQ.

3. Select the lowest total cost from step 2. Its quantity is the minimum-cost order quantity.

This technique can be tedious, however, es-

pecially when there are many break points in the price. Kuzdrall and Britney have suggested a new method that assumes that the price discount schedule for the vendor's product is composed of fixed costs (setup costs) as well as variable costs.[4] It then calls for the use of regression analysis to estimate these fixed and variable vendor costs. Using this information, the method then dictates several well-defined steps to develop a "critical interval" in which an EOQ of least total cost is identified.

There are numerous instances where the EOQ cannot easily be calculated from a formula or even a computer algorithm. In such instances, the framework of total variable costs is essential for keeping things straight. Consider Situation 5-2.

Discussion of Gonder-Odell Manufacturing Company

We have observed that deciding how much inventory is optimal involves balancing the costs

TABLE 5-4   Order size cost calculations (Gonder-Odell Manufacturing Company)

ORDER SIZE	ORDERS PER YEAR (given 5000 unit usage)	PURCHASE COST	ORDER COST	TRANSPORT COST	HANDLING COST	CARRYING COST	TOTAL COST
50	100.00	$125,000	$1000.00	$1500	$500	$ 125	$128,125.00
100	50.00	112,500	500.00	1000	250	225	114,475.00
500	10.00	110,000	100.00	1000	250	1100	112,450.00
1000	5.00	110,000	50.00	1000	250	2200	113,500.00
400	12.50	112,500	125.00	1000	250	900	114,775.00
600	8.33	110,000	83.30	1000	250	1320	112,653.30

that increase with order size against the costs that decline with increases in order size. In the simple case we first considered, only carrying costs and order costs varied with changes in the order size. Deciding upon the optimal inventory in that case involved merely finding the order size that minimized the sum of carrying and order costs. The basic EOQ formula was derived in just this spirit.

The situation facing the Gonder-Odell Manufacturing Company is not nearly so simple. In particular, carrying costs and order costs are not the only ones that vary with changes in the order size; purchase costs, transport costs, and handling costs also depend on the order size. The total of all the variable costs associated with changes in the order quantity would thus involve summing up all of these costs. They are displayed and totaled in Table 5-4 for a variety of order sizes. Note that the carrying costs reflect the actual purchase price of the units and not some generalized or average figure, and that they assume a steady draw upon the inventory so that the average inventory is half the order size.

An examination of Table 5-4 reveals that an order size of 500 and average inventory holdings of 250 minimize the total variable costs. This result is not so surprising because (1) the lowest price starts with the 500 order quantity, and (2) carrying costs rise more rapidly than order costs fall, suggesting that the company should carry as little inventory as it can. These two factors combine to yield 500, the lowest end of the lowest price category, as the optimal order quantity.

The table, except for the order size of 50, looks only at order sizes ending in even hundreds. We need not look at 501 or 499 as possible optimums because of the structure of the transport and handling costs. Non-even-hundred orders involve special transport and handling cost rates for the odd pieces, and these cost increases wipe out any carrying cost or order cost savings such quantities could bring. Put another way, the graph of total variable costs against various order sizes is a discontinuous one that follows the general pattern of Figure 5-7.

This discontinuity, coupled with the inclusion of so many variables in the calculation, makes the determination of an optimal order size something of a trial-and-error process, although in some cases a computer program can search for a solution. No neat formulas as we derived before can lead us easily to an answer. All we can do is converge on an answer in much the same manner as the table does.

CHOOSING BETWEEN PERIODIC REORDER AND REORDER POINT INVENTORY SYSTEMS

These then are the major elements of both the periodic reorder and the reorder point inventory

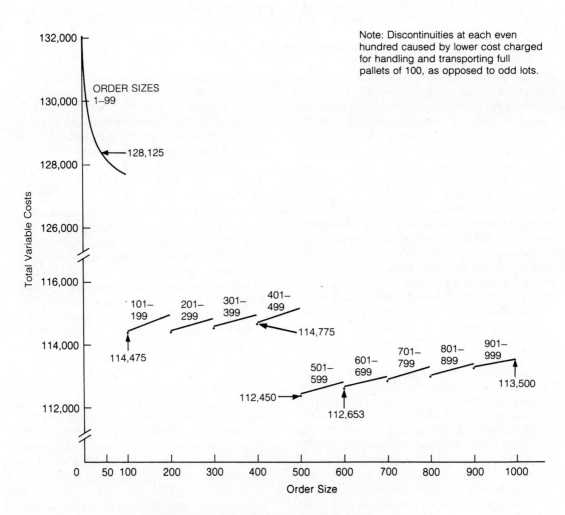

FIGURE 5-7 Total variable costs graphed against order size.

systems. Both, remember, are non-time-phased systems. Situation 5-3 will help us consider why one might institute one system rather than the other.

Discussion of Driscoll Lumber Company

Aubrey Driscoll's three categories of items serve as a useful starting point for a discussion of the

pros and cons of either a periodic reorder system or a reorder point system.

1. *Demand seasonality.* The calculation of an order quantity for a reorder point inventory system implicitly assumes that demand is steady. That is, the minimization of total cost generally assumes that over the relevant time period the draw on the inventory is constant. Thus, using an annual demand

SITUATION 5-3

DRISCOLL LUMBER COMPANY

Spurred by some informal conversation at a recent Lions Club luncheon, Aubrey Driscoll was reflecting on the way in which he stocked items for his lumber company. Together with his brother, Burney, Aubrey owned and operated the Driscoll Lumber Company in Devine, Texas. Devine, a small town southwest of San Antonio, depended largely on cattle ranching and peanut farming for its livelihood. The Driscoll Lumber Company was a major retailer of lumber, hardware, construction materials, and ranching supplies (corral gates, posts, barbed wire, fencing) for the area surrounding the town.

The Lions Club discussion caused Aubrey to think of dividing his inventory of goods into distinct classes, some of which might be ordered better through a periodic reorder system rather than the standard "order when low" system that prevailed in the lumberyard now. As Aubrey saw it, his stock could be classified into several major categories:

1. *Seasonal vs. nonseasonal demand.* The lumber and hardware that the Driscoll Lumber Company sold followed no seasonal pattern. Housing construction and repair in South Texas could be maintained in winter, due to the region's mild climate. Sales of barbed wire and steel fencing, however, were more likely in the late fall and winter, as ranchers and farmers shifted their attention from the raising of peanuts, hay, and other crops to the repair and construction of fields, pastures, and corrals.

2. *Items easily counted for inventory and items more difficult to count.* Most of the items the lumber company stocked were easily counted for inventory. Lumber, plywood, roofing material, cement, and the like were kept in open bins in the company's shed; low levels of any of these items were immediately obvious from just a quick

glance around the shed. Some items, however, were more time-consuming to count, particularly those that came in many different sizes, shapes, or grades. Some hardware items such as pipes and fittings were among these as well as special bolts stored in small compartments. Glass was another such item because it often had to be cut to order, and keeping track of the usable remains was difficult.

3. *Ordered lumber vs. rolling lumber.* Most of the lumber Aubrey Driscoll sold had been ordered about 30 days in advance. What was shipped to Driscoll Lumber Company was exactly what had been ordered, usually in packaged bundles of standard lengths and a fixed count of pieces. Frequently, however, West Coast sawmills specializing in Douglas fir, spruce, hemlock, and other softwoods dispensed with filling specific orders. Instead, the mill would fill railroad boxcars with just what it was sawing at the time, set the boxcars rolling on the rails toward various regions of the country, and rely on lumber brokers to sell off the boxcars before they reached the end of the line. Retail lumber companies could often enjoy significant purchasing discounts by buying lumber in this way, although it frequently meant that some lengths or grades would be overstocked for a time.

To Aubrey Driscoll's way of thinking, these were the major categories of items that he inventoried. He wondered whether he should continue to order all of them only when they were low (a reorder point system) or whether he should make periodic checks of at least some items and order variable quantities (a periodic reorder system). Which items seemed more suitable to one system or the other?

figure to calculate an order quantity is inappropriate if marked demand seasonality exists. While one could calculate different EOQs for different seasons, it is often simpler to use a periodic reorder system for those items whose demand is seasonal. Other things being equal, the Driscoll Lumber Company would be better advised to use a reorder point system for its lumber and hardware (nonseasonal) and a periodic reorder system for barbed wire and steel fencing (seasonal). If the lumber company placed barbed wire and steel fencing on a reorder point system, it might risk carrying too little inventory in fall and winter and too much the rest of the year.

2. *Ease of taking inventory.* A reorder point system requires that the inventory be monitored constantly. If inventory is difficult or expensive to take, a reorder point system is less desirable. At the Driscoll Lumber Company, lumber and other open-bin items are easily inventoried and thus can be maintained under a reorder point system. Glass and certain hardware items, however, are tough to inventory and thus argue for a periodic reorder system.

3. *Price discounts.* The possibility of price discounts on West Coast "rolling lumber" and their irregular timing disrupts both periodic reorder and reorder point inventory systems. Deciding whether or not to buy such lumber, once offered, demands a quick inventory of existing stocks and a computation of how much of the purchased lumber will be used during the ensuing time frame. In a sense, this computation lies outside the routine workings of either inventory system. The fact that an inventory of the existing stocks is required suggests that such price discounts are perhaps more compatible with a reorder point system, but they are still compatible with a periodic reorder system.

Considering all of these features then suggests that the Driscoll Lumber Company may be best off using a reorder point system for its lumber and larger hardware supplies and a periodic reorder system for its small, hard-to-inventory hardware items, its glass, its barbed wire and fencing, and similar items.

In more general terms, a periodic reorder system has a relative advantage over a reorder point system when the costs of taking a physical inventory are high or when there are savings in regard to information (such as seasonal data), production scheduling, price discounts, or transport costs from ordering items on a regular basis. If these cost savings are not significant, however, a reorder point system has the striking advantage of being able to minimize the total variable costs associated with changing order quantities. Broadly speaking, the economics of inventory control favor the reorder point system but only when the important, practical costs of inventory control and administration are not significant.

The saving grace in all of this is that failing to calculate the precisely optimal order quantity under any inventory system is not likely to be devastating. The costs of various order quantities are, in most instances, fairly near one another. In other words, a graph of inventory costs against various order quantities is likely to be shallow (saucer-shaped, as in Figure 5-8), rather than steep (bowl-or cup-shaped). Making some sensible decisions about inventories to get oneself "into the ballpark" is thus more important than landing on precisely the best order quantity. It has been said that order timing is more important than order quantities.[5]

While prevalent in both manufacturing and nonmanufacturing businesses, non-time-phased inventory systems, like the periodic reorder and reorder point systems described above, are perhaps best suited to retail and wholesale situations (Driscoll Lumber Company), where the source and precise timing of demand is seldom known with much certainty. These conditions often apply to manufacturing as well, but there are many manufacturing businesses that know far more about the source and timing of demand for their products, and hence for the parts that make up their products. It is in these in-

FIGURE 5-8 Inventory costs graphed against order quantities.

stances of known or easily provided demand that the time-phased inventory system, such as material requirements planning, makes good sense.

Safety Stocks

Safety stocks are useful in managing inventories precisely because companies do not know in advance exactly what the demands made on them will be. As long as replenishments to an inventory cannot occur immediately, the lead time necessary for delivery of the replenishment order is an uncertain and problematic period of time. Consult Figure 5-9. At time T_1, there was a delivery of inventory that replenished the stock up to the level of Q. At time T_2, it was decided to place another order. This new order could have been placed because a reorder point had been struck (level R of inventory) or because T_2 was the appropriate, periodic time to review the status of inventory (per a periodic reorder inventory system). The order is expected to arrive at time A, so that the lead time is the time between T_2 and A.

During this lead time, most anything can happen. If demand proceeds at its usual, expected rate, when the order arrives inventory

should be depleted to point B. The safety stock, however, will not have been used. If demand is lighter than expected (something that one might think occurs about 50 percent of the time, if demand is a statistical creature with a distribution that is symmetrical about the mean), then at time A, inventory would stand somewhere between points B and C. If, on the other hand, demand is heavier than expected (typically, another 50 percent probability) the safety stock will have to be employed. During the lead time, the quantity AB could be used up before a stockout occurred.

Levels of Customer Service

At issue, then, is how much safety stock should a company hold? How much is enough or desirable? This is sometimes described in terms of determining the level of customer service. There are many, somewhat different measures for customer service, however. Some are more appropriate for some uses than others. Two specific measures of customer service bear mention:

1. The percentage of orders covered by the inventory, or equivalently, the probability of not stocking out. This measure indicates the probability that the company will not stock out during any given order cycle time period. A 95 percent service level, by this measure, indicates a 5 percent chance of failing to fill one or more orders during any given time period. This measure is fairly easy to work with statistically.

2. The percent of all items ordered shipped on time. This is a measure of items and not orders, and it has intuitive appeal. While similar to measure 1, this measure has some significant distinctions. Indeed, the mathematical correspondence between the measures is not a simple one, because stockouts can involve orders for any number of items.

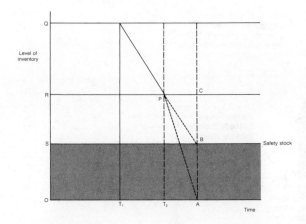

FIGURE 5-9 The usefulness of safety stock.

For this reason, to match a 95 percent service level by measure 1, measure 2 generally has to be greater than 95 percent. Despite the complex mathematical relationship between the two measures, for many items, rough correlations between the two measures can be devised empirically.

Let's return to the issue of determining the desired level of customer service, as measured by either measure. The discussion of Figure 5-9 and previous comments suggest several factors that ought to influence the size of any safety stock:

1. How frequently the order is placed. The larger the quantity ordered at any time—and thus, the less frequent the exposures to potential stockouts—the greater the level of customer service provided.

2. Lead time. The longer the lead time, other things being equal, the more safety stock is desired. Shorten lead times and safety stocks can be lowered.

3. Stability of demand. The more erratic the demand, the greater the safety stock has to

be to maintain a given level of customer service.

4. Relative costs of stockout versus inventory carrying. The greater the penalty to the company of not having enough inventory relative to the cost of holding inventory, the more safety stock is desirable.

For the most part, companies settle on a particular safety stock and accompanying level of customer service on a trial and error basis. A service level is established, and then, over time, performance against that service level is monitored as well as customer satisfaction with delivery. If performance is satisfactory, then the safety stock can be lowered somewhat and performance again monitored. By focusing on the service level, companies can improve their performance dramatically over rules-of-thumb approaches to safety stock that merely pick a given period's demand as the safety stock. By adhering to service levels and tracking them, useful adjustments to the safety stock level can be made, based on demand stability, frequency of order, length of lead time, and stockout versus inventory carrying costs.

Continual trial-and-error adjustments to safety stock levels have a lot to recommend them, especially given an environment of change. There are alternative schemes for setting safety stocks. One fairly simple scheme merits attention as a means to estimate what level of customer service to shoot for, namely the use of the *critical fractile*.

The Critical Fractile Approach

This approach to setting the level of safety stock essentially picks out a suitable level of service based on a trade-off of stockout costs and inventory carrying costs. The chosen level of service then gets translated into a "safety factor" that can be multiplied by the computed stan-

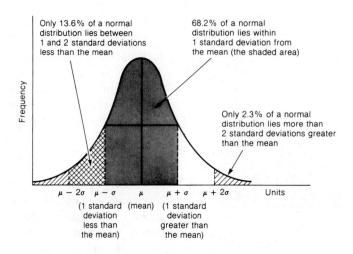

FIGURE 5-10   The normal distribution.

dard deviation of the distribution of demand to yield the extent of safety stock. Let us work through this process in reverse in order to understand it better.

Many distributions of demand can be approximated by the normal distribution, the familiar bell-shaped graph pictured in Figure 5-10. The two parameters needed to describe a normal distribution are its mean and its standard deviation. Naturally, a low standard deviation represents a very tight, stable demand, while a large one represents a more erratic demand. No matter what the value of the standard deviation, however, with a normal distribution, there are standard percentages of the distribution that fall within X standard deviations of the mean. This fact permits us to make the correspondence between the percentage of demand covered by a certain size of safety stock (one measure of the level of customer service discussed earlier) and the number of standard deviations above the mean the inventory represents (the safety factor). Some relevant safety factors to use, given a normal distribution with a 0 mean and a standard deviation of 1, are as follows:

COVERAGE OF EXPECTED DEMAND (%)	
99	2.326
97.5	1.960
95	1.645
90	1.282
85	1.038
80	0.843

Thus, if the distribution of demand is normally distributed with a mean of 50 and a standard deviation of 14, then a 90 percent level of coverage (that is, a 90 percent level of customer service) would be given with an inventory of

$$50 + 14(1.282) \approx 68 \text{ units}$$

of which 18 units constitute the safety stock itself.

The critical fractile calculation helps production managers decide upon an appropriate level of service so that the corresponding safety factor can be applied to the standard deviation of the distribution of demand.

Common sense insists that the level of customer service be higher if the cost of carrying too little inventory and thus stocking out greatly exceeds the cost of carrying too much inventory. The former cost is commonly called the "cost of being under" or the cost of underage (C_u) and the latter is commonly called the "cost of being over" or the cost of overage (C_o).

The suitable percentage coverage that a company ought to seek for its inventories subject to uncertain demand is approximated by the following formula:*

$$\text{critical fractile} = \frac{C_u}{C_o + C_u}$$

*The ratio of $C_u/(C_o + C_u)$ is the critical fractile (or percentile). While technically it applies only to single-period holding of inventories and linear costs of underage and overage, it is a useful enough approximation to be applied more generally.

The basic argument underlying the derivation of the critical fractile is, once again, incremental in origin. Suppose we arbitrarily select q^* as the best level of inventory there could be. It must be true then that we receive an incremental gain by inventorying q^* as opposed to one unit more or less (that is, either $q^* + 1$ or $q^* - 1$). This being the case, we can write formally the following inequality:

(1)
$$C_u[P(d > q^*)] \le C_o[P(d \le q^*)]$$

By stocking q^*, the expected expense of being under when demand is greater than q^* (the cost of underage times the probability that demand is greater than q^*) must be less than or equal to the expected expense of being over (the cost of overage times the probability that demand is less than or equal to q^*); otherwise, it would make sense to stock another unit so that one is not caught being under. Similarly, we can write the following inequality:

(2)
$$C_u\{P[d > (q^* - 1)]\} \ge C_o\{P[(d \le (q^* - 1)]\}$$

By stocking q^*, the expected expense of being under when demand is greater than $q^* - 1$ must be greater than or equal to the expected expense of being over; otherwise, it would make sense to stock one unit less in order to save some money.

Using the fact that $P(d > q^*)$ is equal to $[1 - P(d \le q^*)]$ we can rewrite inequality 1 as

(3)
$$C_u[1 - P(d \le q^*)] \le C_o[P(d \le q^*)]$$

or

$$C_u \le (C_u + C_o)[P(d \le q^*)]$$

or

(4)
$$\frac{C_u}{(C_u + C_o)} \le [P(d \le q^*)]$$

In similar fashion we can rewrite inequality 2 as

(5)
$$\frac{C_u}{(C_u + C_o)} \ge \{P[d \le (q^* - 1)]\}$$

Inequalities 4 and 5 suggest that $C_u/(C_u + C_o)$ is the relevant ratio for picking off the point in the cumulative probability distribution that corresponds to the optimal level of inventories, q^*.

A more thorough explanation of the critical fractile, and that on which this explanation is based, can be found in Barbara B. Jackson, *The Critical Fractile Model*, Note 4–175–058 of the Intercollegiate Case Clearing House, 1974.

This formula meets the test of common sense in that if the cost of carrying too little and stocking out is high relative to the cost of carrying too much, then the suitable percentage coverage will be high. The formula also makes sense in that it cannot reach 1 in value nor can it fall to zero; it must range in between, just like the range for cumulative probability.

What are costs of underage and costs of overage? Let us consider the costs of overage first since they are a bit easier to think about. The costs of overage are all the costs that would be incurred by carrying one extra unit of inventory for the time period needed to avoid the stockout. These are the costs of holding inventory that were discussed previously:

- Finance charges (opportunity costs)
- Storage and handling costs
- Insurance and taxes
- Obsolesence and shrinkage

As an example of the cost of overage, this cost for a year could be 30 percent of the cost of the product, calculated as 15 percent for financing costs (such as the company's prevailing borrowing rate or perhaps the rate that it expects to earn on any cash freed up by reducing inventory), 10 percent for physical costs, and 5 percent for the risk of obsolescence. In most cases, however, buffer inventory would be vulnerable to depletion for only a short time before the next delivery was due. If the period of vulnerability were only one to two weeks, the cost of overage for the relevant period for this example would be approximately 1 percent of the cost of the product.

The cost of underage is the penalty incurred by failing to have a unit of inventory on hand when demand calls for it. At worst, typically, the cost of underage is the lost contribution to profit and overhead incurred because the unit was unavailable for sale. Again, the concept of opportunity cost intrudes into our thinking—here, in the form of contribution forgone. Forgoing all of a unit's contribution assumes that the buyer goes away empty-handed and will never again return to purchase the item. Frequently, however, stocking out of an item does not mean all of a lost sale, especially if the purchaser is willing to substitute another item for the one out of stock (another color, another model, another size) or if he or she agrees to come back when the item is received again in stock. Market research can frequently determine a reasonable expectation for this cost of underage.

As an example of the cost of underage, the contribution per unit might be 40 percent of the revenue the company receives from it; the probability that the unit will be forgone forever might be 50 percent; the probability that some other unit (with contribution of 30 percent) will be substituted might be 30 percent; and the probability that the customer may return later for it might be 20 percent. In such a case, the cost of underage could be estimated as an expected value of the contribution forgone.

$$.5(40\%) + .3(40\% - 30\%) + .2(0\%) =$$
$$.5(40\%) + .3(10\%) + .2(0\%) = 23\% \text{ of the cost of the product}$$

Costs of underage generally greatly exceed the costs of overage for most relevant time periods.

Let us then calculate the critical fractile for this example. The relevant inputs are:

$C_o = 1.15\%$ (30% annual rate for a two-week period)
$C_u = 23\%$

Suppose, as well, that the demand during the period is expected to follow the normal distribution with a mean of 50 and standard deviation of 10.

Critical fractile (percentile)
$$= 23/(1.15 + 23) = 0.95$$
Safety factor corresponding to
a percentile of 95% = 1.645

SITUATION 5-4

DIMARZO COSTUME COMPANY

The DiMarzo Costume Company rented theatrical costumes of all sorts to theater groups, colleges, schools, churches, and the like. During the Christmas season, one of the most popular costumes (aside from Santa Claus) was Frosty the Snowman. (Data on orders placed for Frosty the Snowman costumes over all 20 years of the company's history are given in Table 5-5.) The company could not detect a trend in orders over the years; orders seemed to be fairly random. The company, however, wanted to be able to fill about 95 percent of all its orders for Frosty and wondered how many costumes it should stock at Christmas.

TABLE 5-5   Past demand for frosty the snowman (DiMarzo Costume Company)

YEARS AGO	DEMANDED	YEARS AGO	DEMANDED
1	411	11	296
2	347	12	382
3	412	13	473
4	385	14	320
5	441	15	423
6	402	16	354
7	395	17	512
8	370	18	389
9	480	19	378
10	416	20	392

The size of the buffer or safety stock is then

$$(1.645)(10) = 16.45 \text{ units}$$

The size of the inventory at the start of the period should be the expected average withdrawal from inventory plus the buffer stock:

$$50 + 16.45 = 66.45 \text{ units}$$

To reinforce this discussion of safety stocks, consider Situation 5-4.

Discussion of the DiMarzo Costume Company

Given no discernible trend in the demand over the years for Frosty the Snowman costumes, the DiMarzo Costume Company can let the past 20 years be its guide in selecting the number of Frosty costumes it should stock.

A Historical Count Approach

The easiest, if not the most scientific, way to select an appropriate stock level so that the company can expect to cover 95 percent of the orders placed on it is to make a count of the data. The company could expect that a stock level at or above the highest number demanded over the past 20 years would be too high. Company history shows that in 95 percent of the years (19 of 20) demand was less than 512 but not more than 480. It would seem reasonable, then, to select a stock level between 480 and 512.

A Statistical Approach

A more formal way of selecting an appropriate stock level is to apply some statistics to the data.

The mean of the distribution of demand for Frosty the Snowman costumes is 398.90 and the sample's standard deviation is 50.63. These summary statistics (sample mean and sample standard deviation) are *estimates* of the unknown true population mean, μ, and the unknown true population standard deviation, σ, which underlie the demand for costumes at DiMarzo Costume Company. Often, we do not know how the full population of observations is distributed, and we must depend on samples from that full population to draw inferences about the population itself. Such is the case at the DiMarzo Costume Company. The sum-

FIGURE 5-11   Frequency distribution of monthly sales for DiMarzo Costume Company.

mary statistics, $\bar{X}$ and S, can help us condense the Table 5-5 data into a more easily digested bar graph of the frequencies with which the data fall into various classes. Figure 5-11 displays such a bar graph. For intelligibility, the classes are set at 25, about half of the standard deviation, and the figure is centered on 400, which is just above the true mean of 398.90.

Figure 5-10's bar graph can be approximated by a normal distribution. We know that the Table 5-5 data fall roughly into a normal distribution pattern since (1) 70 percent of the 20 observations fall within one standard deviation of the mean (i.e., 14 of the 20 observations fall between 350 and 450) versus 68.2 percent in a true normal distribution, (2) 20 percent of the 20 observations fall between one and two standard deviations from the mean versus 27.2 percent in a true normal distribution, and (3) 10 percent of the 20 observations fall beyond two standard deviations from the mean versus 4.6 percent in a true normal distribution. It seems reasonable then to presume that the demand for Frosty the Snowman costumes is normally distributed with a mean of 398.90 and a standard deviation of 50.63.

In a normal frequency pattern, the top 5 percent of the distribution falls above the value of + 1.645 standard deviations from the mean. In

this case, we can presume then that 95 percent of the demand for Frosty costumes will fall below

$$398.90 + 1.645(50.63) = 482.19$$

We can take this figure, 482 or 483, as a suitable stock level to assure ourselves that 95 percent of our expected orders can be serviced.

If we were content to have only 90 percent of the expected orders serviced, then the proper stock level would be

$$398.90 + (1.282)(50.63) \approx 464$$

because the top 10 percent of the distribution falls above the value of + 1.282 standard deviations from the mean.

Trends and Aggregation

The DiMarzo Costume Company had to worry only about stocking Frosty the Snowman costumes for one peak time during the year. Furthermore, there were no clear trends in the demand over the years. The task of calculating an appropriate inventory level for uncertain demand is complicated further when trends are involved or when time periods are aggregated. Consider the following modifications of the procedures we have used to date for coping with demand uncertainty:

1. *Trends.* If sales have grown (or declined) over time, the distribution of demand shifts rightward (or leftward) along the X-axis of units demanded. In the simplest case, the distribution itself remains the same and merely shifts position; the mean thus changes, but the standard deviation remains the same. In more complex cases, the distribution changes along with the shift, changing both the mean and the standard deviation. When trends are involved, therefore, it is important to ascertain whether the shape of the distribution is changing along with its mean.

2. *Time period aggregation.* Suppose we wanted to shift the horizon for a periodic reorder system from one month to three months. All the calculations about the appropriate level of inventory to hold were based on a distribution of demand for a month. How do things change if we are to define everything now in terms of three months? If demand follows a normal distribution, is the mean of the new distribution simply three times as large? What about the variance? If we assume a normal distribution for the demands and if those demands in any month are independent of one another (a not unreasonable assumption), then the mean of the new three-month distribution will be three times the one-month mean, and the variance will also be three times greater. The standard deviation, however, will be $\sqrt{3}$ times the old standard deviation because it is the square root of the variance. Thus, if the one-month mean is 50 and the standard deviation is 10, the new three-month distribution can be expected to have a mean of 150 and a standard deviation of

$$10\sqrt{3} = 17.3$$

In general terms, under the assumptions of normal distribution and independence of demand, both the mean and the variance are additive.

MATERIAL REQUIREMENTS PLANNING: A DESCRIPTION OF ITS OPERATION[6]

Earlier, material requirements planning (MRP) was introduced as a way to manage inventories by anticipating their use. As explained there, the basic philosophy of an MRP system is to time the procurement and/or fabrication of the specific items comprising a particular product to synchronize with that product's master production schedule. Given a firm schedule of when and how many of particular finished goods are desired, an MRP system details which component parts ought to be purchased/fabricated in what quantities and at what times.

In order to meet this desirable goal and some other standard functions, a material requirements planning system must continually keep track of:

1. *Master production schedule of end products.* These data "drive" the entire system. Often the system also keeps track of which orders are associated with which demands in the schedule (commonly called "pegging").

2. *Bills of materials for each product and, indeed, each product variation,* so that the demands for individual component parts can be detailed.

3. *Inventory status of each component part.* How many of each part are on hand and how many are scheduled to be received prior to use?

4. *Lead time status of all parts to be purchased or fabricated* so that their availability is timed exactly to meet anticipated needs.

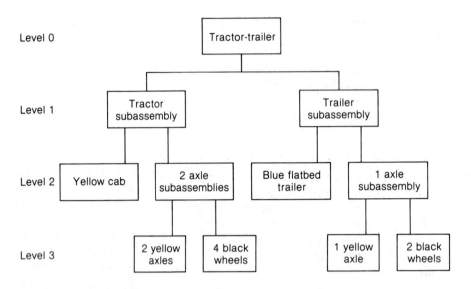

FIGURE 5-12   The composition of a toy tractor-trailer.

5. *Product construction standard times and schedules.* This information details how long (in standard hours) particular tasks can be expected to take and indicates when specific parts or subassemblies will be needed in order to meet the established master schedule for the end product. This information is useful for scheduling materials as well as for assessing the capacity of the factory to produce the contemplated product mix.

6. *Routings of parts to particular workcenters.* These routings indicate which workcenters (machine tools, assembly lines, departments) are involved in the manufacture of each product or product variation. This information is critical to the capacity planning function for which an MRP system can be used. This adaptation of MRP is discussed later in this section.

7. *Standard costs.* Given standard costs for particular parts and subassemblies, an MRP system can be used to calculate inventory investments and to estimate product costs for any modification to the bill of materials' product structure. This adaptation of MRP is also discussed later in this section.

To illustrate how this information gets used by, and processed through, an MRP system, let us ponder a very simplified example: a toy tractor-trailer. This toy tractor-trailer consists of (1) a yellow plastic tractor cab to which is attached two yellow plastic axles and four black plastic wheels (the wheels must first be mounted on the axles and then the axles snapped into place underneath the cab), and (2) a blue plastic, flat-bed trailer (which also has a yellow axle on which two black plastic wheels, identical to those under the tractor cab, are mounted). A "product structure" diagram of the tractor-trailer and its component parts might look like Figure 5-12.

Figure 5-12 serves as the *bill of materials* for the product. Notice that it can be depicted in

	Week					
	1	2	3	4	5	6
Toy Tractor-Trailers	6	10	3	12	15	8

FIGURE 5-13 Master production schedule for the toy tractor-trailer.

Lead Time = 1 Week	Week					
	1	2	3	4	5	6
Gross Requirements						
Scheduled Receipts						
Projected Available Balance 18						
Planned Order Releases						

FIGURE 5-14 Inventory record for axle subassemblies of the toy tractor-trailer.

a series of levels. These levels structure the product into various subassemblies and detail the components of each subassembly. Such a breakdown and structuring enables us to keep separate track of inventories of tractor, trailer, or axle subassemblies and their components. We will see the usefulness of this.

Figure 5-13 is a *master production schedule* for tractor-trailers over the next six weeks. The six-week production horizon is generally somewhat arbitrary and could be extended or shortened as a matter of company policy. In any event, it represents a *firm* commitment to make so many tractor-trailer units by such-and-such a time. Exactly when during the course of the week the tractor-trailer units are desired depends on the convention used. For example, the call for 10 units in week 2 can mean that 10 units should be shipped the first day of the week or the last day of the week or even the midpoint day of the week. The choice is entirely the company's. For our example, let us adopt the convention that the week's master scheduled output is to be shipped on the final day of the week. The time period of a week is used here since it is the most popular for scheduling purposes; but time periods of a month, a day, or something else could be used. The same MRP logic applies in any case.

An inventory record for axle subassemblies is provided in Figure 5-14. Note that there are 18 axle subassemblies (black plastic wheels mounted on yellow axles) on hand that can be used to meet any immediate needs. Any other axles will take at least a week to assemble as the lead time statement in the record indicates. Similar inventory records and lead times exist for all component items and subassemblies for the product.

The value of an MRP system is its ability to determine quickly how many more axle subassemblies (or whatever) to order and when those orders ought to be placed. To do this, the material requirements planning system ties the various inventory records to both the bill of materials and the master production schedule. Such a tie is depicted in Figure 5-15, which shows the level-by-level link between tractor-trailers, tractor subassemblies, and yellow cabs.

It is worth devoting some attention to Figure 5-15 and what underlies it. Level 0 simply reproduces the master production schedule found in Figure 5-13. The "planned order releases" for the tractor-trailer units constitute "gross requirements" for the tractor subassemblies of level 1. That is, the need to ship, say, six toy tractor-trailers at the end of week 1 (the current week) places a demand for six tractor subassemblies for week 1. Two of the required six tractor subassemblies can be supplied out of existing inventories on hand (which we know

FIGURE 5-15 Linked inventory records in an MRP system and a partial explosion of requirements.

because the bill of materials has been structured into subassemblies and thus we can keep track of them), but that leaves us four tractor subassemblies short, as indicated by the "−4" in the "on-hand" row. This shortage in turn leads us to take action—namely, to order the four yellow cabs that we will need to manufacture that subassembly. This planned order release at level 1 is translated into a gross requirement at level 2, which keeps track of the yellow cabs. Thankfully, four yellow cabs are

on hand, and this order can be met out of existing inventories.

At every level, the net requirement for a part or subassembly in any period is calculated in the same way.

Net requirements for a = Inventory on hand from
given period   the previous period

+ quantity on order for delivery in the given period

− gross requirements for the given period

In our diagrams, the net requirement is written in the row labeled "projected available balance." When this net requirement is negative, then some action must be taken (an order placed) if production is not to fall behind schedule. When it is zero or positive, all is well, at least for the time being.

A material requirements planning system can trace out in advance the net requirements for subassemblies or component parts at all levels. Figure 5-16 does such a tracing of requirements for both level 1 (tractor subassemblies) and level 2 (yellow cabs) under the assumption that all shortages of tractor subassemblies trigger planned order releases in the same way as traced out in Figure 5-15. On level 2 the projected available balances (net requirements) accumulate, since no orders have yet been released.

Calculating the planned order releases for the yellow cabs is not as straightforward as calculating the planned order releases for the tractor subassemblies since the yellow cabs can be fabricated only with a lead time of one week. Thus, for example, if the need for 10 yellow cabs in week 2 is to be met, an order for 10 cabs must be placed in week 1. Figure 5-17 follows through with this logic, depicting the required planned order releases for level 2.

As yet, no entries have been made in the row labeled "scheduled receipts." These receipts,

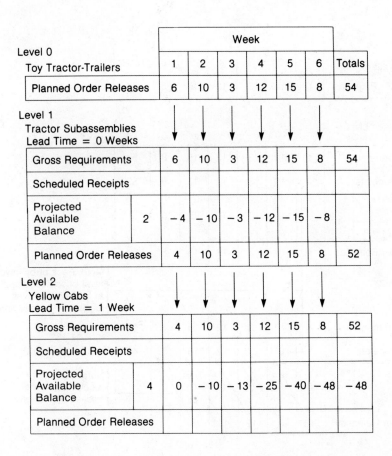

FIGURE 5-16   Net schedule requirements implied by the master production schedule (receipts not yet accounted for).

Level 2 Yellow Cabs Lead Time = 1 Week		Week						
		1	2	3	4	5	6	Totals
Gross Requirements		4	10	3	12	15	8	52
Scheduled Receipts								
Projected Available Balance	4	0	− 10	− 3	− 12	− 15	− 8	
Planned Order Releases		10	3	12	15	8		48

Note: 1 week lead time for order releases.

FIGURE 5-17   Planned order releases when lead time must be accounted for.

	Week						
Level 0 Toy Tractor-Trailers	1	2	3	4	5	6	Totals
Planned Order Releases	6	10	3	12	15	8	54

Level 1
Tractor Subassemblies
Lead Time = 0 Weeks

Gross Requirements		6	10	3	12	15	8	54
Scheduled Receipts		4	►10	3	12	15	8	52
Projected Available Balance	2	0	0	0	0	0	0	
Planned Order Releases		4	10	3	12	15	8	52

Note: Receipt by lower level becomes receipt at next higher level, lagged by its lead time.

Level 2
Yellow Cabs
Lead Time = 1 Week

Gross Requirements		4	10	3	12	15	8	52
Scheduled Receipts			10	3	12	15	8	48
Projected Available Balance	4	0	0	0	0	0	0	
Planned Order Releases		10	3	12	15	8		48

Note: Delivery or receipt lags order release by the lead time.

FIGURE 5-18   Scheduled receipts implied by the master production schedule and by the planned order releases.

however, are linked directly to planned order releases. As soon as an order is "released," it becomes a scheduled receipt. Its "receipt" position in the time phasing diagram is determined by its expected lead time. Thus, the net requirements implied by the master production schedule, as indicated in Figure 5-16, can be rewritten in terms of scheduled receipts, assuming no complications with the indicated lead times. Figure 5-18 displays this. Note that each of the planned order releases has been transferred to the scheduled receipt square for the appropriate week. The projected available balances also reflect the emergence of a series of scheduled receipts.

In practice, of course, planned order releases can be expected to "mature" and be released one at a time, as in Figure 5-15, rather than in entire batteries, as Figure 5-17 may lead one to believe.

Before going on to introduce some "wrinkles" (such as how to plan when the same type of part is used in more than one subassembly) to this basic MRP logic, let us review its fundamental steps:

1. The master production schedule is the data introduced to the MRP system that "drive" it. All the entries and actions taken must be in agreement with the master production schedule. This schedule is assumed by the MRP logic to be correct and "frozen" over some time period.

2. A detailed bill of materials for all products and product variations must also exist, and it should be structured in successive tiers to reveal subassemblies as well as individual component parts. Given the master production schedule and the relevant bills of materials, an MRP system "explodes" the bills of materials through successive tiers to calculate how many parts or subassemblies of a particular type are required to satisfy the master production schedule.

   MRP logic permits the computation of net requirements by adjusting the gross requirements for a particular subassembly or part by the number of units already on hand and those that are expected to be received.

3. The timing for planned order releases depends on the expected lead times for procuring/fabricating/assembling component parts or subassemblies. Orders are actually placed in anticipation of their need, as dictated by the master production schedule and the derivative explosion of the bills of materials.

The data requirements for the computer files that handle the processing for an MRP system are voluminous and include:

- Master production schedules for the weeks indicated

- Bills of materials for all products and product variations
- Existing inventory levels for all parts and subassemblies
- Lead times for all parts and subassemblies
- Orders placed but not yet received (so-called open orders)
- Routings of parts to particular work centers
- Standard costs for particular parts and subassemblies

The processing of an MRP system—the explosion of the bills of materials, the updating of the inventory file records, and the releasing of orders and spotting of scheduled receipts—can be an irregular event (say, once a week) or can proceed all the time. If an MRP system is run at distinctly spaced intervals, the system is said to be regenerative, because the computer file records on master schedules, bills of materials, inventory levels, lead times, and open orders are updated ("regenerated") in their entirety all at once. Such a regeneration conserves computer resources, but it also runs the risk of letting the information on which the entire MRP system depends deteriorate over time.

A net change MRP system, on the other hand, permits the information in any computer file on the system to be updated. More importantly, it also permits the consequences of that updating to be followed through, be they changes in planned order release dates or changed quantities of an item on hand or something else. A net change MRP system uses more computer resources, but it maintains the timeliness of the system. Of course, for a net change system to operate effectively, all the consequences of any transaction in any computer file must be traced to their ultimate conclusion. Records must be tied or "chained" to one another both upward and downward by special "pointers." By following these pointers, a net change MRP system

FIGURE 5-19 Dealing with common parts in an MRP system.

is updated by a series of partial "explosions" rather than by calling for the large, infrequent, full explosion of a regenerative MRP system.

"Wrinkles" to Add to the Basic MRP Logic

Common Parts

In our example of the toy tractor-trailer, the black plastic wheels and the yellow plastic axles are used in both the tractor and the trailer subassemblies. When it is time to review the net requirements for wheels and axles, we must be sure that the gross requirements from both tractor and trailer subassemblies are added together. The explosions of the bill of materials must be careful to keep track of all the instances where a certain part or subassembly is called for. Figure 5-19 shows the demand for black plastic wheels in various weeks emerging from both tractor and trailer assembly. Note that two wheels are needed for each axle assembly and that a tractor uses two axles and a trailer just one.

Same Parts Used at Different Levels

Although it does not happen in our toy tractor-trailer example, it is easily possible for a part to be used at both level 2 and level 3, say, of a product structure for a bill of materials. Trying to keep track of all the demands for such a part is awkward (and expensive for the computer) if some simplifying convention is not adopted. In most instances, this problem is solved by structuring the bills of materials in a way that places all of the same parts or subassemblies at the same level. In Figure 5-20, for example, part A, which could have been placed in two different levels of the bill of materials' product structure, is depicted as occurring all at the lowest level possible. In this way, the MRP computer program encounters it at only one level and sums up its requirements there.

FIGURE 5-20 Bill of materials' product structure dealing
with the same part on potentially different levels.

Level 2 Yellow Cabs Lead Time = 1 Week Lot Size = 15		Week						
		1	2	3	4	5	6	Totals
Gross Requirements		4	10	3	12	15	8	52
Scheduled Receipts			15		15	15	15	60
Projected Available Balance	4	0	5	2	5	5	12	
Planned Order Releases		15		15	15	15		60

FIGURE 5-21 Lot sizing in an MRP system.

Lot Sizing

Up to this point, material requirements planning has been used to place orders that represent precisely the number of units of anticipated use, no more and no less. As we have seen elsewhere in the discussion of materials management, price discounts or some other feature may make it advisable to purchase more than the anticipated need. This possibility may make it desirable to use some economic order quantity reasoning along with the batch-for-batch (lot-for-lot) anticipatory philosophy of MRP. Figure 5-21 displays how planned order releases would look, given a specific lot size to order rather than a lot-for-lot order scheme.

The MRP logic also makes it explicit that if total inventory costs are to be minimized, this must occur on a period-by-period basis, as more information is revealed about future needs, costs, and item availabilities. In practice, being so precise about minimizing a changing total inventory cost may not be worth the effort, but some lot size approximations can be built into an MRP system. Let us consider some of these lot size techniques.

The common lot size technique for MRP is to place orders for only what is anticipated—a technique known as *lot-for-lot*. By using lot-for-lot lot sizes, no remnants of inventory are purposely accumulated to be carried from one period to another. This is an attractive feature, and, as we shall see in later chapters, consistent with the "Japanese" philosophy of manufacturing. Lot-for-lot is less attractive when there are significant order or setup costs that cannot be reduced or when there are frequent and significant instances where delivery is unreliable, orders get canceled or expedited, or delivery quantities are not accurate. These adverse occurrences can be eliminated (and are in "Japanese-type" companies); but to the extent they exist, lot-for-lot suffers.

EOQ lot size reasoning can be applied in MRP systems. There may be well-defined order or setup costs, price breaks, or other costs that can be balanced against inventory carrying costs. An EOQ formula (or computer algorithm) can be developed and used. One problem with using such an approach, however, is exactly what to use for D, the demand. Should the demand amount (and the concomitant carrying cost percentage) be defined for the next month? the next three months? the next six months? the next year? or longer? There is no clear-cut answer, and the choice of a time horizon will alter the calculation. In general, the less uniform the demand over time, the worse any EOQ calculation performs.

There are several lot size techniques that try to skirt this time horizon problem while still balancing setup or order costs against carrying costs. These techniques allow the time horizon for which the order applies to vary from order to order. Thus, these techniques may call for one order to cover the next three periods and a subsequent order to cover the succeeding four periods. The several methods used to determine both lot sizes and the time intervals between orders differ, often trading off simplicity against optimality. We will describe two such techniques: least total cost and part-period balancing.

Least Total Cost (LTC). This technique chooses the lot size and order interval for which the setup/order cost per unit and the carrying cost per unit are most nearly equal. This goal is similar to the rationale of the EOQ model and argues that the setup/order costs and inventory carrying costs for all lots within the time horizon will be low (if not minimized) if these costs per unit are equal.

In its calculations, the LTC technique uses what is known as an *economic part-period (EPP)*. A part-period is one unit of inventory carried for one time period. An economic part-period is that quantity of inventory which, if carried for a single period, would result in inventory carrying costs equal to the setup or order cost. For example, if the one-period carrying cost is 10¢ per unit and setup costs are $15, then the economic part-period is 150 units ($15/$.10).

The least total cost technique calls for a lot size and order interval whose part-period cost falls closest to the EPP. Suppose, then, that the EPP is 150 units, as above, and the net requirements over the next 12 periods are as follows:

Period	Net Requirements	Period	Net Requirements
1	20	7	
2	35	8	35
3		9	
4	25	10	50
5		11	
6	30	12	

Total net requirements: 195
On-hand inventory: 0
Lead time: 0

TABLE 5-6 Lot sizes by part-period

PROSPECTIVE LOT SIZE	PART-PERIODS IN EACH TIME PERIOD						CUMULATIVE PART-PERIODS
	1	2	3	4	5	6	
20	0						0
55	35	0					35
80	60	25	25	0			110
110	90	55	55	30	30	0	260

What is the lot size suggested by the LTC technique for period 1? The answer is 80, as shown in Table 5-6. The lot size of 80 yields a cumulative part-period sum that lies closest to the calculated economic part-period of 150. For that reason, it is the preferred lot size.

It should be noted that LTC does not typically develop an optimal lot size, in the sense that total inventory cost is minimized. Its rationale depends on equating setup/order costs per unit with inventory carrying costs per unit, and that rationale is optimal only when the mathematical functions describing those costs are friendly, as was noted with the basic reorder point model.

Part-Period Balancing. This technique has the same rationale and same computations as the least total cost technique, but it adds a look ahead/look back procedure. The LTC technique chooses lot sizes one at a time, with no attention paid to what might be a proper lot size in future periods. In the previous example, the lot size of 80 would last through period 4; the LTC technique does not look ahead to see what lies beyond period 4. The total costs over the full time horizon could, in fact, be lowered by either increasing or decreasing the lot size choice for period 1, given an investigation of the next lot size choice in the future. In part-period balancing, one peeks at the next lot size decision and adjusts the initial lot size accordingly. A look ahead might indicate that the initial lot size should be increased to cover an additional period or two; a look back might indicate that the initial lot size should be decreased to cover fewer periods.

Part-period balancing can lower total inventory cost as compared with LTC. However, because it does not look ahead or back over the entire time horizon, it cannot be certain of lowering total inventory cost relative to LTC or other techniques, let alone minimizing total inventory costs.

Choosing a Lot Size Technique. The choice of a lot size technique is complicated by the fact that most MRP systems involve product structures (bills of material) that are several levels deep. The introduction of lot sizes other than lot-for-lot into the first level of the product structure can greatly complicate the lot size choices for lower levels. How complicated matters can get depends on the lot size choice itself, the complexity of the product structure, the degree of change permitted in the net requirements, and the degree of commonality of parts. Simulations of different lot size choices under various conditions have not resulted in clear recommendations for MRP users.

Having non-lot-for-lot lot size choices within a multilevel product structure also is likely to bloat inventory more than might be expected. The more complex the product structure, the more likely inventory will be bloated by most lot size techniques.

Safety Stocks

An MRP system can also accommodate safety stocks of items. In general, it is best to think of safety stocks of finished goods—"kits" of component parts—rather than individualized safety stocks for all of the component parts themselves. The accounting is easier if the safety stocks are thought of, and even actually held, in that way. The existence of safety stocks, however, goes somewhat against the grain of the material requirements planning philosophy, since safety stocks cannot be thought of in terms of time phasing for anticipated use. Companies also run the constant risk that their managers, once discovering the presence of safety stocks, will adapt their own decisions to use up the safety stock early and for purposes for which they were not intended.

Safety Lead Times

A common way to cushion an MRP system against any chronic irregularities in the deliveries of either purchased or fabricated parts is to tack on some extra time to the stated lead times. Otherwise, according to this view, chronic delivery problems might result in excessive expediting or rescheduling. Of course, this situation points up the usefulness of dependable delivery schedules. One frequent means of introducing safety lead times is to add a week (the standard time bucket) to a part or subassembly as it moves from one level in the bill of materials' product structure to the next higher level. Thus, a subassembly that resides in level 2 of the product structure and would otherwise be available immediately for assembly into a level 1 subassembly is given a lead time of one week for "safety's sake."

Material Requirements Planning As a Management Tool

A main function of an MRP system, of course, is to trigger purchases and factory orders so that they can meet projected production require-

ments. When all is working smoothly, an MRP system can do just that. However, the test of any materials management system comes not in fair weather but in foul. Events in a materials manager's life invariably go awry. It is in coping with the unexpected and in planning the future that an MRP system can often earn its own way.

A material requirements planning system can serve as a useful management tool in a variety of ways: to make schedules and revise them, to plan capacity, and to measure performance.

As a Scheduling and Schedule-Revising Device

Not only can an MRP system detail what should be ordered when, but also it can indicate how and when late items will affect other aspects of production. It can signal which orders now awaiting delivery ought to be expedited and how any tardiness will alter the existing production schedule (for example, how much final delivery will be delayed or which demands will now be placed in subsequent weeks). Similarly, if advance supply delivery or higher yields or some other positive development occurs, an MRP system can signal which orders to de-expedite or even cancel.

When such positive or negative developments strike, an MRP system can automatically reschedule orders (or, more often, indicate to the materials manager the necessity for rescheduling orders), moving them either forward or backward. For example, the spoilage of some inventory or the breakdown of machinery (both of which may reduce the number available in the future) can trigger the rescheduling of an order in the proper week to avoid a stockout. Unexpected developments could even lead to a change in the master production schedule or in the lot size permitted. Typically, an MRP system identifies a range of possible actions to be taken by the materials manager.

Oliver Wight, one of the pioneers and chief advocates of MRP, referred to MRP as a "simulated shortage list."[7] Traditionally in many companies, the true schedule of production was determined by a combination of what was due out to customers and what parts were available. If parts showed up short, quickly arranged meetings had to be held and immediate decisions had to be made about expediting the parts, if possible, and rescheduling the entire production schedule to accommodate the shortage. By simulating the shortage list well ahead of time, materials managers can take action to rectify potential shortages and/or reschedule production and other materials deliveries before real trouble occurs. The factory is then supplied with what it needs when it needs it. This is not to say that materials will never again have to be expedited or the production schedule adjusted on short notice; problems will always occur and have to be dealt with. With MRP, however, the factory requires less frantic expediting and less tumultuous production rescheduling and does so with less inventory (Wight's estimate is one-fourth to one-third less) than before, because the factory will not be short of parts it needs and overstocked with parts it does not need and perhaps did not even know it had.

It has been observed that when a shortage list dictates the true production schedule, the value of any agreed-upon master production schedule diminishes greatly. The MPS cannot be used to "push" materials out into the factory; instead, the shortage list must be relied on to "pull" materials and production orders through. With a well-functioning MRP system, however, the MPS assumes its rightful place as "driving" production: materials can be "pushed" out into the factory in accordance with the master production schedule without being sidetracked by rescheduling to accommodate parts shortages.

The benefits of a smooth production schedule are numerous. Already cited are the inventory savings that can result. Labor productivity is enhanced by removing expediting, parts shortages, and the destruction of machine or line setups. Foremen are freed from expediting to work on quality, methods, worker relations, and the like. Unnecessary overtime is avoided. Vendor and supply logistics premiums are reduced. Having realistic production schedules and not having materials shortages to blame poor performance on means that workers and managers alike can be evaluated on the things they should be evaluated on (quality, meeting schedules and budgets) without having to sort through so many excuses.

As a Capacity Planning Device

An MRP system can be enlarged to cope with capacity requirements, not just materials requirements. It does this by combining several types of information: (1) the planned production schedule and the materials required to meet it, (2) the time requirements to fabricate/assemble all parts and products, and (3) the particular workcenters in the factory through which those parts and products travel. By knowing how long any part or product can be expected to be worked on (its standard hours) and where all parts or products have to be processed (their routings), an MRP system can predict the workload at any work center in the factory. This predicted workload (in hours), given the planned master production schedule, existing inventories, and any lot size conventions, can be compared with the planned (or possible) hours for the workcenter and any deviations can be noted. For example, if the predicted workload is more than the planned (or possible) hours for the workcenter, then either capacity would have to be increased (perhaps through overtime, machine adjustments, and/or subcontracting) or the MPS would have to be modified to permit a balance of production needs and capabilities. Similarly, if the predicted workload is less than the planned (or possible) hours for the workcenter, resources (such as labor time) could be freed for use elsewhere without damaging the factory's delivery performance.

By using the deviations (variances) of predicted versus planned/possible workloads as feedback on the master production schedule and material needs, an expanded MRP system can be said to "close the loop" between material needs and capacity needs. Not only can materials be planned, but work hours can be planned as well, meshing both with the MPS. The master production schedule can then be realistically deemed feasible, and the MRP system can even be used to dispatch the day's or week's production assignments to the factory's workcenters.

Using an MRP system in this "closed loop" way to calculate capacity requirements—termed *capacity requirements planning*—is the most sophisticated means of assessing whether the factory has the capacity in the short run to meet expected demands on it. There are several other procedures to accomplish the same purpose, but they are somewhat less sophisticated and use less data. These procedures were discussed in Chapter 4.

As a Performance Measuring Device

If we go one step further and assign standard costs to parts and products, we can use the closed loop MRP system to generate financial figures on production and inventories that management can live with. This further expansion of the MRP system has been dubbed *manufacturing resource planning*, or *MRP II*. Companies that use MRP systems effectively in running their operations (those that close the loop, and those that use it for financial or business planning) are often termed *Class A users*.

The use of MRP as a capacity planning device and as a performance measuring device highlights the possibilities of using MRP for "what if" analysis. Demands of various types can be simulated as well as capacity modifications or other changes. Such simulation can be an exceedingly useful planning aid.

The Success of MRP

The potential and promise of MRP have fired the imaginations of managers at many companies. Yet, the actual success rate of MRP to date has disappointed many observers. The failings of many companies to earn the full benefits of MRP can be traced to a lack of appreciation for the diligence that an MRP system requires. As we have seen, the data requirements of an MRP system are massive. If the system is to work well, the data must be accurate and up-to-date. Think of what this means: accurate forecasts of demand, with no last-minute changes allowed; precise bills of materials showing all variations and a formal change mechanism for any engineering change orders; regular cycle counting of inventory so that the on-hand balances as shown are accurate; accurate lead times for vendors; accurate standard times, standard costs, and routings for each part; integrity with material usages and scrap rates, usually requiring a restricted access storage area with consistently good tracking of material flows in and out; and a realistic understanding of what production capacities are.

Accomplishing all these tasks requires management, at all levels, to understand MRP thoroughly, and to commit themselves to data integrity and all the nitty-gritty tracking and cross-checking that is required to maintain that integrity.

The success of MRP can be stirring, however. Situation 5-5 describes Black & Decker's Tarboro, North Carolina, facility and its experience with MRP.

SITUATION 5-5

THE BLACK & DECKER CORPORATION

Materials Management at the Tarboro, N.C. Plant

The Tarboro facility is part of Black & Decker's U.S. Power Tool group. The plant manufactured products for that group and also for the Household group. It was the lead plant for injection molding of plastic parts and for the manufacture of cord sets, battery packs, transformers, and chargers that were sent to a number of B & D manufacturing plants worldwide. Major products manufactured at the Tarboro facility included jigsaws, sanders, cordless drills, nailers, staplers, cordless hand-held vacuum cleaners, car vacuums, and car lights.

The manager of production and inventory control at Tarboro supervised both staff people and the hourly employees who worked in the storeroom. Production and inventory control was subdivided into three major areas, each with its own manager.

- *Inventory Control.* Under its manager were an inventory planner, records maintenance clerk, an inventory verifier, and a secretary.
- *Production Control.* Reporting to its manager were scheduler/expediters for injection molding, cord sets, welding, winding, assembly, and master scheduling.
- *Storeroom.* Under its supervisor were receiving and shipping clerks and materials handlers.

Purchasing responsibilities were not assigned to the manager of production and inventory control; purchasing was operated as a separate entity, with buyers, an expediter, and a secretary. Despite the organizational distinction between purchasing and materials management, the two departments worked closely together.

Outline of the Materials Management Systems

Black & Decker—Tarboro operated an MRP system called PACE (Planned Action and Constant Eval-

uation), which the company had developed in the 1960s. As a net change MRP system, PACE was updated daily. Future production requirements could be shown in PACE as far as one year in advance. Forecasting these production requirements was the responsibility of each group's logistics staff, which controlled all finished goods for that group. Thus the factory's responsibility for any product ceased when it left the factory; the group's logistics function assumed the carrying costs for all finished goods. The PACE system, however, distinguished between "requirements" that stemmed from the 52-week forecast of the group's logistics function, and "allocations" that resulted from firm orders for the product.

The PACE system had been used at Tarboro since the plant started in the early 1970s. However, its usefulness was not fully realized until several years later, when the materials control system (MCS) was added. The MCS was a real-time computer-based system that tracked materials. Records from the receipt of all materials—whether purchased from the outside, shipped from other B & D plants, or manufactured at the Tarboro facility—were kept, as were records of the issue of all materials (both raw materials and work-in-process) from the stockroom. The MCS kept track of all materials in the stockroom by aisle number, bin number, and height within the bin. It could assign received materials from one bin to another. MCS dictated that withdrawal take place from the bin with the fewest pieces and designated its destined point of use as well.

As a high-volume plant, B & D Tarboro produced hundreds of thousands of units of output a year. Stockroom workers did not count precisely either vendor receipts or the units of materials on any release of an order. Thus, at any time, an order might contain more or less than the number of pieces entered into the MCS. Nevertheless, the integrity of the system was excellent, as was evident in reports on materials usage and correct count variance. The production workers could count on receiving enough materials. It helped that scrapped pieces or faulty

Message	Total
Parts with credit on-hand balance	0
Allocations three weeks past due	73
Manufacturing orders three weeks past due	18
Manufacturing orders without shop paper three weeks past due	0
Purchase orders three weeks past due	3
Transfer orders three weeks past due	0
Service and Subsidiary allocations three weeks past due	2
Manufactured parts without components	0
Manufactured parts without op file	2
Interplant parts without components	0
Parts coded U, R, or S with planned orders	0
Parts with status out of phase late	155
Parts with status out of phase early	299
Parts not correctly counted within the last year	32
Obsolete parts with components	0
Obsolete parts with status	0
Obsolete parts with op file	0
Total on-hand inventory balance	34,252,578

Note: Contrast how few exceptions there are relative
to the total number of parts on hand.

FIGURE 5-22 Inventory analysis recap sheet.

pieces were reported back to the stockroom and adjustments were made to the MCS data files. The plant had not had to shut down to take a physical inventory since 1972. Pieces in the system were, however, counted regularly: A level items (high use, high value) four times a year; B level items twice a year; and C level items (low use, low value) once a year. Verifying the cycle counts and modifying the appropriate data bases were the chief responsibilities of the inventory verifier.

The MCS meant a great deal for the integrity of the MRP system at the Tarboro facility. Before 1974–1975, inventory turns (that is, annual sales divided by the value of average inventory held, a ratio that indicates how rapidly inventory can be viewed as turning over in a year's time) at Tarboro were only about five per year, a low number considering that the plant did not have to carry any finished goods inventory and made high-volume products. Without the MCS, it was impossible to maintain the high degree of record integrity required by the plant's high volume. The discipline provided by the MCS helped immensely to clean up the plant, so much so that by the fall of 1985, inventory turns at Tarboro were up to about 36 per year, a dramatic improvement.

Keeping the Materials Flow Clean

For the production and inventory control department, the key to keeping the flow of materials clean was the investigation of the exceptions to smooth operation. These numerous exceptions were detailed weekly in the inventory analysis recap sheet (Figure 5-22). The exception reports summarized on that sheet were carefully investigated. If they had not been investigated religiously, the integrity of the plant's MRP system would have gradually melted away; such attention to detail was essential. A description of these exception reports follows:

1. *Parts with credit on-hand balance.* This report detailed (1) which parts were shown to have been issued to the factory already but for which there was no record of receipt and/or (2) which parts had incorrect on-hand balances to begin with. This kind of error used to be widespread but had been curtailed by MCS. The MCS could not issue anything that was not shown to be already on hand. The MCS required a mandatory flow of materials from receipt to inspection to location in the stockroom and only then to issuance.

2. *Allocations three weeks past due.* This was an important exception report. It showed which allocations (that is, component demands triggered by firm orders for a product) had not yet shown up as completed. Such an inventory status could occur for several main reasons:

   - The allocation was not accurate but had not been changed. Acting on the allocation could result in the procurement of materials unnecessarily.
   - The product had not been built, implying that the materials issued for it were still on the factory floor, and the factory was behind schedule in making it. This condition could demand expediting on the factory floor.
   - The product had been built but the parts were not shown as issued. This situation could occur if extra material from other orders had not been returned to the stockroom. An MCS report on completed manufacturing orders for which components had not been issued was a tip-off to this problem.

3. *Manufacturing orders three weeks past due.* Whereas allocations referred to the component parts of the manufacturing order, the manufacturing order was for the tool itself. This exception report was like the allocations three weeks past due, but it referred strictly to the manufacturing orders themselves. This condition could demand expediting.

4. *Manufacturing orders without shop paper three weeks past due.* This report showed the manufacturing orders for which the paperwork to trigger, and follow up on, the job had not yet been issued.

5. *Purchase orders three weeks past due.* This report listed the items that were to be supplied by an outside vendor but were late. This condition could require expediting by the vendor.

6. *A transfer order three weeks past due.* A transfer order referred to a part made at another Black & Decker plant and used at Tarboro. This condition could require expediting of manufacturing at another Black & Decker plant.

7. *Service and subsidiary operation three weeks past due.* Some allocations were destined for either Black & Decker service or Black & Decker subsidiaries. These allocations could show up as manufacturing orders past due, or they could indicate parts that had been made but had not been pulled from the stockroom and allocated to either B & D service or a B & D subsidiary. The MCS helped greatly here because when allocations were loaded into the PACE program, they were automatically loaded as well into the MCS. MCS automatically triggered an issue whenever a service or subsidiary order was received into the stockroom. This kind of error had therefore become very rare.

8. *Manufacturing parts without the components.* This report notified the production planners of the dangerous situation when no components were structured to an end-item part. For one reason or another, the bill of materials had been skipped. This report was a check on the construction of bills of materials by engineering and on the translation of those bills into the PACE program.

9. *Manufacturing parts without operations files.* An operations file was a process sheet that indicated the labor-hours needed to make a particular part. It was essential to the capacity planning capability of the PACE system. This exception report listed the parts for which the

capacity planning system would not function because no labor-hours were shown or because of some other reason.

10. *Interplant parts without components.* In the Black & Decker MRP system, parts could be structured and exploded to other plants. This report noted all those products or parts whose components were unidentified at other B & D facilities.

11. *Parts coded U, R, or S with planned orders.* This report listed the parts that were being phased out of production by one of three methods: (1) they were being used up because of a change in the bill of materials—a U part, (2) they were destined for rework—an R part, or (3) they were scrapped—an S part.

12. *Parts with status "out of phase late."* This report listed the parts that were scheduled to arrive too late to satisfy the scheduled parent item. These parts were also listed on the inventory status sheets, which were routinely generated for parts that were past due.

13. *Parts with status "out of phase early."* This report listed the parts that were scheduled to arrive before the required date of the parent item. Action should be taken to reschedule those parts so that they will not be out of phase.

14. *Parts not correctly counted within last year.* Parts were classified according to the standard ABC system with A parts scheduled for cycle counting four times a year. Thus, every three months all A items would be physically counted and reconciled to the inventory records. B items were cycle counted twice a year and C items once a year. This report indicated any parts that might have been overlooked by the formal cycle count program.

15. *Obsolete parts with components.* This report listed the parts that were now obsolete but that showed components still active in the system. Thus a purging of these obsolete components was required.

16. *Obsolete parts with status.* This report listed the obsolete parts for which there was some demand. This report was largely superfluous,

because any problems with an obsolete part would have been tracked by other means.

17. *Obsolete parts with an operations file.* This report listed the obsolete parts for which an operations file was still maintained. This report, too, was largely superfluous.

Just-in-Time Manufacturing at Tarboro

While Black & Decker—Tarboro's managers were firm believers in MRP, they were also advocates of "just-in-time" manufacturing techniques as being particularly appropriate for their high-volume operation. They had gone far in merging JIT concepts with their MRP system. Their various efforts in this regard could be described as falling into one of three major categories: (1) production planning, (2) production control, or (3) the process itself. Let us examine the plant's JIT and MRP innovations in these terms.

Production Planning Innovations

As mentioned earlier, purchasing and materials management worked closely together. In recent years the vendor base had been reduced from 400 separate vendors to just 250. Many vendors were now the single sources for various items, with contracts let for terms of one to three years. For 60 percent of the vendors, accounting for 75 percent of purchased item value, there were no purchase orders typed. Instead, each week vendors were sent an MRP system-generated document (see Figures 5-23 through 5-29) that displayed the plant's requirements and current forecasts. For these vendors, purchasing controlled only the pricing and quality assessment for the items procured. The production and inventory control department actually released orders and did any expediting.

It used to be that the plant's MRP system was operated with a safety lead time of one week, as a kind of "cushion" for production. In addition, one week lead times were customarily added for each level in the bill of materials. To speed things along, however, the plant had structured its bills of material to be as "shallow" as they could be (they used as

FIGURE 5-23 Inventory status for the new power tool.

Notes:

1. This is the Inventory Status sheet for a new product (variously termed in what follows as "new power tool," "power tool," or "tool"). This report was generated in the week beginning October 28, 1985, which was shop week 504 in the Black & Decker system. The new power tool is a category 1 package assembly (a manufactured product), as opposed to a category 2 (purchased part) or a category 3 (raw material). The tool carries part number 50141740; the initial 5 indicates that Black & Decker plant 5 (Tarboro) makes the product.

2. The tool is measured in pieces (code 50 = pieces) and is classed as an A item in the plant's ABC inventory system. The last effective engineering change notice was number 01807, but an engineering change notice is pending (ECN pending = P).

3. Black & Decker—Tarboro plans the assembly of the power tool for three weeks out from the current week. Thus, quantities "on order" are shown out as far as week 507, but only planned orders are shown for any higher numbered weeks. Normally, for package assemblies, the "on order" quantity exactly matches the "requirement" quantity. In week 506, however, an error was made that triggered a planned order for 500. In week 508, the "availability" quantity goes significantly negative; week 508 is the week immediately outside the planning horizon.

4. The inventory status sheet shows a significant number of tools past due. This is a legitimate past due situation caused by the newness of the product. As yet, the factory had not been able to produce tools at the planned

rate. It remained about a week behind. If the rate could not be increased soon, the production planners would have to "open a hole in the schedule" somewhere to allow the factory to catch up. A hole could be opened by reducing the requirement(s) in future week(s). The reduced requirements in weeks 509, 513, and 514 were caused by the approaching Thanksgiving, Christmas, and New Year's holidays, respectively.

5. The bottom portion of the Inventory Status sheet was reserved for what was termed "pegging" information. These figures indicated the orders that together composed the demands for the power tool in particular weeks. The pegging information indicated the status of the order (for example, R = requirement, S = shop paper issued, U = planned order), the shop week it was due, the applicable part number (in this case, simply the tool's part number), the lot number assigned to that week's production (note that the lot number corresponds to the last two digits of the shop week, indicating that there was no lead time offset), the model number of the part or product, and the quantity ordered.

The past due amount of 18,257 is simply the sum of the quantities ordered for weeks 496, 499, 502, and 503. These orders had not been fully closed out. Observe that the orders for weeks 496 and 499 involve model 03. Nearly all of the other orders relate to models 00 or 01.

FIGURE 5-23   (continued)

FIGURE 5-24   Inventory status for the plastic bags.

Notes:

1. This is the Inventory Status sheet for part 0076384, a plastic bag that is part of the power tool's package assembly. This is a purchased part (category 2), measured in pieces, and a C item in the plant's ABC inventory system. This report is for shop week 503, a week earlier than that shown for the tool itself. This part was last cycle counted in shop week 485. Currently, there are 7,750 bags on hand.

2. This part has a purchase lead time of 7 weeks (Lead Time, component = 7). One can see the effect of this by noting that the "availability" row does not go consistently negative until week 510, 7 weeks out from the current one. The planned order for 8657 that was generated in the current week exactly matches the negative availability in week 510. This part is still formally planned for 3 weeks out; no allocations (firm orders) are shown past week 506.

3. This part was planned with a lead time offset of 1 week for the power tool. This is evident by reference to the pegging information. For example, under the requirements section, there is a requirement for 1767 bags for the tool (part number 0141740) for shop week 506. This requirement, however, is attached to lot number 07, which for the package assembly does not fall due until shop week 507. This same one week offset can be observed with other orders for the power tool in the requirements section of the pegging information.

4. The 7-week purchase lead time and the 1-week lead time offset total 8 weeks of advance notice for any planned orders. This can be seen in the planned orders section of the pegging information. There is an 8-week difference between the shop week indicated and the week implied by the lot number.

5. Note that in week 506 there is both a requirement and an allocation shown. These demands for plastic bags come from different final products, however. The 1767 unit requirement is linked to a new power tool order, while the 10,000 unit allocation is for some other product (part number 0001690).

6. There is a past due quantity of 440 plastic bags that is linked to an order that was for shop week 500. Probably these 440 plastic bags are no longer needed. The order for week 500 was probably filled by overissues previously made. If the order for week 500 has been closed out (and that can easily be ascertained), then these 440 past due units will need to be purged from the system. These units would show up in the exception reports (discussed later) as "allocations three weeks past due," a signal indicating the need for some reconciliation.

FIGURE 5-24   (*continued*)

few levels as possible). More recently, the plant's materials management people had formally modified the time offsets to permit either a whole week, no offset at all, or a fractional week offset (one-half week). This latter modification involved the creation of *dummy allocations,* which were in essence phony orders that were a fraction of the average weekly demand for the next quarter. By removing the traditional one week of safety lead time and replacing it with the phony order, inventory could be controlled more tightly (less than a full week's inventory was actually held).

Considerable care was taken in devising the master schedule, so that it was realistic and would not necessarily lead to materials expediting or rescheduling. While orders were launched in the traditional way (that is, the system "pushed" materials and work orders onto the factory floor), the assembly accomplished was according to well-established assembly rates and not to due dates.

Production Control Innovations

Traditionally, the storeroom at the Tarboro plant had been a key point of control. Materials were checked into the storeroom and then checked out, as needed, to the factory floor. While providing control over what the plant had in stock, where, and how much, a storeroom does impede the flow of materials straight through to an assembly line, and it costs money to operate. In an effort to streamline the flow of materials, the Tarboro plant was modifying the PACE and MCS systems to facilitate "backflushing." With backflushing, the storeroom would be eliminated as a point of control; materials would be received and entered onto the system but would only be relieved in the accounting system when they showed up as part of the finished goods. The new system would identify materials as either in the storeroom or on the floor. In addition, the plant was adopting more standard containers for parts and more standard stocking points on the factory floor.

508 SEGMENT II / IMPROVING EXISTING OPERATIONS

Notes:

1. This is an Inventory Status sheet for part 0141733, a bearing retainer, that is also a component of the new power tool. It is a longer purchasing lead time component (12 weeks), as can be seen by the difference of 12 weeks between the current 503 week's planned order for 11,102 units and the negative availability of 11,102 in week 515.

2. This report is of particular interest because it relates to a part whose inventories are reduced through the device of fractional week offsets. This is one of the means by which just-in-time manufacturing was fostered by the Tarboro plant's materials management group. The fractional week offset took the form of a phony order (P000000 in the allocations section of the pegging information) that was a fraction of the average requirements over the next 13 weeks (in this case, ½ the average). The requirements lot numbers matched with the shop weeks, as if the entire order was expected to be filled. The phony order, however, acted to give the factory a bit of buffer time, although not a whole week's worth, as was the case for plastic bags.

3. The current week's availability is 20,898 units, determined by adding the on-hand balance of 44,461 to the current week's on order quantity of 27,000 (which includes the 12,000 on order past due) then subtracting the current week's allocation of 50,563 (which includes the allocation of 35,563 past due).

FIGURE 5-25   Inventory status for a bearing retainer.

10/12/85 WEEK 503 **INVENTORY STATUS** CODE- A FOR 50086392-04   I N D I V I D U A L - P A R T   REQUESTED BY   ORDER# 522 80   NAME   DEPT. NO.

CATEGORY	PART NUMBER OR RAW MATERIAL CODE	DESCRIPTION	UNIT OF MEASURE	ABC CODE	FAMILY CODE	CLASS CODE	BUYER CODE	STANDARDIZATION CODE	LAST EFFECTIVE ECN NUMBER	CLASS OR FAMILY						DATE OF LAST C/C	DATE LAST TRANS	ECN PEND	LOC
2	50C86392-04	GEAR 7504 TY6	50	B	♦♦♦		80		64019							500	502	5	

PAGE	LEAD TIME		PRODUCTION LOT SIZE	SCRAP FACTOR	SAFETY STOCK	MINIMUM PURCHASE QUANTITY	PURCHASE CONVERSION QUANTITY	NUMBER ORDERS LAST YEAR	NUMBER ORDERS YEAR TO DATE	USAGE LAST YEAR	EST	USAGE YEAR TO DATE	TOTAL STANDARD COST	SET-UP COST PER LOT	RUN COST (COST EACH LESS SET-UP)	QUANTITY BALANCES			LOCATION
	S/A	COMP														ON HAND	RECEIVED	STAGED	
↑	6	1	0C					32	2	53222C		25625				27800			5

	PAST DUE	CURRENT WEEK	WEEK-504	WEEK-505	WEEK-506	WEEK-507	WEEK-508	WEEK-509	WEEK-510	WEEK-511	WEEK-512	WEEK-513	WEEK-514	WEEK-515
REQUIREMENT						600	20000	20000	12000	20000	20000		16C00	20000
ALLOCATIONS	13910	2891C	15000	2CC0C	195C0							20C00		
ON ORDER			150C0	20C00	20000	20000	20000	12C00						
AVAILABILITY		1110-	1110-	1110-		1210-	1210-	1210-	1210-	21210-	41210-	61210-	61210-	77210-	97210-
PLANNED ORDERS									1210	20000	20000	16000	20000	20000

	WEEK-516	WEEK-517	WEEK-518	WEEK-519	WEEK-520	WEEK-521	WEEK-522	WEEK-523	WEEK-524	WEEK-525	WEEK-526	WEEK-527	WEEK-528	WEEK-529
REQUIREMENT														
ALLOCATIONS	2C0C0	20C0C	15000	20C00	20000	2000C	10000	15C00	15000	15000	12C00	4000	15C00	15000
ON ORDER														

A. Before review by materials planner.

10/19/85 WEEK 504 **INVENTORY STATUS** CODE- A FOR 50086392-04   I N D I V I D U A L - P A R T   REQUESTED BY   ORDER# 521 80   NAME   DEPT. NO.

CATEGORY	PART NUMBER OR RAW MATERIAL CODE	DESCRIPTION	UNIT OF MEASURE	ABC CODE	FAMILY CODE	CLASS CODE	BUYER CODE	STANDARDIZATION CODE	LAST EFFECTIVE ECN NUMBER	CLASS OR FAMILY						DATE OF LAST C/C	DATE LAST TRANS	ECN PEND	LOC
2	50C86392-04	GEAR 7504 TY6	50	B	♦♦♦		80		64019							500	503	5	

PAGE	LEAD TIME		PRODUCTION LOT SIZE	SCRAP FACTOR	SAFETY STOCK	MINIMUM PURCHASE QUANTITY	PURCHASE CONVERSION QUANTITY	NUMBER ORDERS LAST YEAR	NUMBER ORDERS YEAR TO DATE	USAGE LAST YEAR	EST	USAGE YEAR TO DATE	TOTAL STANDARD COST	SET-UP COST PER LOT	RUN COST (COST EACH LESS SET-UP)	QUANTITY BALANCES			LOCATION
	S/A	COMP														ON HAND	RECEIVED	STAGED	
↑	6	1	0C					32	3	53222C		42650				45541			5

	PAST DUE	CURRENT WEEK	WEEK-505	WEEK-506	WEEK-507	WEEK-508	WEEK-509	WEEK-510	WEEK-511	WEEK-512	WEEK-513	WEEK-514	WEEK-515	WEEK-516
REQUIREMENT				500		20000	12000	20000	20000	20000		16000	20000	20000
ALLOCATIONS	11965	26965	20000	19600	20000									
ON ORDER			2559	20C00	20000	20000	120C0	21C00						
AVAILABILITY		18576	1135	1035	1035	1035	1035	2035	17965	37965	37965	53965	73565	93965-
PLANNED ORDERS									17965	20000		16C00	20000	20000

	WEEK-517	WEEK-518	WEEK-519	WEEK-520	WEEK-521	WEEK-522	WEEK-523	WEEK-524	WEEK-525	WEEK-526	WEEK-527	WEEK-528	WEEK-529	WEEK-530
REQUIREMENT														
ALLOCATIONS	2C0C0	15000	20000	20C0C	2C000	10000	15000	15C00	15000	12000	4C00	15000	15C00	150C0
ON ORDER														

B. After review by materials planner.

Notes:

1. Panels A and B represent the situation before and after a materials planner has reviewed the status of a purchased gear (part number 0086392) that is also a component of the new power tool. Panel A displays shop week 503 and Panel B, shop week 504.

2. The part has a purchasing lead time of 7 weeks, so that the week of interest for Panel A is 503 + 7 = 510. A decision has to be reached for that week. There is a negative availability in the current week, but that is of no large concern because there is a phony order for 7885 in week 501. Quantities on hand plus on order should satisfy all demands until week 510.

3. Panel B depicts the situation the following week. An order for 21,000 units has been placed for week 510. The negative availabilities of the previous week have been resolved. The allocation of 6025 units for week 502 (in Panel A) has been closed out, as have all but 4000 units of the allocation of 15,000 for week 503 (contrast Panel B with Panel A). The open order of 15,000 units for week 504 (Panel A) has been closed out as has all but 2559 units of the open order for 20,000 for week 505 (Panel A).

4. Note that most orders shown in these and other inventory status reports are lot-for-lot. Indeed, most of Tarboro's lot size decisions were lot-for-lot, perhaps with some smoothing done (such as searching out two weeks and producing the average of two weeks' total demand rather than a strict lot-for-lot). It was really only for C class items that EOQ quantities (calculated separately) were sometimes used.

FIGURE 5-26 Inventory status for a purchased gear.

```
PART NUMBER 50086392-04 GEAR 7504 TY6                          PAGE  2 OF  2
     2 CAT                SERV ONLY      36,741   TOTAL O/H        0  UNINSPECTED
    50 U/M                SHELF DAYS     36,741   AVAILABLE        0  DEVIANT/REJ
   -55 AREA/DPT           FAM GRP             0   REWORK      95,559  BAL DUE PO
   080 BUYER        0 INS STATUS             0   LOST             0  BAL DUE MO
   500 WK CC    10/21/85 LAST TRANS          0   FLR STOCK   69,800  B DUE ALLOC
              COST                           0   WIPBIN QTY
MFG NBR      DESCRIPTION   DUE TO   REQUIRED    ISSUED   BAL DUE    FLR STK   STAT
014174004  NEW POWER TOOL  504 89    15000       4800     10200          0   START
014174005  NEW POWER TOOL  505 89    20000          0     20000          0   START
014174006  NEW POWER TOOL  506 89    19500          0     19500          0   OPEN
000373001  S/A GEAR PIN    506 89      100          0       100          0   OPEN
014174007  NEW POWER TOOL  507 89    20000          0     20000          0   OPEN
YOUR INQUIRY IS NOW COMPLETE
1) PAGE FORWARD BY DEPRESSING PA1 KEY, OR 2) ENTER PART NUMBER, OR
3) OVERLAY TRANS CODE (AND ENTER OPTIONAL PARAMETERS) FOR NEW TRANSACTION
M007 5008639204
```

Notes:

1. This is a part number inquiry (M007) that is part of the capability of Black & Decker's MCS. This inquiry is for part 0086392, the gear that the before and after planning reports refer to. What is shown is a printout of the second CRT screen shown in this inquiry. (Most of these inquiries are real-time ones made on the CRT without the need for printed copy.)

2. The top portion of the inquiry identifies the part and gives information on its category (purchased part = 2), its unit of measure (pieces = 50), the department it is used in (55), who buys it (80), its last cycle count (week 500), its last transaction (10/21/85), the total on hand (36,741) total available for use (36,741), the balance due from purchase orders (95,559), and the balance due from allocations (69,800 − the sum of the Balance Due column in the lower portion of the report). The standard cost has been suppressed, and no units are shown tied up as rework, lost, floor stock, work-in-process bin quantities, uninspected, or deviant/rejected.

3. The bottom portion of the inquiry shows the status of the orders to which the part in question (the gear) is linked. Two orders—lots 04 and 05—for weeks 504 and 505 have been started. Only when an order has been started will the MCS system permit the storeroom to issue parts against it. The inquiry shows that only lot 04 has had parts issued to it, 4,800 of the 15,000 required. The remaining orders indicate what has been formally planned (3 weeks out from current week) and what their statuses are. Note that one is for a product other than the new power tool.

The previous screen (page 1, not shown here) lists the status of orders for weeks prior to 504. Many of those listings would show closed orders, held orders (for the phony orders), and other started orders.

FIGURE 5-27   Part inquiry for the gear in Figure 5-26.

Process Innovations

As important as these innovations in production planning and control were the innovations that Black & Decker—Tarboro had made in the production process itself. There were numerous instances where operations that historically had been done off-line in batches had been linked together to form a more continuous flow operation. The cordset area was a cardinal example. The previously separate and dis- joint operations—(1) cutting the cord to length and stripping its outer layer, (2) preparation of the cord for the plug, and (3) molding the plug—were combined into a single line flow layout. As a result, inventory had been reduced from five days to one, space had been cut in half, quality feedbacks were more timely, and material handling had been reduced by two-thirds. Similar stories were being told elsewhere in the factory.

```
ORDER # - PLT 5    REF NO 0141740    LOT 03      PART # 5014174000      PAGE  2
    15,000   TOT ORDER QTY              0  1ST OP QTY     DUE WK: 503  MATL WK: 503
    15,000   BAL DUE QTY                0  STKPILE QTY    DESC: NEW POWER TOOL
         0   RECEIVED QTY                                 STATUS:   STARTED 10/08/85
                                                          TO DEPT: 89
PART NBR       DESCRIPTION   CAT BUY STAT  REQUIRED    ISSUED   BAL DUE      AVAIL
50129146-00 PALLET MARKER    2 096 STRT        104        41        63        3625
50129863-46 45X47 S/A PAL'T  2 030 STRT         51        51         0           5
50140672-71 S/A FIELD        2 040 STRT      15000     10206      4794        3662
50140683-00 BEARING SLEEVE   2 096 STRT      15000      9910      5090       22000
50140994-00 BRUSH            2 093 STRT      30000     30000         0       70946
50140996-00 SPRING BRUSH     2 094 STRT      30000     30000         0       35000
50140998-00 HOLDER BRUSH     2 094 STRT      30000     30000         0      119206
50141291-00 SCREW            2 093 STRT      15000     15000         0           0
50141434-00 WASHER           2 096 STRT      15000      7500      7500       52000
50141731-01 SWITCH           2 093 STRT      15000      4250     10750           0
50141733-01 BRG RETAINE      2 094 STRT      15000     15000         0       36900
50141733-02 BRG RETAINE      2 094 STRT      15000     15000         0       41900
50141736-02 BRUSH RING       2 094 STRT      15000     15000         0       23865
50141738-00 HOUSING ASM HAL  2 094 STRT      15000     12662      2338        7104
1) PAGE FORWARD BY DEPRESSING PA1 KEY, OR 2) ENTER ORDER #, OR
3) OVERLAY TRANS CODE (AND ENTER OPTIONAL PARAMETERS) FOR NEW TRANSACTION
M006 5014174003
```

Notes:

1. This is a job status inquiry (M006) for the new power tool (part number 0141740) for lot 03. This is page 2 of that inquiry, which shows the status of various parts that go into the assembly of the tool. Other pages would list other parts comprising the tool's bill of materials. Lot 03 is for 15,000 units, and it was started on 10/8/85.

2. The parts listed in the bottom portion of the page are all purchased parts. All have been "started," and all have had at least part of their requirements issued. Most parts have been completely issued to the lot. Six parts still have some balance due, and what is available to issue is also listed. Such a report suggests what needs to be done in order to complete the lot.

FIGURE 5-28 Job status inquiry for the new power tool (see Figure 5-23).

Setups, particularly in the injection molding department, had been dramatically reduced. This reduction had occurred for several reasons: new equipment had been purchased, special racks and other aids had been designed, procedures had been changed to do as much as could be done while the machine was running, special quick change devices had been added to the equipment, and automated materials handling equipment had been put in place.

Some foolproofing devices (*bakayoke* in Japanese) had been added. For example, an electric eye system had been devised to ensure that all the literature (directions for use, warranty) that should be included in a package was in fact put in. A buzzer would sound whenever a bin of literature was inadvertently passed over.

By these innovations in production planning, production control, and process design, the Tarboro plant had taken great strides in merging the benefits of a well-run MRP system with the benefits of just-in-time production.

```
                         BLACK & DECKER MFG COMPANY        10/19/85
      BUYER-NO                    TARBORO
      PWP-CODE       ORDER STATUS FOR TRI COUNTY INDUSTRIES    589000

   PART NBR    DESCRIPTION    WEEK    DATE    PO NBR       QTY


                            522  02/24                  50 PLANNED
                            523  03/03                  50 PLANNED
                            524  03/10                  50 PLANNED


   * * * * * * * * * * * * * * * * * * * * * * * * * * * * * * * * *


   5012961463 41X45 S/A PAL  504  10/21  96545000         7
                             511  12/09                   4 PLANNED
                             515  01/06                   5 PLANNED
                             516  01/13                   5 PLANNED
                             518  01/27                   4 PLANNED
                             519  02/03                   4 PLANNED


   * * * * * * * * * * * * * * * * * * * * * * * * * * * * * * * * *


   5012961471 43X43 S/A PAL'T 504 10/21  96544204       111
                             506  11/04  96555806       300
                             508  11/18  96550608       200
                             509  11/25  96501909       150
                             510  12/02                 125 PLANNED
                             511  12/09                 140 PLANNED
                             512  12/16                 123 PLANNED
                             513  12/23                  20 PLANNED
                             514  12/30                 118 PLANNED
                             515  01/06                 140 PLANNED
                             516  01/13                 123 PLANNED
                             517  01/20                 140 PLANNED
                             518  01/27                 144 PLANNED
```

Notes:

1. This is a repetitive purchasing report issued on 10/19/85 to Tri County Industries, one of Black & Decker—Tarboro's vendors. This is one page of the full report. It lists two of the parts (different size pallets) that Tri County Industries provided to the plant.

2. For each part, this report lists the due date and shop week and information on its status. For example, for the first part listed in full (5012961463) an order for 7 has been confirmed, due 10/21. The purchase order number (96545000) is given. All the other quantities are not confirmed; they remain "planned." They lie outside the purchasing lead time established for the part. Nevertheless, the quantities shown well into the future are extremely helpful to the vendor, providing a visibility on Black & Decker's needs that would not otherwise be available.

   Black & Decker "owns" the vendor's material for 8 weeks' worth of orders. If there are changes in the plant's needs within that time frame, the vendor does not suffer for the expenses incurred for material. If the vendor is late with an order, however, it is the plant's option to cancel that order, and the vendor swallows that cost.

FIGURE 5-29   Repetitive purchasing report on Tri-County Ind.

The Cost of MRP[8]

The substantial benefits conferred upon an operation by a well-run MRP system are not reaped without some significant expenditures for hardware, software, data base development, and user training. Hardware costs are generally the easiest to estimate and the ones most subject to reduction (at least in real terms). Depending on the complexity of the system, annual lease costs for hardware for MRP can run between $50,000 and $600,000. Software costs are also subject to considerable variation. Wight estimated software lease expense at between $15,000 per year at the low end and $300,000 initial cost plus $30,000 per year maintenance at the high end. Wight also estimated the cost of programming and data base development (such as bills of material, routings, inventory records) at between 6 and 14 worker-years of effort. Users must be trained as well; that expense can vary tremendously, depending on the extent of training and whether instruction is live or via videocassettes.

The typical length of time to install an MRP system is about 18 months.

Choosing MRP or the Two Non-Time-Phased Inventory Systems

Although an MRP system radiates many desirable qualities, it does so at a cost. The question still persists as to when a company should adopt an MRP system and when it should stay with a less versatile but less expensive non-time-phased system. Consider Situation 5-6.

SITUATION 5-6

HEWITT-EVERETT DIVISION

The Hewitt-Everett Division of Winchester International, Inc. manufactured automatic weighing and measuring equipment, which was used primarily by agricultural cooperatives for mixing feeds and fertilizers. The equipment released selected quantities of grain, nutrients, or fertilizer into a hopper for either bulk or bag loading. The heart of the product—and the toughest part to make—was the release mechanism, for it had to be both sturdy and exact. Much of the rest of the equipment was sheet metal; forming it presented no particular difficulties.

Over the past year, Hewitt-Everett had modified the release mechanism to include a new electronic sensor and control system. This electronic system was more rugged, more versatile, and quicker than the mechanical system it replaced. Its introduction had strengthened the product in the market, and sales were running strong.

Hewitt-Everett offered its weighing and measuring equipment in over 70 varieties of sizes and configurations. Since this equipment was bulky and rather expensive, no finished goods inventories were kept. Rather, production proceeded on an order-by-order basis. For the 70-odd different equipment offerings, however, there were only eight different release mechanisms required, which simplified matters considerably. A like number of electronic sensor and control systems were needed as well.

The sole supplier of the electronic sensors and controls was another division of Winchester International, which specialized in the original equipment electronics market. Hewitt-Everett was delighted with the product's quality; but recently, as sales continued their steady upward climb, deliveries from this other Winchester International division had lagged. The late deliveries were causing increasing concern among Hewitt-Everett's management because they were stretching out Hewitt-Everett's own cycle time in fabricating its weighing and measuring equipment. If the company's cycle time were stretched much further, the company would lose its ability to compete for many of the late fall orders, a prime order-taking period. That is, if the company could not deliver its equipment by late winter in time for spring planting, it was in danger of losing any order placed after the first of November.

As a remedy for this disturbing situation, a group of managers within the company had been lobbying Mike Hewitt, the company's founder and still its president, for the introduction of a material requirements planning system that might even cross division lines within Winchester International. The essence of their argument was that Hewitt-Everett needed to give its sister division more time to react to the order for sensors and controls. At present, when Hewitt-Everett received an order, only the assembly department was notified of model and quantity. That department was then responsible for placing a subsequent, derivative order with its suppliers, including the department making the release mechanism. The release mechanism department, in turn, was responsible for placing an order with the sister division. The managers lobbying Mike Hewitt thought that two to three weeks could be saved by notifying the sister division directly of the equipment orders as they were received, instead of waiting for the domino effect of department-by-department ordering. They reasoned that a material requirement planning (MRP) system could coordinate this materials ordering procedure much more quickly and efficiently than the present set of procedures could. They estimated that establishing an MRP system would cost Hewitt-Everett about $100,000 and that maintaining it would cost about $25,000 per year.

To Mike Hewitt, this sounded like a lot of money, but he also recognized that something clearly had to be done to shorten the cycle time in manufacturing. (Some figures on product cost and quantities are given here for the latest year.)

Units sold	420
Present growth rate of unit sales	9%
Average unit cost	$13,500
Average standard cost of release mechanisms	$ 3,100
Average transfer price of electronic sensors and control systems	$ 1,250

Discussion of Hewitt-Everett Division

The lobbying effort directed at Mike Hewitt is well intentioned. An MRP system stretching across division lines at Winchester International does promise to reduce the production cycle time of the release mechanisms that have been at the root of management's present concern. It could well reduce that cycle time by the two to three weeks its proponents claim could be shaved off. There would probably be other benefits as well, such as better control over other components of the automatic weighing and measuring systems the division sold.

Installing a material requirements planning system, however, is not the only way by which the division's production cycle time could be reduced. An alternative worthy of consideration is a simple one—namely, providing a buffer stock of the sensors and controls that have been delivered tardily. The Hewitt-Everett Division could then draw immediately on this "decoupling" inventory and at the same time place an order with the sister division that would result in the restocking of the buffer inventory. Since only eight different sensor and control systems are required anyway, the inventory would not have to be that large and diverse to be effective.

Either the MRP system or the buffer inventory plan would succeed in eliminating the waiting associated with the present system of one department or division placing orders on other departments or divisions. Choosing between the two rests largely on the costs of each. The expected MRP system expenses are already provided. What must be estimated are the carrying costs of the buffer inventory.

Calculating the Carrying Cost of the Buffer Inventory

Although the particular quantities of each of the eight sensor and control systems needed would depend on the expected pattern of demand, for a back-of-the-envelope calculation we might expect to have to inventory four weeks of production, on the average. The company's inventory carrying cost percentage is not quoted in the situation, but 25 percent is not likely to be far off the mark. The expected annual inventory carrying cost would then be:

$$420 \text{ units/year} \cdot 4 \text{ weeks/52 weeks} \cdot$$
$$\$1250 \text{ cost per system} \cdot 25 \text{ percent carrying cost}$$
$$= \$10,100 \text{ per year in carrying costs}$$

This cost is only slightly more than a third of the annual expense of maintaining an MRP system. The required weeks of inventory could be doubled and the buffer inventory costs would still be less than the MRP system's. Thus, the side benefits of the MRP system would likely have to be significant for an MRP system to be preferred.

In addition, it is likely that the time needed to install a formal, computerized material requirements planning system could be significantly longer than the time it would take the sister division to build up an inventory of sensor and control systems. MRP systems typically take many months to install and debug. Although a buildup of a buffer inventory would not be quick, especially considering the recent pattern of late deliveries, at least some inventory could be built up with the next order placed on the sister division.

All things considered then, the simpler, less sophisticated, buffer inventory approach to cutting down on the division's production cycle time appears to be the preferred solution to Hewitt-Everett's present concerns.

When Implementing an MRP System Is Less Desirable[9]

As the workings of a material requirements planning system were described in this chapter, a tremendous amount of data must be accumulated and updated continually—master production schedules, bills of materials, inventory status, production cycle times, materials needs at each stage of the production cycle, supplier lead times, routings of parts, and standard costs. The more easily a company can check off the data in its master schedule, bills of materials, and the like, the more likely that it has its production well under control. Simply going through the exercise of assembling such data in preparation for the implementation of an MRP system is a tremendous learning experience for most companies and suggests a host of useful changes in operations. There is no denying that the MRP philosophy can pay huge dividends to plant management.

On the other hand, there are some circumstances under which implementing an MRP system taxes company resources too much to be worth the effort. The Hewitt-Everett Division situation is one where the benefits of an MRP system do not mesh well enough with the problem to justify its use in preference to a decoupling inventory. In other instances, an MRP system is not justified because of data accumulation and updating difficulties and costs.

For example, in situations where the master production schedule is not known with certainty well in advance, an MRP system is harder to justify. An MRP system works best when products are made to stock and not to order, when large buffer stocks of finished goods exist, and when sales are not very sensitive to abrupt seasonal or cyclical swings.

A material requirements planning system is likewise tougher to implement when bills of materials for products are not stable. An MRP system is best off when the number of new product introductions over time is modest, when there are few engineering changes released, and when there is little or no tinkering on the shop floor by engineers or others.

In a similar vein, an MRP system is likely to run more smoothly and be more effective when the process itself is stable. That is, when the process is not new or state-of-the-art itself, and when it is not likely to exhibit significant variances in product yields and quality, an MRP system stands a better chance. Also, if the time periods when various inputs are used in the process are well established, implementing an MRP system is easier. Lastly, an MRP system is best off when supplier lead times are known and dependable.

MRP systems have been criticized in some quarters as inadvertently contributing to the maintenance of long production cycle times for products (that is, long time periods for the manufacture of products from initial materials acquisition through final inspection). The argument here is that because MRP systems build in excessive safety lead times and inventories, they unwittingly impede innovations that would push the process toward faster production cycles and toward running with only the slimmest stocks of inventory. Indicative of these innovations are the process advances achieved by running families of parts together, using group technology (where equipment is dedicated to a certain family of parts), and employing the just-in-time production methods of the Japanese (see the Chapter 4 discussion on production control). Although MRP systems have, no doubt, impeded some moves to more rapid production cycle times, the experience of plants like Black & Decker—Tarboro with just-in-time techniques of materials management suggests that MRP can be more flexible than might have been thought.

In sum, the material requirements planning approach to materials control has many attractive features and can be a significant unifying force for all of a company's manufacturing. Yet, it has to be embraced with some caution; other means may lead a company to the same ends at less expense in time, money, and headaches.

This concludes the discussion of both anticipatory (MRP) and non-time-phased inventory systems (periodic reorder and reorder point) for managing stocks of items in either raw mate-

rials or finished goods inventories. We push on now to a discussion of managing work-in-process inventories.

MANAGING THE WORK IN PROCESS

As should be abundantly evident from the situation at the Hewitt-Everett Division, inventory systems (especially those of an anticipatory nature) are inextricably interwoven with planning and controlling production itself. This is nowhere more evident than in managing work-in-process inventories, for it is here that managers must keep alert to the interactions of the process and inventory.

How can work-in-process inventories build up? The process descriptions of Segment I help to isolate some general reasons. Among them are production bottlenecks, line changeovers, parts shortage, and uncoordinated production control.

Production Bottlenecks

As we have already observed, the production bottleneck is a classic explanation for the buildup of work-in-process inventories and the bane of the job shop in particular. When bottlenecks occur, good inventory management means taking a close look at the balance of capacities in the process. In particular, if demand has increased or if the mix of products going through the shop or the production methods or equipment has changed, a careful process flow diagram-type analysis can work wonders for diagnosing the problem and suggesting possible solutions.

Line Changeovers

Again, as noted in Segment I, the typical line flow process is a rather inflexible agent for producing a broad mix of products. Often, different products must be run separately and serially on the line. Thus, if the company is to offer a complete product mix, inventories must be built up for each product in turn. Naturally, the more inflexible the line flow and the more dependent the company is on a small number of lines, the greater the inventory buildup is apt to be. In this case, the impact of the process on inventories can be dramatic. Frequently, a company's flexibility is enhanced by establishing production lines that are smaller but more numerous rather than production lines that are fewer in number and larger in size.

Parts Shortage

A classic and all-too-common explanation for the buildup of work-in-process inventories is the lack of one or more parts for completing a unit. In many continuous and line flow processes, the lack of a part would shut down operations altogether; but in other processes parts shortages can frequently be worked around, and are, especially when pressure for delivery is exerted. Unfortunately, although working around a parts shortage may be the quickest way to manufacture a given unit, an entire operation that works in this way reduces productivity considerably. Invariably, extra time is spent figuring what to work around, how to do it, placing work-in-process in limbo somewhere on the factory floor, fetching it for rework, figuring out how to proceed again, actually reworking the unit, and interrupting ongoing operations all along the way. Often, by having to cope with parts shortages and the factory floor difficulties they pose, the company suffers the consequences of poor raw materials inventory management. For many operations, the stockout penalty for a part in raw materials inventory does not include the many petty but cumulatively significant problems that a parts shortage can introduce to the factory floor.

More frequently still than a faulty raw materials safety stock decision, a parts shortage develops because of delivery problems with a supplier. The purchasing department may have ordered enough and may have given the supplier sufficient notice considering past delivery performance, but the supplier simply falls down on the job. There may not be a lot the manufacturer can do in such a situation. We have already discussed (1) the make-buy option, which is sometimes a way out of chronic delivery problems, (2) the multiple supplier option, which can help to assure deliveries as well as reasonable prices, (3) the working with a supplier to improve its production capabilities and quality performance, and (4) the development of systems (such as MRP) that can give suppliers as much visibility into the future as the customer company enjoys.

A fifth means of coping better with such a situation may be the division of attention within the purchasing department to supplies of various kinds. One popular way of dividing up the responsibilities for ordering, monitoring, and expediting supply deliveries is the ABC system described earlier. Different people can be assigned to each group. The A group people, for example, might keep close check on the delivery status of their items, mainly the ones where delivery is likely to be a problem. The C group people are probably dealing with commodity items where their concerns are less with delivery and more with price differences by vendor, price discounts for large volumes, and EOQ-type calculations. (With an MRP system in effect, however, an ABC system is usually redundant; the speed and comprehensiveness of an MRP system makes it fairly easy to treat a C item like an A item.)

Uncoordinated Production Control

As we have seen from Situation 5-6, there can be a mismatch in the product mix processed in different segments of the operation, especially when broad, changeable, and/or variably demanded product mixes are involved. This mismatch in production signals can be purposely sought (the "decoupling" inventory in the Hewitt-Everett situation) or it can be inadvertent. In either case, a work-in-process inventory builds up. Note that this reason for an expansion of work-in-process results not from a production bottleneck per se, because the aggregate capacities of different segments may match up very well. Rather, this work-in-process inventory develops because one segment's output, on a specific product-by-product basis, does not match in the short run a succeeding segment's output needs. In the longer run, of course, unless there is obsolescence, the two segments will produce matching product mixes. The challenge here lies in understanding when production and inventory control is better served and more effective with a work-in-process inventory that buffers segments of the full production process and their information needs from one another, and when such an inventory is merely taking up space, swallowing financing dollars, and confusing and disrupting operations.

One common way that inadvertent work-in-process accumulates in this way is when one portion of the process demands a substantially different setup expenditure than another portion. The typical reaction to a high setup cost is to make the run long. While such a strategy often makes good sense, it is not always the best course of action. Long runs may build up too much inventory for too long a period and risk stockouts of items with more pressing demands. The balance of setup costs against inventory expenses and stockout penalties ought to be done in every case.

Another common way that uncoordinated production control can stack up undesired work-in-process inventory is when expediting within the factory rages out of control. As more and more rush orders are placed on the factory floor, the regular flow of the process becomes increasingly disrupted. This raises work-in-process inventory and lowers productivity (labor time per unit increases). Existing machine setups are likely to be broken repeatedly, necessitating time-consuming rework of the setups themselves. As Segment I's process descriptions revealed, rush orders are incompatible with line flow and continuous flow operations. In job shop and batch-flow operations, production control policies become critical. This is not to imply that rush orders should not be permitted. Rather, it is an admonition that a company whose work-in-process inventories seem to be ballooning ought to look carefully at the extent of rush orders within the process and whether a restructuring or expansion of the process, a different means of production scheduling, or a segregation of rush orders might be a more effective way to maintain both productivity and service levels.

PART THREE
ISSUES IN LOGISTICS[10]

Logistics is chiefly concerned with the movement of products to markets and of materials to manufacturing facilities. Entwined with the actual movement of material, of course, is its storage and handling. Logistics has been a frequently neglected aspect of operations, but one whose potential impact on costs and profits is greater than most realize, as evidenced by the figures in Table 5-7. Total distribution costs, as shown there, are roughly as high a percentage

TABLE 5-7   Distribution costs as a percentage of sales dollar

	OUTBOUND TRANSPOR-TATION	INVENTORY CARRYING	WARE-HOUSING	ADMINI-STRATION	RECEIVING AND SHIPPING	PACK-AGING	ORDER PRO-CESSING	TOTAL
All manufacturing companies	6.2%	1.3%	3.6%	0.5%	0.8%	0.7%	0.5%	13.6%
Chemicals and plastics	6.3	1.6	3.3	0.3	0.6	1.4	0.6	14.1
Food manufacturing	8.1	0.3	3.5	0.4	0.9	—	0.2	13.4
Electronics	3.2	2.5	3.2	1.2	0.9	1.1	1.2	13.3
Paper	5.8	0.1	4.6	0.2	0.3	—	0.2	11.2
Machinery and tools	4.5	1.0	2.0	0.5	0.5	1.0	0.5	10.0
Pharmaceutical	1.4	—	1.2	0.7	0.5	0.1	0.5	4.4
All other	6.8	1.0	2.9	1.2	1.4	0.4	0.4	14.1
All merchandising companies	7.4%	10.3%	4.2%	1.2%	0.6%	1.2%	0.7%	25.6%
Industrial goods	5.9	13.7	2.9	0.7	0.2	2.0	1.0	26.4
Consumer goods	8.1	8.5	4.0	1.3	0.9	0.9	0.5	24.2

SOURCE: Data from B. J. LaLonde and P. H. Zinszer, *Customer Service: Meaning and Measurement* (Chicago: National Council of Physical Distribution Management, 1976).

of sales as direct labor costs, and, for the most part, more amenable to cost cutting.

In managing logistics, several issues loom of central concern:

1. What should be the structure of the distribution system? Where should various inventories, especially finished goods inventories, be held within the system?
2. Which geographic locations make sense as stocking points?
3. How much inventory should be held at each location?
4. How should the flow of goods throughout the distribution system be coordinated? Which products should be treated in which ways?
5. Which modes of transportation should be used?

Ford Motor Company's service parts network, as mentioned in the service tour of Howard Ford, is a good example of these key issues in logistics. Recall that Ford's distribution system had three tiers to it: the national distribution center in Detroit; various regional dis-

tribution centers, such as Atlanta; and various local distribution centers, such as Charlotte. One can expect that the most commonly used parts were abundantly stocked in the local distribution centers, but that uncommon, rarely used parts were available routinely only from the regional or national distribution centers. As that service tour related, there were several ways orders could be placed with the parts network, some calling for wider searches and faster deliveries than others.

To discuss these logistics issues in greater depth, they can be organized into three broad categories: (1) distribution system structure and operation, (2) distribution center location, and (3) transportation mode choice.

DISTRIBUTION SYSTEM STRUCTURE AND OPERATION

In deciding how the distribution system should be structured, a critical decision turns on how centralized or decentralized the system ought to be. Should the company keep its inventory in just a few locations, or should it disperse its goods into a number of regional or metropolitan areas? This question can be a subtle one, and an answer to it depends on balancing the costs and benefits of centralization versus decentralization.

The Argument for Decentralization

The argument in favor of dispersing inventories in a number of locations is clear and compelling, namely that customer service can be greatly enhanced. The time it takes to fill an order can be cut markedly if sales and service people can call on a nearby facility. Fewer errors are likely to be made as well, because field people can be in close, informed touch with the distribution center. Sales may even be stimulated if customers react favorably to knowledge of a facility nearby dedicated to serving them.

Moreover, delivery time can be reduced, not only because the order may be filled more quickly, but also because there is less distance to travel and swift modes of transportation can be used. This contraction in delivery time means that safety stocks can be reduced because fewer days of uncertainty need to be covered.

The Argument against Decentralization

Despite all the aid decentralized distribution can promise field sales and service people, it can be costly. Transportation and handling expenses typically increase with decentralization. Decentralization can also lead to an expansion of inventory to be carried and a loss of control over that inventory. These points against decentralization are argued in greater detail in the following discussions.

Transportation and Handling Expenses

How do the costs of transporting and handling a product differ between a centralized strategy, where the customer is served directly, and a decentralized strategy, where the customer is served through various tiers? The answer is not clear-cut, because there are costs that cut both ways. Naturally, the fewer the number of intervening locations, the lower the transportation expense, suggesting that centralization and direct customer shipments are more economical. On the other hand, shipment of small quantities is invariably more expensive than shipment in bulk, and often, the replenishment of decentralized distribution centers can be done cheaply through bulk shipments. This point argues for at least some decentralization. How these conflicting costs total up naturally depends on the situation—what the full truckload versus less-than-truckload rates are, where the customer is, where the distribution centers are, and how much the order is for.

Often, however, the telling expense is in the handling. If the product has to be handled from one tier of the distribution system to another, additional costs are incurred. These can swamp any cost savings attributable to freight consolidation.

Administering Decentralized Distribution

Inventory spread among a number of facilities is more difficult to keep track of than when it is in one or just a few facilities. Record-keeping is more voluminous and thus subject to error. Swaps between facilities may be so informal that records are not even entered. Moreover, the sales and service people may become so possessive of "their" facility that a hoarding mentality takes over, especially with items that are scarce and that a central authority may want to call in for allocation somewhere else. Such items may purposely become "lost" in the distribution system.

Irregular Demand and Buffer Stocks: The Law of Large Numbers

The demand in any one region of a company's market area is likely to follow a more irregular pattern than the company's overall demand. Greater-than-average demand for a particular product in one region may well be balanced by below-average demand for the same product in another region. Thus, the buffer stock that a centralized facility would have to carry is likely to be considerably less than the sum of the buffer stocks of decentralized facilities, for the same level of protection against stockouts. This result is a variation of the "law of large numbers." The variance of demand for a single, large service center will almost always be proportionally less than the variance of demand faced by smaller, dispersed service centers offering the same coverage against stockouts.

Scattered Warehousing and the Optimal Inventory Calculation

The logic of our EOQ calculation can be applied to the case of many, scattered warehouses versus a single, large warehouse. Much as we derived earlier, let

D = expected period demand over the entire company
i = inventory carrying cost percentage
S = cost per order
C = variable cost per unit of inventory
N = number of scattered warehouses, all of the same size

From our calculations before for the simple case where carrying cost and order cost were the only costs that varied with changes in the order quantity, the optimal order quantity, Q, was found to be

$$(1) \qquad Q = \sqrt{\frac{2\,SD}{iC}}$$

Now let's consider a small warehouse, one of N identical warehouses that the company operates. The demand that each small warehouse will face during the period is D/N. We can substitute this into our formula to find the optimal order quantity, $Q^\star$, for the small warehouse.

$$(2) \qquad Q^\star = \sqrt{\frac{2S(D/N)}{iC}}$$

But there are N small warehouses and so the total of all the order quantities would be

$$(3) \qquad N \cdot Q^\star = N\sqrt{\frac{2S(D/N)}{iC}} = \sqrt{N}\sqrt{\frac{2SD}{iC}}$$

We can substitute equation 1 in to find a relationship between $Q^\star$ and Q, namely,

$$(4) \qquad N \cdot Q^\star = \sqrt{N}\sqrt{\frac{2\,SD}{iC}} = \sqrt{N}\,Q$$

Thus, merely by dispersing inventory in N facilities and allowing each to optimize its order quantities under a reorder point inventory system, we find that the order quantities demanded of the factory—and by implication inventories since in this case average inventory is $Q/2$ or $Q^\star/2$—increase by the square root of the number of warehouses. If we establish four small, identical warehouses instead of one, and if we follow a reorder point system for each one, then inventories will be double what they would be if we established a single warehouse.

This argument is meant to be more suggestive than exact. The regional warehouses of most companies are not organized so that individual reorder point systems prevail. But they are organized differently in many cases precisely to avoid the heavy inventory burden that the line of reasoning sketched above leads to.

Tiered Inventories and Pipeline Momentum

Many distribution systems are tiered. They have a centralized inventory that sits above a number of regional inventories; these, in turn, sit above local, metropolitan inventories. In

TABLE 5-8   Tiered inventory system and disjointed decision rules—the steady state

TIER	ITEM	AMOUNT
A (Local)	Beginning inventory	40
	Sales in week	20
	Ending inventory	20
	Desired inventory	40*
	Order on the next tier	20
B (Regional)	Beginning inventory	40
	Sales in week	20
	Ending inventory	20
	Desired inventory	40*
	Order on the next tier	20
C (Companywide)	Beginning inventory	40
	Sales in week	20
	Ending inventory	20
	Desired inventory	40*
	Order on factory or to be absorbed by buffer stocks	20

NOTE: Weekly sales demand at level of tier A is 20.

*Twice the demand of 20.

some of these systems, the central inventory feeds products to the regional inventories, and the regional inventories feed the local ones. This kind of division can work quite well. However, if the decision rules for holding inventory are disjointed rather than coordinated, such a tiered system can lead to substantial swings in demand and somewhat higher levels of inventories than a completely coordinated system.

To illustrate what is meant, think of an inventory system of three tiers and each tier is mandated to hold two weeks' worth of demand. For a weekly demand of 20, then, the corresponding levels of inventory and orders on the next tier would look like Table 5-8. Note that in each tier the desired inventory is twice the weekly sales, and orders on the next tier proceed accordingly. Observe, however, what happens when demand falls by a single unit (5 percent) at the level of tier A (the local level) and stabilizes there (at 19). The period-by-period adjustments implied by the myopic decision rule

of "hold two weeks' worth of sales in inventory" are traced in Table 5-9.

As the table shows, this tiered inventory system with its myopic replenishment rule takes four periods to settle into a steady state. What is more, the orders placed on successive tiers become more and more erratic and vary wildly from period to period. When the initial demand reduction occurs, it is covered by the inventory already in the pipeline and no orders are placed on the factory. However, the pipeline's inventory is soon depleted and the next period's factory order is huge. This is an example of the "pipeline momentum" that can afflict a tiered inventory system or tiers of suppliers in a multilevel supply network. Not only does it cause great variability in period-by-period demands on each tier, but it can sometimes cause more inventory to be held, over time, than necessary.

Avoiding the whiplash of this pipeline momentum effect calls either for more coordination among the tiers (so that tier C can adjust immediately to the problems tier A is experiencing) or more foresight in the lower tiers (so that these tiers can anticipate the erratic demands that will be placed on them). In either case, avoiding the pipeline momentum effect means junking the myopia that is implied by a seemingly innocuous decision rule like "hold two weeks' worth of sales in inventory."

In any event, this pipeline momentum effect can be one more argument against a decentralization of distribution centers.

Distribution System Operation

No matter how the network of distribution centers is configured, there are several ways to link the operations of the distribution centers to customer demand. Three major techniques are used to operate distribution systems, all variations of the familiar reorder point, periodic reorder, and MRP techniques already discussed.

TABLE 5-9   Tiered inventory system and disjointed decision rules—reaction over time to 5 percent demand reduction

TIER	ITEM	PERIOD 0	PERIOD 1	PERIOD 2	PERIOD 3	PERIOD 4
A	Beginning inventory	40	40	38	38	38
	Sales	20	19	19	19	19
	Ending inventory	20	21	19	19	19
	Desired inventory	40	38	38	38	38
	Order on the next tier	20	17	19	19	19
B	Beginning inventory	40	40	34	38	38
	Sales	20	17	19	19	19
	Ending inventory	20	23	15	19	19
	Desired inventory	40	34	38	38	38
	Order on the next tier	20	11	23	19	19
C	Beginning inventory	40	40	29	46	38
	Sales	20	11	23	19	19
	Ending inventory	20	29	6	27	19
	Desired inventory	40	22	46	38	38
	Order on factory or to be absorbed by buffer stocks	20	0	40	11	19

Let us examine their application to distribution systems.

1. *Reorder Point.* Using a reorder point technique is a straightforward, very decentralized way to operate a distribution system. Each distribution center has its established reorder point levels for the products it handles. When they are replenished by the next level up in the distribution network, which could be another distribution center or a factory, the replenishment is an economic order quantity's worth, typically using either past demand or a future projection as its basis.

This technique is decentralized because the inventory records are maintained strictly at the distribution centers and not by some central authority. Often, the setting of reorder points and economic order quantities is left to the individual distribution centers. This decentralization of information and decision-making tends to bloat the level of inventory in the system and to make any allocations of temporarily scarce inventories

difficult to achieve. It is sometimes said that the reorder point technique "pulls" inventory out into the field.

2. *Base Stock.* The base stock technique is essentially a periodic reorder technique. With this technique, the distribution center is replenished on a regular, periodic basis. The various inventories held are brought up to levels that are expected to hold up, with a given level of customer service, until the next replenishment arrives. The replenishment is thus of variable quantity.

The base stock technique is a more centralized one because the resupply point requires information enough to assemble periodically what each distribution center needs to tide itself over until the next replenishment. The information processing required of the base stock technique is thus greater than that of the reorder point technique, but the field inventories are likely to be lower and better coordinated. This technique "pushes" inventory out into the field, rather than "pulls" it. (Note that the push or pull associated with distribution networks is different from the push and pull associated with production control within a factory.)

It is interesting to note that the typical just-in-time manufacturing relationships with vendors call for frequent, periodic replenishments of inventory to bring the factory inventory back up to some base stock level (the level dictated by the number and size of the standard containers used in the process).

3. *Distribution Requirements Planning (DRP).* DRP is analogous to MRP in that the levels of inventory in the field are tied to projected, time-phased demand. The projected demand works like the gross requirements line of an MRP inventory status record, and the conventional MRP logic can be applied to determine how much inventory should be supplied to each distribution center and when it should be shipped. This approach is often also termed the "time-phased order point."

Much as with MRP, various lot sizing techniques can be applied, often to group differently timed needs together to ship replenishments economically. And, like MRP, rescheduling can be accomplished easily if forecasts or actual demands change.

Of course, DRP is more information-intensive than either the reorder point or base stock techniques. It can also be linked to MRP in the following way: The demands forecast for individual distribution centers can be summed and used as a basis for the development of a master production schedule, the schedule that drives an MRP system.

costs, and this makes it a much easier decision than plant location, which is dealt with in Chapter 7. The distribution center decision lends itself to some mathematical analysis, and numerous studies for companies have been done using mathematical techniques to zero in on low-cost locations.

The heart of the decision is finding the location (or set of locations) that minimizes the cost of transporting goods to customers. Doing this analysis requires information on the quantities demanded by all customers, the quantities that can be supplied from each distribution center, where those customers are located, and the freight rates applicable from the contemplated locations to each customer. Different locations will offer different distances and hence transportation costs to customers, and a systematic way to examine these costs is called for. Simulations can be performed and are often most appropriate for complex, many-factor decisions. For simple cases, however, linear programming or one of its offshoots is often the most effective tool. One special case of linear programming is termed the *transportation method.* It is introduced in the discussion on linear programming in Appendix B of Chapter 4.

Variations on the simple transportation problem permit the distribution center to be subject to fixed as well as variable costs. Consult a book on operations research topics for a discussion of the sophisticated methods employed to solve these more true-to-life problems.

It should be stressed, however, that for most companies the solution given by these mathematical techniques is frequently modified by some qualitative considerations that could not be incorporated into the formulation.

DISTRIBUTION CENTER LOCATION

The location decision for distribution centers is dominated by consideration of transportation

TRANSPORTATION MODE CHOICE

Transportation mode choice tends to be a very specialized field of inquiry. Mode choice decisions require reams of very detailed information on transport costs and delivery times by mode for different classes of shipments characterized by weight, volume, and specialized shipping requirements (such as refrigerated trucks, open flatcars, pressurized compartments). Less than truckload or less than carload rates tend to be very different from full truckload or full carload rates. Mode choice is further complicated by a proliferation of rates. A company's traffic department cannot merely think of truck, rail, water, or air but must think in terms of common truck carrier, owner-operator trucks, own fleet trucking; regular rail service, piggyback (truck-rail) service; ocean, lake, or river barges; commercial jet shipping or private jet shipping; and a number of other variations. Rates and deliveries vary, as does the impact of federal and state regulation, which can for no good reason dictate substantially different shipping rates from seemingly equivalent shipping points or different rates between two points depending on which direction shipment is made.

Other than to note some of the many peculiarities that afflict the nation's transportation system and thus the mode choice decisions of companies, this text will leave to more specialized and detailed treatments this issue of transport mode choice.[11]

PART FOUR
ORGANIZING THE MATERIALS FUNCTION

This chapter began by calling attention to the three major divisions of materials management, procurement, materials control (which includes both inventory control and production planning and control), and logistics. In traditionally organized companies, these three functions often report to three different department heads—procurement to a general manager, materials control to a manufacturing manager, and logistics to a marketing manager. In the last decade, however, considerable organizational restructuring of the materials function has occurred, elevating the importance and visibility of the "materials manager" within the corporate organization.

Four organizational variants have emerged in many companies, and they seem to be about equally popular. Borrowing from Miller and Gilmour, these variants follow the organization charts depicted in Figure 5-30 and are labeled, respectively:[12]

- *Integrated approach.* All materials functions report to a single materials manager.

- *Supply-oriented approach.* The materials manager assumes authority over procurement and materials control, leaving logistics to report elsewhere.

- *Distribution-oriented approach.* The materials manager assumes authority over materials control and logistics, leaving procurement to report elsewhere.

- *Manufacturing-oriented approach.* The materials manager assumes authority over procurement and logistics, leaving materials control to report directly to a manufacturing manager.

The choice of organization appears very much to depend on the types of materials problems that the company is experiencing. If the problems straddle the traditional bounda-

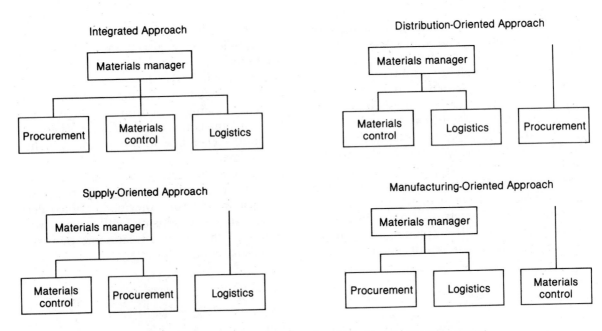

FIGURE 5-30   Four possible organization charts for materials management.

ries of procurement, materials control, and logistics, then it is much more likely that a materials manager will be assigned to oversee the functions in question. For example, if the company is having difficulty deciding how to balance inventory carrying costs against volume discounts from purchasing in quantity, a materials manager who oversees both procurement and materials control may help to resolve the issue. Similar types of problem overlaps across the traditional functional lines explain many of the recent materials management reorganizations that have been sweeping across the industrial landscape.

QUESTIONS

1. How does the situation at Dulaney Toy Company illustrate the main principles of procurement and the principles of a make-buy decision?

2. Outline clearly how the inventory needs of the job shop vary from those of the continuous flow process.

3. Compare and contrast the purpose and natures of the anticipatory and nonanticipatory approaches to inventory management.

4. Of what value is the concept and application of the critical fractile model to a situation of demand uncertainty? What else

is involved in deciding inventory level under demand uncertainty?

465 5. In what ways do the periodic reorder system and the reorder point system differ from each other? Be specific and use graphs where 473 relevant.

6. "The key thing about the determination of an economic order quantity within a reorder point inventory system is not the formulas themselves." What, then, is the key determinant, and how is this determinant manifested in the example of the Gonder-Odell Manufacturing Company?

487 7. A material requirements planning system must continually keep track of numerous elements. What are these, and how are they exemplified at Black & Decker—Tarboro?

8. Review and summarize the fundamental steps in material requirements planning. Make sure you include the data requirements for computer files for such a system. What are some of the most common complications that can arise in such a system?

9. What are some of the factors that influence the decision whether to go with an MRP or a non-time-phased system? Give an example.

10. How can work-in-process inventories build up? How can you cope with them?

11. What are some of the advantages and disadvantages of a decentralized distribution strategy? How would you quantify them?

12. What are the most popular variants or organizing the materials function?

PROBLEMS

1. Joe Little had been assigned the task of designing and acquiring 12 engine oil containers for the Major Motors Corporation. The containers were to have a capacity of 110 gallons plus; they had to be able to be moved by forklift trucks and to be stored on existing racks. The containers were needed to make the handling of the oil easier and the engine oil-fill operation more efficient. A preliminary analysis indicated that the estimated cost savings would generate a payback within six months at most.

Joe's design required only basic "metal bending" and welding processes, and these processes were part of the plant capacity of Major Motors. Joe received bids from three external shops and summarized them as follows:

Vendor	Cost per container	Delivery
1	$565	In six months
2	$578	Maybe in two months, but in four months for sure
3	$535	In one month, but this vendor had a reputation of not meeting delivery dates and of taking shortcuts

Joe's next step was to make an analysis of having the maintenance and machine shop departments fabricate the containers in-house. The following figures were the result:

Material	$294
Labor @ $7 per hour wages + $7 per hour fringes = $14 per hour to shear, bend, assemble, and weld; 3.5 hours for maintenance; and 6.5 hours for machine shop	140
Factory overhead @ 2.5 × direct labor = $17.50 per hour	175
Total per container	$609

His analysis also indicated that the maintenance workers could be allowed to work on the containers only in their spare time because their primary function was to keep the plant operating. The machine shop had a backlog of orders, but the necessary work could be squeezed in within the next month.

Analyze the various alternatives for Joe and discuss the various implications of the nonquantified information.

2. The Digital Watch Company had demand for the year of 1200 units. It found that its average order cost is $9 per order and its carrying cost is $0.10 per unit per year. What is its economic order quantity; should it wish to calculate it?

3. Digital has found that it can order watchbands from an outside vendor on the following price schedule:

Order quantity	Price
500 or less	0.50
501 or more	0.45

With demand and cost information from problem 2, what is Digital's economic order quantity?

4. Digital's inventory manager has taken an introductory course in production/operations management and, given a recent increase in the banks' prime lending rate, now feels she can more accurately estimate carrying cost at 30 percent of the purchase price. From the information in problems 2 and 3, what is Digital's economic order quantity for watchbands?

5. Digital Watch has found that it can produce watchbands at a rate of 4000 per week, and that demand is 2400 per week (assuming 50 weeks). Digital's setup cost is $9 per run, and its carrying cost remains $0.10 per unit per year.
   a. What is Digital's economic production quantity?
   b. For how many weeks will Digital produce at a time?
   c. How many production runs will be made in a year?
   d. What is Digital's maximum inventory?
   e. What is Digital's average inventory?
   f. If you had a choice, how would you manage this situation? Would you use an economic production quantity? Why or why not?

6. Under what conditions and process types would you make certain that your director of purchasing is one of the two or three best talents you have on your staff? Under what conditions do you not care so fervently?

7. Under what conditions would you be wary of using the critical fractile method, as outlined, to handle demand uncertainty in nonanticipatory inventory models?

8. React to the following statement. "None of these inventory systems, be they anticipatory or non-anticipatory, can divorce themselves completely from some attention to the speed at which inventories are drawn down."

9. Lee Plastics, a small injection-molding plastics company, did custom work for local businesses. It did not like to hold any inventory of resin but felt that it had to in order to react instantly to customer orders. (Vendor lead times were short, usually less than a week, but sometimes even that was too long.) The prices the company had to pay for its resins declined with the quantity ordered, which also argued for ordering more than needed and keeping the rest in inventory. Acetal was a typical resin that the company used about 100,000 pounds of during a year. It was available at the following prices for the following quantities:

	Resin Price	Transportation and Handling
Under 2000 lbs.	$2.69/lb.	$.25/lb.
2001–4000 lbs.	1.68/lb.	.21/lb.
4001–6000 lbs.	1.57/lb.	.18/lb.
6001–13000 lbs.	1.51/lb.	.15/lb.

Placing orders more frequently was not a problem and any extra costs were negligible. Transportation and handling varied with the size of the order, because small orders were somewhat more of a nuisance to handle. The costs ranged as in the table. The cost of carrying and storing the resin was about 20 percent of the purchase value.

How much should Lee Plastics buy at a time?

10. After examining the following information on watches, derive the planned orders for watchbands, using lot-for-lot order sizing.

Watches

Period: 1 2 3 4 5 6 7 8 9 10
Demand: 10 20 40 0 50 30 30 40 50 30
On-hand inventory: 50 units at the beginning of period 1

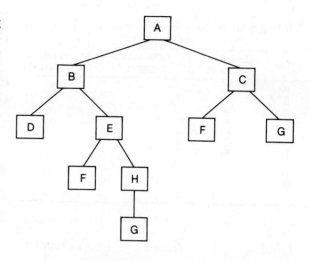

FIGURE 5-31   Components of product A.

Outstanding orders: 30 units to arrive at the beginning of period 3
Lead time: one period

Watchbands

Usage: one per watch
On-hand inventory: 0
Outstanding order: 0
Lead time: two periods

11. Information on product A is shown in Figure 5-31 and Tables 5-10 and 5-11. Using this information and lot for lot as the order sizing rule, derive the planned orders for part F.

12. What is a "closed loop" MRP system? How would you try to measure its benefits for a plant? Its costs?

13. The following list gives the parts for a particular product, indicating their level in the product structure. Higher numbered levels fit into the next highest level's subassembly. Also indicated are the number of parts needed each time one unit of the next highest level's subassembly is made.

TABLE 5-10   Factors in the production of product A (problem 11)

ITEM	LEAD TIME (weeks)	HOW MANY USED	ON-HAND INVENTORY
A			40
B	2	2	30
C	3	2	60
D	2	1	80
E	3	1	50
F	2	2 (1 in E, 1 in C) 2 (1 in C, 1 in H)	30
G	1	1	20
H	1	1	10

TABLE 5-11   Master schedule for product A (problem 11)

WEEK	REQUIREMENT	WEEK	REQUIREMENT
1	20	11	20
2	40	12	50
3	10	13	40
4	30	14	0
5	25	15	10
6	30	16	20
7	15	17	15
8	0	18	45
9	80	19	0
10	30	20	30

Level	Item	Quantity
1	A	1
2	B	2
2	C	2
1	D	2
2	E	1
3	F	1
3	G	1
2	H	2
3	I	4
3	J	4
1	K	3

Draw the product structure tree. How many of each part do we need to make 20 of the product in question?

14. If each level in problem 13 means a safety lead time of one week, what would the inventory status report look like for parts E, G, and J assuming demands for the product of 10 in week 5, 20 in week 8, and 15 in week 10?

15. The weekly demand for a selected product appears to be normally distributed with a mean of 200 and a standard deviation of 30. The lead time for producing the product is generally one week and orders can usually be produced on demand at little or no additional cost. The inventory carrying charge per unit per month is $8. The unit's price is $300, of which $70 is the estimated contribution per unit. How many units should be stocked?

How would your answer change, if at all, if the extra cost to produce the order on demand were $500?

How would your answer change, if at all, if the lead time increased to two weeks?

16. What is the appropriate expression for total cost and the solution for the economic order quantity when back orders are possible, although with some penalty attached? The problem can be represented as in Figure 5-32, where Q is the order quantity to be optimized, H is the maximum inventory on hand at any one time, t_1 is the time when no stockouts occur, and t_2 is the time when stockouts occur. Note that angles A and B are the same. The number of order cycles in any year is

$$N \text{ (order cycles)} = \frac{D \text{ (annual demand)}}{Q \text{ (order quantity)}}$$

17. How would the lot sizes be chosen by part-period balancing under the following circumstances? Setup cost is $60, an inventory carrying cost per unit per period is 40¢,

Quantity

H A Q

t_1 t_2 B Time

FIGURE 5-32 Order quantity when back orders are possible (problem 16).

and the schedule of net requirements is as follows:

Period	Net Requirements	Period	Net Requirements
1	30	7	50
2	60	8	30
3	45	9	60
4	15	10	15
5	60	11	40
6	45	12	50

Total net requirements: 500

What would the lot sizes be like without the "look-ahead, look-back" features of part-period balancing?

18. The master production schedule at Harris, Inc., is as follows:

Master Production Schedule

	Week 1	Week 2	Week 3	Week 4
Product 101	10	15	20	15
Product 102	4	10	5	12

Component 151 is used in both products (1 unit of the component in each). Component 151 is available in lot sizes of 50 with a purchasing lead time of one week. Currently, there are 20 units of component 151 in inventory and an open order (scheduled receipt) for 50 more (its lot size) due at the beginning of Week 2. No safety stock is held.

Complete the MRP record for component 151 as of the beginning of Week 1

19. *Harris, Inc., continued.*
During Week 1 the following things happened:

(1) The open order for 50 turned out to contain only 45 on delivery.
(2) The shop scrapped 3 units of component 151 and drew out 3 replacements.
(3) A customer cancelled 2 units ordered for Week 2.
(4) The Week 5 orders are for 18 Product 101's and 10 Product 102's.
(5) A 3-unit order for 102 has been moved up from Week 4 to Week 2.
(6) The production planner released an order for 50, due in Week 2.

Week	1	2	3	4
Gross requirements				
Schedule receipts				
Projected available balance				
Planned order releases				

Week	1	2	3	4
Gross requirements				
Schedule receipts				
Projected available balance				
Planned order releases				

Complete the now-current MRP record for component 151 as of the beginning of Week 2.

What actions should the production planner responsible for component 151 take?

20. The Dunnick Tool and Die Company had the following product structure for one of its products, the X27.

a. Complete the following MRP records for Parts F and M given the indicated gross requirements, a lead time of one week for part F and one week for part M, lot-for-lot order quantities, and no safety stock.

b. Suppose lot-for-lot order quantities are forsaken in favor of lot sizes of 15 for Part F and 30 for Part M. How would

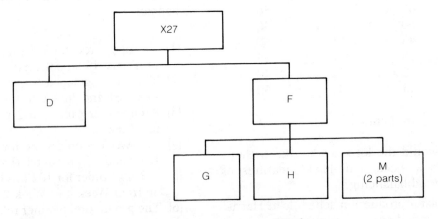

Part F		1	2	3	4	5
Gross Requirements		12	14	10	19	22
Scheduled receipts		22				
Projected available balance	0					
Planned order releases						

Weeks

Weeks

Part M	1	2	3	4	5
Gross Requirements	42				
Schedule receipts	40				
Projected available balance	13				
Planned order releases					

the MRP records in part *a* of the question change?

21. Show the buffer stock needed by a centralized warehouse is likely to be less than the sum of buffer stocks needed by decentralized warehouses. Assume independent demand in two geographic areas described by the following:

Units Demanded During Period	Demand Probability
0	0.2
1	0.6
2	0.2

What would be the expected loss in sales if only 2 units were held in inventory, either as 2 units in a centralized warehouse or 1 unit each in the two decentralized warehouses?

SITUATION FOR STUDY 5-1

TIFFANY TIRE COMPANY

George Blimpo has recognized that his distribution operation is consistently carrying too much inventory. He wonders whether he can reduce that inventory by implementing some sort of inventory system.

Tiffany Tire Company is a small midwestern distributor of radial tires. It is composed of three retail outlets and one warehouse. The warehouse buys its supply of tires directly from the factory and supplies only the three retail outlets. Also, the three dealers buy only from Tiffany's warehouse.

Table 5-12 shows last year's demand for tires, by month, for the three dealers. As you can see,

demand has remained fairly constant over the last three years. The variations in demand are random rather than seasonal or part of a trend.

Table 5-13 shows the results of a study done last year to determine inventory costs for the dealers and the warehouse. The differences in cost are due to the locations of the dealers and the warehouse. For example, Dealer 2 is located in downtown Detroit and the cost of renting storage space is much higher than it is in Mt. Vernon, Illinois, where Dealer 3 is located. Also, the dealers have higher carrying costs than the warehouse because of the transfer pricing policies of Tiffany; the dealers are paying a higher

TABLE 5-12   Demand for tires
(Tiffany Tire Company)

MONTH	DEALER		
	1	2	3
January	400	600	500
February	300	800	400
March	200	400	900
April	600	300	600
May	800	500	200
June	600	300	600
July	300	400	800
August	200	500	800
September	400	600	500
October	350	650	500
November	250	350	900
December	600	600	300

TABLE 5-13   Inventory costs
(Tiffany Tire Company)

DEALER	ORDER COST	CARRYING COST (per tire per year)	LEAD TIME (months)
1	$90	$1.60	1
2	45	2.20	1
3	60	0.90	1
Warehouse	150	0.75	2

price per tire than the warehouse. A similar explanation could be given for the differences in order cost.

George expects that the demand and cost estimates shown in these two tables are representative of what will happen in the future.

What would you recommend that George do to develop a new inventory system for the dealers and the warehouse, given that the existing system is just an educated guess?

REFERENCES

1. Some useful sources on procurement include:

Corey, Raymond E. "Should Companies Centralize Procurement?" *Harvard Business Review* 56, no. 6 (November-December (1978): 102.

Heinritz, Stuart F., and Paul V. Farrell. *Purchasing: Principles and Applications.* 6th ed. Englewood Cliffs, N.J.: Prentice-Hall, 1981.

Leenders, Michiel R., Harold E. Fearon, and Wilbur B. England. *Purchasing and Materials Management.* 7th ed. Homewood, Ill.: Richard D. Irwin, 1980.

Shycon, Harvey N., and Christopher R. Sprague. "Put a Price Tag on Your Customer Servicing Levels." *Harvard Business Review* 53, no. 4 (July-August 1975): 71.

2. See Michiel R. Leenders, Harold E. Fearon, and Wilbur B. England, *Purchasing and Materials Management,* 7th ed. (Homewood, Ill.: Richard D. Irwin, 1980), pp. 170–81 for a good discussion of the functions and forms of inventory.

3. Good sources of additional information on nonanticipatory approaches include:

Backes, Robert W. "Cycle Counting—A Better Way for Achieving Accurate Inventory Records." *Production and Inventory Management* 21, no. 2 (Second Quarter 1980): 36–44.

Buffa, Elwood S., and Jeffrey G. Miller. *Production-Inventory Systems: Planning and Control,* 3d ed. Homewood, Ill.: Richard D. Irwin, 1979.

Dickie, H. Ford. "ABC Inventory Analysis Shoots for Dollars, Not Pennies." *Factory Management and Maintenance* (July 1951).

Hadley, George, and T.M. Whitin. *Analysis of Inventory Systems.* Englewood Cliffs, N.J.: Prentice-Hall, 1963.

Peterson, Rein, and Edward A. Silver. *Decision Systems for Inventory Management and Production Planning.* New York: John Wiley & Sons, 1979.

Plossl, George W., and W. Evert Welch. *The Role of Top Management in the Control of Inventory.* Reston, Va.: Reston Publishing Co., 1978.

Plossl, George W., and Oliver W. Wright. *Production and Inventory Control: Principles and Techniques.* Englewood Cliffs, N.J.: Prentice-Hall, 1967.

Starr, Martin K., and D. W. Miller. *Inventory Control: Theory and Practice.* Englewood Cliffs, N.J.: Prentice-Hall, 1962.

Vollmann, Thomas E. *Operations Management: A Systems Model-Building Approach.* Reading, Mass.: Addison-Wesley, 1973.

Vollman, Thomas E., Berry Williams, and Whybark, D. Clay, *Manufacturing Planning and Control Systems,* Homewood, IL., Dow Jones-Irwin, 1984.

4. See Paul J. Kuzdrall and Robert R. Britney, "Total Setup Lot Sizing with Quantity Discounts," *Decision Sciences* 13, no. 1 (January 1982), pp. 101–12; and R. R. Britney, P. J. Kuzdrall, and N. Fartuch, "Note on Total Setup Lot Sizing with Quantity Discounts," *Decision Sciences* 14, no. 2 (April 1983), pp. 282–91.

5. George W. Plossl, *Production and Inventory Control: Principles and Techniques* 2d ed., Prentice-Hall, Inc. (Englewood Cliffs, NJ: 1985), p. 97.

6. Some useful sources on MRP include:

Hall, Robert. "Getting the Commitment of Top Management." *Production and Inventory Management* 18, no. 1 (1977): 1–9.

Miller, Jeffrey G., and Linda G. Sprague. "Behind the Growth in Materials Requirements Planning." *Harvard Business Review* 53, no. 5 (September-October 1975): 83–91.

Orlicky, Joseph A. *Material Requirements Planning: The New Way of Life in Production and Inventory Management.* (New York: McGraw-Hill, 1975).

Papesch, Roger M. "Extending Your MRP System into Your Vendor's Shop." *Production and Inventory Management* 19, no. 2 (1978): 47–52.

Schroeder, Roger G., et al. "A Study of MRP Benefits and Costs." *Journal of Operations Management* 2, no. 1 (October 1981).

White, Edna, et al. "A Study of the MRP Implementation Process." *Journal of Operations Management* 2, no. 3 (May 1982).

Wight, Oliver W. *MRP II: Unlocking America's Productivity Potential.* Williston, Vt.: Oliver Wight Ltd. Publications, 1981.

7. See Oliver W. Wight, *The Executive's Guide to Successful MRP II* (Englewood Cliffs, N.J.: Prentice-Hall, 1982).

8. This section owes much to Oliver W. Wight, *The Executive's Guide to Successful MRP II* (Englewood Cliffs, N.J.: Prentice-Hall, 1982), pp. 27–35.

9. A good discussion of many of the points about implementing an MRP system is found in Robert W. Hall and Thomas E. Vollman, "Planning Your Material Requirements," *Harvard Business Review* 56, no. 5 (September-October 1978), pp. 105–12.

10. For additional information on logistics, see James I. Heskett, Nicholas A. Glaskowesky, Jr., and Robert M. Ivie, *Business Logistics: Physical Distribution and Materials Management,* 2d ed. (New York Wiley, 1973) and Ronald H. Ballou, *Business Logistics Management: Planning and Control,* 2d ed. (Englewood Cliffs, N.J.: Prentice-Hall, 1985).

11. An issue related to mode choice is the determination of when deliveries ought to be expedited, perhaps by using a faster, more expensive mode of transportation. See D. P. Herron, "Managing Physical Distribution for Profit," *Harvard Business Review* 57, no. 3 (May-June 1979) pp. 121–32.

12. Jeffrey G. Miller and Peter Gilmour, "The Emerging Materials Manager," working paper 79-17 of the Graduate School of Business Administration, Harvard University (January 1979). Jeffrey G. Miller and Peter Gilmour, "Materials Managers: Who Needs them?" *Harvard Business Review* 57, no. 4 (July-August 1979): 143–53.

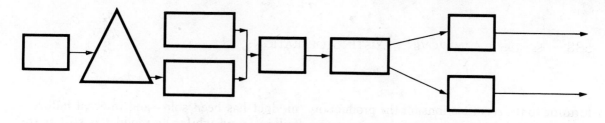

CHAPTER 6
MAKING QUALITY HAPPEN

This chapter will explore what quality is and what is required to make it happen in a factory or service operation. In a sense, this chapter should have been the first in this segment about improving existing operations; its importance merits such attention. The discussion of how quality happens in an operation, however, demands a prior understanding of many of the features of the production or service delivery process, and thus it comes at the end of this segment, as a capstone.

PART ONE
APPRECIATING QUALITY

Everybody wants high quality. The worker or the executive who proclaims the need for low quality has yet to be found. More than this, managers consistently trumpet quality's role in their marketplace successes; quality is often acknowledged as a competitive prerequisite. Yet, despite the acknowledged importance of quality, it is probably the most misunderstood concept about operations.

What Quality Means

When we think about a "quality" product, most of us probably think of how good the product looks, how sturdy it is, whether it performs many functions, how luxurious it may be, how reliable it is. Judging quality for many of us is an exercise in assessing a host of subjective criteria about beauty, luxury, and performance. According to this perception of quality, Rolls Royce and Mercedes mean quality cars, Nikon means quality cameras, Hewlett-Packard means quality calculators, Calvin Klein means quality designer jeans, and Henredon means quality furniture.

Unfortunately, these popular perceptions of quality are not what quality professionals and enlightened managers mean by the term. *Quality* means only one thing to such people: conforming to the specifications for the product or service as laid down by engineering and management. If a product meets the specifications, then it is a quality product, be it a Ford Escort or a Cadillac Seville, a Kodak pocket camera or a top-of-the-line Minolta. Whereas to the popular mind, quality is a subjective judgment about the merits of one set of product or service specifications versus another, to the quality professional and to the manager, quality is simply whether or not the product or service conforms to the specifications for it.

Of course, a product can have specifications or design features that leave it prone to failure or quick breakdown. To the quality professional, it is not a contradiction that a quality product (in the sense that it was made to all the documented specifications) would perform shabbily due to a set of lousy specifications. Making quality happen in the organization, then, means making products or delivering services according to the specifications and, if the specifications are found wanting by the consumer or manufacturing, causing them to be changed formally. The means by which a product's "fitness for use" can be assessed and redefined is discussed in Part Two of this chapter.

By defining quality as conformance to specifications, one removes the subjective elements about what quality may be and replaces them with objective and quantifiable ways of gauging it. Moreover, once one quantifies quality, one can then think about attaching some costs to it.

The cost of quality becomes the cost to the company of doing things wrong, of not conforming to the specifications. When viewed this way, the cost of quality takes on an importance that goes beyond many managers' thinking about product costs. The cost of doing things wrong includes the cost of product failure to the company (often companies distinguish between external failure—failure found once the product has been sold—and internal failure—failure found while the product is still at the factory), the cost of trying to detect those failures before they are delivered, and the cost of preventing those failures in the first place. Table 6-1 lists key items in each of these cost areas. These costs can total 15 to 20 percent of a company's cost of sales.

If a company is to avoid most of these costs of quality, then it must produce the product or deliver the service correctly the first time, and every time. To do this, however, everybody in the organization must be convinced that things have to be done right the first time. It is a cop-out to say that quality is the strict province of the quality control department or that quality problems start on the factory floor. In fact, they are more likely to start in places other than the factory—in product design, manufacturing engineering, industrial engineering, training, purchasing, customer order processing, or elsewhere. W. Edwards Deming, one of the grand old men of quality management and the man after whom Japan's Deming Prize for quality is named, insists that management is responsible for 85 percent of the quality problems in a factory; workers are responsible for only 15 percent.

As companies work diligently on quality, they often discover that not only do their total costs of quality decline but that the compositions of those costs of quality shift. Typically, the failure costs shrink in level of importance while prevention costs expand.

IMPROVING QUALITY

Quality in an operation is improved only when everybody involved—those who handle the product and those who do not—become aware that their tasks can affect quality and that they may need to redirect their procedures and habits toward preventing mistakes. The goal, of

TABLE 6-1   Elements in the cost of quality

FAILURE COSTS	DETECTION COSTS	PREVENTION COSTS
External failure costs:	Process capability measurement (e.g., control charts)	Design reviews
Consumer affairs (dealing primarily with customer complaints about quality)	Product acceptance	Engineering drawing checks
	Prototype inspection and tests	Engineering quality orientation program
Field service (mostly repair of what should have worked)	Receiving inspection and tests	Engineering specifications reviews
Product liability (insurance and settlements)	Supplier surveillance	Preventive maintenance
	Work-in-process and finished goods testing and inspection	Process capability studies
Product returns, recalls, and corrective action costs		Product qualification
Warranty costs		Quality audits
Internal failure costs:		Quality orientation programs
Downtime due to defects		Supplier evaluations
Engineering change orders		Supplier quality seminars
Purchasing change orders		Tool and machines control
Redesign		Worker training and cross-training
Retesting		
Rework in factory or service operations		
Scrap		

course, is to have no quality problems, to have every product be perfect. The achievement of this goal, however, requires significant changes in management and worker attitudes and a relentless pursuit of all the small things that can ruin quality by causing work not to be done properly the first time.

A controversial step toward this goal of a perfect product is to discard traditional points of view about making mistakes. There is a big jump from making perfection a "goal" to making it a "standard," but it is felt by many that such a change of attitude is essential to significant improvements in quality. According to this view, the standard is "zero defects" for everybody associated with the operation. A zero defects standard does not say to all concerned merely that they are to do the best they can; rather, it says that everyone is *expected* to produce with zero defects or *change* the procedure so that they will get zero defects produced. All

the causes of errors or potential errors must be removed and the operation changed so that everything is done right the first time, every time. This means that workers and managers must analyze mistakes to determine why particular defects were introduced into the product or the service. Why were parts missing? Why were the wrong parts delivered? Why were operations missed or put in the wrong sequence? Why did the product fail in the field? Should it be redesigned? Should the materials be different, or should the assembly or test procedures be changed? Why was the wrong part ordered? How can the product's order blank be made foolproof? Are the tolerances in the product too tight to be held by manufacturing? Should new investment in equipment or tooling be made to permit these tolerances?

One could go on and on about the sources of errors. What is critical, though, is that each error must be removed if the product is to be produced with zero defects. This attitude change also affects the traditional roles of management and the workforce; no longer can the workers be seen merely as executing the wishes of management and engineering. Rather, management and engineering have to be viewed as resources to be applied to the solution of quality problems that are, for the most part, known first to the production workers. The workforce can solve many quality problems themselves but should not have to find and remedy all of them. Thus, if the zero defects standard is to be reached, management and engineering must be brought in to help the workforce solve particular problems. Management and engineering should serve the workforce, not the other way around.

The setting of the zero defects standard and the importance of removing all causes of errors in the process have been debated. The debate centers on the various components of the cost of quality as noted above: failure costs, detection costs, and prevention costs. How are these costs of quality related to the number of defects in the product? As the number of defects changes, how do the total costs of quality (that is, the sum of the costs of failure, detection, and prevention) change? Do they rise or fall? Figure 6-1 demonstrates the two opposing views on this issue. According to the traditional view (as represented in Figure 6-1a), the lowest cost is achieved at some nonzero level of defects. The other view (shown in Figure 6-1b) concludes that the zero defects standard is the lowest cost. The difference, of course, is that one side of the debate postulates that the costs of prevention and detection increase substantially as one gets closer and closer to zero defects. Supporters of this view reason that there have to be some diminishing returns from error removal as more and more errors are found and fewer errors persist. The last errors are thought to be the toughest to find and correct. The other

A. The traditional view.

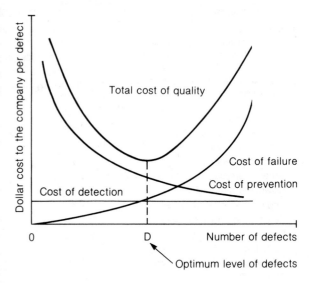

B. The zero defects view.

FIGURE 6-1 The debate on the optimum number of defects.

school of thought states that the causes of defects in the product are so simple, although numerous, that it takes no more expenditure to remove the last cause of error than to remove the first. It may take longer to determine what that last source of error is, but, so this school of thought goes, the steps to correct it are likely to be rather simple.

This debate on whether there is, in fact, an optimal level of defects for a product is essentially an empirical debate, but, as yet, no one has done a very good job of estimating what these curves look like. Are they more like panel A or are they more like panel B? In time, we will probably all have a better sense about whether the zero defects standard is truly the lowest cost way to make a product. Philip Crosby and his adherents believe that quality is "free" and that, in fact, the lowest cost way is always to produce the product right the first time.[1] Others are not so sure that quality, at the level of zero defects, is, in fact, free.[2] What the Japanese and others have been teaching us, however, is that the optimal level of defects is far lower than anyone had previously dared to think.

MANAGEMENT ATTITUDES TOWARD QUALITY

There is much less debate about the attitudinal and organizational changes that have to be made to promote conformity to specifications. The importance of making quality everybody's business has already been discussed; a problem in one area of the company can easily overlap into problems elsewhere, with deleterious effects on the quality of the service delivered or the product manufactured. Other attitudes about quality have to be rethought as well. In many non-quality-conscious companies, the identi-fication of product defects too often leads to blame and recrimination, with excuses abounding and managers and workers alike seeking to avoid being singled out for quality problems.

In a quality-conscious company, defects are not the cause for blame, but merely an indication that everyone needs to work together to eliminate the causes of the defects. Moreover, the notion that quality should or must be sacrificed in order to promote delivery or cost goals is replaced by the notion that only by producing a quality product can a company stay competitive and that, over time, costs will be lowered and deliveries improved when the causes of quality problems are identified and remedied. For the quality-conscious company, the cost of quality (failure costs, detection costs, and prevention costs) is known and reported consistently, typically as a percentage of sales or of the cost of goods sold. Hunches about the costs of quality are replaced by definitive statistics kept by the accounting function of the firm. Managers in the quality-conscious firm are evaluated on their quality as measured by the cost of quality.

Other changes are evident as well. Vendors become an important member of the quality team and are educated on what it takes to produce quality products or services that meet the needs of the customer company. The quality department is held in high regard by everyone; it is a leader in thinking about manufacturing and changes to the product or service. Quality control reports not to manufacturing but to a separate manager and thus is not subject to the schedule and cost measures applied to manufacturing performance.

This change in management organization and attitude can be achieved in many ways. Philip Crosby has suggested a 14-step procedure, which he has found effective for a variety of companies in both service and manufacturing environments.[3] Briefly, the Crosby program consists of the following steps, which can be expected to take 12 to 18 months to implement fully:

1. *Obtain the commitment of management.* If company attitudes are to be changed, the very top level of management must be personally involved with sending the right signals to everybody about the importance of quality and the necessity for people to work together to identify quality problems and to solve them.

2. *Establish a quality improvement team.* A team of influential people from various departments within the company is needed to initiate the changes to attitudes and procedures that will ensure that things are done right the first time. This team should have a coordinator who is charged with the staff work needed to implement the team's decisions.

3. *Take quality measurements.* If quality is to be improved, one must have measures of what it was and what it is. Every aspect of the process should be reviewed and measurements taken. Quality is often said to be difficult to measure, especially in service or support aspects; but even in the most unstructured operations some measures can be devised, for instance, by asking managers how they know who to promote.

4. *Estimate the cost of quality.* Given these measures, the cost of quality for the entire operation should be estimated. The initial estimates may prove to be low; many companies find that the cost of quality, before a quality program is instituted, is 15 to 20 percent or more of the cost of sales.

5. *Spread quality awareness.* Share with all employees the measures of quality that have been devised and what quality costs the company.

6. *Encourage corrective action.* This is the first chance that employees get to bring their quality problems to their supervisor for discussion and resolution.

7. *Establish an ad hoc committee for the zero defects program.* This committee investigates the zero defects concept, becomes clear about its meaning, and transmits its importance to the quality improvement team. This committee also plans for the zero defects day when the company and its employees formally adopt zero defects as the standard for their work.

8. *Train supervisors.* All supervisors at all levels of management are informed about zero defects and removal of the causes of errors so that they can explain these topics to their subordinates.

9. *Have a zero defects day.* On this day all employees commit themselves to make zero defects the standard for their work.

10. *Set goals.* Under the guidance of their supervisors, groups of employees establish goals for improving quality in their operations.

11. *Remove the causes of errors.* Workers identify the causes of quality problems and ask for the resolution of these problems by the appropriate group within the operation (such as manufacturing engineering, industrial engineering, personnel, purchasing).

12. *Recognize achievements.* Senior managers recognize those groups and employees who have identified problems and suggested remedies.

13. *Establish a quality council.* This council of the quality professionals in the operation communicates among themselves and to others about the quality program and what remains to be done about it.

14. *Do it over again.* Senior management re-establishes commitment to zero defects, error cause removal, and changes in management attitudes, so that the operation can keep fresh about the need for quality and vigilant about seeking improvements in it.

The Crosby 14-step program is not the only method, of course. Other programs exist, typically associated with other leading figures in the crusade for better quality management: W. Edwards Deming, Joseph M. Juran, and Armand Feigenbaum. While there is much that is common across the various programs available, there are some differences in emphasis and style. For example, Crosby is sometimes criticized for being too much of a "cheerleader." Deming's approach is heavily statistical in nature and draws fire from some quarters for that. The Juran and Feigenbaum approaches are fairly eclectic in their treatment of the subject.[4]

PART TWO
TECHNIQUES FOR MAKING QUALITY HAPPEN

As the management of quality has evolved, the inspection of products to determine which ones meet specifications has been deemphasized by many companies as the prime source of quality conformance. Instead, there has been a concerted effort to improve the design and control of the process. This shift of emphasis is very much in tune with the theme of "making it right the first time." Because of it, troubleshooting can more easily restore a basically stable process to a high level of conformance. If troubleshooting depended on examining the defects detected solely by product inspections rather than process inspections, the troubleshooter would have a tougher job. This person would lose valuable information (especially that from process measurement and instrumentation) and would have to sort through more potential causes of the defects. It would take much longer to trace a symptom of poor quality back to a cause. Thus, it is in everybody's interest to shift the emphasis for quality control away from the examination of poor quality products and toward the examination of the process itself.

This part discusses mainly techniques that can be applied to the process rather than techniques for sorting good products from bad.

Such techniques (such as acceptance sampling) are called for in some circumstances, but techniques that deal directly with the process should have a greater impact. Three major questions will be addressed here, all related to keeping quality conformance high: Is the product design adequate? Is the process adequate? Is inspection adequate?

Is the Product Design Adequate?

Perhaps the most basic concept of quality management is "fitness for use"; this notion largely governs all the subsequent techniques used to manage quality. Fitness for use is simply the extent to which the product, as designed, serves the real purposes of the consumer. What is it about the product that has value for the consumer? Conversely, what about the product has low value for the consumer? By carefully analyzing a product's fitness for use, managers and engineers can be sure that a product is designed expressly for its purpose. A product can be underdesigned or overdesigned and thus inappropriate for the use to which the consumer puts the product. This same philosophy is part of the attitude of value engineering mentioned in Chapter 3.

Stages of Product Development

How can a new product under development meet this overarching criterion of fitness for use? Most companies have a well-defined series of steps through which their new products pass. The best companies also promote close and continuing contact among the various functions that get intimately involved with new product introductions. The nature of the cross-function contact may vary among no formal teams, formal teams chaired by manufacturing with responsibilities upstream in the design phases of the product, formal teams chaired by engineering with responsibilities downstream in the transfer of the product to manufacturing, and special buffer managers between engineering and manufacturing. Whatever the form, it is generally acknowledged that close, sustained contact promotes better new product introductions. The stages of product development, briefly, include:

1. *Concept development and feasibility.* This stage in product development is devoted to thinking through the initial notions about the new product. Is it technically feasible? Is it cost effective to develop? This phase gets engineering and marketing attention for the most part and can take a lot of time.

2. *Detailed design.* Once a new product has been deemed feasible, the detailed engineering of it must take the concept as originally developed and make it capable of being produced.

3. *Prototype.* Given the initial specifications for the product, the first units of the product need to be built and tested. In this stage, the product may perform poorly and the concept may be scrapped or the design may be reinitiated. In many companies the prototype is created by engineering; although there may be some concern for manufacturing procedures and equipment in the construction of the prototype, often the production management does not get intimately involved with the new product at this stage.

4. *Manufacturing prototype.* At this stage the product is evaluated by manufacturing for its manufacturability. Typically, design changes are made at this point to simplify the manufacturing process, change materials, make use of existing manufacturing equipment or strengths, and merge the new product with any existing products. This stage may involve experimentation with new processes in pilot plant operations. Preproduction lots of the product are made, trying as much as possible to simulate all aspects of the product's manufacture in a plant so that any potential problems can be identified early, rather than after full-scale production has begun.

5. *Full-scale production.* This is the transfer of the new product to manufacturing's full control and its production in existing manufacturing facilities.

6. *Post-release design changes.* Many products require design changes as suggested by customer use and manufacturing experience once the product has been released into full-scale production. Such design changes may be minor, but there still needs to be a mechanism to accomplish them.

At each of these six stages there are means by which problems with the product under development can be identified. In the early stages there are reviews of the concept and the design. Later, there is a test of the prototype under various conditions. There are tests also of the manufacturing prototype, some done in-house and some done with consumers in trial marketing. In all cases, good records of product failure and process problems should be kept.

Reliability, Maintainability, and Safety

Keeping good records enables companies to use some quantitative techniques to improve product development, particularly in the areas of product reliability, product maintainability, and product safety. Let us consider each of these.

- *Reliability.* There are a number of measures of the reliability of a product. The classic one is "mean time between failures," the average time between successive failures of a product that can be repaired. Variations on this measure include the "mean time to failure," which is the average time before a failure of a nonrepairable product or the average time until the first failure of a product that can be repaired, and the "mean time between maintenance," which is the average time between specified maintenance activities. Other reliability measures include failure rates—that is, measures of the number of failures that occur for a given unit of time. Related to failure rates are "lifetime" measures, such as the "mean life" of the product, which is the average amount of time the product can be used before it wears out or is in need of major overhaul. A variation is the "median life," the time period during which half of the units of the product produced would have failed.

  These measures for reliability are important for setting standards for performance that the product, as designed and manufactured, must meet and also for helping to assess where the quality problems are in the product. Such analyses of reliability may lead to redesigns to make aspects of the product "redundant" or to change its materials or manufacturing procedures to enhance reliability.

- *Maintainability.* Maintainability refers to how easily the product can be maintained by the consumer. The measures of maintainability generally refer to the "mean time to repair," the downtime needed for either scheduled or unscheduled maintenance, and the cost of maintaining the product over time. As with the measures for reliability, these measures may be used not only as goals for product design and manufacture but also as evidence in an analysis of what it takes to make maintenance simple and inexpensive.

- *Safety.* Good product safety can scarcely be stressed enough. Good safety management means some hardheaded analysis of the product, its design, and its manufacture. Safety has to be quantified, just like reliability and maintainability. Typically, various classes of hazard are identified, from catastrophic to negligible. The potential for the product to cause such safety hazards has to be realistically assessed and new product designs or methods developed.

IS THE PROCESS ADEQUATE?

The enviable quality reputation of the major Japanese manufacturers can be traced largely to the careful attention they give to process control. In particular, they have been innovative about quality in the manufacturing system as a whole. More will be said about this in the Chapter 10 discussion of the Japanese manufacturing philosophy. Suffice it here to introduce some of the basic considerations about production system adequacy for quality.

A number of useful checks of the full manufacturing system should be done before a new

TABLE 6-2   Quality and dominance in the process

TYPE OF DOMINANCE	CHARACTER	SAMPLE PROCESSES	PROCESS CONTROL SYSTEM(S)
Setup	Process is stable and reliable; if setup is correct, product is correct	Many machine shop operations, printing	First and last piece inspection
Machine	Process subject to some drift	Papermaking, packaging (such as beer), plastics injection molding	Control charts (such as $\overline{X}, R, X, P$)
Operator	Skill of operator is critical to quality of product, foolproofing important	Apparel, fast food service, repair shops	Control charts (such as, P,C), acceptance sampling
Component	Process is stable, but quality of product is dependent on quality of components	Most auto assembly and other assembly processes	Incoming inspection, acceptance sampling

product is released for production. One of these is the so-called tool tryout, during which new tools or pieces of equipment are formally put through their paces. As much as possible, this tryout should simulate actual manufacturing conditions, and the units produced should be examined carefully to make sure that the tool or piece of equipment is operating as planned. Tool tryouts are essentially trial runs of individual work station capabilities. It is important also to have some trial runs where all aspects of the manufacturing process become involved. Such trial runs are important to uncover quality problems that may build up from one workstation to another or that involve components or materials handling or some other aspect of the process outside the purview of the worker at an individual workstation.

Depending on the type of process involved, the production of quality usually depends on a particular aspect of the process to a much greater degree than on other aspects of the process. That is, one aspect of the operation dominates others and, if quality is to be produced, that aspect of the operation must be controlled properly.* Ta-

ble 6-2 indicates four types of dominance in the process, the kinds of production processes that typically are associated with each type, and the process control systems that can be used to keep track of process quality under each of these types of dominance. Some of these process control systems will be explained in greater detail later.

Process Capability Measurement: Determining What's Important

For almost any product, we can make out a long list of specifications as to its size, shape, material content, color, functional characteristics, and so on. All of those specifications can be measured and tolerance limits for those measures established. The performance of the process in manufacturing the product to meet these specifications to within the tolerances established is a gauge as to the process's capabilities. Fortunately, it is almost always the case that only some of the specifications have to be held to truly tight tolerances in order for the product to be "fit for use". Often, the important specifications are known from the design phase of

---

*This concept of dominance owes much to Juran.

product development and the process itself can be designed to meet these specifications readily. Sometimes, however, problems with the product surface either in inspection or out in the field and demand special attention for their elimination.

It makes sense in these instances to make use of Pareto analysis. *Pareto analysis* is simply the categorization of the various problems identified and the development of frequency distributions for them. Such frequency distributions can quickly reveal what kinds of problems seem to be the most important and are thus worthy of extended effort to solve. Pareto analysis can lead to the establishment of supplementary specifications for the product that, if met by manufacturing, can avoid the problems detected. Typically, data for a Pareto analysis is reasonably easy to collect, and collection is frequently done by operators and/or inspectors over the course of several days or several weeks, the time frame, of course, dependent on the frequency of problems and the output rate of the process. Pareto analysis is an extremely useful tool in isolating the "vital few" problems from the "trivial many," to borrow a phrase from Juran.

Another useful tool for determining what's important is the *chronological run chart*, a graph of some measured characteristics plotted in the order of manufacture. Having this plot in chronological order identifies trends in the data that might be missed if just a calculation of the mean or median or standard deviation is performed. Chronological run charts differ from control charts (discussed later) in that they cannot demonstrate conclusively that a process is under statistical control, but they can offer strong evidence that something about the process has changed. Consult Figure 6-2, a run chart of the percent defective. It displays two suspicious measures, the span between time units 10 and 18, and the span between time units 21 and 30.

What makes these two places suspicious is that the percent defective stays on one side of the median for at least 8 units of time in a row. That is akin to flipping a coin and having it come up 8 heads in a row. It is so unlikely that it suggests a specific cause; for the section consistently below the median something very good was at work, while for the section consistently above the median something adverse was operating. These suspicious patches are persuasive indications that the process is not under control and that the specific causes of the two suspicious patches ought to be researched.

Process Capability Measurement: The Control Chart

If the process is to produce quality products, its capabilities have to be measured periodically so that management can be sure that it is performing as planned and is not drifting away from quality manufacture. In the last 50 years or so, a statistical means of assessing process capabilities has come to the fore—namely, the use of control charts[5] to measure the adequacy of a particular process.

Control charts are used to separate random causes of variation in product quality from nonrandom, "assignable" causes of poor quality (operator error, faulty setup, poor materials). Assignable causes often demand a lot of work to remedy, but remedied they can be.

Typically such remedies may involve better training, more precise directions, improved fixtures, different materials, improved tooling, and the like. When these remedies are put in place, the process's capabilities are immediately improved; the assignable causes of poor quality have been removed. What remains is random variation in quality.

Control charts are of two general classes: variable control charts and attribute control charts. A *variable control chart* plots some spe-

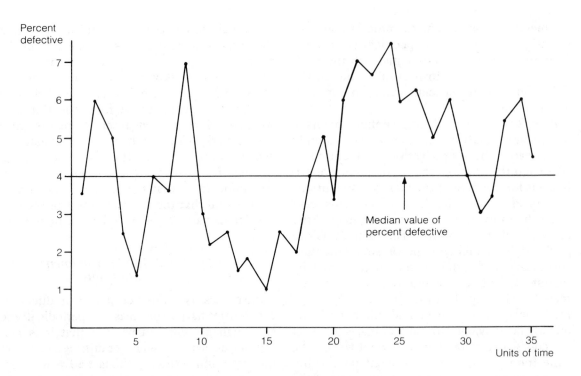

FIGURE 6-2   A chronological run chart.

cific measure along the Y-axis (such as lengths, diameters, pressures) and various sample numbers along the X-axis. The most common variables charts are $\bar{X}$ and R charts. The $\bar{X}$ chart plots the average of the measurements taken on each sample, and the R chart plots the range of measurement within each sample. *Attribute control charts*, on the other hand, typically deal with the "defects" of whatever kind in the samples taken. They can provide useful summary data about the process, but may have to be supplemented by the use of specific variables (for example, length, weight, pH, temperature) if particular explanations about the causes of the defects are to be tested. Indeed, these two classes of control charts can be used at the same time, in cooperation with one another. Table 6-3 compares some of the basic variations.

Variable control charts can, in fact, be set up with an almost limitless number of quality characteristics measured on the Y-axis. In developing control charts, it is thus important to distinguish the process characteristics that are most apt to be associated with defects (the vital few) and not to worry about other aspects of the process that, by all indications, appear under control (the trivial many). The characteristics chosen for study should logically be associated with remedies that can be taken. Often, Pareto analysis can be helpful in identifying the variables to plot.

Variable Control Charts

Once it has been decided to develop a variable control chart, and the characteristics to be plotted have been picked, the next task is to con-

TABLE 6-3 Major types of control charts

TYPE OF CHART	STATISTICAL MEASURE PLOTTED ON THE Y-AXIS	COMMENTS
X̄	Small sample averages of particular measurements	The most common control chart; indicates change in central tendency of process
R	R = Maximum-minimum values of small samples of measurements (R stands for range)	Frequently accompanies X̄ chart; indicates when a significant loss (or gain) in uniformity has occurred
X	Individual measurements, not averages	Less sensitive than the X̄ chart; useful only when small samples cannot be taken conveniently and one observation per lot is all that is possible
P	P = Fraction defective	Most useful when "go, no go" decision is needed; can help tell when to apply pressure for quality improvements; uses "attributes" data, not measurements data
C	C = Number of defects	Most useful when all samples are the same size and the number of defects possible is large but the likelihood of any single type of defect is small; avoids proliferating X̄ or X charts in such situations; another "attributes" data control chart

struct the chart itself. Consider the $\bar{X}$ chart first (Figure 6-3). Typically, that chart's mean line is the average of past data, at least 50 data points worth. The $\bar{X}$ chart always uses samples for its calculations, because samples are much more efficient in detecting shifts in process capability. Control limits for the $\bar{X}$ chart, for example, apply to sample averages, not individual values. Three standard deviations on each side of the mean line are usually used as control limits because that ensures that random causes alone would indicate false alarms in only 0.3 of 1 percent of the cases (99.7 percent of a normal distribution lies within 3 standard deviations of the mean).

With today's calculators and computers, it is easy to calculate the standard deviation of a set of sample means, and such calculations should be used. Historically, however, that calculation was more time-consuming, and some formulas were developed to estimate the upper and lower control limits using the grand average (the av-

erage of the sample averages) and the average of the sample ranges. Those estimation procedures are still in use, and for the sake of completeness, they are presented here.

$\bar{X}$ chart upper control limit

$\bar{X}$ chart lower control limit

$$= \bar{\bar{X}} + 3\sigma_{\bar{x}} \approx \bar{\bar{X}} + A_2 \bar{R}$$

$$= \bar{\bar{X}} - 3\sigma_{\bar{x}} \approx \bar{\bar{X}} - A_2 \bar{R}$$

Where $\bar{X}$ = grand average (average of the sample averages), $\sigma_{\bar{x}}$ is the standard deviation of the sample means, $\bar{R}$ is the average of the sample ranges, and A_2 is the estimating factor that varies with the size of the samples being taken. It is found in Table 6-4. Of course, the preferred means of computing the control limits now is not to use this short-cut estimation, but rather to calculate the standard deviation of the sample means straightaway.

With the R chart, the mean line is precisely $\bar{R}$, the average of the sample ranges, and the

FIGURE 6-3   Sample $\overline{X}$ and R control charts.

TABLE 6-4   Factors for estimating control limits in $\bar{X}$ and R charts

NUMBER OF OBSERVATIONS IN SAMPLES TAKEN	FACTORS FOR $\bar{X}$ CHART FROM $\bar{R}$, (A_2)	FACTORS FOR R CHART	
		LOWER LIMIT D_3	UPPER LIMIT D_4
2	1.880	0	3.268
3	1.023	0	2.574
4	0.729	0	2.282
5	0.577	0	2.114
6	0.483	0	2.004
7	0.419	0.076	1.924
8	0.373	0.136	1.864
9	0.337	0.184	1.816
10	0.308	0.223	1.777

Source: J. M. Juran (ed.), *Quality Control Handbook* (New York: McGraw-Hill, 1979), Table Y, Appendix II.

control units (1) can be calculated from the sets of samples taken, or (2) estimated from $\bar{R}$ itself.

R chart upper control limit

$$= \bar{R} + 3\sigma_R \approx D_4 \bar{R}$$

R chart lower control limit

$$= \bar{R} - 3\sigma_R \approx D_3 \bar{R}$$

Where σ_R refers to the standard deviation of the sample ranges, and D_3 and D_4 are estimating factors also found in Table 6-4. Again, the preferred technique these days is to calculate the standard deviation of the sample ranges straightaway.

A process is in statistical control if it has no points outside the control limits and no suspicious looking runs (portions where there are many points on one side of the mean line) or where there is a definite trend that suggests the process is drifting out of control.

A process that is operating in statistical control has no variation produced by specific, traceable causes (typically termed *assignable causes*) that usually can be remedied economically; all its variation is due to random causes. Thus, its variation is at a minimum, given the process technology applied. If one wants to improve a process that is in statistical control (that is, reduce the spread of the control limits), one has

to change the process technology. One implication of this truism is sometimes startling to managers: If the process is out of control but yet tighter tolerances are desired, managers should not immediately go and buy new, replacement equipment. Rather, the managers should seek to uncover and remove the assignable causes of variation. Buying new equipment could be a very expensive way to tighten tolerances, and success in doing so is not ensured. Working on getting the process under statistical control is the suggested prelude before any creative, and perhaps costly, engineering and equipment revamping of the process.

As process changes are made, the control chart can be updated. A new mean and new, tighter control limits can be calculated. By continual improvement, variation in the process can be reduced. At some point, then, the process may be in such good control that managers can forgo using a control chart for the particular variable of concern. Instead, periodic quality audits can confirm whether the process continues to produce high-quality items. Sometimes, only first- and last-piece inspections of a batch of parts/products need to be performed.

The control chart is thus a way station on the road to quality—an important way station, but nevertheless just a way station. It is of little value when the process is known to be out of control, and it may be too time-consuming to keep up when the process is known to produce perfect pieces. The importance of the control chart lies in distinguishing random variation from variation caused by specific, traceable factors that can be remedied. As the process gets worked on, the control chart is a record of the process's capability.

Naturally, the worth of any machine's capabilities are appreciated only in relation to the engineering specifications required. If a machine that is in statistical control can work to tighter tolerances (on the order of two-thirds to three-quarters of the tolerance specified by design engineering), all is well. The machine will likely produce almost all good items. Those items produced should not undergo 100 percent inspection but should only be audited (sampled) from time to time. If, on the other hand, the machine cannot hold tighter tolerances than about three-quarters of the design tolerance, then some different tack ought to be followed. There are four major alternatives to try in such a case:

1. Improve the machine if you can. Try different tooling, speeds, feeds, and so on.

2. Shift the item to a different machine, if that is possible.

3. Get the engineering staff to approve a looser tolerance, if they are willing.

4. If all else fails, sort good items from bad through 100 percent inspection until you can redesign the product, or purchase a new, better machine, or in some other way improve the capability of the process relative to the design tolerances.

Attribute Control Charts

So far, the discussion has centered on $\bar{X}$ and R charts, the major examples of variable control charts. Mentioned above was the other major class of control charts, attribute control charts. Attribute charts typically plot "defects" of one sort or another. These charts have to suffice when there is no clear measure to make or where there are multitudes of defects possible, but with no single one of sufficient frequency to develop a variables chart on. The two major types of attribute charts are the P chart, which tracks the percent defective in the samples taken, and the C chart, which tracks the number of defects in the samples taken. The samples taken for attribute charts are usually greater than those used for $\bar{X}$ and R charts by at least an order of magnitude.

Attribute charts make the assumption that defects get produced in much the same way that "heads" turn up when coins are flipped. That kind of a process is generally termed a *Bernouilli process*, and there are two, similar statistical distributions that model Bernouilli processes: the binomial distribution and the Poisson distribution. These distributions make it easy to determine mean lines and control limits for attribute control charts.

The P chart assumes a binomial distribution of the percent defective created by the production process, where $\bar{p}$ is the mean percent defective and the standard deviation is

$$\sqrt{\frac{\bar{p}(1-\bar{p})}{n}}$$

where n is the size of the sample taken. Thus, the control limits are defined as

P chart upper control limit
$$= \bar{p} + 3\sigma_p = \bar{p} + 3\sqrt{\frac{\bar{p}(1-\bar{p})}{n}}$$

P chart lower control limit
$$= \bar{p} - 3\sigma_p = \bar{p} - 3\sqrt{\frac{\bar{p}(1-\bar{p})}{n}}$$

The P chart has wide applicability and is particularly useful in controlling specific kinds of defects that may occur.

The C chart plots the number of defects in a sample and is applicable when the likelihood of any single type of defect is small but where there may be a large assortment of different types of defects possible. The C chart assumes that defects arrive at the process much like phone calls arrive at a telephone switchboard. The distribution that captures this phenomenon best is the Poisson which is a particularly friendly distribution since its standard deviation is merely the square root of its mean. The mean line on a C chart is simply $\bar{c}$, the mean number of defects. The control limits are given by

$$\text{C chart upper control limit} = \bar{c} + 3\sigma_c = \bar{c} + 3\sqrt{\bar{c}}$$

$$\text{C chart lower control limit} = \bar{c} - 3\sigma_c = \bar{c} - 3\sqrt{\bar{c}}$$

Attribute control charts, such as P and C charts, should be interpreted in the same way as variable control charts. If the process is operating in statistical control, as demonstrated by a the control chart, then all the variation is produced by random causes and not by assignable causes. If the percent defective is to be lowered, the process itself has to be changed.

To understand better the use of control charts and other aspects of quality management, consider the following situation.

SITUATION 6-1

STROH BREWERY COMPANY REVISITED, WINSTON-SALEM BREWERY, QUALITY ASSURANCE

The quality assurance department at the Winston-Salem brewery of Stroh operated round the clock 7 days a week and employed 38 people. Quality assurance operated three separate labs at the brewery; two chemical labs (brewing and microbiology) and one physical lab (packaging). All aspects of the brewery's operations were checked systematically every day. Quality assurance wanted to make sure not only that beer shipped from the plant met the company's high standards but also that the process by which the beer was brewed and packaged was operating under control and consistently within specifications. Quality assurance viewed itself as the early warning station for the check of product and process conformance to the company's dictated specifications. There were a dozen or so manuals, several feet thick in total, that detailed the tests and specifications for product and process quality.

The Brewing Lab

The brewing lab was the larger of the two chemistry labs at the plant. The brewing lab was charged with testing each batch of beer at every stage in its brewing cycle, from the development of the wort through fermentation and aging in the ruh and government cellars. The work in the lab was divided among various technicians: alcohol technicians, government cellar technicians, water technicians, and so-called weekly technicians. The alcohol technicians were charged mainly with chemical analysis of samples taken from wort production, fermentation, and the various storage cellars. The government cellar technicians operated more in the filtering area and the finished cellars, checking air and carbon dioxide content, clarity, and pH every time a tank was emptied and every time the packaging lines called for a brand change. The water and weekly technicians were concerned chiefly with more specialized checks of the quality of water and other inputs (although malted barley was checked by the Detroit staff before shipment to North Carolina) and of miscellaneous items.

As an example, consider the alcohol technician's job in more detail. This person checked a number of things: specific gravity, refractive index, original gravity (a measure of the percentage of fermentables in the wort at the start); real extract (a measure of the amount of solids left in the beer), alcohol percentage,

VDK (a measure of the amount of an undesirable yeast by-product remaining in the beer), pH (an acidity measure), color, sodium and calcium concentrations, bitterness units (a measure of the amount of hops in the beer), foam pour (a measure of the time it takes for the foam head of the beer to collapse 1 inch when poured at a given temperature and at a specific height), foam cling (a measure of how much the foam head on a beer clings to the surface of the glass—the more it clings, the better), and haze abuse (a measure of the clarity of the beer). For all of these tests there were detailed procedures and specifications that the plant had to meet.

The test for original gravity, for example, was performed about 300 times each day, 100 or so on each shift. Whenever one of the 750 barrel tanks that were used for fermentation or aging was pumped so that the beer traveled to the next stage in the finishing process, a sample of about 250 ml was taken. This sample had to be tested within an hour or so of the pumping of the tank. This test took about 15 minutes and consisted of (1) warming the sample to 25°C, (2) passing the sample through filters, (3) reducing the temperature to 20°C, (4) placing a small portion of the filtered beer in a refractometer to determine its refractive index, and (5) comparing the weight of another portion of beer with the weight of water to determine its specific gravity. Given a certain refractive index and a certain specific gravity, the original gravity, alcohol percentage, and real extract could be calculated.

The results of such tests were promptly transmitted to the brewhouse, where corrective measures could be taken, if necessary. For example, if the sampled beer was light on original gravity, so-called heavier beer from an accumulator tank could be combined with it to return the sampled beer to within specifications. Most "out of spec" conditions could be remedied by repumping and remixing the beer in question. There were only two major conditions that could not be remedied: mixing two types of beer inadvertently and too high a sodium content. The latter condition was unlikely but could result from faulty cleaning of a tank. Each time a tank was emptied, it was cleaned with a dilute solution of sodium hydroxide, which was then neutralized with phosphoric acid and rinsed with water. If this cleaning was not done properly or if caustic soda was inadvertently added to a tank, the level of sodium in the beer would be too high and the beer would have to be discarded.

The brewing lab was also charged with analyzing beer that had already been distributed. Stroh employed a number of buyers who regularly bought beer in liquor stores and supermarkets and sent it back to the plant for analysis. This analysis was mainly a check on the stability of the beer over time;* tests were done on its clarity, foam duration and cling, and taste. The brewing lab also did an abuse test on a sample of each week's production. In this test, various cans and bottles of beer were alternately heated to 140°F. and cooled to freezing over the course of a week, thus simulating all the abuse beer could encounter before it was consumed. Clarity checks were then run.

As a check on the workings of the brewing lab, once a month the Detroit quality assurance staff sent two of the same samples to each Stroh plant for analysis. The plants submitted their results to Detroit, where the corporate quality assurance staff scrutinized the results. Any plant whose quality assurance tests were not accurate enough was so informed, and measures were taken to improve its procedures. Once a year there was a complete audit of the procedures and records of the lab. A team from Detroit came for a full week and evaluated all phases of quality assurance, not only in the brewing lab but also in the microbiology and packaging labs.

Microbiology Lab

The microbiology lab was adjacent to the brewing lab and was responsible for bacteria and yeast counts on all stages of the process. In essence, the microbiology lab was responsible for checking that the bacteria and yeast counts in the water used in the process, in the process equipment (tanks, pipes), in the air in the plant, and in the finished beer itself were within designated limits. Any deg-

---

*On each can and bottle were special codes that indicated exactly when and where the beer was packaged. For example, the code 5242 8745 on a can of Stroh's indicated that the beer was packaged in 198(5) on day 242 of the Julian calendar (August 30) by the eighth plant (Winston-Salem) on line 7 in the forty-fifth quarter-hour of the day (between 11:00 A.M. and 11:15 A.M.).

radation of the equipment or the materials could harm the quality of the beer, and so checks were made every day on the brewery's microbiology.

The Packaging Lab

The packaging lab was located just off the packaging floor. Its mandate was to check the filling and packaging of beer into cans, bottles, and kegs. The work of the packaging lab could be divided into monitoring three major areas: (1) the activities of the packaging floor, (2) the canning and bottling processes, especially the seaming of cans and crowning of bottles, and (3) the filled cans, bottles, or kegs.

Monitoring operations on the floor meant, in large measure, keeping track of the equipment and making sure that it was working properly to produce a product that met various physical specifications. These specifications included the following:

- The proper positioning of labels and their smooth and wrinkle-free placement on bottles

- The operation of the mechanisms that detected and removed from the line cans or bottles that were not filled to the proper levels

- The torque on twist-off bottle caps

- The proper temperature and water flow in the pasteurizers

- Leaking due to improper lid placement on cans or improper crowning of bottles

- The proper coding on cases and cans and bottles

- Sanitation of the filling and closing machines

Seams were examined every four hours, when twelve cans in a row were removed from each line. Twelve cans were removed because that was how many heads were on the seaming machine that placed the lid on the filled can of beer. For each can, a number of measurements were taken, some with the micrometer (such as seam height, seam thickness, depth of the countersink). The seam was also rated visually (tight or loose). The lids were then removed from the cans, and the seams were analyzed under a magnifying apparatus to check the overlap of the "body hook" (the flange on the can itself) with the "cover hook" (the edge of the lid crimped over). This careful examination was a check on the strength of the seal on the can and its ability to maintain a tight, leak-proof seal. Other measures were taken as well, including a test for metal exposure (an examination of the thickness and coverage of the coating on the inside of the aluminum can).

The accuracy of filling was checked every two hours for each line. At that time three containers were withdrawn and investigated for carbon dioxide content, air quantity, and the accuracy of the fill. The data derived from these samples were used to compile process control charts. Figure 6-4 is a process control chart for air quantity and carbon dioxide content. This chart is for bottling line 1, where 12 oz. bottles are filled, for the four days of October 22–25, 1985. Although data for both air quantity and CO_2 content are gathered, only the air quantity control chart graphs are shown. Those graphs are the classic $\bar{X}$ and R graphs. The key parameters for the two graphs are given in the box labeled "control data." As seen there, the overall mean is 0.42 ml of air in the bottle with upper and lower control limits of 0.56 ml and 0.28 ml, respectively. The mean range is 0.14 ml, with an upper control limit of 0.36 ml and a lower control limit of 0. The specifications for air quantity are well above the upper control limit. Those specifications (in the upper right corner) call for a sample average of no more than 1 ml of air and an individual sample reading of no more than 1.45 ml of air.

Below the control data lies the information taken for each sample. Note that the samples were taken at two-hour intervals, for the most part. Samples were also taken immediately after each change from one tank to another. This changeover was a source of nonrandom variation and thus was watched carefully. Note that the 2:20 P.M. changeover on October 22, involving Old Milwaukee (OM) beer from tank 24 caused a real spike in this control chart. (This chart was specifically chosen to reveal an out-of-control situation.) The notation on the chart indicates that the supervisor (Mr. Zegan) was notified and that the beer was "held for inspection" (HFI) under HFI number 125. In fact, what happened was that 98 cases of beer were held for inspection, and upon a thorough audit, 97 cases were later released as good product. Because of the attention of the workforce to such control charts, the process was typically halted before bad product was produced. The cost of held beer at Winston-Salem was only 1

A. October 22 through 10 P.M. October 23.

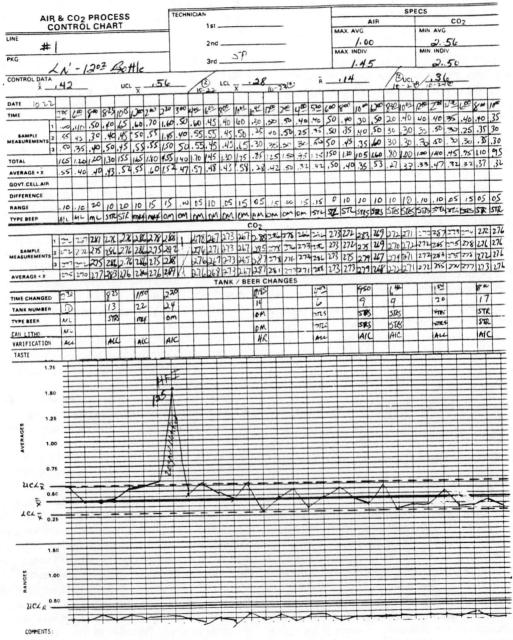

FIGURE 6-4 Air and CO_2 control charts, as used at Stroh's Winston-Salem plant.

B. October 23 through 2 A.M. October 25.

AIR & CO₂ PROCESS CONTROL CHART

TECHNICIAN			SPECS	
1st _____			**AIR**	**CO₂**
2nd _____		MAX. AVG.	MIN. AVG	
3rd _____ SP		1.00	2.56	
		MAX. INDIV.	MIN. INDIV.	
		1.45	2.50	

LINE: #1

PKG.: LN-12oz Bottle

CONTROL DATA:
$\bar{\bar{X}}$ .42 $\textcircled{\scriptsize 10-24}$ UCL $\bar{X}$ $\textcircled{\scriptsize 10-25}$ LCL $\bar{X}$ .28 $\bar{R}$ .14   UCL$_R$ .36

DATE																		
TIME	12⁰⁰	1⁴⁵	4⁰⁰	6⁰⁰	4³⁵	11⁰⁵	12⁰⁰	1³⁰	4⁰⁰	4⁵	6⁰⁰	8⁰⁰	10⁰⁰	12⁰⁰	2⁰⁰			
SAMPLE MEASUREMENTS 1	.30	.35	.40	.40	.30	.40	35	.45	50	.25	40	.35	40	30	.40			
2	.30	.40	.45	40	.30	.40	45	.45	45	.25	.50	40	60	30	.40			
3	.35	.45	.40	50	.25	.45	40	.45	55	45	.50	40	.40	45	40			
TOTAL	.95	120	1.25	130	85	1.25	120	1.35	150	.95	1.40	1.15	140	105	160			
AVERAGE = X	.32	40	.41	43	.28	.42	.40	.45	50	.32	.47	.38	47	.35	40			
GOVT. CELL. AIR																		
DIFFERENCE																		
RANGE	05	10	.05	10	.05	.05	.10	.00	.10	.20	.10	05	20	15	0			
TYPE BEER	STR	STR	STR	STR	STL	STR	STR	STR	STR	STL	STL	STR	STR	STR	STR			

Air - .44   CO₂ - 2.75   44 - 45 checks

CO₂

SAMPLE MEASUREMENTS 1	263	279	272	275	280	284	277	272	267	270	267	262	272	272	270			
2	274	279	274	269	282	283	277	272	272	270	263	274	272	272	272			
3	274	270	270	273	279	284	283	278	272	265	264	268	172	272	270			
AVERAGE = X	270	276	272	273	282	284	279	274	270	268	265	265	272	272	271			

1 High #1 25
AFI

TANK / BEER CHANGES

TIME CHANGED	1³⁰	7¹⁵	1¹¹												
TANK NUMBER	23	3	6												
TYPE BEER	STR	STR	STR												
CAN LITHO	STR	STR	STR												
VARIFICATION	AIC	AIC	AIC												
TASTE															

COMMENTS:

FIGURE 6-4   (continued)

FIGURE 6-5   A taste test form. (*Courtesy of Stroh Brewery Company*) cent per barrel, a level many times lower than the industry average.

The succeeding portions of both the X̄ and R charts document a process that is in good statistical control.

Taste Test

Every Thursday afternoon a panel of tasters at the Winston-Salem brewery assembled to sample Stroh beers that had been sent from all the other company breweries. This test usually involved tasting three beers at a time and marking a sheet such as found in Figure 6-5. The results of this taste test were pooled with those from the taste tests done at other locations within the company. Any clearly and widely perceived deficiencies in a brewery's beer were carefully investigated and corrective measures taken. The Winston-Salem plant also tested other beer brands against Stroh to assess Stroh's quality and distinctiveness. The taste panel at the plant was qualified every year. This was done by having the Detroit staff send to the plant samples that had been "spiked" with chemicals to make the beer more hoppy, more bitter, more malty, or otherwise different than usual. A taster who did not adequately perceive these characteristics was removed from the taste panel.

The Winston-Salem brewery took pride in the quality of its beer and its packaging. Just about anything concerning the product or the process that was quantifiable was checked every day at the plant. The plant was committed to conforming precisely to the requirements established by the staff in Detroit.

Investigating and Correcting Causes of Quality Problems

Identifying quality problems through the use of control charts, of course, is not enough. Their causes must be researched and corrective measures taken. Space does not permit a thorough discussion how quality problems should be investigated and corrected, but several observations can be made.

1. *You are only as good as your data.* There is nothing like good, meaningful data for tackling quality problems. Sometimes the data appropriate for investigating a problem are routinely collected, say, for posting on a control chart. Other times the data of interest may not be readily available or subject to significant errors. If this is the case, the first step is to understand where the problem may be coming from (for example, particular product types, particular segments of the process) and how important it is (vital, trivial). Once these things are understood, the kinds of data appropriate to the problem's study are usually apparent. Collecting them may require (1) measuring aspects of the process or the product; (2) keeping track of defects and their characteristics; (3) tracing particular defects to times, lines, or machines; and (4) noting any changes or conditions in the process and its materials, equipment, and/or labor. The accumulation of these data may require a substantial investment in quality monitoring equipment and gauges and specific procedures. Some experiments may have to be conducted.

2. *Be systematic in the investigation.* One of the aids to quality problems investigation that has been particularly effective for the Japanese is the "fishbone" diagram, which tries to be explicit about the causes and effects in the process. (See Figure 6-6.) Explicit diagrams of this type are reminiscent of the process flow and information flow diagrams considered earlier in this text. They, too, were means of making explicit what might otherwise be missed.

3. *Make the process foolproof.* Once the cause of the quality problem has been found, often the corrective measures that should be taken are designed to make the process foolproof. Foolproofing may come about through a change in the process technology, product

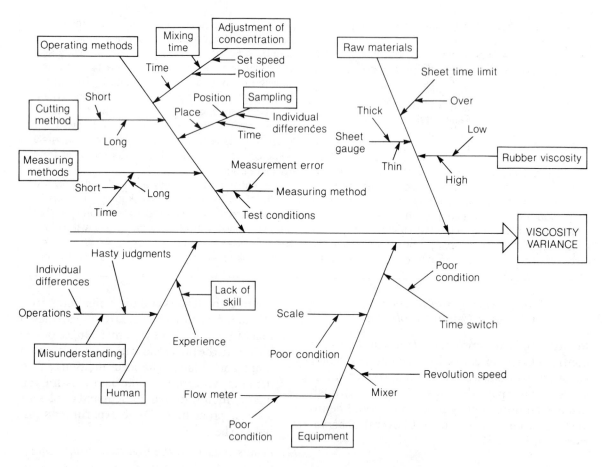

FIGURE 6-6 A fishbone diagram for splicing cement viscosity for radial tires. (From Cole, *Work, Mobility, and Participation*, p. 146)

design, or methods and procedures. Such foolproofing may call for special product design or for the use of particular foolproofing fixtures, alarms and cutoffs for machinery, multiple signals or identity codings, optical magnification or remote control viewing, formal countdown procedures, or a host of similar devices. The trick is to change the process and/or the product so that the only way to make it is the quality way.

Sample Sizes and the Operating Characteristic Curve

It is beyond the scope of this text to deal thoroughly with the issue of how big a sample to use in generating a control chart of a specific type. We can only hope to appreciate some of the difficulties and subtleties involved. All sampling involves some risk. Indeed, there are two types of errors that can be made:

- Type I error: Rejecting a sample (or lot) when it in fact meets specifications. This is sometimes called the producer's risk, and it is usually designated by α. A 5 percent chance for this to occur is typical.
- Type II error: Accepting a sample (or lot) when it in fact does not meet specifications. This is sometimes called the consumer's risk and it is usually designated by β. A 10 percent chance for this to occur is typical.

These errors can be depicted on what is known as an operating characteristic curve (see Figure 6-7). There is an operating characteristic (OC) curve that can be associated with every sampling plan devised. The OC curve depicts the trade-offs inherent in a sampling plan between errors of type I and errors of type II. A type I error may cost the company money, but it is a type II error that causes ill will with customers. For this reason, most sampling plans try especially hard to limit type II errors, even at the expense of type I errors.

Figure 6-7 is an example of an operating characteristic curve where the true proportion of defectives is 5 percent of the lot. Ideally, one would like to have an operating characteristic curve that looks like the dashed line rectangle in the figure, bounded by a 1.0 probability on the Y-axis and by 5 percent defective on the X-axis. This is an unattainable goal, barring 100 percent inspection, and this reality forces us into balancing type II errors against type I errors.

The shape of an operating characteristic curve depends primarily on the sample size taken (n) and the acceptance number (i.e., the allowable number of defects in the sample) denoted by C. In general, the more critical one wishes to make the inspection—that is, the smaller the areas for both type I and type II errors—the larger the sample size and the acceptance number need to be.

FIGURE 6-7   An operating characteristic curve.

Is the Inspection Adequate?

The task of setting up and keeping control charts on the process is a type of inspection. As stated earlier, this type of inspection needs to be encouraged because it focuses on the process, not on the product. There are a host of other types of inspections, with different purposes attached to each. Table 6-5 summarizes some of these types of inspections and their purposes.

Adequate inspection, first and foremost, involves the establishment of clear operational standards for assessing an item's quality. There should be as little ambiguity as possible about what constitutes good quality. Often it is difficult to specify objective, measurable criteria, but it is an important step toward adequate inspection, and it has the added benefit of helping the workforce, as well.

TABLE 6-5   Basic types of inspection

MAJOR USE	TECHNIQUE APPLIED	COMMENTS
Process control	Control charts	Can be used to examine the variability of the process along selected measured dimensions. Serves as an indication of "drift" in the process due to specific, assignable causes. Logs are often kept to help track down causes of out-of-control operations as indicated by control chart.
		Can be used with standards (tolerances) given as a base against which future operations history can be compared.
Sorting good items from bad	100% inspection	Usually done at the end of the process but often done as well for selected vendor purchases and at selected points in the process, particularly in front of expensive processes. Often the focus for advances in automated testing.
		The types of defects detected can be analyzed as guides for improving the process.
Rating product quality	Product audits	Tests, sometimes destructive of the product, are designed to determine the seriousness of various defects.
Distinguishing good lots from bad lots	Acceptance sampling	Used to classify whether a lot of material is acceptable or not. Often used for incoming inspections of vendor material. Measurements are made of the discrete units of lot or the specimens are taken from batch and the percentage defective is compared with the standard derived from prior data.
Inspecting inspectors	Comparison of performance versus actual	Defects detected by inspector (person or machine) are compared with actual number of defects in what was inspected. Can involve defects "planted" by a quality control group.

Although there are a variety of issues involved in inspection, two of particular interest are how much inspection will be done and where inspection ought to be located in the process.

How Much Inspection?

At issue is whether, out of any lot, all items ought to be inspected (100 percent inspection), whether no items ought to be inspected, or whether a sample of items ought to be inspected. Let us explore the rationales for each of these alternatives, in turn.

100 Percent Inspection

The 100 percent inspection method is essentially a sorting operation to distinguish good items from bad ones. It can be a costly means of inspection, of course, and, in those cases, it is typically justified only if the cost of having a bad item in the product (or a bad product itself) is relatively high. 100 percent inspection is most prevalent at the finished goods stage of the process, or where product safety is a high priority.

If inspection can be made automatic, the cost of 100 percent inspection plunges. In such circumstances, 100 percent inspection of important product characteristics becomes very attractive. Many high-volume consumer goods companies such as the Stroh brewery in Winston-Salem use automatic inspection equipment.

If there are multiple inspectors, each inspecting all of the items, it is sometimes said that the inspection is 200 percent, 300 percent, and so on. Having such multiple inspection draws fire from experts such as Deming as wasteful and inefficient. They contend that 200 percent inspection is often less effective than 100 percent inspection because the inspectors may not feel obliged to sort out every defect, relying instead on "the other guy."

No Inspection

More and more, as the movement for just-in-time production has taken hold, and as companies have become devoted to managing quality by concentrating on the process, incoming materials from trusted vendors have been placed into production without inspection. Companies have been asking themselves why it should be necessary for items that have been inspected as finished goods in one factory to be reinspected as incoming material at the next. If one is confident in the vendor's process and inspection procedures, material ought to bypass incoming inspection.

Of course, not all companies feel free enough to accept their vendors' output without inspection, but the list is growing. In these cases, often the vendor ships along copies of the control charts relevant to the product, to demonstrate that its production process is in statistical control. In these cases, too, there are periodic audits and other checks to make sure that customer and vendor are in tune with one another, but routine inspections are dispensed with.

Acceptance Sampling

By far the most predominant current practice for inspecting incoming materials is to use a sampling procedure. (Sampling may also be used elsewhere in the process.) The idea is to sample from the entire lot of items shipped and to determine from the inspection of the sample whether to accept the shipment or to reject it. There are several, widely utilized sampling plans, including two World War II-vintage military standard procedures (Mil. Std. 105D, an attributes sampling plan, and Mil. Std. 414, a variables sampling plan) and the Dodge–Romig sampling plans (also for attributes).

Associated with any sampling plans are one or two quality indexes that serve to categorize the sampling plan as more or less stringent. Two quality indexes merit mention:

1. Acceptable quality level (AQL). The acceptable quality level is associated with the operating characteristic curve characterizing the sampling plan and its type I error (producer's risk). The AQL is a standard representing the maximum percent defective in the lot that can be considered satisfactory. It has no firm mathematical definition except that the probability of accepting the lot should be very high if its percent defective lies within the AQL set. See Figure 6-5 for a typical positioning of an AQL. The AQL exists as a standard for accepting a lot that has been sampled. It should not be confused with the "zero defects" production standard for quality, nor should it be forgotten that under any sampling plan, of no matter what AQL, some lots will be accepted with an AQL worse than the standard (type II error).

2. Rejectable quality level (RQL). The rejectable quality level, sometimes also termed the *lot tolerance percent defective (LTPD)*, is also associated with the operating characteristic curve characterizing the sampling plan, but it refers to the plan's type II error (consumer's risk). The RQL or LTPD is the defect level standard that defines what is unsatisfactory and should therefore be rejected. As with the AQL, there is no firm mathematical definition. Often, the RQL or LTPD is set so that if the percentage of true defects is high, the probability of accepting the lot is no more than 0.10.

Between the AQL and the RQL lies a region of ambiguity where the lot cannot be accepted straightaway but where it cannot be decisively rejected either. Sampling plans have been devised to deal with this ambiguity. The base case sampling plan is termed "single sampling." In single sampling a single, reasonably large sample is taken and the lot is either accepted or rejected, depending on the sample's findings. Generally, a more economical means of passing judgment on a lot is first to take a small sample that can be used straightaway to accept some lots and reject others. With such a sample, however, there will be times when the sample finding will be just too borderline on which to base an accept/reject decision. In these cases, another sample is taken and added to the first. With this now larger sample, the accept/reject decision is made. This is called "double sampling". This notion of double sampling can be extended to include repeated sampling, embracing more than two draws from the lot. In "sequential sampling," repeated draws are made until an ambiguity about acceptance or rejection fades away with ever larger sample sizes.

Sampling plans like Mil. Std. 105D specify how large a sample to draw, (or indeed whether multiple samples ought to be drawn), how many defects will be tolerated in the sample before it is rejected, and how the sampling plan ought to be modified for different levels of performance, good or bad. These specifications naturally vary with the tightness or looseness of the AQL chosen and the size of the lots that are to be inspected.

In recent years, acceptance sampling has come under increasing criticism. Some critics object that sampling plans permit rejects at some "acceptable quality level," when the goal should be not to have any in the lot in the first place.

Others note that acceptance sampling can be costly and often is not cost justified. These critics do well to call attention to the fact that acceptance sampling is sometimes misapplied.

In this regard, it is useful to investigate the economics of inspection so that we can determine when it is advantageous to inspect 100 percent and when it is advantageous not to inspect at all.[*] Some assumptions are in order:

1. Every product made gets tested at some point in the process (such as the final test), and if any defective part/item is in it, the product will fail inspection.
2. There are no inspection errors.

Define the following costs:

k_1 = cost to inspect one part that goes into the product

k_2 = cost to dismantle the product, repair it, reassemble it, and test it again once it has failed inspection due to a defective part

k = average cost to test one or more parts in order to find a good replacement part for one that has shown up defective.

p = average percent defective in the lot of parts

The cost per part of 100 percent inspection is

Cost 100% = $k_1 + kp$ [the cost to test one part and replace it if needed]

and the cost per part of no inspection is

Cost 0% = $p(k_2 + k)$ [the cost of repairing the product once it was discovered bad and then of replacing the faulty part]

The difference in the two costs is

$$\text{Cost}_{100\%} - \text{Cost}_{0\%} = k_1 - p\,k_2$$

[*]This discussion follows Deming, op. cit., p. 267 ff., although others have also dealt with this issue.

The breakeven point between 0 percent and 100 percent inspection is thus when

$$p = k_1/k_2$$

If $p > k_1/k_2$ then 100 percent inspection is merited, and if $p < k_1/k_2$ then no inspection is merited.

One cannot be assured that the average percent defective in a lot will be precisely p from one lot to another. Naturally, if there is wide divergence in the percent defective from one lot to another, then the decision rule of looking at k_1/k_2 becomes less of a guide. What can be said is if the worst lot has a $p < k_1/k_2$, then no inspection should be done, and if the best lot has a $p > k_1/k_2$, then 100 percent inspection should be done. For situations in between acceptance sampling makes particular sense.

It should be stressed that neither acceptance sampling—not anything else, for that matter—is a substitute for close working ties with a vendor. To the extent that a vendor's quality can be improved to a level of known statistical control, then acceptance sampling can fade away.

SOME DO'S AND DON'TS IN THE DEMING MANNER

W. Edwards Deming has been a very influential figure in quality management circles. It is perhaps fitting, then, to conclude this chapter on quality by presenting some key points of his (as I have interpreted them), in do's and don'ts form. Some of these precepts of Deming are controversial. They are stated baldly, in most cases. Nevertheless, all of these do's and don'ts make us think of better quality management practices.

Do's of Quality

1. Do plot the points in a chronological run chart or other statistical chart. Trends may be evident in the data. Use all the information you can.

2. Do give lots of education and training in statistical quality control to workers and managers at all levels in the organization.

3. Do change the foreman's role from one of orientation to and evaluation on the quantity of output that flows through his department to a role whose orientation and evaluation is based on quality.

4. Do stimulate teamwork among the functions of marketing, design engineering, and manufacturing.

5. Do drive out fear in the workforce by not laying off anybody because of quality improvement gains.

6. Do inspect material, either by 100 percent inspection or by no inspection at all. (See previous section for discussion of this.) Acceptance sampling, for the most part, is a thing of the past and is usually more expensive.

Don'ts of Quality

1. Don't expect slogans to work. They usually demoralize the workforce in the long run. (Deming is not a fan of Zero Defects Days or of banners flying in the factory's rafters.)

2. Don't pay workers according to any incentive scheme that is based on the quantity of work accomplished (piecerates). In fact, don't even have time standards for work known to the workforce. (This is an extremely controversial point of view, but is based on Deming's belief that any encouragement of quantity over quality is to be avoided.)

3. Don't award business to the lowest bidding vendor, unless you know that the low bid is because the vendor has the best process capabilities.

4. Don't have multiple inspectors; it just dilutes the responsibility.

5. Don't study defects from a process that is in statistical control; you won't learn anything, because the variation is random.

6. Don't buy any equipment unless you already have the process under statistical control. Why complicate the task with more uncertainty and expend funds for something that may not even be needed?

QUESTIONS

1. How could one resolve the debate about whether quality is "free" or not?

2. Which measures of reliability and maintainability are applicable under what conditions?

3. Which kinds of control charts are most effective for the kinds of situations faced by each of the company operations depicted in Segment I of this text?

4. Which kinds of inspections are most applicable to the six processes described in Segment I of this text?

5. What are some of the main ways in which quality can be controlled and improved? Does adding another quality check always benefit an operation? What are some different kinds of quality checks?

6. Define the following terms and discuss their significance for and application to quality control:

   a. mean
   b. variance
   c. normal distribution
   d. type I error and type II error
   e. double sampling

PROBLEMS

1. Choose some popular or fashionable products or services. What does the average person say about their quality? How would you go about measuring the quality of these products or services?

2. To some, "zero defects" has meant only a propaganda slogan for motivating worker effort to improve quality performance. How does Crosby's view of zero defects differ from that?

3. Which of Crosby's 14 steps do you think would meet with the greatest resistance at a typical company? Why?

4. Table 6-6 presents sample measurements on a process. Is this process under control? Construct an $\bar{X}$ and R control chart to see.

5. Piedmont Electronics manufactures some complex communications equipment (such as multiplexers) that can be regarded as the joining and testing of various subassemblies. Currently, only after final assembly is the primary functional testing done. At issue is whether some testing of individual subassemblies ought to be done before final assembly, and if so, which type of testing should be done. Here are some data to consider:

TABLE 6-6   Sample measurements on a process (Problem 4)

				SAMPLE NUMBER					
1	2	3	4	5	6	7	8	9	10
0.100	0.101	0.102	0.104	0.095	0.107	0.104	0.112	0.097	0.106
0.098	0.103	0.103	0.101	0.099	0.102	0.110	0.108	0.106	0.110
0.102	0.100	0.100	0.105	0.103	0.100	0.101	0.105	1.100	0.101
0.100	0.099	0.104	0.103	0.106	0.097	0.098	0.101	0.108	0.105

- Final assembly costs about $35 of labor and materials per unit.
- The functional test after final assembly passed two-thirds of the units. The other third went to repair. Repair cost an average of $30 per unit received. About one-fourth of the units were scrapped right away. Of the remaining units, all were final tested again and about half passed. The others were scrapped.
- The final testing and shipping cost $25 per unit.
- Each year 1000 units of this model were manufactured.
- One possible test of the subassemblies would cost $20,000 in equipment and promised to identify 60 percent of the potential problems.
- The other possible test of the subassemblies would cost $12,000 in equipment but promised to identify only 40 percent of the potential problems.
- Should Piedmont Electronics install the new equipment for testing the subassemblies? Which possible test should be implemented?

6. The Pork & Rind firm decided to go ahead with the production of the Puffy Cheezies (see problem 7 in Chapter 4), and they need to set up quality control inspection stations. The process flow is from mixer to gun to oil spray to oven and finally to packaging. The cost to put each ounce through each process (i.e., the value added for each process), the expected percentage rejected, and the costs to inspect are in Table 6-7. The tests after the mixer and the oiler require the use of the lab. The other tests are visual only. Where would you suggest that inspectors be stationed?

7. Turnum and Down (T&D) have an automatic screw machine set up to run small brass shafts for a customer. The shaft diameters are supposed to be 0.375 ± 0.0025 inches. T&D have determined that the machine is capable of generating the shafts to size normally distributed with a standard deviation of 0.0005 inches.

   a. A sample mean has been taken with a value of 0.377 inches. What action should be taken?

   b. Three sample means of 0.3755, 0.376, and 0.3765 inches have been measured. What action should be taken?

   c. Three sample means of 0.376, 0.3745, and 0.377 inches were taken immedi-

TABLE 6-7   Quality control considerations (Problem 6)

PROCESS	VALUE ADDED	EXPECTED PERCENTAGE REJECTED	COST TO INSPECT ALL ITEMS
Mixer	$.04	10%	$.02
Gun	.005	3	.01
Oiler	.015	2	.04
Oven	.005	8	.01
Package	.01	4	.005

*Per ounce of Puffy Cheezies.

ately after a new load of brass raw material was started. What action should be taken?

d. Three measurements were taken of 0.3755, 0.3744, and 0.364 inches. What action should be taken?

e. One sample mean of 0.3766 inches was measured. What action should be taken?

8. What quality control practices mentioned in the chapter are evident in the operation of the Stroh Brewery plant in Winston-Salem?

9. At the Jackson Paint Company, paint chip cards with the proper color matches were used as an important marketing tool. The following data was available on rejects of paint chip cards for poor color match. Samples of 50 were taken at any time. Is the instrumentation used to match colors of cards to standards under control?

Rejects by Sample

	Sample Number											
	1	2	3	4	5	6	7	8	9	10	11	12
Percent of chip cards failing color match	8	6	6	12	14	8	10	6	4	10	12	6

10. Should there be 100 percent inspection or no inspection of the component that evidences the following characteristics?

Average percent defective in the lots delivered	4%
Cost of inspect one part	$0.25
Cost to dismantle product, repair it, and test it again, given failure due to a defective part	$3.50

11. The operator of a machine that sprays vitamins on flakes of breakfast cereal is concerned about quality. Every so often during his shift he measures how much vitamin mixture he has dispensed. If his measure is high, he readjusts the spray so that less comes out, and if his measure is low, he opens up the spray nozzle so that more is dispensed. What would you say about the quality practices of this operator?

12. Joe ran a small transfer line and Walt inspected the output of that line. Joe was paid an incentive wage that was tied to the output of the line. Walt was instructed to identify all the bad parts produced. Comment on this situation. How would you change things, if at all?

SITUATION FOR STUDY 6-1

APOLLO MOTOR COMPANY, OMAHA PLANT

The Omaha Plant of the Apollo Motor Company had the worst quality rating of any of the company's plants. Besides, labor relations were exceedingly acrimonious and the plant was filthy. Attitude surveys of the workforce indicated exceedingly low morale. It was clear to Mike Garrett, the new plant manager, that without some improvement in productivity and quality the plant was sure to be closed within a year.

The plant had been making pickup trucks and Garrett knew that a new model of pickup truck was on the drawing boards at Apollo Motor's design center. The plant that would assemble this pickup truck had not yet been chosen, but Garrett thought that if the Omaha plant could somehow show significant quality improvement, it could be chosen.

The trick, of course, was how to do it. How could he turn around this plant? How could he instill quality in the work done there? How should his job change, how should the job of his supervisors change, how should the jobs

of the workers change? If the Omaha plant was to show improvement, it had to do so soon.

REFERENCE NOTES

1. Philip B. Crosby, *Quality Is Free* (New York: McGraw-Hill, 1979). *good book*

2. Joseph M. Juran and Frank M. Gryna, Jr., *Quality Planning and Analysis*, 2d ed. (New York: McGraw-Hill, 1980).

3. Crosby, *Quality Is Free.*

4. Philip Crosby, *Quality Is Free* (New York: McGraw-Hill, 1979). Joseph Juran and Frank Gryna, *Quality Planning and Analysis* (New York: McGraw-Hill, 1980)
W. Edwards Deming, *Quality, Productivity, and Competitive Position* (Cambridge, MA: MIT-Center for Advanced Engineering Study, 1982).
Armand Feigenbaum, *Total Quality Control* (New York: McGraw-Hill, 1983).

5. For more on control charts, consult a source such as *Quality Control Handbook* by Joseph M. Juran (ed.), 3d ed. (New York: McGraw-Hill, 1979). *good book*

III

DECIDING FUTURE OPERATIONS

The policies and decisions discussed so far in this text have dealt mainly with short-term time horizons and with only modest alterations in the size, design, or scope of operations. In this segment of the text, some costly and fundamental longer-term decisions affecting operations are confronted.

This segment consists of Chapters 7 and 8, each dealing with a different kind of major change.

- *Capacity change.* Managers must periodically consider whether production capacity is sufficient and how any new capacity should be planned, developed, and started up.

- *Technological change.* Technology is always marching forward; this march often has implications for a company's products and/or production processes. This chapter introduces issues in the management of technological change and outlines some of technology's promises and pitfalls.

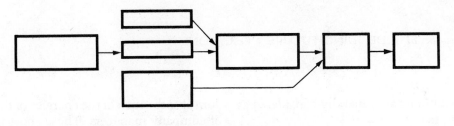

DEALING WITH CAPACITY CHANGE

In Segment II of this text, which dealt with improving an existing operation, a number of short-term measures to increase an operation's capacity were discussed. Among such measures were:

1. Overtime.

2. Second or third shifts.

3. A more level production rate over time for the purpose of building up finished goods inventory for peak periods of demand.

4. Altering the product mix or the production schedule to reduce setups of machines or work groups and thereby to coax more production out of the operation.

5. Adding more labor to an existing stock of capital—for example, by rebalancing a line flow process.

6. Improving information or materials movement within a process—for example, by introducing material requirements planning systems or decoupling inventories.

7. Modest investments, product redesigns, process modifications, or management innovations that decrease manufacturing cycle times, freeing resources for additional ca-

pacity. Many of these measures, with possible long-term implications as well, will be discussed more thoroughly in the subsequent chapter on technological change.

8. Subcontracting products or pieces of the production process. This measure is frequently not an immediately implemented change; it can remain a long-term policy of the company as well as a short-term one.

These measures, either separately or in combination, can have dramatic effects on a plant's capacity. Most of them, however, are short-term substitutes for securing additional space and equipment for production. Overtime, shift-work, revamped production scheduling, and some others can often meet peaks in demand, but they usually cannot be sustained over a long period of time. Improvements to the process, product design, information, or materials handling systems, although desirable long-term policies in themselves, are often incapable of boosting production enough to eliminate a plant's need for more space in the face of sustained increases in demand. Although a company normally looks first to such a list of short-term means of adding capacity, more substantial space additions are generally considered at the same time.

This chapter will concentrate on the three "bricks and mortar" choices for adding capacity: (1) on-site expansion of an existing facility, (2) the establishment of a new branch, and (3) the relocation of an existing operation to larger quarters. Among the issues that surround these choices are:

- How much should any capacity expansion be?
- When should it be timed?
- Where should it be located?

The discussion of these issues and choices comprises the agenda for this chapter. After discussing the basic elements behind the size and timing of capacity expansion in a manufacturing enterprise, we will examine similar issues in a service industry. Finally, we will consider, in more depth, the decision whether to add capacity on site or to establish a new branch or to relocate to larger quarters, and the decision of where to place a new facility.

The decision about contracting capacity is every bit as involved as the decision about increasing capacity—and markedly more difficult for most managers to make. While most of the chapter will deal, implicitly if not explicitly, with capacity expansion, some portions will treat plant closing and contraction as well.

AN OVERVIEW OF CAPACITY PLANNING

In most companies, most short-term measures to increase capacity (1) can be planned for in a matter of weeks, (2) involve only limited sums of corporate capital, (3) are studied at the plant (rather than the corporate) level, and (4) originate and are carried through in an informal way. Although they are the concerns of top management, such short-term capacity measures sel-

dom absorb much of the energies of the top rank of company managers. These short-term measures are apt to be too routine and too devoid of strategic importance to demand the careful study of the layers of management that sit above the particular concerns of individual plants.

Longer-term, bricks-and-mortar capacity expansions occupy top management time to a much greater degree. This is because they involve considerable expense, far above the spending authority of even the chief executive officer, and they often have strategic and competitive implications for the company. Moreover, the initiation of capacity expansions is apt to be the result of a formal companywide planning and review procedure rather than the result of a plant's reaction to day-to-day demands.

A typical planning and review procedure is an annual exercise that looks five years into the future. (Five years is the typical number. Highly capital-intensive companies like those in the chemical and steel industries may choose 10 years; more consumer-sensitive industries like apparel or fast growing industries like electronics may choose three years.) This exercise is driven by a marketing forecast for each year (and quarter, perhaps) of the planning horizon and for each product produced. Available production capacities are estimated as well and the two are meshed together to determine to what extent capacity is in surplus or in deficit. Naturally, both marketing and production estimates are much more nebulous the further into the future the company looks.

More than simply identifying capacity shortfalls and their likely timing over a multiyear horizon, the planning exercise concentrates on alternatives for dealing with such shortfalls. The on-site expansion of certain plants, the character, size, and region for possible new branch plants, or the relocation of some plants may be considered as viable alternatives for coping with capacity shortfalls. The review of the submitted plans normally comes to some tentative

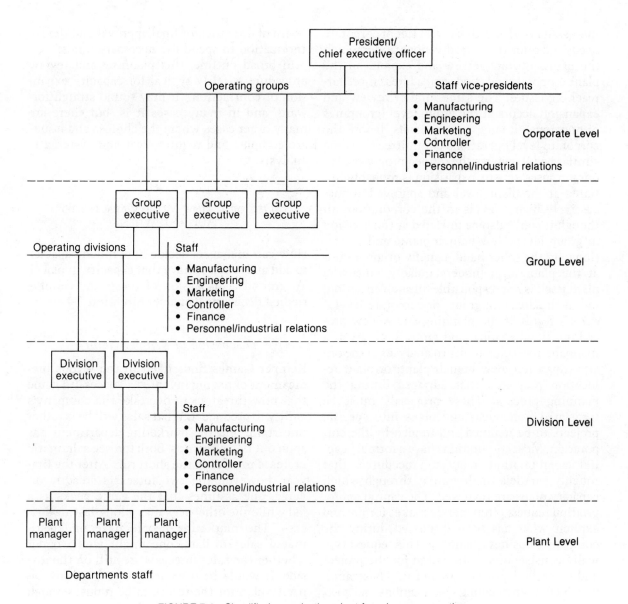

FIGURE 7-1   Simplified organization chart for a large corporation.

decisions about which avenues for remedying capacity shortfalls ought to be shelved, at least for the time being. It is unlikely that firm commitments will be made on any specific proposal but the waters will be tested on many.

The planning and review procedure generally works from the bottom up. (See the organization chart in Figure 7-1.) While the particular individuals involved vary from one organization to another, generally plant managers and their staffs work out the lowest tier of corporate needs and priorities. The divisions under which the plants operate review and expand on the plant proposals and needs and address more far-reaching issues. The same kind of review and expansion occurs at the group level (groupings of divisions), if such a level exists, before the corporate level operations committee (or some similar body) reviews the refined proposals. For our purposes, on-site expansion is probably initiated at the plant level and approved at successively higher levels in the corporation, although it could also be initiated at the division or group level. New branch plants and relocations, on the other hand, usually originate not at the plant level (understandably, since the plant itself is not responsible for such an action) but at the division, group, or corporate levels.

As a result of the planning and review procedure, the divisions (and groups) are given a mandate to develop in-depth analyses of the on-site expansion, new branch plant, or plant relocation proposals that surfaced during the planning process. These proposals must be translated from ideas and plans into specific projects to be manned and funded by the corporation. Most corporations have a formal "capital appropriation request procedure" that roughly parallels the hierarchy through which capacity plans are reviewed. The capital appropriation request often merely makes formal and explicit what has been discussed during the company's business planning. This request typically consists of a justification for the project and some in-depth analyses of it. These analyses include engineering specifications and cost/timing estimates; specific size, product, equipment, worker and manager requirements, and location decisions; and an economic analysis (sometimes called a capital budgeting analysis). The appropriation request, after it has been completed and approved at the group and division levels, makes its way to the company's

board of directors for final approval and the authorization to spend the necessary funds.

In broad outline, this planning and review procedure is fairly typical for capacity expansion or contraction.[1] It may sound straightforward, and in many cases it is, but there are many other cases where the choices and issues are complex and require clear and systematic analysis.

Deciding How Much Capacity to Add and When

How can managers decide how much capacity to add and when to have that capacity in place? To ground a discussion of these uncertainty-riddled decisions, consider Situation 7-1.

Discussion of Kemper Games

Kemper Games finds itself in the joyous predicament of having invented a successful game that now threatens to overtake the company's ability to produce it. What sales will be is rather uncertain, and the marketing department has spun out two scenarios. Both foresee a dramatic increase in sales in the short run. After the first year, however, the two forecasts steadily diverge; one assumes that the game peaks as a fad while the other sees it as a long-lasting success. The marketing people have underestimated sales to date; one might well wonder whether the sales forecasts are still on the low side. It would be reasonable to expect any capacity plan for the future to be robust enough to cope with another sizable increase in forecasted sales.

The first order of business is to assess whether all three courses of action being considered (expansion, third shift, and subcontracting) are feasible, given the prevailing market forecast. Subcontracting seems feasible since no mention

SITUATION 7-1

KEMPER GAMES, INC.

The latest sales figures were very encouraging. Laura Kemper, president and chief executive officer of Kemper Games, Inc., could not help but smile. After four essentially static years, Kemper Games looked like it was headed for an absolutely fantastic sales year that would carry the small company into the top ranks of the growing game industry. The reason behind this success was Kemper's latest entry in the market, "Bungle, The Game of Life Styles." Laura, an inveterate games player herself, had developed the game over the past two years with her husband, Peter, who headed the company's product development department. The company had introduced it about six months ago.

Bungle was an adult board game for two to six players. The game produced no winners—everybody lost. This outcome apparently struck a responsive chord in adults of every age and income group. The game's early success had set Peter Kemper to the task of developing a successor game, Deluxe Bungle, which would soon be ready for production. Deluxe Bungle was played by two-person partnerships (such as couples). In playing Deluxe Bungle, not only did everyone lose, but partners were encouraged to turn against one another. Peter had high hopes for the game, although no marketing study had been made as yet.

Bungle's success, however, was soon going to create capacity problems at Kemper Games. The factory could reliably produce about 900 sets per day in two shifts and inventory stood at 3000 sets. The magnitude of the problems anticipated depended in large measure on the particular forecasts for the game's sales (see Table 7-1). The range in the forecasts was due mainly to variations in the assumptions used. Low estimates derived from regarding Bungle as a fad that would soon pass. Higher estimates regarded Bungle as a long-running staple, like Monopoly.

The forecasts influenced not only the size of any additions to capacity but also the nature of those additions. Laura Kemper confronted several choices concerning capacity:

TABLE 7-1   Forecast of Bungle's sales by upcoming quarters (Kemper Games, Inc.)

QUARTER UPCOMING*	FORECAST 1† (sets/day)	FORECAST 2‡ (sets/day)
1	600	600
2	750	750
3	1050	1050
4	1500	1500
5	1200	1500
6	900	1500
7	750	1500
8	500	1500

SOURCE: Marketing Department.
*The company plans for 62 days of production each quarter.
†Forecast 1 assumes that Bungle's sales are merely a fad that will peak in quarter 4 and gradually taper off.
‡Forecast 2 assumes that Bungle's sales will parallel those of Boggle and Pente. After rising like a fad, they will sustain themselves at a high level.

1. Kemper Games could expand on-site (enough space and lead time were available to do so), or it could lease nearby space to satisfy forecasted requirements. Table 7-2 includes some cost estimates for the various space additions corresponding to the forecasted sales figures. The space could be used for any of Kemper Games' products since nearly all of them required printing, plastic fabrication, gluing, and assembly. Costs for the additional equipment and working capital needed to reach various output levels are also included.

2. The company was going to operate two production shifts in the upcoming first quarter, doubling production from its current rate of 450 sets per day. A third shift was a definite alternative. Wage premiums would have to be paid, though, to attract a suitable workforce and supervisory personnel. In addition, productivity was expected to be less in the third shift, because the workforce quality would probably be lower than that prevailing in the first two shifts and because only a skeletal staff would supervise production. A 25 percent wage premium over first-shift operations was expected as well as an effective

TABLE 7-2   Cost estimates for on-site expansion and leasing options (Kemper Games, Inc.)
A. Costs of on-site expansion (Present space allocated to Bungle production is 40,000 square feet.
Current two-shift production capability is 900 sets per day.)

ADDITIONAL PRODUCTION RATE PER DAY OVER TWO SHIFTS	SQUARE FEET REQUIRED	ESTIMATED COST (PLANT)	ESTIMATED COST (EQUIPMENT) AND WORKING CAPITAL
300	15,000	$225,000	$ 75,000
450	20,000	300,000	100,000
600	24,000	360,000	120,000
750	27,000	405,000	175,000

B. Costs of leasing the only nearby existing facility:

20,000 square feet or less—$7.00 per square foot per year
More than 20,000 square feet—$6.50 per square foot per year

output rate of 90 percent of the first shift. Labor constituted 40 percent of a set's variable cost of $2.40.

3. Kemper Games had so far manufactured all its games in its own facilities. However, the company could subcontract the manufacture of the entire game or of certain components (such as the printing of the board, the cards drawn as part of the game, the plastic pieces). The convenience of subcontracting was costly. According to one estimate, the 40 percent contribution margin that Kemper Games enjoyed on the $4 factory price of Bungle (the retail price was $7.95, just about a 100 percent markup) would be eroded to 20 percent through subcontracting the entire game.

It was also possible for Kemper Games to reduce or even to eliminate its need for additional capacity by pricing the game higher. However, Laura had decided to accept a lower margin than was the norm in the industry, and thus a lower retail price, in order to spur sales of Bungle and to spread the Kemper Games brand name. The initial marketing report for Bungle with estimated sales at different

retail prices is reproduced as Table 7-3. Currently, sales for quarter 1 were running about 60 percent ahead of that market forecast.

Laura felt if Kemper Games was to have enough time to act on the on-site expansion option, she would have to act within the week. Any new on-site construction, begun now, was not likely to be available until the start of quarter 4. Inventory would have to be built up in the interim, which Kemper Games would be able to carry at a rate of 10¢ per unit per quarter.

TABLE 7-3   Marketing report on sales by price category (Kemper Games, Inc.)

RETAIL PRICE	CORRESPONDING FACTORY PRICE	SET SALES PER DAY·
$ 7.00	$3.50	420
8.00	4.00	360
9.00	4.50	315
10.00	5.00	285
11.00	5.50	260
12.00	6.00	240

·Set sales per day are estimated at 6 months after introduction.

was made of any constraints impeding potential subcontractors. In gauging feasibility, then, it is largely a matter of testing the third shift and expansion alternative.

Let us test the expansion alternative first. Any expansion on site begun now would not be ready for production until the fourth quarter. In the meantime, two shifts would have to suffice.

TABLE 7-4   Inventory buildup under the on-site expansion alternative
(Kemper Games, Inc.)

QUARTER	DAILY DEMAND	DAILY PRODUCTION	DAILY INVENTORY BUILDUP OR DEPLETION	CUMULATIVE INVENTORY ON DAILY BASIS FOR QUARTER
1	600	900	+300	+300
2	750	900	+150	+450
3	1050	900	−150	+300
4	1500	1500	0	+300

TABLE 7-5   Inventory buildup under the third shift alternative and forecast 2
(Kemper Games, Inc.)

QUARTER	DAILY DEMAND	DAILY PRODUCTION	DAILY INVENTORY BUILDUP OR DEPLETION	CUMULATIVE INVENTORY ON DAILY BASIS FOR QUARTER
1	600	1305	+705	+705
2	750	1305	+555	+1260
3	1050	1305	+255	+1515
4	1500	1305	−195	+1320
5	1500	1305	−195	+1125
6	1500	1305	−195	+930
7	1500	1305	−195	+735
8	1500	1305	−195	+540
9	1500	1305	−195	+345
10	1500	1305	−195	+150
11	1500	1305	−195	−45

Fortunately, two shifts begun now will be enough to carry Kemper Games until the fourth quarter, with some to spare. Inventory would be built up in the first two periods and depleted in the third. If the on-site expansion involves 24,000 square feet, the corresponding production rate is 600—just enough to combine with the two-shift rate of 900 per day to meet a continued demand for 1500 units per day. Table 7-4 summarizes how demand would be satisfied under the on-site expansion alternative. As the table makes clear, immediate implementation of the second shift leaves the first quarter buildup as an inventory cushion of 18,000 units (calculated as 300 units extra per day times 62 days)—12.5 percent of expected demand over the first three quarters. Such a cushion is welcome and by no means too large, given the possibly explosive sales for the game.

Let us turn our attention now to the feasibility of a three shift operation. The third shift is expected to be more costly and less efficient than either of the first two shifts, chiefly because of the quality of the labor and the skeletal staffing of supervisory positions. Specifically, only 405 units (calculated as 450 times 0.9) are expected during each third shift. With this in mind, we can construct an inventory buildup table like Table 7-4, using the larger forecast estimates. As is plain from Table 7-5, the third shift can produce enough inventory early on, if implemented in quarter 1, to tide the corporation over until quarter 11. For the short term, then, a third shift is clearly feasible, although over the long term, if the second forecast prevails, a third shift would come up short of capacity. In that case, only on-site expansion would serve.

On the other hand, if forecast 1 prevailed, on-site expansion just for the Bungle game would be overkill because it would be necessary only for quarters 4 and 5. What seems to be suggesting itself is a wait-and-see approach to on-site expansion. A third shift appears to be the best way to meet short-term demand; a decision on on-site expansion can be deferred until the popularity and longevity of Bungle in the marketplace can be ascertained more precisely, perhaps even as late as quarter 7.

Although just this analysis of the feasibility of each of the options may be persuasive to many, a carefully documented decision is still far off. The economics of the decision have yet to be discussed.

Compared with the expansion alternative, both the subcontracting and third shift alternatives leave the corporation with less contribution (that is, dollars allocable to profit and to pay for overhead) per unit produced. By subcontracting, Kemper Games loses half of its 40 percent contribution margin on the $4 factory price of Bungle. Thus, the contribution per unit from subcontracting declines to

$$\$4.00 \cdot \frac{.40}{2} = \$.80 \text{ per unit}$$

from the present $1.60 per unit.

By going to a third shift, the 25 percent labor premium Kemper Games has to pay will also cut into the contribution per unit produced. In this case, we need to calculate the third shift increase in labor costs (composed of variable costs, labor content, and the shift premium) and subtract this amount, along with the variable costs for the first and second shifts, from the factory price:

$$\$4.00 - \$2.40 - (\$2.40 \cdot .40 \cdot .25)$$
$$= \$1.36 \text{ per unit}$$

Given that the third shift is feasible for the short term and that its contribution per unit

produced is much higher than the subcontracting option, it is clear that the subcontracting option should be dropped from further consideration. Of course, the subcontracting of just a part of the Bungle game is a possibility, but that option has not been developed sufficiently within the corporation to address it here.

It remains to investigate the economics of expansion versus third shift operation. After all, if adding capacity is cheap, Kemper Games may be better off holding excess space for a while, until Deluxe Bungle or some other game can fill up the space, no matter which Bungle forecast prevails. As noted, expansion can come either by building an addition to Kemper Games' original structure or by leasing some space very close-by. Let us resolve the build-or-lease issue before examining the economics of the expansion/third shift decision.

Because a build-or-lease decision would possibly prevail only for a demand pattern like forecast 2, let us assume forecast 2 for the purposes of the analysis. In order to meet that forecast, an additional 600 units per day will be needed, implying a space requirement of an additional 24,000 square feet. The estimated cost to build and equip this area of plant comes to $480,000— $360,000 for the plant and $120,000 for the equipment. In return for this investment comes the ability to earn a stream of contribution from the manufacture of Bungle. At a contribution of $1.60 per unit and production of 600 units per day, the investment pays itself back in 500 working days.

Although it is nice to see a payback so short, the most persuasive way to analyze the economics of capacity choice is to use net present value (NPV) analysis, sometimes referred to as discounted cash flow analysis. Almost all of the largest and most sophisticated companies employ the net present value technique in their capacity planning decisions.

---
* ASIDE *

Net Present Value (NPV)

The technique of net present value grows out of that pervasive concept of opportunity cost. For an investment of such and such a size, a corporation expects to generate a stream of earnings that extends into the future. But, by investing so many dollars in that particular investment project, the company forgoes the opportunity of earning a return on those same dollars by putting them in some money market instrument to earn interest or by using them to finance another income-generating project. In order to decide, then, whether to undertake an investment, a corporation needs to ascertain whether that investment will likely generate a stream of income whose value over time would be greater than bank interest earnings or the return from other investment projects not undertaken.

Put in other words, because income-generating investment opportunities exist, there is a time value to money. That is, having a dollar today is worth more than having a dollar tomorrow because today's dollar enjoys the opportunity of being put to work to finance an investment that will generate a stream of dollars into the future. How much more is today's dollar worth than tomorrow's dollar (apart, of course, from inflation, which is another matter altogether)? It depends, as we might expect, on the return that can be earned from investments.

This rate of return, usually called the *discount rate,* typically varies from company to company and industry to industry, because some companies and industries are generally more profitable than others. In any case, the discount rate is at least as high as the interest rate available from the financial markets, because all companies have the opportunity of placing their cash in some money market instrument.

How can the discount rate be used to value the worth of a dollar tomorrow? Suppose r is the discount rate. A dollar (the principal) invested today at the day-to-day rate of return r would be worth

$$\$1 + (r \cdot \$1) = \$1(1 + r)$$

tomorrow. Put another way, tomorrow's dollar is worth only $1/(1 + r)$ of today's dollar; it has a "present value" of

$$\$1\left(\frac{1}{1 + r}\right)$$

How much is a dollar worth two days from now? Even more than today's dollar is worth tomorrow because it has the opportunity of earning interest on tomorrow's interest as well. More formally, a dollar invested today at the day-to-day rate of return r would, in two days, be worth

$$\begin{array}{ccc} \$1 & + \quad (r \cdot \$1) & + \quad r[\$1 + (r \cdot \$1)] \\ \text{(principal)} & + \text{(tomorrow's} & + \text{(the return 2 days} \\ & \text{return on} & \text{from now on} \\ & \text{today's} & \text{tomorrow's total)} \\ & \text{dollar)} & \end{array}$$

$$= \$1 + 2r + r^2 = \$1(1 + r)^2$$

Put another way, a dollar received two days from now is worth only $1/(1 + r)^2$ of today's dollar. Its "present value" is

$$\$1\left(\frac{1}{(1 + r)^2}\right)$$

As we should expect, a dollar received three days from now is worth $1/(1 + r)^3$ of today's dollar, and so on for successive days.

How can we use the discount rate to value a stream of income, such as would be generated by an investment? Suppose the investment returned a dollar tomorrow and a dollar the next day. How much should we value the investment? Essentially we have already solved for this value. It is merely the sum of the present value of a dollar received tomorrow and the present value of a dollar received two days from now. Hence, the value of the stream of dollars received tomorrow and two days from now equals

$$\$1\left(\frac{1}{1 + r}\right) + \$1\left(\frac{1}{(1 + r)^2}\right)$$

It is easy to see then that the value today (the present value) of a dollar received in each of n days is simply

(1) $\$1\left(\dfrac{1}{1+r}+\dfrac{1}{(1+r)^2}+\dfrac{1}{(1+r)^3}\right.$
$\left. +\ \dots\ +\dfrac{1}{(1+r)^n}\right)$

What would be the value of a dollar received beginning on day 3 and extending to day n? Obviously, it is

$$\$1\left(\dfrac{1}{(1+r)^3}+\ \dots\ +\dfrac{1}{(1+r)^n}\right)$$

but the ability to add and subtract present values implies that this figure can be computed as the present value of a dollar received from tomorrow through day n less the present value of a dollar received tomorrow and the next day. This ability to add or subtract present values comes in handy when computing them.

It is important to understand how the present value calculation is affected by changes in the discount rate and the time horizon chosen:

1. The higher the discount rate, the lower the present value of any stream of income. Income received in distant periods is particularly hard-hit by high values of r, since $(1+r)$ is raised to successively higher powers.

2. The longer the time horizon over which income is to be received, the higher the present value of any income stream. As the horizon stretches on, however, less and less is added to the present value, other things being equal.

We have discussed net present value and the discount rate in terms of days. Of course, usually the discount rate is quoted on an annual basis, and the cash flows associated with the investment are grouped into yearly accounts.

In calculating net present values one can choose between two conventions:

• Nominal (currently prevailing) rates of discount and nominal cash flows. Under such a convention, the cash flows in more distant years are swollen by in-

flation; even in a situation of no growth in unit volumes, dollar volumes show growth at the rate of expected price inflation for the product. The rates of discount, in turn, can be regarded as the sum of some inflationless "real" rate of discount and a premium reflecting the expected rate of general price inflation.

• Real (inflation-adjusted) rates of discount and real (constant dollar) cash flows. Under such a convention, inflation is netted out of both cash flows and discount rates.

In most simple situations, either convention will yield the same qualitative results. In some cases, however, when particular cash flows can be expected to grow over time according to different rates of inflation, only the first convention (nominal discount rates and cash flows) is flexible enough to allow divergent inflation expectations. What one wants to avoid, of course, is the use of real, constant dollar cash flows and a nominal discount rate, because then future cash flows will be needlessly penalized.

The actual calculation of net present values is accomplished by evaluating the expression

$$\text{cash flow}_0 + \dfrac{\text{cashflow}_1}{1+r}+\dfrac{\text{cashflow}_2}{(1+r)^2}+\ \dots\ +\dfrac{\text{cashflow}_n}{(1+r)^n}$$

where the subscripts refer to the year (or period) of interest. This calculation can be done term by term (the only option when the cash flows are all dissimilar) or many terms at a time if a cash flow remains the same over a number of periods and can be factored out. Many calculators are programmed to calculate present values, and tables exist with (1) the present value of a dollar received in a certain period given such and such a discount rate and (2) the present value of a dollar received each period for so many periods at such and such a discount rate.

In investment decisions, if the calculated net present value is positive, the corporation can expect to increase its worth by undertaking the investment. If the net present value is negative, the investment should not be undertaken, at least on economic grounds. (There may be other factors to consider in making such a decision.)

TABLE 7-6   A comparison of cash flows (Kemper Games, Inc.)

YEAR	CASH OUTLAY (−) OR RECEIPT (+)	
	ON-SITE EXPANSION	LEASING
0	− $480,000	− $120,000
1	+ $ 59,520	+ $ 82,080
2	+ $238,080	
3	⋮	⋮
4	⋮	⋮
5	+ $238,080	+ $ 82,080

Using NPV to Assess the Build/Lease Choice at Kemper Games, Inc.

For simplicity's sake, let us pursue the Kemper Games situation by following the convention of using real, constant dollar cash flows and real rates of discount.

To build an on-site expansion of 24,000 square feet requires an initial outlay of $480,000. For this investment, the company expects a contribution four quarters out of

$$\$1.60 \text{ contribution/unit} \cdot 600 \text{ units/day}$$
$$\cdot 62 \text{ workdays/quarter}$$
$$= \$59,520 \text{ contribution/quarter}$$

and a stream of annual contributions after that of $238,080 (4 · $59,520) per year in real terms. Although different assumptions can be made about the relevant discount rate on the investment and the proper time horizon, we may want to use especially high rates of discount (in real terms) and a short time horizon because the games business is faddish and uncertain. Arbitrarily, then, let us select a real discount rate of 15 percent (very high) and a time horizon of only five years. The cash flows involved in this investment, excluding taxes from consideration, are shown in Table 7-6.

The net present value of this stream at 15 percent is $162,800. Kemper Games can thus expect to make money on this investment. But, we still must compare it with the leasing option

to see which would bring the higher expected increase in the company's worth.

Leasing 24,000 square feet of space at $6.50 per square foot per year comes to an annual expense of $156,000. This cost cuts into the $238,080 annual contribution, although leasing eliminates the plant expense of $360,000. The cash flows involved with leasing (again excluding taxes from the calculation) are also shown in Table 7-6.

The net present value of this stream of cost and contribution at a discount rate of 15 percent is $155,150. Because this figure is less than the $162,800 present value of the build on-site option, the economics say build rather than lease, although there is not much difference between the two.

Third Shift Operation Versus Building On Site

We can now turn to the economics of third shift operation versus building on site. Suppose forecast 1 prevails. A three-shift operation can meet the sales demand for the five quarters Kemper Games will need in order to determine whether forecast 1 or forecast 2 correctly gauges the market. Thus, for the first year and for the first quarter of the second year, there will be a stream of contribution from the units sold. There will also be a stream of inventory carrying charges (given as 10¢/unit/quarter) for the units actually produced. It is the sum of the net present values of these streams that we are interested in.

Note that because forecasted needs in excess of 900 units per day, which is the two-shift capacity, occur only in quarters 3, 4, and 5 of forecast 1, the contribution to be reaped from the third shift occurs only in those quarters. Nevertheless, because third shift production should begin in quarter 1 and last through quarter 5 before being dismantled, inventory

TABLE 7-7   Contribution and cash flows
(Kemper Games, Inc.)

| YEAR | CASH OUTLAY (−) OR RECEIPT (+) | | TOTAL |
	CONTRIBUTION	INVENTORY CARRYING CHARGES	
0	$0		
1	+ $63,240	− $29,760	+ $33,480
2	+ $25,296	− $22,630	+ $ 2,666
3	$0	− $ 7,965	− $ 7,965

will accumulate all through that period. Accumulated inventory must be financed and this is a charge to be considered. This reasoning suggests that both the second and third shifts should be discontinued in quarter 6 so that the excess inventory can be drawn down. This may well be an optimistic action, especially if demand continues at a somewhat higher rate than anticipated by forecast 1. More than likely, only the third shift would have to be discontinued, but for purposes of the calculation, let us stick strictly to forecast 1. We can summarize these flows of contribution and costs as shown in Table 7-7.

The net present value of this stream of cash flows at a 15 percent discount rate is $25,900. This figure confirms that even with the high inventories that are maintained under the option of instituting a third shift, the decision is a profitable one for Kemper Games. It is not hard to see that if forecast 1 prevails, building a plant just to get over the peak demands of quarters 3, 4 and 5 is not advisable. Contribution is raised from $1.36 to $1.60 per unit, but the volumes demanded are so low that total contribution, undiscounted, comes to barely over $100,000 and the total investment required is almost $500,000. Thus, if forecast 1 prevails, a third shift operation is preferred.

Suppose forecast 2 prevails, however. How different are the results? We already know that three shifts can provide only enough inventory to last through quarter 10 and that, with a lead

time of three quarters necessary for the build option, a decision on building a plant expansion can be delayed only until quarter 7. Since Kemper Games must build at some point if forecast 2 prevails, the question then can be rephrased as "If forecast 2 prevails, should Kemper Games build now or later?"

If the corporation builds now, it faces an immediate outlay of $480,000, contribution of $59,520 in quarter 4, and a stream of $238,080 per year in contribution thereafter, as we saw in Table 7-6. The net present value of this stream of cash flows is $162,800.

If the corporation builds later, say beginning in quarter 7, three shifts would be maintained through quarter 10 and inventory carried throughout that period. The extent of the required inventory buildup is already documented in Table 7-5, and the inventory carrying expense for any quarter is simply the quarter's cumulative inventory on a daily basis multiplied by 62 days per quarter and the 10¢/unit/quarter inventory charge. Table 7-8 develops the contribution attributable to sales from third shift operation in the first year, namely $12,648 in quarter 3 and $50,592 in quarter 4. Because demand remains constant at 1500 units per day in forecast 2, the $50,592 figure is maintained in all subsequent quarters. In summary form, these flows of contribution and cost, including the cash outlay for the plant expansion in year 2 and the resulting cash flow from it, are shown in Table 7-9.

TABLE 7-8   Contribution attributable to sales from third shift operation (Kemper Games, Inc.)

YEAR	QUARTER	CONTRIBUTION FROM UNITS SOLD FROM THIRD SHIFT	CUMULATIVE INVENTORY ON DAILY BASIS FOR QUARTER, FORECAST 1	INVENTORY CARRYING CHARGES ON THIRD SHIFT PRODUCTION
1	1	0	+705	$4371
	2	0	+1260	7812*
	3	$12,648†	+1515	9393
	4	50,592	+1320	8184
2	5	25,296	+1425	8835
	6	0	+975	6045
	7	0	+675	4185
	8	0	+575	3565
3	9	0	+475	2850
	10	0	+375	2325
	11	0	+275	1705
	12	0	+175	1085

*Calculated as (1260 cumulative inventory held per day of that quarter, from Table 12–5) · (62 days/quarter) · ($.10 inventory carrying charge per unit per quarter)
†Calculated as [(1050 − 900) = 150 units/day of third shift production sold] · (62 days/quarter) · ($1.36 contribution/unit)

TABLE 7-9   Contribution and cost flows from build later option
(Kemper Games, Inc.)

YEAR	CONTRIBUTION	CASH OUTLAY (−) OR RECEIPT (+) INVENTORY CARRYING COSTS AND INVESTMENT COST	TOTAL
0	$0		
1	+$ 63,240	−$ 29,760	+$ 33,480
2	+$202,368	−$500,646	−$298,278
3	+$220,224	−$ 3,069	+$217,155
4	+$238,080	$0	+$238,080
5	+$238.080	$0	+$238,080

The net present value of this stream of cash flows at a discount rate of 15 percent is $200,850. Because this figure is higher than the NPV for the build-now option, the economics argue for deferring the on-site expansion and filling the gap in the meantime with a third shift operation.

Under both forecasts, a strategy of using three shifts until at least quarter 10 is preferred. Not only is it feasible but the economics, under the assumptions made, are superior.

Are there any arguments for a build-now strategy? Although none of the noneconomic arguments may be strong enough to cause the abandonment of immediate three-shift operation, there are several reasons why on-site expansion may have to be undertaken sooner than quarter 7:

1. If Deluxe Bungle is introduced to the market, and if its sales parallel those of Bungle, Kemper Games may need considerably more capacity than three shifts could ever hope to provide.

2. The marketing department seriously underestimated Bungle's appeal, and there is no

assurance that its sales estimates now are correct. Of course, this is a difficult task, at best. If sales are understated again, however, Kemper Games could quickly fall short of capacity.

3. The economics advise establishing a third shift at the same time as a second shift is being established. The addition of so many new workers so quickly is bound to have a serious impact on productivity. The company's managers simply cannot be expected to train two new shifts of workers without considerable start-up difficulties and monumental exhaustion. The capacity plan should allow for the especially low productivity both the second and third shift can be expected to suffer for two or three quarters.

These three considerations ought to temper our enthusiasm for the third shift alternative. Although they may not deter the establishment of a third shift in the near term, they should keep us alert to the need for additional production space.

Lessons from Kemper Games, Inc.

It should be clear from this discussion that even a relatively simple capacity situation, such as that faced by Laura Kemper, can be surprisingly complex in its analysis. No wonder then that most corporations take months developing and reviewing capacity plan proposals!

As we have seen, there are some critical features to the typical capacity plan and its analysis: the forecast, gauging capacity, the transition to increased space, economic analysis with net present value, dealing with risk, and noneconomic considerations.

The Forecast

The driving force behind the typical capacity planning exercise is a forecast or group of forecasts of sales in the upcoming quarters and years.

In most companies, the forecast itself is not the particular responsibility of the production or operations managers, although they might have a hand in it. More often, the marketing department for a particular product or product line is charged with forecasting sales.

Forecasting the long term is frequently very uncertain, especially if the market is not well defined or the product is new or highly dependent on the fortunes of a hard-to-predict national economy. Over the years, forecasting techniques have become increasingly sophisticated, although one must admit that an entire arsenal of mathematical techniques may fall short of a single person's "gut feel" or refined intuition. (See the Chapter 4 discussion of forecasting.)

Gauging Capacity

As we found earlier in this text, production capacity can be very ambiguous, subject to a host of influences. Nevertheless, capacity planning requires some appraisal of present capacity and what can be done to increase capacity by a given amount.

The Transition to Increased Space

As Kemper Games' situation makes clear, it is one thing to recognize the need for increased space in the long term and quite another to manage the transition from the present to that long-term goal. Capacity increases often come in lumps, and in such circumstances managers must devise short-term policies to ease the operation into that capacity increase. At Kemper Games that meant a third shift but in other situations it may mean subcontracting, an inventory buildup, price adjustments to modify demand, overtime, line rebalancing, or something similar.

The nature of this transition, coupled with the needs of the forecast, often determines the timing of a capacity increase. As we saw in Kemper Games, the ability of a third shift to meet demands in the short run enabled the corporation to delay the construction of an on-site expansion until the sales pattern for the admittedly difficult-to-predict Bungle game was known with considerably more certainty.

Economic Analysis with NPV

Finding an economic justification for a particular capacity proposal is an important step in advancing that proposal through approval and implementation. Because capacity plans are almost always multiyear in outlook, the time value of money becomes an important consideration in any economic analysis of a project. With Kemper Games, the technique used to analyze the multiyear economics was net present value, sometimes called discounted cash flow.

The use of present value calculations is clearly superior to the simple, and still widely used, payback calculation. Payback is simply the breakeven computation of when a project's income exceeds the investment. Unfortunately, the payback calculation ignores (1) the time value of money (that is, the fact that income earned in later years is not equivalent, dollar for dollar, to income or expenditures incurred beforehand) and (2) the pattern of expenses and income over time. Thus, wherever the pattern of income and expenses becomes at all irregular, the payback calculation is apt to yield wacky results.

For more subtle reasons, net present value is also preferable to a sophisticated technique called *internal rate of return (IRR)*. The IRR method solves for a rate of discount that yields a net present value of precisely zero. As might be expected, for most purposes the NPV and IRR methods yield identical results, but there are some offbeat cases where the IRR method can lead to erroneous conclusions and where NPV is considered superior. Finance texts describe the particular cases where the two methods diverge; all that the operations manager has

to know is that the net present value technique will always yield a proper figure by which investment projects can be compared. That figure is the gain in the corporation's worth that is likely to result by undertaking the investment.

In any analysis of the economics of a project, assumptions have to be made. It is usually worth exploring how the economics vary under different assumptions. This kind of sensitivity analysis can be applied to (1) the time horizon of the project, (2) the cash flows expected in any year, and (3) the rate of discount to be applied to the cash flows. The sensitivity of a project's net present value to such factors is important because the risks involved with a project may be great; whether it should be chosen may rest on how "robust" its economic value is, given a host of different assumptions. Sensitivity analyses help to identify the projects that entail high risks as well as high returns.

Dealing with Risk

A corporation's capacity decisions are among the more uncertain it faces. While there is no sure-fire way to handle riskiness, it usually is helpful to know whether adding capacity is cheap or expensive and what penalties the corporation faces by having either too much or too little of it. If, for example, capacity is rather cheap to add and falling short of it would forgo substantial contribution, the corporation is probably better off to carry an excess. Many job shops and batch flow processes involve relatively little capital investment and considerable labor intensity. In such processes, it is often the case that some excess capacity can usefully be kept for peak periods of demand and left idle the rest of the time. Its use during the peak periods generates more than enough contribution to finance it for the remainder of the year.

Noneconomic Considerations

Although the economics of a capacity project are important, it is a narrow-minded manager who bases his or her decision solely on the economics. Three nonquantifiable (or at least difficult to quantify) factors deserve special mention:

1. *The impact of particular choices of capacity and facilities on existing operations.* The transition to enlarged capacity or to a new facility can be time-consuming and troublesome; it is seldom as smooth as either hoped for or planned. It often pays, however, to make some allowance for the impact of a new project on the existing operation. For example, in the Kemper Games situation, the introduction of the second and third shifts simultaneously is bound to involve an extra amount of chaos. How much is problematic, but its presence should be considered in the decision.

   The nature of these impacts on existing operations is varied. Frequently, a capacity or facilities change will alter the character and extent of materials handling and movement within the company. Marketing and/or sales may have to adjust to such a change as well. Often, too, the start-up of the new capacity saps engineering and management attention from the existing operation. Other impacts abound as well, many peculiar to the company or the investment itself.

2. *The competitive reaction of others in the industry to the capacity change.* Many capacity projects cannot be investigated in a vacuum, since their desirability rests in part on how competitors meet a company's particular decision on new capacity. This is particularly true of oligopolistic industries and those that are sensitive to transportation costs. How a competitor reacts may greatly affect the market in a geographic area or the market for a particular product line.

3. *Flexibility and new capacity.* In fast-paced industries, where new products, markets, and marketing approaches are routine, production must stay flexible. The choice of a capacity project in one form or another may hinder or help the company's ability to keep abreast of the latest developments. Flexibility is very difficult to quantify, but its importance to a firm's continued success can be immense.

Common Pitfalls in Dealing with Capacity

The capital appropriation request procedure as outlined at the beginning of this chapter has recently come under increasing attack.[2] The procedure is frequently seen as too rigid in practice and too narrow and confining in its outlook. How ironic it is that purchasing, which accounts for half of the cost of goods sold in many companies, and hiring, where lifetime decisions are often made, are management activities that are taken almost casually in many companies, whereas plant managers are often required to jump through hoops to justify capital expenditures for equipment that may be fairly inexpensive when compared with a worker's capitalized stream of earnings.

Some companies do tend to look at manufacturing choices involving large expenditures as isolated decisions, not as interrelated parts of an overarching manufacturing strategy (see Chapter 10 for a discussion of manufacturing strategy). This approach narrows the focus for many capital appropriations. This narrowed focus, coupled with the need for appropriation requests to win approval by the corporation's financial department, leads to several problems with these procedures:

1. Many corporate procedures for capital appropriations are typically used, or even intended, for the study of additional capacity,

not replacement capacity. As a result, what needs to be done to shore up existing operations and to keep them fully competitive is sometimes overlooked or not examined very critically.

2. The procedures too frequently stimulate a weak and/or narrow list of alternatives to be investigated. Although the stated corporate policy may be to promote fresh, even radical, ideas, in practice the options that are considered tend to be conservative and may even be specifically slanted to what the general manager thinks (or is believed to think by the group making the study).

3. Capital appropriation plans are typically excursions into uncertainty. Benefits from new plant, equipment, or process configurations—especially radical ones—tend to be more elusive to quantify than are costs. As a result, options that are safe (such as on-site expansions as opposed to new plants, known technologies rather than fledgling technologies) often have an inherent advantage, although they may be the worst choices for the company in the long run.

4. To get around the biases of narrowness and uncertainty, project teams that really believe in change often end up fudging their data. Games are then sometimes played between project teams and the corporate level managers who must decide on the appropriations. It is understandable then that capital appropriations that have to meet a certain hurdle rate (rate of discount) often end up with project proposals whose rates of return are just over those hurdle rates. Some companies deliberately set their hurdle rates high as a way to insist that new capital projects end up better than existing capital projects. Too often, however, setting these high rates simply stimulates more creative fudging of the data.

From my point of view, capital appropriation projects should be evaluated in the context of the company's formal manufacturing and competitive strategies. Thus, individual projects would be seen as involving interrelated pieces of manufacturing, capacity, and technology. The key question for the decision would be how the individual project fits with the manufacturing plan. This is not to say that the economics of net present value should be ignored. Rather, this point of view argues for all the right kinds of benefits to be included in the calculations. It also argues for the hurdle rates to be realistic and for post-audits of projects to be done so that project teams and top management can recognize the numbers problems that one can fall victim to in developing capital appropriation requests.

CAPACITY IN A SERVICE INDUSTRY

Most services are provided (1) on demand, (2) with interaction between the customer and someone who conveys, and often provides, the service, and (3) without any inventories to help smooth out the supply task. Under such circumstances it is not difficult to understand why capacity planning and choice are a critical element in the management of service industries. As background for a discussion of capacity management of services, consider Situation 7-2.

Discussion of Quaker City Squash

The situation Dick Murnane finds himself in illustrates many of the unique problems with which service firms have to wrestle, most of which are doggedly difficult to quantify.

The first-cut economics of this situation are actually quite straightforward. For each court, Quaker City Squash now receives $8 per half-hour or $16 per hour of use. There are five hours

SITUATION 7-2

QUAKER CITY SQUASH, INC.

So far it had seemed easy, but now Dick Murnane, president of Quaker City Squash, Inc., faced the first tough decision of his young business career: should he expand operations and, if so, how? For the past two years, Quaker City Squash, located in the business district of Philadelphia, had been selling half-hour blocks of time on its six squash courts to anyone willing to pay the $8 fee. Squash is a racquet sport generally played indoors by two people and is similar in style to handball. It had been enjoying growing popularity, especially at universities. Once out of college, however, players typically had to join downtown clubs to gain access to squash courts. The club fees were invariably high and covered more than just squash.

Sensing this latent demand, Dick (a former college varsity player himself) used some of an inheritance to purchase a building downtown and convert it into six air-conditioned squash courts, locker and shower rooms, several offices, and a bar and grill area where a bartender/short-order cook served drinks and a limited selection of sandwiches. Business boomed. Soon after opening, Dick extended the hours of operation so that now play began at 7 A.M. and continued to 10 P.M. every day but Sunday. Further, Dick hired a teaching pro who was now drawing a fine salary from teaching and from restringing squash racquets. The squash pro was regarded as a definite asset to the operation. Even the bar and grill was making money by doing a brisk luncheon and cocktail business.

From all Dick could tell, Quaker City Squash attracted mainly young (under 40) professionals who worked in Philadelphia's business district. Most had been introduced to squash while in college or in graduate school and were looking for a way to stay in shape. Over 90 percent of the clientele was male. The peak hours lasted from 11:30 A.M. to 2 P.M. and from 4:30 P.M. to 7 P.M.; it was rare when a court was open during those times. Average usage outside these hours ran about 50 percent. The same 50 percent usage prevailed all of Saturday as well. Standard practice was to reserve a court at least a day in advance, although no reservations except permanent ones (a year's worth of time at a particular hour and day of the week) were accepted for any more than a week in advance. There were no assigned or permanent lockers; players brought their clothes and racquets with them.

With business going so well, Dick naturally pondered the opening of another Quaker City Squash Center. Two different options presented themselves:

1. Open another center in the business district, much like the one currently in operation. A building suitable for the necessary remodeling was available in another portion of the downtown area. It could be purchased for $300,000 and the remodeling for six courts could be done for $275,000. Operating expenses (salaries, utilities, necessary maintenance, taxes) could be expected to run about $115,000 per year, the same rate as at the existing squash center. This new squash center would cater to the same market as the old one; but because it would be located in a different part of the business district, it would appeal to a different group of young professionals.

The available building was somewhat larger than the existing center, and that posed some special problems. Dick could add another court, but that would mean paring some space away from the locker rooms and the bar and grill. Or, Dick could expand the locker room space (some of the permanent reservation holders had been clamoring for their own lockers at the existing facility and would gladly pay for them) and/or expand the space of the bar and grill, making it fancier, perhaps adding a waiter, and permitting the kitchen to expand its limited menu in hopes of attracting more players after their games or of catering to a small band of squash "addicts" who might use the squash center as their own "club." The costs seemed roughly comparable; that is, $40,000 more would pay for either the additional court, or the expanded locker room ($10,000) and an expanded bar and grill (between $20,000 and $35,000 depending on decor and modifications to the kitchen).

2. Alternatively, Dick could open a squash center in one of Philadelphia's suburbs. Demand in the suburbs was more spread out and so only a smaller center, say three courts, could be supported at any one location. Building in the suburbs was likely to be considerably cheaper than remodeling a downtown building. For a suburb along the fashionable Main Line, construction estimates, including land, averaged about $200,000 for a three-court squash center. Operating expenses were also likely to be proportionately lower, the best estimate being $48,000 per year.

Much less predictable was suburban demand for the courts. Dick had no good feel for how strong any one of several trends would be and what each would mean for the operation:

- Would a suburban location shift demand to more women players than was true of downtown? Was that demand strong enough so that Quaker City Squash should offer nursery services?

- Would the peak demand period shift from lunch to, say, the early evening, as was true for many indoor tennis clubs?

- Would the time pattern of play support opening up later than 7 A.M. and extending play to 11 P.M. or even midnight?

- Three courts would not support a bar and grill, as in the downtown squash center, but Dick wondered whether some vending machines ought to be substituted.

- Three courts would not support a full-time teaching pro. Dick wondered whether a part-time pro would be necessary, say in the morning, teaching mainly women.

A further concern of Dick's, no matter which alternative was finally chosen, was how competition would affect all of his operations. Not only was there the threat of new squash centers opening up in either the business district or the suburbs, but there was also the threat of the downtown clubs introducing "squash only" privileges at special rates. Dick wondered whether adhering to the same strategy and being first in the market was sufficient, or whether he should try to "lock in" his clientele by offering memberships like the clubs.

of each weekday when all the courts are occupied; for the remaining 10 hours per day and for all of Saturday only half of the courts are occupied. These figures imply a weekly revenue of $5520 ($920 per court) and a yearly revenue of $287,040, assuming the same level of use as now exists. We can use this revenue figure together with the investment sum required ($575,000) and the expected operating costs of $115,000 per year to analyze the economics of another downtown location. The cash flows in real terms for that investment over, say, 10 years are shown in Table 7-10.

The net present value of the investment (10 years at a high real rate of interest of 15 percent) is a handsome $288,430. We can also calculate the average usage level that must be sustained if the investment is to have a net present value of at least zero. The annual revenues would have to be $229,570 per year to have an NPV of zero and this in turn implies an average usage rate of 51 percent. Any rate higher than that and the NPV turns positive.

In similar fashion, the economics of the suburban location can be calculated. The investment comes to $200,000 with expected annual operating costs of $48,000. If the revenue per court remains the same as downtown with five hours of peak play and 10 hours of 50 percent usage, weekly revenues will total $2760 and the yearly revenues will come to $143,520. The cash flow pattern is shown in Table 7-10.

TABLE 7-10   A comparison of cash flows (Quaker City Squash)

YEAR	NEW DOWNTOWN LOCATION		TOTAL	SUBURBAN LOCATION		TOTAL
	CASH OUTLAY (−)	RECEIPT (+)		CASH OUTLAY (−)	RECEIPT (+)	
0	− $575,000			− $200,000		
1	− $115,000	+ $287,040	+ $172,040	− $ 48,000	+ $143,520	+ $95,520
2	.	.	.	.	.	.
.	.	.	.	.	.	.
.	.	.	.	.	.	.
10	− $115,000	+ $287,040	+ $172,040	− $ 48,000	+ $143,520	+ $95,520

The net present value of this suburban investment (10 years at a real rate of interest of 15 percent) is $279,390, which is almost as high as for the new downtown location. In fact, shortening the time horizon or raising the discount rate makes the suburban location relatively more attractive. The economics, then, do not argue much in favor of one location over the other.

What must guide the decision are a number of other considerations, most of which are exceedingly difficult to quantify. They are what make the capacity decisions of service industries, in many cases, relatively more troublesome than those of manufacturing enterprises. Among these considerations are the mesh of marketing with operations, competitive reactions, demand modification, and nonspace capacity adjustments.[3] These four considerations can all shape thinking about the need for and the design of capacity in service industries. Although their economic impact is frequently difficult to assess, their importance to the success of any service firm's operation can be crucial. At the same time, deciding what should be done about each is quite a burden. As we shall see, the course Dick Murnane should follow with Quaker City Squash is far from evident.

The Mesh of Marketing and Operations in Planning Capacity

Should Quaker City Squash's courts be centrally located in the business district or should it decentralize its capacity? The juxtaposition of marketing and operations is critical in this regard. Is growth to be found in the suburbs? Which is more convenient: squash near home or squash near work? How much a part of the game is camaraderie, and is camaraderie more likely to flourish at a downtown location? Will significant numbers of women be attracted to the game if courts are situated in the suburbs?

Because capacity is often the "product" in a service business, or at least intimately linked to the service provided, knowledge of why a customer purchases the service is a critical item in the plan for the design of new capacity. This is something Dick Murnane must ponder; the answers are by no means obvious.

Related to the issue of increasing the right kind of capacity is the concern about whether new capacity will undercut the service provided by already existing capacity. At Quaker City Squash, will a new downtown location divert players away from the existing downtown site, or will players refrain from downtown play during the day to play at the suburban location in the evening? To answer these questions, one needs knowledge of the customers, where they come from, and why.

Another aspect of the close marketing/operations bond in a service firm's capacity planning is the need to keep balance in the mix of elements which make up that capacity. For example, at Quaker City Squash there is the opportunity to build a seventh court, although at the expense of the locker rooms and grill. Alternatively, a private locker room could be installed and the bar and grill expanded.

If one assumes that the new court will attract use just like any of the other courts, the economics are much more likely to support a squash court than to support private lockers or added space in the grill room. What must be questioned is whether a new court, coupled with smaller locker and grill room space, would actually add enough revenue to warrant its construction. It is conceivable that usage would adjust itself not to the number of courts provided but rather to the locker room and/or grill room space. In that case, adding a seventh court would be a disastrous move since total patronage would actually fall.

Competitive Reactions

We have already discussed the importance of gauging competitive reaction for capacity planning in manufacturing companies. Because capacity decisions (how much, of what type, and where) are so critical to a service firm's competitive stance, the reactions of competitors are usually even more significant in service industries. At Quaker City Squash, for instance, competitive reactions may take the form of other squash centers being opened in downtown Philadelphia or they may be policy changes at some of the existing clubs (say, the inauguration of separate squash memberships for special fees). In any event, competition can quickly change the earnings potential of all of Quaker City Squash's operations.

Modifying Demand

When a bottleneck is reached in the provision of a service (for example, during the noon hour at Quaker City Squash), often that bottleneck can be relieved, at least temporarily, by manipulating demand in various ways through pricing policies and service policies.

Pricing can be used as both carrot and stick to shift the extent and the timing of demand. High prices can shut off demand or shift it into other time periods. Low prices can stimulate demand. Whether a price cut will actually lead to more revenue as well as greater patronage depends on how sensitive the demand by patrons is to price changes. If changes of X percent lead to changes in the quantity demanded of more than X percent, the demand is said to be *price elastic* and revenues can be increased by cutting price. If an X percent change in price leads to a less than X percent change in the quantity demanded, the demand is termed *price inelastic* and revenues can actually be increased by raising price. Ascertaining whether demand is in fact price elastic or price inelastic is often hit or miss, however, and it is usually under pressure—severe lack of capacity or embarrassingly excess capacity—that prices are altered significantly.

The extension of existing services and/or the provision of ancillary or complementary services can also have a substantial impact on demand. In terms of the Quaker City Squash situation, the teaching pro, the bar and grill, the private lockers, nursery care, the reservation system, and other extras may all have important implications for demand. One or more of them may be instrumental in attracting demand or in shifting demand from peak times to off-peak times. The reservation system is clearly a tool to apportion demand among peak and off-peak periods, and the timing of the teaching pro and nursery services could also have a bearing on broadening demand away from the peak periods.

Adjusting Capacity without Altering Space Requirements

At Quaker City Squash, space means capacity, but there are a variety of other service indus-

SITUATION 7-3

TIGHE PRINTING COMPANY

"Maybe sometimes you can be too successful," Ruth Tighe mused to herself. The Tighe Printing Company, of which Ruth was president, had enjoyed substantial growth. Ruth was increasingly concerned, however, that continued sales increases simply could not be accommodated without increased space.

The Tighe Printing Company specialized in high volume printing of magazines, catalogs, and business forms. The regional sales of magazines like *Newsweek* and *McCall's* were run on Tighe presses and constituted the bulk of company sales. Timeliness, as could be expected, was essential to the company's success. The company was located in downtown New Haven, Connecticut, in a six-story structure built in 1923. Founded by Ruth's grandfather 10 years before then, Tighe Printing was the building's first tenant. The company bought the structure in 1935.

As the company grew after World War II and thus required more space, it started displacing other tenants. By the late 1960s, the company had taken over the entire building, all 75,000 square feet (11,500 square feet on each of the six floors and 6000 square feet in the basement). In 1972, again pressured by space needs, the company leased 15,000 square feet in the building next door and knocked out a wall in between. Now even this space was fully utilized.

Ruth Tighe was convinced that she would have to decide soon how she was going to structure the company's growth. The possibility of starting afresh with either a new branch facility or a relocation was appealing, albeit more expensive. Ruth would have to weigh these relative benefits and costs.

Ruth Tighe confronted a choice from among three alternatives:

1. *Continued expansion in the neighborhood.* A building two doors down from Tighe Printing and on the other side of the street was up for either sale or long-term lease. The building was four stories high with a basement, occupying 55,000 square feet. A likely rent would be $2.25 per square foot per year. The asking price for the building was $700,000.

2. *Establishment of a branch plant.* Rather than keep all its production space close together, Tighe Printing could locate a satellite plant elsewhere in the city or in the suburbs. This new branch could house a new press or two and could concentrate on a certain type of printing.

3. *Relocation of the entire operation.* Rather than break up existing operations into two distinct locales or continue a more or less haphazard expansion around the company's main building, Tighe Printing could sell its old holdings and equipment and move the entire operation in one piece to larger quarters, purchasing new equipment in the process. Exclusive of new machine purchases, a move itself was likely to cost $200,000.

Newly constructed space for either a branch or a move would cost $18 per square foot or more, depending on location. Rents for suitable, existing space could vary from $2.20 per square foot per year to $3.50 per square foot per year. The higher values would secure space in newer, one-story structures.

As Tighe Printing was now, operations there left much to be desired. In particular, the movement of goods and information was worsening. The growth of the enterprise through all seven levels of the main building separated departments that logically should have been placed side by side. Work-in-process had to be handled almost twice as often as necessary, and, besides being time-consuming, led to more routing errors than Ruth Tighe, at least, felt should be the case. Intrafactory transportation was slow, limited to a single elevator. Because there were only two loading docks, the delivery of paper and other raw materials was often held up to give priority to shipments out of the building. Deliveries often had to be taken at odd hours. In addition, more and more materials and output were being stored outside the plant, sometimes expensively.

The constraints of the building also meant that many of the latest innovations in the printing industry such as phototypesetting and the faster and larger electronic web presses had to be forgone. Furthermore, space constraints made it impossible to reap the advantages of running machines close to one another in tandem and sorting entire magazines or forms on the spot—advantages in terms of production scheduling, production control, and workforce assignments.

tries in which capacity can be increased modestly by employing several techniques:

- Using part-time workers for peak times.
- Increasing efficiency via methods improvements, labor specialization, labor cross-training, and the like.
- Inducing consumers to provide some of the service themselves (e.g., salad bars at restaurants).
- Sharing equipment or other resources with firms or organizations in the same or a related industry.

ON-SITE EXPANSION, BRANCH ESTABLISHMENT, AND RELOCATION

Once a company's managers agree that new capacity ought to be erected to satisfy expected future demand, they still face deciding how that new capacity ought to be implemented. Should on-site expansion, the opening of a new plant, or the relocation of an existing one prevail? This decision lies at the heart of Situation 7-3.

Discussion of Tighe Printing Company

Growth is forcing the Tighe Printing Company to seek more production space, and Ruth Tighe has to choose from among three means of adding that space: expanding locally, placing some operations in a new branch, and relocating to a larger facility. Of these options, expanding locally is the lowest cost one, at least in terms of initial dollar outlay. A building of 55,000 square feet can be purchased for $700,000 or leased for about $125,000 a year. That much space in new construction would cost about $1 million or more to build and over $200,000 a year to lease. Relocating would cost an additional $200,000.

Although a local expansion may be inexpensive in the short run, it may be frightfully expensive in the long run, especially if it locks Tighe Printing to outmoded technology, high materials handling costs, and other detriments to an effective operation. There are indications in the situation that some of this is occurring already. What then are the relative advantages of on-site expansion, new branch establishment, and plant relocation?

The Relative Advantages of On-Site Expansion

On-site expansion is by far the most popular way of adding production space. Its low cost (often no new land acquisition costs), the relatively short time lag associated with it, and its status as a "known quantity" make it appealing. By expanding on-site a company is assured of keeping its labor force intact and it does not have the difficult task of weeding out products or pieces of the production process for isolation in another plant.

Often, too, on-site expansion is viewed as a way to achieve the benefits of economies of scale. This is an elusive concept, however, and it merits some discussion of its own.

∗ ASIDE ∗

Economies of Scale[4]

It is frequently stated that large companies enjoy a competitive edge over small companies because of the inherent advantages of economies of scale. The phrase has a strong appeal, and large companies with sizable plants have a certain aura about them. General Electric or IBM is no stranger to the observation that

TABLE 7-11   Defining the differences in unit costs

PLANT	CAPACITY	VOLUME PRODUCED	PROCESS TECHNOLOGY	MANUFACTURING COSTS PER UNIT PRODUCED
A	100— Difference	100— Difference	Type X	$1/unit
B	100 in capacity;	40— only in	Type X	Higher than
	same	volume		$1/unit
	volume to			
	capacity			
C	200— ratio	200	Type X—	Lower than
			Difference	$1/unit
			only in	
			process	
			technology	
D	200	200	Type Y—	Much lower
				than $1/unit

its continued cost competitiveness is the result of its size. The phrase draws nods of recognition, yet few people can define it and fewer still have thought critically about it.

All too often you hear a company president nonchalantly say something like, "If we increase the size of our operations in this plant, we'll naturally enjoy some economies of scale." There is nothing natural about economies of scale and certainly nothing to be nonchalant about.

Confusion with the term is understandable because it serves as an umbrella for a number of real but quite distinct concepts. Because it is an umbrella term, *economies of scale* often loses its usefulness in making management decisions on plant size.

Volume, Capacity, and Process Technology

How do economies of scale relate to plant size? The standard definition declares that economies of scale are reaped whenever higher output volumes lead to lower unit costs. However, the definition only seems to be clear.

Consider four different plants, all in the same industry. Plants A and B are physically identical in every respect. They differ only in that Plant B produces just a fraction of the volume of Plant A, perhaps because Company A's marketing efforts are much more effective than Company B's. Plant C is similar to Plant A in layout and equipment but is twice the size. Plant D, on the other hand, incorporates an entirely different

process technology from the other three and can produce twice what Plant A can produce.

I draw these examples to distinguish among the concepts of volume, capacity, and process technology. As Table 7-11 shows, Plants A and B share the same capacity and the same process technology, although their actual volumes differ. Plants A and C share the same process technology, although not the same capacity; Plants C and D share the same capacity but not the same process technology.

These concepts of volume, capacity, and process technology are important because they all relate to economies of scale. We will discuss these three specific types of economies.

Economies of Volume

The higher volume Plant A will enjoy lower unit costs than Plant B because it can spread its fixed costs (overhead, capital costs, machine setup costs) over a greater number of units. If by *scale* we mean *volume,* then the difference in unit costs between Plants A and B can be an economy of scale.

For some people, however, this "spreading of fixed costs" seems too trite an example to be labeled a "scale economy," and so they dismiss it. These people then modify the definition of a scale economy to exclude economies that are really *economies of volume.*

Economies of Capacity

As the table shows, Plant C's unit costs are lower than Plant A's and thus much lower than Plant B's. Plant

C's increased capacity permits it to carry proportionately less raw materials inventory. This may be due to the familiar "economic order quantity" result that optimal inventories need increase only as the square root of volume and not proportionately with volume.

On the other hand, because Plants A and C share the same technology, Plant C is not likely to enjoy a proportionately lower work-in-process inventory, but its finished goods inventories may well be proportionately lower. For example, suppose Plants A and C both make two different products. If Plant A has only one production line that it must change over from one product to the other, it will have to build up proportionately more finished goods inventory to cover its demand than Plant C, which can afford to manufacture each product on a separate, dedicated line. Plant A needs to carry enough of an inventory of its first product to tide itself over while it makes its second product. Plant C need not worry about this problem.

In addition to these inventory-associated economies, Plant C will have an advantage over the smaller Plant A, as its increased capacity allows the luxury of more spare equipment and maintenance capabilities or of additional and useful overhead functions. If scale means "capacity," then any differences in unit costs between Plants A and C can be appropriately called economies of scale.

Economies of Process Technology

As we can see, Plant C enjoys some cost advantages over Plant A. However, Plant D enjoys even lower costs—for two major reasons: capital-for-labor substitution and labor specialization. Plant D has automated more (substituted more capital for labor) than Plant C. Using more, better, and different equipment, Plant D has been able to produce as much as Plant C, but it employs fewer workers. As a result, its costs are lower. The increased automation at Plant D may or may not be an advance in the state of technology, but the increase in capital certainly alters the process in Plant D as compared with Plant C. Moreover, often a company cannot make small additions to its plant's stock of equipment and space; large additions (frequently termed "indivisibilities") have to be made and are perhaps the classic explanation for economies of scale. Such indivisibilities are usually substantial alterations to a plant's process technology and so are

more than just scale changes. They are changes in process technology, and should be recognized and managed as such.

One particular substitution of capital for labor merits special mention. The geometry of processes that deal with free-flowing materials (chemicals, molten metals) often permits output to vary according to the volume of its capital equipment, while the costs (construction and/or operating costs) vary according to surface area. This is the frequently quoted "6/10 rule," which argues for large-process technologies. The rule is so named because it was found that for chemical plants a doubling of volume leads to only a 6/10 increase in surface area and thus costs. An oil refinery is one such example. Output depends greatly on the sizes of tanks and pipes, but construction and maintenance costs depend more on surface area of the material that surrounds the oil held inside. For most other (non-free-flowing materials) operations, however, such cost advantages are much less significant.

Plant D also has lower unit costs because it has altered its process technology to specialize its labor for particular tasks. In order to make its process more continuous, jobs are "deskilled." That is, instead of large numbers of highly skilled workers each doing a number of operations to form the product, the process is organized to link together less skilled workers doing a small number of specific operations. The time and responsibility any one worker devotes to a particular product is reduced in an effort to increase productivity through repetition and specialized competence. The pace of the production process shifts from worker discretion to management option. The car assembly line is a classic example of labor specialization and management (that is, mechanical) pacing.

To reiterate, both capital-for-labor substitution and labor specialization alter process technologies. Thus, if by scale we mean "process technology," then we can appropriately call these two means of cost reduction "economies of scale."

Avoiding Ambiguity

As pointed out in the preceding paragraphs, the term "economies of scale" suffers from irredeemable ambiguity. It can take a variety of meanings depending on one's interpretation of "scale" as volume, capacity, or process technology. Even then, there are a variety of ways to effect the economies. Instead of inviting confusion by using the term "economies of scale," people should think of volume, capacity, and process technology separately.

Plant Size Decisions over Time

The plant size decision depends on the careful balancing of a number of alternative technologies, costs, and risks. Over time, these alternatives become more and more blurred. Technological advance is unpredictable, and it is not clear whether new capital equipment with smaller or with larger break-even volumes will predominate. Lots of new technology is sophisti-cated, expensive, and large scale; and yet microcomputers and some machine tools are persuasive examples of some small-scale technological change.

In sum, "economies of scale" is vague enough to provide easy justification for any number of decisions on plant capacity. Because it is so vague, its usefulness to managers is minimal. Instead, two areas should be carefully scrutinized: (1) the cost reductions a company can achieve through specific changes in a plant's volume, capacity, or process technology and (2) what those changes mean for management control, logistics, inventories, and the ability to respond to product or process innovations.

✱

Return to the Issues at Tighe Printing

These cautions about economies of scale notwithstanding, on-site expansion sports some very attractive features. Nevertheless, it is not an all-purpose remedy for production space shortages and there are a host of circumstances where either a new branch or a relocation would be preferred.

The Disadvantages of On-Site Expansion: Building the Case for Branching and Relocation

Although frequently attractive, on-site plant expansion can usher in a host of diseconomies as well, particularly if on-site expansion has been a repeated practice. For example, as more and more production space is added on-site, the layout of the plant typically becomes less and less optimal. Rarely is an entire plant reconfigured during an expansion; rather, only portions of the plant get shifted around. The result, over time, is that departments, once close together, become separated. Materials handling and storage become more difficult, with more chances for delay or error. Managers find themselves isolated from one another and/or from the work groups they are supposed to oversee. In short, intraplant transportation and communication become strained and this strain is likely to have detrimental consequences for product delivery and quality.

Staying at the same site often postpones the introduction of new process technology as well. Old equipment is kept in use, old methods are followed, and the advantages of new equipment and techniques are forgone, with consequences for both future costs and product innovation.

Continued on-site expansion means that more and more workers and, often, more and more products, must be managed. Such a layering of expanded responsibilities creates real complexities for managers at all levels. The existing cadre of managers may be asked to supervise more than they are readily capable of, thus lessening the attention certain problems should receive. With more products and output from the same plant, decisions on the levels, composition, and uses of inventories are likely to become more difficult and prone to error. Decisions on production control—what and when to produce, how to sequence it through the factory—are likely to become vastly more complex as well. As more and more products are added to the factory, the cost accounting system is likely to become more arbitrary and thus less helpful.

With more products in the plant, management runs the risk not only of complicating

TABLE 7-12 Advantages of branches and relocations to on-site expansion

PROBLEM AREA	NEW BRANCH PLANT	PLANT RELOCATION
Plant layout and materials handling	Radical improvements possible with operations placed in branch; some possibilities of improving base plant as operations are placed in branch	Radical improvements possible
New process technology	New technology for branch possible; likely that base plant will keep much of old technology	Scrapping of old plant, equipment, and methods possible; new technology can supplant it readily
Production and/or inventory control	Can mean radical change to production control procedures and policies in new plant, though not much change to be expected for old plant; inventories can build up by adding branch	Can mean radical changes to production and inventory control; inventory levels not likely to be affected
Managerial impact	Additional managers needed to open and run branch; staff demands increased to coordinate plant interactions	Old set of managers can generally run new plant without stretching themselves too thin
Product proliferation	Can easily manage new products, especially if branch plants are organized as product plants	New products less easily managed
Size of workforce	Keeps workforce levels at all plants under desired ceilings	Little or no effect on workforce size
Financial burdens	Extra overhead demanded to cover more than one location, new plant start-up expenses	Moving costs, new plant start-up expenses
Ease of meeting future growth	Relatively easy; geographic growth met best with new market area plants, product introductions with product plants, and vertical integration with process plants	Not easy; shares many future capacity problems with on-site expansion alternative

supervision, inventory, and production control systems and the like, but also of placing incompatible demands on managers, workers, and systems. For example, products produced in low volumes, but with special performance features, demand a different mode of management, worker effort, and control systems than products produced in high volumes with few special features. If both are manufactured in the same facility with common management, workforce, and operating policies and systems, the likely result is that both products will suffer in the individual dimensions (price, performance, delivery) that make a product competitive.

Besides this incompatibility problem, the addition of more workers to an existing site is apt to require the increasing formalization of the workforce-management relationship. The workforce is less apt to identify strongly with the company, and labor relations within the plant may become strained. Old management concessions to the workforce may come back to haunt operations. With increasing size, the plant is more likely to become a target for unionization, if it is not already organized.

For these reasons, continued on-site expansion becomes less and less desirable. The alternatives—the establishment of a new branch plant and plant relocation—can avoid many of these long-term and frequently subtle pitfalls of on-site expansion, although their abilities to surmount certain of these pitfalls differ. Table 7-12 outlines some of the relative advantages of new branches and relocations.

New branch establishment, for example, is at a relative advantage if the plant's problems run more to product proliferation, workforce size, or meeting expected future growth. By branching, a company can avoid overloading one plant with either too many products or too many workers. At the same time, the new branch can exploit the latest production technology and the most sensible plant design. The operating policies and systems of the branch can also be meshed carefully with the product(s) chosen for manufacture and with the competitive priorities attached to them.

Plant relocation, on the other hand, is at a relative advantage if the plant's problems are more involved with plant layout, materials handling and storage, new process technology, production and inventory control, and lack of management depth. Relocation, by definition, means closing one facility and opening another at roughly the same time, which means that relocation can readily scrap old capital, technology, and policies for new. Thus, relocation gains in standing when the plant's problems are less related to large size and more to process technology and control.

Return to Tighe Printing Company

From the description of Tighe Printing's problems, it would seem that relocation is best able to remedy them. The company's present site and building are contributing to poor materials and information flow, excessive outside warehousing, and delayed introduction of production process improvements. The time appears appropriate to abandon the company's history of incremental expansion on site in favor of the more radical approach of relocation. New branch establishment appears to be a less attractive solution since some economies are possible by running nearby machines in tandem. Production scheduling seems to be facilitated by bunching the printing presses at the same site.

Tighe Printing has not performed any quantitative study of the likely opportunity costs of maintaining the existing plant in the face of what the company could do at another location. Some such study would be warranted. However, the implications of the qualitative aspects of the situation, which have already been discussed, are unlikely to be reversed, as the study may show.

SITUATION 7-4

TIGHE PRINTING COMPANY (REPRISE)

After considerable thought, Ruth Tighe decided to relocate her growing printing company. Only by abandoning the old six-story structure the company had grown up in, she reasoned, could the company keep abreast of the latest technological changes that were making over the printing industry. New and sufficient single-story space appeared to be the answer. What remained to decide was where the space ought to be located.

After some preliminary scouting by the company's vice-president for operations, four options presented themselves (excluding, of course, the ever-present option of continuing to search for

sites). A summary of site-related costs is included in Table 7-13.

1. Long Wharf Industrial Park in New Haven. Tighe Printing could maintain its home in New Haven by moving less than a mile to some vacant land in the nearly complete Long Wharf Industrial Park. Only one parcel of land of suitable size was left, a five-acre site. Assuming single-story construction, having only five acres would restrict the plant space to 110,000 square feet. (Property covenants in the park restricted plant size to no more than half the area of the site.) Nevertheless,

TABLE 7-13   Site-related costs for plant relocation (Tighe Printing Company)

COST ITEM	SITES			
	LONG WHARF	EAST HAVEN	HAMDEN	NEW HAMPSHIRE
Land price per acre	$70,000/acre (for 5 acres)	$18,000/acre (for 10 acres)	$12,500/acre (for 12 acres)	$6,000/acre (for 12 acres)
Estimated cost of building plus land	$2.8 million (110,000 square feet to be built)	$2.1 million (Asking price for 140,000 square feet)	$2.3 million (110,000 square feet to be built)	$1.9 million (110,000 square feet to be built)
Estimated remodeling costs		$.3 million		
Labor costs		Essentially invariant across sites		
Transportation costs		Essentially invariant across sites		
State income tax	9.1%	9.1%	9.1%	0%
Local property tax (% of real value)	4.0%	3.5%	3.2%	3.3%
Insurance per year— fire, etc. (now $10,000/year)	$15,000	$15,000	$17,000	$21,500

the site provided free parking for Tighe's 220 employees and the certainty that none of the plant's workers would leave as a result of the move. Long Wharf was served as well by bus as was the company's old plant. Construction was likely to take 15 to 18 months.

2. Relocate to an existing plant site in East Haven. In East Haven, about four miles east of the old factory, Tighe Printing could move into a factory building that had been vacated six months before by a machine tool manufacturer. Some renovation was going to be necessary, estimated at $300,000. The company could move in within five months. The plant housed 140,000 square feet on 10 acres of land. Thus, although the plant was more than large enough for the company's needs now, there was also the possibility of expanding on site in the future.

The plant was not served by bus, but parking was ample. Ruth Tighe would have to think about alternative means (company bus, car pools) by which all of the plant's present workers could get to work. Ruth expected that some workers might not want to commute across the Quinnipiac River Bridge to East Haven. The area, however, was as densely populated as most neighborhoods in New Haven itself, and reports indicated that labor availability in the area was excellent.

3. Relocate to available land in Hamden. Another site was available about 11 miles north of the old factory in Hamden. A 12-acre site was available there in the Hamden Industrial Park, with all utilities provided. Construction would take between 12 and 15 months, it was estimated. Bus service was available to the plant, but it was very sporadic, coming only every 60 minutes. Parking would be no problem, and the proximity to two expressways in the area would shorten commuting for at least some workers. There was surely a number, say 15 to 25 percent, who would not relocate with the company.

4. Relocate to a 12-acre site near Manchester, New Hampshire. Because most of Tighe Printing's business involved magazine or business forms and catalog contracts with national concerns, and because the transportation involved was the U.S. mail, the company was not necessarily tied to a location within the New Haven metropolitan area. Of course, the company would lose some of its local clients, but with the continuing growth of southern New Hampshire, there was apt to be enough new business to pick up whatever slack existed.

New Hampshire was alluring for two reasons: (1) New Hampshire levied lower taxes—no income tax and comparable property and other taxes, and (2) New Hampshire was closer to

Ruth Tighe's ski lodge and summer home in Vermont.

Picking up stakes and moving so far from New Haven would not be without cost, however. Few of the plant's workers could be expected to move to New Hampshire; some of the plant's managers might also jump ship. Labor was available in southern New Hampshire, but the recent word that Ruth Tighe had heard was that labor was becoming increasingly tight, especially for skilled positions. There certainly were not going to be any labor cost savings.

Moving would not be easy for Ruth Tighe herself or for her family. Her husband, an accoun-tant, could find a new job in New Hampshire fairly easily, but a move could be more disrupt-ing to her two teenaged daughters.

Moving to New Hampshire would probably cost an additional $75,000 over the local move estimate of $200,000. Construction time for the plant was estimated at between 12 and 15 months.

Ruth Tighe wondered which of these four sites, if any, she ought to choose. Net sales in the present year were about $12.7 million and net income be-fore taxes stood at about $675,000. Tighe Printing's present site was valued at roughly $1 million.

Discussion of Tighe Printing Company (Reprise)

The economics of this location decision are very similar to the economics of the Kemper Games situation. The time horizon is long, and varying cash flows will be associated with the different years of each of the alternatives. Table 7-14 por-trays some cost flows and their illustrative net present values. A time horizon of 20 years is assumed as well as a discount rate of 15 percent. Note that the cost flows represent marginal changes. That is, only costs that differ across locations are included in the calculation. The present values of the cost streams, then, are useful only to compare with one another. A more thorough inclusion of costs and expected revenues could have been done; in that case, the present values could be compared not only with one another but with zero as well, giving some indication of the worth of the investment as well as the relative desirability of each site.

Table 7-14 reveals that New Hampshire would be the lowest cost site by quite a bit, over $800,000 of present value. Ruth Tighe must ask herself whether the abandonment of the com-pany's present workforce and market area would be less costly over the long pull than this site-specific cost advantage. For sure, developing a new workforce and searching out at least some

TABLE 7-14   Cost flows and net present values (in millions of dollars) (Tighe Printing Company)

SITE	INITIAL INVESTMENT			YEARLY EXPENSES THAT DIFFER ACROSS SITES		INSURANCE	PRESENT VALUE OF COST STREAMS*
	LAND	BUILDING	OTHER	INCOME TAX	PROPERTY TAX		
Long Wharf	$.350	$2.8	0	$0.061	$0.126	$0.015	$4.414
East Haven	$.180	$2.1	$0.3†	$0.061	$0.090	$0.015	$3.619
Hamden	$.150	$2.3	0	$0.061	$0.078	$0.017	$3.426
New Hampshire	$.072	$1.9	$ .075‡	0	$0.065	$0.0215	$2.588

*Present value calculations assume real cash flows, a real discount rate of 15 perent, and a time horizon of 20 years
†Represents the cost of renovating the available East Haven building
‡Represents the incremental cost of moving to New Hampshire. All relocations will cost at least $200,000 but the one to New Hampshire will cost $275,000.

new sales contracts will cost the company something. For example, a training cost of $4000 per employee for each of the company's 200 plus job positions would itself wipe out the cost advantage of the New Hampshire site.

Because Tighe Printing has been thriving in New Haven, there are no strong pressures to cut costs, and there is every incentive to keep the company's workforce and customer base intact. There is not much to choose between the East Haven and Hamden sites. Both are measurably cheaper than the Long Wharf site and would retain most of the company's employees. The Hamden site offers potentially more space for expansion, but the East Haven site could be available 7 to 10 months earlier. It probably would be better to move earlier rather than later, but either Hamden or East Haven would be well worth the investment. The Long Wharf site should probably be avoided. Not only is it expensive, but its possibilities for expansion are modest at best, and building on the site would take even longer than building in Hamden.

Tighe Printing Company's situation is representative of many companies, as will be discussed in the next section.

The Nature of Location Decisions[5]

Plant relocations are overwhelmingly made by small, growing plants (often independent of particular suppliers, markets, or labor sources) that are pressed for more production space. They move to larger, modern quarters and in the process alter their production technology, sometimes in fundamental ways. The vast majority of relocations are over short distances (less than 20 miles), which help to ensure labor force continuity and the retention of customer and supplier contacts. To a lesser degree, relocations also occur to consolidate two or more plants into a single new facility, and to escape from high site costs (wages, land values, taxes). As one might expect, however, it is the plant whose profits are hurting the most that sees relocation chiefly as a means to lower costs. These plants are also the ones who are most likely to move further than 20 miles in search of these lower costs.

Plant relocations are trauma-filled experiences for many managers and so are apt to be avoided if at all possible. Only about a third of the relocations seriously contemplated are actually carried through; actual relocations occur at a rate of only 3 percent per year for manufacturing establishments of all sizes, and less than 1 percent per year for plants of at least 100 employees.

More common, especially within larger companies, is the establishment of new branch plants. Each year, on average between 3 and 6 percent of the existing stock of plants is added as new branch plants; of branches contemplated, more than two-thirds are actually established, double the rate of relocations.

New branches start out small—only 40 percent, on the average, of the size of their sister plants—and are simply organized. They are less apt to be unionized and more likely to enjoy simple logistics. While likely to be located in modern facilities with the latest technology, they are also frequently dependent on the corporate services provided by the plant or plants from which they were spun off. The products they make are commonly mature ones, technically well established, with few engineering changes necessary, although for a quarter to a third of new branches the products and/or technology is brand new.

Multiplant Manufacturing Strategies[6]

Analysis of new branch plants and of the base plants from which they typically spring reveals that the new branch plant fits into a prescribed place in a multiplant company's scheme of things. Four general types of multiplant manufacturing strategies seem to prevail in the operating division of large companies. Behind each one are some compelling cost or managerial reasons.

The Product Plant Strategy. Perhaps the most popular strategy is the product plant strategy where distinct products or product lines are manufactured in separate plants, each plant serving the company's entire domestic market area.

The product plant strategy permits each plant to concentrate on a limited set of products, generally within a well-defined market niche. This concentration has the advantage of permitting the plant management to select the process technology, equipment, labor force, manufacturing policies, and organization that are consistent with the particular competitive priorities (cost, performance, product flexibility, speed of delivery) associated with the plant's products. In this way, the company can avoid much of the complexity and congestion that plague many oversize, multipurpose factories. In addition, if there are any economies of scale to be reaped, a product plant strategy can take advantage of them. Product plants can also take advantage of any raw materials or worker expertise that are specific to particular geographic areas.

A product plant strategy is likely to correspond to a decentralized manufacturing organization with a relatively small staff at the corporate level. Plant locations may be far-flung, but more often they are clustered within one or two broad regions of the country. Within such a strategy, a significant challenge to management lies in recognizing when a plant has become too large. What constitutes "too large" varies from industry to industry, technology to technology, and company to company; but the most frequently quoted figures lie between 500 and 1000 employees, with few companies stating figures in excess of 2000.

Companies in many industries can divide operations according to a product plant strategy because the products manufactured are many and varied. About 60 percent of the Fortune 500 companies follow a product plant strategy. For smaller companies, the product plant strategy is even more prevalent.

The Market Area Plant Strategy. Under this strategy, plants are designated to serve particular subnational market areas. The plants themselves manufacture all or most of the corporation's product line. The market area plant is perhaps the classic notion of the branch plant. When freight costs are important because of high product weight or volume relative to value, it makes sense to spread plants apart geographically. This is all the more true if products are consumed over wide areas, and if the market requires a quick response by manufacturing.

A market area plant strategy is likely to require more corporate coordination than the product plant strategy. The corporate staff is likely to be larger and to carry considerable clout. By the same token, plant managers are less likely to be able to act autonomously. A different management challenge confronts the market area plant—namely the sequencing and regional authority of new plants. For instance, should an East Coast company's second plant be in the Midwest, West, or South, and how should the market be split between plants? If the second plant is placed in the West, where and when should a third plant be sited?

The national breweries are classic examples of market area plants, as are many glass, can, paper converting, food, and building products companies. All involve products consumed in quantity everywhere and subject to significant transport costs as a fraction of product value.

About 30 percent of the Fortune 500 companies follow a market area plant strategy.

The Process Plant Strategy. Rather than separate their products into individual plants, some companies, notably those with complex products, separate their production process into various plants. These plants are often viewed as feeders to one or more final assembly plants. A process plant strategy is less prevalent than the others, occurring in less than 10 percent of Fortune 500 companies, for example.

Like the product plant, the process plant exists to simplify an inherently complex and confusing managerial situation. For complex products like automobiles, large machine tools, and computer systems, a number of plants become involved in making components of the completed product. The manufacturer typically faces a rash of make-or-buy choices for many of these components, but to be able to produce one or another of these components competitively may require different raw materials, labor skills, control systems, or management skills and organization. This difficulty, coupled with the already discussed diseconomies introduced by large size, argues for a division of the complete manufacturing process into stages, with separate plants for each stage. For any one stage, however, there may be economies of scale. Diverse manufacturing requirements explain why some plants may be located in the South or the Far East (for lower labor costs), or in resource- or expertise-rich areas (such as "Silicon Valley" in California), or merely in a separate location, to provide surrounding plants with a special service that would be uneconomic for them to provide for themselves. This stage-by-stage division may lead to many feeder plants shipping to one or more assembly plants, or to one or a few feeder plants (for a critical component, say) shipping to many other manufacturing plants.

In any event, the concept of plant separation to simplify operations persists.

The process plant strategy is even more demanding of high-level corporate coordination than the market area plant strategy. The process plant strategy is generally accompanied by a manufacturing organization that is highly centralized, technically well versed, and responsible for the control and coordination of materials and product between plants. For this reason, process plants are often located within an easy commuting distance of one another.

The General-Purpose Plant Strategy. Some companies do not establish specific plant charters. Rather, plants are prized for their flexibility in adapting to constantly changing product needs. Defense contractors, among others, are typical companies following a general-purpose plant strategy.

The general-purpose plant strategy demands a considerable degree of centralized control. Coordination of plants is a real management challenge, as is the smooth staging of transitions in plant use and in employee assignment.

Site Selection

Once a multiplant manufacturing strategy has been decided on and plant size picked, site selection follows. The multiplant strategy frequently can say a lot about the choice of region. For example, clustering of plants in a particular region of the country is most apt to occur under the process or general purpose plant strategies and is least likely under the market area strategy. The choice of where within a region to locate, however, is sometimes very straightforward and sometimes baffling.

Many people, including some location consultants, try to simplify the decision making by introducing elaborate rating schemes that quantify everything imaginable about a particular location. Much of this is false rigor. There are, of course, a number of costs that can usefully be estimated—among them expected labor costs, construction, rental, or remodeling costs; taxes and other government payments; transportation cost savings or penalties for both inputs and finished goods; expenditures for needed services such as energy, pollution control, roads, sewerage, water, and parking; insurance costs; moving costs; and expected plant start-up inefficiencies or time delays due to start-up or to governmental approvals. Often one or just a few of these costs are so important that they can control the entire site selection process. The six controlling considerations that occur most often (in about two-thirds of the cases involving major manufacturers) are labor costs, avoiding labor unionization, proximity to markets, proximity to suppliers or resources, proximity to another company plant, and quality of life (variously defined) in the area. Although costs such as these may be important to evaluate, (and linear programming can help assess the impact of transportation costs), they do not tell the complete story and sometimes they do not differ enough to ground a location choice strictly on their merits. A company should not expect any quantitative analysis to isolate a single area or site that stands alone as clearly optimal. Rather, a company should expect that a number of sites will show more or less the same cost structure.

Often the next phase of site selection is an exploration of the intangible and qualitative features of a location that could be expected to contribute to the company's competitive success. Although these factors may be difficult or even impossible to quantify, they are no less real; companies should resist the temptation of letting hard numbers drive out reasoned but qualitative analysis. The intangibles can be of many varieties: risks associated with any of the quantitatively evaluated costs or the sales potential of the site; the area's prevailing "business climate" (which means different things to different people but mainly long-term competitiveness); educational and training strengths of the area; attitudes of the workforce toward productivity, change, and unionization; the aesthetic and cultural attributes of the area (important aspects for attracting and holding managers); the cooperation of the local and state government for resolving public service or other public matters faced by industry; the commuting distances of workers and managers; and the impact of other, perhaps competitive, industries in the area. Frequently, a careful point-by-point comparison of these difficult-to-quantify factors against the real demands a particular product, area, or process will make on the manufacturing function can argue decisively for a particular site. A site need not rate high on all factors, but it should rate high on those that truly make a difference for the plant's competitiveness.

The company should be prepared as well for location analyses that, at the end, do not favor one site over another. If careful analysis reveals no preferable option, a company should not feel guilty that a seemingly inconsequential item tips the scale toward one site. After all, in such a case the company stands to gain or lose little by the location choice itself.

Plant Closings

An inescapable and always unpleasant fact of corporate life is the plant closing. It is one of the most difficult decisions that operation managers face. Closings can be forced on companies in a number of ways, but the most common are poor production technologies, layouts, and materials handling; lack of sales volume; and competitive pressure on price. Many plant closings cannot be avoided, but some may be put off by careful attention to the roles the plant can play at various stages in its corporate life (start-up, maturity, decline). Planning for the plant's various roles well ahead of time can save much anguish.[7]

QUESTIONS

1. Why is Kemper Games described as being in a joyous predicament? What are some of the tactics Kemper explores for getting out of its predicament? How might Kemper's experience be generalized for other companies' benefit?

2. Define and discuss the following concepts:
   a. net present value
   b. discount rate
   c. the effect of changes in the discount rate and the time horizon on the present value calculation
   d. the difference between real and nominal rates

   How do these concepts fit into Kemper's procedure for deciding whether to build or to lease?

3. What role does long-term forecasting play in the capacity plan and its analysis?

4. Summarize and discuss the six main lessons that can be learned from Kemper Games' dilemma.

5. For service industries, what are the main factors involved in decisions about capacity?

6. The term *economies of scale* covers a multitude of concepts. What are some of the more important concepts? How do they relate, if at all, to issues of capacity and expansion?

7. Review three of the relative advantages of branches and relocations vis-a-vis on-site expansion.

8. "Maybe sometimes you can be too successful," comments Ruth Tighe about the progress of her printing company. Are there times when this can be true for a company? In considering the four distinct options, does Tighe look at all aspects of the decision? Support your answer.

9. Summarize and discuss the importance of the various multiplant strategies mentioned in this chapter.

PROBLEMS

1. Hal operates an automotive repair shop. He has the opportunity to purchase another auto repair shop across town. This shop has been generating about $60,000 in annual profit after taxes and he feels, with the new demand and better management, he can increase this to $68,000 or $70,000. The present owner is asking $210,000 for the business. To help him decide whether this would be a profitable purchase for him, Hal has made the following estimates:

Life of the business	20 years
Internal cost of capital	10% real rate
Extra annual expenses Hal foresees	$20,000 for another manager's salary

Analyze Hal's problem and make a recommendation.

2. The Calway Cab Company currently operates a fleet of 27 cabs in a medium-size Midwestern town. The firm is considering expanding the fleet. They feel that each

additional cab will generate less clear profit annually than the last additional cab. They have estimated that the twenty-eighth cab will generate $4000 per year and that each additional cab will generate 5 percent less than the previous one. Each cab has a purchase value of $11,000 and a trade-in value of $5000 at the end of two years. The company has an internal cost of capital of 15 percent. Ignoring taxes, how many new cabs would you recommend that they purchase?

3. Emil Gaines owns and operates Consolidated Salvage yards. Emil has a scrap compressor that does not have the capacity to maintain the level of production required. In deciding whether to buy a new compressor, Emil has compiled the following data:

Depreciated value of old compressor	$17,000
Market value of old compressor	$ 1,000
Price of new compressor	$65,000
Installation costs	$ 4,000
Economic life	10 years
Salvage value	$ 1,000
Required rate of return	12%
Estimated annual cost savings	$13,000

Ignoring taxes, answer the following questions:

a. Should Emil purchase the new compressor?

b. What is his actual rate of return?

4. The Carl Bodkin Electronics firm manufactures an assortment of consumer electronics, including C.B. radios. The firm has a standardization program and they have standardized 95 percent of their control knobs. Each of these knobs costs 39¢ when bought at an annual volume of 808,000. The firm's managers have completed a make-or-buy analysis and feel they can make the knobs at a cost savings of 13¢ each. They are currently analyzing two different potential processes:

	Process A	Process B
Installed cost	$35,000	$45,000
Annual operating cost	$ 9,000	$ 6,000
Economic life	4 years	5 years

Ignoring taxes, what is your recommendation and why?

5. Discuss the appropriate management level that should gather information and make the decision regarding the three "brick and mortar" choices for adding capacity presented in the chapter.

6. Discuss the length of the review and planning procedures for various industries. Do those who use longer planning periods have better forecasting methods?

7. What kinds of alternatives should a planning group consider for meeting shortfalls?

SITUATION FOR STUDY 7-1
CENTRAL LOUISIANA OIL—HANKS C WELL

The Hanks C well had been shut in for 45 days. This gas well in central Louisiana was leased to Central Louisiana Oil. This well was old and the gas pressure in it had declined significantly over the years. At present the pressure was too low to lift the water that was also in the well and so the gas could not be recovered by conventional means. Under the terms of the lease,

TABLE 7-15   Expected cash flows (Central Louisiana Oil—Hanks C Well)

OPTION	INVESTMENT NOW		CASH FLOW DIFFERENCES FROM BASE CASE		YEAR 3
			YEAR 1	YEAR 2	
Small diameter tubing	$43,000	(costs)	Base case	–	–
		(sales)	Base case	–	–
Gas lift	$33,000	(costs)	$44,000	$44,000	$46,000
		(sales)	$150,000	$80,000	$60,000
Beam pumping unit	$74,000	(costs)	$44,000	$45,000	$47,000
		(sales)	$150,000	$80,000	$60,000*
		(salvage)	–	–	$49,000

*This option will generate higher sales than projected here.

Charlie Clotfelter, the production manager for the field where the Hanks C well was, had only 15 more days to get the well going again. If time ran out before production could be resumed, Central Louisiana Oil's rights to the lease would terminate and the owners of the land and its mineral rights could negotiate with another production company.

Before the well had been shut in, Clotfelter had tried all of the conventional means of increasing gas pressure to no avail. He was now faced with three major options involving larger capital expenditures:

1. Smaller diameter tubing could be dropped down the well's shaft, causing the gas to travel faster up the tubing and thus probably to lift the slug of water. Such a scheme would cost $43,000 and could be expected to work, but perhaps not for long. Eventually the pressure in the well would decrease even more and the smaller diameter tubing would not be able to lift the water.

2. Natural gas could be forced into the well between the existing tubing and the outer casing of the well shaft. This gas would join with the natural gas from the well to create enough pressure to lift the slug of water. This operation promised to keep production going longer than that with the smaller tubing and it cost only $33,000. To ensure that operations would start up within the next 15 days, a right-of-way to a compressor unit on a neighboring lease would be needed immediately, but the two leases were not clear about whether this right-of-way could be obtained easily. Clotfelter was hopeful that it could be, but he was not certain.

3. A beam pumping unit could be installed on the well. The pump would lift the water out of the well and thus free the well to produce its natural gas. This operation would cost $74,000 in capital expenses, some of which could be salvaged after, say, three more years of well operation. This option also had the potential for generating more gas than either of the other options. Whether, in fact, it could produce more gas depended on what kinds of geologic structures were below ground.

The expected cash flows over the next three years are given in Table 7-15. Charlie Clotfelter wondered what actions he should take to resume the operation of the Hanks C well.

SITUATION FOR STUDY 7-2
MIDWEST BRANDS, FAST FOOD

Joel Huber had recently joined the corporate staff of the Fast Food Division of Midwest Brands. The company operated about 300 restaurants in the Midwest. Rather than standardize these restaurants, management had allowed about 30 different sizes and layouts to develop over the years. Joel's immediate concern was with a restaurant where the local management wanted to add 40 seats without expanding the kitchen. The dining area currently seated 112, and the restaurant was doing a booming business during lunch and dinner peak hours.

Management at this division had been rather lax. Little systematic data was kept on the operation and use of the restaurants, and there were no guidelines on the steps to take in expanding a restaurant's seating capacity. It was Joel's job to study this request for expansion, using some systematic analysis. He wondered, first, how the decision ought to be structured and, second, what data he ought to collect to analyze it properly.

CASE FOR STUDY
JUNG PRODUCTS, INC.

It was September 1973 and Bob Conway, president of Jung Products, had recently been informed that Hamilton County intended to condemn and raze his company's downtown Cincinnati factory to construct a new courthouse and jail.* In the course of company planning, Bob had considered the advisability of a new location for his company's manufacturing facilities, but with this action by the county, relocation would be unavoidable. Rather than feeling relieved, however, at having Hamilton County make the relocation decision for him, Bob realized that he was beginning to face a

series of decisions about where, when, and how to relocate his growing business.

A Brief Company History

Jung Products was founded in 1917 by George H. Jung, Jr., who pioneered the use of elastic knit fabric for an arch brace and later (1930) for an ankle brace. Under the brand name "Futuro" (1936), Jung became a leading manufacturer of elastic supports of all kinds, selling to the public through drug and shoe stores, and also producing private label goods (pads, athletic sup-

---

*Hamilton County's right of eminent domain enabled it to condemn Jung Products' present site. Once its present site was condemned, Jung Products would be paid a fair market value for it as determined by independent appraisals of the property, subject to appeal if Jung Products felt the appraised value was too low. The county would also pay the costs of moving up to 50 miles away from downtown Cincinnati.

porters) for the major sporting goods houses. After a hiatus during World War II caused by the shortage of rubber, the company resumed its growth, gradually adding products such as elastic stockings and consolidating its leadership of over-the-counter sales of elastic health supports.

In 1948, George Jung, Jr., died, and management of the company was assumed by the former advertising manager, H. M. Stuckenberg. Bob Conway had married into the Jung family; he joined the company in 1958. When Mr. Stuckenberg retired in 1962, Bob was able to succeed him.

Under Conway, Jung Products continued to expand its health supports (Futuro) and sporting goods (Grid) product lines at the rate of one or two products a year. In 1969, building on its strength in drugstore distribution, the company introduced an entire line of convalescent products (canes, crutches, bedpans, wheelchairs), which it sold through drugstores under the Futuro Patient-Aids brand name.

Even as Jung Products was broadening its product offerings, it began to integrate backward by acquiring or establishing three companies:

- Rampon Products, Inc., of Asheboro, North Carolina. Rampon was a manufacturer of elastic knitted products and fabric, which Jung Products acquired in 1965. Besides supplying Jung Products with elastic knit fabric, Rampon also produced men's support hose and women's support stockings and pantyhose. About 40 percent of Rampon's dollar output was currently supplied to Jung Products' Cincinnati operations.
- J.R.A. Industries of Asheboro, North Carolina. J.R.A. was established in 1969 as a further step backward in process integration. J.R.A., situated next door to Rampon, manufactured the elastic "thread" used in knit-

ting elastic products. About 20 percent of J.R.A.'s production was used as raw material by Rampon.
- Theradyne Corporation of Jordan, Minnesota (near Minneapolis). In September 1973, Jung Products had only recently acquired the Theradyne Corporation, a leading manufacturer of wheelchairs and related products. Theradyne would continue to market its products under its own brand name in addition to supplying items for the Patient-Aids product line.

The Market for Jung Products

Jung marketed about 130 products in a wide assortment of styles and sizes. This total could be broken down into the three product lines roughly as follows: 30 products in the elastic Health Supports line, 75 products in the Patient-Aids line, and 25 products in the Grid (private label sporting goods) line. (Table 7-16 traces sales over the past 10 years.)

Other than its sales to the major sporting goods companies (Wilson, Rawlings, Spalding, and MacGregor), Jung Products sold almost exclusively through drugstores. About 70 percent of its sales went through drug wholesalers and about 30 percent through drugstore chains. Jung was the dominant company in over-the-counter sales of elastic health supports and convalescent products in the drugstore. Jung's sales were international. Sales were broken down by region as follows:

3%	Cincinnati metropolitan area
8%	elsewhere in the Ohio-Kentucky-Indiana region
20%	elsewhere in the Midwest
59%	nationally, other than in the Midwest
10%	international

Bob Conway could cite a number of reasons for Jung's success. The company took pride in its ability to supply its wholesale customers quickly

TABLE 7-16 History of gross sales (Cincinnati operations only of Jung Products, Inc.)

YEAR	HEALTH SUPPORT AND GRID	PATIENT-AIDS	TOTAL
1963	$ 5.12*		$ 5.12*
	11.6%†		11.6%†
1964	5.71		5.71
	12.3		12.3
1965	6.41		6.41
	15.4		15.4
1966	7.41		7.41
	6.2		6.2
1967	7.87		7.87
	19.2		19.2
1968	9.38		9.38
	8.8		26.8
1969	10.22	$1.68*	11.89
	17.4	49.2%†	21.9
1970	11.99	2.50	14.49
	3.0	61.2	13.0
1971	12.35	4.03	16.38
	17.5	46.1	24.5
1972	14.50	5.90	20.40

*In millions.
†Annual growth rate.

and dependably. Such service meant that the wholesalers could provide same-day delivery to their retail accounts without having to keep excessive inventories. Jung's products were also among the most sophisticated and innovative on the market. Many company resources were devoted to advancing product designs. Jung had been innovative in merchandising as well. In the 1950s the company had been the first to introduce a health supports "department" to the drugstore. Jung enjoyed broad distribution through drug wholesalers, most of whom featured Futuro products, and the company's sales force made regular calls on retailers nationwide. Jung was not, however, the low-price producer, but the market was not too price sensitive.

The Production Process in Cincinnati

Jung's downtown Cincinnati operations consisted of two adjacent buildings, one of six stories and the other of two stories. Except for some packing and some hosiery production, all man-ufacturing was done in the larger structure. This factory produced about 60 of the company's 130 products; others were either made by Jung's subsidiaries or subcontracted. The Cincinnati operation produced 20 of 30 items in the Health Supports product line, 25 of 75 items in the Patient-Aids product line, and 15 of 25 items in the Grid product line. Considering the variety of styles and sizes, the factory was responsible for a huge assortment of products. However, the production process was not complex.

The products manufactured in the Cincinnati factory could be classified into two groups: brown goods and white goods. Brown goods generally comprised those items that were worn on exposed areas (knees, elbows, ankles—as braces; most of the Health Supports line and some of the Patient-Aids line were brown goods. White goods generally consisted of items that were worn under clothing as supporters; all of the Grid line and some of each of the other two product lines were white goods.

The production of these classes of products differed because only brown goods contained latex, which required special treatment. All production was in batches, generally of 200 items each, a convenient number for handling the materials. Brown goods production started with assembly of raw materials, which in most cases, was simply the woven or knit elastic fabric generally supplied by Rampon Products. The fabric was then cut according to various patterns. To secure the severed latex in the cut fabric, the edges of the fabric were painted with liquid latex and then placed on racks to dry. Drying was rapid, and the batch of latexed fabric was then put into movable bins (laundry carts) and delivered to the people who sewed fabric pieces into the designated shape. General-purpose industrial sewing machines were used for this task. For many products, only one workstation of sewing was required; others demanded several workstations. After the material had been sewn, the seams were pressed using special machines. Sometimes trimming was also required. The then finished goods were packed into boxes and dispatched to the warehouse. The warehouse was an important operation because most orders from drug wholesalers and drugstore chains called for a mix of products delivered within a matter of days. Products had to be sorted carefully, and all orders filled had to be tracked reliably.

White goods manufacture was very similar to that of brown goods except that the latex application and materials pressing steps were unnecessary. Despite this simplification, white goods fabrication was in general more complicated (i.e., more operations were done on each item) and thus demanded more cutting and sewing time.

In 1973, Jung Products employed approximately 200 people at its Cincinnati location. This largely female labor force was drawn from all over the Cincinnati metropolitan area, in-cluding northern Kentucky, and did not reside primarily in any one portion of that area. Labor turnover in the plant stood at about 10 percent a year, which was low for the garment industry; many workers had been with the company for years. Absenteeism was also low, averaging about 6 or 7 percent. All the plant's workers were represented by the Amalgamated Clothing Workers Union. Management relations with the union were well established, cordial, and constructive.

Jung Products filled its orders from a finished goods inventory of all its products. In general, the company liked to have two to four weeks of expected sales on hand as inventory. Because sales were somewhat seasonal, the actual volume of desired inventory fluctuated during the year. Production was geared to replenish this inventory.

On average, materials accounted for 60 percent of a product's sales price and labor accounted for 15 percent. Jung Products drew its supplies from many sources. By value:

10% from the Cincinnati metropolitan area
15% from elsewhere in the Ohio-Kentucky-Indiana region
20% from elsewhere in the Midwest
50% from national sources outside the Midwest, principally the South (Rampon Products) but also from cities like New York and Philadelphia
 5% from international sources

About 1.1 percent of net sales was spent on freight charges for incoming raw materials and about 3.6 percent on freight charges for outgoing finished goods.

Company History Related to Relocation

Since World War II, Jung Products had owned* and occupied at least a portion of the six-story building at 312 East Court Street in downtown

---

*Ownership of the building was legally by Ione Corp., a Jung family real estate holding company that was a subsidiary of Jung Products.

Cincinnati. As sales and operations expanded, the company took over more and more space within the building until, by 1960, all six floors were devoted exclusively to Jung Products. As growth continued and as the Patient-Aids product line was being introduced, the company, in 1968, acquired an adjacent two-story structure (311 Central Parkway), which until 1970 served mainly as Jung Products' offices and as its sole warehouse and shipping department.

At that time, space requirements forced the company to seek additional warehouse space. None was available in the downtown area and, instead, Jung bought 10,000 square feet at Colerain and Alabama Avenues, about five miles from the Court Street plant. Into this warehouse was moved the packing, finished goods storage, and shipping for the Patient-Aids product line. The need for even more warehouse space the next year, 1971, forced the company to lease 10,000 square feet at Colerain and Alfred Avenues, a half mile or so from the Colerain and Alabama warehouse. The storage and shipping of the Grid product line was transferred to this location. By September 1973, then, Jung Products occupied a factory and three warehouses, each warehouse handling and shipping a different product line. What made each situation even more uncomfortable was the overlap of customers; all the customers who purchased Patient-Aids products also purchased Health Supports products. Too often a customer who had placed a single order would receive two shipments the same day, one from each warehouse, and have to pay freight on both. Jung Products' growth was creating some major logistics problems.

For Carmine Dell'Aira, the vice-president of operations, dealing with the growth of the company was a high-priority concern. Carmine had joined Jung Products in 1970, shortly after the Colerain and Alabama warehouse became operational. He soon realized that the company's growth plans implied almost a doubling of space requirements from about 80,000 square feet to about 150,000 square feet from 1970 through 1975. Because of the division of warehousing activities, Carmine's chief concern was the smooth handling of customer orders. And as the Colerain and Alabama facility was soon to be overtaxed, he did not relish the prospect of four warehousing operations for one factory.

Carmine's initial thinking was to establish eventually a distribution center large enough to handle orders for all Jung's product lines. The more he thought about the distribution center, however, the more convinced he became about the good sense of relocating all of the company's operations. Carmine's conviction was beginning to command Bob Conway's attention more and more. As Carmine saw it, a relocation would permit Jung to:

1. Obtain more space in both the factory and the warehouse, and thus allow for needed additional buffer inventories of finished goods.

2. Expedite order handling by combining all warehousing activities, erecting new double-decker gravity flow racks in the warehouse, and using new trucks and carts to move merchandise. Real productivity gains in warehousing could be realized.

3. Improve materials handling and shorten cycle times in the factory by transferring operations from six separate floors tied together by one slow elevator to only one or two floors.

4. Enlarge raw materials orders to take advantage of possible volume discounts.

5. Provide space for the manufacture of new products. One candidate operation for a new plant was the assembly of aluminum parts for walkers and other items in the convalescent product line, which would permit Theradyne to concentrate on its special competence with chrome-plated steel.

6. Provide space for the future growth of Jung Products.

The notion of leaving the central business district was, for personal reasons, particularly tough for Bob Conway. Bob's family had been long-time residents of Cincinnati, and Bob was deeply involved in civic affairs.

The new facility, wherever it was located, would be owned outright by Ione, Jung Products' real estate holding company subsidiary. If Ione was not to incur high taxes on the capital appreciation of the Court Street site, the capital gain had to be applied to the purchase of new quarters. For this reason, leasing space was not a real alternative for Jung Products. Jung would probably seek industrial revenue bond financing from whichever town was chosen.*

Decisions to Be Made

Forced now by Hamilton County to relocate Jung Products, Bob Conway began considering the choices he had concerning (1) when the company should move, (2) where it should move, and (3) how he ought to organize the company to make the move.

Timing Options

Even though the county had formally announced its intention to condemn Jung's present site, the company was not required to move for several years. Would it benefit Jung to be among the first industries in the area to relocate, or would it be better to wait until other companies had relocated and had perhaps smoothed the way administratively for the county's handling of the matter? Carmine Dell'Aira's memos on space requirements advised that Jung Products would

run short of space by 1975 if nothing was done and if growth proceeded according to plan. Given the county's decision and assuming the validity of Dell'Aira's project space requirements, Bob Conway believed that the company should be settled in its new facility by the end of 1974. Of course, if sales did not meet forecasts, relocation by 1975 would not be needed. More importantly, Jung Products had the distinct options of operating for a time in somewhat cramped quarters or of opening another branch operation. What did not appear to be a possibility was second-shift operation. Because of local industry practice and the limited availability of trained workers and supervisors, second-shift operation was judged not practical.

How much time that left Conway now in September 1973 was problematic. If he decided to build a new plant, construction was likely to take at least a year. If he decided to move into an existing structure, the move could be made in a matter of months, depending on how much remodeling was required. Thus, the longer Bob delayed the decision, the fewer the choices of location and the greater the risk of compounding operations problems in the factory and the warehouse.

Local Options

Carmine Dell'Aira, working with some industrial realtors in Cincinnati, had done some preliminary investigation of suitable sites. All prices for space to be constructed were based on an arbitrary 100,000 square feet, even though Carmine knew that if Jung Products built on its new site, it would build much more than 100,000 square feet. Dell'Aira's work put four distinct options before Bob Conway, in addition to the option of spending more time and effort to search for additional sites. The options

*An industrial revenue bond is a local municipal bond floated, at a rate substantially lower than corporate issues due to its tax-exempt standing, to pay off the debt incurred by the town in developing a site and in building a plant for a particular manufacturer. The manufacturer then pays off the bond's principal, interest, and servicing costs through its lease rental payments to the town. Up to 100 percent of a project's costs can be financed in this way.

TABLE 7-17   Comparison of four sites Jung Products, Inc.

ITEM	QUEENSGATE II	MARIEMONT	FLORENCE, KY.	ASHEBORO, N.C.
Build or buy?	Build	Buy	Build	Build
Plant space used to base estimated prices on	100,000 sq. ft. on 7 acres	215,000 sq. ft. on 6¾ acres	100,000 sq. ft. on 14 acres	100,000 sq. ft. on 17 acres (owned by subsid.)
Land price per acre	$65,000	(in quoted price)	$9,500	$4,000
Total estimated or quoted for land and building	$1.5M	$1.2M	$1.35M	$1.2M
Remodeling needed	—	$.75M	—	—
Highway access	Excellent	Fair	Good	Fair
Served by public transit?	Yes	Yes	Yes, but very poorly	No
Taxes				
Real property (% of actual value)	1.71%	2.65%	1.2%	3.065%
Inventory (% of actual value)	2.3%	2.65%	1.2%	3.065%
Local income tax	2%	0.5%	0%	0%
State income tax	8%	8%	5.8%	6%
Tax holiday (on property taxes)	No	No	First 10 years	No
Labor costs relative to Cincinnati area	—	—	—	Same
Suspected labor availability	Excellent	Good	Fair	Fair to good
Materials freight savings relative to Cincinnati area	—	—	—	$18,000/yr.
Finished goods freight costs relative to Cincinnati area	—	—	—	Unknown
Insurance	$12,500/yr.	$12,500/yr.	$20,000/yr.	$20,000/yr.
Possibility of industrial revenue bonds for financing	Probable	Certain	Certain	Certain
Expansion possible?	Possible but rules somewhat restrictive; city demanded immediate and full development of all land purchased	Only modest, once building fully occupied	Substantial	Substantial

Dell'Aira had discarded were sites and structures that were the wrong size or layout or that would clearly cost Jung Products more than he knew Karl Davis, the company's financial vice president, would be willing to pay.

1. The Queensgate II Industrial Park, on the site of the old Crosley Field in downtown Cincinnati, about a mile and a half from the Court Street plant. At this time, the city of Cincinnati was developing a new industrial park in the west central portion of the city. Jung Products could build a facility in that park.

2. The former American Standard plumbing fixture factory in Mariemont, Ohio, a well-established suburb about eight miles east of downtown Cincinnati. This building was part of an older and fully developed industrial park and lay just beyond the Keebler cookie factory. Although still structurally sound, the building was in horrendous condition—the floors oozed oil and many repairs were needed. The building had been vacant for over a year and this suggested that the owners might accept a lower bid for it.

3. The Northern Kentucky Industrial Park in Florence, about 18 miles to the south and west of downtown Cincinnati, on the fringe of the metropolitan area. Space for construction was available in this large and growing industrial park.

4. Asheboro, North Carolina, near Greensboro. The opportunity to move from the old location also presented Bob Conway the opportunity to move onto the property of his subsidiary suppliers in North Carolina. The moving costs would, of course, be higher if this site were chosen since the county would reimburse Jung Products for only the first 50 miles of the move, but Jung would benefit from decreased raw materials freight costs and the opportunity to mold Jung's operations more closely to Rampon and J.R.A. Industries.

Aspects of these four sites are compared in Table 7-17.

Actually Moving the Company

Apart from deciding when and where Jung Products should relocate, Bob Conway was concerned that the actual move be made smoothly. Among the issues he felt needed resolving were:

- What management committees should be formed?
- When and how should the union and the workers be informed of the move?
- What management-labor committees should be formed?
- How should operations be staged in the move to ensure unbroken service to Jung Products' customers?

Although these issues were subordinate to the actual relocation decision, Bob felt that they needed to be addressed quickly so that a coordinated plan for the move could be implemented.

REFERENCE NOTES

1. For an extended description of the decision-making mechanism for capacity expansion or contraction, see Joseph L. Bower, *Managing the Resource Allocation Process* (Homewood, Ill.: Richard D. Irwin, 1972).

2. See, for example, Robert H. Hayes and William J. Abernathy, "Managing Our Way to Economic Decline," *Harvard Business Review* 58, no. 4 (July-August 1980), pp. 67–77, and Robert L. Banks and Steven C. Wheelwright, "Operations vs. Strategy: Trading Tomorrow for Today," *Harvard Business Review* 57, no. 3 (May-June 1979), pp. 112–20.

3. These considerations regarding capacity expansions are discussed in Earl Sasser, "Matching Supply and Demand in Service Industries," *Harvard Business Review* 54, no. 6 (November-December 1976), pp. 133–40.

4. This section on economies of scale is adapted from an article of mine entitled "Before You Build a Big Factory," *Harvard Business Review* 54, no. 4 (July-August 1976), pp. 100–104.

5. Many of the statistics cited here on location are derived from Roger W. Schmenner, *Making Business Location Decisions*, Englewood-Cliffs, N.J.: Prentice-Hall, 1982.

6. Another useful reference on multiplant manufacturing is F. M. Scherer et al., *The Economics of Multiplant Operation* (Cambridge, Mass.: Harvard University Press, 1975).

7. See Roger W. Schmenner, "Every Factory Has a Life Cycle," *Harvard Business Review* 61, no. 2 (March-April 1983): 121–29.

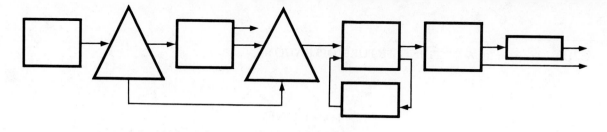

DEALING WITH TECHNOLOGICAL CHANGE

The management of technological change may well be the least-developed aspect of operations management. Companies of wildly different philosophies and organizations have been successful innovators. No one model of technology management has so far been recognized as head and shoulders above the others. And yet everyone realizes that technological advance is critical to a country's continued economic growth. By one estimate, technological innovation was responsible for 45 percent of U.S. economic growth between 1929 and 1969.[1] In addition, high technology companies grow quickly in both sales and employment.

This chapter introduces some of the ideas that people have put forward as important to successful innovation and some of the issues that continue to be debated.

What is technological change? There is debate even on this. Are new products evidence of technological change? How about minor modifications to existing ones? Do new machines constitute technological change? How about bigger (or smaller) revisions of existing ones? We can readily recognize new, far-reaching process technology changes (such as Henry Ford's moving assembly line, computer process controls in papermaking), but what about small alterations in an existing process that are more on the scale of line

rebalancing? Merely trying to answer these questions can give us some feel for the debate.

The ambiguity associated with technological change is sometimes resolved by recognizing that both product and process changes can be either radical or incremental. The debate itself over which product innovation is significant or which process modification is radical is evidence of the belief many share that radical or significant technological change is somehow different and that it demands different modes of thinking and management to make it work. Hence, trying to identify what is or is not radical or significant is a worthwhile endeavor. Even though we may think of technological change as a continuum from "irrelevant" to "momentous," successful innovators, so some people argue, should treat one end of the continuum differently from the other.

The significance of the distinction between radical and incremental change laps over into the chief managerial issues that companies confront about technology. These issues can be classified into two major groups:

- What are the sources of technological change?
- How should new technology (product or process) be evaluated and implemented?

These critical questions form the twin themes of this chapter.

PART ONE
SOURCES OF TECHNOLOGICAL CHANGE

When we think of technological innovation, we often distinguish between product innovation (new product introductions) and process innovation. While conceptually distinct, the two are often related. Abernathy and Utterback have suggested one such relationship between product and process innovation.[2] Figure 8-1 captures the major points of their idea.

In the early portion of a product's life, product design is critical. A product's early users are almost always more interested in product performance than in price. Considerable product redesign is undertaken to make the product even more useful and desirable for its users. Abernathy has referred to this early phase of product technology as the search for the "dominant design."[3] Dominant designs are those products that "make a market," such as Ford's Model T car, the DC-3 airplane, the Xerox 914 copier, Kodak's "Brownie" camera and the IBM PC. In this early going, the production process is most apt to be a job shop or a near-job shop.

As acceptance of the dominant design proceeds, however, cost reduction becomes increasingly important. Process innovation—geared primarily to lowering costs, increasing yield, and gaining production speed—commands management attention. Changes become less and less radical as the product, the process, and the organization become more and more standardized. The production process edges closer to the continuous flow end of the process spectrum. At the same time, both product and process become increasingly vulnerable to a radically different offering of similar function by some producer outside the traditionally defined industry (for example, an electronics company like Texas Instruments making watches).

In this view, then, product and process innovation are both aspects of broad technological advance and of the shift in market characteristics, over time, that usually accompanies such advance.

PRODUCT INNOVATION

New products spring from someone's research and development (R&D), but the question is whose and how can such R&D be stimulated. Some companies are renown for generating new products from within (such as DuPont, Intel, 3M, Corning Glass), and the management emphasis in such companies focuses on how the research labs can keep up their rich traditions. Other companies are forced (or perhaps choose) to generate their new product offerings from different sources—sometimes copying others' new products, sometimes acquiring the rights to the product, sometimes acquiring the innovating company itself.

Investigating new product innovation in depth is beyond the scope and purpose of this text. Suffice it here simply to note that this is a topic where our ignorance is vast and one likely to stir continued debate.

PROCESS INNOVATION

The sources of process innovation are similarly perplexing. Some innovations stem from a company's own work (occurring in conjunction with new product innovation), some stem from advances made by equipment or materials suppliers, and some result from copying or acquiring the technology developed by others.

Although the sources of process innovation are often baffling, the character of process in-

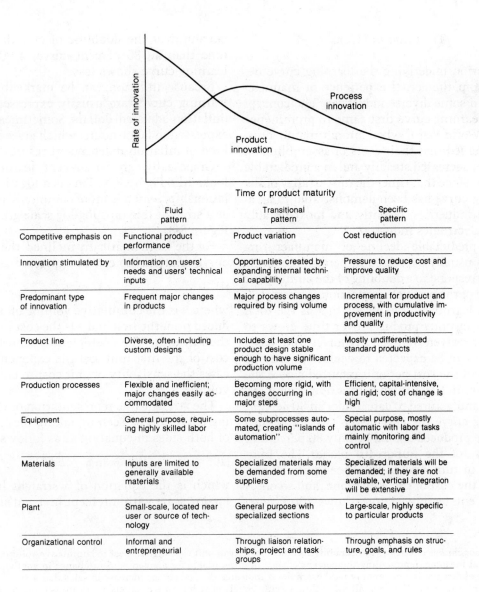

FIGURE 8-1   Level and type of innovation. (From Abernathy and Utterback, "Patterns of Industrial Innovation," p. 40)

	Fluid pattern	Transitional pattern	Specific pattern
Competitive emphasis on	Functional product performance	Product variation	Cost reduction
Innovation stimulated by	Information on users' needs and users' technical inputs	Opportunities created by expanding internal technical capability	Pressure to reduce cost and improve quality
Predominant type of innovation	Frequent major changes in products	Major process changes required by rising volume	Incremental for product and process, with cumulative improvement in productivity and quality
Product line	Diverse, often including custom designs	Includes at least one product design stable enough to have significant production volume	Mostly undifferentiated standard products
Production processes	Flexible and inefficient; major changes easily accommodated	Becoming more rigid, with changes occurring in major steps	Efficient, capital-intensive, and rigid; cost of change is high
Equipment	General purpose, requiring highly skilled labor	Some subprocesses automated, creating "islands of automation"	Special purpose, mostly automatic with labor tasks mainly monitoring and control
Materials	Inputs are limited to generally available materials	Specialized materials may be demanded from some suppliers	Specialized materials will be demanded; if they are not available, vertical integration will be extensive
Plant	Small-scale, located near user or source of technology	General purpose with specialized sections	Large-scale, highly specific to particular products
Organizational control	Informal and entrepreneurial	Through liaison relationships, project and task groups	Through emphasis on structure, goals, and rules

novation is less so. Moreover, an understanding of the character of process innovation carries with it some important lessons about how productivity can be enhanced.

A useful touchstone for a discussion of the nature of process innovation is the empirical phenomenon typically referred to as the "learning curve."

The Learning Curve[4]

The notion underlying the learning curve derives from the actual experience of manufacturers in some diverse industries. The concept of the learning curve first came to prominence before World War II when aircraft manufacturers observed that their costs of assembling an airplane decreased steadily and in a predictable fashion. Since that time, the universality of the learning curve has been demonstrated in a variety of industries, recently and most notably in the electronics industry.

The predictable decline of manufacturing costs is usually expressed in percentage terms that correspond to a doubling of the cumulative volume of the product in question. Thus, an 80 percent learning curve means that as the total number of units produced over time grows to twice any given number, manufacturing costs per unit can be expected to decline to only 80 percent of the cost per unit incurred before the doubling. If 100 airplanes of a new type have been manufactured to date, under an 80 percent learning curve the cost of the two hundredth airplane produced should be only 80 percent of the cost of the hundredth plane. The hundredth, in turn, should have been only 80 percent of the cost of the 50th plane, and so on. A 70 percent learning curve shows more cost-cutting over the doubling of cumulative volume than an 80 percent curve; a 90 percent learning curve shows less.

Because inflation can be markedly erratic, learning curves are usually expressed in real (inflation-adjusted) dollars. Sometimes they are expressed in labor-hours, which gives the same kind of inflation-independent result.

Graphically, an 80 percent learning-curve looks like Figure 8-2. This is a logarithmic relationship, which is more commonly portrayed as a straight line on a log-log scale grid such as Figure 8-3.

For the mathematically inclined, the learning curve relationship can be expressed as

$$(1) \qquad y = ax^{-b}$$

where x is the cumulative volume of units produced from the first and y is the cost to produce the xth unit. The coefficient a represents the cost of the first unit and the exponent b indicates the sensitivity of unit cost to cumulative volume.*

The straight line representation of the learning curve can be seen by taking the logarithm of both sides of equation 1, as follows:

$$(2) \qquad \ln y = \ln a - b \ln x$$

which is the equation of a straight line on a log-log scale with intercept $\ln a$ and slope $-b$.

---

*This exponent b is referred to by economists as the elasticity of unit cost with respect to cumulative volume. *Elasticity* has special meaning, representing the percent change in one variable for a given percent change in another. The price elasticity of demand is a commonly used example; it indicates the percentage increase in sales that a given percentage decrease in price will stimulate, all other things being equal. That b is in fact an elasticity measure is seen by taking the logarithm of equation 1 and differentiating with respect to ($\ln x$) as follows:

$$y = ax^{-b}$$

$$\ln y = \ln a - b \ln x$$

$$\frac{\delta(\ln y)}{\delta(\ln x)} = -b = \frac{\dfrac{\delta y}{\delta v}}{\dfrac{\delta x}{\delta x}}$$

FIGURE 8-2   Learning curves portrayed on a conventional graph.

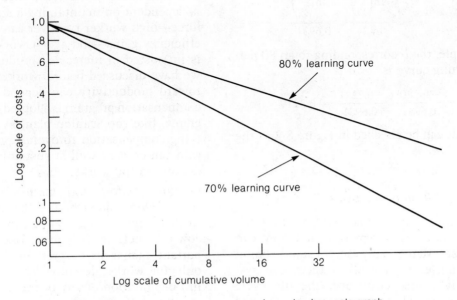

FIGURE 8-3   Learning curves portrayed on a log-log scale graph.

It should be made clear that b is not 0.8 for an 80 percent learning curve; there is, however, a relatively simple correspondence between b and the percentage figure that labels the learning curve. This relationship can be derived as follows.

Let $y_1 = ax^{-b}$ and let y_2 be the unit cost for double the cumulative volume of x. The fraction y_2/y_1 would be 0.8 for an 80 percent learning curve, 0.7 for a 70 percent learning curve, and so forth.

(3) $$\frac{y_2}{y_1} = \frac{a\,(2x)^{-b}}{ax^{-b}} = \frac{a2^{-b}x^{-b}}{ax^{-b}} = 2^{-b}$$

This equation gives the percentage learning curve for every choice of elasticity, b. We can easily turn this equation around to give the elasticity, b, that corresponds to every percentage level of learning curve.

$$\frac{y_2}{y_1} = 2^{-b}$$

$$\ln\left(\frac{y_2}{y_1}\right) = -b \ln 2$$

$$b = \frac{-\ln\left(\frac{y_2}{y_1}\right)}{\ln 2} = \frac{-\ln\left(\frac{y_2}{y_1}\right)}{0.6931}$$

For example, the b corresponding to an 80 percent learning curve is

$$b = \frac{-\ln(.80)}{0.6931} = \frac{+0.2231}{0.6931} = 0.3219$$

This result can be checked in Figure 8-2 as the slope.

Composition of the Learning Curve

So much for the mathematics. What does the learning curve really represent and how can it be of use? Many, many factors stand behind the learning curve and all of them can systematically reduce costs over the life cycle of the product. These factors can be grouped into major categories: workforce-related factors, process modifications, and product modifications. The workforce-related factors, are more short run in character and distinguish, for some, the learning curve from the broader notion of the "experience curve." The experience curve is also a relationship between cost and accumulated volume, but it is generally associated with longer term factors dealing with process and product modifications as well as factors related to the workforce. Nevertheless, the terms "learning curve" and "experience curve" are often used interchangeably.

Workforce-Related Factors

- *Worker learning on the job.* This was the initial explanation for the results of the pre–World War II aircraft manufacturers, and for some people, this is what the learning curve represents. Cost decreases attributable to gains in worker efficiency through practice are generally quickly exhausted. That such cost reductions can be sustained over time is dependent on maintaining a stable workforce—high worker turnover can annihilate efficiency gains—and also a workforce that is interested in increasing productivity. As we have discussed before, worker attitudes toward productivity can depend on which compensation program is adopted. Some programs, like the Scanlon plan, by purposely tying compensation to overall productivity gain can do very well at sustaining cost reduction in the workforce.

- *Employee effort and management pressure.* Plain, old-fashioned hard work by workers and managers alike can keep costs down. Sometimes it is overlooked how important management pressure can be not only for worker learning but also for the full exploitation of any of the other factors in this list. Learning curve results frequently have an uncanny knack of matching learning curve expectations, and so we should not discount the impact of management pressure.

- *Workforce organization.* Akin to worker learning and effort is the organization of the workforce. A systematic training program, a thoughtful division of labor, and a considered plan for job mobility and advancement all have a role to play in lowering costs and in keeping them low over time.

Process Modifications

- *Methods improvements.* Included as methods improvements would be shortcuts in machine setup or operation, changes in the sequencing of a product through the factory, improvements in production and/or inventory control, and the introduction of production aids such as jigs, fixtures, or patterns. These and other changes in methods can sometimes improve the yields of "good product" in the process and reduce the scrap involved.

- *Capital-for-labor substitution.* This is a classic means of lowering costs—substituting machine operations for tasks formerly performed manually.

- *Capital-for-capital substitution.* This means of reducing costs involves the replacement of existing plant and equipment with plant and equipment of more recent vintage. The new equipment is frequently more versatile, faster, more durable, and/or cheaper to operate with capabilities that exceed the existing models. The new equipment may be either larger or smaller than that which it replaces and for this reason more desirable.

- *Vertical integration.* By broadening the span of its process, a manufacturer can often lower its costs, although this is not always the case. This topic is discussed in more detail in the next chapter.

- *"Pure" technological change.* By "pure" technological change I mean the more radical redesigns of the production process that are brought about by breakthroughs in engineering or basic research. Examples abound in almost every industry—continuous casting in steel, computerized typesetting in printing, process control equipment in many industries, freeze drying methods in food processing, to name a few. For these changes new equipment must be designed, and so "pure" technological change usually includes capital-for-labor and capital-for-capital substitution as well. But pure technological change is usually much more than these kinds of substitution, for it involves a rethinking about how a particular product is made. Generally it triggers a host of changes throughout the production process, from changes in worker training and methods and in production and inventory control to changes in the company's handling of capacity requirements.

  Pure technological change, in this sense, will be the center of discussion in Part Two of this chapter.

Product Modifications

- *Product design.* A frequent source of cost reduction is product redesign. Often a product can be simplified in its design so that its manufacture becomes significantly trouble-free. As was discussed in Chapter 3, the term "value engineering" has been coined to describe this critical look at a product's construction and how it can be altered to lower manufacturing costs. Products as diverse as automobiles, television sets, and digital watches have all undergone significant value engineering in recent years.

  Not only does product redesign reduce manufacturing cost; it often enhances a product's performance and this, in turn, is valued in the marketplace. If product performance is what the market buys, this kind

SITUATION 8-1

NASHVILLE FIRE EQUIPMENT COMPANY

Mal Getz, president of the Nashville Fire Equipment Company, was in the midst of contract negotiations with the business agent of the union that had recently won the right to represent his company's employees. The union, as one of the points it wanted to negotiate, had broached the concept of regular wage increases as so-called "improvement factors." The union argument was that because workers over time produce more with the same amount of human effort (due to such things as technological progress, better tools, methods, processes, equipment, and worker cooperation), they ought to be rewarded with regular wage increases.

Mal recognized this union point of negotiation as one based on the learning curve principle, and different in character from the typical wage increase to keep up with the cost of living. Mal had to admit to himself that the improvement factor was founded on sound reasoning. Moreover, Nashville Fire Equipment had been benefiting from the learning curve over the last several years, and Mal knew that the union would almost certainly be able to document that fact. It seemed likely then that management would have to agree to negotiate "improvement factors" for the next three years, the term of the contract.

The difficulty was that Mal was at a loss as to how to estimate what labor savings the company could legitimately expect over the next three years, and thus what improvement factors the company ought to consent to.

The company had recently been rejuvenated by the introduction of an articulating hydraulic boom (known within the industry as a "squirt"), a new product and technique for fire fighting that permitted the quick, pinpoint spraying of water into otherwise inaccessible places. The squirt had been winning increasing acceptance in the fire departments that served as the company's customer base and now accounted for most of the company's sales. Nashville Fire Equipment's squirt was a patentable modification of a similar product that the Seiver Company had licensed Nashville Fire Equipment to make. Table 8-1 documents various times, production volumes, and worker hours associated with the squirt. Over the next year Mal Getz expected to continue to employ 50 workers on the squirt. He wondered whether the table data, coupled with the learning curve concept, could form the basis for a recommendation on suitable improvement factors.

TABLE 8-1   Production times, volume, and worker times for the Squirt (Nashville Fire Equipment Company)

WEEK	CUMULATIVE UNITS PRODUCED AS OF THAT DATE	HOURS NEEDED TO MANUFACTURE FIRST UNIT OF WEEK
2	1	4000
10	7	2550
38	25	1850
70	65	1500
150	180	1170

of product redesign can even be placed in the category of cost reduction. Semiconductor memory for computers is an example where product performance improvements have been a significant feature in the cost and price decline of the "product" purchased—the storage of a given unit of information in computers and related products.

• *Materials substitution.* Akin to product redesign is the use of different, possibly new, materials in place of other materials in the product. The substitution of aluminum for steel, plastic for glass or metal, metal for wood, and so on can lower the total costs of manufacture with relatively few design changes to many products.

Summary

As the length and breadth of this list makes clear, the learning curve phenomenon is founded on a wealth of strong influences. What is not so clear is how the regularity of the learning curve can be used as a planning and decision tool. Consider Situation 8-1.

Discussion of Nashville Fire Equipment Company

It is easy enough to calculate the learning curve implied by the brief list of data in Table 8-1. The learning curve calculated is depicted in Figure 8-4. (See also the Aside.) Mal Getz could use this finding of an 85 percent learning curve to grant an "improvement factor" to the company's workforce on, say, an annual basis payable at the end of the next year.

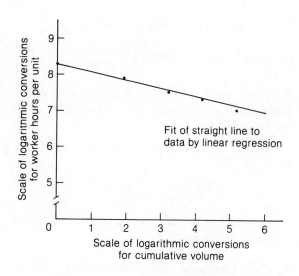

FIGURE 8-4 Learning curve for Nashville Fire Equipment Company's "Squirt."

✳ ASIDE ✳

Fitting a Straight Line to the Company's Data

Fitting a straight line to the data of Table 8-1 involves converting those data to logarithmic form (Table 8-2) and then applying the technique of linear regression to the converted data. Linear regression, part of most computer software statistical packages and even found on many calculators, is merely a procedure for choosing the straight line that minimizes the sum of the squared vertical distances between the data points and the fitted line.

The equation of the fitted straight line to the converted (natural logarithm) data, as found by linear regression, is

$$(1) \begin{pmatrix} \text{natural} \\ \text{logarithm} \\ \text{of hours} \\ \text{needed} \end{pmatrix} = 8.293 - 0.237 \begin{pmatrix} \text{natural} \\ \text{logarithm of} \\ \text{cumulative units} \\ \text{produced} \end{pmatrix}$$

TABLE 8-2   Conversion to logarithms of data in Table 8-1

CUMULATIVE UNITS PRODUCED	NATURAL LOGARITHM CUMULATIVE UNIT PRODUCED	HOURS NEEDED	NATURAL LOGARITHM OF HOURS NEEDED
1	0.00	4000	8.29
7	1.95	2550	7.84
25	3.22	1850	7.52
65	4.17	1500	7.31
180	5.19	1170	7.06

or put in the nonlogarithmic terms of $y = ax^{-b}$

(2) (hours needed) $= 4000 \cdot \left(\dfrac{\text{cumulative units}}{\text{produced}}\right)^{-0.237}$

Converting this estimate of b (0.237) into the appropriate label for the learning curve is accomplished by equation 3 above:

(3) $\dfrac{y_2}{y_1} = 2^{-b}, \; 2^{-0.237} = .85$

Thus, the data of Table 8-1 imply an 85 percent learning curve.

✳

Return to Calculating an Improvement Factor

One procedure for calculating an improvement factor is as follows:

1. Calculate how many labor-hours will be spent on the product over the course of the next year.
2. Estimate how many more units of the product are expected to be manufactured during that number of labor-hours.
3. Using the formula, compute the expected labor-hours for the unit that will be manufactured in exactly one year from now.
4. Compare the labor-hours per unit then with the present labor-hours per unit. The labor rate can then be adjusted to reflect the lower labor-hours that will be spent on each unit in a year's time.

For the Nashville Fire Equipment Company, following this procedure entails these calculations:

1. 50 weeks · 50 workers · 40 hours/week = 100,000 labor-hours for the next year.

TABLE 8-3   Estimate of labor-hours needed to produce a particular Squirt (Nashville Fire Equipment Company)

NUMBER OF UNITS PRODUCED	ESTIMATED LABOR-HOURS NEEDED TO PRODUCE THAT UNIT*
1	4000.0
180	1170.9
181	1169.4
182	1167.9
183	1166.4

*From learning curve estimated in Figure 8-4.

2. To get an estimate of how many more units can be made in 100,000 labor-hours, we have to use the 85 percent learning curve we calculated in the Aside. Each successive unit will require slightly less labor. We could generate a table (Table 8-3) like Table 8-1. Using Table 8-3 we could sum up the individual times, starting with unit 181, until their sum reaches 100,000. By referring to the table, we could then discover the corresponding number unit on which the 100,000th labor-hour was spent.*

If we did this, we would find that the 100,000th labor-hour was spent on the 270th

---

*Fortunately, we do not have to perform this calculation, although it takes a little integral calculus to avoid it. The labor time spent between the mth unit and the nth unit is approximated by the integral of the learning curve function evaluated between m and n. Since the learning curve function is a monomial, the integral is easily evaluated. In particular, labor time between mth and nth units

(1) $= \displaystyle\int_{m}^{n} y\,dx$

unit. That is, exactly one year from now, if the Nashville Fire Equipment Company continues on its 85 percent learning curve, its workers will be working on the 270th squirt.

3. Over the course of the year it will have produced 90 (270 − 180) squirts. The 270th unit will require only

$$y = 4000 \, (270)^{-0.237}$$
$$= 1060 \text{ hours to complete}$$

This situation shows the phenomenal power of learning. It took the Nashville Fire Equipment Company three years to produce its first 180 squirts; in a single year's time, if its 85 percent learning curve is maintained, it can expect to produce almost half that amount.

4. At present, 1170 labor-hours are needed to produce the latest unit, the 180th. From the above calculation, in a year's time only 1060 hours will be required, which is only 90.6 percent of the present labor input. With this productivity advance, if the price of the squirt remains the same (a rather big if), the company can afford to pay its workers 1.10 (1/ 0.906) times as much in a year's time and still enjoy the same profit margin it now does. This figure of 1.10 thus provides a ceiling on the improvement factor that Mal Getz has to decide upon.

Applying the Learning Curve

The forgoing series of steps demonstrates how the learning curve can be used as a planning device. Here the learning curve was used to calculate an "improvement factor" for labor, but it could also have been used to figure out by what date a given number of units will have been produced or to guide labor hiring practices to fulfill a certain commitment by a given date. The learning curve can be particularly useful

---

where y is the learning curve estimate of labor time needed to produce any unit x. We can then use the formula for the learning curve to substitute for y:

$$(2) \qquad = \int_m^n ax^{-b}dx$$

Then we factor out the constant a:

$$(3) \qquad = a \int_m^n x^{-b}dx$$

Taking the integral, then, yields

$$(4) \qquad = a\frac{x^{1-b}}{1-b}$$

which can be evaluated at n and m and subtracted to reveal the labor time spent between units.

We can apply this formula to figure out how many squirts the Nashville Fire Equipment Company can be expected to make in a year. We know that 100,000 labor-hours will be spent during the next year. The company has already manufactured 180 squirts according to the learning curve that was derived as

$$y = ax^{-b} = 4000x^{-0.237}$$

Stepping through equation (4), we have

$$100,000 \text{ hours} = \int_{180}^n 4000x^{-0.237} \, dx$$

in tracking and in planning new product introductions.

However, a larger issue than the mere mechanics of the learning curve is whether the concept can be applied at all to situations like that of the Nashville Fire Equipment Company. What are the weak points in using the learning curve for such situations?

As a glimpse back at Figures 8-2 and 8-3 reveals, the learning curve is keenly sensitive to position and slope, which are determined respectively by the coefficient *a* in equation 1 and by the exponent *b*. We ought to ask the question then whether the first squirt made by the company in week 2 of Table 8-1 should be viewed as the absolute first unit or not. As was mentioned in the situation, Nashville's squirt is a patentable modification of a similar product that the Seiver Company had licensed Nashville Fire

Equipment to make. It could easily be argued that the first unit should not be the squirt itself but the Seiver Company's licensed product. The impact of such a change can be dramatic. Suppose, for example, that Nashville Fire Equipment's first squirt is viewed as the 31st unit for purposes of computing the learning curve. The latest unit would thus be the 210th. The refigured learning curve would be

$$y = 21,850x^{-0.570}$$

which translates to a 67 percent learning curve and drastically different results.

Perhaps the company's early experience with a similar licensed product brought down its labor-hours per unit much more quickly than could otherwise be expected; what is learned from producing one product can frequently be transmitted to those working on another prod-

where n is the as yet unknown number of the unit to be worked on in exactly one year's time.

$$= \frac{4000_x{}^{1-0.237}}{1-0.237}$$

evaluated at n and 180 and subtracted as follows:

$$= \frac{4000n^{0.763}}{0.763} - \frac{4000(180)^{0.763}}{0.763}$$

$$= 5240n^{0.763} - 275,410$$

Rearranging terms and dividing through yields

$$\frac{100,000 + 275,410}{5240} = n^{0.763}$$

$$71.64 = n^{0.763}$$

Taking the natural logarithm of both sides enables us to solve for n:

$$\ln(71.64) = 0.763 \ln n$$
$$\ln n = 5.6$$

which implies

$$n \approx 270$$

uct within the company, or even from within one company to another. In that case, the learning curve the company could anticipate over the next year would be much less steep than the currently calculated 85 percent curve. Moreover, what learning curve rate would be appropriate may be very unclear, especially at the outset. Much of the issue of "technological forecasting" revolves around the appropriate choice of the learning curve elasticity, b, for various new products and which influences on that rate are likely to be important.

These doubts about the position and slope of the learning curve are not easily resolved and argue for great caution. Mal Getz may well be able to grant an "improvement factor" to his workers, but one somewhat less than 110 percent of the current rate seems prudent.

Situation 8-1 underscored the conflicts that can arise in the use of standard times. Technological change and learning will often improve worker times and erode the standards established. Making adjustments, especially if wages are tied to performance relative to the standard, can be tricky.

Strategic Use of the Learning Curve Concept

This concern for the applicability of the learning curve phenomenon to short-term, tactical decisions of a corporation extends as well to longer term, strategic decisions. The strategic impact of the learning curve is nowhere more evident than in the electronics industry—particularly in the growth and behavior of one company, Texas Instruments. Texas Instruments has had a reputation as a tough competitor whose strategy has been to generate huge sales volumes by repeatedly cutting prices. The company has sought the sales leadership in all the markets it has entered, using low prices to generate volume and using volume, via learn-

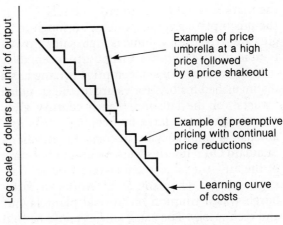

FIGURE 8-5 Pricing strategies and the learning curve.

ing, to generate cost (and price) reductions. Texas Instruments has been reputed to relish industry shakeouts, and such companies are generally feared as competitors.

One tactic that some companies have used with success to deter the entry of newcomers to a market and to stimulate a continual shaking out of an industry is *preemptive pricing*. Preemptive pricing is based on the expectations of the learning curve. Prices are set and announced at low levels, often with slim margins, and it is expected that volume production will stimulate enough cost reduction that total profits will become acceptably high. This kind of pricing is in distinct contrast to the practice of maintaining, for as long as possible, high prices in the face of declining costs, perhaps inviting a massive shakeout as more and more competitors enter the market under the existing price umbrellas.

These divergent strategies are represented pictorially in Figure 8-5. Note that although the initial profits are higher under the price maintenance umbrella strategy, because prices are higher the market is not likely to grow rapidly. Under the preemptive pricing strategy, although margins are often thin, volume is high, sales growth is rapid, and total profits can be quite acceptable.

In many industries, preemptive pricing has a distinguished history. For example, the so-called "trusts" of the late nineteenth century grew quickly and grew large by keeping prices low and using technology to cut costs. Rockefeller's Standard Oil refineries were models of the state of the art—the largest and fastest around. Carnegie's Edgar Thomson Steel Works in Pittsburgh was a triumph of rational plant layout and technology. The same stories could be told of sugar, tobacco, and the other trusts. In each of these cases, the first producer to get volume up and to force technological advance in process design was the one that traveled down the learning curve the first, forcing others out of the industry by pricing low and accumulating profits all the while.

It is no coincidence that all of the trusts of the nineteenth century were in commodities. Commodity manufacturers do not have to worry about new product introductions or product modifications undermining sales of their particular products. Commodity manufacturers can concentrate on cost reduction without fearing what competitors will market to counter their own product lines. The power of the learning curve phenomenon is greatly weakened by continual product model changes or new product introductions. These throw the company onto new learning curves or back up old ones.[5] Consumer taste-sensitive industries are thus much less able to compete successfully with preemptive pricing than are more taste-invariant industries.

This fact suggests that the strategic implications of the learning curve are best exploited by particular classes of companies. Whether a company can adopt preemptive pricing and exploit the learning curve phenomenon successfully depends to a great degree on how it values a dollar received today versus a dollar tomorrow. Preemptive pricing defers its rewards more than traditional price maintenance because it must wait to foster growth in the market and because it stimulates an immediate and ongoing shakeout in the industry. Thus, preemptive pricing is relatively more attractive when some or all of the following features are true:

1. The expected product life is long.
2. The product is standardized, like a commodity, with little risk that consumer tastes will suddenly turn against it.
3. The expected growth of the market is rapid.
4. The apparent slope of the learning curve is steeper, since the learning curve in that instance can constitute a substantial barrier to the entry of other firms into the industry.
5. The product is not patent protected.
6. The company is not particularly strapped for cash.

To the extent these features are true, preemptive pricing (implied by the learning curve) can act to gain market share in a growing market and thereby command considerable profits.

PART TWO
EVALUATING AND IMPLEMENTING NEW TECHNOLOGY

We are all well aware that new discoveries are constantly making old knowledge obsolete. We take for granted that new technologies will someday, somehow transform whatever operation we care to name. The certainty of technological advance, however, does little to quell the uncertainties many managers feel about coping with it. Too often, managers abandon technology and the issues surrounding it to the engineers and scientists who are with it day to day. They fear that they need to understand the technology in all its details in order to manage it, and that fear can be paralyzing.

Managers need not be paralyzed by technology. Indeed, if technology is not to run the business, they must learn to manage technology. According to Wickham Skinner's insightful views, some inquisitiveness and the willingness to reason by analogy can be exceedingly helpful in coming to grips with process technology change.[6] The kind of inquisitiveness required to begin understanding technology is precisely the same kind of inquisitiveness that runs through Segment I's plant tours: What happens to the material during the process? How do machines or workers transform it? How does the new technology differ from the old? Where is the new technology vulnerable to breakdown or error? The manager need not fully understand the science behind the new technology, but he or she should be able to understand it by analogy or in some other way visualize what the technology does.

Armed with this knowledge, the manager can pose some basic, but tough, questions whose answers are critical to the effective management of new technology.

1. *What will it cost?*   This, of course, is a favorite question of managers. Costs involved with new technologies can include procurement cost, installation, debugging, maintenance, materials handling, operating costs (labor, utilities, material), and overhead assignable to it.

2. *What will it do?*   There are several key issues riding with any process change, among them: capacities involved, range of products affected, tolerances held, reliability offered,

product characteristics performed, scrap/rework and energy saved. These issues, in essence, define the potential for the new technology.

3. *What will it require?*   What will adoption of the new technology mean for direct labor skills, maintenance, setup, quality control, scheduling, inventory levels, materials needs, space, layout, and production control? These are the skills and the systems that support the existing process and must also support any new technology.

4. *How certain are the costs, potentials, and requirements of the new technology?*   This, too, is a familiar managerial question that can be useful in defining the "bounds" of the technology. Here is where some sensitivity analysis can be very informative.

Skinner's questions help make the management of technology more systematic. They can often lead the way to an understanding of exactly what management must do well to have the new technology succeed, and that is valuable information indeed.

The remainder of this part of the chapter addresses new product introduction and process innovation and concludes by discussing some recent developments in manufacturing technology.

New Product Introduction

For most operations, there are new products to be made or new services to be delivered nearly all the time. Making the introduction of a new product or service go smoothly, however, takes some planning and effort. The merit of the new product or service should be assessed so that priorities and resources can be properly assigned. And engineering should make a smooth and timely transfer of the new product or service to the operations people. This section addresses such requirements and how companies have coped with them.

Assessing the Technological Fortunes

Spotting the product designs that will be commercially successful is an uncertain business at best. It has been suggested that a new "technological winner" must score high on a mix of separate criteria.[7]

- *Inventive merit.* How important are the scientific advances in the product?

- *Engineering merit.* Does the engineering of the product fully exploit the scientific advances made? Must many changes be made?

- *Operational merit.* What will the product mean to company operations and organization? Will major revamping be required?

- *Market merit.* Is the product innovation what the market wants and will pay for?

To the extent that a product's inventive merit is strong, its marketing features attractive, and any required engineering and operational changes either slight or fully anticipated, a new product is likely to be a commercial success. A failure in any of these dimensions can spoil an otherwise promising product.

Pinpointing a promising technological advance is unavoidably subjective, but some research suggests that many of the uncertainties involved can be usefully quantified.[8] A number of these approaches to forecasting the success of a new product use the Delphi method, combining an expert panel with probability measures. Each panel expert is asked to indicate his or her own view of an R&D project's success. These opinions are collected, tabulated, and usually reviewed again by the expert panel, which can then revise its initial probability selections. Such assessments can be made at regular intervals over the years required to research and develop a new product.

Such assessments of the probability for success of various R&D projects can be important inputs to the management of these projects, identifying those that need attention and governing in part how resources can be controlled and apportioned among projects.

Managing New Product Introduction to the Factory

The search for a dominant design as well as a general broadening of product offerings requires that new product designs be introduced into the factory. Of course, this change is not so wrenching for a job shop process as for a flow process, but in any case it demands special coordination among product engineers, industrial engineers, and operations people.

Ensuring cooperation between engineering and manufacturing is frequently no mean trick; distrust and animosity between the two functions is too often the rule. Resentment of engineering by manufacturing may be caused by real, or perceived, incidents such as:

- Engineering is later than scheduled with the design, but manufacturing is still expected to get the first units to the market according to the initial schedule. Engineering is perceived by manufacturing as not being punished for taking too long.

- Engineering goes over budget at will, but manufacturing is held to its budget with religious fervor.

- Manufacturing is not consulted about the new product while it is in the design phase and yet has to accept a design that may please the engineer but is needlessly difficult to fabricate, assemble, and/or test.

- Engineering changes to designs, parts, and methods are needlessly frequent; it is as though engineering staff cannot make up their minds. Yet manufacturing is expected to react instantly.

- Engineers seem to have a penchant for specifying items that are hard to purchase and/or require a long lead time, although a little ingenuity could have made use of off-the-shelf items that are easily obtained.

For its part, engineers may gripe (and rightly) about the manufacturing group's inertia, single-minded attention to cost factors, needless devotion to existing equipment and methods, and so on.

A new product introduction, to be smooth, must bridge this chasm of mistrust. Companies have tried this feat in many ways. A popular way to build trust and cooperation is to establish a task force composed of engineering and manufacturing people who are charged with planning and implementing the new product introduction. This task force is typically chaired or led by engineering. Depending on the situation, manufacturing may be involved early in the product design or later. Exactly when manufacturing should be involved is seldom clear. If it is involved while the product design is little more than a dream, manufacturing is likely to have little to contribute. If it is involved only later, manufacturing may suggest changes in the design that are expensive, if not impossible.

Other times, no formal task forces are assigned. Engineering and manufacturing departments must then coordinate through normal channels. Sometimes either engineering or manufacturing will create a liason team, charged with coordinating the new product introduction. Sometimes top management will interpose its own liaison team to act as a buffer and referee between the two functions.

None of these means of new product introduction necessarily dominates the others in all situations. Some companies keep alternating the way they do things or permit different mechanisms in different divisions.

INNOVATION OF THE PRODUCTION PROCESS

The introduction of process innovations is even less well delineated than new product introduction. As mentioned at the start of this chapter, incremental change is often thought to offer different management problems from radical change. It is frequently felt that continual, small improvements in the process technology can be stimulated by company reward systems or company grants for the pursuit of new ideas, such as are found at companies like 3M. Or, they can be induced by increased management pressure, through work restructuring programs to call forth worker modifications, or by compensation schemes like the Scanlon plan, which ties pay increases to productivity gains. The factors cited earlier as influencing the learning curve can all account for incremental changes in process technology. Further, implementing incremental change can often be done without placing great demands on management's coordinating abilities.

Radical changes to the process technology are more problematic. More money and greater risk are involved, as well as the need to coordinate many people in various company departments. What leads to success in such an endeavor is not known with certainty, but analyses of some radical process innovations seem to uphold these general principles:

- The suggested process change must fit the company's business goals and thereby foster the commitment of the company's top management.

- The company must have a realistic idea of what the innovation can do well and should not get swamped by trying to innovate everywhere at once.

- Some attention should be given to how the innovation may be resisted by workers, consumers, or government.

- Any test should be made in a setting that is representative of the company's business and environment.

- A strong individual—sometimes termed the "change champion"—should act as both catalyst and critic for the innovation and its implementation.

A flavor for these views on managing innovation can be sampled in the following description of Giant Food Inc. of Landover, Maryland, and its leadership position in laser beam scanning at supermarket checkout counters.

Giant Food Inc.: Laser Beam Scanning at the Checkout Counter

Giant Food Inc. was the leading grocery store chain in the Baltimore-Washington area. As of early 1983, it operated 132 stores in Maryland, Virginia, and the District of Columbia. Only Safeway Stores was in a position to challenge Giant's dominance of this regional market.

Since Giant Food's introduction of self-service grocery shopping to Washington, D.C., in 1936, the company has maintained a reputation for innovation. It was a pioneer in frozen foods in the 1940s and self-service meat departments in the early 1950s. Throughout the late 1950s and the 1960s the chain developed such concepts as combining food and general merchandise and a pharmacy in the same store. Giant Food has also been a leader in consumer advocacy. The company's consumer advisor in the early 1970s was Esther Peterson, the first appointed assistant to the president for consumer affairs (under

FIGURE 8-6   A sample universal product curve (UPC) symbol. As with all such symbols, the first five digits represent the manufacturer; the second five digits represent the item. Price is not included in the symbol.

Lyndon Johnson). Under Peterson's direction, Giant Food adopted a "consumer bill of rights" and led the way in unit pricing on aisle shelves, calendar dating of perishable commodities, disclosure of nutritional information on the package, and the marketing of recycled paper products. More recently, the company has adopted one of the first semiautomated grocery warehouses to be developed.

Giant Food's tradition of innovation is no more readily appreciated than in its leadership in the application of laser beam scanning to checkout counters. The company was far and away the nation's technological leader in scanning, having installed it in all its stores by August 1979, the first food store chain to do so.

Scanning and its Benefits

With laser beam scanning the cashier does not have to key in the price of any item that is marked with the special universal product code (UPC) symbol. This symbol, pictured in Figure 8-6, uses bands of lines of varying thickness to represent both the manufacturer and the precise product to be scanned. The product with its attached symbol is drawn over a window in the checkout counter, which houses a low-energy laser beam scanner. This scanner "reads" the UPC, matches the product with its price, which is on file in an in-store minicomputer, and prints out a tape that identifies both product and price (see Figure 8-7).

The now recognized advantages of checkout counter scanning are numerous. These advantages are generally divided into so-called "hard savings" and "soft savings." The hard savings refer to benefits such as:

- Quicker checkout of an order, enabling the store to maintain or improve its checkout service with fewer lanes and cashiers, and better scheduling of both.

- Faster and more accurate end-of-shift balancing of each cash register.

- Elimination of the weighing, bagging, and pricing of produce in the produce department and its transfer to the checkout counter where it can be done more efficiently and more accurately.

- Avoidance of the expense of replacing mechanical cash registers.

- More economical ordering of groceries by stores from headquarters.

These hard savings alone are enough to make scanning very attractive. As of June 1978, Giant Food estimated that these savings totaled $6634 per month for a store doing $160,000 worth of business each week. This kind of saving was enough to ensure a payback of between two and four years, depending on the size of the store. More than this, Giant Food estimated that another $2745 could be saved each month if individual items did not have to be marked with price labels and updated periodically, because a scanning system operates without any keying in of prices. Item price-marking has been the one controversial feature about laser beam scanning. The company, although aware of the

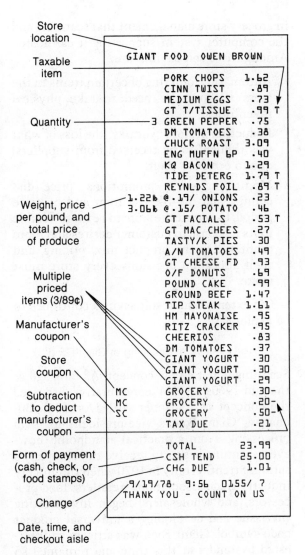

FIGURE 8-7 An annotated sample register tape from a laser-beam-scanning checkout.

savings it could realize if items did not have to be price marked, nevertheless continued to put prices on all its store items in conformance with the demand of some consumer groups.

The soft savings from scanning at the checkout counter refer to some fundamental changes in grocery store management that scanning and the computer system supporting it can foster. Among these soft savings are:

- Automatic reordering of certain items in the store without the need to take physical inventories.
- Reduction in store "shrink" (the loss of what was thought to be received from suppliers) due to errors or theft.
- Monitoring sales, promotions, price discounts, and the like by item and by time period, to permit the store to be more flexible in its response to customer desires and more profitable in the product mix, pricing, and shelf allocation decisions every store must make.

The extent of such soft savings continues to be explored.

The Genesis of Scanning at Giant Food

Scanning is not a new concept. As long ago as the mid-1960s, an IBM representative discussed the concept of a scanner with Donald R. Buchanan, Giant Food's vice-president for data processing. From a practical standpoint, however, scanning began to receive the company's serious attention only in 1970 when the grocery industry trade associations (retailers, food processors, and wholesalers) began investigating the issue and developing a universal product code symbol. Giant Food was strictly an interested bystander at this time and remained so through the selection of the universal product code symbol design in 1971 and the first test of a scanning system by Kroger in its Kenwood, Ohio, store in 1972–73. Buchanan did visit with scanner manufacturers throughout this period, but no commitments were made.

As study results began to appear both from the Kroger test and from tests by the scanner manufacturers, Buchanan began getting a gut feeling that the benefits of scanning would outweigh the costs. On an informal basis, he and selected others from data processing and operations began to study the matter more intensely. In early 1974, Buchanan became convinced that the equipment manufacturers were serious about scanning (IBM had announced its 3660 Supermarket System in November 1973) and that Giant should undertake a study of its own. This view was bolstered by the long-term trend for increasing wages in the industry and thus rewards for those grocery chains that could reduce the labor intensity of store operations. Furthermore, Giant Food's stores were high volume stores, the ones analysis suggested were most favorable to the scanning technology.

Buchanan brought his idea for a test store to the attention of Giant Food's executive vice-president, Israel Cohen, and its president, Joseph Danzansky.* After hearing about the proposal and its potential, Cohen and Danzansky approved the test. At this point the informality of the scanning idea gave way to the formality of committing the company's funds to it. Buchanan was given responsibility for the project.

In March 1974, Buchanan appointed a seven-member team, reporting directly to him, and charged them with (1) designing the new "front end" (as the checkout counter area was called), (2) choosing the equipment manufacturer(s) for it, (3) developing the computer software to control the scanning process and the information it provided, and (4) installing the prototype system in the test store. The team leader was recruited from the banking rather than the grocery business and had a strong background in data processing. Four other members of the team

---

*Cohen is now president and chairman. Danzansky is chairman emeritus.

had data processing backgrounds, three of them with experience at Giant Food. These technical people included a systems programmer, a senior systems analyst, and two other analysts/programmers. In addition, a store manager and an assistant store manager were assigned permanently to the team.

Buchanan deliberately sought a wide mix of experience for the team and also generous staffing, an indication of Cohen's and Danzansky's commitment to the project. Team motivation was high because the entire team recognized that it had significant control of the direction scanning would take at Giant Food. The team reported each week or so to Buchanan. It was originally desired to house the team at Giant's headquarters in Landover, Maryland, but space constraints there forced the team to rent some space adjacent to a Giant Food store about six to eight miles from headquarters.

In an associated development, Esther Peterson met with a group of consumers and consumer groups to discuss scanning and its role in a supermarket. The results of these meetings were fed to the team.

Team Operation and the Severna Park Store

Early in the team's deliberations it was decided to use IBM equipment in the test. There were a variety of reasons for the choice. Giant Food was already a satisfied IBM customer, and it was felt that IBM was committed to the scanning technology. It was reasonable to expect that IBM was going to be around for the long pull and, if IBM were true to form, it would place enough people on the project to make it seem as though Giant Food had hired some private consultants. As it turned out, later in the project some IBM people became, in effect, members of the team, although by that time it was clearly a Giant Food operation.

It was decided as well that the test of scanning proceed in a new store so that the project would not disturb in any way existing operations. A new store planned for Severna Park, Maryland (a relatively affluent southern suburb of Baltimore) was chosen. The team trained all of the labor at the new store; Giant Food's operations group assisted the team and was itself trained in this new technology. In fact, the team nearly lived at the store for months, both before and after its opening. The scanning at Severna Park was viewed primarily as a development effort to investigate scanning technology, the systems needed to operate it, the hard cash savings attributable to it, and customer reaction.

The Severna Park store opened in late January 1975. The opening data had been pushed back somewhat by the construction people because the parking lot could not be laid in time. Although the team felt they could have met the original store opening date, they breathed a sigh of relief. Actually, the team was overprepared for the store's opening, having spent nearly a year in planning and preparation.

Most grocery stores enjoy a gala grand opening, preceded by a lot of advertising. In contrast, the Severna Park store opened 10 days before its grand opening and with no advertising. The store thus underwent a shakedown with just the people who wandered into it and without the crush and hoopla attending most store openings. The preview opening consisted of a number of media events and a series of explanatory sessions, held three times a day over several days, directed to groups such as the print media, the electronic media, consumer groups, teachers, suppliers, the financial community, Giant Food employees, and labor officials.

The Severna Park store test was designed to be as pure a test of the benefits and operation of scanning as could be devised. The store thus opened without any prices on individual items. Shelves were marked with a new descriptive unit price label and a scanning unit was set up in the front of the store for customers to use. The controversial nature of item pricing was evident soon enough. Even though customer response was enthusiastic, organized consumer groups began to register their complaints, even before the store's opening. The store was picketed, and bills were later introduced into the Maryland and Virginia legislatures to require item pricing.

Except for this consumer group reaction, the results from the Severna Park test were promising. Giant officials spent large amounts of time at the store gauging results. Cameras had been mounted to film the checkout process and time-and-motion studies were made of the film.

Taking Scanning Past the Test Phase

To this point, no one had given any indication of commitment beyond opening the test store. It was Cohen who announced a few months after the opening of the Severna Park store that a second scanning test installation should be used when the company opened its next store— a unit in Glen Burnie, Maryland, in August 1975. It was decided to put prices on all items in the Glen Burnie store. This meant that Cohen's faith in scanning was strong enough not to let the program die in the face of the recession the United States was suffering at the time. This decision also helped set a pattern of placing scanning in the new stores that Giant was scheduling to open.

Cohen's decision to go ahead with scanning in the new Glen Burnie store had an immediate impact on the choice of an equipment manufacturer. At this time, only IBM was offering full-scale scanning equipment. NCR was offering a point-of-sale terminal that could be upgraded at a later time to scanning, but scanning was not yet available. Thus, IBM equipment was chosen for Glen Burnie and would prove to be the model for all of Giant's subsequent scanning stores.

The team responsible for the Severna Park store went ahead with the installation of scanning at Glen Burnie and the training of people there. The experience at Severna Park paid off in an easier and trouble-free installation at Glen Burnie. The benefits seen at the Severna Park test were duplicated at Glen Burnie under its mildly different conditions.

During this time, Giant Food's managers were still somewhat surprised by the extent of consumer group activity against scanning without item pricing. While the company had managed, just barely, to argue the state legislatures of Maryland and Virginia out of mandatory item pricing, management was still very sensitive to consumer reaction. With this in mind, the company agreed to abide by the results of a Michigan State University study of scanning and price recognition. In early 1976, the study reported that there was some loss of price awareness in some consumers when scanning was used without item price marking. Giant Food thereby instituted item pricing in all its planned scanning stores as well as the Severna Park store. This finding was a blow to the company, but Giant publicly stated that they would abide by the results of the study. However, the benefits that Giant Food saw for scanning—both hard and soft savings—appeared to outweigh its costs, even when the savings in item pricing costs were excluded.

As it became more and more clear that scanning at the checkout counter would be a way of life for all of Giant Food's new stores and any that were undergoing extensive remodeling, the company's operations department became more and more involved with this transition in the company.* A point-of-scale

---

*In fact, because of the business advantages that Giant Food saw in scanning, an early commitment was made to install scanning not only in new stores but in all company stores. The first conversion of an existing store occurred in October 1975.

installation committee was formed with Buchanan as chairman. The committee consisted of an IBM representative, a manager from the company's construction department, a contract electrician involved in the installation, the vice-president of operations, the company's two zone managers, a personnel manager, and two members of the data processing department. This installation committee was charged with making a smooth transition in all stores and existed apart from the original data processing department team. This committee reviewed time schedules for phases of the installation, reported on installation progress, and ironed out coordination problems among the company departments that were becoming increasingly responsible for individual pieces of the scanner installation program.

At the same time the nature and composition of the original team changed. It dropped from seven members to six, retaining four of the original group, including the team leader. It was now called the data processing department field support team; its duties became more mechanical, directing and troubleshooting the installation process rather than evaluating it.

A point-of-sale steering committee, chaired by Buchanan, was appointed by Cohen in 1978. This group's purpose was to investigate the soft savings achievable through scanning. Little had been done on this at the beginning of the project, but with an increasing number of stores with scanning and an entire system of information created, it was decided to exploit such possible benefits.

The point-of-sale installation committee met for about two years (1976–77) and then disbanded. The field support team and the point-of-sale steering committee continued to operate into 1979. The installation of scanning in Giant Food stores became routine. A store could be converted to scanning with only about a week's notice.

When more than 60 percent of its stores used scanning, Giant Food's data processing department began merging the control systems for both scanning and nonscanning stores. As new scanning stores were instituted, separate data files for prices, inventory, costs, and the like were established to support them. As the new scanning system grew, it became more and more desirable to merge it with the former control system.

Over time there has been a drop in the real costs of installing scanning. Checkout counter stands are no longer the custom products they were in the first scanning stores. The number of grocery items marked with the Universal Product Code symbol has also grown; at the beginning of 1979, 95 percent of dry and frozen goods were marked. Source marking of pharmacy items has lagged behind these other items. Naturally, produce, meats, and seafood must continue to be marked at the store.

Giant Food's leadership in computerizing the grocery store has continued. In 1982, Giant Food announced it would study 11 more applications of computers in its stores. These applications range from computerized assistance to determine how a side of beef is to be butchered to an "electronic order book" for produce and direct store delivery from selected vendors.

Lessons from Giant Food

Giant Food Inc. is in no way responsible for the following views and presentation. They remain solely the responsibility of the author.

It is easy to observe how Giant Food's experience clearly reflects the general principles stated earlier:

1. Laser beam scanning at the checkout was seen early on as fitting particularly well into Giant Food's stores. Those stores were generally large and high volume, and it was in large, high volume stores that the most sig-

nificant benefits for scanning were expected. Moreover, Giant Food's top managers, Cohen and Danzansky, recognized this affinity and gave the entire project their very strong backing. The company's rich history of innovation no doubt helped establish change as the norm for the company, and so projects like scanning would not be opposed on irrational grounds.

2. Donald Buchanan and the project team did not hold unrealistic ideas about what scanning could do. Nor were all the possible uses of scanning explored at once. Rather, the team's mandate was a comparatively modest one: to develop a scanning system that worked and to place it in a test store so that some hard savings could be analyzed.

3. Some resistance to the innovation was encountered, but the company was flexible enough to overcome it.

4. Both the Severna Park and Glen Burnie stores used for the tests of scanning were typical of most Giant stores, especially the new ones. The tests were thus as representative as the company could make them.

5. In Donald Buchanan, Giant Food had a strong "change champion" who acted (1) to stimulate the company's thinking about scanning, (2) to organize a diverse project team and give it direction, (3) to isolate the team so that it could do its job without distraction, and (4) to support the team within the company so that team decisions stuck.

These general principles, of course, may not explain all of Giant Food's success in innovating laser beam scanning at the checkout counter. Other factors may have played an important and as yet undetected role. Nevertheless, these principles apply to Giant Food; what is more, they seem to carry over from one successful innovator to another. Furthermore, many stalled innovations or outright failures have neglected one or more of these general features of successful innovation. These principles bear careful consideration.

Recent Developments in Manufacturing Technology[9]

During the last decade or so, manufacturing technology has changed tremendously. There is now a dizzying array of sophisticated, electronics-based equipment to choose from. Consequently, factories of the future are likely to look very different from the factories of the present. The changes involve nearly every aspect of factory operation:

- *Materials.* New plastics, alloys, composites, powdered metals have been developed.

- *Inventory control.* Bar coding of parts and work orders, computerized parts storage and retrieval are commonplace today.

- *Materials handling.* Automatic guided vehicles, new kinds of conveyor systems, many with scanning equipment for bar codes are some recent changes.

- *Testing.* Automated testing equipment using X-rays, ultrasound, radioactivity; automatic gauging, including robotic gauging are two types of equipment innovations.

- *New hardware.* The plethora of new computerized systems is described next.

- *New means of controlling and linking hardware together.* Some techniques for improved control and communications are also described next.

Hardware Advances Affecting Continuous Flow and Line Flow Operations

As this text has already discussed, continuous flow and line flow operations are more capital-intensive than other kinds of processes.

Historically, that capital intensity has been in conveyors for materials handling and special-purpose equipment designed expressly for the process and plant being considered. With the march of technology, this equipment has become faster, more versatile, and more capable of producing quality products. Conveyors now have the ability to scan products and packaging for bar code identification and route items to different places by code. Equipment has been filled with sophisticated sensors and process controls that permit increased speed of operation while maintaining quality control. Automatic inspection equipment also acts to maintain quality.

Robots have been introduced in many line flow operations, often to perform under particularly nasty conditions, such as heat, noise, danger. Welding robots, painting robots, and "pick-and-place" materials handling robots are the most frequently observed types. Some of the more advanced robots, those capable of some assembly operations and those able to "see" and "feel" the work they handle are less prevalent.

Some technological proponents are so enthralled with the latest, flexible automation that they disparage the traditional, inflexible, "hard" automation that has characterized continuous flow and line flow processes for years. Yet, if a company can live with inflexibility, as is the case with most companies employing continuous or line flow processes, then "hard" automation and transfer lines (a linked series of machines that work on material that is clamped into position) are often the cheapest and most reliable equipment to operate.

Hardware Advances Affecting Job Shop and Batch Flow Operations

Some of the most intriguing recent changes in production technology have affected job shop and batch flow processes, which have not tra-ditionally been the objects of technological innovation. These changes have, in many instances, altered these processes so that they function more like line flow or continuous flow ones.

Let's tour some of the major innovations and the alphabet soup that their introductions have cooked up. Of comparatively long standing is the numerically controlled (NC) machine, which is capable of altering workpiece feed, workpiece position, and tool speed and orientation through the use of prepunched paper or plastic tape. NC machines are particularly prevalent in metal working functions like turning, milling, drilling, grinding, punching, and the like. NC machines can often perform jobs faster and more accurately than manually operated machines, but the tapes require programming, sometimes at considerable expense.

Much more recent has been the development of the CNC (computer numerically controlled) machine, which allows the operator to punch in the various specifications and controls for the job and eliminates the need for prepunching a tape. A CNC machine is thus more flexible than an NC machine. In addition, many CNC machines can change tools automatically, selecting the next tool from a rotating inventory of tools. The next generation of machines are DNC (direct numerical control) machines. DNC ties together a CNC machine with a computer (known as a controller) that directs its movements.

The capabilities of CNC and DNC machines constitute one pillar of CIM (computer integrated manufacturing). The ideal for CIM is the creation and design of new parts on a computer, the translation of those designs into instructions usable by CNC and DNC machines, and the activation of actual production using those instructions.

Other pillars for CIM are CAD (computer aided design) and CAM (computer aided manufacturing). CAD capabilities have progressed rapidly in recent years. In essence, CAD hardware and software enables the design engineer to do mechanical drawing without a drafting table, and to do it better. With CAD, parts can be created, their dimensions changed easily, various geometric views checked out, and the parts tested for fit, stress, and other features without the necessity for any expensive, physical prototype. This can be an enormous saving of time and expense.

CAM (computer aided manufacturing) has been less widespread. CAM is also a more ambiguous subject. For some, CAM has a fairly limited scope, applying only to the use of the computer to generate instructions for CNC or DNC machines or for designing tools, fixtures, and layouts or for preparing or analyzing quality control data. For others, CAM is broader, even to the point of taking the CAD-generated design and following it through to the finished piece.

To date, linking CAD with CAM and the potential of CIM have yet to be realized in many manufacturing situations. Also in its infancy is flexible manufacturing system (FMS) technology. FMS combines the group technology layout and parts family concepts discussed in Chapter 2 with DNC technology. With FMS, a series of DNC machines are grouped together and linked with automatic materials handling equipment, all under the direction of a controller. In essence, then, FMS is a more fully automated example of group technology. A part is started in one machine, perhaps necessitating an automated tool change. Once finished, the part is automatically removed and transferred to the next operation. The part proceeds from one machine to the next, all without human intervention—even for setup. Such a system is capable of running independently, say at night, without workers to monitor it. All actions are taken as result of the controlling computer program. A key advantage of an FMS is that it can switch to making completely different parts.

Small lots, or even single parts, can often be easily run through the system. There are still comparatively few true FMS's in operation throughout the world, although their numbers are growing rapidly. To date, they have not been as flexible as their proponents have trumpeted. Often the effort to get the system up and running on the initial small family of parts is so exhausting for the engineers and managers involved that they are reluctant to broaden its role. Nevertheless, many FMS adopters are pleased with the technology.

We are already seeing glimpses of the factories these technological advances may lead to in the future. For example, the Messerschmitt plant in Augsburg, West Germany, uses a flexible manufacturing system to produce a center section of the Tornado fighter plane. This flexible manufacturing system, costing in excess of $50 million, links 28 NC machine centers, an automated tool flow and changing system, an automated workpiece transport system. A computer then controls the movement of workpieces, the changing of tools, and the operation of all the machines. The efficiencies this system has permitted are remarkable. The machines in this system cut metal about 75 percent of the time, an unheard-of percentage in more manual systems. Lead time for production of the fighter plane is only 18 months, compared with the almost 30 months for similar planes produced by more conventional techniques. The flexible manufacturing system has reduced the number of NC machines required by 44 percent, the personnel required by 44 percent, floor space by 30 percent, and throughput time by 25 percent.

The Kamo works of the Niigata Converter Company in Japan is another example. Of its 200 machine tools, 15 are capable of running unmanned at night and these 15 account for 29 percent of the output of the plant. On average, these machines are cutting metal half of each 24-hour day. Still another example is Fujitsu Fanuc. In one of its factories there are 29 manufacturing cells with wire guided materials handling and automatic storage. During the day shift, the operations runs with 19 workers and at night with only one. Only Fujitsu's assembly operations remain labor intensive; still, 100 workers account for about $75 million in sales, about five times as productive as a conventional plant producing the same output mix.

This automation has occurred in the United States, too. Allen-Bradley, Inc., of Milwaukee has developed a $15 million, completely automated assembly line for making contactors and relays (starters and controllers for industrial electric motors) in various models. The assembly line consists of 26 stations where nearly 200 different parts are installed in just 45 minutes. Each hour 600 units are produced, but the lot run can easily be as small as a single unit. Bar codes help the system differentiate one product model from another. The line can make products in 2 different sizes and with up to 999 possible combinations of parts, without slowing for changes. Quality is aided in part with 3500 automatic inspection steps. Not surprisingly, Allen-Bradley is now the lowest-cost producer in the world.

Not all factories will become so automated, but increased automation does seem to be a clear trend. It is likely that, with time, many factories will replace more and more of their direct labor with automated equipment.

Managing the New Technology

Day-to-day manufacturing problems are becoming more the problems of white-collar workers (engineers and managers), rather than solely the problems of blue-collar workers. Machines will increasingly do the dirty work.

This is not to say that manufacturing is likely to become easy to manage well. Rather, we can expect that a different set of problems will demand attention. More processes are likely to need sophisticated engineering skills on a regular basis. This may mean shortages of engineers or of technical assistants such as programmers. The heightened need for engineering may also trigger more conflicts within the company—clashes between engineering and manufacturing, purchasing, marketing, and finance. There may be more conflicts between different kinds of engineering (such as design versus process engineering).

With technological advance, management's responsibilities are apt to be modified in various ways:

- The means by which new technologies (such as CAD/CAM) are evaluated financially may need to be changed, because present procedures (including net present value techniques) tend to discriminate against the new technological advances.[10] Although the costs are all captured, the benefits of such advances are often so diffuse and hard to quantify that they escape traditional procedures.

- Because companies are more likely to have to live with technological change on a continuing basis, a company must become more attuned to feedback on its technological choice. No longer may companies simply study and choose technology as if it were a one-shot deal.

- Because of the recent advances for job shop or batch flow processes, many companies are going to have to reconceptualize these processes and the planning and control systems for them. Particular attention will have to be paid to the management of transition within the company. Items like training and dealing with workers who feel threatened by technological advance may take on added emphasis. These issues have already been faced by many continuous flow process companies; their experiences have and will serve as models for others.

- At a strategic level, a key decision is the choice of which technologies to pursue and when. Many companies have failed to detect the change of technological winds—vacuum tube makers that discounted semiconductor advances, chemical companies that discounted materials changes, pinball machine makers that discounted video games. The antennae must always be up and searching for new developments, if merely to defend the company's interests.

In regard to the last mentioned change, a company must be well aware of the limits to its own technological prowess so as not to be blinded when the promise of something better rolls around. Ten signals that can tip off a company to the imminent approach of a technological limit have been identified.[11]

- Top managers have an intuitive sense that the company's R&D productivity is declining.
- R&D is missing more and more of its deadlines. This trend is often misinterpreted as a signal that the department is losing effectiveness, when in reality improvement is becoming more difficult to achieve.
- Typically, as limits are approached, process improvements are easier to attain than product improvements (as we noted at the start of this chapter).
- The creativity of R&D is perceived as having declined.
- There is disharmony among the R&D staff.
- Replacement of R&D leaders or staff brings little or no improvement.

- Profits come from increasingly narrow market segments.
- Market share in a specialized market niche is lost. This signal is particularly important when market share is lost to a smaller competitor.
- There is little difference in returns despite spending substantially more—or less—than competitors over a period of years. When significant variations in expenditures produce no significant differences in performance, the technology is near its limits.
- Smaller competitors are taking radical approaches that "probably won't work." If they do work, larger competitors may suddenly become smaller ones.

The company that is alert to such signals can start to assess more radical revisions to its product offerings and process capabilities.

CONCLUDING REMARKS

Clearly, in the future a manager will have to spend more time dealing with technological change. As was noted in Part Two, no one model for technology management has emerged as superior. However, as we have discussed, some management practices can enhance the probability of success when faced with technology changes. Of prime importance is an awareness of issues and complications associated with the adoption or avoidance of new products and processes. This awareness includes recognizing that different changes—incremental versus radical, product versus process—require varying management methods. Also, managers need to learn not to rule out possible technology paths too quickly and they need to keep up on the basics.

QUESTIONS

1. What do you understand by the term *technological change?*
2. What are the mathematical assumptions behind the learning curve? What does learning represent for manufacturing?
3. What is linear regression and of what relevance is it to the Nashville Fire Equipment Company? Give three examples of other situations in which the concept would be useful and applicable.

4. What are some uses of the learning curve in long-term strategic decisions?
5. Analyze and discuss the relationship between product innovation and process innovation, providing a concrete example from your own reading or experience.
6. In what ways does Giant Food's introduction of scanning into its grocery stores illustrate the general principles operating behind radical process innovations?

PROBLEMS

1. Summarize the procedure for calculating a learning curve. Of what use is this procedure?
2. It has been observed that preemptive pricing strategies are more useful in certain situations than in others. What are the characteristics of these situations?
3. How can changing the product design result in a technological change?

SITUATION FOR STUDY 8-1
Kid Klothes, Inc.

Bob Stifler is president of Kid Klothes, a small family-owned apparel manufacturer for children. He was contemplating the acquisition of some new technology in an effort to keep his company competitive in the cut-throat world of apparel. Children's clothes were highly cost sensitive; mothers did not wish to spend a lot of money outfitting their children, yet children's clothes contained all of the pieces and seams to sew as large clothes, effectively constraining many of the cost savings possible. Labor was a significant variable cost in the manufacture of children's clothes, accounting

for as much as 35 percent of the cost of goods sold. Any savings on the direct labor making up a child's garment would help make that clothing more price-competitive in the marketplace.

Bob was especially interested in applying some of the latest technology to the fabrication of children's clothes, particularly the use of automated sewing machines and of automated fabric cutters. The investments in this new technology were sizable. An automated cutting system of the type Bob felt was necessary cost $300,000, and programmable automated sewing machines with edge guides cost $15,000 each. The best estimates predicted the automated cutter could replace 14 full time cutters. The automated sewing machine could, on average, double the output from a conventional sewing machine. The average shop wage was $6 per hour.

Bob wondered what he should know before making this decision. What were the things he should be leary of about this new technology, and how should he assess it? He had to act quickly or else forfeit the chance to use this new technology for the next seasonal peak in production.

SITUATION FOR STUDY 8-2
MEDICAL HOSPITAL

Medical Hospital is a large regional hospital located in Weatherford, Oklahoma. Included in the hospital is a large pharmacy. Recently, the pharmacy has been experiencing long lead times for filling prescriptions, and the pharmacy manager, Patricia Pritchard, is anxious to find a solution to the problem. The main difficulty occurs during night hours and weekends when the regular pharmacists are off duty.

During the evening shifts (3 P.M. to 11 P.M.) and weekends, the pharmacy is staffed by technicians. The technicians are trained in pharmacy procedures but are not pharmacists. They are allowed, however, to fill prescriptions. Due to the time of the shift and the requirement of working every other weekend, it has been very

difficult to find highly motivated and trainable people to work full-time. Most people preferred to work days and wanted weekends off. Many who were hired were slow to learn the job.

An alternative to hiring full-time technicians was to hire students from a nearby pharmacy school on a part-time basis. Each student worked about 20 hours a week, and so twice as many employees were needed to fill all the slots. Most pharmacy students could be expected to work a maximum of two to three years because once they finished their pharmacy program, they were not happy to be technicians. Also, some of the students would tie their work to the school calendar, and turnover was high in May, August, and December. The result was that from

TABLE 8-4 Orders filled per hour (Medical Hospital)

EMPLOYEE	WEEK 1	WEEK 2	WEEK 3	WEEK 4	WEEK 5	WEEK 6
A	8	12	12	15	18	20
B	6	11	12	14	16	18
C	7	12	14	16	16	16
D	8	10	10	14	14	18
E	12	18	20	21	21	22
F	5	8	10	11	12	14
G	6	8	10	13	15	16
H	8	10	13	15	17	19
I	9	10	12	12	14	16
J	10	12	15	17	19	21

two to five technicians (an average of three) were new every four months. Usually technicians were brought in at a rate of two per week and were trained on the job as well as by a course taught by the pharmacists.

Patricia had noticed not only that productivity was low, but also that the cost of training technicians was high. She had heard that the learning curve concept had been applied in manufacturing and wondered whether it could be applied to the pharmacy's product, a filled order. Pat defined an order as having three medications, the average. If an order had six medications, it was counted as two orders. On an average night 55 orders were processed. The normal maximum speed for an employee was around 20 to 24 orders per hour.

Patricia decided to study, for several weeks, the speed with which 10 technicians filled orders. The shift supervisor collected information on orders filled correctly by these technicians. It was easy to identify each technician's work, as they were required to initial each order filled. Table 8-4 shows the results of this study in orders filled per hour, and Figure 8-8 shows the learning curves for three of the 10 employees.

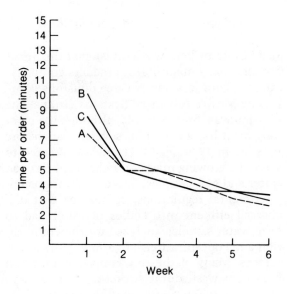

FIGURE 8-8   Learning curves for technicians A, B, and C.

Now that Patricia had this information, she was uncertain how it could be used to help reduce the cost of training new employees, and how she could help reduce her turnover problem.

CASE FOR STUDY
MEAD COMPUCHEM
THE ETHERNET DECISION

It was June 1982. Howard Magid, vice-president of operations for Mead CompuChem, stared out his window at the threatening clouds. His plane reservations for a trip to the West Coast next week had just been confirmed. Howard wondered what he would hear there from Finnigan Corporation and Hewlett-Packard. What these companies' engineers had to say might help Howard decide what should be done about the Ethernet project.

Background on Mead CompuChem

Mead CompuChem was a division of the Mead Corporation, a major forest products company. CompuChem was one of three divisions comprising Mead's Advanced Systems Group. The division was three years old, although the planning for it had gone on for several years before its start in 1979. The division was created to serve the growing market for chemical tests on water and soil samples. Because of various environmental regulations, companies that discharged effluent into bodies of water had to have water samples analyzed for the composition and concentrations of various known pollutants. Many of the soil samples came from hazardous waste dump sites; they were used to determine the composition of the material buried at the site. Rather than analyze the samples themselves, companies often contracted laboratories to do the analyses. Mead CompuChem serviced commercial customers as well as the Environmental Protection Agency. (Mead CompuChem's lab in Research Triangle Park, North Carolina, was just down the road from one of EPA's main laboratories.)

Since its start with four employees, the division had grown to 89 people at Research Triangle Park and another 16 at a newly opened satellite regional facility in Chicago. Sales had increased more than threefold in 1981 and were expected to double in 1982.

The concept at Mead CompuChem was to make a line flow process out of what historically had been treated as a small batch operation. Analyzing environmental samples for pollutants was not new. Traditionally, such analyses demanded the use of specialized machines called gas chromatograph/mass spectrometers (GC/MS). These delicate scientific instruments cost about $120,000 each. Typically, pollution analysis would be done by a Ph.D. chemist operating such an instrument and interpreting its results. Mead Corporation foresaw that with the increase in environmental regulations mandating pollution testing, this small-sample approach could be altered to make it a much more systematic line flow process. With specialization of duties and attention to the flow of materials, Mead CompuChem could do in three weeks and at much lower cost what it took traditional chemists six weeks to do.

A Description of the Process

Mead CompuChem was strictly an analytical laboratory. It did not collect samples for its clients nor did it interpret the results. It simply provided the client with a chemical analysis of which pollutants occurred in the samples and in what concentrations. The client could order a variety of tests. For water samples, a deluxe test would detect and determine the concentrations of 128 "priority" pollutants—including acids, bases, pesticides, volatile chemicals, metals, cyanides, and phenols. The most popular analysis detected 113 organic chemicals that were priority pollutants. In addition, on a special quotation basis, CompuChem could provide analytical services to a customer's specifications.

To a client requesting sample analysis CompuChem would send a patented container with decontaminated bottles and jars of various sizes in which to put the collected samples. The client would ship the container back to Mead CompuChem by air freight. Upon receipt of the container, documentation was initiated to indicate what kinds of analyses were desired, what procedures would be required, where the analyses and their preparation steps would be performed in the lab (there were 23 work stations), and the time each work station had to perform its task (without violating EPA-mandated analysis procedures or making the final report late to the client).

After the order was entered into the computer routing and scheduling system, the samples were prepared for analysis. If a water sample was to include analysis of volatile chemicals, no preparation was required other than to refrigerate it. For all other tests, the sample was prepared by a process called *extraction*, which concentrated any chemicals in the sample so that they could be analyzed. The equipment in the extraction lab was designed to concentrate organic constituents from water and soil samples. Once extracted, the small vials of concentrated samples were ready for the gas chromatograph/mass spectrometry lab.

In an analysis by GC/MS, one to five microliters of a sample solution were injected into a gas chromatograph injection port. Here the sample was volatilized and entered the chromatographic column, where differences in the chemical nature of each compound in the sample caused a separation of compounds. Each compound entered the instrument's ion source (through a special pressure balancing interface), where it was bombarded by electrons. This bombardment caused the molecules to fragment into a characteristic pattern of smaller charged particles called ions. These ions were then separated according to their mass-to-charge ratio and detected in sequence by an electron multiplier. The signal generated by the multiplier was proportional to the abundance of each fragment ion and could be used to generate a "mass spectrum" for each compound in the sample. To identify the component, the instrument's computer data system compared the spectrum of the unknown material with a library of compounds. If the system could not make a match, a skilled chemist looking at a printed mass spectrum was sometimes able to identify which compounds produced specific peaks in that mass spectrum and the levels at which they were present. For some unknowns, however, the mass spectrum information was not sufficient to identify the compounds.

While reasonably simple in concept, the GC/MS technology was extremely sophisticated. Furthermore, the data produced by such an in-

strument was so voluminous (15 to 25 megabytes of data per day per instrument) that each of CompuChem's 18 GC/MS machines in Raleigh/Durham and each of its six machines in Chicago required its own minicomputer to accumulate the data and reduce it to a form that could be analyzed.

In a typical run, the GC/MS took about 45 minutes to perform the chemical analysis and to accumulate the data. During this time, the minicomputer could perform two distinct tasks—the foreground (or primary) task and the background task. The foreground task was always the accumulation of raw data for the run in progress. The background task could vary. Important background tasks included (1) "quantitation," whereby the raw data from the previous run underwent some calculations and were summarized; (2) printing; and (3) searches, whereby specific characteristics of the previous run were compared with a library of such characteristics in order to help identify the compounds. Occasionally, a sample was so complex that the background tasks on the previous run's data, particularly printing, could not be accomplished in the 45 minutes devoted to accumulating data on the current run. To give the minicomputer time to catch up, a new sample injection was postponed 15 to 20 minutes. This kind of delay was especially prevalent with semivolatile analyses, where it occurred for between 20 and 40 percent of the samples.

After a run had been made on the GS/MS, the run results were reviewed by an assistant manager, usually a shift later. The results as reviewed were sent to the report integration section, which collected all the analyses done for a client's order and integrated them into a single report. The resulting documents were then transmitted to the quality control section, which looked for any irregularities in each run and determined whether any problems existed. When there was a problem, the results could usually be corrected by reevaluating the origi-

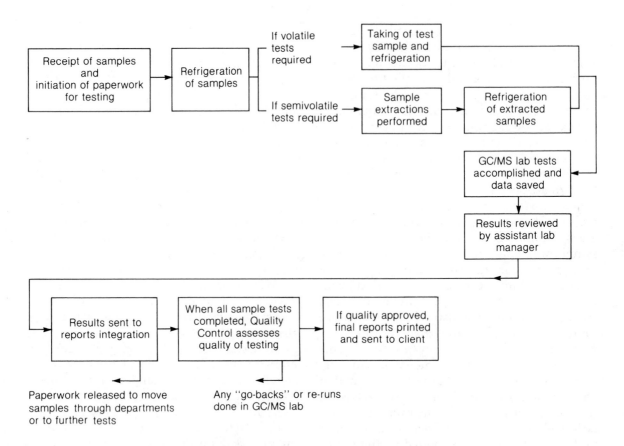

FIGURE 8-9   Simplified process flow for Mead CompuChem.

nal data, although sometimes samples had to be rerun. Quality control typically saw the results three to four days after they had been run. Once quality control approved the run, a final report was generated. Figure 8-9 presents a process flow diagram for CompuChem's operation.

The Research Triangle Park GC/MS lab housed 18 machines. They were run 24 hours a day on three shifts. Not all of them were necessarily busy during each shift; that depended partly on the volume and mix of work entering the lab. Two of the machines were used only for R&D. One shift of four machines was dedicated to product development—special analysis aside from the mandated environmental

work or perfecting new procedures before their introduction into the production laboratory; these machines could be pressed into service during the second and third shifts if they were needed because of work volume or downtime on other machines. The remaining 12 machines were used routinely for production. They were grouped into four stations of three machines each. Two stations concentrated on the analysis of volatiles, and two on the analysis of semivolatiles; samples for the latter had undergone preparation in the extraction lab.

At the start of each eight-hour shift, by EPA mandate, each machine had to be "tuned." This tuning was almost an art and typically took about an hour. Tuning ensured that the machine was operating properly and was detecting all that it should be detecting and that the results would be reproducible by other machines in other laboratories. To tune a machine, the technician ran a standard solution of known compounds through the machine to see whether the machine detected all the compounds in this solution and at the correct concentration levels. A blank sample containing pure water, for example, would also be run to make sure that the machine was being completely purged of contaminants between runs.

A single technician handled three machines (a work station) at a time. Each of the machines would be set up for a particular type of procedure. Because a setup could take several hours, it was advisable to run together as many samples requiring the same procedure as possible. During any eight-hour shift, the technician in charge of a work station was exceedingly busy. The tasks might include retrieving a sample from the refrigerator, "shooting" it into the machine, monitoring data acquisition, initiating the software programs that reduce the data, monitoring the summary tables, starting the printing of the reports on the run, setting up the machine for different procedures, tuning a machine, performing an initial data review, or initiating preventive maintenance.

Quality Control

Ensuring that the GC/MS was operating properly and that the results it derived were accurate was a complicated endeavor. Not only did the machine need to be tuned every eight hours, but each sample had to be specially prepared. To calibrate the machine's results so that the concentrations of pollutants could be accurately determined, special concentrations of standard chemicals not normally occurring in nature were "spiked" into every sample. These special compounds at their known concentra-

tions provided the standards with which to compare the pollutants in a sample. Naturally, it was desired that the GC/MS detect all the surrogates spiked into each sample. If, for example, the level of a particular surrogate was too low, something was wrong. Perhaps the instrument was faulty. Or perhaps something about the chemistry of the sample led the surrogate to be "lost" chemically.

Determining the cause and extent of any GC/MS failures was a key duty of the four workers in the quality control section. To be assured that all was well, the quality control section entered (1) pure blanks into the system, (2) blanks spiked with standard compounds, and (3) already analyzed samples spiked with known concentrations of specific compounds. About 10 percent of the volume run through the lab consisted of blanks, and one of every 20 consisted of a blank or a sample spiked with known concentrations of particular compounds. Given such care, most runs went smoothly and presented no problems. However, about 5 to 10 percent of all samples needed to be rerun because of problems, and about 5 percent required the reevaluation of the raw data produced by the machine.

To provide this capability of reevaluating raw data, all the runs done by the lab were saved on magnetic tape. This archive also permitted clients who had questions about the analysis to look at the data in raw form. Unfortunately, the GC/MS were not equipped to generate magnetic tapes. To generate a tape, the disk pack from a GC/MS had to be removed and placed on another computer system that would dump its contents onto a magnetic tape; the disk pack could then be replaced and reused. It took about 15 minutes to remove a disk pack, transport it to the tape back-up apparatus, locate another disk pack, put it back onto the GC/MS, and have the machine ready for a new analysis. Approximately every 5 to 10 runs, the disk pack was filled and required the back-up procedure.

Thus, for each machine in the lab, between 15 minutes and half an hour every shift were spent backing up the run results.

In addition to authorizing controls (blanks) through the GC/MS the quality control section examined the outcomes of all the tests. Reports were not released without quality control's approval.

Current Problems and the Promise of Ethernet

The effective utilization of CompuChem's resources suggested that the company was better off when (1) all of its GC/MS were tuned and accumulating data, as opposed to being untuned or processing/printing data; (2) all computerized information was used by computers only and printed out on high-speed printers, as opposed to forming the basis for manually typed reports and the manual use of computer-generated data; and (3) there was little lag in the availability of data by quality control or by other areas of the business. These points can be explained more completely:

1. *Machine availability.* The extreme complexity of the instruments used in the GC/MS lab and the need to have them tuned every eight hours placed real constraints on the business. Naturally, the greater the fraction of any shift a machine was devoted to running samples and accumulating data, the more profitable it and the lab were. Time spent tuning a machine and waiting for hard copy printouts to be developed was essentially unproductive. If machines could be tuned more quickly or if data processing by the GC/MS themselves could be avoided, then the lab could be more productive.

   In addition, the constant starting and stopping of the disk drives was beginning to cause the physical deterioration of the units. Several head crashes (i.e., hardware failures that lost all the data on a system by destroying the recording medium on the disk) were occurring each quarter, costing about $400 in hardware costs and two hours in lost machine time each, if the parts were in stock. In addition, each head crash destroyed the data from one or more runs and these samples had to be repeated. Thus, instrument downtime required for repairs was increasing and the mean time between failures was dropping.

2. *Use of machine-generated data.* At several points in the CompuChem process, computer-generated data were printed into hard copy reports and manipulated manually before a final report was sent to the client. It was recognized that the process would be more productive if, every time data were generated by the computer, they could be saved for subsequent computer use and not lost. Two segments of the process were particularly important in this regard:

   - The final reports that were sent to clients included data that the GC/MS had generated. However, because these data were saved only on tapes or on hard copies, the final report could not easily use that information. Efficiency would be enhanced if the word processors that printed the client reports could tap directly into the GC/MS generated data. In that way, the report writing operators would not have to enter significant results manually into final reports.
   - A computer system (the laboratory management system) scheduled jobs in particular labs and their work stations. However, the results of each step in the process had to be entered manually onto the laboratory management system and the paperwork for each job had to be reis-

sued. If the output of one segment of the process could be saved on the central computer, then the data entry step could be eliminated and the paperwork describing each job's routing would not have to be reissued. This would save some effort in production control.

In addition, because of manual transcription of data, erroneous information was sometimes placed on the various computer systems in the laboratory. If basic data could be entered only once and the results automatically accumulated in that file, adequate safeguards could be installed to ensure that the error rates were almost zero.

3. *Time lags for information.*   Quality control suffered a lag of three or four days before it could review a run's results. This lag imposed some extra cost on the system. For example, in about 5 percent of the cases, Quality control ordered a "go-back," a re-analysis of the data accumulated by a GC/MS. Under the current system, a go-back necessitated a transfer of data from tape to disk and then the remounting of the disk pack onto the GC/MS. All told, a go-back cost about an hour of various people's time. Some go-backs could be avoided if more hard copy were generated by each run, but the generation of this hard copy would consume operator time and GC/MS time. The time lag for quality control also raised concerns about the propagation of incorrect procedures or machine operation. If such faulty operations could be identified early, savings would result.

The technology called "Ethernet" showed promise of solving some of the problems inherent in CompuChem's current operations. Ethernet is a local area network technology developed by Xerox Corporation and licensed to users at a nominal fee. This technology permitted computers and other data processing equipment to exchange data at fantastically high speeds, on the order of 10 million bits per second. Theoretically, an Ethernet network could connect all of CompuChem's GC/MSs with other computers and peripheral devices such as tape drives and larger disk pack storage units. In such a system the GC/MS machines could "pitch" data to larger and faster computers that could "catch" the data and manipulate them faster than could the minicomputer within each GC/MS machine. The GC/MSs would no longer be stand-alone units but would be tied to each other and to a series of computers that could service the data much more efficiently. No longer then would the GC/MS minicomputers tie up instrument time merely processing and printing hard-copy reports. No longer would disk packs have to be dismounted and remounted in order to save data on tape. No longer would quality control have to wait three or four days for the hard copy results of particular runs; instead, it could review a given shift's data within minutes of that shift's completion. In fact, quality control could even monitor a machine's performance as it was collecting data. Individual GC/MSs could pitch packets of freshly accumulated raw data onto Ethernet, which could then feed that data to a dedicated computer for quantitation, printing, search, and other analysis. The potential of Ethernet was exceedingly enticing. (See Table 8-5 for a summary of the benefits anticipated with an Ethernet network.)

The Situation with Finnigan

Finnigan Corporation was a small, but highly regarded, one-product company located in California's Silicon Valley. It had designed and produced all the GC/MSs used at CompuChem. To develop an Ethernet network, these machines had to be linked to an Ethernet cable

TABLE 8-5 Potential savings from an Ethernet Network

ITEM	PRESENT OPERATION	ESTIMATED BENEFIT FROM ETHERNET
Quality control		
1. Identifying GC/MS malfunction (occurs about once a month)	4 worker-days	Only one worker-day likely
2. Go-backs	5% of runs; 1 hour spent on each go-back	Go-backs eliminated; data already on-line
3. Reruns	About 5–10% of all runs	Savings probably less than 10% of current cost of reruns
4. Special requests for hard copy output by QC section	Occurs in about 10% of runs; requires about 1 minute of print time to produce	Special request eliminated; data already on-line
5. Effort by QC section	Base case for comparison	Twice the checks could be accomplished in half the time
Product control		
1. Report integration	Paperwork on routing, procedures, and timetable reissued after each lab performs its tasks	Only one set of paperwork need be issued; all tracking could be done on-line
2. Scheduling	Done by lab managers and operators; slack in schedule estimated at 20% of capacity	Could be done entirely by computer; slack in schedule could be reduced
3. Final report	Clerks need to enter numerical results into word processing	Savings estimated at 70% of two clerks' time
GC/MS lab operations		
1. Instrument "up-time"	Instruments up about 60–70% of the time they could be available for data accumulation (i.e., tuned and functioning)	Instruments could be fully utilized for data accumulation once tuned
2. Archive function	About 16 worker-hours per day; inadvertent slack in shift schedule	4 hours per day; turnaround would improve (more runs per shift)
3. Reliability	Frequent handling of disk packs results in some problems with data integrity	Reliability would improve
4. Reviewer time	Recurring problems not caught early	Quick availability of data may eliminate these problems. Savings in worker-hours (by the reviewer of run results) estimated at 10–15%

*Estimates based on departmental information.

with the appropriate hardware and software to permit each machine to pitch data onto the Ethernet network. (The development of Ethernet also meant configuring the Ethernet so that it was compatible with the HP3000 minicomputer whose planned use was as the "catcher" of the summary data the GC/MSs pitched. This problem was one Mead CompuChem had to address.) The hardware involved a modem board that permitted data to be trans-mitted outside the minicomputer built into each machine. The software was to organize the data into "packets" so that they could be pitched effectively onto the Ethernet network.

CompuChem's idea about using Ethernet was not new. In June 1981, CompuChem had approached Finnigan about the applicability of Ethernet. At that time an agreement was reached that Finnigan would develop the modem and write the software. This agreement was very favorable to CompuChem: Finnigan agreed to install the required hardware and software with no advance payment and with the stipulation that CompuChem had no financial obligation if the network did not meet its specifications.

Finnigan had estimated that 90 days would be required to complete the task. However, it was eight months before Finnigan returned to CompuChem with a prototype. This prototype included a modem board and some software. The prototype did succeed in transmitting data from the previously stand-alone equipment to a computer that could catch the data. However, it took too long and thus was not acceptable. In fact, the old procedure of removing the disk pack and physically carrying it to another computer to be mounted and processed onto tape was faster than the Finnigan prototype. Finnigan acknowledged the failure of its prototype to meet requirements and promised to return with an improvement. In June 1982, four months after the unsuccessful debut of its prototype, Finnigan had yet to return with a workable system. Howard Magid did not know whether Finnigan was close to a solution or whether the company had abandoned hope of developing the software necessary to use an Ethernet network effectively. Although the financial agreement was favorable to CompuChem, the absence of a financial stake in the venture did significantly reduce CompuChem's leverage with Finnigan. Howard did have a favorable opinion of Finnigan's technical capabilities in general, however, and had faith in the leader of Finnigan's software efforts.

Short-Term Options

Howard had identified four options:

1. *Wait for Finnigan.* If Finnigan was successful in remedying the present problems within a reasonably short time, then all was

well. The hardware changes that Finnigan was making would probably cost CompuChem about $100,000. When Finnigan would succeed, however, was not known; it could be next week, or never. It was not clear either when CompuChem would know that Finnigan had failed. Finnigan could, of course, state that it had abandoned the project, but Magid thought that unlikely. Rather, he thought that Finnigan would put this project on the back burner, claiming to CompuChem that it was working on it slowly but surely.

CompuChem did not require the use of the Ethernet network right away. The current economic recession had affected CompuChem's business. Sales for 1982 were originally forecasted to be three times 1981 levels, but in June it looked like sales would only double them. This decline offered the company some breathing space, because it was only with high volumes that the capabilities of the Ethernet system to augment capacity were seen most clearly. Although no one knew when the recession would break, Howard thought that it would be autumn before volume picked up substantially and the lab would again clog up with work.

2. *Use what Finnigan had already done and jerry-rig the rest.* CompuChem could take the eight modems already developed by Finnigan, reimburse Finnigan for the $30,000–$40,000 that their development probably cost, and use those modems to link groups of two or three GC/MSs via "hard wiring" to minicomputers to process some of the data from each machine and to do the tape archive of each run. This option would abandon the Ethernet network in favor of a much less sophisticated approach. CompuChem would lose the ability to review data on-line, which quality control had wanted. However, the major features desired—keeping the machines up longer, saving the transfer of disk

packs for archival purposes, and using computer-generated summary information directly in the preparation of final reports—would all be saved. This fix of the problem would be a custom job, but it would be fairly inflexible and would duplicate only a fraction of what Ethernet's total potential promised for the company over the years.

3. *Go to a third party and try to save the Ethernet concept.*   Under this option, the modem hardware that Finnigan had already developed would be used, but CompuChem would try to save the concept of an Ethernet by going to a software expert to develop the software for linking the Finnigan GC/MSs to an Ethernet (such as placing the data into "packets" and making the network connection). In essence, this option would do for CompuChem all that Finnigan was supposed to do but apparently could not. This option would be more expensive than the first two, requiring about $100,000 for hardware and about $50,000 for software.

Both this option and the second one ran some risks. It could be that Ethernet and related technologies simply could not be married effectively with GC/MS. By choosing either option 2 or option 3, CompuChem risked throwing away lots of money. Another risk was associated with fixing any problems with the Finnigan instruments. If software deficiencies or errors were identified, Finnigan would provide remedial software to solve the problem. However, both options 2 and 3 called for modifications in the Finnigan software. Hence, any software problems might be seen as related to the adaptation of the software, not with anything that Finnigan had been responsible for. Thus it was safer to have Finnigan entirely responsible for all hardware and all software, because the company would ensure that the instrument was capable of meeting specifications. By choosing either option 2 or option 3, CompuChem risked losing Finnigan's expertise in solving any software problems that cropped up.

To make matters worse, a large portion of the program code for the instrument was undocumented. Modifications were difficult, if not impossible, without the close cooperation of the Finnigan "gurus" who understood the guts of the system.

4. *Do nothing.*   CompuChem could abandon its search for a solution to this problem and run the operation more or less as it was. The cost of this option was opportunity costs, which were fairly negligible at low volumes but increased substantially as volume grew. Howard Magid felt that with high volumes an Ethernet network could save between $50,000 and $100,000 per year in staff salary costs in quality control, data processing, and elsewhere.

Long-Term Considerations

Mead CompuChem was currently depreciating the Finnigan machines it owned in three years. Thus, next year, in 1983, the first group of six Finnigan machines would be fully depreciated. CompuChem did not have to use Finnigan machines. Hewlett-Packard also made a GC/MS and was expected to announce its latest models in September. According to advance reports, these models would permit local area network communication (HP's own design, not Xerox's Ethernet) between machine and Hewlett-Packard minicomputer. Howard Magid viewed this as a favorable development, because Hewlett-Packard had an excellent reputation and was considered by many to announce new machnes only after technical problems had been solved. Thus, CompuChem could wait a year or so and start acquiring Hewlett-Packard equipment that would have a local area network already developed for it and serviced by the company. This approach was consistent with CompuChem's decision to purchase HP3000 minicomputers to drive the laboratory management system. Hewlett-Packard GC/MS equipment had not been originally chosen because the Finnigan equipment was easier to tune and operated more smoothly. It was hoped that the new Hewlett-Packard GC/MS would be closer to Finnigan's performance.

More fundamental to the long-term prospects of Mead CompuChem was the impending decision about the kinds of chemical tests that the company would perform in the future. Lee Myers, Mead CompuChem's president, thought it likely that the company would pursue larger markets than those spawned by environmental regulations. For example, markets for very esoteric testing in toxicology or chemotherapy could be entered easily. These markets, however, required higher volumes, quicker turnarounds (day, not weeks), and lower unit prices than the environmental analysis business, although their data needs for each test would be much less. If CompuChem were to enter this market, it would probably need analytical instruments different from GC/MSs. With an Ethernet network, however, even new instruments could be linked with GC/MSs and computers to provide a very flexible analysis system.

Lee Myers expected that this strategic decision for CompuChem would be made in the next six months. His goal was to have the environmental business be less than half of the division's total sales in three or four years.

REFERENCE NOTES

1. *Business Week* (July 3, 1978): 47.

2. William J. Abernathy and James M. Utterback, "Pattern of Industrial Innovation," *Technology Review* 80 no. 7 (June–July 1978): 40–47.

3. Abernathy, *The Productivity Dilemma*, Johns Hopkins University Press, 1978.

4. For some additional information on the learning curve, see David L. Bodde, "Riding the Experience Curve," *Technology Review* 78, no. 5 (March–April 1976, pp. 53–59); Winfred B. Hirschmann, "Profit from the Learning Curve," *Harvard Business Review* 42, no. 1 (January–February 1964), pp. 125–39; William J. Abernathy and Kenneth Wayne, "Limits of the Learning Curve," *Harvard Business Review* 42, no. 5 (September–October 1974), pp. 109–19.

5. For an elaboration on this point using the auto industry, especially the interplay between Japanese imports and the domestic manufacturers, see W. J. Abernathy, K. B. Clark, and A. M. Kantrow, *Industrial Renaissance* (New York: Basic Books, 1983). This book argues that technological advance and the character of the marketplace have rejuvenated the technological aspects of product design and competiton within the automotive industry.

6. This discussion draws heavily from Chapter 6 "Technology and the Manager," in Wickham Skinner, *Manufacturing: The Formidable Competitive Weapon*, (New York: John Wiley & Co., 1985).

7. George R. White and Margaret B. W. Graham, "How to Spot a Technological Winner," *Harvard Business Review* 56, no. 2 (March–April 1978).

8. H. U. Balthasar, R. A. A. Boschi, and M. M. Menke, "Calling the Shots in R&D," *Harvard Business Review* 56, no. 3 (May–June 1978); William E. Souder, "Analytical Effectiveness of Mathematical Models for R&D Project Selection," *Management Science* (April 1973).

9. Information on recent developments in manufacturing technology is sometimes available in the popular press. See Richard N. Foster, "A Call for Vision in Managing Technology," *Business Week* (May 24, 1982), p. 24, Gene Bylinsky, "The Race to the Automatic Factory," *Fortune* (February 21, 1983), p. 52; Gene Bylinsky, "A New Industrial Revolution Is on the Way," *Fortune* (October 5, 1981), p. 106; M. Eugene Merchant, "The Factory of the Future," a speech by Merchant, the principal scientist for manufacturing research of Cincinnati Milacron Incorporated; Thomas M. Hout and George Stalk, Jr., "The Big Revolution on the Factory Floor," *Wall Street Journal* (July 12, 1982), p. 18.

10. Bela Gold, "CAM Sets New Rules for Production," *Harvard Business Review* 60 no. 6 (November/December 1982): 88–94.

11. These signals were identified by the consulting firm of McKinsey and Co. as reported in *Business Week* (May 24, 1982), pp. 26, 28.

IV

OPERATIONS STRATEGY AND ORGANIZATION

The last segment of this text pulls together the various elements of operations policy that have been discussed so far and molds them into a view of what constitutes operations strategy. The first chapter of this two-chapter segment deals with vertical integration. Companies are repeatedly confronted with opportunities to broaden the scope of their operations by becoming their own suppliers or by taking their products closer to the consumer. They are faced as well with opportunities to narrow this scope. These are make-or-buy issues writ large, and this chapter discusses the considerations relevant to decisions about vertical integration. The second chapter in this segment, and the last one in the book, pulls together the various elements of operations policy that have been discussed so far and molds them into a view of what constitutes operations strategy. This chapter deals with the multitude of choices managers face and how they can be gathered into a consistent and convincing operations strategy.

DEALING WITH OPPORTUNITIES FOR VERTICAL INTEGRATION

The sequence of activities that bring a good or service into being and then to market is frequently a long one. Very often, the companies involved in the sequence confront some intriguing choices about how much or how little of that sequence to involve themselves with. Take gasoline for example. There are at least six broad stages involved in manufacturing and marketing gasoline: (1) exploring for and purchasing the mineral rights to the land under which the oil lies, (2) drilling the well and pumping oil from it, (3) transporting the crude oil from well to refinery, often by pipeline or tanker, (4) refining the crude oil into a multitude of petroleum products, (5) transporting refined gasoline from refinery to storage tanks (tank farms) and thence to service stations, and (6) selling gasoline at the service station pump. A company can decide to engage in just one of these six activities or to straddle two or more of them. Indeed, there are companies that engage in just one activity and there are companies that engage in all of them.

At issue in this chapter is how to decide the extent of a company's commitment to portions of the full sequence of production and distribution activities for any good or service. In the common terminology, it is a decision about the degree of vertical integration that a company should seek. The decision is complex, influenced by a number of factors.

FACTORS IN THE VERTICAL INTEGRATION DECISION

As an introduction to some of the factors that can guide vertical integration decisions, consider Situation 9-1.

SITUATION 9-1

RICH CLOVER DAIRY

Perhaps it was time to close this chapter in the dairy's history. All Ralph Maynard knew was that it would be an emotional ending, if it came to that. Ralph, president of the Rich Clover Dairy and son of its founder, faced the decision whether to close the dairy's own farm. The farm, located in the lush, rolling countryside north of one of the city's reservoirs, had been the dairy's showpiece for over 40 years. Rich Clover's prize herd of guernsey cows was pastured there and the dairy had used this fact to advantage in marketing itself as "the dairy with cows." (Most other dairies had no cows of their own; they bought milk from dairy farmers, processed and bottled it, and then sold it under their brand name. Rich Clover bought most of its milk from area dairy farmers but produced its own guernsey milk.) Many of the area's families had made a point of bringing their children to the dairy to see the cows and bulls, the twice-daily milkings, and the egg-laying chickens. The farm no doubt contributed not only to the dairy's image among local people of being devoted to quality but also its position as the area's second largest dairy.

Times were changing, however, and Rich Clover was not immune. Although the dairy's sales had continued to grow with the development of the area, the nature of those sales had changed drastically. Where 20 years ago, two-thirds of the dairy's sales were from home deliveries, now they barely accounted for 20 percent. The slack had been taken up by increased sales to grocery stores (Rich Clover was a leading supplier to local chains and Mom-and-Pop independents) and by the founding of the dairy's own convenience stores, which were open from 7 A.M. to 11 P.M. and sold a variety of grocery items in addition to dairy products.

Other changes had some significant implications for the farm itself. The area's continued growth had spread population and housing farther and farther from the downtown. The farm, once a considerable trek out into the country, was now much more within the fringe of the area's growth. Land prices were escalating and the dairy could reap a handsome profit by selling its 1500 acres.

In addition, the farm raised only guernsey cows, which were known for their very rich milk. The dairy's "top-of-the-line" milk (8 percent of sales), "Golden Guernsey," was supplied almost entirely by the farm's herd. With changing lifestyles, however, milk rich in butterfat was steadily losing market share to nonfat and low fat milk. Ralph Maynard could foresee the day when the farm's herd would be forced to supply milk for other than the Golden Guernsey line—the dairy's highest margin product. As it was, 20 years ago the herd had been able to produce only half the dairy's need for guernsey milk; the milk from other guernsey herds had been purchased then to make up the other half.

Ralph could foresee other changes at Rich Clover. The dairy's receiving and bottling plant, located in the city, was over 45 years old. Although periodically modernized, the bottling plant was neither as efficient nor as fast as the latest plants other dairies boasted. Moreover, traffic around the plant had become increasingly snarled, in part because the plant's loading operations were more suited to traditional, small milk trucks than to the larger, refrigerated trailers that could better supply grocery and convenience stores. The relocation of the dairy's bottling operations was a choice Ralph could sense he would have to face in the years to come. First, he thought, the farm's future should be addressed.

Discussion of Rich Clover Dairy

Ralph Maynard faces several challenging decisions. Traditionally, the Rich Clover Dairy has been vertically integrated (at least with respect to guernsey milk). Of concern now is whether the dairy ought to remain so. The potential for either selling the land to developers or relocating the bottling plant forces this decision upon Maynard.

Given its current degree of vertical integration, a company usually needs to make three decisions about which way to go:

1. Should the company stay put or should it move toward more or less vertical integration? If the latter, should it change its degree of *backward integration* (integration toward the source of raw materials) or *forward integration* (integration toward the final consumer)?

   Rich Clover Dairy is more vertically integrated than most dairies: backward integrated into its own herds and forward integrated into its own convenience stores as well as home delivery. The decision the dairy faces regarding as farm is whether to stay put or decrease its backward integration.

2. How far backward or forward should the company go in its vertical integration?

   Rich Clover Dairy decided years ago to move backward all the way to ownership of cows and land. It could have chosen to stop short of so deep a backward integration by not owning cows or land or both.

3. What balance among activities should the company seek? How complete should its backward or forward integration be?

Although Rich Clover Dairy became backward integrated into the production of guernsey milk, it did not produce all the milk it needed; it still bought heavily from area dairies. This incomplete vertical integration (sometimes referred to as *partial or tapered integration*) can provide many of the advantages of vertical integration but without some of its disadvantages. Although partial integration is sometimes deliberately chosen by companies, it often occurs simply because capacity increments can be "lumpy," inevitably causing an imbalance in capacities among the segments of a process.

An important feature of a reasoned analysis of these decisions, especially their long-term aspects, involves an assessment of the economics of vertical integration. That is, where in the entire span of activities that a company can choose to perform are the rates of return to invested capital high and where are they low? This important question is often very difficult to answer. We can get a handle on it by taking a brief excursion into the realm of economics and the concept of an "economic rent."

✱ ASIDE ✱

Economic Rents and Vertical Integration

A sure way to riches is to offer a product or service that is both in demand and scarce in supply. In such situations the price people are willing to pay is often very much higher than the costs of bringing the product or service to market. The difference between the two is termed an *economic rent*.

Land is the classic example of an economic rent. Certain categories of land, say land with oil underneath it, are in at least relatively fixed supply. That is, even over several years, the known quantity of oil land does

not vary greatly (although vary it does). As long as oil companies bid higher for the use of the land than housing developers or commercial interests, owners would be willing to offer their land for drilling. A higher bid brings no further change in behavior from the landowners; all they can say, no matter how high the price, is "Yes, go ahead and drill." What they receive from the oil company is an economic rent.

To aid our understanding, we can graph this situation (Figure 9-1). The quantity OS is the land available.

FIGURE 9-1   Economic rent.

FIGURE 9-2   Economic quasi rent.

SS' is the supply curve, which is vertical, indicating that a higher price offered for the use of the land will not induce any more production. Production is fixed at the OS acreage level. DD' is the demand curve, indicating the price the oil company would pay for various quantities of land offered. OP is the per acre price that the company is willing to pay for the services of OS acres of oil land. The OP price is the economic rent in this situation of a production input that is in rigid supply. The landowner reaps a total economic rent of OSP'P, which can be a considerable sum.

Few inputs are in rigid supply, of course, but many come into temporarily rigid supply. Owners of these inputs can in these short-lived cases earn what is called a *quasi rent*. Figure 9-2 illustrates this case. Here, increases in the price offered will induce more of the input to be supplied, as we can tell from the rising supply curve, marked MC because it is really the marginal cost curve for the input. The demand curve intersects the supply curve at F, thus establishing the level OE as the price for the input. The input could be purchased, however, for any price higher than OA,

because any price higher than OA would cover the average variable costs of the owner of the input. In the long term, however, we could not count on having the input supplied if the price did not exceed OC, which is the level at which average total costs are covered. The difference, of course, is that some fixed costs must be covered in the longer run, if not in the short run.

Quasi rents are pure rents in the short run, although in the longer run they must go to pay off fixed costs; otherwise the input would have to be withdrawn. In Figure 9-2, the total quasi rent is ABFE. The quantity ABDC represents the fixed costs that must be paid off in the longer run, whereas CDFE represents pure economic profit.

What do rents and quasi rents have to do with the economics of vertical integration? Rents and quasi rents are important because they often indicate where rates of return are high. Because scarcity brings about rents and quasi rents, it often pays to ask where scarcity lies in an industry. Find scarcity, and you often find a road to riches.

---   *   ---

Returning Home With the Cows

Back to Ralph Maynard's responsibilities at the Rich Clover Dairy. Where does scarcity exist in

dairying? Where do the bucks and the high rates of return lie? According to Maynard, dairy cows are not scarce, and so we should not expect large rates of return from owning a herd of guernsey cows, at least not for their milk production. (Their marketing clout because of the slogan "the dairy with cows" is a different question.) This is an argument then for selling the farm.

If scarcity and high rates of return do not lie with owning cows, where do they lie? The answer to this is less than clear-cut, but the Rich Clover brand name and its quality image appear to be what is "scarce." The industry is one where the retailing end of the business is likely to be a much more important factor than the origin of the milk. Whatever else, a dairy wants to maintain its strength as a bottler and marketer.

This seat-of-the-pants case against a dairy's owning its own herd is insufficient by itself to decide the matter, because the immediate issue is more concerned with whether it is better to hang onto the farm for a few more years in anticipation of even higher land prices in the area or to sell the farm now and invest the cash in some other income-generating alternative. Once again, the decision involves a marginal analysis. Will the land price gains outweigh the expected net benefits of relocating the dairy and adopting a more efficient bottling technology? The strict economics of the decision rest on these calculations, which are less a matter of vertical integration and more a matter of investment analysis.

This divergence of project economics (hold land or relocate the bottling plant now) from industry economics (where the economic rents are) is an intriguing one, common to many vertical integration situations. The industry economics are likely to govern the long-run earnings of a company, but individual decisions in the short run are likely to be made on narrower grounds. In this instance, Rich Clover Dairy is likely to be better off without its own guernsey herd in the long run, but land speculation in the short run may well advise keeping the farm at least a few more years. What managers need to be vigilant about is that the sequence of short-run decisions made is consistent with the long-run economics of the industry. We shall return to this theme in further discussions about vertical integration.

Another purely operational concern with implications for vertical integration centers on the balance of capacities between stages of the production process. Over the years at the dairy, the herd of guernsey cows had been insufficient to supply all the Golden Guernsey milk demanded. If recent trends persist, however, the herd will soon provide more than enough milk to meet the declining demand for Golden Guernsey milk. The farm's excess milk would then have to be mixed with other, lower profit margin milk, or else production would have to be cut back. Thus, just because the product mix demanded of the dairy has changed, the attractiveness of vertical integration, already suspect, is eroded further. The capacities of the farm and the bottling plant simply do not match as well as they used to, and the dairy risks forgoing contribution because of this mismatch.

It was mentioned earlier that the Rich Clover farm had, at least historically, aided the company's marketing efforts and its quality image. This remains an argument for maintaining the farm. There may be other ways, of course, of promoting a quality image. For instance, assuming the dairy is relocated, the sight and advertising of a new bottling plant with all the latest, fastest, and cleanest equipment could well make up for whatever tarnishing occurs to the Rich Clover image as a result of selling the farm.

THE ADVANTAGES OF VERTICAL INTEGRATION

The arguments brought to bear against vertical integration at Rich Clover Dairy notwithstanding, vertical integration can be very attractive. For one thing, integration either backward or forward may lead to the location of the profit-enhancing economic rents in the industry.

Let us pursue our oil industry example further and delve into the history of the industry in the United States.[1] The oil industry did not begin fully integrated but rather integrated backward and forward in piecemeal fashion. In fact, the Standard Oil Company, and later the Standard Oil trust, did not seek vertical integration until it was forced to.

After the discovery of oil in western Pennsylvania in 1859 came a decade of remarkable advance in refining technology that led to low-cost, high-speed continuous flow refineries. John D. Rockefeller's Standard Oil Company in Cleveland came to the fore in the early 1870s because it was the largest and fastest refinery. At that time, the industry was being racked by excess capacity and price cutting. Industry associations sprang up but were essentially toothless in enforcing prices on their members.

In trying to add discipline to the loose cartel of refiners, Rockefeller struck a bargain with the railroads that gave Standard Oil and its associates significant price breaks in exchange for the steady use of large numbers of rail tank cars. This arrangement was beneficial to both Standard Oil (lower transport costs) and the railroads (better scheduling of railcars). The lower rail rates were enough to discourage future investments in refineries and to keep existing refineries in the cartel. Rockefeller had succeeded in discovering a way to protect the economic rents he and others in the Standard Oil group enjoyed—namely, by ensuring that refining capacity remained scarce.

Some oil producers soon found a way around Rockefeller's railroad arrangement, however. Using the innovation of the long-distance oil pipeline, some crude oil producers (Standard Oil did not own any crude oil production) in western Pennsylvania were able in the late 1870s to bypass the railroads to bring crude oil to the

East Coast for refining, and at a lower cost. These producers then integrated even further forward by building their own refineries because pipelines were even better than railroads at maintaining an even flow of crude into continuously operating refineries. It did not take long for Rockefeller and Standard Oil to realize that the scarcity (and the economic rents) in the industry had shifted. The scarcity of refining capacity was no longer protected. What was scarce was low-cost transportation of crude oil from oil field to refinery. Standard Oil moved quickly to build its own pipelines and then to relocate its refinery capacity in the markets that could now be easily served by pipeline. By the early 1880s, low-cost crude oil transportation was no longer scarce. Standard Oil's economic rents from refining were once again secure.

In a few years, these economic rents were again threatened, this time by the oil wholesalers to whom Standard Oil sold its product. Once small and widely dispersed, the wholesalers began to build large storage facilities, selling large quantities over wider areas for lower unit costs. The larger scale of individual wholesalers gave them increased market power and began shifting the scarcity away from refining capacity to storage and marketing. Again, Standard Oil reacted swiftly to this threat and protected its economic rents by creating its own national sales organization and buying out the wholesalers.

This action brought protection for only a few years until it was realized, with the decline in production in the western Pennsylvania fields, that crude oil production was itself the source of possible scarcities and economic rents. Standard Oil then moved to purchase oil-producing properties to ensure crude oil supplies and any economic rents to be gathered due to periodic constrictions in supply. By the early 1890s then, Standard Oil was a completely integrated company, able to protect itself against the threat of any scarcities.

The point of this brief recapitulation of the fascinating early history of Standard Oil is to spotlight the importance of scarcity and economic rent to vertical integration decisions. So long as no scarcities existed, Standard Oil was content to remain less than fully integrated. But when scarcities arose, Standard Oil was forced to dispel them or face an erosion of its own profitability. Standard Oil's history raises another interesting point: Scarcity and economic rents can be tremendously mobile. That fact became painfully obvious in the oil industry once again with the Arab oil embargo of 1973. The Arab oil states reaped stupendous economic rents. Since then, however, there have sometimes been gluts of crude oil, with the likely result of throwing scarcity and economic rents back on refining capacity.

Indeed, Ashland Oil thought that this was the case. As the chairman of Ashland was quoted in a *Business Week* article (September 4, 1978, p. 99): "If our refineries don't have crude oil, no industry runs in those areas and no commercial enterprises operate. . . . The government will not allow such a situation to exist." Ashland Oil cut back its oil exploration and production but increased its refining capacity, precisely because it felt the economic rents lay in refining. Other oil companies disagreed, of course, with this assessment and stepped up their exploration programs because they felt the economic rents lay in the production of crude oil.

In sum, a major attraction of vertical integration is its ability to control the reaping of economic rents and quasi rents. It does this by assuming all the relevant profit margins in the chain of production and distribution activities that bring a good or service into being and off to market. By controlling the key features of an entire production/distribution system, the vertically integrated company can cut its costs and at the same time control scarcities so as to help maintain prices and reduce the threat of new

capacity to the industry by raising any barriers to entry.

There are some other strong motives for vertically integrating that relate to exercising control over the industry or process:

1. Providing better control over the quality of suppliers and/or end products.
2. Providing better control over the delivery performance of supplies and/or end products.
3. Possibly protecting the company against the exploitation of any proprietary technology it may have that may not be patentable.

These three motives are defensive ones for a corporation, much as Standard Oil's actions were defensive. Companies that pride themselves on quality, delivery, or technology are sometimes compelled to provide their own supplies or take their products closer to the consumer. Vertical integration is often seen as one way to maintain reliability in quality, delivery, or technology, although it may not be the only way. Suppliers, however, can frequently be managed successfully to provide consistently dependable deliveries of quality products. Much recent management attention has been devoted to this task, as was indicated in Segment II of this text and will be underscored in the next chapter. Maintaining reliability probably contributed to Rich Clover Dairy's establishment of its farm, a motive borne out by the dairy's successful cultivation of a quality image.

Other motives address cost advantages that can sometimes be enjoyed because of vertical integration:

1. The transactions costs between process stages can be saved, as can middleman profits. This cost-related point is allied with the notion of economic rents, because those activities that post high middleman profits or

for which transactions costs are high are also likely to yield impressive economic rents.

2. Process planning, especially when it encompasses technological change, can encompass two or more process stages, leading to advantageous product designs and process designs.

3. By linking process stages directly, materials handling can be improved.

4. By linking process stages directly, production scheduling and control can often be made smoother and better coordinated. Inventories are less likely to build up unnecessarily between process stages.

5. The company can assure more complete use of company resources or by-products that might otherwise be difficult to sell (such as using agricultural waste as fuel in an electricity cogeneration project, where a boiler produces heat to produce process steam *and* drive an electric generator).

6. The extra costs incurred by a company for inducing a supplier to take on a risky endeavor (termed a "risk premium") may be reduced to the extent that the demand on an in-house supplier can be at least as steady, if not more so, than the demand on an outside supplier.

7. Information about the market may be easier to gather. Marketing may be more effective, product differentiation more successful, and the prices charged higher.

THE PERILS OF VERTICAL INTEGRATION

As attractive as vertical integration can be, there are also a host of perils associated with it. The situation at Rich Clover Dairy uncovered a couple of them:

1. Integration into some links of the production/distribution chain may be uneconomic because economic rents are not likely to reside there. For instance, the dairy's backward integration into the ownership of guernsey cows was not likely to provide the dairy with control over scarcities, and so high rates of return on such an investment were unlikely.

2. Vertical integration may induce problems in achieving a balance of capacities among portions of the production process, particularly if the product mix is subject to considerable change. At Rich Clover Dairy, the farm was coming into greater and greater imbalance with the bottling plant since Golden Guernsey milk was passing out of favor.

There are other possible perils with vertical integration, as may surface in Situation 9-2.

SITUATION 9-2

MATHESON SEMICONDUCTOR CORPORATION

Matheson Semiconductor Corporation, located in the "Silicon Valley" of California, was a young but growing firm with a remarkable reputation for innovation. Rod Matheson, the company's founder, was a near-legend in the electronics industry for his ability to crack seemingly impossible engineering problems.

Recently, Matheson had done it again, solving much of the yield problem associated with the "bubble memory," a revolutionary way to store electric charges by using layers of garnet crystal. Bubble memory was an alternative way to store charges; RAM (random access memory) silicon chips or CCDs (charge-coupled devices) were other ways. Matheson Semiconductor was not the only company working on bubble memories; Texas Instruments, Intel, National Semiconductor, and IBM were among the other, larger companies that had research and development projects devoted to them. With this breakthrough, however, Matheson Semiconductor was clearly in the lead in what promised to be a very large market.

Heretofore, Matheson Semiconductor had been a supplier of semiconductor devices to the original equipment market. It did not manufacture products for the end-user.

The top tier of management at the company was concerned that Matheson Semiconductor keep its lead in bubble memories. Given the well-documented effects of the learning curve, management stressed the importance of quickly establishing sales for the product. At issue was how best to stimulate sales. A substantial number of end-users, to be sure, would order the bubble memory immediately. However, it was not at all evident that the large mainframe computer manufacturers (IBM, Burroughs, Sperry-Univac) or even the minicomputer makers (Digital, Data General, Hewlett-Packard) or personal computer makers (Apple, Commodore) would switch immediately to bubble memories.

Some of these companies were tied up with their own R&D projects for bubble memories, CCDs, or RAM, and they might be reluctant to jettison them for Matheson Semiconductor's version. Others might want to wait out the technology a while, refraining from redesigns of their own equipment and eagerly awaiting the arrival of still newer technology that might dominate bubble memories.

It had been suggested that Matheson Semiconductor might best help its own cause by going straight to the end-user market with add-on memory units compatible with either IBM or Digital Equipment Corporation computers, or both. This step into forward integration would take some engineering work and some entirely new manufacturing expertise, but the market potential was very enticing.

Management was split on the issue. Marketing, and to a lesser extent, manufacturing, were behind the move to integrate forward. Marketing was eager to conquer new territory; manufacturing, though somewhat cautious about the new demands expected of it, was eager to see costs drop as volume rose. Engineering, on the other hand, was dead set against the proposal, largely because it relished its state-of-the-art position in semiconductor electronics and did not want to be bothered with the more "pedestrian" engineering involved with computer applications.

It looked more and more like the issue was Rod Matheson's alone to resolve.

Discussion of Matheson Semiconductor Corporation

The allure of high and steady sales volumes for the bubble memory is certainly a strong one. The same sort of allure attracted many semiconductor manufacturers like Texas Instruments, Rockwell International, and National Semiconductor into the hand-held calculator market in the early 1970s. Not all of those companies would admit that the experience was a good one, however. There are many perils to vertical integration, and the type of situation Matheson Semiconductor finds itself in is indicative of many of them.

The prominence of the learning curve concept in industries like electronics has fostered a chicken-egg phenomenon: innovations like the bubble memory cannot break into new markets unless their costs are lower, and their costs will not be lower unless their markets are large. The pressure, then, is to seek out as many applications as possible to get production volumes up. Vertical integration has been among the means employed, despite the fact that the scarcity almost certainly lies in the expertise and production of the innovation (the bubble memory) and not in the application.

The alternative is to manage around the vertical integration. That is, instead of integrating backward, the company can try to manage its suppliers better; and instead of integrating forward, the company can try to manage its customers better. What does this mean? In the case of Matheson Semiconductor, it might mean a stepped-up campaign to locate and to convince a computer hardware manufacturer that the bubble memory would be an ideal means of adding on memory to an existing computer, perhaps enticing the manufacturer more with some of the cost savings from learning curve advances. In the case of backward integration, managing suppliers better might mean deliberately seeking out multiple suppliers to ensure both delivery and reasonable cost or it might mean selecting a single supplier and working to coordinate production planning, process design, and quality needs between the company and the supplier. Of course, a company will not be able to manage around vertical integration all the time—companies often have to settle for limited product applications—but it is an attractive alternative.

What about managing vertical integration should a company be sensitive to?

The Flexibility Issue

Vertical integration will almost surely make a company less flexible to react to changes in products, production processes, and production volumes. By layering another full step of production or distribution on the company's existing operations, it is nearly certain that the coordination of change will be more difficult and the evaluation of managerial performance less objective. It is to be expected that as vertical integration broadens, the probability increases that at least some product, process, or volume changes cannot realistically be made at all. The company locks itself in more and more.

At Matheson Semiconductor, for example, forward integration into add-on memory units may constrain the company to produce bubble memories of a certain type for a lot longer than a company so eager to stay on the technological frontier may want to. The classic example of how vertical integration, coupled with a constant drive to lower costs (the learning curve), combined to halt product flexibility is the Model T car of Henry Ford.[2]

Ford was fully integrated in 1927, with processes specifically designed to manufacture almost all of the Model T's parts. From 11 cents of capital investment per sales dollar in 1913, Ford integrated backward and forward to the point where in 1926 each dollar of sales was backed by 33 cents of capital investment, representing such vertical integration as a steel mill, a paper mill, a railroad, a glass plant, and others. Starting in the early twenties, however, car buyers' tastes began changing perceptibly. The Model T, an open car design, was being beaten in the marketplace by heavier, more comfortable, closed body cars. Ford tried to modify the Model T to include these features being pioneered by General Motors but could not do so successfully. At last, Ford bit the bullet as its sales shrank. In 1927, it had to close its River Rouge plant for remodeling, but the inflexibility of Ford's process at the time was so great that the remodeling lasted almost a year! From that time on Ford's leadership in the automotive industry was relinquished to General Motors.

Vertical integration can influence process change as well. With so much more invested in the process, integrated producers are less likely to scrap a production technology and somewhat more likely to "patch up" the existing one—not so much because they are ignorant of sunk costs but because individual pieces of the process tend to come up for review and action rather than the entire process itself.

The question for a company contemplating vertical integration is whether inflexibility really matters or not. For many companies, products and demands are standard enough and stable enough that a loss of flexibility is of little concern. For other companies, however, flexibility is of central importance, and for most of these companies significant vertical integration carries with it many perils.

Effect on the "Core" Business

How does a move toward vertical integration affect the nature of the company's "core" business? Increasing the span of production a company takes upon itself raises a couple of questions about the management tasks in operations.

1. Will the move to more vertical integration tend to draw a company out of the particular niche in which it finds itself most competitive? This concern is related to the balance of capacities issue that surfaced in the Rich Clover Dairy situation. Often there exist imbalances in the capacities between stages of a production process. Since management abhors excess capacity almost as much as nature abhors a vacuum, pressure for "doing something" with the excess capacity arises. This "something" may well turn out to be incompatible with the company's core business, the reason for the vertical integration in the first place. For example, a pharmaceutical company's backward integration into chemicals may leave the company with excess chemical production capacity. The company may then seek to sell other chemicals on the side. Over time, the side business may grow, leaving the pharmaceuticals division at odds with the chemicals division for the capacity it was originally supposed

to have by right. At this point, the company is no longer a pharmaceuticals company—it has been pulled out of its niche.

2. Will managing a move toward greater vertical integration place new costs or risks on the company? If so, are these costs or risks acceptable? Often, an increase in vertical integration is quite costly and it raises the level of output at which the company breaks even. With a higher breakeven volume, the company faces increased pressure for sales and greater vulnerability to a downturn in the market or to cyclical sales. The company must assess what the higher breakeven volume may be and whether it poses any real problems.

Other Perils

Besides financial cost and risk, vertical integration can place strain on a manager's capabilities and on the management organization. The coordination of an integrated operation is frequently different from and more difficult than the coordination of operations within a narrow portion of the process. Concern for production control, logistics, and inventories tends to be much more intensive. Authority must cut through all layers of the operation. This typically places managers in roles different from what they are used to and strains the prevailing organization of those managers. Frequently, a different set of managerial skills must be mastered and the organization modified before vertical integration can be made to work well. These changes can be costly.

To return to Situation 9–2, Matheson Semiconductor has good reason to fear forward integration in this instance. It is probably a company ill-prepared to handle a great deal of coordination across manufacturing, although the engineering-manufacturing coordination is probably well oiled. What is more, vertical integration is likely to weaken its position on the frontier of semiconductor electronics by drawing talent away from the most technically demanding tasks and lessening the company's flexibility.

Vertical integration raises both barriers to entry in an industry (protecting economic rents as mentioned earlier) and barriers to exit (implying that a company cannot easily get out of the business if it wanted to). The expense of vertical integration, which can be substantial, is thus somewhat risky if the ability to exit the industry quickly is valued highly.

A RECAPITULATION

Before making some closing observations about vertical integration, it is useful to summarize its attractions and perils.

Attractions of Vertical Integration
Control-Related Attractions

- Vertical integration can insulate that which is scarce in the span of possible company activities, and thus what is apt to yield desirable economic rents. This is a defense against technological or other shifts of bargaining strength that can work to the disadvantage of the nonvertically integrated company.
- Barriers to entry into the industry may go up as a result of an integration move, thus discouraging potential competition. (This point is closely allied to the previous one, being an "offensive" strategic move rather than a "defensive" one.)
- A vertically integrated company may improve its control over the delivery and quality of suppliers.

- Vertical integration can protect against exploitation of proprietary (but not patented) technology.

Cost-Related Attractions

- Closer linking of process stages can aid materials handling.
- Process planning, especially with respect to technological change, can encompass both process stages, leading to advantageous product designs and process designs.
- Production scheduling and control can be made smoother, more coordinated.
- Transactions costs and middleman profits can be saved; "contracts" between process stages may be simplified.
- Supplier risk premiums can be reduced because demand on in-house suppliers can be expected to be at least as steady, if not more so, than demand on outside suppliers.
- Information about the market may be easier to gather; marketing may be more effective, product differentiation more successful, and the prices charged higher.
- More complete use can be made of company resources or by-products that would otherwise be difficult to sell (for example, cogeneration of electricity instead of selling agricultural waste).

Perils of Vertical Integration
Control-Related Perils

- An integration move can be away from scarcity and desirable economic rents into operations with a lower rate of return to invested capital.
- Vertical integration can lead to an imbalance of capacity among process stages. Trying to cope with this (such as by raising return to

the capacity investment) can draw a company out of its competitive niche in a market.

- The sometimes equally effective choice of managing suppliers or customers better (demanding required aspects of delivery, quality, or price; or communicating needs better about schedules, technology, product change, etc.) can be overlooked.

- Flexibility for change in materials, products, technology, process design, or production volumes can decrease—rendering a company less nimble, or even less willing to compete. As a result, a company can fall behind technologically.

Cost-Related Perils

- Trying to overcome any barriers to entry that existed in the industry being integrated into can be expensive.

- The breakeven volume of production may go up, leaving the company more susceptible to economic fluctuations.

- Exit barriers for the company may go up, implying that the company cannot easily get out of the business if it wanted to.

- Management talents and organization can be strained by the demands of vertical integration for coordination. The costs of overhead, planning, and logistics can rise markedly. Efforts and talents may become fragmented if coordination is not attended to.

- Performance evaluation of process stages may become less objective as process stages become more "captive" to one another.

VERTICAL INTEGRATION IN THE LIFE CYCLES OF PRODUCTS AND PROCESSES

When we first examined vertical integration in Segment I of this text, we noted that it is most prevalent in products that are standardized and produced in large volumes by processes that have rigid patterns of flow. In terms of the product-process matrix (Figure 2–1), vertical integration is characteristic of the lower right-hand corner.

In observing the behavior of industries, we should expect to find then that changes triggering both product standardization and process simplification are apt also to trigger vertical integration in the industry. The firms that are fully integrated are likely to hold a tremendous edge over their nonintegrated competitors.

Watches

A fascinating example of this tendency has recently been played out in the watch industry.[3] Historically, the watch industry was extremely fragmented. Separate groups of companies fabricated watch movements, cases, and other components, assembled them into watches, and distributed them. The Swiss watch industry, for example, consisted of many small components fabricators and assemblers.

Enter the age of the quartz movement. This innovation at once improved time-keeping accuracy and simplified watch construction. Quartz movement watches, powered electronically, have fewer parts than mechanical watches. This fact in turn forced watchmaking away from labor-intensive assembly and permitted the introduction of automated equipment. Getting the most from the automated equipment, however, generally meant scheduling longer production runs than the watch industry was used to; this, in turn, meant standardizing designs. There was a risk, of course, that even the modest standardization that occurred would have been resisted by the market, but the advent of the quartz movement electronic watch apparently has been novelty enough. Bulova, for example, reduced the number of basic model series it manufactured from 18 to three.

The acknowledged leader in quartz watches, Seiko of Japan, was a vertically integrated company from the start. It was therefore able to exploit the quartz movement invention (originally Swiss) and develop it further under its own R&D group. Seiko's success has forced a rash of vertical integration moves within the industry that have simplified watchmaking's logistics, cycle times, and labor input. Bulova is integrated and the Swiss industry, historically so fragmented, has clustered into large watch combines.

The Swiss companies like Longines and the U.S. company Bulova still are impressive trademarks in the industry and are relatively the strongest names in jewelry and department store sales. Whether the trademark will remain so influential (that is, whether it will be the source of economic rents) is a matter of some debate. Some believe that the rents are now to be had in production.

Fiber Optics

Vertical integration's impact on the fledgling fiber optics industry is also likely to be fascinating. It is now technologically possible to manufacture telephone cables that use strands of pure glass to transmit light pulses (instead of copper wires that conduct electrical impulses). The industry's manufacturing requirements can be divided into three major segments: (1) manufacture of the optical fiber itself, (2) manufacture of telephone cable using this optical fiber, and (3) manufacture of the electronic equipment that sends and receives the light pulses sent along the cable (e.g., transmitters, multiplexers, repeaters).

This division of the industry is analogous to the division of the traditional telephone transmission business: copper producers, cable producers, and transmission equipment makers. In this traditional business, there are companies that concentrate on one portion (such as just copper producers or cable producers) and some that overlap two portions (for example, Anaconda produces both copper and cable, Western Electric produces both cable and transmission equipment). Furthermore, the traditional copper cable telephone transmission industry is so well established that even small independent telephone companies can engineer their own systems, choosing equipment and cables from a number of different suppliers.

As time goes by, this diversity of suppliers may also apply to fiber optics telephone transmission, as telephone companies of all sizes begin to master the fiber optics technology. However, some observers feel that the only strong competitors in this new industry will be those that are vertically integrated. In the United States, only AT&T Technologies is totally vertically integrated. Due to some fortuitous cross-licensing of technology between AT&T and Corning Glass Works, AT&T Technologies is able to manufacture its own optical fiber as well as cable and electronic transmission equipment. Several Japanese companies have combined, under government auspices, to accomplish a similar degree of vertical integration. There still remain, however, some companies that are not vertically integrated: Corning Glass Works makes only optical fiber, although under substantial patent protection; Siecor, a joint venture of Seimens of West Germany and Corning Glass Works, makes only cable; and an assortment of companies manufacture the electronic equipment needed.

At issue as this industry develops is whether the successful companies will be those that are vertically integrated or those that are not. Where will the economic rents lie and what will it take to protect a company's position in this industry? There is much speculation now. Time, as always, will tell.

QUESTIONS

1. Define and discuss the relationship between vertical integration, economic rents, quasi rents, and scarcity.

2. Summarize and give examples of the main advantages of vertical integration.

3. How does the dilemma of the Matheson Semiconductor Corporation illustrate some of the dangers that can attend vertical in-tegration? Can you think of some of your own examples?

4. Vertical integration almost always affects the nature of a company's core business. Why is this?

5. Think of a life cycle of products and proc-esses similar to that of the watch industry. What part does vertical integration play in that life cycle?

PROBLEMS

1. What market conditions should exist for a firm to consider vertical integration?

2. What are the methods of vertical inte-gration? Discuss the relative merits of each.

3. How does the management coordination task change with greater vertical integra-tion?

4. Give an example of a situation where the reverse of more vertical integration would probably be the better strategy.

5. "Vertical integration will almost surely make a company less flexible to react to changes." Discuss this statement, supporting your points with examples from your reading and/ or your own experience.

SITUATION FOR STUDY 9-1
DEVINE NUTS REVISITED—
THE SHELLING PLANT DECISION

Two years ago, the profit margin Devine Nuts received for grading and drying peanuts was cut in half by inflation and other factors. The past year was even worse, causing Frank Coyne to wonder why he had chosen this line of work. Frank did notice, however, that the shellers to whom he sold his loads of graded and dried pea-nuts seemed to be doing well enough, even dur-ing the past two years. This observation sparked him to assess the possibility of building his own shelling plant. If Frank were to do this, Devine Nuts would be the sole middleman between the farmers who brought harvested peanuts to the company for grading and drying and the peanut processing companies (for example, peanut but-ter manufacturers, candy companies) that pur-chased bagged shelled peanuts of particular sizes (jumbos, mediums, splits) from shellers.

Devine Nuts' grading and drying operations were located in three south Texas towns within about 30 miles of each other: Devine, Pearsall, and Charlotte. Pearsall was the most centrally located of the three and the logical choice for a shelling plant. Devine Nuts could easily purchase some land contiguous to its holdings in Pearsall on which to build the new plant. Having a shelling plant in Pearsall would be particularly attractive to area farmers. Currently, peanut growers had to haul their harvests 250 miles or more north to shellers at a cost of about $26 per ton in transportation expense. (The prevailing average price of a ton of farmer's stock was $550.) Since a ton of farmer's stock consisted of only 75 percent peanut kernels, some of the transportation expense of hauling peanut shells, stones, and debris 250 miles could be removed by having a shelling plant for the local area. Given this transportation advantage, Frank Coyne was confident that the shelling plant could easily attract 10,000 to 12,000 or more tons of peanuts each year. The peanut growing season in south Texas was the longest in the nation; even so, Frank expected that 80 percent of the year's peanuts would be delivered within a six-week span.

Spurred by the potential for a shelling plant in the area, Frank had obtained some estimates of the costs of erecting and running a new shelling plant. The total costs (land, plant, equipment) for a sheller with a rated capacity of 10 tons per hour (and an effective capacity probably higher than that) were estimated to be $1.25 million. The expected variable costs per ton of farmer's stock were as follows:

Labor	$16
Bags	$20
Utilities	$ 3
Insurance, taxes, inspection fees, lab fees, and other overhead	$16
	$55 per ton

Frank felt that, for the time being, a fee of about $90 per ton could be charged for the shelling. Devine Nuts, of course, could and did buy farmers' harvests and then resell them to peanut brokers or peanut processing companies. To Frank Coyne's way of thinking, however, it was imperative that Devine Nuts not speculate in peanuts. Even if it meant having to settle for a few pennies less per pound, Frank wanted to be sure that every ton Devine Nuts purchased from farmers was quickly sold to someone else.

Before he could commit to building the shelling plant, Frank had some other concerns that needed to be addressed. One was simply the operation of the plant itself; neither he nor any of his sons had managed an operation like it. Another concern related to customer deliveries. Frank knew that some peanut processors bought their tonnage in large batches but wanted delivery stretched out over several months. If such purchases were the rule, Devine Nuts would have to store shelled peanuts, a somewhat perishable commodity, for longer than they had ever stored peanuts before, with all the added costs of carrying them, insuring them, and storing them. Finally, and not least, came the matter of financing this venture. The local Pearsall bank seemed willing to lend, but only for a maximum five-year period and at rates that were expected to be two percentage points above prime (currently running at 11 percent).

Frank wondered whether he should go on with the sheller venture or simply hope for better profit margins in the existing business. How many tons would Devine Nuts have to shell to break even every year? He needed to decide soon or risk missing the next shelling season altogether.

REFERENCE NOTES

1. For the history of the U.S. oil industry, see Alfred Chandler, Jr., *The Visible Hand: The Managerial Revolution in American Business* (Cambridge, Mass.: Harvard University Press, 1977).

2. See William J. Abernathy and Kenneth Wayne, "Limits of the Learning Curve," *Harvard Business Review* 52, no. 5 (September-October 1974), pp. 109–19.

3. See, for example, "Seiko's Smash," *Business Week* (June 5, 1978).

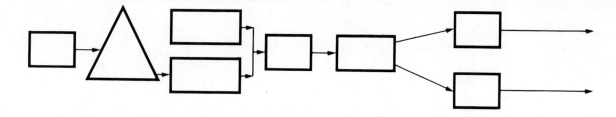

OPERATIONS STRATEGY

It is time to draw together the topics we have discussed so far into a unified view of operations and how operations can be used as an effective competitive weapon for the corporation. This chapter contains two parts, the first dealing with manufacturing strategy and the second dealing with service operations strategy.

PART ONE
MANUFACTURING STRATEGY

As should be clear by now, manufacturing managers have a wealth of choices in the means by which they can influence the manufacture of goods. Let us review these choices, which have been introduced separately before.

OPERATIONS CHOICES

Operations choices can be segregated into three broad categories: (1) technology and facilities, (2) operating policies, and (3) operations organization. Let us review these categories and choices in turn.

Technology and Facilities

These choices frequently involve large capital expenditures and long periods of time. These are the big decisions that do much to define the type of process employed.

1. *Nature of the process flow.* Is the flow of product through the plant characterized as rigid, with every product treated in the same way? At the other extreme, is the flow a jumbled one, with products routed in many different ways through the factory? Or, does the flow of product through the process fall somewhere in between?

    Are segments of the process tightly linked to one another, or are the connections between process segments loose? How quickly can materials flow through the process?

    Is the process a "pure" one or is it a hybrid of different process types?

2. *Vertical integration.* How much of a product's value is a direct result of factory operations? Should production involve more (or less) integration backward toward raw materials or more (or less) integration forward toward customers? Can it involve more (or less) of either of these?

3. *Types of equipment.* Is the equipment used general purpose in design or special purpose? Can any special-purpose, seemingly inflexible equipment be linked together in innovative ways to yield production systems that are themselves more flexible than the equipment comprising them?

   Is the equipment meant for high speeds and long runs, or not? How flexible is it for changeovers in products/models? How quickly and easily can such changes be accomplished?

   What possibilities exist for linking one piece of equipment with another for balanced and quicker throughput?

   Is the equipment operator-controlled or automatically/computer-controlled? Is its performance monitored by operators or by computer?

   Can the equipment be speeded up or slowed down to match production needs?

   Does the equipment demand substantial nonoperation support (maintenance, repair, software, setup, tooling)?

   Can the company build or modify its own machines? Does it have close ties to equipment manufacturers?

4. *Degree of capital or labor intensity.* To what degree has the equipment and/or technology permitted labor value to be driven out of the product or service? How important could reduced labor value in the product be to costs, yields, or sustained levels of "production to specifications" (good quality)?

5. *Attitude toward the process technology.* To what extent does the company pioneer advances in process technology? Is the company a leader in that regard or a follower? How closely does it track other process improvements?

   How committed is the company to research and development? What mix is sought between the two?

   How close is the alliance between manufacturing and engineering? To what extent are efforts made to design products so that they are easily manufactured? How are design and manufacturing teams organized for new product introductions?

   Are engineering change orders numerous? To what can they be attributed? How disruptive to the process flow are they?

   What investments are made in manufacturing engineering and industrial engineering relative to product design engineering?

6. *Attitude toward capacity utilization:* How close to capacity (defined as best as possible) does the company desire to operate? How willing is the company to stock out of a product because of too tight capacity?

   Does capacity generally come in significant chunks? What can be done to keep capacity well balanced among segments of the process?

7. *Plant size.* How big does the company permit any one plant to grow? To what extent are either economies or diseconomies of scale present?

8. *Plant charters and locations.* Does it make sense to assign different product lines, product processes, or geographic markets to particular plants? How do the plant locations chosen mesh together into a multiplant operation?

Operating Policies

Once the process technology and facilities have been selected, management must still decide on a host of features concerning how the process technology is used. Three broad segments of such operating policies present themselves: loading the factory, controlling the movement of goods through it, and distribution.

Loading the Factory

1. *Forecasting.* To what degree is the plant's output mix known with certainty before raw materials must be gathered or equipment or personnel assigned? To what extent must forecasts be relied on to determine which raw materials ought to be ordered and which equipment/worker capacity reserved, and how much of each?

   How reliable have past forecasts been? Does manufacturing second-guess marketing's demand forecasts? Should it?

   What techniques work best for forecasting requirements?

   Is there a long product pipeline that risks pipeline momentum problems and heightens forecasting needs?

2. *Purchasing.* Given the decision on the plant's degree of vertical integration, what does the plant make for itself and what is purchased from outside suppliers? How are suppliers chosen? What kinds of contracts (for example, long-term or spot) are sought?

   Is purchasing formally integrated with forecasting and/or order taking? How much visibility is granted suppliers about the company's expected future needs? Are orders on suppliers made through an MRP system or other informal means? Or are formal purchase requisitions required?

   How important is supplier quality compared to price in determining how suppliers

are chosen? How is supplier quality monitored? How well does this monitoring work? What supplier improvement programs, if needed, have been adopted?

3. *Supply logistics.* How frequently, from where, and by what mode of transportation do raw materials arrive at the plant? How sensitive are costs to changes in these factors?

   How readily can materials be received, inspected, and stored? Is vendor quality good enough to dispense with incoming inspection? Is vendor delivery reliable enough and frequent enough to be able to feed the plant's production needs without large raw materials inventories?

   How is materials handling accomplished within the plant? How much is automatic and how much is manual? What controls are used?

4. *Raw materials inventory system.* How much inventory of raw materials is held? What system is used (material requirements planning, reorder point, periodic reorder)? How does the inventory level vary with demand, price discounts, supplier lead time changes, supply uncertainties, or other factors? What triggers the replenishment of the raw materials inventory?

   How are materials controlled in the stockroom? Are records accurate enough to be relied on without ceasing production for physical inventories? Is all scrap reported?

   Are materials placed into "kits," or are they fed directly to the shop or line?

5. *Production planning.* Are goods manufactured to customer order or to forecasts, or are they manufactured to stock some finished goods inventory? Is inventory permitted to be built in advance to cover peak period demands and thus smooth out

production, or does production try to "chase" demand, with little or no buildup of inventories?

How are workforce needs planned for? How are model or product line changes planned for? How far in advance can changes be routinely made to the general production plan? How disruptive to the process is any expediting or rescheduling? Are routine allowances made for such situations?

Controlling Movement Through
the Factory

1. *Production scheduling and inventory control.* What triggers the specific production of goods: orders, forecasts, or reference to a finished goods inventory? How do factors like the pattern of demand and product costs influence any trigger level of finished goods inventory? How are specific departments, lines, work centers, and the like scheduled? What factors of the process, the pattern of demand, or product variations and costs affect the schedule?

What determines specific priorities in the jobs awaiting work in a department? How much expediting is permitted? How much rescheduling?

What or who determines the specific priorities of work: an MRP system, foreman discretion, specific rules, simulation results?

Does instituting an MRP system make sense for the plant? How much fluctuation or stability exists for bills of materials, vendor reliability on delivery, production cycle times? What levels of accuracy and integrity exist for inventory counts and records, for production/rework counts and records for scrap? What kinds of exception reports and follow-through stand to be most helpful?

2. *Pacing of production.* Is the pace of production determined by machine setting, worker effort, management pressure or dis-

cretion, or some combination? How readily can the pace be altered?

3. *Production control.* How much information, and of what type, flows within the production process, both from management to the workforce and from the workforce to management? How easily can product variations, engineering change orders, product mix changes, or production volume changes be transmitted to the workforce? How soon can management react to machine breakdowns, parts shortages, or other disruptions of the normal flow of product and process on the plant floor?

How are machines, workers, materials, and orders monitored? What "early warning signals" are looked to? What remedies are routinely investigated?

4. *Quality control.* Does everyone in the organization truly believe that quality (performance to specification) is his job, not simply the function of a quality control department? What mechanisms and cooperative forums exist to assure that "work is done right the first time"? How closely linked are design engineering, manufacturing/industrial engineering, quality control, workforce training and supervision, maintenance, and production scheduling and control?

How is quality checked, both of process and product? How many checks are made at different steps in the process? How much authority is given to quality control personnel?

5. *Workforce policies.* What are the skill levels required of various jobs throughout the process? How are they trained for? Is the work content of jobs broad or narrow? Is cross-training of workers desirable? How do workers advance in the factory (by job classification, different jobs, changes of shift, into management)?

How and how much are workers paid? Are any incentives, wage or otherwise, built into the process? How are workers' achievements and ideas encouraged and recognized?

How does management feel about unionization? What actions concerning unions does it take?

What is the age and sex composition of the workforce?

What opportunities exist for job enlargement and job enrichment? Is there a place for quality of work life projects? How else can the workforce be encouraged to participate in the management of the operation?

Distribution

1. *Distribution.* What are the channels of distribution? How are they filled? What are the trade-offs between service and inventory costs?

2. *Logistics.* What are the benefits and costs of various geographical patterns of warehousing and distribution? What modes of transportation make sense? How should they be managed?

Operations Organization

1. *Operations control.* Are the major operating decisions retained centrally or dispersed to individual plant units? What kinds of decisions rest primarily with the plant?

How is the plant evaluated? What biases might that method introduce?

2. *Talent.* Where within the organization are the best people put? What talents are most prized for the smooth and continued successful operation of the process?

CONSISTENCY IN THESE OPERATIONS CHOICES

These choices—and all operations must make them either explicitly or implicitly—define to a great degree what the corporation's production process looks like and how it operates. Furthermore, these choices are a significant explanation of how well an operation is running or could be expected to run. This is an important point; let us consider it in greater depth.

In Segment I of this text, we discovered that for each broadly defined type of process (job shop, batch flow, line flow, continuous flow), certain characteristics of the process hang together and define what that process is. For example, one would expect a job shop to be characterized by such operations choices as general-purpose equipment, broad work content of the jobs workers perform, production to order, and lots of information flowing within the shop. If these features were not all present, one would have good reason for suspecting that the particular process being investigated was not a pure job shop. Similarly, one would expect a continuous flow operation to be characterized by operations choices such as special-purpose equipment and capital intensity, production to stock rather than to order, machine pacing of production, and at least some dependence on the forecasting of demand. Deviations from this list would also raise questions about the purity of a continuous flow operation.

We can proceed a step further. Not only do certain broad characteristics of any process hang together, but they *should* hang together. The operations choices outlined above should be carefully matched up to be consistent with one another. In most instances, deviations from the model and consistently defined process should be changed because they run a serious risk of acting at cross purposes to the other elements of the process. For example, a "job shop" whose workers are limited by their training or by management edict to perform only a few, very specific tasks risks losing a great deal of flexibility and scheduling ease compared to a job shop with broad work content to the job. Such a process choice risks establishing workers as well as machines as regular bottlenecks to shop capacity. Clearly, in this case, worker tasks ought to be expanded.

To cite another example, a line flow operation that permits many or significant engineering changes on a regular basis risks losing the benefits of production speed, lower labor value in the product, and low work-in-process inventories. The products of a line flow process should be fairly standard; if they cannot be, the other elements chosen for the process ought to be seriously examined and the process altered to make it less line flow and perhaps more batch flow.

To say that certain broad characteristics of any process should hang together as a consistent whole is not to say that *every* operations choice mentioned above can be unambiguously assigned to a specific process. Picking the process does not at the same time mean that *all* of the operations choices we discussed above are automatically determined. A company typically can exercise a great deal of latitude in selecting the specific elements of its production process. The job shop and the continuous flow process, which lie at either end of the process spectrum, are probably more constrained to specific choices of process elements than are batch or line flow operations. In other words, the job shop and continuous flow processes must, in general, be consistent over a greater range of process element choices than either a batch or line flow process. Nevertheless, considerable choice is possible in defining almost any process.

Recall also from Segment I that different challenges to management are inherent in different types of production processes and in the

SITUATION 10-1

PORTERFIELD GLASS COMPANY, GLASS CONTAINER DIVISION

The Porterfield Glass Company's Glass Container Division was almost exclusively a manufacturer of bottles for beer, soft drinks, and other beverages. The technology of glass bottle making was well known and not subject to radical advances. Basically, all that was required to fabricate a bottle was to (1) melt down sand, lime, and soda ash, usually with natural gas, (2) purify the resulting molten glass mixture, (3) suck up a portion of the molten glass into the molds of a rotating bottle-forming machine, (4) treat the molded bottle in a tunnel-like annealing oven, and (5) do any required printing on the bottle. All the equipment was specific to bottle making.

There were substantial cost advantages with increased size because of energy saving in melting and because larger, more efficient bottle-molding machines could be dedicated to specific bottles without wasting any time with mold resetting. Different colors or glass types had to be manufactured in separate batches.

The company's major customers (breweries and soft-drink bottlers) were scattered across the country but were concentrated in the major metropolitan areas. These bottlers did not like to inventory bottles, primarily because they were bulky, and so demanded at least daily shipments—even shipments three or four times a day to feed their typically multi-shift bottling operations. For such service these bottlers were willing to enter into long-term contracts and to provide lead time of a month on all orders.

process elements that make them up. Here, too, the job shop and continuous flow processes are more clear-cut in what they demand of management. For the job shop, scheduling workers and machines, bidding for new jobs, handling materials, and maintaining the flexibility to manufacture a great variety of goods are paramount to management. For a continuous flow process, management's challenges are completely different. What is demanded is care with the planning of capacity and new process technology and with the management of materials from suppliers to the plant and from the plant to the customers. The challenges to management for batch or line flow operations are less well delineated, since both must be concerned with the balance of capacities within the process, product flexibility, worker motivation and training, and product design. There are shades of stress on these challenges, but the distinctions between them are more blurred and less clear-cut.

Selecting Consistent Elements of a Production Process

Selecting the component elements for a manufacturing or service operations company is not a trivial task. Situations 10-1 and 10-2 offer some practice in describing how an operation ought to be organized.

Discussion of Porterfield Glass Company

The previous section on operations choices provides a framework for selecting a production process suitable for Porterfield Glass Company's Glass Container Division. Let us then follow the choices outlined in that section.

Technology and Facilities

Although the glass containers made by the division are most likely specialized (shape, qual-

ity glass, color, printing) for the individual customer, each bottle goes through identical steps in the process. Different glass recipes or bottle molds may be used, but the process itself does not vary by customer order in any significant way. The pattern of the process flow can be rather rigid then. As suggested in the situation itself, the equipment is special purpose. Combined with the rather rigid process flow, this feature suggests a considerable degree of capital intensity to the process.

The division could well be vertically integrated to a great degree, with the company owning and controlling its own sand pits and limestone quarries, particularly if demand is large. On the other hand, the raw materials that go into making glass are so common, so readily available, and used in so many other ways that it is hard to believe that backward integration into sand, lime, or soda ash supply would be very attractive. The rate of return to the company's capital is almost certainly as high or higher in bottle-making as in the supply of raw materials for glassmaking. The delivery of such commonly available materials is surely reliable enough to remove delivery as an argument for the division's maintaining control over its own raw materials.

The fact that supplies are so readily available and easier to ship than bottles themselves is an argument as well for locating close to customers and not suppliers. Because customers demand a steady stream of bottles into their plants, it is clearly advantageous for the company to locate its plants close to its largest customers, if that can be arranged. Plant size should be determined in large measure by customer needs. The plant should be large enough to incur some of the cost advantages there are in energy savings and mold resetting, but after some threshold level, additional cost advantages from increased size are not likely to be large. As it is, the plant should be constructed purposely with capacity in excess of long-term customer contracts. Otherwise, the division risks poor delivery performance during a customer's demand peak, which may endanger the entire contract. The division should track customer markets fairly closely so as to anticipate needed capacity expansions. Technological changes are not likely to be important to the industry, as suggested in Situation 10–1—apart, of course, from a possible redefinition of the business to encompass plastic bottles, too. This implies that the division can successfully follow, rather than lead, process innovation in glass bottle manufacture.

Operating Policies

The loading of the factory is likely to be dominated by the continual output demands of the long-term customer contracts. Raw materials supplies, which are bulky, are probably best shipped by rail or barge on at least a weekly basis, and perhaps more often. The inventory of raw materials is apt then to be replenished on a regular basis, the quantity of each replenishment being enough to bring the desired buffer stock up to some desired level (in a periodic reorder system). The buffer inventory itself is likely to be large because (1) stockouts of materials could jeopardize any contracts and (2) the raw materials are of low value anyway. Heavy investment in forecasting is probably not required; the long-term customer contracts are great aids in determining plant material needs with enough lead time so that deliveries are not jeopardized.

Production should be to customer order and a "chase" type strategy should be followed in planning production over the short term. With long-term customer orders and customer willingness to provide sufficient lead time, production planning of workforce size, hours, and schedule should be fairly straightforward. The schedule, in practice, should not vary much from month to month. There are likely to be advantages in batching orders that use the same glass, though in different shapes or sizes. Changing products—glass or molds—should be a routine matter requiring a very standard directive from management. The quicker and more routine the product changeovers, of course, the more profitable the entire process. Except for changeover periods, the pace of production is determined solely by machine speeds. Information is largely one-way, from management to the workforce, except for sounding the alarm when a machine breaks down.

The workforce is likely to divide into two skill groups. Highly skilled, highly paid labor is likely to be required for troubleshooting equipment repair, for maintaining the equipment, and perhaps for controlling the glass making itself so that it conforms to the "recipe." Other tasks are likely to be unavoidably narrower in content and therefore suitable for lower skilled, lower wage labor. With the equipment largely pacing production, incentive pay schemes are inappropriate. Rather, all workers should be paid by the hour. Opportunities for either cross-training or worker advancement outside the rather narrow and well-defined departments making up the process are relatively scant. Job advancement is likely to be mostly shift changes or relief work. Unionization is likely to make little impact on operations.

Quality of the product is largely a matter of the proper functioning of the equipment. Quality control is best accomplished by sampling output and using control charts to identify problems or potential problems in the process.

Manufacturing Organization

Within a division like the Glass Container Division, authority is best left centralized. Plants are not autonomous, but are much like one another. The central staff should control the larger decisions on technology and facilities, leaving the plant responsible for dealing with day-to-

SITUATION 10-2

COWLES COMPUTER CORPORATION

Cowles Computer was a small but rapidly growing maker of medium-size digital computers (minis and superminis, in the trade's jargon, rather than personal computers or mainframes). Sales were doubling every year and prospects for sales growth in excess of 50 percent a year remained strong. Cowles manufactured computers for so-called end use, that is, for use by customers without any further modification. The end-use market could be contrasted with the original equipment manufacturer OEM market, which dealt with computers that would be included in other products (such as large machine tools). Customers typically wanted different special features added to the basic computer that they purchased. Thus, part of any computer sold looked like all others, and part was unique.

In its product development, Cowles stressed the development of software (e.g., programs, operating language) rather than hardware. Thus, although technically its computers were not particularly advanced or fast, they were extraordinarily versatile and could communicate directly with all other models of Cowles computers. Cowles had been introducing more and more advanced computer systems at a rate of about one new model a year, a fast pace even for the industry.

The assembly of a computer from its component pieces and its subsequent testing, although a complex task, did not require vast scale or particularly sophisticated equipment. The secret to performance lay in the engineering.

day operating problems, personnel, and equipment maintenance. The plant is best evaluated as a cost center.

Within the plant, management talent in the plant engineering department is critical. At the division level, management talent should be directed to the choice and development of equipment and process technology, because the division's future rests largely on these.

Summary

Glass container manufacture, as should be clear by now, is largely a continuous flow process and it shares a host of traits with other continuous flow or near-continuous flow hybrid processes. In fact, the bottle-making process is very similar to the bottling process itself, as the description of the Stroh brewery operation in Tour E makes evident. There simply is not a lot of room in such processes for much deviation in the process characteristics and challenges. More deviation is possible in other types of processes, as Situation 10-2 reveals.

Discussion of Cowles Computer Corporation

Again, using the framework developed in the section on operations choices, the operations at Cowles could be selected, in rough fashion, as will be described.

Technology and Facilities

Compared to Porterfield's Glass Container Division, Cowles confronts a much more jumbled flow to the process because a certain amount of product customizing must be done. This need for a degree of product variation, coupled with the quick pace of new product introduction, places a premium on Cowles's ability to remain flexible. This product flexibility, in turn, has important implications for the design of the production process. The equipment for the most part should be general purpose and production labor-intensive. Significant vertical integration should be resisted, particularly since the company does not aspire to be a leader in computer hardware. The company ought to be aware of process technology advances in other companies but need not be a leader itself.

The company's enviable rate of growth will probably keep capacity utilization chronically high; but because a minicomputer is far from being an item one buys off a store shelf, some stockouts can be tolerated. Without any real economies of scale, the determination of plant size depends more on keeping plant operations simple. Where plants are to be located depends on how individual plant charters are established. If the full production process is broken apart in pieces, then it makes sense to locate all the plants close to one another. If, on the other hand, complete, assembled computers of different types are chartered for each plant, then the plants can be located farther away from each other. Given the high degree of new product introduction, however, Cowles may want to keep its plants close together no matter what the charter chosen. In this way, communication and troubleshooting are improved.

Operating Policies

The need for product flexibility carries over to the definition of plant operating policies. The loading of the factory, for example, should reflect the speed at which the market can demand one mix of output rather than another. Long-term supply contracts for all but the most basic and unchanging parts are inappropriate. The raw materials inventory system presents some real challenges. Product obsolescence argues for a low level of raw materials inventory; yet the long manufacturing cycle time one can expect with a complex product like a computer argues for larger inventories to avoid waiting for supplier deliveries. These contrasting forces argue for the importance of forecasting sales. If, in fact, the product customization done involves the latter stages of production, forecasts can be useful in triggering production of the basic

component parts of Cowles's computers. Hence, a periodic reorder inventory system may be appropriate. The complexity and ever-changing engineering of computers and the needs of later-stage product customization argue against installing a very elaborate MRP system to control raw materials inventory. The transport of supplies can almost certainly be handled by truck and air at economical enough rates.

As mentioned above, the manufacturing cycle may be divided between the early stages, where production can be initiated by reference to the forecast and a derived production plan, and the later stages, where the necessary product customization can be indicated only by order. These kinds of separable demands on the production system admit the possibility of production control through the use of a decoupling inventory. As we discussed, such an inventory has the advantage of shortening the response time of the process by simplifying the flow of information required to meet orders. While the later stages of the process react to individual orders, the process's early stages are initiated by observing the level of products of different kinds in the work-in-process inventory, which "decouples" the stages. It is the drawing down of inventory that sparks new production in the standard component portion of the process. This procedure smooths the output rates of the component part of the process, although the customizing stages must still chase demand more. These customizing stages require more information, such as product variations to be made and engineering changes. They may also require that information flow back to management from the workforce, because new engineering will need to be evaluated and delivery times adjusted for special orders.

Generally speaking, the workforce must be skilled, because it will be called upon to perform different and changing tasks on the continually evolving product line. Considerable cross-training is advised. Some standard jobs may permit incentive pay schemes, but for those jobs that are changeable, hourly pay is recommended. Worker advancement to new positions or areas in the factory may be encouraged as a way to spread expertise in the rapidly growing company. Cowles may also be well advised to be wary of possible unionization and to be particularly attentive to worker needs and requests. Unionization may bring an increasing inflexibility to the process, which might handicap future efforts at new product introduction or product mix change.

An important task is the establishment of quality controls and tests. With such a complex product, many things can go wrong. Testing is likely to be time-consuming but it must be done on all units. The series of tests established must shrewdly diagnose problems but with a minimum outlay of time and before large new chunks of value are added to the computers manufactured.

Manufacturing Organization

The company's manufacturing organization is somewhat dependent on the plant charter choice. If plants make their own complete computers themselves, they can be fairly autonomous, with a full resident staff. However, if the plants are feeders to one another, a strong corporate staff must coordinate the activity. Talent within the organization is best centered in engineering (the company's comparative advantage), production control, and quality control.

The Impact of Competitive Priorities on Operations

Too many managers falsely believe that manufacturing's goal should be low-cost production in every instance. While being the low-cost producer is often a very advantageous position, there are many other ways to compete successfully in most industries. Products can be differentiated from one another too readily and markets have too many niches in which companies can position their products. In one sense, this marketing diversity takes the heat off operations people to cut costs continually; but in another sense, it broadens the role of operations within the company, because operations must now react to different sets of competitive demands.

What is more, the competitive demands that can be placed on manufacturing are diverse and numerous. These eight competitive demands, sometimes termed manufacturing tasks, can be organized into three distinctly different groups. These groups are (1) product-related concerns, (2) delivery-related concerns, and (3) cost concerns.

Product-Related Concerns

1. Product performance—whether the product's design or engineering permits it to do more or better than comparable products.
2. Product reliability and workmanship—apart from differences in product design, whether the quality of materials and workmanship enhances the product's value and increases its durability and reliability.
3. Product customization—how adaptable the operation is to meeting special customer specifications.
4. New product introduction—how readily the operation can bring out product variations or completely new products.

Delivery-Related Concerns

1. Speed of delivery—the time between order taking and customer delivery.

2. Delivery reliability—apart from the speed of delivery, how close actual delivery is to any quoted or anticipated delivery dates.
3. Volume flexibility—how readily the operation can switch production rates on some or all of its products.

Cost Concern

• Cost to produce—the traditional burden on manufacturing to become the low-cost producer, generally related to higher volumes and less customization.

Which of these competitive demands takes priority at a company depends on several forces: the economics of the industry, particular competitive pressures, government mandates and incentives, the company's own resources, and the company's culture and attitudes. What is important to recognize is that operations can be subject to different, and changing, competitive demands. Determining priorities for competitive demands frequently is challenging. Marketing managers typically want the company to compete along all aspects. They can recognize competitors that cater to each "manufacturing task," although no one competitor competes across all dimensions. Determining the competitive demands the firm will concentrate on (essentially, translating the business unit strategy into clear manufacturing tasks) often is very difficult.

The Limits to Operations

Some companies compete primarily on each one of these competitive dimensions. Scattered among the low-cost producers are others that emphasize product performance features (Porsche cars, Hewlett-Packard pocket calculators) or product workmanship (Rolls Royce cars, Ethan Allen furniture) or any of the other characteristics mentioned. What is crucial to recognize, however, is that no one product and no one production operation can compete across all competitive dimensions with equal vigor. A company must choose which competitive dimensions it wants to rank high and which must necessarily rank lower. A production operation, like anything else, cannot be all things to all people.

To reinforce this truism, consider what it would take to design and operate a manufacturing operation that ranked cost, speed of delivery, and product customization all with the highest priority. One simply cannot concoct an operation that could do justice to even these three competitive dimensions; an internally consistent set of operations choices could not be made that satisfied all three goals. For example, the highly capital-intensive special-purpose machinery that could imply low-cost products and speedy deliveries blocks the more labor-intensive, high information needs for a high degree of product customization. By the same token, considerable product customization with rapid delivery could not be accomplished at low cost.

That a production operation cannot perform equally well across all eight of the competitive dimensions listed above may seem to be a totally reasonable, even intuitively obvious proposition. In a sense it is. However, there are many operations managers for whom the truth of this proposition is not evident. These people like to wear buttons with the word "hero" emblazoned on them; they regularly seek more demands on their operations or at least do not refuse such demands. The following scenario is typical.

The manufacturing operation is humming along nicely until the marketing department starts reciting so-called "customer complaints" about product delivery or quality. The manufacturing manager feels compelled to react quickly to this pressure, and he or she makes certain adjustments to the process without really examining the longer-term implications of the short-run actions. After a time, the finance department confronts manufacturing with the "corporation's" desire to reduce inventory carrying costs or capital expenditures. In an effort to appease the finance people, manufacturing shaves inventory or tables some spending plans. Step by step, as manufacturing gets tugged and pulled by such forces, whatever consistency existed among the numerous operations choices discussed above starts to unravel. With the introduction of inconsistencies to operations, much of the competitive potency of operations is diluted.

The Concept of Manufacturing Focus

What is needed then is a determination from top management of what corporate strategy means for manufacturing—an evaluation of the importance of the eight "manufacturing tasks" cited earlier. Once manufacturing is clear about what is demanded of it, it can go about choosing the technology, facilities, operating policies, and organization that are at once internally consistent and consistent with the declared corporate strategy and competitive priorities. The importance of these consistencies has been argued forcefully and persuasively by Wickham Skinner.[1] Skinner terms this consistency of choice manufacturing "focus." For him, focus is a top-down kind of idea that must start with an explicit statement of the corporation's objectives and strategy. This statement must then be translated into "what it means for manufacturing," and the existing operation must be examined, element by element, in a kind of manufacturing audit of the existing facilities, technology, and operating policies. Only then can the corporation think of altering any of the elements that do not mesh with the explicit statements of corporate strategy and its meaning for operations. The goal of factory focus is to have all of the operation—right down to the first-line supervisors and all of the workforce—pulling in the same direction, the direction implied by the proclaimed corporate strategy. Focus also implies that manufacturing should be well coordinated with marketing, finance, personnel, engineering, R&D, and other departments.

Manufacturing choices (technology and facilities, operating policies, organization) are going to be made one way or another. In companies that appreciate manufacturing strategy and factory focus, however, these choices are made explicitly, under top management's direction—and not implicitly, by leaderless managers and workers on the factory floor.

Focus is designed to avoid situations where manufacturers have geared up to do well what the corporation does not need done and then do poorly on the task on which the corporation's success really depends. Or, commonly, too many conflicting tasks are asked of the same operation, caused, for example, by product proliferation or by a blind acceptance of "professionalism" in functions like engineering, inventory control, finance, or quality control. The result too often is that no tasks are accomplished very well.

Consider Situation 10-3 on the next page.

Discussion of Matthew Yachts

This situation with Matthew Yachts is a common example of product proliferation that has begun to sabotage an otherwise smoothly operating production process. How does the apparently innocuous addition of one more type of yacht to a boatyard that makes all kinds of yachts anyway sabotage operations?

SITUATION 10-3

MATTHEW YACHTS, INC.

Matthew Yachts, located in Montauk, Long Island, manufactured sailing yachts of all descriptions. The company had begun by building custom-designed yachts for a largely New York-based clientele. Custom-designed yachts still accounted for three-fifths of Matthew's unit sales and four-fifths of its dollar sales and earnings. Over the years, as Matthew Yachts' reputation for quality design and workmanship spread, sales broadened to cover all of the Eastern Seaboard.

In an effort to capitalize on this increased recognition and to secure a piece of the fastest growing market in sailing, Matthew Yachts began manufacturing a standard, fixed design craft. Matthew attacked only the high end of this market, as the boat measured 37 feet long. Nevertheless, even this end of the market was more price sensitive and less conscious of performance than Matthew Yachts' custom design customers were.

All of the company's yachts were manufactured at the Montauk plant, and shared the same equipment and skilled labor force. Custom designs were given priority in scheduling, and the new boat was rotated into the schedule only when demand slackened. As sales of the fixed design boat increased,

however, scheduling the new boat on a regular basis became necessary.

Matthew Yachts were built basically from the bottom up. Fabricating hulls was the first step. Increasingly, fiberglass hulls were demanded for their speed and easy maintenance. Afterward came the belowdecks woodworking, followed by the fiberglass and woodworking on the deck itself. The masts were turned and drilled separately. Masts and hull were then joined and the finish work completed.

Over the past year, as the fixed design craft continued its steady increase in sales, costs and deliveries began to slide precipitously, especially on the fixed design yachts. During this period, when push came to shove, construction of the fixed design craft always yielded time and resources to the higher profit margin custom designs. As a result, many fixed design yachts were strewn around the yard in various stages of construction. Moreover, space in the existing shipyard was becoming scarce, and a plant expansion of one sort or another appeared inevitable.

The company wondered whether it should stay in the business of building fixed design yachts and, if so, how it should continue.

To understand this situation, let us trace through some plausible consequences of adding the fixed design yacht to the yard. First of all, we should recognize that the custom work and the fixed design work were very different from one another. The competitive priorities for the two diverge greatly. For the custom work, competitive demands such as product customization, product performance, and product reliability and workmanship are critical; cost and delivery are much less important. For the fixed design craft, on the other hand, cost and delivery carry relatively more weight, and features like product performance are not nearly so important. These differing competitive priorities

place conflicting demands on the production process.

The traditional custom work requires a skilled workforce, broad job content, a tremendous amount of information transmittal through the process, and great attention to the scheduling of work, among other things. The boatyard is a job shop. Into this job shop has been thrown a product that is more standard, sold in higher volumes, and susceptible to price competition. Ideally, it should not be manufactured with a job shop type of process but with one that is more like line flow. Such a process would use more and more special-purpose equipment, narrower worker tasks balanced against one another to stabilize the pace of work through the yard, a materials inventory and handling system that removes most responsibility for worker ordering or handling of materials, a lower skilled workforce, and more explicit quality checks in the process, among other things.

When the two different kinds of yachts are manufactured in the same boatyard, costs on the fixed design yacht naturally climb over expectations. The workers are obviously treating its construction with the same care and methods that they use for the custom yachts. Deliveries too tend to be long and to grow longer, because the present process is not organized to reduce work-in-process inventories or manufacturing cycle times and the lower margins on the fixed design yachts relegate them to second priority whenever the going gets tough.

The pressing space problem at the boatyard indicates that now is a convenient time for seeking "focus" at the yard by splitting the two product lines and manufacturing them in separate facilities with separate equipment, workforces, and controls. The new, fixed design yacht is probably best produced in a new boatyard, possibly located a considerable distance from Montauk, where a new workforce and more specialized equipment and controls can be devoted to the task. Space problems could be relieved at the same time focus is achieved.

The separation of product lines and manufacturing facilities (perhaps in plants-within-the-plant) so that only one set of competitive demands is addressed at a plant is a tremendously compelling idea. For Matthew Yachts it means maintaining the match of a job shop process to the custom yachts it was originally designed to manufacture. It also means the match of a new process, more like a line flow, to the standard design, higher volume yachts. In principle, the need for separation to achieve "focus" is clear, and yet there may be good reasons to resist separation, even perhaps in the case of

Matthew Yachts. It is to these resistances to focused manufacturing that we now turn.

Resistance to Focused Manufacturing

Although focused manufacturing is an enormously appealing and "clean" concept, it can meet with some resistance. Focus is rooted in the many inevitable trade-offs managers must make about their facilities, technology, and operating policies. It states that there is no one "right" set of policy decisions; choice depends on how one competes. Focus manufacturing's strength lies in the recognition that production choices abound and in the conviction that they should be tied together for best results. What is often overlooked, however, is that focused manufacturing is itself just one choice among the many that companies confront; while appealing and powerful, it is no cure-all. Like everything else, it is subject to trade-offs.

Consider these cases where focused manufacturing may be resisted by managers, perhaps justly so:

- A single factory produces two distinct product lines, each serving a different type of market. One product line's sales are buoyant and growing, while the other's are shrinking, increasingly vulnerable to competitive attack. Within the factory, minimal separation seems warranted, but splitting the lines cannot be done easily by installing a plant-within-the-plant because (1) production space on site is already cramped and (2) the existing and rampant job bumping between product lines would be difficult, if not impossible, to eliminate without totally disrupting the workforce. Focused manufacturing thus recommends a completely new plant for a product line that is in trouble. Moreover, the new plant will incur some one-time start-up costs and an ongoing overhead structure.

Here lies the resistance. Do the benefits of focused manufacturing actually outweigh the known costs of new plant construction, start-up, and staffing? And for a product with a possibly shaky future?

- Two different products are manufactured in the same factory. Sales for each are seasonal and offsetting; one product's demand peak nearly matches the other's trough. Nevertheless, the competitive demands on each product are vastly different. One must be produced to rigid specifications, and so worker attention to detail must be paramount. For the other product, quality is not crucial; speed of delivery is. The workforce, inculcated with the importance of caring for product quality, cannot change its ways sufficiently to make the factory a very successful manufacturer of the second product.

  Here lies the resistance. Do the benefits of focused manufacturing outweigh the costs not only of establishing a new plant but of carrying seasonally slack capacity in both plants?

- A new plant is being started up to specialize in the high-volume products of a high-technology company. The plant's capital-intensive component supply department could be constructed specially for the products to be placed in the factory—in a sense, focused for just those products. If this were done, the department would forgo the opportunity to supply other, more sophisticated products of the company. But, a more general-purpose design of the department would add 25 percent to capital expenses. Product lives in the industry are short, and nobody knows what the next set of high-volume products will be.

  Here lies the resistance. Do the benefits of designing the plant to be focused, including the capital expense savings, outweigh the technological rigidity that focus may imply for the factory's future?

Similar manufacturing situations are not uncommon, and they offer some perplexing options for managers. Evaluating the forces pushing either for or against focused manufacturing is not a clear-cut endeavor, since a variety of difficult-to-measure factors must be balanced against one another. In fact, assessing what factory focus really means in a given situation can be vexing. Nevertheless, merely understanding the pushes and pulls on focused manufacturing may help to ease managers' burdens in confronting this type of situation.

Analyzing Factory Focus

How does focus help? What should a manager look for as predictable consequences of focusing a factory? Focus can help in a variety of ways (although not in all instances):

1. *Improving the flow of materials and product within the company.* Often the first sign of confusion in a factory shows up in plant logistics—late or misdirected materials or product, incorrect order taking or order filling of either materials or product, and increasingly complex production scheduling. In such a situation, focusing by product or product group often makes sense, because by organizing in that way, plant logistics can be simplified and thus improved.

2. *Reducing production throughput times.* Often, by separating products and at the same time pulling together portions of the production process, a focused factory can reduce its production throughput times. This fact in turn implies reduced work-in-process inventory, fewer rush orders and disruptions to ongoing operations, less expediting asked of suppliers, greater potential capacity, and perhaps, lower finished goods inventories.

3. *Increasing job specialization and product identification.* By concentrating on a limited number of products or processes, work-

ers and managers may more easily find ways to redefine procedures and methods to smooth the flow of manufacturing even more. Especially if the workforce can identify with and take pride in the specific product manufactured, the company may benefit from more suggestions for product and cost improvements.

4. *A clearer cost accounting system.* By streamlining operations, the cost accounting for a product or process is simplified, and the simplifications often means better pricing decisions and improved capacity utilization.

5. *Better reaction to production gone awry.* Factory focus means ingrained operating routines and corrective measures that can simplify and smooth the factory's reactions to nonstandard, potentially troublesome developments.

In any individual case, of course, these advantages to focus may be present in greater or lesser degree. Furthermore, the ability to measure their impact varies widely. Nevertheless, managers may do well making some estimates of their strength so as not to fall victim to the syndrome of hard numbers driving out reasoned, but qualitative analysis.

As the examples introduced above make clear, there are a number of arguments against focused manufacturing. These, too, vary in the ease by which they can be quantified. A company's ability to focus its manufacturing may be constrained by:

1. *Idle machines.* In separating products that use the same machinery, a company risks running certain machines at much less than their rated capacities. Thus, a lower volume of output must absorb the fixed costs of the machinery. Fortunately, the sensitivity of to-

tal costs and earnings to this increase in fixed cost is relatively easy to calculate.

2. *The savings of placing differently cyclical or seasonal products of diverse characters within the same factory.* As with idle machinery, the costs of focusing operations through product separation, measured in terms of increased inventory building and possibly increased hiring and firing of labor, can frequently be handled quantitatively.

3. *New plant construction with increased overhead.* A more difficult constraint to analyze involves a focusing of operations that, for one reason or another, demand a totally new factory with an accompanying overhead structure rather than the designation of plants-within-plants. Such a radical change is sometimes mandated because of growth of the product lines affected and insufficient room to expand on site. Sometimes it is mandated by the need to develop an entirely different kind of workforce or to get out from under outmoded work rules and practices that could not be modified easily at the old plant. In a sense, then, new plants are mandated generally only when the penalties of maintaining production in a single facility are great.

Even with the plant-within-plant option, overhead will probably increase because of separate supervision, production control, and materials handling. These costs too can be deterrents to focused manufacturing.

4. *"Deserting" an existing workforce.* In separating products or processes for their own plants, some layoffs of an existing labor force may be necessary, at least temporarily. This is never a happy prospect, even if improvement in workforce practices is one of the reasons behind such a move to focused manufacturing.

5. *Production rigidity.* A more subtle, but nevertheless important, possible constraint on the focusing of manufacturing is the threat of rigidity it poses for production. By segmenting the operations for each of a string of products, for example, one runs the risk of losing the ability to react quickly to some new product or new process innovations. The new independence of each product may lock the company into a much less fluid structure than what it was used to. It makes sense then for companies that experience a large share of product or process innovation to be leery of a strict segmentation of products or portions of the production process. In fact, focused manufacturing would itself argue for a concentration on the creative, technological function in these kinds of companies anyway, because that is how many such companies compete. This is an important point. Focused manufacturing, and good manufacturing strategy, do not argue necessarily for a segregation of products. It may make more sense to segregate portions of the process or particular skills within the company. The guiding principle is always consistency with the acknowledged manufacturing tasks.

A common threat that emerges from these possible constraints on focused manufacturing is that change—reflected in sales growth, decline, or uncertainty—is an enemy of factory focus. When products with different competitive demands are continually introduced, when the mix of products sold frequently shifts, or when seasonality or cyclicality abounds, then the costs of complying with factory focus become high and the benefits of focus less clear-cut. Thus, the firm that is growing in sales and product offerings and is in constant need of cash is often the one that confronts the balancing of factory focus against other aspects. Since the costs of focused manufacturing may outweigh

its benefits, managers must be careful to resist the enticement of hard number costs overshadowing a more nebulous evaluation of benefits. Further, they must be vigilant in continually testing whether focused manufacturing can fit into their situations; for, as easily as focused factories can lose their focus with change, nonfocused factories can acquire the need for it. In our judicial system, we have found that it works best if one is presumed innocent until proven otherwise. In manufacturing, it can be argued, it is better to seek focus until proven otherwise.

REVISITING THE PRODUCT-PROCESS MATRIX

These notions of manufacturing focus, change, and resistance to focus can be reinforced by drawing upon the product-process matrix that was introduced in Segment I. As will be recalled, the product-process matrix related the character of a plant's products—one of a kind vs. commodities—to the character of the process flow—jumbled vs. rigid, loosely linked vs. tightly linked. Figure 10-1 reproduces the product-process matrix as it was introduced in Segment I (Figure 2-2).

As it was first discussed, the product-process matrix was devoid of any dynamic features. It was merely a handy box in which to categorize the range of production processes we have considered in this text. As should be evident by now, the typical manufacturing operation must deal constantly with change and with the threat of change. It is natural, then, to expect a number of companies to undergo considerable movement within the product-process matrix. The learning curve, for example, represents a constant pressure to move along the matrix diagonal down and to the right.

Movement within the product-process matrix is not likely, however, to be precisely along the diagonal. Such a smoothly modulated

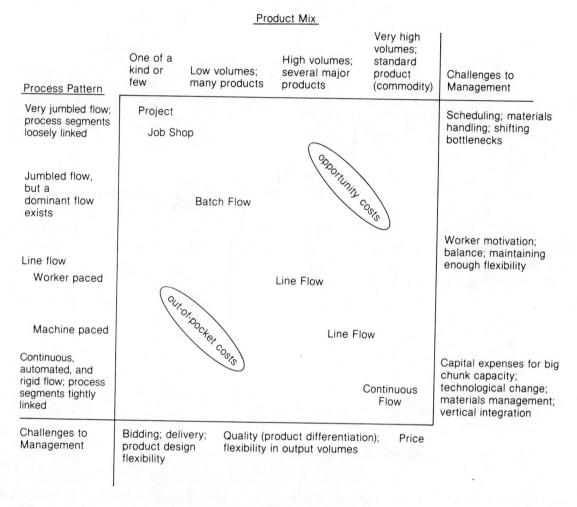

FIGURE 10-1   A product-process matrix.

movement is difficult because many process and product changes tend to be abrupt, at least, that has been true of much change in the past, particularly in the continuous flow process industries.[2] A smoothly modulated diagonal movement is also made difficult by the fact that companies tend to concentrate their efforts at any one time on either a large product change or a large process change. Movement along the diagonal requires simultaneous product and

process change, which is a complex management enterprise. Thus, rather than smooth movement along the diagonal, companies undergoing change are more apt to demonstrate steplike movements within the matrix, such as depicted in Figure 10-2.

In charting their movement over time within the product-process matrix, companies can generally choose to remain above or below the diagonal, since it is unlikely that they can

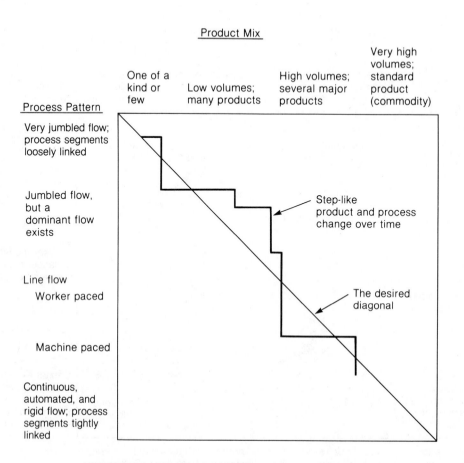

FIGURE 10-2   Movement within the product-process matrix.

remain on it. Is a path over time that lies predominantly above the diagonal any better than a path that lies predominantly below it? The question is a meaningful one and aims at the heart of corporate as well as manufacturing strategy.

As noted in Segment I, the area of the product-process matrix that lies below the diagonal is characterized by out-of-pocket expenses. This area is where the rigidity and capital intensity of the process are relatively further advanced than the acceptance (the increasing commodity aspects) of the process's products. A company whose decisions position it below the diagonal places significant pressure on its marketing people to drum up the sales volume needed to sustain its relatively further advanced process characteristics. Otherwise, the high costs incurred in financing a process change that is significantly capital-intensifying are likely to lower the company's profits. What such a company would like to see is continuing sales growth that brings the company's position within the matrix back to the diagonal, for only the diagonal represents a perfect match of process and product characteristics. In a sense, the diagonal represents those "patches" of the matrix where focused manufacturing is best achieved.

The area above the diagonal, as also noted in Segment I, is characterized by opportunity costs. Here, the process's characteristics are relatively less advanced than is product acceptance. The company's profits suffer, not because high investment in plant and equipment must be paid off, but because process advances could manufacture the product for less. By having its process lag behind its product acceptance, the company forgoes the opportunity to earn more. By positioning itself above the diagonal, the company places pressure on its manufacturing people to lower costs.

A strategy that consistently positions a company above the diagonal of the product-process matrix is essentially a conservative one; the company risks the loss of dollars that could have been made rather than the loss of dollars already earned. As we observed before, opportunity costs are every bit as real as out-of-pocket ones, but the conservative firms would rather lose potential profits by lagging behind in production technology than incur certain, out-of-pocket expenses for advances in the process. While the road to high profits has no shortcuts and lies in keeping both out-of-pocket and opportunity costs low, the shortcut to bankruptcy lies in incurring out-of-pocket expenditure. Incurring opportunity costs is simply a longer and more tortuous road to bankruptcy, as the company gets left in the dust by faster moving companies.

An analogy to one of my favorite sports may serve as a useful characterization of the "strategy paths" companies can choose to follow. Think of the company as a golfer teeing up in the upper left of the matrix (see Figure 10-3). The company/golfer is pondering a shot down the diagonal of the matrix, the center of the fairway for our purposes. Like all golf-

ers, the company/golfer cannot expect to hit the ball straight; he's probably going to put some hook or slice on the ball. Knowing what swinging a certain way will do to the ball, our company/golfer compensates. If he expects to hit a slice, he aims left of the center of the fairway; if he expects to hit a hook, he aims right. It just so happens that the physics of golf dictate that a hook shot is apt to travel further than a slice, since the hook puts an overspin on the ball that makes it roll more when the shot strikes the fairway. In contrast, the slice puts an underspin on the ball that dampens the roll of the ball. The hooked shot, then, is apt to travel farther, but is also more apt to run into the rough if not properly struck. The sliced shot is safer because its roll, once on the fairway, is less, but the shot sacrifices distance.

The "slice" is the conservative company's path through the matrix, risking only opportunity costs. The "hook" is the more adventurous path through the matrix, which risks out-of-pocket expenses. Both kinds of "shots" can be successful, ending up with the company/golfer lying on the diagonal (center of the fairway). The hook, while riskier, is also a more likely way to leave other companies/golfers in the dust, far back up the fairway.

The masters of the hook strategy in this era of manufacturing have been the Japanese. The leading Japanese companies have made significant inroads in all international markets, primarily at the high-volume-product end of the product mix spectrum. These companies have led with their manufacturing capabilities that stress high-quality conformance at low cost; the pressure in these companies is on their marketing arms.

The manufacturing philosophy lying behind the hook strategies of the major Japanese companies is the topic of the following section.

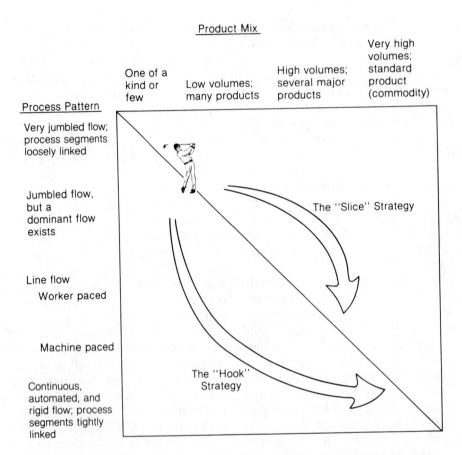

Product Mix

FIGURE 10-3 Strategy paths through the product-process matrix.

JAPANESE MANUFACTURING PHILOSOPHY[3]

The resounding worldwide success of many Japanese businesses over the last decade or so has forced companies of every stripe to take notice. A host of industries—from steel and automobiles to cameras and consumer electronics—have been dramatically affected by Japanese manufacturers. The impact has been all the more striking when one considers that as recently as the 1950s, the words "made in Japan" were synonymous with shoddy merchandise.

Ironically, the world's reception of Japan's shoddy merchandise immediately after World War II laid the groundwork for today's broad acceptance of the quality and reasonable price of Japanese goods. In essence, Japanese industry diagnosed its problems and embarked on far-reaching changes that lifted the competitiveness of many Japanese companies to new highs. With improved quality as their goal (quality being defined, as in Chapter 6, as "conformance to the requirements"), major companies in Japan have reworked their manufacturing choices so that quality in manufacturing is supported at every turn.

To understand how the Japanese have realigned their manufacturing strategies to produce quality merchandise and to become effective worldwide competitors in manufacturing, it is useful to contrast Japanese manufacturing philosophy with what can best be described as the "received tradition"—the precepts under which at least some companies in the United States and other countries have implicitly operated. This tradition, like the Japanese manufacturing philosophy, has evolved over time. It should, however, be considered not as a carefully constructed "philosophy" of manufacturing, but as a series of policies that have sprung up willy-nilly in response to the barrage of demands routinely made on Western manufacturing—demands particularly for quick delivery and for customization of the product. Also important to the development of this tradition has been the ascendency of short-run financial measures by which to gauge the performance of business units in Western companies.

The distinctions then between the received tradition and the Japanese manufacturing philosophy are best seen as contrasts in the policies derived from distinctly different competitive strategies: on the one hand, preoccupation with delivery, customization, and the short run; on the other hand, preoccupation with quality. That so many manufacturers worldwide are studying the Japanese is testament to the effect quality has had in the competitive arena. If this philosophy had not been so effective, manufacturers here and elsewhere would not now be studying it so diligently.

The Japanese manufacturing philosophy, as portrayed in this chapter, is a philosophy applicable to the high-volume, consumer good-based, readily recognizable Japanese companies. It is not a philosophy for the Japanese job shop. To be even more particular, this philosophy is consistent with only a certain set of competitive demands (per the discussion earlier in the chapter). Specifically, the Japanese manufacturing philosophy presented rates cost, reliability and workmanship, and delivery reliability as more important, with customization, speed of delivery, and volume flexibility as least important. As the United States has come to learn, much of the consumer goods industry competes in just this way, but these competitive priorities are far from universal. In reading the discussion, one should bear this in mind.

The received tradition is not very flattering to the companies that have unwittingly adopted its tenets. However, one should not get the impression that all Western manufacturers subscribe to it. In fact, there are many Western companies whose policies have long been similar to those that we will describe here as "Japanese."

This analysis contrasts the Japanese manufacturing philosophy with the "received tradition" via 16 precepts. Each contrasting pair of precepts will be presented, with a discussion first about the received tradition (designated RT) and then about the Japanese manufacturing philosophy (designated JMP). Some of these precepts will review what has already been said about the Japanese elsewhere in this text. By placing them all together here, I hope to encourage your understanding of how the pieces of Japanese manufacturing practice fit together into an overarching "philosophy."

1. Quality

RT: It costs money to make quality products.

This precept states that conforming to the requirements is often difficult and thus costly. According to the received tradition, there is a real, acknowledged trade-off between cost and quality; one cannot expect to be both the low-cost producer and the producer with the highest quality ratings. This precept contrasts starkly with the Japanese philosophy.

JMP: Quality is free.

In their campaign to improve quality, Japanese manufacturers have shown the world that, in the long run at least, working to improve quality can actually lead to reduced costs as well. Doing things right the first time ensures not only quality products but also low-cost ones, as was discussed in Chapter 6. The differences in the cost of comparable U.S. and Japanese goods are not fully explained by differences in wage rates or governmental policies. For example, after detailed study of Japanese and U.S. automakers, a former director of corporate manufacturing engineering for Chrysler put Japan's cost advantage, per comparable car, at $1700 (circa 1980) and attributed most of the difference to "adversarial labor relations, excessive inventories, lagging productivity, and inferior quality performance" in the United States.[4] The typical Japanese compact or subcompact (circa 1982), was assembled in 14 worker hours (vs. 33 for a comparable U.S. car), its engine was built in 2.8 hours (vs. 6.8 for a U.S. engine), and its body parts were stamped out in 2.9 hours (vs. 9.5 for the U.S. car).[5]

2. Expertise

RT: Engineers and managers are experts. Workers serve their desires.

This received tradition acknowledges that charting the direction for the company is the responsibility of its management and engineering staff. These people are highly educated and are paid to be take-charge types. Workers are the means by which the directions set by these managers and engineers are fulfilled.

JMP: Workers are experts. Managers and engineers serve them.

According to the Japanese philosophy, if the company is to do things right the first time, it is the workers who have to do it. It is the workers who have to build quality in—workers on the line actually fabricating or assembling parts, workers testing the items, workers handling orders, workers handling materials. Under this philosophy, it is the workers who know the problems that are encountered in getting things done right the first time. They know what the problems are although they may not know exactly how to solve them. Managers and engineers under this philosophy provide the wherewithal and skills to work on the quality problems identified by the workforce. Many of the initiatives taken in the quality-of-work-life and quality circle movements are in this spirit. These initiatives put the worker at the center of change in the organization and view management and engineering as aids for the eyes, ears, and minds of the workforce—not simply as the authorities from which orders come for directing the movements of the hands and feet of the workforce.

3. Mistakes

RT: Mistakes are inevitable and have to be inspected out.

The received tradition recognizes the truism that all of us are imperfect and that we are liable to make mistakes in our work. If these mistakes are not to reach consumers, then we have to inspect products to rout out any that contain defects. The process should be designed therefore to make it fairly easy to identify products that have defects and to have those defects remedied (in a rework station) if possible and, if not, to have the defective products scrapped.

JMP: Mistakes are treasures, the study of which leads to process improvement.

Under the Japanese philosophy, mistakes are not inevitable. Recognizing that a defect exists is not enough, nor is purging any defects by some final inspection. This philosophy goes beyond the received tradition by holding to the view that every mistake is an opportunity to understand why the process is not foolproof. By tenaciously investigating every defect and its cause, one can gradually, bit-by-bit and project-by-project, improve the process so that it does not create defects. In this philosophy, zero defects is not just a goal but a standard obtainable by diligent investigation of the errors created in the process.

To adhere to the standard of zero defects, the Japanese company tries to sustain a "habit of improvement," with all aspects of the company engaged in continual efforts to improve product designs and process performance. Here, again, the workers are viewed as experts. Only they, once trained and equipped, can monitor all aspects of the process. To do such monitoring well, however, requires clear and compelling measures of product and process quality that are well communicated to all those associated with the process. (Charts and displays tracking quality measures are everywhere in Japanese factories.) Japanese workers are responsible for correcting their own errors, which they are often also required to uncover through 100 percent inspections of completed parts. To make it easy to identify defects, considerable time, thought, and expense are devoted to developing foolproof devices and automatic defect checks (termed *bakayoke*) that monitor product and/or process characteristics continuously.

Not only are workers expected to monitor quality and to correct their mistakes (no rework stations upon which to discard faulty work), but also they are frequently part of any study of process improvements. Workers are schooled in the use of statistical techniques and cause-and-effect analysis (such as in the "fishbone" chart). Quality circles are one forum for the use of these skills in the workforce.

The Japanese typically reject certain notions about the acceptance sampling of lots. Why sample lots of completed parts or products when you would like to be sure that every piece is perfect? Only 100 percent inspection is desirable in that case. Inspection of every piece is particularly appropriate if the process is relatively "unstable" (that is, not highly automated or lacking a long history of operation). With "stable" processes, sampling may occur, but it usually involves sampling the first and last pieces, to be assured that the process has not inadvertently wandered off course.

4. Inventory

RT: Inventory is useful—it keeps production rolling along.

The received tradition recognizes that inventory can buffer a manufacturing process from defects and other problems (parts shortages, late vendor delivery) that could otherwise cause the operation to grind to a halt. Inventory is like grease for the process, enabling it to keep functioning despite adversities.

JMP: Inventory is evil—it hides problems that should be allowed to surface.

According to the Japanese philosophy, not only does inventory cost you money to carry and take up space, but it also lets you trade off that which is not perfect. If the process is to be refined continually so that it turns out only perfect products, then all the problems in the process must be identified and worked on. If excess inventory exists in the process, then there is a temptation to avoid working to perfect the process, and thus problems that should be uncovered are not. The Japanese term *jidoka*, meaning "making things visible," is at odds with the notion of inventory. What better way to focus everyone's attention on the need for quality than to have the process rigged so that there is no place to hide? Banish inventory and you expose nonquality work.

Japanese managers often refer to a flowing stream as a parable for production. Water does not always flow evenly and at the same pace everywhere along a stream. Water sometimes gets trapped in deep pools, blocked by rocks and other obstacles that sometimes remain hidden under the surface. These rocks and obstacles impede the smooth, swift flow of the stream. In this parable, the flowing stream is the flow of materials in the process. The pools of water are inventories, and the rocks in the stream are the imperfections in the process (such as quality problems: problems fostered by distrust such as double orders, extra safety stock, poor maintenance). If the stream is to run fast and clear, the rocks and obstacles must be removed. To accomplish this, however, the water in the stream has to be lowered so that even the hidden rocks are exposed.

The meaning of the parable is inescapable. To uncover the imperfections in a process, inventories should be lowered. Otherwise, those imperfections are likely to remain hidden from view, and the process will never be smooth flowing.

The Japanese recognize, of course, that some inventory usually is necessary and that no process can run with no work in process. But they would argue that the quantity of inventory that is minimally required is generally much smaller than anyone thinks. Running a process with little work-in-process inventory is no small task; keeping product moving through the system in Japan often is done by applying considerable pressure to the worker to perform at the set rate so that other workers are steadily supplied with product to work on.

This pressure is sometimes deliberately applied by either removing inventory from the system or shifting selected workers off the line and into other work. Such "experiments" to see how the operation copes are done to uncover the bottlenecks and quality problems in the process. In some operations, there are lights above each worker that can be lit when a worker falls behind or when quality is jeopardized (a yellow light signals that a worker cannot keep up the pace without making errors; a red light signals that something fundamental is wrong and the process should be stopped). An operation with few yellow lights lit may indicate that too much labor or inventory is available, and management may react by removing workers from the line or tightening up on inventory until more yellow lights are lit. Red lights are valued because under them treasures of mistakes are found.

5. Lot Sizes

RT: Lot sizes should be economic.

As noted in Chapter 5, good inventory management principles involve balancing the cost of carrying inventory against other costs involved in (1) setting up production, (2) granting price breaks for volume purchases, or (3) dealing with other variable costs associated with changing the order or production quantity. The simplest example of this balancing of costs is characterized by the celebrated economic order quantity formula:

$$EOQ = \sqrt{2DS/iC}$$

In the received tradition, manufacturers can fill in the variables in the equation (that is, demand for the period, setup cost, prevailing interest rate, and variable cost of the product) and solve for the economic order quantity. This is straightforward, impeccable logic.

JMP: Lot sizes should be small, preferably one.

In contrast, according to the Japanese manufacturing philosophy, the EOQ equation, although thoroughly logical, is not seen as an expression to solve for some economic order quantity. Rather, the Japanese see the formula as a mandate to lower setup costs, because if EOQ is to be low, the setup costs should decline. The Japanese have made tremendous investments in reducing the time required for each changeover in the factory and making sure that machine setups can be done quickly and routinely. The difference between the changeovers in many Japanese factories and those in conventional U.S. factories is like the difference between a typical motorist changing a flat tire and the pit crews operating at the Indianapolis 500. Whereas the typical motorist may take 15 minutes to do the job, the pit crews at Indianapolis may take 15 seconds.

In Japan there are stories told of tire-curing molds changed in 10 minutes (as opposed to the three or four hours U.S. manufacturers typically take) or of car panel stamping presses changed in 10 minutes (as opposed to 6 hours in some U.S. car manufacturers). The Japanese strive for "single setup" (that is, single-digit or less than 10-minute setup) or even "one-touch setup" (less than 1 minute).

How do they accomplish this? Not too differently from the pit crews at Indianapolis, and, usually, nothing fancy has to be done. Some precepts apply to setup reduction. Among them:

1. Approach setup reduction with the same techniques of industrial engineering and methods improvement that are routinely applied to operator tasks. This means documenting how the setup is done now (videotaping is popular) and then looking for ways to eliminate steps, improve the times of other steps, and make any adjustments either trivial or automatic. It means establishing a procedure and looking to improve it all the time.

2. Do as much of the setup as you can while the machine is still running. Have all materials ready for the setup so that the machine is down for as little time as possible. To foster this "external" setup reduction, workcenters are often designed so that setup materials can be stored close to the workstations. Attention may also have to be paid to preparing for the next setup carefully (cleaning, sharpening, adjusting) well before the next setup is required.

3. Modify the operating equipment to permit easy setup and little adjustment. This can mean designing cartridge type connections, color coding, multiple connection pins or plugs, and similar measures.

4. Know what you want the machine to be set up for. Do not make the machine any more general purpose than you need to. This means understanding what kinds of parts are going to be assigned to it and what kinds of tools and fixtures are to be used.

5. Let one person do as much of the setup as possible. This may mean designing special carts for storing tools/fixtures/attachments, perhaps at the same height as the machine, so that physical effort is reduced.

6. Practice doing the setup. Practice is as important for reducing setup times as it is for reducing operator process times.

With quick setups and small lot production, the level of inventory can be kept lower for two reasons: (1) inventory need not accumulate at work stations into large lots to be transported later to other work stations, and (2) with quick changeovers, the process becomes more flexible. Production can be scheduled to match, often precisely, the current mix of demand for product variations. No longer must orders be filled out of inventories that are kept solely because expensive setups dictate long production runs. Orders can be filled by a very responsive production process.

6. Queues

RT: Queues of work in process are needed to be sure that machine utilization stays high.

The received tradition recognizes that machines represent a substantial investment and that they can best earn their return if they are kept busy. Thus, having a queue of work in process in front of each machine is a way to make sure that the machine will stay busy, earning its keep.

JMP: Once in motion, always in motion. Production should be just in time; there should be no queues of work in process.

Under the Japanese philosophy, if inventory is evil and if lot sizes are to be small, all materials have to keep moving through the process continuously. For that to happen the process needs to be tightly coupled. This may make it vulnerable to disruption, but only by tight coupling can the performance of the process be made visible to all and the success or failure of segments of the process be easily determined and traced.

In the Japanese philosophy, quality and just-in-time (tightly coupled) production are closely linked. Just-in-time production uncovers problems quickly, permits feedback to the workforce that is timely and meaningful, enhances the interdependence of workers and process segments, raises worker motivation and pride, and gives new meaning to cross-training. When these things happen, quality is worked on and improved; rework and scrap are reduced. The factory's systems created to cope with low quality or high inventories are no longer required and can be phased out. Productivity measures show great increases.

With improved quality, inventories can be reduced even more, space saved (space in Japan is scarce anyway), and the process made even more tightly coupled. Thus, quality consciousness and just-in-time production often feed one another, lowering costs even as quality conformance improves.

For some U.S. managers, unfortunately, just-in-time production is simply an excuse for berating vendors. For these managers, going just-in-time means forcing the vendor to hold all the inventory and blaming the vendor for any quality problems encountered. In reality, just-in-time production is less a vendor policy than it is a prescription for linking together elements of the process, so that materials are seldom required to sit idle. To the extent that a factory can make its future materials needs highly visible to vendors and that the vendors themselves can improve their own process capabilities, then just-in-time production can be applied to the entire manufacturing pipeline, and inventories for all firms in the pipeline can be reduced. Some managers inappropriately make procurement policy step one in a shift toward just-in-time production. In fact, procurement changes should follow a plant's conversion to just-in-time operation, with all that conversion means for process redesign; production control; quality management; and leveled, steady, and highly visible production plans.

7. The Value of Automation

RT: Automation is valued because it drives labor out of the product.

In the received tradition, most appropriations for new capital are justified primarily by the labor savings that they generate. Automation is thus seen primarily as a capital-for-labor substitution.

JMP: Automation is valued because it facilitates consistent quality.

Under the Japanese philosophy, machines are seen as a means to perform tasks the same way every time. This view assigns a value to automation that is over and above any labor savings that may occur; labor savings are secondary to the ability of automation to make the process perfect.

This point of view also implies that automation does not have to be sophisticated to be valued. Many Japanese machine tools are simple, in-house creations of the company that are designed for a single purpose. Robots, mainly of an unsophisticated type, are widespread. This last point has received much press. While generally impressed with the numbers of robots, some observers have downplayed the Japanese commitment to robotics because the robots in use there are less sophisticated than some had thought. These people argue that Japan is not as much in the forefront of technology in robotics as some would have it. To me, this criticism misses the point. The Japanese use lots of robots; if one values producing quality, then the extent of Japanese robotics should be praised, because those robots help improve the quality of the products being produced.

8. Sources of Cost Reduction

RT: Cost reduction comes by driving labor out of the product and by having high machine utilization.

In the received tradition, the two most analyzed elements of manufacturing cost are labor wages and capital equipment expense. Considerable engineering and management effort is devoted to assessing how the direct labor component of a product can be lowered or whether machines of various types will be utilized enough to justify their capital expenditure. In line flow processes, line balancing is frequently management's chief concern. The dynamics of process change are seldom considered explicitly.

JMP: Cost reduction comes by speeding the product through the factory.

In contrast, in the Japanese philosophy, there is no particular focus on wages or capital ex-

penditures. Just-in-time production can reduce inventory and space; but more importantly, it leads to a clean, tightly coupled process that means fewer inspectors, less rework, lower warranty costs, and the like—all the things that argue for quality being free. In addition, the more tightly coupled the process is, the less it is victim to some of the disagreeable characteristics of the job shop—excessive shop paperwork, resignation to bottlenecks, acquiescence to multiple routings, and tolerance of expediting. If a manufacturer works at reducing the product's cycle time through the process and thus at making the process more tightly coupled, there is no need to worry about anything else—not about direct labor costs or machine utilization. Those costs will take care of themselves.

Concern for speeding a product through the factory leads to explicit concern for the dynamics of process change. As noted earlier in this book, many processes are hybrids, mixes of job shops or batch flows with line or continuous flow processes. Some of the genius of the just-in-time production mentality is that it forces companies to think how such hybrids can be modified to become more purely line or continuous flow.

Some Japanese companies have taken intermediate steps to modify job shop processes into continuous flow processes (what Schonberger terms automated production lines).[6] One such step is to create dedicated production lines that abandon strict lot-by-lot processing by "overlapping" production (releasing segments of a lot early, as happens frequently when orders are expedited in job shops or batch flow processes). If volumes are high enough, the process sequence can become a completely dedicated line, relieving much of the strain and paperwork of coordination that afflict job shops and batch flow processes and decreasing work-in-process and buffer inventories.

Another intermediate step involves the physical merger of processes such as happens in group technology, where selected families of parts are grouped together and assigned to a given, dedicated series of machines and workers.

A third intermediate step toward a continuous flow process is the creation of mixed model processing, where the drive for flexibility in the line's production transcends the more specialized concern for line balance at all costs. Mixed model processing attempts not only to mix the assembly of different models in small sequences (preferably a different one each time), but also to mix any subassembly and fabrication, so that work-in-process or buffer inventories are reduced to a minimum throughout the entire process.

Although these steps between job shop and continuous flow process cannot be made in every instance, the Japanese have demonstrated how important it can be to press continually for process changes that transform hybrid operations into more smoothly flowing process types.

9. Material Flow

RT: Materials should be coordinated and pushed out into the factory.

Most conventional materials management systems authorize production by releasing information about the order to be worked on to both the factory floor and the materials stockroom. The materials stockroom, then, provides the materials for production, and the factory floor knows ahead of time what materials will be coming. This type of system prevails in operations that require several different manufacturing departments to work on the product. The idea is to coordinate materials and to bundle them in advance of their need by the factory so that the factory departments involved will have their materials ready for use. In practice, this often involves the accumulation of materials for a set period of time, be it a day or a week or so, giving the supervisors on the factory floor the ability to select which jobs they will perform first from among the bundled materials available. As discussed earlier in the text, much of the shop floor control function revolves around the precise scheduling of work to be done by different areas of the factory. In such a conventional system, the materials function can be seen as driving the pace of production in the factory.

JMP: Materials should be pulled through the factory.

Under the Japanese philosophy, in order to ensure that no work-in-process queues exist, the production schedule and the shop floor control system must have the "downstream" operations triggering the initiation of work in the "upstream" operations. Otherwise, there is a greater risk of accumulating work-in-process inventory ahead of any slow operations in the process. By this philosophy, providing a unit more than is demanded is as bad as providing a unit less than demanded. Under such a philosophy, there can still be an MRP system that explodes requirements through the bill of materials but it must not authorize the release of an order to the factory floor; only processes downstream can act to release such orders. The most famous example of this type of "pull" system is that operated by Toyota Motor Company, the kanban system, discussed in Chapter 4. It should be remembered that the kanban system works well only when demands are fairly stable, when the production schedule is frozen for fairly long periods of time, and when few, if any, irregularities in product models have to be coped with.

Production planning is one of the toughest factors in a pull system. Planners must take care not to introduce too much change nor to press production so much that there is no slack in capacity. Yet, on the other hand, the process needs to be kept reasonably flexible and free of sizable pockets of excess capacity. A master production schedule (and final assembly schedule) that meets these criteria is often a delicate thing to concoct.

10. The Role of Overhead

RT: Overhead functions are essential.

At the same time that the received tradition pushes for lower direct labor cost and higher machine utilization, it often implicitly acknowledges the requirements for overhead functions (such as purchasing, industrial engineering, production scheduling, inventory control, quality control, materials handling). Much of this overhead is dedicated to either coordinating aspects of the process or studying it. Although manufacturers operating under the received tradition may grumble about overhead rates that in recent years have soared to 500 percent or more of direct labor, typically they don't take positive action to arrest such growth in indirect labor.

Not only does the received tradition promote the growth of "staff" versus "line" management, but also the people picked for such staff assignment are apt to be trained for their "specialty" and desire little, if any, rotation into other staff or line assignments.

JMP: Any labor that does not directly add value to the product is waste.

Japanese manufacturers have a fervor about ridding the process of extraneous labor. This may be done, for example, by some simple materials handling schemes (one worker positioned close enough to another to hand over the product). More importantly, the whole push for getting the process clean and functioning perfectly results in fewer inspectors, fewer rework stations, less scrap to be handled, and simpler production schedules.

Moreover, the Japanese are much more committed to limiting the size of any staff and to rotating managers through many different kinds of jobs, rather than promoting specialization. Through just-in-time production and the tight coupling of the process, many of the coordination tasks needed in job shop/batch flow processes are eliminated. The Japanese also require more thought and study from their line managers and workers than happens with many U.S. companies. The Japanese can get away with adding such burdens to their line people, because the process itself is simplified and smoothed so that managers and line workers do not have to fight fires continually. Managerial time is viewed as better spent improving the process *permanently* rather than trying to get a "hot" order through.

11. The Cost of Labor

RT: Labor is a variable cost.

Under the received tradition, labor is one cost that can be forgone when demand drops. In many industries, layoffs are a hard fact of life; although Western companies to not like to lay off their people, it is expected to occur when times are tough.

JMP: Labor is a fixed cost.

The notion of lifetime employment in Japan has received much attention in the popular press. In fact, lifetime employment is a reality for only a quarter or so of the Japanese workforce, and only then in the very strongest companies, those which in the last decade or so have become household words in the United States. In such companies, during downturns in demand, workers may be put on special maintenance assignments or a considerable degree of subcontracting may be brought in-house. Supplier firms that are less strong are made to suffer proportionately more than the large companies that guarantee employment for their workers and managers. Despite this caveat, lifetime employment remains a goal for even the weaker companies in Japan. The benefits of lifetime employment are clear both for society as a whole and for the companies involved. The dedication of the workforce is generally high, although this dedication is becoming less strong in today's Japan.

The chief implication of the Japanese view of fixed labor costs pertains to the attitude that the company holds toward personnel. When workers are lifetime employees, the company is forced to take seriously its hiring, training, cross-training, management development, job rotation, and career path counseling. Personnel departments in Japan are strong; their work is not ignored, nor are end runs made around them, as happens in so many Western companies.

12. Machine Speed

RT: Machines are sprinters, and pulled hamstrings are to be expected.

According to the received tradition, machines are expensive and if they are to return that expense (and more), they must run at capacity. Breakdowns may then be expected. Moreover, in the received tradition, large, multipurpose machines are valued more than specialized, less flexible machines.

JMP: Machines are marathon runners, slow but steady and always able to run.

According to the Japanese philosophy, machines should be run only as fast as they can turn out perfect pieces consistently. Machine speeds in Japan are often not set as high as they could be, and more importantly, preventive maintenance is performed religiously. Too often, the U.S. practice is to perform maintenance "when we can get to it," rather than at definite times that may be inconvenient for the production delivery goals set for the process. The best maintenance people are too frequently assigned to the false heroics of fixing equipment that has broken, rather than devising and accomplishing better preventive maintenance procedures.

The freedom to perform religiously systematic preventive maintenance and daily machine checks in Japanese factories comes in large part from the practice of deliberately planning for less production than is theoretically possible. Rather than put pressure on the process to produce at capacity, the Japanese provide for the slack required for maintenance, process improvement, and the like. What the Japanese sacrifice in lost output, they more than make up for in reduced machine downtime, higher yields, less rework, and the like.

The Japanese also do not fear using specialized equipment, often of their own devising. Such equipment is frequently lower cost, slower, and more inflexible than is typically contemplated by U.S. companies. Yet, for the Japanese company, such equipment is valued because it may help make the process more tightly coupled; its use, along with that of other inflexible equipment, can result in a production *system* that is at once more flexible, quicker to respond, and less subject to breakdown than a production system that is built around a large, multipurpose, and expensive piece of equipment. As noted earlier in this text, many small production centers or production lines are typically easier to schedule than one large one, and inventories can be kept lower at the same time.

13. Procurement

RT: Procure from multiple vendors.

Vendors in the received tradition should be managed with an eye toward the benefits of competition. Vendor should be set against vendor so that the resulting competition keeps prices low and service attractive.

JMP: Procure from a single vendor.

The Japanese view their suppliers as extensions of their companies. They are part of the company, to be worked with to improve their quality and to guarantee their delivery to be "just in time." Price is not viewed to be nearly as important as quality or delivery dependability. As the reasoning goes, why risk compromising quality and threatening just-in-time production for a minor break in price?

In many U.S. companies, the purchasing department is a burial ground for those who could not succeed elsewhere in the organization. To the Japanese, on the other hand, purchasing is a critical function, since much of management in Japan consists not so much of organizing people within a company as organizing other companies to do the work. There is less vertical integration for the most part in Japan (for example, materials as a percentage of the cost of goods sold is about 80 percent for Toyota versus about 50 percent for General Motors), and this leaves the management of suppliers and subcontractors as a very important endeavor.

The activities of a Japanese purchasing department have much less to do with the price negotiations and vendor qualifications engaged in by purchasing departments operating within the received tradition. Rather, the purchasing department's mandate is to support product quality and just-in-time production. This implies developing long-term contracts with suppliers for whom the company's business is significant, encouraging suppliers to produce and ship in small lots of exact quantities, demanding frequent deliveries, encouraging supplier process quality so that incoming inspections are eliminated, providing minimal part specifications to suppliers so that supplier talent and value engineering can be devoted to improving one's own product performance and cost, and insisting on reliable transportation. (Because of Japan's rough terrain, reliable transportation often means stimulating suppliers close to the company plant.) For the United States, frequent deliveries are increasingly made by trucks modified for lots of less-than-truckload shipments. These trucks then enter a fixed route cycle of pickups and deliveries, much like a bus route.

14. Expediting

RT: Expediting and "work around" are ways of life.

If, as in the received tradition, delivery and customization are viewed as essential to one's competitive success, one must then be able to cope with the whims of consumers. Many of the factory's systems are developed with expediting in mind, and much of the time of the factory's managers is spent expediting material from suppliers, expediting orders through the factory, and scrambling to devise ways to work around the materials that are not yet there.

JMP: Expediting and "work around" are sins.

The surest way to destroy just-in-time production and quality is to change continually the production scheduling or the engineering documentation on the product. In the Japanese philosophy, rush tags and engineering change orders are inventions of the devil. Instead, production schedules are set well in advance. They are frozen for longer periods than is the case in U.S. companies, and production is run with less chasing of demand and more of a level production strategy. If some product variety and customization have to be forgone, so be it. To do otherwise compromises quality too much.

This is not to say that Japanese companies cannot provide a wide range of products. Their concern for quick changeovers and small production lots permits greater product variety and flexibility than one might think. The configuration of production lines (U-shaped rather than straight line), the cross-training of the workforce, and concern for keeping the entire process tightly coupled argue for considerable changes in worker job assignments and enhanced flexibility in Japanese factories. Yet, marketing whims are less apt to disrupt the Japanese company than one that accepts the received tradition.

15. Housekeeping

RT: Work means getting your hands dirty.

Just as factories under the received tradition accept mistakes as inevitable, they also often accept dirt and untidiness as the price one pays to get the product out on time.

JMP: Buddha and Confucius like things clean.

This statement is a variation on "Cleanliness is next to godliness." Cleanliness, according to the Japanese philosophy, goes hand-in-hand with the notion of making things visible. The cleaner and the more organized the factory floor, the better able the workers will be to identify problems in the process and call everyone's attention to them.

16. Horizons

RT: Quick and dirty often has to be "good enough."

In the received tradition, results are often expected, even demanded, in a relatively short time. Much of the corporation's attention is spent on making sure that the quarterly income goals are met. This concern naturally laps over into manufacturing philosophy and the pressures on plant managers. Short-term goals often carry more weight than long-term goals, and short-term results that deviate somewhat from long-run plans may set off a premature redefinition of the entire long-term strategy.

JMP: Patience is more than its own reward.

For the Japanese company, largely because of Japan's system of industrial organization that, for example, permits banks to own stock, stock prices and shareholder happiness are much less important than market share and other longer-term goals. This attitude implies that patience will prevail as the process is purged of its problems and the workforce becomes accustomed to performing to the standard of zero defects. Similarly, capital appropriation request procedures may not be viewed as nearly so high a hurdle as is sometimes the case in U.S. companies.

In Conclusion

These precepts from the received tradition and the Japanese manufacturing philosophy, as I interpret them, are listed for comparison in Table 10-1. What should be evident from examining them is that the different motivations for these contrasting philosophies have yielded some points of view about manufacturing that often radically differ from one another.

A caveat is in order. Although the Japanese manufacturing philosophy has proven to be very effective for a number of Japanese companies, mainly in high-volume, repetitive industries, this philosophy may not be applicable in all its particulars to diverse sets of businesses, even in Japan. Yet for many companies it does portend a better way. Many U.S. companies have recently adopted this type of philosophy and have been very satisfied with the changes that it has brought to their operations. The precepts listed in the table can be applied in any country or culture. We can expect to see and hear more about them as time goes on.

SOME ISSUES AFFECTING MANUFACTURING STRATEGY

There are, of course, many issues that can have a significant impact on manufacturing strategy. This section deals with two that have been the

TABLE 10-1 Japanese manufacturing philosophy vs. the "received tradition": 16 precepts

THE RECEIVED TRADITION	JAPANESE MANUFACTURING PHILOSOPHY
1. It costs money to make quality products.	1. Quality is free.
2. Engineers and managers are experts. Workers serve their desires.	2. Workers are experts. Managers and engineers serve them.
3. Mistakes are inevitable and have to be inspected out.	3. Mistakes are treasures, the study of which leads to process improvement.
4. Inventory is useful—it keeps production rolling along.	4. Inventory is evil—it hides problems that should be allowed to surface.
5. Lot sizes should be economic.	5. Lot sizes should be small, preferably one.
6. Queues of work-in-process are needed to be sure that machine utilization stays high.	6. Once in motion, always in motion. Production should be just in time; there should be no queues of work-in-process.
7. Automation is valued because it drives labor out of the product.	7. Automation is valued because it facilitates consistent quality.
8. Cost reduction comes by driving labor out of the product and by having high machine utilization.	8. Cost reduction comes by speeding the product through the factory.
9. Materials should be coordinated and pushed out into the factory.	9. Materials should be pulled through the factory.
10. Overhead functions are essential.	10. Any labor that does not directly add value to the product is waste.
11. Labor is a variable cost.	11. Labor is a fixed cost.
12. Machines are sprinters, and pulled hamstrings are to be expected.	12. Machines are marathon runners, slow but steady and always able to run.
13. Procure from multiple vendors.	13. Procure from a single vendor.
14. Expediting and work around are ways of life.	14. Expediting and work around are sins.
15. Work means getting your hands dirty.	15. Buddha and Confucius like things clean.
16. Quick and dirty often has to be "good enough."	16. Patience is more than its own reward.

subject of some debate: (1) what technology may mean for the focused factory concept, and (2) what contributes to advances in productivity.

Technological Advance and the Focused Factory

Some observers of the recent change in manufacturing technology discussed in Chapter 8 have remarked that technological advance may soon make the focused factory concept obsolete. These observers take note of (1) how successfully the Japanese have maintained product flexibility while moving down the product-process matrix diagonal and (2) the promise the latest technologies (for example, CAD/CAM, flexible manufacturing systems, DNC) hold for improving the product cycle times through job shop and batch flow processes. With such

change, they reason, the factories of the future will be able to make customized products as easily as mass-produced ones. No longer then, according to this view, will factories have to be focused for specific products or process types.

This is an interesting proposition, and one that will bear keeping in mind as the years go by. The new technologies, coupled with better production scheduling techniques, are likely to close some of the gap between job shop and continuous flow processes. New technologies will not, however, be able to close all of the gaps between the various process types distinguished in this text. So long as there are relative differences between the various process types, the notion of factory focus will remain useful. If focused factories are able to outperform more general-purpose ones, even by a small margin, it will pay to adopt them.

Productivity

Since 1970, U.S. productivity, measured as real GNP (gross national product) per worker, has not been advancing at its historical (post-World War II) pace. This falloff in the rate of growth of productivity has puzzled many observers, and no definitive explanation has yet emerged. A number of possible explanations have been advanced, however. Among them are some traditional, macroeconomic explanations:

• Low levels of business investment, caused perhaps by increased uncertainty in the economy.

• The phenomenal increase in energy costs, causing many companies to turn to less energy-intensive production technologies but with no compensating increase in output.

• More pervasive government regulations, which have required huge "nonproductive" capital outlays for pollution control equipment.

• Shifts in employment away from agriculture and manufacturing and toward the service and government sectors, where productivity increases may be harder to come by.

• Increased reluctance to lay off workers when business turns down.

• Decline in the willingness to work hard, caused perhaps by high marginal income tax rates and/or too "socialist" a welfare system.

• Demographic shifts toward younger, less-skilled workers.

Some people say that these macroeconomic explanations do not hold much water because, among other reasons, they do not explain cross-country variations. These critics put forth other explanations:

• American management has been too enamored of short-run return and has failed to plan effectively for the long run. It has, according to this view, failed to invest in new capital and technology and has given up on new product innovations.

• There is a tension between productivity (as exemplified by the learning curve) and the customization, product variety, and new product introduction that are common to many marketing strategies. Marketing demands for flexibility, so this argument goes, cut into the national rate of growth of productivity.

• The data on productivity are unreliable, especially for service industries. Output in many cases may not be valued properly, and there may be some problems in accounting for the quality and learning of the workforce.

How this debate will be resolved is unclear. We have much yet to understand about how the national figures on productivity are affected by changes at the plant level. At the plant level, concern for declining productivity is much less evident than it is in Washington. For many plants, productivity gains are being reaped regularly, although there are questions that could be asked about the reliability of plant data, just as there are questions about the reliability of the national data.

Productivity Measures

Chapter 3, which discussed workforce management, introduced the widely used labor efficiency measure (standard hours/actual hours), which is often used also as a productivity measure. This efficiency measure and its cousin, the effectiveness measure, are not classic productivity indices. That is, they do not represent a ratio of output to input, which is the standard definition of productivity. In addition, labor efficiency is a partial measure of productivity; it relates only to labor and not to capital or materials. Nevertheless, movements over time in this efficiency measure are likely to be highly correlated with movements in any other, more direct measure of labor productivity. These direct measures might be units per labor-hour, tons per day, or something similar.

There are many other measures of productivity in use. Most of these are partial measures. The inventory turn ratio, for example, is a measure of the productivity, broadly construed, of dollars invested in inventory. Value added per employee, gross margin, and ratios of indirect labor are other widely used measures.

While one can gripe that partial measures of productivity do not balance labor and capital productivity, partial measures do have their place. They are usually easy to calculate and readily understandable by workers and managers alike. When the measure indicates that performance is off, people can generally explain what happened easily. Because people typically pay attention to things that get measured and rewarded, the choice of productivity measure to track is not a casual one. The measure should capture something that managers feel is important to company competitiveness. Nonetheless, the measure chosen is less important than the company's prevailing manufacturing strategy. If the strategy adopted is a good one, productivity cannot help but improve.

Productivity Policies

Productivity is a complex phenomenon. There is a host of anecdotes about what contributed to a particular factory's or company's productivity advance, and many stories differ completely. For some people, productivity means hardware advance. For others, it means motivating people. For some it means simplifying the organization, while for others it's synonymous with quality management. Some say it's

value engineering. Yet others say it may be methods improvements and industrial engineering. Thus, the plant manager who is faced with a mandate to improve productivity is confronted with a great diversity of options. They can be dizzying and confusing, and the plant manager who attempts to undertake all of them at once risks doing none of them well.

At issue, then, is which of the many potentially conflicting policies the factory should adopt. Are there some policies or programs that are more fundamental than others for a factory of a certain character? Simplicity has long been a cardinal management tenet, so it would be advantageous for plant managers to be clear on what should be stressed in order to improve productivity.

Some recent research and thinking on this matter* suggests that reducing throughput time in the factory—the time between when materials are available to work on and when the product is finished, inspected, and ready to be shipped—is a strong candidate as a simple, unifying "banner" for plant managers to proclaim. Reducing throughput time can only be done effectively if quality is pursued (rework avoided), work-in-process inventories are lowered, bottlenecks are addressed, process segments are linked together, and production schedules are feasible. Throughput time reduction, as a goal, helps to focus managerial attention on these important policies.

This kind of effort, of course, smacks of Japanese manufacturing philosophy and just-in-time manufacturing principles. Throughput time reduction, more than automation per se, seems to be a more effective way to improve productivity. Much has been made of the differences between the highly technical approaches General Motors is taking to drive its

*See Roger W. Schmenner and Randall L. Cook, "Explaining Productivity Differences in North Carolina Factories", *Journal of Operations Management*, vol. 5, no. 3 (May, 1985), pp. 273–89.

costs down and the low-tech approach taken by NUMMI, the joint GM-Toyota venture in Fremont, California, that builds the new Nova. The NUMMI venture has been highly productive without big investments in the latest hardware. It is more evidence that throughput reduction, rather than automation per se, might be a better "driver" of productivity advance.

Organizing Manufacturing[7]

In the discussion of manufacturing strategy earlier in this chapter, a recurrent theme has been the search for operations choices that were at once consistent with one another and consistent with the perceived competitive demands that manufacturing must meet if the corporate strategy is to be advanced. A second theme has valued simplicity—no conflicting goals for a factory, single-mindedness of purpose and of worker and management tasks.

These rubrics for the selection of a plant's operating characteristics follow through as well in the definition of the management organization that oversees and coordinates operations. Consistency and simplicity should anchor the manufacturing organization.

How can an organization be consistent and simple? To begin to answer this question, let us analyze two distinct ways to organize an operation's management: the product-centered organization and the process-centered organization.

The Product-Centered Organization

At its simplest, the product-centered organization resembles a traditional plant-with-staff organization, which is repeated at higher and higher levels to control groups of plants and then groups of products and/or product lines.

Customarily, individual products or product lines are placed in their own plants and managed exclusively by a product-oriented group of managers. Figure 10-4 offers a schematic representation of a product-centered organization.

Authority in this kind of organization is spread among the products and forced down within each product organization. Each product group is a small but independent company.

So far, this type of organization has been associated exclusively with products and product lines. Equally valid would be an association with geographic market areas. Here, instead of independent product companies, the company is independent within the boundaries of a certain geographic area. Most commonly, these separate geographic divisions of manufacturing involve foreign operations; but for some companies, domestic operations are organized with considerable authority placed at the regional level. Although it is more complete to describe such organization as product/market-centered, for ease of exposition I will continue to call it a product-centered organization, leaving the market-centered variation implicit.

A product-centered organization is most often found in less complex, perhaps more labor-intensive production processes that do not rely on vast economies of scale or on the latest or most sophisticated equipment. Rather than be dominated by cost reduction, tight controls, and formal planning cycles, the product-centered organization is much more attuned to product mix flexibility and innovation. Consumer goods companies are often product-centered in organization.

The product-centered organization is appealing because it is "clean," responsibilities are well delineated. Performance within the organization is easy to evaluate, because usually product groups are established as profit centers. Plant managers are important in the company and are often charged with responsibility for

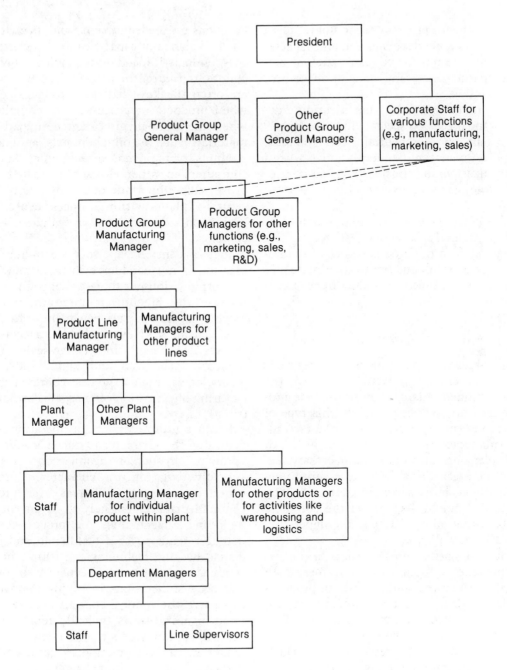

FIGURE 10-4   Organization chart typical of a product-centered manufacturing organization.

decisions about process technology, plant equipment, product development, and capacity as well as more routine concerns such as personnel, maintenance, and production control and scheduling.

The product-centered organization demands—and breeds—a special kind of manager: independent, entrepreneurial, well rounded. Junior-level managers frequently move within the organization and must be tracked continually as they take on new or different responsibilities.

The corporate staff is relieved of much of its duties, particularly day-to-day operations. The corporate staff in the product-centered organization is often small and left to coordinate policies and personnel across product lines or geographic regions.

The Process-Centered Organization

Instead of breaking apart product lines for their own plants and manufacturing staffs, the process-centered organization breaks the process apart into distinct pieces. In this type of organization, most often several plants combine to manufacture the final product, although a multiplant operation is not a necessary feature of the organization. It is necessary to delineate responsibilities in manufacturing not by product line but by segment of the complete manufacturing process. Hence the appelation "process-centered."

Because an entire series of plants or process segments must be coordinated to ensure smooth changes in the mix and quantities of products manufactured, the process-centered organization must be strongly centralized. This centralization of authority contrasts sharply with the decentralization that prevails in the product-centered organization (see Figure 10-5).

In addition to providing coordination, the centralized authority is often absorbed with decisions on needed capacity and its character, on the balance of capacities in the entire process, on logistics, and on technological change and its impact on the process. These decisions are often the key challenges to management when products or processes are complex, as when the company is oriented to particular materials (such as, oil, chemicals, agricultural products) or to advanced technology (such as, computers or other electronic products). Because such important decisions are retained centrally, plants within a process-centered organization are nearly always evaluated as cost centers.

Such a centralized, process-centered organization is not conducive to rapid new product introduction nor to vast swings in volume because the pipeline momentum and geographic separation between plants often lead to sluggishness. Nevertheless, if aspects of a process can benefit from large-scale or particularly specialized and rapidly advancing technologies, then a process-centered manufacturing organization offers a substantial contribution.

Because authority in the organization is kept centrally, the character of the managers who "grow up" in such an organization tends to be very different from the character of product-centered managers. Whereas the product-centered manager is likely to be an entrepreneur and a generalist, the process-centered manager tends to be a technician and a specialist. Because technologies within a process-centered organization are frequently so complex and because decisions involving them are so expensive, the young manager in a process-centered organization is typically removed from the substantial production decisions that are made. Instead, the young manager usually undertakes a rather technical and frequently long apprenticeship. At the end of the apprenticeship, however, lies the opportunity to make de-

FIGURE 10-5   Organization chart typical of a process-centered manufacturing organization.

cisions of a substantially larger magnitude than most product-centered managers make.

Table 10-2 lists the major operating differences between product-centered and process-centered manufacturing organizations.

There are no strong arguments for consistently favoring one type of organization over the other. In terms of total manufacturing costs, neither organization could always be expected to dominate. The process-centered organization, for example, can best manage economies of scale or situations where tight controls are desirable; but at the same time, the process-centered organization is likely to increase over-head and logistics costs. It may also experience longer production cycle times and larger inventories, because it is less flexible in general than the product-centered organization.

Because of the staff specialization within a process-centered organization, technological change is often fostered best under such an organization. The central staff is apt to be highly expert, aware of technological alternatives, trends, research, and the experiences of other companies in the industry. This is a clear advantage of the process-centered organization, because the exploration of technological advance in a product-centered organization may

TABLE 10-2   Differences between product-centered and process-centered manufacturing organizations

	PRODUCT-CENTERED	PROCESS-CENTERED
Profit or cost responsibility: where located	Product groups	Central organization
Size of corporate staff	Relatively small	Relatively large
Major functions of corporate staff	Review capital appropriations requests	Coordinate decision making with marketing
	Communicate corporate changes and requests	Make facilities decisions
	Act as clearinghouse for personnel information, management recruiting, purchasing, used equipment, management development programs	Set personnel policies
		Set purchasing policies
		Review logistics-inventory management
	Evaluate and reward plant managers	Coordinate production schedules
	Select plant managers and manage career paths—possibly across product group lines	Decide whether to make or buy and whether to vertically integrate
		Recruit future plant managers
		Review plant performance, cost center basis
Major responsibilities of plant organizations	Coordinate decision making with marketing	Use materials and facilities efficiently
	Make facilities decisions (subject to marketing)	Recruit production, clerical, and lower management workers
	Make purchasing and logistics decisions	Train and develop future department and plant managers
	Schedule production and control inventory	Respond to special requests from marketing within limited ranges
	Decide whether to make or buy	
	Recruit management	

be hit-or-miss. Some corporate staffs may take on the responsibility, or a separate research division may sponsor the needed research and development. In any case, major technological issues are often removed from the line operations of the typical product-centered organization.

A process-centered organization may also enjoy a relative advantage when it comes to managing the purchasing function, because such an organization can often win volume discounts. These economies may or may not accrue to a product-centered organization. In some product-centered companies, purchasing is split between the product lines and a central purchasing staff for the very reason of securing volume discounts.

Choosing the Organization: Product, Process, or Some Combination?

As they have been introduced so far, the product- and process-centered organizations are polar opposites in some important respects, and they can be expected to place fundamentally different demands on the company—different policies and practices, measurement and control systems, managerial attitudes, kinds of people and career paths. The question arises then in any given situation as to whether a product-centered organization should be put in place, whether a process-centered organization should be preferred, or whether some combination of the two ought to prevail. To explore this question consider Situation 10-4.

SITUATION 10-4

STE ELECTRONICS CORPORATION

Rich Charles, vice-president for operations at STE Electronics, swore that the San Jose plant was built on quicksand and that any week now, on a visit there, he would be sucked under with no more than a muted gulp for his last breath. It was a constant wonder to him why he wasn't having nightmares about the plant.

STE Electronics Corporation, headquartered in San Francisco, was a small but growing company manufacturing specialty electronics equipment for the process machine industry and for the Department of Defense. The company was organized around two divisions: the industrial products division with its manufacturing facility in Livermore, and the defense products division with its manufacturing facility in Bakersfield. Supplying both of these divisions was the San Jose plant, which made power supplies and printed circuit boards.

As Rich Charles saw it, the San Jose plant was a battleground over which the industrial products and defense products divisions waged an intermittent war. Charles himself was some sort of umpire who would periodically award the spoils of victory to one division's "army" or the other's. There were continual skirmishes between the two divisions concerning the allocation of the San Jose plant's capacity. Each division wanted priority to be given the delivery of its power supplies or printed circuit boards. Both products were critical components of the company's range of electronic equipment, and the failure to deliver on time could seriously interrupt each division's production schedule. Nevertheless, both divisions were playing games with orders on the San Jose plant. In an effort to ensure delivery, both divisions would over-order from San Jose and at the same time pretend they needed every unit they ordered, and quickly at that.

To make matters worse, the defense products division would continually harass San Jose about product quality. This was understandable, too, for the defense products division had to produce to exceedingly precise specifications. The industrial products division was not under as stringent pressure.

Delivery and quality concerns flared up periodically as skirmishes, but there was a pitched battle every year at transfer price setting time. Each division was evaluated as a profit center but the San Jose plant was evaluated as a cost center. Because materials costs were a substantial fraction of product cost, each division had the incentive to keep the transfer prices they paid for their power supplies and printed circuit boards low. But, because San Jose's total costs had to be covered, there were fevered sessions where the allocation of San Jose's overhead expenses were argued over, each division trying to throw them onto the other. Rich Charles did not enjoy these sessions.

Charles had a measure of compassion for the San Jose plant and its management. They were always caught in the crossfire, and it was only the concerted efforts of the cadre of old engineers who ran San Jose that kept things moving as smoothly as they did. However, in not too many years most of the San Jose management were slated for retirement, and Rich Charles was concerned that no young heirs apparent seemed to be rising to take charge of the plant. Charles knew that the young talents in the company were shying away from the San Jose operation, both because of the divisional crossfire and because the product divisions were viewed as the "fast track" within the company. Charles himself had come up mainly through the industrial products division and his predecessor had headed the defense products division. It was no wonder that STE's young managers viewed San Jose as a dead end for their careers.

Rich Charles had pondered closing the San Jose operation and spinning off the power supply and printed circuit board production to each division, but he had shied away from this option. San Jose did realize some economies from the scale of its operation and its breakup would be costly and would spread the existing expertise too thin. What Charles really wanted to think about was some alternative organization of manufacturing that might lighten his burden and that of his staff in dealing with San Jose and its interactions with the product divisions. As it was now, San Jose housed only about a quarter of the company's manufacturing employees, but it accounted for well over half of his time and the time of his staff. The plant needed persistent guidance on matters such as forecasts, production control, and inventories.

Discussion of STE Electronics Corporation

We can picture the manufacturing organization at STE Electronics as in Figure 10-6. As Rich Charles is only too aware, this kind of organization places distinctly different demands on him and his staff. The profit-center product divisions view the central staff as umpires and as little else. They do not approach the control staff for much day-to-day support, but rather remain in their nearly autonomous worlds. The San Jose plant makes much more use of the central staff, mainly because the central staff cannot afford to risk seeing San Jose "on its own." The plant is too important to the smooth operation of the entire company.

For this kind of situation, Hayes and Schmenner argue for either a product-centered organization or a process-centered one, but not the combination that is evident as STE Electronics. The corporate staff cannot function properly when so many conflicting demands are placed on it. Just as the role or charter for each plant must be clear and simple, so must the role or charter for the central manufacturing staff. Hayes and Schmenner propose a test for such "organizational focus," as they put it: How easy would it be to fragment manufacturing, say, if forced to by the antitrust division of the Justice Department? If the operations could be fragmented easily, organizational focus has been achieved. If too many parts of the organization become entangled so that fragmentation is difficult, they argue, the organization is not focused.

What then should Rich Charles do at STE Electronics? Clearly, the suggestion to break up the San Jose plant and to toss a chunk of it to each of the product divisions is sound, at least organizationally. Apart from that, Charles may be well advised to formalize the relationship between San Jose and the product divisions. This

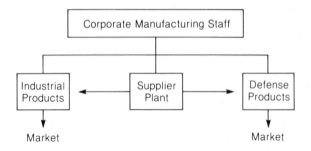

FIGURE 10-6 The manufacturing organization at STE Electronics.

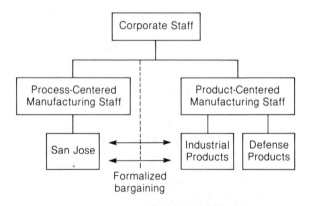

FIGURE 10-7 A revised organization chart for STE Electronics.

organization can be accomplished by insisting that transactions between each product division and the San Jose plant be carried out at "arms length"; San Jose could enter into contracts with each division and could maintain the right to refuse compliance with a division request, just as the divisions would be free to seek outside suppliers. This approach argues for an organization that is more subsidiary than divisional. To maintain this organizational formality, the corporate staff could be divided into two parts, one aiding and overseeing the San Jose plant and the other coordinating the two product divisions. By seeking this separation, the two organizations assume a more equal status and eliminate the conflicting roles that the corporate manufacturing staff had to play.

A revised organization chart might look like Figure 10-7. As for Rich Charles himself, he might have to choose sides, occupying a role either at the head of the product-centered staff or at the head of the process-centered one. He, too, should not have to occupy the middle ground.

PART TWO

SERVICE OPERATIONS STRATEGY

Part One of this chapter opened by reviewing a whole series of operations choices faced by manufacturing managers. Service operations managers, of course, face a similar list of choices. Table 10-3 outlines some major ones.

Furthermore, just as manufacturing choices work best when they are consistent with each other and with the competitive priorities implied by the business strategy, so too do service operations choices. Service business competition can be as cut-throat as any, perhaps more so, because barriers to entry are frequently lower for service businesses. The service business with inconsistent operations choices, is often quickly weeded out.

Service businesses can no more be all things to all customers than can manufacturers. The concept of factory focus has easy parallels in the service arena. A number of the criticisms leveled at various service companies reflect concern over too many different kinds of services offered or a failure to achieve the operational synergies touted when the merger or acquisition was first undertaken. One cannot assume that the "formula" that has been so successful in one service business will necessarily carry over to another service business, even if that business is merely a segmentation of the old one.

REVISITING THE SERVICE PROCESS MATRIX

Strategic Changes in Service Operations

The classification of service businesses into four categories—service factory, service shop, mass service, and professional service—can be used to investigate what has happened strategically to service operations over time. The most salient development in many service businesses has been vast segmentation and diversification. Services that were once clearly service shops or mass service firms are no longer so clearly labeled. Service firms are spreading themselves out across the service matrix. Some examples are instructive:

1. One of the classic changes has involved the development and evolution of fast food. The traditional restaurant could be positioned as a service shop with relatively high customization and interaction for the consumer and a middling labor intensity. The elegant gourmet restaurant may even be classed as professional service. On the other hand, with the advent of fast food, interaction and customization for the consumer has been dramatically lowered, as has the labor intensity.

TABLE 10-3   Key choices for service operations

I. Technology and Facilities

Type of facility and equipment (Used by customers themselves? How? How attractive do they have to be? How are they used during a peak versus a nonpeak situation? General-purpose versus special-purpose equipment? Anything proprietary about equipment or its use?)

Layout (Job shop-like? Fixed position? Other?)
Location (How critical to attracting customers?)
Size of the facility
Geographic spread of any multiple facilities
Degree of labor intensity
Attitude toward capacity utilization (Facility for the peak demand or not?)

II. Operating Policies

A. Planning the Operation

Forecasting (Extent required? Type used?)
Logistics and inventory system used for materials employed
Manpower planning
Schedule setting (Can service provision be "leveled" in any way?)
Demand management for peak and off-peak times

B. Controlling the Operation

Labor issues—hiring, training, skill levels required, job content, pay, advancement, unionism
Accounting controls used
Checklists developed
Foolproofing designed into the layout and the equipment
Quality control audits and policies
What triggers provision of the service and the pace of the operation (Customer? Forecast?)
Production control (How does information flow within the operation? What is on track? What is not? How can anything gone amiss be fixed? How can any changes be implemented?)

C. Operations Organization

What is kept at the individual unit level, and what is centralized?
Where is talent held in the organization?

For the classic fast food companies, the change has been from a service shop to a service factory. This has left the restaurant business with a wide diversity of operations types.

2. Another interesting innovation within the service shop quadrant has involved hospitals. The new kinds of hospitals developed by Humana, Hospital Corporation of America, and others are different in type from the traditional community hospital or university medical center. The traditional hospital (and especially the university medical center) is geared to treat any disease, and thus, invests in all of the latest equipment and technology for diagnosis and treatment. This

new breed of hospital customarily deals with the more routine kinds of medical treatment; often such care facilities do not include intensive care units and other high expense units for very sick or dying patients. Those patients are referred to larger and more well-equipped hospitals. For its part, the new type of hospital offers much lower cost service that is convenient for the consumer. The new hospital thus offers less customization but also a higher degree of labor intensity.

3. Another series of changes has occurred in some of the services characterized as "mass service." Retailing offers some interesting examples. The expansion of catalog stores

(such as Best's or Sharper Image), warehouse stores (such as Toys 'R' Us), mailorder sales (such as L. L. Bean), and brand-name discounters (such as Loehmann's) has broadened the traditional retailing operation toward a lower degree of labor intensity, largely by providing less than department store-type "full service." On the other hand, the proliferation of boutiques and specialty operations within stores like Bloomingdale's is evidence for a different kind of change, one where interaction and customization are stressed, often with higher labor intensity (more than "full service"). By being more "professional" (frequently with salespeople on commission), such stores hope to convert more browsers into buyers.

4. The deregulation of commercial banking and financial services has also created some intriguing strategic changes for operations within the mass service quadrant. Automation in commercial banking (automatic teller machines, electronic transfers, and other new technological advances) has pushed aspects of commercial banking to lower labor intensity. Indeed, credit card operations and check clearing are now placed in their own facilities, often at quite a distance from the commercial banks themselves, and they do essentially the kind of work that one would expect in a service factory. This kind of change is evident in some other financial service companies. One of the justifications given for the acquisition of Lehman Brothers Kuhn Loeb by Shearson/American Express was the fact that the trading operations of Lehman Brothers could be easily absorbed by slack capacity in the backroom operations at Shearson.

However, even as technological advances have helped commercial banking become less labor intensive, there is a move to customize some services even more. The "unbundling"

of financial services brought on by such deregulation milestones as the removal of interest rate ceilings on certificates of deposit, the cessation of fixed brokerage commissions, the demise of Regulation Q (which placed ceilings on interest payable by commercial banks), and the first steps toward interstate banking has promoted this development. Many of the services that have been acquired by the "financial supermarket" companies are essentially services that will give those companies greater interaction with and customization for consumers. The increasing menu of services from the traditional brokerage houses may cause the old-time broker, who tried to be all things to his or her client, to become an anachronism.

Moving Toward the Diagonal

Given the importance of focused operations and the quickening pace of segmentation and diversification of service businesses, understanding the dynamics of service process change can be very helpful. There are several observations about these dynamics that bear attention. The first observation is that many of the segmentation moves that service businesses have made, as were just discussed, have been *toward* the diagonal that runs from the service factory to the professional service firm. Figure 10-8 illustrates this point. But why is this the case? What is it about the diagonal that is so attractive for existing services? The unifying thread in these moves toward the diagonal seems to be *better control*, although the kinds of controls needed differ from the service shop side of the diagonal to the mass service side.

On the mass service side, control often relates to labor costs and efficiency; these services are constantly trying to get a grip on their labor scheduling and productivity. With mass service, plant and equipment are rarely con-

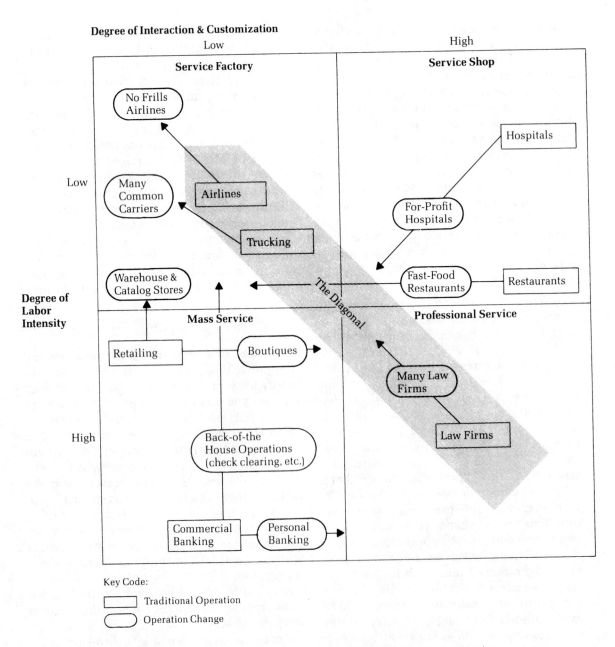

Degree of Interaction & Customization

Low   High

Service Factory   Service Shop

No Frills Airlines

Hospitals

Low

Many Common Carriers   Airlines

For-Profit Hospitals

Trucking

Degree of Labor Intensity

Warehouse & Catalog Stores

The Diagonal

Fast-Food Restaurants   Restaurants

Mass Service   Professional Service

Retailing   Boutiques

Many Law Firms

High

Back-of-the House Operations (check clearing, etc.)

Law Firms

Commercial Banking   Personal Banking

Key Code:

☐ Traditional Operation

⬭ Operation Change

FIGURE 10-8 Strategic operation changes within the service process matrix.

straints. In retailing, for example, labor is a critical variable cost, so scheduling labor is an important activity. The recent increased use of point-of-sale terminals has permitted sales tracking of different items throughout the day. Such information, in combination with selling cost (wages paid divided by sales for any period—a productivity measure) is tremendously useful to workforce scheduling. Such information also helps inventory control, of course. Moves toward more customization, such as the department store boutique and its commission salespeople, can also be understood as moves toward increased control of the selling situation itself with concomitantly higher revenues, profits, and productivity.

On the other side of the diagonal, the service shop frets about control of the service itself. In the service shop, plant and equipment are frequently constraining. Thus, there are concerns for how frequently unpredictable jobs (such as autos for repair, health care patients) can be sequenced through areas with expensive capital equipment. Control is affected as well by great uncertainty about when and how people know that the service is satisfactorily rendered. Hospitals, for example, have a high proportion of fixed costs and thus worry a great deal about capacity utilization. Current debates about whether administrative staffs or medical staffs should dictate the utilization of hospital resources (particularly given changes in reimbursement practices) are, at core, debates about resource control. One can thus understand pressures to provide less customized and/or interactive service (fewer tests, more ambulatory care).

The service factory and the professional service firm suffer less from loss of control. This is not to say that control is not an issue for both of these service types, but with the professional service firm, the high degree of interaction and customization is at least matched with a high

degree of labor intensity and a tremendous amount of skill in the workforce. Control is a much more individual affair, relatively free of constraints of plant or equipment. The service factory, on the other hand, can plan its "process" to foster more control; in this regard the service factory shares many of the benefits that manufacturing operations enjoy. The process defines the service and the flow of the process is relatively smooth. The labor needed is well known for given levels of demand and scheduling of labor, plant, and equipment is fairly straightforward.

Even though there are forces on existing operations to move toward the diagonal, we should not be alarmed that all service shops or mass service operations will become extinct. Many operations will be able to adhere to their traditional operations choices, and marketing pressures for increased customization and the generation of completely new services are likely to replenish the supply of service shops or mass service operations that are pressed to transform themselves. Witness, for example, the upsurge of luxury airplane travel or luxury hotel accommodation. These are new services that are being rendered to particular market niches. The change recently in how computers are sold, with more mass outlets as opposed to individual salespeople, is another example.

Moving Up the Diagonal

A second observation on the dynamics of service processes centers on some of the service business already located on the diagonal. The professional service firm and the service factory are not immune themselves from strategic changes. Of those services that have changed their positions within the service process matrix, most have moved up the diagonal. Consider the changes that have occurred within many law firms over the last decades. The growing staffs of paralegals and other lower-cost labor and the increasing specialization of what many law firms do has driven many firms within that professional service industry toward lower labor intensity and less customization (that is, less full service). Similarly, other professional service firms have invested in equipment, much of it for word processing or data processing.

In a similar vein, the deregulation of trucking and air travel has brought significant change to those service factories. Deregulation of trucking has forced many of the old line common carriers to invest dramatically in breakbulks and additional freight terminals so as to do better with less-than-truck-load shipments. While these capital investments have meant increased barriers to entry by competitors to these trucking firms, these firms can no longer afford to offer so customized a service for their clients. They are more specialized and offer fewer services. Their pricing structures have been changed to encourage the clients to ship in particular ways. This has meant movement up the diagonal for most of the common carriers.

A similar story can be told of the airlines. Deregulation encouraged their operations to shift to hub and spoke systems. All of the major airlines have changed their operations in this way so that a number of "pushes" can be made from their major airport hubs during any day. Where once competition was on time of day and the elegance of service, competition these days is more on price and less on the number of flights and their timing during the day. Thus, for most airlines, the result has been both less customization in what they offer the consumer and lower labor intensity, because significant investments have been placed in the hubs.

Just as movement toward the diagonal does not necessarily mean that service shops and mass service firms will cease to exist, the move up the diagonal does not necessarily mean that professional service firms will all become small service factories. There will always be some firms that will be able to remain successfully with high labor intensity and high interaction and customization, and there will be new professional services rendered that, at least initially, will demand a combination of high labor intensity and high interaction and customization.

QUESTIONS

1. Three categories of decision making or policy making define to a great degree what the corporation's process looks like and how it operates. Summarize the main aspects of each category.

2. Why is consistency valued so highly in the production process choice? To defend your position, provide examples that you know about from your own experience or reading.

3. Compare the main operational features of the Porterfield Glass Company with those of Cowles Computer Corporation.

4. What are four of the main competitive demands that can be placed on manufacturing?

5. For a corporation, what are the principal advantages and disadvantages of factory focus? What are the main areas of resistance to focus?

6. "Movement within the product-process matrix is not likely to be precisely along the diagonal." Discuss the theory behind this statement, paying particular attention to what it means to be above or below the diagonal.

7. Name the two clear ways to organize an operation's management. What advantages does each offer? For what kind of operation? How does one choose? Provide an example for your discussions.

8. Discuss the factors or concerns that should be considered in selecting the elements of a production process.

9. Discuss the competitive demands on manufacturing. Can a manufacturing manager expect to perform equally well in all of the demand aspects? Why?

10. What is meant by the term *focused manufacturing* and why is it an important concept?

PROBLEMS

1. "Inflexible, special-purpose machinery can be as much a part of a flexible manufacturing system as flexible, general-purpose machinery." Comment on this statement.

2. Hewlett-Packard, in its Puerto Rico plant that assembled display terminals, adopted a concept that the company termed "focused flow." Instead of building many different terminal models at the same time, it sequenced production serially so that at any one time the factory of 275 employees assembled only one model of terminal.

    What do you see as the advantages to such a strategy? What are its disadvantages?

3. In Situation for Study F-1, Tom Stoddard was attempting to use production and operations management in the house construction industry. Where was his operation located in the product-process matrix? Relate the theoretical concepts of the product-process matrix to Tom's actual process.

4. The home construction industry has for many years tried to get from the top left-hand corner to the bottom right-hand corner of the product-process matrix. What progress in this direction has been made in your local area? Why is this so?

5. Bob Leone's company manufactures a material that significantly lengthens the life of fluorescent bulbs. This material is patented, but the patent will run out in five years. Demand for the material is growing at a rate of 25 percent a year as the major fluorescent bulb manufacturers use it in more and more of their product offerings. What manufacturing choices would you recommend to Bob to help him cope with this situation?

6. U.S. auto manufacturers are faced with some monumental production challenges—the need to produce more small cars, the need to increase gas mileage on all their cars, and the need to meet emissions control standards. What kind of manufacturing changes would you suggest to meet these challenges and still keep autos affordable? Be sure to consider items such as product design, product line breadth, purchasing, vertical integration, process technology, capacity balance, and workforce policies.

7. You are a maker of skateboards, one of the latest crazes in the United States. What manufacturing choices would you make to serve this market, which is expected to grow by 450 percent over the next year? Support your choices. What manufacturing strategy underlies your analysis?

8. What parallels do you see in the dynamics of the product-process matrix and its service counterpart? What clear distinctions exist?

SITUATION FOR STUDY 10-1

STAR TRUCK CORPORATION

Tom Horn had just been appointed vice-president of operations for the Star Truck Corporation and had moved to the corporate headquarters in Atlanta. Tom had most recently been plant manager of the Star Truck plant in Little Rock, Arkansas. The firm had decided to build a new truck plant in the Midwest and had taken an option on 20 acres in an industrial park just outside Dayton, Ohio. Tom's first job as vice-president was to coordinate all the design aspects and managerial concerns to make sure the new plant operated in an efficient and effective manner and made a high contribution to the firm. Tom thought he could rely heavily on his experience at the Little Rock Star Truck plant, plus his education, to bring this assignment to a successful conclusion.

The trucks that were built at the Little Rock plant, as well as those to be built at the Dayton plant, were the diesel tractor portion of highway tractor-trailers (the "18-wheelers" of CB and TV renown). The tractors were the "cab over"—flat in front and no hood. Basic production followed this format:

1. The running gear (including engine, transmission, axle, brakes, and suspension systems) was purchased from name brand suppliers and adapted to suit the particular requirements of the buyer.

2. The frame rails were purchased with prepunched bolt holes in the front. The remaining holes were drilled on semiautomatic machines with patterns, again to suit the configuration ordered by the buyer.

3. The cab was the single component that most distinguished the Star Truck from every other manufacturer's. The cab was entirely assembled in the plant from components both made in the plant and purchased.

4. There were a number of variations on the truck design from which a buyer could choose to individualize or customize a truck.

Star manufactured to order and felt comfortable with a 90-day backlog—much shorter, and the firm felt uneasy about sales; much longer, and they felt that buyers would go to the competition. Although the firm did occasionally sell trucks to dealers for floor models, the usual sales was to the individual owner-driver through a local dealer. The firm would negotiate lower prices for stripped-down models to fleet operators when necessary to absorb slack capacity. Tom would allow no more than three fleet buyer's trucks to be scheduled in the plant at one time. He thought it best to intersperse these multiple orders in with the typical single-unit orders. Star Truck's reputation as the "limousine" of trucks was enhanced by the fact that the buyer had such a wide selection of designs and accessories from which to choose, compared with the limited selection offered by larger volume manufacturers. The truck sales price ran from $70,000 to $120,000—typically higher than that of the competition. However, this higher price apparently did not deter buyers.

To get a better grasp of the whole, Tom made the following attempt to identify, define, and categorize the various departments and work centers.

- *Machine shop.* Did precision machining of component parts, usually in batches to inventory. Occasionally built and repaired simple tools, jigs, and fixtures for both itself and other areas. Would also, at times, do precision machining for the maintenance department. Employees were highly skilled machinists.

- *Maintenance department.* It kept the plant and equipment operating; also included the janitorial function; assembled and installed new machines and processes. With the exception of janitors, the maintenance crew was made up of highly skilled craftsmen such as electricians, maintenance welders, and millwrights. On many of the jobs, more than one trade or skill was involved. Maintenance jobs were scheduled in order of priority: (1) breakdowns, (2) building or installing a new process (once project funds were approved, the investment was charged to the plant; Tom thought it was not too smart to have a $100,000 machine sitting idle in the receiving area), and (3) preventive maintenance (coordinated with machine/process availability and maintenance department slack).

- *Press department.* This contained a variety of brake and punch presses, metal shears, metal rolls, spot welding, metal routers, and metal saws. The machines were used to fabricate a large assortment of component parts from aluminum cab "skin" to support brackets. The parts were made in batches to inventory. The employees were semiskilled machine operators.

- *Production welding area.* Workers assembled and welded various component parts, which were run in batches to inventory requirements. The welders were skilled production welders.

- *Paint areas.* These were scattered throughout the plant.

  The smaller component parts were hung on a conveyor line, which transported them through an automatic washer and "static" paint process for undercoat paint. The parts were run in batches through the identical process. The one employee required for this process was very low skilled.

  Each finished cab was primed and baked, then given its unique set of colors and trims by painting and baking each color or trim stripe; each color or trim required a separate trip through the paint booth and oven. Each cab was scheduled to match up with the correct truck chassis.

  The truck wheels were painted in a separate paint booth near the truck line. Again, each set of wheels, usually numbering 10, was painted to order, although white predominated. The wheels were also scheduled to match the production build schedule.

  The chassis or remainder of the truck was painted and baked on the assembly line. The line passed through a paint booth and oven.

  The painters in these operations were skilled production painters.

- *Frame rail drilling.* All the common holes on the front three-foot portion of the truck rails were prepunched by a vendor. The remainder of the holes (about 75 percent) were drilled on two semiautomatic drilling machines. Both rails of a set of two had the same pattern with the exception of a few holes. The rails were thus clamped together and drilled two at a time. The rails were scheduled and drilled to suit the plant build schedule. The workers were skilled machine operators.

- *Assembly processes.* These included frame assembly, suspension assembly, transmission to engine assembly, drive shaft assembly, cab assembly, cab trim, door assembly, and wheel tire assembly. These minor assembly operations fed into the major truck assembly operations. Each of these operations performed the same basic set of tasks

FIGURE 10-9   Major processes to be incorporated into the new Star Truck plant.

on each unit, as on an auto assembly line. The major difference at Star Truck was the fixtures and tooling that were necessary for each set of possible combinations. For example, the axle/suspension/brake assembly required an inventory of welding fixtures. Another oddball operation was the drive shaft assembly. The product engineers emphatically declared they could not consider all the variables that would enable them to predetermine drive shaft lengths. Therefore, each drive shaft was custom fit as the truck chassis was pulled along the assembly line, thus precluding many of the economies that would have been possible otherwise.

Figure 10-9 is a schematic representation of most of the productive processes with which Tom had to be concerned in trying to design the new plant. Ancillary functions such as shipping, receiving, and materials management Tom neglected for the moment. He felt that if he could get a firm grasp of his problem with the processes described above, then he could fit in the others.

1. What concerns or considerations would you have if you were Tom?
2. What do you suggest that he do?

SITUATION FOR STUDY 10-2
HERRIESTON CORPORATION

The plastics division of Herrieston Corporation had sales of $53 million and produced a variety of plastic parts out of 12 plants scattered throughout the South and the Southeast. In the late 1960s researchers at DuPont Corporation developed a new bottle made of plastic that was shatterproof, 11 times lighter than the comparable glass bottle it could replace, and capable of storing liquids for three months without loss of flavor or carbonation.

The plastics division, seeing this development as an extremely attractive growth opportunity, seized upon this idea by proposing to purchase a number of machines that could utilize this technology. The costs of this technology were significant. If the division were to place a two-liter bottle-making machine in each of the 12 plants, the cost would be $13 million in capital outlay. Having machines in each of the geographically scattered plants was attractive from the standpoint of servicing local markets but unattractive from the standpoint of introducing new technologies to plants that performed many different kinds of operations. Relatively few of the plants shared any commonalities with the new technology and

those commonalities were simply the manufacturing of milk bottles. One decision facing the division was how big an investment to make and whether the new plastic-bottle-making machines ought to be introduced to the existing plants of the division or whether new plants in selected areas ought to be constructed.

Most of the costs of bottle making were in materials. Plastic resins, being oil derivatives, were much more expensive per pound than the raw materials of glass fabrication. Glass making, on the other hand, was much more energy-intensive than the making of plastic. The two-liter plastic bottle was a good choice to start off producing because its ratio of product volume to plastic was much higher than the similar ratio for smaller bottles. Still, as the plastic bottles were currently engineered, materials costs were of concern relative to glass bottles.

What should Harrieston's strategy be? How big an investment should it make in two-liter plastic bottles? Where should this investment be made? What strategies for manufacturing, especially in the future, should be adopted?

REFERENCE NOTES

1. See Wickham Skinner, *Manufacturing: The Formidable Competitve Weapon* (New York: John Wiley & Sons, 1985), which brings together a number of Skinner's articles that appeared first in the *Harvard Business Review*. Another exceedingly useful book on manufacturing strategy is Robert H. Hayes and Steven C. Wheelwright, *Restoring Our Competitive Edge: Competing Through Manufacturing*, (New York: John Wiley and Sons, 1984).

2. See Alfred Chandler Jr., *The Visible Hand: The Managerial Revolution in American Business* (Cambridge, Mass.: Harvard University Press, 1977).

3. Some useful readings on Japanese manufacturing techniques and philosophies include:

Clark, Rodney. *The Japanese Company.* New Haven, Conn.: Yale University Press, 1979.

Drucker, Peter F. "Behind Japan's Success." *Harvard Business Review* 59, no. 1 (January-February 1981): 83–90.

Drucker, Peter F. "What We Can Learn from Japanese Management." *Harvard Business Review* 49, no. 2 (March-April 1971): 110–22.

Hall, Robert W., *Zero Inventories,* Homewood, IL. Dow Jones—Irwin, 1983.

Hall, Robert W., *Attaining Manufacturing Excellence,* Homewood, IL: Dow Jones—Irwin, 1987.

Hayes, Robert H. "Why Japanese Factories Work." *Harvard Business Review* 59, no. 4 (July-August 1981): 56–66.

Juran, Joseph M. "Japanese and Western Quality: A Contrast in Methods and Results." *Management Review* (November 1978): 27–45.

Schonberger, Richard J. *Japanese Manufacturing Techniques: Nine Hidden Lessons in Simplicity.* New York: The Free Press, 1982.

Schonberger, Richard J. *World Class Manufacturing: The Lessons of Simplicity Applied.* New York: The Free Press, 1986.

Wheelwright, Steven C. "Japan—Where Operations Really Are Strategic." *Harvard Business Review* 59, no. 4 (July-August 1981): 67–74.

Yoshino, Michael Y. *Japan's Managerial System: Tradition and Innovation.* Cambridge, Mass.: MIT Press, 1968.

Yoshino, Michael Y. *Japan's Multinational Enterprises.* Cambridge, Mass.: Harvard University Press, 1976.

4. *Fortune* (February 8, 1982): 38.

5. Ibid., p. 35.

6. Richard J. Schonberger, *Japanese Manufacturing Techniques: Nine Hidden Lessons in Simplicity* (New York: The Free Press, 1982).

7. This section is based on Robert H. Hayes and Roger W. Schmenner, "How Should You Organize Manufacturing?" *Harvard Business Review* 56, no. 1 (January-February 1978), pp. 105–18.

INDEX